MW00528758

Handbook of
SYSTEMS
DEVELOPMENT
1999

Paul C. Tinnirello, *Editor*

AUERBACH

Boca Raton   London   New York   Washington, D.C.

Acquiring Editor:	John Wyzalek
Project Editor:	Carol Whitehead
Marketing Manager:	Rod Bell
Cover design:	Dawn Boyd
PrePress:	Carlos Esser
Manufacturing:	Carol Slatter

Library of Congress Cataloging-in-Publication Data

Handbook of systems development / Paul C. Tinnirello, editor. --1999
   ed.
       p. cm.
   Includes bibliographical references and index.
   ISBN 0-8493-9979-3 (alk, paper)
     1. Applicaton software--Development--Handbooks, manuals, etc.
  I. Tinnirello, Paul C.
  QA76.76.D47H34   1999
  005.1–dc21   98-35521
                                                     CIP

No claim to original U.S. Government works
International Standard Book Number 0-8493-9979-3
Library of Congress Card Number 98-35521
Printed in the United States of America 1 2 3 4 5 6 7 8 9 0
Printed on acid-free paper

Contributors

PHILIP L. ARTHUR, *IBM Dallas Systems Center-based Consultant, Roanoke TX*

C. WARREN AXELROD, PhD, *Corporate Information Systems, Carroll McEntee & McGinley, Inc., New York NY*

ILIA BIDER, *Project Manager and Senior Consultant, Prolifics, London UK*

BEN A. BLAKE, *Professor of Computer and Information Science, Cleveland State University, Cleveland OH*

BIJOY BORDOLOI, *Assistant Professor of Information Systems and Management Sciences, University of Texas, Arlington TX*

BILL CAMARDA, *Freelance Technology Writer and Editor, Ramsey NJ*

PATRICIA L. CARBONE, *Principal Staff Member, Mitretek Systems, McLean VA*

DALE COHEN, *Electronic Messaging Team Project Manager, R.R. Donnelley & Sons Co., Chicago IL*

KEN DOUGHTY, *Principal Consultant, O'Driscoll & Doughty Associates, Brisbane Australia*

RICHARD T. DUÉ, *President, Thomsen Dué and Associates, Ltd., Edmonton, Alberta Canada*

LEN DVORKIN, *President, Italex Consulting, Inc., Thornhill, Ontario Canada*

ADAM FADALLA, PhD, *Assistant Professor of Computer and Information Science, Cleveland State University, Cleveland OH*

THOMAS FLEISHMAN, *Vice President and Director of Information Services, Kaiser Permanente Medical Care Program, Pasadena CA*

DAN FOBES, *Software Architect, Yardley PA*

LOUIS B. FRIED, *Vice-President, Information Technology, SRI International, Menlo Park CA*

DAVID FRIEND, *Chairman, Pilot Software, Inc., Cambridge MA*

MICHAEL L. GIBSON, *Professor of Management, Auburn University, Auburn AL*

IDO GILEADI, *Manager, Deloitte & Touche Consulting Group and Lecturer, Ryerson Polytechnic University, Toronto, Ontario Canada*

FRANK GRIECO, *Manager of Information Systems Audit, Brisbane City Council, Brisbane Australia*

CARL STEPHEN GUYNES, PhD, *Professor, College of Business Administration, University of North Texas, Denton TX*

GILBERT HELD, *Director, 4-Degree Consulting, Macon GA*

LUKE HOHMANN, *Vice-President of Engineering, SmartPatents, Inc., Mountain View CA*

DAVID K. HOLTHAUS, *Software Specialist, Nationwide Insurance Enterrpise, Columbus OH*

DOUGLAS B. HOYT, *Certified Computing Professional, Founding Member of the Institute of Management Consultants, Hartsdale NY*

RAFFAELA IBBA, *Project Leader, Finseil Group and Treasure Grupo Utenti Function Point Italia, Rome Italy*

PAUL J. JALICS, PHD, *Professor of Computer and Information Science, Cleveland State University, Cleveland OH*

LEE JANKE, *Consulting Manager, Unidata Professional Services, Denver CO*

BRIAN JEFFREY, *Managing Director, International Technology Group, Mountain View CA*

LEON A. KAPPELMAN, *Department of Business Computer Information Systems, College of Business Administration, University of North Texas, Denton TX*

WOLFGANG KELLER, *Senior Manager, Software Design & Management, Ltd., Munich Germany*

YOUNG-GUL KIM, *Assistant Professor of MIS, Graduate School of Management, Korea Advanced Institute of Science and Technology, Seoul Korea*

RALPH L. KLEIM, *Co-founder, Practical Creative Solutions, Redmond WA*

BERNARD S. KLOPFER, *Management Consultant, EMS, Inc., Weirton MA*

WILLIAM N. LEDBETTER, PHD, *Professor of Management, Tuskegee University, Tuskegee AL*

RICHARD J. LEWIS, JR., *eCom Connections and Miami University, Oxford OH*

DAVID LITWACK, *President, dml Associates, Fairfax VA*

DAVID H. LONGSTREET, *Independent Consultant, Memeber of the International Function Point User Group Board of Directors, Blue Springs MO*

JOE LUCHETSKI, *University of Texas, Arlington TX*

IRWIN S. LUDIN, *Co-founder, Practical Creative Solutions, Redmond WA*

JACK T. MARCHEWKA, PHD, *Assistant Professor of Management Information Systems, Department of Operations Management and Information Systems, Northern Illinois University, DeKalb IL*

VICTOR MATOS, PHD, *Associate Professor of Computer and Information Science, College of Business Administration, Cleveland State University, Cleveland OH*

JACK MCELREATH, *Managing Partner, Consulting and Systems Integration, Computer Sciences Corp., Waltham MA*

PREM N. MEHRA, *Senior Architectural Engineer, Microsoft, Corp., Redmond WA*

SANTOSH K. MISRA, PHD, *Associate Professor of Computer and Information Science, Cleveland State University, Cleveland OH*

NATHAN J. MULLER, *Independent Consultant, Huntsville AL*

CRAIG S. MULLINS, *Platinum Technology, Inc., Oakbrook Terrace IL*

POLLY PERRYMAN, *Independent Consultant, Stoughton MA*

STEVEN RABIN, *American Software, Atlanta GA*

T. M. RAJKKUMAR, *Associate Professor, Department of Decision Sciences and Management Information Systems, Miami University, Oxford OH*

TOM L. ROBERTS, JR., *Assistant Professor, College of Business Administration, Middle Tennessee University, Murfreesboro TN*

PATRICIA L. SEYMOUR, *Principal and Founder of Technology Innovations, Danville CA*

DUANE E. SHARP, *President, SharpTech Associates, Mississauga, Ontario Canada*

MICHAEL SIMONYI, *Systems Architect, Etobicoke, Ontario Canada*

DANIEL L. SPAR, *Consultant, Transarc Corp., Falls Church VA*

J. WAYNE SPENCE, *Business Computer Information Systems Department, College of Business Administration, University of North Texas, Denton TX*

STANLEY H. STAHL, *Managing Partner, Solution Dynamics, Los Angeles CA*

ANDREW J. SWADENER, *Consulting Manager, Unidata Professional Services, Denver CO*

BHAVANI THURAISINGHAM, *Lead Engineer, Center for Integrated Intelligence Systems, The MITRE Corporation, Bedford MA*

WILLIAM M. ULRICH, *President, Tactical Strategy Group, Aptos CA*

WAYNE R. VINCENT, *Sun Microsystems, New York NY*

JAMES A. WARD, *Independent Consultant, Hoboken NJ*

LARRY WHIPPLE, *Senior Programmer/Analyst and Project Manager, The Corporation of The Church of Jesus Christ of Latter-Day Saints, Salt Lake City UT*

BRYAN WILKINSON, *Director of Information Systems Audit, Teledyne, Inc., Los Angeles CA*

Contents

Introduction

THE DEVELOPMENT OF APPLICATION SOFTWARE remains one of the most demanding and challenging activities in the computing industry. Continuous advancements in technology, compounded with aggressive business competitiveness, has fueled an extremely difficult and often overwhelming development atmosphere. Rapidly evolving technologies, such as e-commerce or component objects, exemplify both the opportunities and complexities for building tomorrow's advanced systems. Adding to this challenge has been the serious shortage of skilled workers who can competently fulfill the software development mission.

IT professionals who work in the application development environment are struggling with the pace of such change as well as the stress of integrating new applications within the framework of existing systems. Concurrently, there is continuous demand for better control and accountability of IT expenditures. Furthermore, there has been more pressure for software professionals to acquire business related knowledge without sacrificing technical savvy. Clearly, accomplishing the diverse challenges of application development requires maturity, adaptability, and perseverance.

This edition of the handbook has been updated to reflect the latest information and strategies involved with application development. It builds on the strengths of earlier editions by providing a vast array of real world and practical knowledge from development experts. I have endeavored to preserve continuity with the experiences that many development managers share about software development, including my own experiences. Thus, the collective set of chapters offers a compelling portfolio of all facets of the application development process.

Application development technology trends in the last year continue to emphasize the critical and urgent need of reducing the overall time to bring applications to production. Section I, "Management and Planning," Section II, "Development Strategies," and Section IV, "Programming Techniques," each review the practical and realistic aspects of new development methods including multitiered client server, object-oriented development, and Internet-based systems. Although these newer development methods are gaining widespread acceptance, there are significant risks to those organizations that are not prepared to examine the technology from all sides. Thus, the opportunities that may be gained from a new type of technical advancement can be lost due misunderstanding or poor strategy.

Exploiting the massive amount of accumulated data within an organization's information framework has also been a serious business challenge to development managers. Section V, "Database Functionality and Design," Section VI, "Operating Platforms," and Section VII, "Networking and Connectivity" provide numerous procedures for capitalizing on the vast amount of stored information. Organizations that aggressively pursue methods for effective information extraction will be better prepared to meet the economic challenges of the revolutionary e-business world.

Year 2000 date compliancy is still focusing much attention on the issues that surround deployed application systems. Section VIII, "Testing Software Applications," Section XI, "Supporting Existing Software," and, Section XII, "Post Development Administration," cover important details regarding applications that migrate from development to the production environment. Given the accelerated pace of development, many applications are quickly transferred into production mode without rigorous testing or control mechanisms.

Regardless of the numerous challenges that surround development, there is always an abundant array of new and exciting opportunities that are enabled via new technology. Section III, "Tools, Tips, and Practices" and Section IX, "Quality and Productivity Initiatives" offer valuable information about leveraging new technology to help meet business goals and objectives. This includes breakthrough tools that take advantage of code reuse and advanced object-oriented technology.

Sustaining the necessary awareness of business and technology events is becoming more burdensome each day. Finding the time to investigate and explore various development paths is often compromised by the hectic pace of today's IT environment. Section X, "Leveraging Staff Resources," provides useful guidelines for those who manage or lead development teams. Isolating oneself from business and technology trends is extremely risky. While it is often important to maintain the status quo, it is equally, if not more, important to stay near the edge of the future.

The factors that lead to successful application development is not happenstance. Accomplishment requires the maturity of experience, a keen sense of adaptability and the commitment to perseverance. Possessing these talents does not guarantee success, but without such skills the development effort is even more arduous. Unfortunately, there are no exact blueprints for the development process, nor is there a singular style or procedure. Despite what may be published or taught, application development also requires a broad spectrum of technical and managerial wisdom as well as the ability to seek out new methods and alternatives. Furthermore, these skills must be synchronized with the business climate of a given organizational environment.

Managing the application development process is a delicate balancing act of people, technology, and corporate culture. Achieving the necessary skills for this challenge is an unceasing process. Perhaps this may explain the high failure rate of many development projects or the burnout rate of many software managers. I recognize the difficulty of mastering the various demands that these three segments impose on the application development function. Fortunately, many of the chapters in this handbook provide insights that can ease the burdens associated with development.

Keeping pace with needs of programming staff has become more formidable, especially in a tight labor marketplace. Career uncertainty seems to loom about as the result of new and specialized software technologies. Satisfying the interests of highly qualified professionals and concurrently motivating those who lumber in older technologies is no easy task. Yet, without the necessary development talent, organizations risk the loss of business opportunities. While outsourcing techniques can assist some application needs, it cannot accommodate all of the issues that face today's development requirements.

Determining the value of technological advancements is more complicated as each year passes. The flurry of predictions and expectations about hardware and software trends is often confusing, if not misleading. It is important to maintain the status quo without losing an edge on the future. But at what cost? Not all new technology is ready for rigorous production demands. And many software managers are thrust into decisions regarding new development tools without the benefit of benchmarks or pilot projects.

Development managers are no longer isolated programming servants in hiding. In fact, the trend for closer integration of business and technical expertise is an accepted prerequisite for IT professionals. However, recent shifts in economic conditions have forced many software managers to rethink application development strategies based on business survival and corporate mood. Making the appropriate decision could be more "politically correct" than "technically correct." This can be especially true as business departments take more responsibility for their own application development.

Although the aforementioned conditions have existed for decades, there is greater intensity and acceleration in today's development environment. Each good decision is a function of quicker responsiveness with the potential of greater return on investment. Likewise, poor decisions can be more perilous. Regardless of the adversities, software development still holds the promise of using technology for the furtherance of business goals. And many application managers are eager to continue the pursuit of fulfilling such goals via successful development techniques.

Effective use of this handbook can best be accomplished if the reader previews the chapters by reading each section introduction. Most sections are organized around the various components and phases of application development. In some instances, the section may represent a subdiscipline, such as database technology, to the overall development structure. Numerous chapters make reference to ideas found in others sections. Some chapters could easily fit into other section areas, so the reader is advised to look at all material when searching for a particular topic or concept. Unlike other books, which have limited scope, this handbook is an ideal tool that encompasses an extensive range of development material. In many ways it can be used as both an encyclopedia and a guidebook. For the reader, this provides a concise source for easy reference.

The daily challenges of application development will remain as long as business needs exist. For those of us who strive earnestly to improve the process, it is never boring or dull. From my own experiences as an application development manager and now as a senior-level IS executive, I am cautious about predictions that suggest quantum improvements to the development process will occur overnight. Instead, I envision strong incremental steps that are supported by commitment and determination. Utilizing the information in this book can leverage the ability to not only survive, but succeed amidst an environment of ongoing change. I hope that the material in this edition will renew your determination, offer opportunity for discovery, and generate enthusiasm for development challenges that lie ahead.

Section I
Management
and Planning

MANAGEMENT AND PLANNING are obvious prerequisites to the complexities associated with application development. Yet, meeting the demands to fulfill projects expeditiously can compromise the most stringent plans. As a result project management and planning practices are being observed more carefully in both large and small corporations. Numerous organizations are assessing the value of all department levels, including the IS area, for productivity, quality, and return-on-investment. Driving this mission has been the increased demand of business competition fueled by globalization of the economy. IS environments are particularly prone to scrutiny due to the increasing expenses associated with development initiatives. Development managers must continually justify the cost of existing technology while assessing the value of new solutions. The dynamics of today's IS climate may not allow for the traditional techniques used in management and planning. In response, some organizations are revamping current management and planning procedures while other organizations are pursuing alternate methods to manage application development activities. Chapter I-1, "Evaluating Project Performance," discusses the various issues that can encumber the successful completion of a typical development project. Identifying these issues can be extremely valuable when determining the appropriate and often necessary tradeoffs during project implementation. Minimizing management overhead can also enable development managers to respond more quickly and effectively to organizational goals and objectives. As a follow-up, Chapter I-2, "Productivity Through Project Management," closely examines three critical variables that impact planning and controlling application development. Work, resources, and time are co-dependent factors that can influence the success or failure of projects. Understanding the dynamics of these variables will help strengthen the role that project management plays in the implementation of new technology. The Year 2000 Crisis has drawn tremendous attention over the last several years. And it will continue to have a significant impact on computing resources long after the next millennium has started. This effort has often been viewed as a large maintenance task by some organizations that have struggled to bring the date conversion under control. But is this just another run-of-the-mill maintenance situation?

1

Chapter I-3, "Project Management Solutions for the Year 2000 Crisis," provides meaningful insight on the benefits of project management as applied to this software dilemma. Despite the publicized debates over the best solution, the Year 2000 Crisis will likely be resolved through judicious management and planning rather than reckless programming endeavors.

Outsourcing continues to gain the interest of those organizations who seek an alternative to internally developed application systems. Development managers are often unprepared, and sometimes unwilling, to objectively evaluate the various outsourcing options available. Recent surveys indicate that reckless outsourcing practices can be volatile in an organization's technology endeavors. Likewise, ignoring outsourcing can be just as dangerous, especially with the shortage of skilled IS professionals. These issues only emphasize the need to carefully assess all sides of the outsourcing marketplace. Chapter I-4, "Managing the Risks of Outsourcing Systems Development," the authors challenge the reader's knowledge about outsourcing alternatives. Although outsourcing alleviates some of the resource issues required for development, there is still a need for project management as a means of ensuring implementation success.

Chapter I-1
Evaluating Project Performance

Ralph L. Kliem and Irwin S. Ludin

OPPORTUNITIES ABOUND FOR INFORMATION SYSTEMS (IS) PROJECTS to go awry, mostly because projects do not operate in a vacuum. A wide range of pressures are placed on them that affect quality, schedule completion, and budgetary performance. The results are often excessive costs, inadequate schedule performance, and poor quality.

A study by Standish Group International, Inc., indicates the following:

- Thirty-one percent of information technology projects are canceled before completion.
- Sixteen percent of projects finish on time and within budget.
- Fifty-two percent of projects overrun cost estimates by 189%.

Obviously, such a poor record affects the bottom line, costing firms thousands, even millions, of dollars. It behooves management, therefore, to assess performance before and during the project — and the earlier the better.

One approach for assessing current and future project performance is to use a ranking method adopted from basic statistical analysis and the work of Jerry FitzGerald (*Fundamentals of Systems Analysis*, New York: John Wiley and Sons, Inc., 1987). This approach, called a project assessment approach, focuses on four key fundamental elements of the project management process: people, quality, schedule, and budget. That information is used to evaluate the application of the basic processes of project management to achieve the goals of a project.

BASIC DEFINITIONS

Before describing the project assessment approach, definitions are necessary to ensure a solid understanding of what to accomplish:

- **Project Management.** The tools, techniques, and knowledge required to manage a project.
- **People.** Individuals required to ensure that a project is completed efficiently and effectively.

0-8493-9979-3/99/$0.00+$.50
© 1999 by CRC Press LLC

- **Quality.** The output from a project that meets customer requirements or standards.
- **Schedule.** The timeline required to complete a project.
- **Budget.** The money allocated to complete a project.

The project assessment approach entails four steps: Gathering background information, performing an assessment and constructing a matrix, conducting an in-depth review, and preparing the report. These steps are discussed in the subsequent sections.

GATHERING BACKGROUND INFORMATION

The person responsible for assessing a project, called an assessor, acquires a good understanding and knowledge of the project. This step involves answering the "Five Ws" and one "How" for a project:

- Why does the project exist?
- What are the major goals and objectives?
- Who are the key players?
- When are the major schedule milestones?
- Where do project activities occur?
- How are tasks executed?

Assessors acquire much of this information through interviews, surveys, documentation reviews such as project manuals and project history files, and database scanning such as archived databases.

CONSTRUCTING THE MATRIX

This step requires considerable planning to execute. Five people are key to successful execution:

- Assessor
- Facilitator
- Subject matter experts
- Selected team members
- Scribe

Assessors. They are responsible for the overall execution of this step and the entire project assessment approach. They usually function as the facilitator for constructing the matrix, although someone else could perform that role.

Facilitators. They facilitate, rather than run, the assessment sessions. They ensure open communications and encourage participation.

Subject Matter Experts. They are the most knowledgeable people on the project. Their knowledge may be technical or operational. The assessor selects them with the concurrence of project leadership (e.g., senior management).

Selected Team Members. They are project participants who are not necessarily subject matter experts but can provide helpful insights during this step. The assessor selects them, too, with the concurrence of project leadership.

Scribe. This person records notes during meetings for this step. He or she is neither the facilitator nor a subject matter expert. He or she may, however, be a team member.

Establishing Guidelines

To conduct an effective second step, the facilitator should remember to:

- Set up the facilities before the session.
- Have adequate supplies on hand.
- Appoint roles (e.g., that of the scribe or subject matter expert) ahead of time.
- Encourage everyone to speak.
- Be objective and noncommittal.
- Ensure everyone agrees on the process and objectives.
- Break frequently.

In addition, participants in the sessions should:

- Come prepared.
- Be tolerant of different views.
- Apply active listening skills.
- Agree on the perspective of ranking and definitions.

After identifying the participants (i.e., the team), the assessor initiates construction of a matrix for the project. The objectives are to identify and rank according to priority the project management processes and goals of the project. This ranking enables determining the existence and importance of processes and goals and how to efficiently and effectively achieve them. The assessment team, not the assessor, determines the basis for prioritization. The team does that through forced choice.

At the conclusion of this step, the assessment team produces a matrix, as shown in Exhibit 1. The matrix in Exhibit 1 consists of rows and columns. The rows represent project management processes, ranked in descending importance. The columns represent the organization's goals, also ranked in descending order. The rows and columns in Exhibit 1 are already ranked according to priority. A brief description of each follows:

- **Assessment.** Determining the environment in which a project occurs.
- **Definition.** Deciding the goals in advance.

Exhibit 1.   How Measures of Success Relate to Matrix

Goal Process	Goal B	Goal C	Goal A	Goal D
Planning	Moderate	Weak	Strong	Strong
Leading	Moderate	Strong	Strong	Strong
Organizing	Strong	Strong	Weak	Weak
Closure	Weak	Strong	Weak	Weak
Controlling	Weak	Strong	Weak	Weak
Assessment	Moderate	Strong	Weak	Weak
Definition	Weak	Weak	Weak	Weak

- **Planning.** Determining what steps to execute, assigning who will perform those tasks, and verifying when they must start and stop.
- **Organizing.** Orchestrating project resources cost-effectively to execute plans.
- **Controlling.** Assessing how well the project manager uses plans and organization.
- **Closing.** Completing the project efficiently and effectively.
- **Leading.** Influencing people to achieve goals and objectives.

Ranking Processes

The ranking of the processes occurs during a group session with the assessor, facilitator, subject matter experts, selected team members, and scribe present. Through forced choice, they rank goals according to descending order via voting. The values for each goal are tallied to determine the importance of each process. Exhibit 2 shows the ranking of processes and how to calculate the ranking.

Exhibit 2.   Ranking of Processes (Example)

Assessment	Assessment	0 + 12 = 12				
Leading 2	3	Leading 2 + 15.5 = 17.5				
Definition 3	2	0	Definition 3 + 5.5 = 8.5			
Planning 4	1	2.5	2.5 2.5	2.5	Planning 9 + 11 = 20	
Organizing 3	2	4 1	4 1	4 1	4	Organizing 12 + 5 = 17
Controlling 1	4	5 0	0 5	3	2 5 0	Controlling 8 + 5 = 13
Closure 5	0	2 3	2 3	4 1	0 5 0 5	Closure 17 + 0 = 17
	12	15.5	5.5	11	5 5	0

6

Exhibit 3.   Ranking of Project Goals (Example)

Goal A	Goal A	0 + 6 = 6			
Goal B	4 ¹	Goal B	4 + 6 = 10		
Goal C	3 ²	2 ³	Goal C	5 + 4 = 9	
Goal D	2 ³	2 ³	1 ⁴	Goal D	5 + 0 = 5
⋮					
⋮					
⋮					
	6	6	4	0	

When conducting the ranking, everyone must agree on the perspective. Is the ranking based on schedule? Budget? Quality? Failure to determine the perspective can quickly lead to miscommunication and misdirection.

Ranking Project Goals or Objectives

Ranking of goals or objectives is conducted the same as processes. Exhibit 3 shows a ranking of goals and how to calculate them.

The columns consist of the major goals or objectives for a project. The goals, ranging from one to dozens, are ranked in descending order. A goal is a broad statement of what the project will achieve; an objective is a specific, measurable benchmark that the project must achieve toward accomplishing goals.

Everyone should agree on the perspective to take when ranking. The same perspective should be used as in ranking processes.

Quadrants

The ranking of processes and goals or objectives enable determination of the importance of the cells, too, by identifying the most important quadrants or "regions" of the matrix. The first quadrant represents the most important goals and processes; the second, the next most important; the third quadrant, the next most important; and the fourth, the least important.

The importance of goals, objectives, and processes is based upon their calculated value resulting from ranking. These values play an important role in determining whether a cell (i.e., the intersection of a goal and a process in the matrix) is very important vis-a-vis other cells, as shown in Exhibit 4.

7

Exhibit 4.   Matrix Showing Quadrants

Goal Process	Goal B (10)	Goal C (9)	Goal A (6)	Goal D (5)
Planning (20)	200	180 1	120	100 2,3
Leading (17.5)	175	157.5	105	87.5
Organizing (17)	170	153	102	85
Closure (17)	170	153	102	85
Controlling (13)	130	117 2,3	78	65 4
Assessment (12)	120	108	72	60
Definition (8.5)	85	76.5	51	42.5

Each cell contains one or more measures of success. A measure of success is a set of activities, tools, expertise, and techniques necessary to complete a project management process to achieve any given goal. There are five high-level measures of success for project planning processes to achieve a goal:

- Does a work breakdown structure exist?
- Are reliable time and cost estimates available?
- Has risk control been conducted?
- Have resources been allocated?
- Does a realistic schedule exist?

A group of internal project management experts can determine the measures of success for any given process. The assessor evaluates the degree of applying a measure of success in a methodical, consistent manner. He or she determines whether a measure for a particular cell is strong, moderate, or weak in its implementation. This judgment is based upon knowledge, experience, expertise, and research abilities. To reduce subjectivity, the assessor creates a range of values that indicate strong, moderate, or weak application of project management processes. For example, a strong application of a process falls within 100% to 75% of the total possible points, moderate application is within 74% to 25%, and weak is below 24%. For example, the degree of a measure of success for the first cell in Exhibit 1 is shown in Exhibit 5.

Weak measures of success in a high-priority section of the matrix indicate an important area for improvement. Consequently, weaknesses in the first quadrant are serious concerns; weaknesses in the lower quadrant are of the least concern.

A wide array of tools exist for constructing the matrix. These tools include graphic, spreadsheet, and word processing software. The keys, of

Exhibit 5. Cell Evaluation Scheme (Sample)			
Strong	**Moderate**	**Weak**	
(3)	(2)	(1)	
– Does a work breakdown structure exist?		X	
– Are reliable time and cost estimates available?		X	
– Has risk control been conducted?		X	
– Have resources been allocated?		X	
– Does a realistic schedule exist?		X	
Total:	3	6	1
Grand Total = Strong [3 * 1] + Moderate [2 * 3] + Weak [1 * 1] = 10			
Maximum score = Strong [3 * 5 line items] = 15			
This project's evaluation = 10/15 = 66%, which falls into the moderate rating			

course, in using the tool are the expertise of the person using it and the accuracy of the information coming out of it.

CONDUCTING AN IN-DEPTH REVIEW

This step verifies the contents of each cell. The assessor verifies to ensure that the contents of the matrix are thorough and accurate. The assessor does that by conducting additional interviews, reviewing documentation, and scanning databases. Good sources for documentation reviews are the project manual, project history files, and archived databases.

PREPARING THE REPORT

When the matrix is complete and its contents verified, the assessor prepares the report, which is presented either as a document or an oral presentation and contains all the basic elements of any business report, including distribution information, background, scope, findings, and recommendations. Eighty to 90 percent of the report, of course, should focus on the findings and recommendations, and it should answer two fundamental questions:

- What is the current state of the project?
- Where is the project going?

In the final report, certain guidelines should be followed. The writer should:

- Allow for revisions.
- Avoid spelling errors.
- Be clear and concise.
- Communicate the contents of the matrix to everyone who needs to know.
- Keep the "big picture" in focus.
- Keep the focus on the matrix.

CONCLUSION

The project assessment approach offers the IS manager many benefits. It can identify which activities are influencing the project in a positive or negative way, and which have only a moderate effect. For example, the approach can determine to what degree schedules are being developed and how achievable they are.

This approach also provides a useful, objective assessment of project disciplines implemented. It minimizes subjectivity. This type of project assessment, for example, evaluates the effectiveness of the project leaders' styles.

The project assessment approach identifies areas to improve project management processes, increasing the opportunity for process improvement. For example, it is possible to identify aspects of updating schedules that can be improved.

The approach also provides an early warning about trouble that looms ahead for a project. Project managers and executives do not have to wait until the morning after disaster strikes. For example, managers can see what it is about the project plan that may fail to achieve a significant goal.

Finally, this method for project assessment provides a database of improvements to apply and warning signals to identify for future projects. No longer does history have to repeat itself. For example, staff can see which problems with the current project could be avoided on future projects of a similar nature.

Chapter I-2
Productivity Through Project Management

James A. Ward

EVERY SOFTWARE MANAGER has been involved in systems development projects that were less than totally successful. A survey by a large consulting firm found that 25% of large projects were canceled, 60% experienced significant cost overruns, 75% had quality problems, and less than 1% of all systems development projects were delivered on schedule and met requirements. This is an awesome waste of an organization's resources.

When faced with a potential systems development disaster, can software managers turn a project around and achieve success? Better still, can they institute measures that prevent projects from failing in the first place, thereby ensuring productive use of systems development resources?

The answer is yes. This chapter offers a prescriptive approach to project control that has been consistently successful in achieving on-time delivery of systems that meet requirements.

KEYS TO GETTING STARTED

The key activities that occupy the project manager at the start of the project are planning and scheduling. These activities must also be repeated when attempting to salvage a project that is heading for disaster.

Project Requirements

Projects can and do fail if requirements are known, but there has never been a complete disaster when all requirements were fully defined, documented, understood, and agreed on by all involved parties. Many projects fail when resources are devoted to doing the wrong things.

System scope, objectives, and requirements must be completely defined, documented, reviewed, and approved. This definition must take place before

0-8493-9979-3/99/$0.00+$.50
© 1999 by CRC Press LLC

the initiation of a project or as the first activity undertaken during project execution. When a project is in trouble, requirements must be revisited, restated, and reapproved.

In addition to defining the scope and objectives of the system to be developed, the project manager must also define the project in detail. This definition addresses the work to be done, the resources devoted to that work, and the time that the effort will take. Management must review and approve this project definition to ensure that resources are being applied productively. Systems development and productivity results from the ability of the project manager to produce the greatest amount of work with the least resources in the shortest possible time.

Work. The work to be performed should be defined in such a way that when it is accomplished, the project will be successfully completed. Although it may sound elemental, this is not always the case. Given the current state of the art of systems development, it is unlikely that any two project teams, attempting to develop the same system within the same organization, would perform an identical set of tasks or activities in the same manner or sequence. It is also unlikely that they would produce the same results. No two systems are exactly alike. Each project defines its own work.

Standardized work processes are essential to systems development success. Stable and repeatable systems development procedures are required if software managers are to effectively plan, schedule, and control work.

Resources. Resources consumed are primarily the efforts of the personnel assigned to the project, but they also include dollars, computer time, purchased software, supplies, and management and support time. Resources may also be defined to include the tools and methodologies used.

Time. Time is defined for this chapter as the elapsed calendar time from the inception of the project to its successful completion.

PROJECT PLAN AND SCHEDULE: RELATING THE KEY VARIABLES AT PROJECT INCEPTION

Once software managers have defined the work to be done, software managers can apply resources over time to accomplish that work. Intuition tells that if one variable is held constant—in this case, the work to be done—then the other two variables can be adjusted in opposite directions. More resources to do the same work ought to take less time.

Intuition is correct, but only within certain limits. Unless project managers understand the dynamic interaction of the three variables of work, time, and resources, the negative effects of these dynamics during project execution will drive the project to disaster.

Resources Versus Time

Resources assigned past a certain level will not shorten project time. Beyond a point, more resources will actually lengthen the time it takes to develop a system. Brooks' Law states that adding resources to a late software development project makes that project later. Even at project inception, this holds true.

Usually, the formula is that no more people can be productively used on a project than the square root of the total amount of estimated worker months needed. If a project is estimated to take 100 worker months (8 1/2 years) of effort, then more than 10 people assigned to the project will not shorten the calendar time it takes to complete the project. Excess resources become wasted or counterproductive.

This dynamic holds true because of the nature of systems development project work. Certain tasks require the output of other tasks. Tasks must be performed in a specified sequence. There is a limit to the number of concurrent tasks that can be performed effectively. After a certain point, tasks cannot be effectively broken down and assigned to more than one person. In addition, the more people assigned to a project, the more overhead is incurred in communications, management, and coordination of activities. If one person had all the requisite skills to complete a 100-worker-month project, that person could probably do so more efficiently and use fewer resources than a larger project team. However, a software manager does not want to wait 8 1/2 years to find out.

The Law of Marginal Utility

The law of marginal utility operates in systems development projects. Accordingly, the second person assigned to a project will contribute less than the first, the third less than the second, and so on. Although each new person makes a positive contribution and thereby reduces the overall calendar time it takes to complete the project, at some point the marginal utility curve turns, and the next person's contribution becomes negative.

The actual contribution of the eleventh person in this example will probably not be negative, but rapidly declining marginal contribution begins at about that point. Therefore, a 100-worker-month project should take at least 10 calendar months to complete no matter how many resources are assigned to it.

Because the productivity of each additional person added to the project will be less than the preceding person's, the average productivity of the entire project team is reduced. In allocating resources, management must achieve the optimal size of the project team that balances resources against time to achieve the most productive mix.

Overall Elapsed Time

If after estimating the total elapsed time for the project, the project will take more than one calendar year to complete, the project manager should seriously think about redefining the project. The project can be broken into phases or define multiple projects. A 144-worker-month (12-year) project is about the largest discrete systems development project you should contemplate tackling.

There are some compelling reasons not to undertake very large systems projects. First, an organization loses its attention span at some point. Other priorities intervene. Resources tend to disappear through either attrition or reassignment.

Second, business conditions change. If a project cannot be completed within one calendar year of its inception, this project risks the delivery of an obsolete system from a business standpoint. Competition is moving more rapidly all the time. The government regulatory climate may change (this applies to virtually any industry). Reduced cycle time is a concept being preached for all products and services. It has always been true for effective information systems.

Third, the larger the project, the greater the risk of failure. Even the best project managers and the best project management methodologies and tools become strained when attempting to control projects that are too large. Degrees of error in planning or estimating that would be easily correctable on small projects can be overwhelming on large ones. A 50% overrun on a project of one worker year can be handled. The same 50% overrun could prove fatal to a 20-worker-year project. Management must have the visibility and the ability to control overruns and cut losses, and that is much more likely on smaller projects.

Many organizations have obviously undertaken very large projects. Chances of success are significantly enhanced when a project is carved up so that a major implementation occurs at least once a year. This method also provides ongoing visibility and organizational commitment to the project.

The Role of Estimates

Every organization has a way of estimating systems development projects. Whether this involves drawing lines on a Gantt chart, applying sophisticated estimating algorithms, or just stating what the dates must be, the project manager either develops or is given an estimate of how long a project should take.

Estimates that are based on fact and are accurate can be a tremendous advantage in project control. Estimates that are no more than a guess or someone's wish can be extremely detrimental. Unless estimates have a real basis in fact and are developed by the individuals actually assigned to do the work, they are best ignored except when reporting progress to management.

The value of estimates is in productively allocating resources and in co-ordination of task interdependencies. Estimates should not be used as evaluation tools. The project manager must be free to adjust plans and estimates on the basis of actual project feedback without having to explain why initial estimates were not totally accurate.

Plans are guides, and estimates are just that—best and most educated guesses about what should happen. The reality is the actual project work that is being performed. If the reality does not always conform to the plan, it is likely that the plan may need some modification.

FACTORS THAT DISRUPT THE BALANCE BETWEEN WORK, RESOURCES, AND TIME

Systems development projects that cannot be completed in one calendar year should be restructured as multiple or phased projects. More than a certain amount of resources assigned to a project will not be productive.

In many organizations, there are other factors that further reduce a manager's ability to productively plan and schedule resources over time to work on systems development projects. These factors work against the ideal relationships between work, resources, and time.

Systems Development Methodology

A systems development methodology consists of two components: a systems development life cycle and a project management methodology. The systems development life cycle (SDLC) is the guide that the project team follows; it defines the tasks that must be performed during the systems development process. Furthermore, it provides for correct ordering and interrelationships between these tasks. An SDLC should provide the stable and repeatable work processes that are essential to productive systems development planning and control. Without this definition, large projects are simply too complex to successfully plan and control.

Project management is not software. An automated project management system will not manage projects. Software is merely a tool to automate some of the functions of project scheduling and status reporting. In the hands of an effective project manager using a proven methodology, software may provide some benefits. However, the chief benefactors of these tools are higher-level management who want to know where resources have been expended.

Without a proven systems development methodology, organizations cannot hope to successfully accomplish projects requiring the effort of more than one or two persons. They can muddle through on smaller projects but are in trouble when they try to tackle anything larger.

Systems Development Standards

A second factor that limits an organization's ability to productively use optimum levels of project resources over time is a lack of standards. People are limited in their ability to work independently on concurrent tasks because no one knows what will be produced by a task until that task has been completed. The quality of the work becomes purely subjective.

Where standards do not exist, management's span of control is reduced. Project managers must directly supervise personnel at a much closer level of detail. A manager may be able to supervise the work of 10 to 12 people on a project for which standards are in force. Without standards, that same manager may only be able to coordinate the efforts of three or four people. For the organization, this has the further negative effect of reducing the contribution of the best people, because they must closely monitor the work of others. Lack of standards usually lowers overall organizational productivity.

Task Splitting

A third factor that reduces an organization's ability to use resources productively is task splitting. By assigning personnel to more than one project, management may think that more things are being accomplished or that resources are being used more productively. In fact, the opposite is true. Task splitting has a negative effect on productivity and efficiency, and this reality should not be ignored.

A person can devote 100% of his or her time to one project. That same individual will be productive only 40% of the time on each of two projects, 20% on each of three projects, and so forth. Deciding among tasks adds coordination and decision time. Time is lost in switching from one task to another. Task splitting is a notorious resource stealer. Dedicated resources are always the most productive.

PROJECT STATUS REPORTING: MONITORING PROGRESS AGAINST THE PLAN

For a project manager, project execution involves monitoring progress against the plan and schedule on a regular basis, recognizing deviations, and taking appropriate corrective action. A project manager is chiefly responsible for ensuring that the work meets all quality standards and that it conforms to requirements and specifications. Providing high project visibility to users and management is also a primary project management task.

90% Done—Or Work Completed, Resources Expended, Time Used

A project manager must invoke regular and formal status reporting. All project team members should report progress against the plan and schedule weekly. This reporting should be done at the lowest task level.

Each week, the project team members should answer the following questions about their assigned tasks:

- Is it done?
- If it isn't done, when will it be done?
- If it is behind schedule, what are the reasons?

The intent of status reporting is to chart real progress and at the same time to verify the efficacy of the project plan, schedule, and estimates. Avoid any reporting of percentage of completion on any task, however, because this reporting is invariably overly optimistic and conveys no real information that the project manager can use. In any event, the tendency to report percentage of completion usually indicates that tasks are too large to be accomplished in a time period in which they can be effectively controlled.

Providing High Visibility

When project managers report status to management and users, they should emphasize deliverable products. Managers should report progress against major milestones and major deliverable products as defined in the project plan.

A project cannot be too visible. High visibility ensures management support. Management meddles in projects when it does not know what is going on. When and if the project hits rough sledding, the project manager will need the support of management to take action. This support must be nurtured through the confidence that comes from keeping management informed.

Reporting Status Frequently

Each member of the project team should have at least one task due for completion each week and on which to report. Under no circumstances should a team member ever have more than two weeks between task completion dates. If this is the case, the project manager should go back to the plan and break the tasks down further.

Management isn't interested in weekly task-level reporting, however. Status reporting that is too detailed (or too frequent) usually obfuscates rather than clarifies project status.

A major milestone or deliverable product should be scheduled each month. Never let a project go more than two months without planning some significant event. The completion of a project phase with a formal report, including submission of the plan for the next phase, dramatizes progress most forcefully. The submission of a major deliverable product that requires management and user review and approval is also a critical event. If at least one of these events does not happen in more than two months, the project should be restructured and replanned.

Recognizing Deviations Early

Equipped with accurate project status information, the project manager can assess progress and detect any deviations or problems at the earliest possible point. An axiom of effective project management is act early, act small. Corrective action can be instituted in small doses and in ways that will not be disruptive.

Upon receiving weekly project team status reports, the project manager must post actual progress against the plan and note any deviations. If the project or some members of the project team are consistently ahead or behind the estimates, think about adjusting estimates accordingly. Minor adjustments in estimates, scheduled task completion dates, and task assignments should be done weekly as the project progresses. These minor adjustments need not be communicated beyond the project team as long as they do not affect the scheduled dates for major milestones or deliverable products.

Identifying Causes of Deviations

In even the best planned projects, deviations will occur. The first place to look for corrective action is in the plan itself.

There will be times in the course of any project when monitoring progress and making minor adjustments to the plan will not be sufficient to keep the project on schedule. This may happen for any number of reasons, and the reasons will undoubtedly influence the actions the project manager may take.

The work may change because of changes in project scope. Resources may be lost to the project. Technology may be poorly understood. The project team may have problems interacting effectively. Computer time may be unavailable. When projects deviate significantly from plan and schedule, the dynamics of the key variables of work, resources, and time will determine the likelihood of success of any action that is taken to get the project back on schedule.

Leaving aside those occurrences that significantly alter the work to be done (such as changes in scope or incorrect requirements definition), the most frequently encountered problem is severe or persistent schedule slippage. The easiest course of action is to admit that estimates were overly optimistic and that the project will simply take more time to complete. However, persistent schedule slippage is more likely to be a symptom of underlying problems than the cause of the problem. Extending project time will not cure these problems and may only allow the project team to dig a deeper hole for itself. It is lack of time that forces most project teams to face the reality of failure.

Instituting Corrective Measures

If the project manager is thoroughly convinced that the problem is simply caused by overly ambitious estimates and schedules, then the schedule should be altered. Otherwise, under no circumstances will increasing resources against the same overall schedule be successful in and of itself.

The project manager must subject a troubled project to detailed analysis, usually with the help of an independent party. Unless the underlying causes of problems are eliminated, the project will only experience greater problems as the project manager (and others) attempt to apply corrective action. Management must be supportive of this process.

Once appropriate corrective action has been initiated, the project manager must then go back to square one and prepare a formal project status report. Bearing in mind that the dynamics of work, resources, and time will be much different from what they were when the project was initially planned, the manager can then develop a new project plan and schedule.

SUMMARY

A predictable pattern results when project managers fail to understand the dynamics of work, resources, and time. First, schedules are extended, usually more than once. When this does not work, resources are added, making problems that much worse. Finally, in an attempt to bring the project to a conclusion, the work effort is cut back, often to the point at which the resulting system no longer meets the requirements it was originally meant to address.

Heroic efforts to meet the original schedule by working large amounts of overtime for extended periods will not work. Error rates will soar, project communication will become increasingly difficult, and teamwork will be severely strained. Often this drives the project into a never-ending sequence of testing and error correction. These consequences often result because of management's inability to distinguish between effort and productivity.

MANAGEMENT AND PLANNING

By understanding and managing the interaction of the key variables of work, resources, and time, the project manager can productively plan and control systems development projects. Potential failures can be turned into successes. New projects can be launched with confidence in the likelihood of success — delivering systems that meet requirements on schedule and within budget and make the most productive use of the organization's systems development resources.

Chapter I-3
Project Management Solutions for the Year 2000 Crisis

Ralph L. Kliem

HANDLING THE YEAR 2000 PROBLEM has all the elements of a project. It looks like a project. It smells like a project. It feels like a project. It tastes like a project. So the only conclusion is that the Year 2000 problem must be a project. That makes it a good candidate for applying the six basic processes of project management. Then, why do most IS shops treat it like any other maintenance activity?

Four Elements of Project

Maintenance activities (also known as housecleaning operations), of course, eliminate problems with or improve an existing system. Often, these activities do not involve a large effort and their impact is restricted to a few subsystems or modules of a much greater system. Typically, they do not involve the release of a complete configuration; the goal is to keep the existing system in working order and implement any changes within a reasonable period of time. Maintenance to an existing system, if well-documented and controlled, should not be costly; its schedule for the revision should not be tight; the level of quality is not rigorous; and the expertise required does not necessitate having it come from the best and the brightest.

The Year 2000 problem is not a maintenance activity. It is a full-fledged project in itself and becomes even more so as the number of interrelationships among components and the size of the overall system increases.

To be considered a project, an issue or problem must involve four key elements:

- Cost
- Schedule
- Quality
- People

The Year 2000 problem involves all four of these elements.

0-8493-9979-3/99/$0.00+$.50
© 1999 by CRC Press LLC

Cost. Addressing the Year 2000 problem requires large sums of money, regardless of how it is calculated. No one knows for sure the degree of impact, but estimates exist. The Gartner Group estimates a worldwide cost from $300 to $600 billion. Other experts say it will cost the U.S. $75 billion alone, costing a typical large company $5 to $40 million, maybe even $50 to $100 million. Some experts have estimates based on lines of code (LOC); each LOC will cost from $.50 cents to $1.50. The reality is that no one really knows the exact cost. What they do know, however, is that it will cost.

Schedule. Addressing the Year 2000 problem has a defined end date for completion. At 12:00:01 a.m. on January 1, 2000, everyone on this planet will enter a new century. Nothing can stop that deadline from approaching.

Yet, few people and organizations feel compelled to do anything. Procrastination has turned many people and organizations into IS couch potatoes regarding the issue. Some experts, like Peter de Jager, estimate that fewer than 35% of North American businesses have started working on the Year 2000 problem. Other experts take a more global perspective, saying that fewer than 20% of the firms in the world have done something.

Quality. The Year 2000 problem is not just a cost or time issue; it's a quality issue, too, that affects small, medium, and large information systems. As the world moves increasingly toward interconnected and distributed systems, quality becomes a greater concern.

The reasons are quite clear. Most systems handle dates in the MM/DD/YY format with the year hard-coded. When performing subtractions and comparisons, for instance, in the year 2000, calculations dealing with time spans, such as interest and actual calculations, can result in data manipulation problems, data loss, and system shutdowns. With the year 2000 being a leap year, the magnitude of the problem increases by affecting banks, insurance companies, and government institutions.

Many people believe that the Year 2000 problem is solely a minicomputer or mainframe issue, especially for ones running COBOL-based and other third-generation applications. Wrong. Even the tiny microcomputer must face the Year 2000 problem. After all, time waits for no one or anything. Users of pre-Pentium microcomputers must face, for example, the year 2000 for applications and data.

The Year 2000 problem cannot, however, be divided conveniently into three distinct categories of problems (microcomputer, minicomputer, and mainframe), but as a big, interrelated one, because all of them are typically integrated thanks to the rise of distributed computing and client/server technology.

An integrated system can "hiccup" over the Year 2000 problem. C/S applications and mainframe databases, for example, can face problems when the former uses two-digit fields for dates and the latter uses four digits. If one system recognizes the Year 2000 as a leap year and the other one does not, the latter will reject the transaction.

People. The year 2000 issue deals with people, especially ones fixing the problem. With a rising demand for systems professionals with expertise in client/server and Internet technologies a concomitant fall has occurred for people having knowledge of "legacy" technologies (e.g., COBOL and Assembler). Many reasons have contributed to this circumstance (e.g., the glamour of the new technologies, the higher levels of pay, career enhancement, etc.). Somehow, the people skilled in the new technology must return to address the Year 2000 problem, whether to develop a replacement system or modify an existing one. Coupled with the need and estimated hourly cost of $55 to $65 per hour for legacy expertise, the importance of managing these people will increase dramatically.

The people factor, of course, goes beyond skills expertise. It is a motivational issue, too. As noted earlier, a sense of denial exists about the foreboding impact that the year 2000 forewarnings. Coupled with denial is procrastination due to laziness, overconfidence, or belief that the Year 2000 issue is a maintenance concern. Like all maintenance issues, the backlog increases along with the accompanying costs. All this becomes important because eventually all companies must face the year 2000 and will have to pay for denial and procrastination at a higher cost and faster pace. Short of destruction of the universe, the Year 2000 issue will turn into a perennial maintenance issue even years beyond that red-letter date, if not addressed early.

PROJECT MANAGEMENT FOR THE YEAR 2000

The Year 2000 issue then has all the makings of a project — time, cost, quality, and people — making it an excellent candidate to apply the six basic processes of project management:

- *Leading.* Leading entails nurturing an environment that encourages people to perform their best in a manner that achieves goals and objectives.
- *Defining.* Defining entails answering the who, what, when, where, why, and how of a project so subsequent activities occur cost-effectively.
- *Planning.* Planning involves determining what must be done and is required to achieve those goals and objectives.
- *Organizing.* Organizing involves establishing a cost-effective infrastructure.
- *Controlling.* Controlling involves ensuring the cost-effective achievement of project goals and objectives and taking appropriate action, when necessary.
- *Closure.* This process entails concluding a project cost-effectively to ensure a smooth transition from development to implementation.

How Project Management Benefits Year 2000 Efforts. These six processes offer the five following advantages:

- They help to determine the magnitude of the effort as well as its business and technical impacts.
- They help to identify priorities as well as assess and manage risks.
- They help to identify the most appropriate route to pursue (e.g., re-engineer or modify the application or system).
- They help in selecting the appropriate technical and business tools and techniques.
- They help to determine the cost of addressing the Year 2000 problem.

The following sections of this article further examine these processes and their benefits.

LEADING A YEAR 2000 TEAM

The importance of this process is often overlooked on projects. Yet, it is the only process that occurs concurrently with all the other processes. Leading involves creating an environment that encourages the best in people and in a way that meets project goals and objectives. It means providing a vision for the project; communicating; keeping motivation levels high; maintaining focus on the vision; being supportive; and encouraging team building.

Creating such an environment is not easy for a Year 2000 project. The Year 2000 problem has the stigma of being mainly a maintenance activity. Many managers procrastinate or operate in denial. Many developers feel the subject is not as glamorous as working on client/server and Internet projects. A tendency also exists to treat Year 2000 projects as entities unto themselves, as if they are something out of the mainstream for IS. Consequently, the "big picture" quickly fades. It is important, therefore, that the project manager keep everyone's focus at an enterprise-wide level. The best way to accomplish that is by ensuring cross-functional representation exists on the team and at meetings.

DEFINING A YEAR 2000 PROJECT

When defining a Year 2000 project, project managers must consider several factors to determine final results. The Statement of Work (SOW) is the tool to do that.

Statement of Work

The SOW is an agreement between the developers and clients on just what the Year 2000 project will achieve, both from business and technical perspectives. Exhibit 1 shows its elements.

Exhibit 1. Statement of Work Elements and Examples

Element	Examples
Introduction	General background information like the age of the relevant applications, their owners and users, their level of complexity, and maintenance history
Goals and objectives	The order of importance for the relevant applications and the desired data error rate for each one
Scope	Whether to re-engineer or modify an existing application or integrate it with a commercial off-the-shelf package
Assumptions	The type and level of support from the vendors, especially if revisions are necessary to their software
Stakeholders	Senior managers, both in the IS and user arenas, responsible for the success of the project and the major tasks that they must perform
Resources	The required type and level of specific programming expertise, such as COBOL, VM, or client/server architecture
Schedule	The completion of important phases of the project, such as conducting an impact analysis or testing
Budget	The maximum direct (e.g., labor) and overhead (e.g., facilities) costs set for the project
Amendments	Changes to any of the above elements (e.g., goals and objectives)
Signatures	By the project manager, chief information officer, and system owner

SOW Benefits. The importance of developing an SOW is readily apparent. It requires some forethought about size as well as business and technical impacts. It encourages assessing and managing risks before it is too late and addressing them later becomes costlier. It also encourages advance thinking about the most appropriate approach to maximize goals and objectives attainment and to minimize lost time and effort. It forces thinking about the business and technical tools, techniques, and processes to employ before taking significant action. Finally, it "irons out" the business issues before the technical activities happen in an uncontrolled manner, making it costlier and more difficult to backup and regroup later on down the life cycle.

PLANNING A YEAR 2000 PROJECT

With a complete SOW, a solid baseline exists to develop plans. These plans define in greater detail the tasks to perform and their sequence of execution. It consists of these six elements:

- Work breakdown structure
- Time estimates
- Schedules
- Resource allocation
- Cost calculation
- Risk management

Although these elements can exist simultaneously, they are easier to understand when discussed separately.

Work Breakdown Structure

Known also as the WBS, it is a top-down, hierarchical listing of tasks that is organized according to "deliverables" or "phases" or both.

For a Year 2000 project, it might be best to structure the WBS according to these major phases:

- Assessment
- Analysis
- Modification
- Conversion and migration
- Validation and testing
- Implementation

Assessment. The assessment phase involves acquiring a solid understanding of the existing environment and the effect Year 2000 changes will have on it. The two basic deliverables from the assessment phase are the description of the current environment and an impact analysis.

The description of the current environment includes tasks like:

- Conduct inventory at the PC, minicomputer, and mainframe levels.
- Identify source code.
- Identify run books and copy books.
- Identify databases.
- Identify reports.
- Identify screens.
- Determine existing capacity needs.

The impact analysis includes:

- Identify the most important applications affected.
- Identify which applications to reengineer or replace.
- Assess the cost and size of the changes.
- Determine the business and technical risks and their priorities.
- Evaluate the operational processes most affected.

Analysis. The analysis phase entails expanding on the details addressed in the impact study. The major deliverable is a requirements and specifications document that describes exactly what is affected and what must be done. The document includes:

- Locate date occurrences in specific source code modules.
- Determine which screen fields to change in an application.
- Determine which data files to modify.
- Identify the impact to job scheduling and report distribution procedures.

- Identify the impact to vendor products, such as storage management systems.
- Identify which source code programs and applications are and are not changeable.
- Identify which reports to modify.
- Determine which documents to update.
- Identify security issues.
- Determine tools to use.
- Coordinate with vendors.

Modification. The modification phase involves making the necessary changes. The major deliverables are the changes to the items identified in the analysis phase, which includes:

- Modify source code programs.
- Update run books and copy books.
- Revise date field in screens.
- Modify data files.
- Update the outlay of reports.
- Modify source code to enable interfaces among system components.
- Modify system logic.
- Establish configuration management and change control.

Conversion and Testing for the Year 2000. The conversion and testing phases are critical. According to the Gartner Group, it may take up half the effort and cost of handling the Year 2000 problem. The major deliverables are conversion and testing. It includes:

- Convert old source code to the new or modified source code.
- Convert data into the new format for processing.
- Upgrade hardware and software.

Testing involves performing tasks like:

- Devise a testing strategy (e.g., regression and aging testing).
- Develop a test plan (e.g., test scripts and performance criteria).
- Create test data sets.
- Identify verification and validation criteria to use.
- Conduct unit testing (e.g., conversion of data and code execution).
- Conduct system testing (e.g., ensuring no corruption of data streams).

Implementation. The implementation phase involves moving the new or modified programs and data into production. The major deliverable is an implementation plan that includes:

- Assign applications and databases go into production first, giving preference to mission critical ones.

27

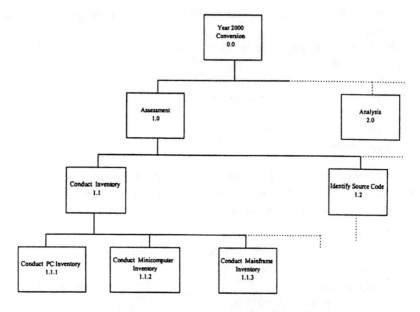

Exhibit 2. Work Breakdown Structure Graph

- Determine the best approach to redeploy the new applications and databases (e.g., parallel implementation).
- Conduct training for the user community.

Work Breakdown Structure Components. Often the work breakdown structure is displayed graphically in a hierarchical manner (see Exhibit 2). The hierarchy reflects a top-down organization, from general (i.e., product or subproduct) to specific (i.e., tasks to build the product or subproduct).

Time Estimates

After tasks have been identified, the next step is to estimate the time to complete them. Estimating time requires looking at several variables (e.g., resource availability, expertise, and complexity) and using that information to calculate the total time, usually in hours and then converted to flow time, to complete it. The three-point estimating technique is the best approach to determine the amount of time to complete a task and it includes these three variables: most optimistic, most likely, and most pessimistic. The most optimistic is the ideal time it would take if everything was perfect. The most likely time is the time that it should usually take under "normal" conditions. The most pessimistic time is the amount it would take under the worst conditions. The figures are then calculated to determine an expected time to complete a task. The calculated time is converted into eight hour units or whatever ever unit desired.

28

Estimating time for tasks on Year 2000 projects should be easier than for unprecedented development projects. The reason is that an understanding of the current systems to modify should exist (if well-documented and under configuration management). Other specific factors to consider when estimating are business and technical constraints (e.g., proximity to the year 2000 and complexity of legacy code, respectively), as well as the availability of expertise in legacy technology.

Risk Assessment

One of the first things prior to developing a schedule is to determine the major priorities of the project. Risk assessment enables doing that by identifying what is and is not important. It involves identifying the components of the system and its risks and ranking both accordingly. Such information presents a better idea of the importance of tasks vis-à-vis one another. Management can then decide whether to modify, reengineer, or replace specific systems. Within applications themselves, risk assessment is just as important for identifying which data, programs, reports, documentation, and interfaces are critical vis-à-vis one another.

Schedules

With the tasks identified, the hours and durations developed, and the priorities established, the next step is tying the tasks together into a logical framework to follow. This framework is a network diagram that shows the dependencies between tasks (see Exhibit 3). It also tells which tasks have float, or the time to slide, before impacting significant dates. Tasks having little or no float represent tasks on the critical path; such tasks cannot slide or because that will impact the project end date. As time approaches the year 2000, the schedule must be compressed, thereby increasing the likelihood of sliding tasks and impacting the project end date.

Resource Allocation

After developing a "straw horse" schedule, resource allocation is the next step. During this step, resources are assigned to balance the need for a realistic schedule with resource availability. Project managers can generate histograms to determine which resources will be overused and which ones will not be fully utilized. Ideally, project managers want a smooth histogram.

On a Year 2000 project, resource allocation involves sharing people on tasks requiring legacy system expertise, deciding the tools (e.g., object-oriented COBOL) to use on specific tasks, and determining the tasks to outsource, if necessary. To generate a sense of responsibility and immediacy to the Year 2000 topic, programmers and other participants should be assigned to tasks in a way that generates a sense of responsibility for

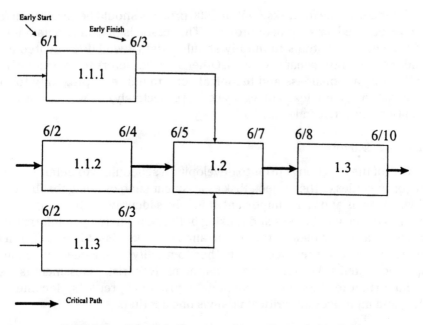

Exhibit 3.   Schedule Framework as a Network Diagram

replacing or updating full applications or categories of related applications (see Exhibit 4).

Calculation

With a leveled histogram, project managers can determine project costs. The key question is: does the schedule allow accomplishing milestone dates within the available budget? If the answer is yes, no revision to the schedule or assignments are necessary. If the answer is no, changes to the schedule or resource assignments must occur. These changes may involve reassigning people, changing schedule logic, and streamlining processes.

Exhibit 4.   Task Table

Tasks	Person	Lopez	Jones	Chen	Ackers
Conduct inventory at mainframe level		Lead	X		X
Conduct inventory at PC level		X	Lead		
Conduct inventory at minicomputer level		X		Lead	
Identify source code		Lead			X
Identify data bases		Lead		X	

The average cost of COBOL programmers is from $55 to $65 per hour, according to some experts. As the year 2000 approaches, this cost will likely increase. It is also likely that as tools become available (e.g., object-oriented COBOL) their tool costs will increase. It is imperative, therefore, that project managers strive to maximize productivity and minimize waste, particularly as the Year 2000 gets closer.

ORGANIZING

Although planning is an essential process and a major part of project management, it is not the only process. Organizing, too, is important. It involves establishing an infrastructure to maximize efficiency and effectiveness. Three principal components entail:

- Team structure
- Documentation
- Meetings

Team structure. Team structure involves identifying a "pecking order" that clarifies roles, responsibilities, and reporting relationships. Developing and publishing organization charts and responsibility matrices are common ways of establishing and building a team structure. Because the Year 2000 problem affects more than standalone systems, it is important that the team structure is cross-functional. This ensures that all affected parties can provide input and, consequently, obtain a sense of ownership.

Documentation. Documentation covers both technical and business materials. Some common documentation include architecture diagrams, procedures, user manuals, source code listings, work flows, and memorandums. Some items may go into a project library, project history files, or project manual, or perhaps all three; especially applicable to Year 2000 projects are process models and architecture diagrams for affected programs and databases.

Meetings. Meetings include setting up three basic types: status review, checkpoint review, and staff. Status review meetings are regularly held to collect information on tasks and major deliverables. Checkpoint review meetings are held at the completion of a major deliverable or upon reaching a milestone date in the schedule. Its objectives are to determine any lessons learned and whether to proceed. Status review meetings are held to regularly share information and experiences. Attendance at the meeting should be highly cross-functional to ensure adequate participation and coverage of the main issues. User involvement is absolutely essential to gain their acceptance of modifications.

CONTROLLING A YEAR 2000 PROJECT

Controlling involves ensuring the project proceeds cost-effectively according to plans. It entails:

- Status collection and assessment
- Change control
- Corrective action

Status Collection and Assessment. On Year 2000 projects, status collection and assessment requires looking at business and technical aspects. Regarding business aspects, for example, it requires collecting and assessing data on schedule performance. Regarding technical issues, for example, it requires collecting and assessing data about the quality of changes to databases and applications.

Change Control. Change control involves capturing, analyzing, and evaluating changes to technical and schedule baselines. It is not only important for the schedule. Changing and recording modifications to data files and date fields in applications also require some change control or configuration management whether in staging or production.

Corrective Action. Corrective action entails taking necessary action to ensure that project goals and objectives are accomplished according to business and technical plans; if not, replanning should occur. For Year 2000 projects, corrective action is especially important when verification and validation of changes to databases and applications have negative results.

CLOSURE

Closure encompasses compiling data, converting data into information, and providing a smooth transition from product development to implementation. The idea behind closure is to develop lessons learned and to ensure that nothing is overlooked as the project concludes. Specific closure activities include identifying what did and did not go well; ensuring people and other resources were managed released efficiently; and conducting reviews to ensure that the goals stated in the SOW were satisfied.

It is especially important for Year 2000 projects to capture lessons learned, particularly for the first application. Subsequent Year 2000 projects can avoid repeating mistakes. Lessons learned should address business (e.g., time availability for project completion) and technical (e.g., testing) issues. Reviews of Year 2000 projects can prove invaluable for capturing lessons learned and identifying oversights and other shortcomings that occurred, particularly to applications, source code, databases, screens, and reports. Releasing maintenance programmers can also prove challenging because as the tasks conclude inactivity begins, thereby losing precious time to work on another Year 2000 project.

CONCLUSION

Historically, the end of a century has often been portrayed as something negative, such as the end of the world coming. It seems that the IS world is looking upon the year 2000 as something even worse than that — a systems maintenance task. As long as that misconception holds, it could be the end of the world for a systems development manager's job. The year 2000 is a systems project and it should be managed as a project by using the following six basic six processes:

- Leading
- Defining
- Planning
- Organizing
- Controlling
- Closure

By applying these six processes to the year 2000, systems development managers will be better able to tackle this massive project because they benefit it in the following ways:

- They help to determine the magnitude of the effort as well as its business and technical impacts.
- They help to identify priorities as well as assess and manage risks.
- They help to identify the most appropriate route to pursue (e.g., reengineer or modify the application or system).
- They help in selecting the appropriate technical and business tools and techniques.
- They help to determine the cost of addressing the Year 2000 problem.

Chapter I-4
Managing the Risks of Outsourcing Systems Development

Ken Doughty and Franke Grieco

THE INFORMATION TECHNOLOGY (IT) OUTSOURCING STRATEGY is usually associated with the contracting out of an organization's entire Information Services (IS) function to an external service provider. There are a number of organizations that are not outsourcing the whole IT function, but only those functions considered to be not "core" competencies. System development is a function often considered to be non-core and therefore outsourced.

Arguably, the decision to outsource should be based on a detailed analysis of the organization's Strategic IT Plan and Corporate Plan. From this analysis it can be determined whether outsourcing conforms with the organization's strategic direction or if it is required to facilitate the organization's IT strategies. The main arguments for outsourcing are the minimization of the risks associated with system development and the maximization of return on investment in information technology (more value for money). Therefore, outsourcing the system development function is considered by many a risk reduction and cost minimization strategy.

The more sobering argument is that outsourcing system development does not eliminate the risks associated with it. However, it transfers some risks to the contractor and exposes the outsourcing organization to new risks.

The factors that may contribute to an outsourcing decision include:

- The development of the Strategic IT Plan, resulting in identification of the system development function as no longer being a "core competency"
- The dramatic increase in the availability of "off-the-shelf" parameter-driven software (e.g., SAP, Oracle Financials, People Soft, BAAN, MAN/MAN/X)

0-8493-9979-3/99/$0.00+$.50
© 1999 by CRC Press LLC

- Previous system development experience by the organization (especially failures)
- Access to "best practice" software development organizations (ISO9000 certification)
- Lack of credibility in the organization's Information Systems (IS) Department
- Accelerated realization of reengineering benefits
- The rising cost of in-house system development
- Reduction in and better control of system development costs
- Lack of adequate infrastructure or resources and skills to develop systems to meet the organization's requirements on time and within budget
- The opportunity to free the organizations resources for other purposes
- Business venture with developers in marketing a product

Executive management are demanding that systems development managers, as part of their mandate, ensure that the risks associated with system development are being minimized. To facilitate this the Information Systems Audit and Control Association (ISACA) recently released a document titled "Control Objectives for Information and Related Technology (COBiT)."[1] This document replaces the Control Objectives, which was the ISACA standard for auditing information technology. COBiT has been developed with a business orientation as the main theme and designed not only to be utilized by auditors, but also, and more importantly, as a comprehensive checklist for business process owners.

COBiT provides a framework for ensuring that an organization has a strong internal control environment for its information technology business processes. COBiT Section Planning and Organization PO9–Assess Risks states that:

> Control over the IT process of assessing risk that satisfies the business requirement of ensuring the achievement of IT objectives and responding to threats to the provision of IT services is enabled by the organization engaging itself in IT risk-identification and impact analysis, and taking cost-effective measures to mitigate risks....

COBiT clearly details the requirement for reviewing the risk management of any information technology project, including systems development. However, limited audit resources and other business related priorities can restrict the ability to adequately cover the development process (i.e., when systems development is outsourced). Therefore, a framework is required to ensure compliance with the professional association's requirements and assists the organization in the risk management of its system development. This includes managing the risks associated with outsourcing system development.

This chapter defines risk management and how it should be applied to system development. Additionally, a detailed risk model and IS audit approach for the risk management of outsourcing software development, utilizing COBiT, is demonstrated.

The model discussed in this chapter provides a control approach that identifies system development risk, risk factors, risk rating, and risk reduction strategies in outsourcing the system development process.

RISK MANAGEMENT

To develop the COBiT approach and its application requires a sound understanding of risk management concepts. Ideally, a systems development manager should use a proven and documented methodology in the application of risk management techniques. For example, the Australian/New Zealand Standard AS4360[2] defines the first generic standard on risk management in the world. The standard defines the following terms:

Risk. The chance of something happening that will have an impact upon objectives. It is measured in terms of likelihood and consequences.

Risk Management. The systematic application of management policies, procedures, and practices to the tasks of identifying, analyzing, assessing, treating, and monitoring risk.

Risk Treatment. The selection and implementation of appropriate options for dealing with risk.

The standard also provides guidelines in its appendices for the following areas:

- Application of Risk Management
- Steps in Developing and Implementing a Risk Management Program
- Generic Sources of Risk and Their Areas of Impact
- Examples of Risk Definition and Classification
- Examples of Quantitative Risk Expressions
- Risk Management Documentation
- Identifying Options of Risk Treatment

Systems development managers can utilize this standard not only in gaining a sound understanding of the risk management concepts, but also in its application.

Systems development managers should also be aware of the other tangible risks associated with project management that may contribute to the failure of the outsourcing software development project. The following risks are project risks irrespective of whether outsourcing is utilized or not; they are included here to provide a checklist of issues to consider during the contract negotiation phase with the preferred outsourcing contractor and during the planning for, and initial setup of any project.

1. Failure to have a clear business objective for the project that is well understood by all participants and stakeholders in the project.
2. Having too large a scope for the project or not having the scope of the project clearly defined.
3. Ineffective project management, which is demonstrated through factors such as:
   - Either no or poor project management methodology or procedures
   - No project management charter or unclear specifying of the role, duties, and responsibilities of the project manager or project team members
   - Multiple project managers, with responsibility for the management of the project not clearly defined
   - Lack of a formal, and regularly updated, project plan
   - Failure to adhere to the project plan
   - The project plan not covering all stages of the project from its initiation through to the postimplementation review
   - Irregular project progress reporting or progress reporting that imparts little real information to the project sponsor and steering committee
   - Authority of the project manager may be implied rather than stated and communicated to all the stakeholders by executive management
   - Project team members may be working independently without any overall coordination, resulting in wasted resources and contributing to the failure of the project
   - Project reporting lines may either be not established, not clear or be to inappropriate management
   - Project monitoring systems may not have been established or developed at the outset of the project
   - Monitoring standards or benchmarks to measure the performance of project management may not be established or may be inappropriate
   - Project reports may not be sufficiently detailed to assist executive management to monitor the progress of the project in terms of work completed against milestones and budgets
   - Insufficient knowledge of project management software to effectively use the software
4. Not having a clearly defined project structure:
   - No clearly defined sponsor/owner for the project at the senior management level
   - Not having the right mix of IT and user staff (stakeholders) on the project team
   - Project team members not having appropriate levels of technical skills and experience

5. The Project Manager and or project team may not have the skills or training to undertake the role. Often the Project Manager is user appointed because he "knows" the current system.
6. Long lead times between project deliverables
7. Uncontrolled or high levels of requests for modifications to the design specifications during the development and implementation phases of the project
8. Failure to control the change management aspects of the project such as:
   - Maintaining user involvement and commitment
   - Redesign of business processes and work practices
   - Changes in the organization structure
   - Training
   - Post implementation support

SYSTEM DEVELOPMENT METHODOLOGY

For the purposes of this chapter it is assumed that the executive management of the organization has made a strategic decision that system development is no longer a core competency. This decision was based on a detailed analysis in developing the organization's strategic IT model.

The strategic IT plan details the IS department's strategic direction from being a system developer and maintenance provider to adopting a "caretaker role" with regard to the organization's current legacy systems. This means that system development of new systems, including the purchase of off-the-shelf software solutions, will be outsourced.

It is important that the organization's executive management "manage" this change in strategic direction from internal system development to outsourced development. A key point to note is: an organization's processes have a greater influence on the culture of the organization than behavior. Therefore, a competent change management process must be undertaken to ensure that there is a cultural and business change that will be accepted by the organization as a whole. If the executive management does not manage the process competently, it may result in the rejection of the outsourcing concept and also cause dysfunctional activities by stakeholders (e.g., System Owners, Users, and the IS department).

Today, systems development methodologies address the issue of risk management, whereas previously risk management in system development was often implied in the process rather than a project task item that had to be addressed, actioned, and signed off. Previously IS management was recommending to executive management to develop or redevelop systems without the support of a risk analysis being undertaken. This exposed the organization to unidentified and unmanaged risk that may have lead to business objectives not being attained.

System development methodologies, for example, APT3 address risk management in the following terms:

Project Initiation

- Responsibilities of all parties involved in the project.
- Deliverables and delivery schedule.
- Acceptance criteria.
- Risk, problem, and change management.
- Standards and procedures to be used.

Identify System Risks. Document the risks at the system level. These risks include loss of systems and/or data caused by hardware malfunctions, human errors, malicious damage, fraud, viruses, unauthorized use, hacking, theft or sabotage.

Assess Probability of Risk Occurring. Examine each identified risk and estimate the potential for its occurrence.

Determine the compounded probability of risks identified occurring. (For example, if there are 200 risks with a possible 1 in 100 chance of occurrence per annum, then there is a probability of 2 risks per annum.)

Assess Risks

- Identify the critical system consequences of each of the risks occurring and place monetary values on them.
- Assess strategic risks and consequences for the business.
- Review the results of the exercise with management and rank the risks.
- Document damage potential, the costs associated with the occurrence of the risks and the overall probability.
- Document the risk management strategies and the likely costs.

Review Current Risk Management Processes

- For each risk, identify the countermeasures currently in place and their annual costs.
- Examine each risk and estimate its probability.
- Examine the effectiveness of the countermeasures.
- Document the current countermeasures, their costs, the risk probability, and the potential costs to the organization.

Determine Overall Risk Management Strategies. Document potential risk management techniques that could be used in place of current practices.

Systems development managers should ensure that the organization's system development methodology addresses not only the risk management process, but also the consistent application of the process throughout the system development life cycle. Further, they have to ensure that the results of the Risk Analysis is complete and accurate and they are to be conveyed to the organization's executive management before the outsourcing of System Development is approved.

MANAGING RISK

Inadequate risk assessment and management may lead to software development projects going "off-the-rails" due to unidentified risks eventuating and being poorly managed. The associated extra costs and time escalations can:

- Detrimentally impact the viability of a software development project
- Lead to failure in achieving strategic business objectives
- In a worst case scenario cause an organization to go out of business

The systems development manager can assist the organization in developing a risk framework by utilizing the COBiT[1] PO9 "Assess Risk Guidelines. By adopting and appropriately applying the COBiT PO9 Guidelines, the systems development manager ensures that a comprehensive coverage of the risks associated with outsourcing software development.

A risk assessment framework should be an intrinsic part of a business continuity plan. The framework would require an assessment of risks that could impact on the organization reaching its business objectives on a regular basis. The assessment should also identify the residual risk (the risk the organization s management is willing to accept). Ideally, it should provide risk assessments for the organization as a whole and for the separate processes including major projects.

The COBiT PO9 Assess Risk Guideline refers to a number of control objectives that need to be addressed in its application. The control objectives are:

1. Business Risk Assessment
2. Risk Assessment Approach
3. Risk Identification
4. Risk Measurement
5. Risk Action Plan
6. Risk Acceptance

Business Risk Assessment

The organization's management needs to identify its role in contributing to the organization's objectives, policies, and strategies when making decisions about risk. These must be clearly understood as they help to define the criteria as to whether a risk is acceptable or not, and the basis of control.

41

COBiT states that management should establish a systematic risk assessment framework.

The organization needs to have policies and standards in place to provide guidance to the staff responsible for risk management. Responsible staff need to be aware of the instances where risk assessment needs to occur and the desirable criteria that should be used.

For example, the size (i.e., monetarily, time frame, impact on the business) a project must be for a risk assessment to be mandatory. Guidelines for the context that should be used, (e.g., strategic context, organizational context or project/process context). In some instances, it may be necessary to assess risk at both the global and project levels).

Risk-Assessment Approach

To ensure a consistent and acceptable standard of risk assessment an approved approach needs to be in place. It should outline the process for determining the scope, boundaries, methodology, responsibilities, and required skills.

There has been a considerable amount of research performed in the area of risk management and assessment. Therefore, management does not need to reinvent the wheel in establishing an approach. In many instances, management only needs to determine what approach is best suited for the business. For example, in developing a risk measurement approach the Australian/New Zealand Standard AS/NZS 4360:1995 "Risk Management" can be utilized.

Exhibit 1 outlines the steps to be followed in developing the risk action plan template for outsourced system acquisition/development projects. It is at a high level and simply follows the COBiT control objective steps.

The AS/NZS 4360:1995 "Risk Management" standard was used as the basis for developing the risk action plan template found later in this chapter. A matrix approach was utilized, as shown in Exhibit 2.

Exhibit 3 is an example extracted from the template.

Risk Identification

There are number of methods of identifying risks, for example:

- Surveys, questionnaires, interviews
- Workshops, discussion groups
- Past history failure analysis
- S.W.O.T analysis
- Documentation and analysis of flows (data, physical etc.)
- Modeling
- Analysis of local and overseas experiences, etc.

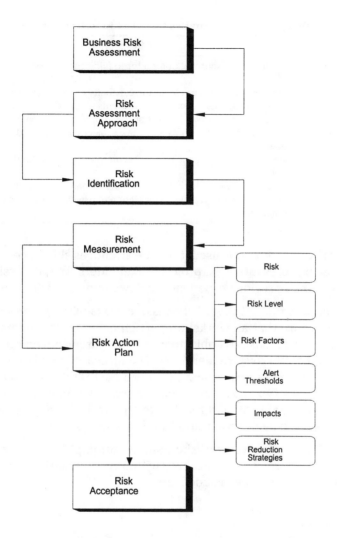

Exhibit 1. IS Risk Approach.

Exhibit 2. Excerpt from the Risk Action Plan Template

Title	Description
Risk	The risk being addressed.
Risk level	A measure of likelihood and seriousness of a risk's impact. It is calculated using the A/NZS 4360 Risk Management Standard.
Risk factors	A list of the elements that collectively contribute to the risk.
Alert thresholds	The symptoms or events that indicate the risk is likely to occur.
Impacts	The specific effects if the risk occurs.
Risk treatments	The strategies that can be implemented to minimize the likelihood or impact of the risk.

Exhibit 3.   An Example Extracted from the Risk Action Plan Template

Title	Description
Risk	Inability of Outsourcing Contractor to fulfill contract requirements
Risk level	H (High)
Risk factors	Outsourcing Contractor loses the capability to continue satisfying contract requirements due to excessive demands placed on its resources (e.g., Customer base grows too fast or the Company loses key resources).
Alert thresholds	Expanding client base. (Winning new project contracts and soliciting large new clients.)
Impacts	The organization's requirements become low priorities for the Outsourcing Contractor.
Risk treatment	Monitor contract schedule/contract performance. Link incremental payments with successful completion of project milestones within a set timeframe.

If a workshop method is used, then the attendees should consist of the project team representatives, project stakeholders, and, if possible, individuals who had previous experience in developing a risk framework.

The auditor's role in the workshop is one of a facilitator. The facilitator's role is to ensure that all workshop participants clearly understand the project's strategic business objectives, and requirements and that a comprehensive list of risks are identified. The attached template provides a good basis for the list. However, it is only a basis and not a complete list suited for every type of outsourced system development project. The risks, risk measurement, and risk treatments will vary depending on the type of project, type of organization, and type of industry.

The risk identification workshop should attempt to identify as many risks associated with the project both within and outside the control of the organization. Areas to be included are

- Threats
- Vulnerabilities
- Strategic directions
- Relationships

Risk Measurement

This risk measurement phase requires the analysis of the likelihood and consequences of each risk identified. The guidelines provided by AS 4360 suggest that the risk level is a function of the likelihood of a risk occurring and the possible impact of the risk if it eventuates. Once the likelihood and impact of a risk are estimated the results are incorporated into a matrix to give the final risk level a value.

The rankings for the likelihood of a risk occurring are detailed in Exhibit 4.

Exhibit 4. A Ranking of the Likelihood of a Risk Occurring

Level	Description	Description
A	Almost certain	The event is expected to occur in most circumstances.
B	Likely	The event will probably occur in most circumstances.
C	Moderate	The event should occur at some time.
D	Unlikely	The event could occur at some time.
E	Rare	The event may occur only in exceptional circumstances.

Exhibit 5. An Example of Likely Events

Level	Description	Description
A	Almost certain	Unauthorized entry through use of poor passwords.
B	Likely	Corruption of backup media due to poor storage conditions
C	Moderate	Theft of equipment due to visitors being unsupervised.
D	Unlikely	Flooding on the top floor of a high rise building.
E	Rare	Physical damage to facilities due to terrorist attack.

Exhibit 6. Ranking of the Consequences of a Risk Occurring

Level	Description	Description
1	Insignificant	Low financial loss; minimal reduction in customer service, staff morale, or operational efficiency; minor impact on cash flow or ability to plan business activities; no or low political impact.
2	Minor	Medium financial loss; medium reduction in customer service, staff morale, or operational efficiency; medium impact on cash flow or ability to plan business activities; medium political impact.
3	Moderate	High financial loss; high reduction in customer service, staff morale, or operational efficiency; high impact on cash flow or ability to plan business activities; high political impact.
4	Major	Major financial loss; major reduction in customer service, staff morale, or operational efficiency; major impact on cash flow or ability to plan business activities; major political impact.
5	Catastrophic	Total financial loss; huge reduction in customer service, staff morale, or operational efficiency; catastrophic impact on cash flow or ability to plan business activities; total political impact.

Exhibit 5 is an example of likely events.

The rankings for magnitude/impact of consequences if a risk occurs are described in Exhibit 6.

Exhibit 7 exemplifies the different categories of risk impact.

Combining the estimated rankings for likelihood and impact from the above tables into another matrix provides a measurement of risk. The final risk measurement rankings are depicted in Exhibit 8.

Exhibit 7. Categories of Risk Impact

Level	Description	Description
1	Insignificant	Nonstakeholders protesting their lack of involvement in the project.
2	Minor	High staff turnover in project teams requiring an increase in training expenditure and lost productive time due to new project team members familiarizing themselves with the project requirements.
3	Moderate	Failure to reach milestones within planned time frame causing overruns in expenditure and key strategic objectives not being achieved
4	Major	Failure of a major IT project to provide the expected results (i.e., the project not yielding expected returns on investment).
5	Catastrophic	Halfway through the project the outsourcing contractor goes into receivership, bringing the project to a halt until all legal issues are resolved and expertise and resources are again organized to continue the project.

Exhibit 8. Measurements of Risk

	Consequences				
Likelihood	Insignificant 1	Minor 2	Moderate 3	Major 4	Catastrophic 5
A (almost certain)	S	S	H	H	H
B (likely)	M	S	S	H	H
C (moderate)	L	M	S	H	H
D (unlikely)	L	L	M	S	H
E (rare)	L	L	M	S	S

H = High risk: detailed research and management planning required at senior levels
S = Significant risk: senior management attention needed.
M = Moderate risk: management responsibility must be specified.
L = Low risk: manage by routine procedures.

Therefore, if a risk is likely to occur and the possible impacts are considered major, then the risk level is regarded as High (H).

Risk Action Plan

In developing a risk action plan the following categories should be covered.

Risk Factors. Risk factors are the basic elements that collectively contribute to the risk. These can be identified, for each risk, during the risk identification phase (e.g., during the workshop).

For example, Risk — the selected outsourced software developer may lose the ability to satisfy its contractual obligations.

The risk factors that may contribute to this risk include:

- Financial difficulties
- Takeover by another company, broken up, and sold off
- Change in the outsourced software developer's strategic direction
- Outsourced software developer decides that there are no longer any benefits to be obtained in continuing with the outsourcing contract arrangement

Alert Thresholds. Alert thresholds, which include events or trends that indicate the probability of a risk occurring, is becoming more likely.

For example, for the risk identified above, rumors of cash flow problems could be an indication of financial difficulties. A ratio analysis of the outsourced software developer's financial statements could indicate possible financial difficulties.

Impacts. The impacts represent the likely result if a risk eventuates.

For the risk identified above, if the outsourced software developer is bankrupted, then the organization has the task of picking up the pieces (i.e., continuing the software development of the strategic business system). This would require either building in-house teams to continue with the project or finding another suitable contractor. Either way the organization would incur losses in time and money.

Risk Treatments/Risk Action Plan. The risk treatments are risk management strategies for minimizing the likelihood of occurrence or the impact on the organization if the risk eventuates.

For example, to minimize the impact of the outsourcing contractor going into liquidation, the outsourcing firm can ensure that an escrow agreement is entered into by all relevant parties. This will provide the outsourcing firm with access to all source code and documentation if such an event occurs.

Alternatively, the outsourcing firm could foster a partnership working relationship. Depending on how critical the system development is, it could provide financial support to the outsourcing contractor, if required.

Risk Acceptance

Once the risk management strategies have been identified, a number of steps are required.

The first being an identification of what risks executive management are prepared to accept (i.e., residual risk). The residual risks are usually those events that have a very low likelihood of occurrence or very low material impact. For example, there is a very low likelihood that the earth will be struck by asteroid one cubic kilometer in size and the impact on the operations of the organization if the petty cash float of $20.00 being stolen is very low.

The remainder of the risks need to be addressed. The implementation of the relevant risk strategies need to planned and costed. If viable (i.e., cost-effective), then the strategies should be implemented. However, if not, alternative strategies need to be developed.

Most important, the responsibility for the implementation of the risk reduction strategies need to be assigned to a manager with the appropriate skills, commitment, and authority.

USING THE TEMPLATE

The successful contractor's responsibilities include:

- The selection of the development tools
- The development of a fully functional system that meets the user's requirements and complies with the strategic IT architecture
- The effective management of the change management process
- The acquisition and installation of the hardware platform and operating system

The hardware and software maintenance was not included within the scope of the development project.

The following is a list of definitions relevant to the template (see Exhibit 9).

- **Developer:** The organization acquiring the product or service
- **Outsourcing Contractor:** The prime contractor, the organization responsible for delivering the product or service
- **Application Developer:** The organization providing the skill and resources to design the application, write the code, and build the database
- **Hardware Provider:** The organization that will provide the computer equipment
- **DBMS Provider:** The organization that provides the database development products
- **Change Management:** The organization responsible for the change
- **Contractor:** Management required to make the implementation of the new system a success
- **Middleware Provider:** The organization that provides the software tool products for the development of the application

1. COBiT — Control Objectives for Information and Related Technology (COBiT); Systems Audit and Control Association (ISACA) — 1996.
2. AS4360 — Risk Management — Standards Association of Australia.
3. APT — APT Methodology, EXECOM, Perth, Western Australia, 1993.

Exhibit 9. The Risk Audit Assessment Template

Risk	Risk Level	Risk Factors	Alert Thresholds	Impact	Risk Treatment
Inability of Outsourcing Contractor to fulfill contract requirements.	H	Outsourcing Contractor loses the capability to continue adequately satisfying contract requirements due to excessive demands placed on its resources (e.g., Customer base grows too fast or the Company loses key resources).	Expanding client base. (Winning new projects and soliciting new customers.)	The organization's requirements become low priorities for the Outsourcing Contractor.	Monitor schedule/contract performance. Monitor acceptance criteria compliance. Prioritize the Developer business with vendor.
		Outsourcing Contractor is no longer commercially viable (e.g., Goes into receivership or liquidation.)	Analysis of financial performance indicates that Outsourcing Contractor will go or goes into receivership.	Restricted access to hardware, source code, and documentation, which has been paid for but is still in the possession of the contractor.	Ensure that the Developer has the ability to take over or acquire critical Outsourcing Contractor's resources in order to keep the project going.
		Outsourcing Contractor changes ownership. The new owners break up and sell off the Contractor's assets and it ceases to exist. The new owner may take action that would relinquish its contractual obligations to the Developer.	News of takeover threats by a corporate raider.	Loss of contractor for system development, maintenance, support, and enhancement	Contract condition that contractor supplied equipment becomes the Developer property on payment and that transfer of ownership is confirmed by the subcontractor. View software acquisition documentation to determine extent of license/copyright ownership by Outsourcing Contractor to see if it may have a detrimental effect.

Exhibit 9 (Continued).   The Risk Audit Assessment Template

Risk	Risk Level	Risk Factors	Alert Thresholds	Impact	Risk Treatment
		Outsourcing Contractor is or becomes fundamentally incapable of delivering (e.g, they lied about their ability).	Deliverables are constantly not met.	Incur costs associated with finding replacement contractors or organizing resources internally.	Contract condition requiring contractor to provide certified financial information on a regular basis for the purposes of evaluating financial performance.
				If Outsourcing Contractor goes into receivership ownership of hardware and software license may revert to subcontractors (This is sometimes a contract condition between prime contractors and subcontractors).	Ensure that Outsourcing Contractor indemnifies the Developer over any action that may arise between Outsourcing Contractor and its subcontractors (e.g., Copyright ownership claims, etc.).
Risk of Outsourcing Contractor losing interest in meeting contractual obligations.	H	Outsourcing Contractor decides to change its strategic direction and no longer wishes to support, maintain, or enhance the product the Developer acquired.	Outsourcing Contractor is sold/taken over.	Loss of contractor for system development or diminished service.	Ensure that the Developer has the ability to veto the transfer of software copyright ownership to a third party (i.e., the Developer should have the ability to stop the sale of copyright ownership to a small unknown company). This should also apply to the transfer of support and service contracts.

Risk	Likelihood	Description	Consequence	Mitigation strategy
Risk of Outsourcing Contractor losing interest in meeting contractual obligations.	H	The product provided matures to a point that it would no longer be financially viable for the contractor to continue enhancing it.	Change in profile of contractor's client base.	Loss of contractor for system maintenance, support and enhancement or diminished service.
				Retender or complete project with internal resources.
				Details of personnel involved in developing and maintaining system.
				The Developer has access to Outsourcing Contractor's marketing strategy and market research material for assessment purposes.
				Ensure that the Developer has the ability to approve key personnel for the project including those employed by subcontractors as well as Outsourcing Contractor.
		The product fails in the marketplace and Outsourcing Contractor loses interest.	Sunset clause of facilities support/maintenance	Incur costs associated with finding replacement contractors or organizing resources internally.
				Ensure that the Developer has the ability to veto the transfer of software copyright ownership to a third party.
			Relationship deterioration between Developer and Contractor.	Loss of contractor for system development or diminished service.
				Ensure that contracts between Outsourcing Contractor and subcontractors are in place and the Developer has access to the contracts.

Exhibit 9 (Continued). The Risk Audit Assessment Template

Risk	Risk Level	Risk Factors	Alert Thresholds	Impact	Risk Treatment
Risk of Outsourcing Contractor losing interest in meeting contractual obligations.					Outsourcing Contractor should commit to providing support for the product for a minimum of five years. (The Developer should not be committed to acquiring Outsourcing Contractor's support for more than one year at a time.) Performance guarantees from contractor signed by a guarantor. Ensure that the Developer has the ability to veto the transfer of software copyright ownership to a third party.
Risk of Application Developer losing capacity or interest for meeting contractual obligations.	H	Application Developer is no longer commercially viable (e.g., Goes into receivership.)	Analysis of financial performance indicates that Application Developer will go into receivership.	Time blowouts, increased costs and loss of expertise.	Outsourcing Contractor must have the ability to acquire ownership of source code copyright in the event that Application Developer go out of business. This should be evidenced by the Developer.

Risk Factor	L	Risk Event	Scenario	Consequence	Treatment
		Application Developer goes into receivership.		Increased costs in product maintenance and support.	Contract condition that permits the Developer unencumbered access to source code and related documentation if Outsourcing Contractor goes out of business.
		Change in management or ownership.	Application Developer decides to change its strategic direction and no longer wishes to support, maintain, or enhance the product.	Increased costs in maintenance and support and a possible loss of access to expertise.	Ensure that there are no legal restrictions preventing the Developer from employing key personnel that worked for the outsourcing contractor.
		Application Developer is sold/taken over.	Application Developer changes ownership. The new owners break up and sell off the Contractor's assets and it ceases to exist.		*(The above three treatments apply to all three risk factors listed in this section.)*
Risk of Hardware Provider losing capacity or interest for meeting contractual obligations.	L	Hardware Supplier goes into receivership.	Hardware Supplier is no longer commercially viable (e.g., Goes into receivership.)	Hardware no longer supported.	Provide support internally.
		Change in management or ownership.	Hardware Provider decides to change its strategic direction and no longer wishes to support, maintain or enhance the hardware the Developer acquired.	Increased costs in supporting and maintaining.	Port system to a new platform.
		Hardware Supplier is sold/taken over.	Hardware Provider changes ownership. The new owners break up and sell off the Contractor's assets and it ceases to exist.	Costs associated in porting to another platform.	Ensure that hardware satisfies open systems standards.

Exhibit 9 (Continued). The Risk Audit Assessment Template

Risk	Risk Level	Risk Factors	Alert Thresholds	Impact	Risk Treatment
				(The above three impacts may apply to all or some of the risk factors listed in this section.)	*(The above three treatments apply to all three risk factors listed in this section.)*
Risk of DBMS Provider losing capacity or interest for meeting contractual obligations.	L	DBMS Provider is no longer commercially viable (e.g., Goes into receivership.)	DBMS Provider goes into receivership.	DBMS Provider no longer supported.	Port to another DBMS.
		DBMS Provider decides to change its strategic direction and no longer wishes to support, maintain or enhance the product the Developer acquired.	There is a change in management or ownership.	Costs associated in porting to another DBMS.	Ensure that DBMS satisfies open systems standards.
		DBMS Provider changes ownership. The new owners break up and sell off the Contractor's assets and it ceases to exist.	DBMS Provider is sold/taken over.	*(The above impacts may apply to all or some of the risk factors listed in this section.)*	*(The above treatments apply to all three risk factors listed in this section.)*
Risk of Change Management Contractor (Change Management Contractors) losing capacity or interest for meeting contractual obligations.	H	Change Management Contractor is no longer commercially viable (e.g., Goes into receivership.)	Change Management Contractor goes into receivership.	Time loss.	Find some one to replace Change Management Contractor.

Risk Factor		Cause	Event / Indicator	Impact	Treatment
Risk of Middleware Provider losing capacity or interest in meeting contractual obligations.	L	Change Management Contractor loses the capacity to provide.	Analysis of financial performance indicates that Change Management Contractor will go into receivership.	Time loss.	Perform change management function internally. Select a change management contractor with sound financial and performance backgrounds. *(The above treatments apply to all risk factors listed in this section.)*
		Middleware Provider is no longer commercially viable (e.g., Goes into receivership.)	Middleware Provider goes into receivership.	Middleware Provider product no longer supported.	Replace Middleware Provider with alternative product.
		Middleware Provider decides to change its strategic direction and no longer wishes to support, maintain or enhance the product the Developer acquired.	Change of management or ownership.	Cost of changing product.	Ensure that product satisfies open systems standards.
		Middleware Provider changes ownership. The new owners break up and sell off the Contractor's assets and it ceases to exist.	Middleware Provider is sold/taken over.	*(The above impacts may apply to all or some of the risk factors listed in this section.)*	*(The above treatments apply to all three risk factors listed in this section.)*
The risk of relationship deterioration between the Developer and Outsourcing Contractor.	H	A dispute between the Developer and Outsourcing Contractor.	A high degree of disputes/unresolved disputes.	Extended delivery times.	Ensure that relationship is built on basis of partnering not an adversarial contract. Neither party should be too restrictive in its demands or lack flexibility in accepting solutions.

Exhibit 9 (Continued). The Risk Audit Assessment Template

Risk	Risk Level	Risk Factors	Alert Thresholds	Impact	Risk Treatment
The risk of relationship deterioration between the Developer and Outsourcing Contractor.			Disputes can occur while trying to reach a compromise over a system functionality; payments; and product/service quality.	Cost overruns.	Good project planning can contribute to a healthy relationship between vendor and purchaser. The project plan should clearly stipulate: - The roles and responsibilities of all parties; - Who the key personnel are for both the Developer and Outsourcing Contractor; - Project time plan; - Channels of communication; - Risk management approach; and quality planning.
				Diminished deliverable quality.	Dispute resolution procedures in contract (i.e., escalation, arbitration, etc.). Nominate an independent mediator, agreeable to both parties, to decide on unresolved disputes.

Risk	Likelihood	Description	Consequence	Mitigation
The risk of having to pay for modifications to the application.	L	Outsourcing Contractor maintains that all modification requests are Developer specific. Therefore the Developer must pay. This may be the case early on in the project life as the Developer will be one of a few customers if not the only one.	Being billed by the contractor for any modifications requested.	Commitment from Outsourcing Contractor that they will provide software version support for at least 18 months for each release. To have access to support, the Developer should not be committed to upgrade each time there is a new release of the product.
			Cost overruns and disputes.	Hourly rates should be stipulated in a contract schedule to cover requested services that are outside the contract. Rate increases should be negotiated and specified in the contract.
				Ensure that there is a formal process for handling modification requests. The process should ensure that quotes are provided, in accordance with schedule rates, and that the request is formally approved by the Developer before Outsourcing Contractor performs any work on the request.
				Dispute resolution clause in contract.

Exhibit 9 (Continued).   The Risk Audit Assessment Template

Risk	Risk Level	Risk Factors	Alert Thresholds	Impact	Risk Treatment
The risk of having to pay for modifications to the application.					Nominate an independent arbitrator to decide on unresolved disputes.
					Contract conditions and monitoring.
The risk of there being misinterpretation of system specifications.	S	Outsourcing Contractor's interpretation of functional specifications may differ from the Developer's.	Disputes between the Developer and Outsourcing Contractor.	Cost overruns and disputes	Ensure that the specifications are adequately defined (use an accepted methodology, etc.)
			Outsourcing Contractor wishing to renegotiate Contract requirements.		Adequate planning and partnership fostering, as for previous risk, to ensure that issues never escalate to a dispute stage.
					Dispute resolution clause in contract.
					Nominate an independent arbitrator to decide on unresolved disputes.

Risk	S	Cause	Consequence	Treatment
Lack of control over deliverable quality.	S	Outsourcing Contractor loses its QA accreditation.	Lack of QA accreditation proof.	The Developer agent should be appointed to evaluate contractor quality assurance systems.
		Inadequate QA acceptance criteria is specified in the contract.	Constant failure of deliverables to meet design review or acceptance criteria.	The contract or project plan should detail quality requirements and acceptance standards.
		Lack of escape clauses in the Contract.	Diminished deliverable quality.	Acceptance criteria should be clearly defined and based on the detailed design specifications.
		Detailed design specifications are inadequate.		Payments should be tied to performance.
				The Contract should contain dispute resolution procedures.
				Contract condition that Outsourcing Contractor maintains its quality accreditation.
				Contract condition to rectify faults "bugs" in system that were not found during the course of reasonable testing.
				(The above treatments may apply to all risk factors listed in this section.)

Exhibit 9 (Continued). The Risk Audit Assessment Template

Risk	Risk Level	Risk Factors	Alert Thresholds	Impact	Risk Treatment
Product licenses restricting the Developer's use of facilities.	S	Changes in legal structure and relationships of the Developer entities.	Business Units become independent corporations. The Developer Units establishing one-stop shops or similar. The Developer extending its network through agents and other facilities. Separate the Developer Entities (Developer gets broken up into more than one Developer).	Facilities licenses restrain use of facilities by other entities. Business or organizational development opportunities constrained.	Contract condition that will allow for the Developer entities and agencies to utilize systems. Contract to indicate that the Developer does not pay for additional costs for extra site licenses or user licenses. Alternatively, the contract could contain formulae for calculating costs associated with obtaining site licenses and user licenses.
Ongoing availability of key contractor personnel (HR plan for key project personnel succession).	H	Outsourcing Contractor may have an inadequate staff training and replacement strategy. Outsourcing Contractor's knowledge base may be sensitive to staff loss.	High staff turnover for contractor. Inability of contractor to meet deadlines.	Time blowouts. Inability to obtain product support, etc.	Identify key resources and implement strategies to maintain their availability (e.g., Ensure that Outsourcing Contractor plan to train and maintain at least four people that are adequately familiar with the product).

Risk		Risk Factor	Consequence	Treatment
Risk of adequate performance criteria and KPIs not clearly specified in contract.	H	Inadequate system documentation maintained by Outsourcing Contractor.	Lack of Contractor accountability.	Outsourcing Contractor to provide information, on a regular basis, of their key project personnel detailing their skills, experience, and background.
				Ensure that the contract does not restrict the Developer from employing key staff that leave Outsourcing Contractor.
				(The above treatments may apply to all three risk factors listed in this section.)
		Inability to define KPIs.	Detrimental impact on deliverable quality.	Base KPIs on detailed system specifications.
		KPIs artificially set too high or too low.	Software deficiencies diminished data integrity.	Use industry standards for setting KPIs.
			(The above impact applies to both of the risk factors listed in this section.)	Expert assistance in defining KPIs.
				Mutually agreed KPIs.
			Disputes with Contractor.	Ability to modify KPIs during course of project.
				(The above treatments may apply to all risk factors listed in this section.)

Exhibit 9 (Continued). The Risk Audit Assessment Template

Risk	Risk Level	Risk Factors	Alert Thresholds	Impact	Risk Treatment
Viability of equity interests (funding the development but not owning the product).	S	No intellectual property rights.		No royalty streams for the Developer and potential loss of revenue. Competitors can easily negate any competitive advantage provided by the technology via acquisition.	Informed executive or policy decision on whether to partake in royalties or not. An affirmative decision could result in a long-term relationship between the developer and the outsourcing contractor.
No apparent risk sharing arrangement with contractor.	S	The contract price does not adequately account for the risks taken and the returns forgone by the Developer.		Contract price too high	Competitive tenders.
Outsourcing Contractor may demonstrate the product to prospective customers and use the Developer as a demonstration site.	M	The Developer becomes a Beta site.	Testing Beta releases of the product on a frequent basis.	Down time due to failure of Beta software.	Restrictions on Beta testing. Stringent testing before allowing any Beta versions into the Developer production environment.

Therefore, there is a risk that a business partnership agreement with the Outsourcing Contractor may cause too much disruption in the Developer.	There are frequent new releases of the product (every six months).	Too many visits from prospective customers. Staff complain that they cannot complete their own work due to customer visits.	Costs associated with staff time taken up demonstrating the product. Overtime costs associated with catching up on work backlogs.	Restrictions on product demonstrations. Contract condition indicating that liabilities to rest with Outsourcing Contractor for any costs or losses incurred by the Developer during testing or product demonstrations.
S Risk of inaction or delay in making decision on project supply contract.	Long periods for decisions to be made.	Evaluation and decision to appoint a contractor takes too long. Complaints received from tenderers.	Damage to the Developer Image. On cost factor added into tenders by any party tendering for jobs in the Developer. Tenders withdrawn. Tender price may be revised upward.	Streamline process for future decisions. Improve process for briefing tenderers.

Exhibit 9 (Continued). The Risk Audit Assessment Template

Risk	Risk Level	Risk Factors	Alert Thresholds	Impact	Risk Treatment
Risk of developing Project in-house.	H	The Developer not currently geared up for developing a system for project type project (inadequate internal skills base and resources).	No suitable Contractors.	Schedule and budget overruns.	Detailed performance measures for all contract deliverables.
			Inability to reach agreement with tenderers.	Requirements unsatisfied.	Detailed planning and an adequately skilled project team.
				High costs	Follow recognized methodology.
					QA and audit reviews.
					Employ or contract into the organization the required skill base and expertise.
					Performance based payment.
The risk of failure in the change management processes	H	System not meeting stakeholder expectations.	Inadequate stakeholder involvement or ownership.	Nonacceptance of the system	Ensure adequate stakeholder involvement and encourage ownership of system.
		System not being used to its fullest potential.	Poor promotion and selling of new system to users/stakeholders.		Monitoring processes.
		System considered a failure and a hindrance to business processes.			QA acceptance of change management.
		Decreased level of service.	Lack of adequate staff training and documentation.		Develop a change management plan that includes communication of issues to all stakeholders and training.

Risk	S	Consequences	Risk factors	Treatments
		No realized productivity or performance gains. Increase customer complaints.	Poor redeployment and retraining planning. Change Management Contractor becomes unavailable.	*(The above treatments may apply to all or some of the risk factors listed in this section.)*
Risk of overcontrol by the Developer.	S	Diminished quality in service and deliverables.	Relationship between the Developer and Contractor is not one of partnership but confrontational. The contract is too restrictive. The Developer's organizational culture is not conducive to a partnership with the Outsourcing Contractor. Too many groups established to review contractor progress and performance. Multiple project managers. No formal communication channels established between the Contractor and the Developer.	Obtain expert advice to ensure that the contract is not too restrictive. Ensure that undue pressure is not placed on the outsourcing contractor (i.e., it is not the Developer's main objective to force the Outsourcing Contractor into receivership). Ensure that communications with the tenderer are through one point. Ensure that a charter contains the explicit authorities defined. It should also contain procedures on how the Developer will deal with Outsourcing Contractor during modifications and after the contract is set. *(The above treatments may apply to all the risk factors listed in this section.)*

Exhibit 9 (Continued). The Risk Audit Assessment Template

Risk	Risk Level	Risk Factors	Alert Thresholds	Impact	Risk Treatment
The Developer's inability to address changing customer needs across a wide range of business processes.	S	Contractor cannot address modification requests quickly so that Developer processes can adjust to meet customers changing needs.	Modifications requests are not addressed in a timely fashion by the contractor.	Cost increases. Time blowouts.	The project functional specifications require that many parameter changes can be performed by the user. This will minimize dependency on the Outsourcing Contractor for implementing system modifications.
					Adequate acceptance testing to ensure functionality.
Security Risks					
• Unauthorized access to the Developer data and equipment.	H	Poor security culture.	Poor access controls at Outsourcing Contractor premises.	Cost overruns.	Outsourcing Contractor must have a disaster recovery capability. It should have insurance to cover Developer equipment on their premises. Back-up processes should be in place with at least one set of copies going off site to Developer-designated premises.
• Malicious intent to undermine project.	H		Poor access controls on the Developer premises.	Time deadlines not met.	Evidence of above requirements must be provided on demand during course of contract.

Risk				
• Disaster recovery planning and risk management during development and implementation phases.	H	Poor Industrial Relations policies or their poor implementation. Lack of Business Continuity Planning and risk minimization strategies by Outsourcing Contractor.	Project failure or termination.	
Risk that the Developer's data provided for development and test purposes or even residing in the production environment could be accessed and used for unauthorized purposes.	H	The Developer not having access to or control over its own data leading to unauthorized access or usage of the data. Ownership clauses not included in contract.	Damage to the Developer's image. Possibility of missed income. Costs incurred to access data or use data in different ways.	Contract to indicate ownership of all data and its usage. Independent audit review of Outsourcing Contractor's logical and physical security.
The risk of functionality changes during the course of the project.	H	Initiation of change requests. The Developer decides on new types of fees, taxes, and rebates. Payment requests from Outsourcing Contractor for unauthorized change requests.	Increases in contract cost. Time blowout for project completion.	Ensure that there is a formal process for handling modification requests. The process should ensure that quotes are provided, in accordance with schedule rates, and that the request is formally approved by the Developer before Outsourcing Contractor performs any work on the request.

Exhibit 9 (Continued). The Risk Audit Assessment Template

Risk	Risk Level	Risk Factors	Alert Thresholds	Impact	Risk Treatment
The risk of functionality changes during the course of the project.					The project functional specifications require that many parameter changes can be performed by the user. This will minimize dependency on the Outsourcing Contractor for implementing system modifications. Acceptance testing to ensure functionality.

Section I – Checklist
Management and Planning

1. Does your organization use a formal project management methodology for all programming activities? If not, what determines the need for using a formal approach.
2. Is project management a necessity in your environment or an optional part of development and support activities?
3. Are you confident about the benefits of project management or are you reluctant to embrace all aspects of the process?
4. When, if ever, should project management procedures be abandoned to meet project deadlines. Does this happen often in your organization?
5. How are project management practices conveyed to IS staff and end-users in your organization? Is there formal training?
6. Does your organization periodically review project management procedures effectiveness? If so, is it done before or after a crisis takes place?
7. Have you ever engaged in nontraditional project management procedures so as to advert difficulties with traditional methods? Does it work?
8. How is the Year 2000 project being managed in your organization? Is it treated as a formal systems project or another maintenance request?
9. From your experience, should development and maintenance activities use the same or different project management methodologies?
10. When does the Year 2000 project terminate in your environment? Is there a formal project schedule for completion?
11. Has your organization identified legacy systems for replacement or reengineering? Which is more appropriate?
12. What is your organization's experience in reengineering older application systems? Is it more difficult or less difficult than expected?
13. In your opinion, how should outsourcing be used effectively? Is it best suited for new development or ongoing support tasks?
14. What pitfalls have you identified with outsourcing IS projects?
15. What analysis methods are used in your organization to determine the appropriate need for or against outsourcing. Is cost always a factor?

Section II
Development Strategies

APPLICATION DEVELOPMENT IS OFTEN VIEWED as the quintessence of computer programming. This perception has been justified by the amount of interest that software development receives from the computing industry. Most notable are in the growing number of vendors who provide hardware and software technology, consulting, and outsourcing services, as well as advancements in academic research. However, this overwhelming level of attention can have a formidable price. In the past, development expenditures have been warranted by the creation of new application systems that improve or enhance business processes. Currently there is concern over the cost to maintain a state-of-the-art development environment. Some organizations are questioning the return on investment for expensive development technology. Since many of the fundamental business systems have already been automated, it may be more difficult to warrant further expense on new applications. Surprisingly, the trend for introducing new development technology continues to escalate, and this in turn can drive the desire to build newer business applications that exploit the advancements in system development. Consequently, development managers are now faced with the additional challenge of justifying new applications, and the technology needed to build systems. Without a doubt, today's application development is more demanding, with little room for errors.

Object-based technology has gained increased acceptance as the development process of choice. In comparison to other methods, object technology has much to offer. As with more traditional development approaches, this technique also requires discipline and commitment to ensure success. Chapter II-1, "The Fusion Method for Developing Object-Oriented Software," examines the fundamental concepts of object-oriented programming, and raises interesting points about the development process. This chapter also provides a hybrid methodology that combines the advantages of earlier object-oriented procedures without losing the essential benefits provided by object components. In conjunction, Chapter II-2, "ObjectDriver: A Method for Analysis, Design, and Implementation of Interactive Applications," offers another perspective on object-oriented development via a new methodology targeted for interactive systems. The premise of this method uses the key constructs of objects, events, activities,

71

and history, to build systems that can meet end-user expectations more thoroughly.

The introduction of the graphical user interface (GUI), almost two decades ago, has been a radical departure from menu screens found in earlier application systems. Since its inception, the GUI has continued to evolve as a critical component of desktop application, especially in client-server and Internet-based systems. Perhaps the great interest in GUI programming is due to the perception that it casts on the application as a whole. If the interface is too busy, the application may be viewed as too complicated. However, if the interface helps users identify business functions, then the application is viewed positively. Chapter II-3, "Creating GUIs Users Can Use: Usability Analysis," Chapter II-4, "Designing Usable User Interfaces," and Chapter II-5, "Building GUIs Users Can Use: Usability Development" are a series of chapters that detail the process of building strong, well-defined, and meaningful interfaces to applications. Many business users appreciate the graphical user interface because it can provide powerful access to an application without being too computer cryptic. At the same time, it can offer greater enhancements to productivity. But graphical development is not as easy as it may appear. Despite the numerous software products available for GUI development, there remains important issues that managers must recognize as part of the overall application development process.

Formal methodologies and procedures are frequently targeted as areas in which to improve software development. Unlike software tools, it is still unclear if development methodologies are best described as art or science. This uncertainty has created much controversy among software vendors, consultants, and professional developers. Chapter II-6, "Effective Systems Development Management: The Experts Advise," provides an informative perspective on the value of development methodologies. This chapter offers various opinions from leading experts about those project phases that can influence the success or failure of application development. Managers will find these opinions helpful in forging a strategy for development in their own environment.

Chapter II-1
The Fusion Method for Developing Object-Oriented Software
Larry Whipple

TECHNIQUES FOR DESIGNING COMPUTER SOFTWARE VARY as much as the innovative uses database managers find for the software once it is put into production. In the early days of computer programming, there were no formalized techniques and managers depended on the experience of their senior developers, who were usually the de facto designers and architects. As time passed, techniques, standards, and guidelines began to emerge to help mold development efforts.

In the days of procedural coding, development methodologies started to be loosely defined. The idea of input-process-output was firmly established as the broad model for all business computer systems. Methods such as structured analysis and design were developed and widely used. Relational databases relational model made their appearance and the days of data-driven development began in earnest. By the mid-to-late 1980s, nearly every large software shop was using some sort of development methodology as a means of delivering on time and within budget.

OBJECT-ORIENTED DEVELOPMENT METHODOLOGIES

Object-oriented (OO) programming has been around for more than two decades but is just now reaching the developer community as a whole. As database managers strive to apply the methodology paradigm to OO development, a number of problems are arising. Traditional techniques that worked well in procedural coding do not translate to OO methodology. Functional decomposition, structured analysis and design, and data-driven design are all having problems fitting into the object world. They tend to focus too tightly on either the data or capability and ignore the inherent inclusion and runtime interaction of both in object systems.

OO-specific analysis and design methodologies were created to address these issues. The Object Management Group (OMG) compiled a list of nearly 30 such OO applications development methods. Although not all

0-8493-9979-3/99/$0.00+$.50
© 1999 by CRC Press LLC

these methods came into widespread use (many were strictly speculative or academic), several attained a certain following and notoriety. Methodology theorists and designers such as Grady Booch, Peter Coad, Ivar Jacobson, James Rumbaugh, and Edward Yourdon all made, and continue to make, significant contributions to OO applications development methodology advances.

With all these techniques from which to choose, the choice itself became problematic because choosing a "wrong" technique could, at best, make the OO system more costly or, at worst, completely disrupt development. In addition, these first-generation OO application development methodologies lacked a cradle-to-grave inclusiveness. While one technique addressed identifying objects, a second searched for interaction between objects, and yet a third dealt with the design and creation of classes. Each excelled in its area but failed to deliver a complete solution.

MAJOR OO INFLUENCES

After extensive research and real-world tests, a team at Hewlett Packard Labs in Bristol, England developed a new method of OO applications development called Fusion. Fusion is an attempt at a seamless union of the best methodologies available. It combines Rumbaugh's object modeling technique (OMT), a formal technique known as pre- and postconditions, a rework of Jacobson's objectory use-case concept, and Beck and Cunningham's class-responsibility-collaborator (CRC) with elements of the Booch method to come up with a hybrid that can lead developers all the way through a complete objective design (see Exhibit 1).

The only piece that might be considered missing is that there is no formal method for creating a requirements document. The assumption is that the requirements will be created by the user. A requirements document is

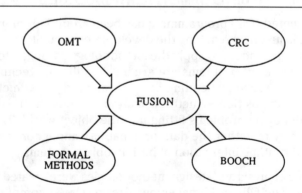

Exhibit 1. First-Generation Object-Oriented Analysis and Design Methods

usually a collection of natural-language statements with appropriate graphics and screen and report designs. Fusion relies on the existence of this document, and thus it is important to make sure it is available.

Since its introduction in late 1993, the Fusion method of object-oriented software development has grown steadily in popularity, which is as much a tribute to its original design as to the evolution of the method. As new users find Fusion, it is molded to fit their needs. It has become successful because of its flexibility. Although it is used extensively at HP, it is also used in the information systems, telecommunications, and defense industries worldwide. A new version of the Fusion methodology that is more architecture-centric and focuses on team development is currently being prepared at HP for release. The new Fusion uses the unified modeling language (UML) for model notation and documentation.

THE FUSION METHODOLOGY

The Fusion methodology is divided into three major phases with multiple deliverables in each: analysis, design, and implementation (see Exhibit 2). The analysis phase defines the interaction of the system with its environment. Various models are produced that describe classes, relationships, operations, and the order in which those operations may occur. The design phase describes how the system will behave. The models delivered by this phase describe how system operations are implemented, how classes refer and relate to one another, and the attributes and operations of the classes. Implementation deals with turning the design into code for a particular object-oriented language. There are checks at the end of each phase to ensure all necessary work has been accomplished and that the appropriate models have been created.

Fusion uses a data dictionary concept to document entity and object names and other important definitions. A sample model is a simplified clinical lab information system designed to assist a technician in testing body fluid samples taken from patients in a hospital and then reporting the results of those tests.

Analysis Phase

The analysis phase is divided into two steps: creation of an object model and creation of interface models (see Exhibit 2). This phase identifies a list of entities from the requirements document. These entities serve as the basis for all the work to come after, so developers should spend the needed time to identify them all. A good technique for identifying entities is to simply pull out all the nouns used in the requirements document that directly relate to system operation. This process typically reveals a great percentage of entities, although usually not all. Additional entities may be revealed by interviews with the user and as a by-product of the analysis and design.

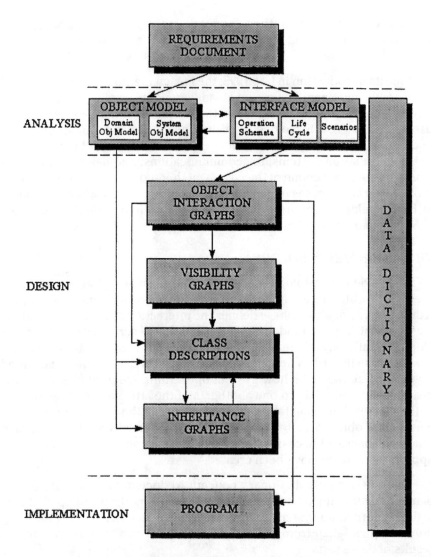

Exhibit 2. A Collection of Models and Documentation Components Delivered in Three Phases

For the clinical lab example, it is useful to start with the following entities: technician, analyzer, sample, patient, test, patient report, and test request.

Object Model. After identifying the initial entity candidate list, creation of the object models can begin. The object model uses a standard entity-relationship diagram notation, including cardinality figures, to document the classes to which the identified entities map. Each box represents a class, and each diamond shape represents the relationship between the

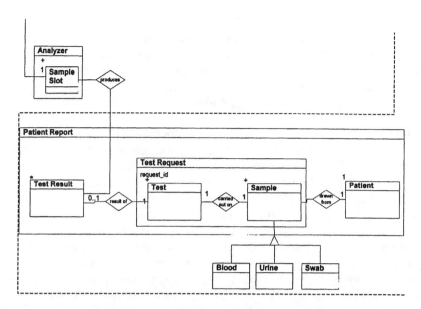

Exhibit 3. The Interaction and Relationships between Individual Objects in the System

classes. Cardinality figures document how many instantiations of a class are required or available in its relationship with another class.

Exhibit 3 shows what a portion of the object model for the clinical laboratory might look like. The test-request aggregate class, where one test is carried out on only one sample, illustrates how cardinality works.

Exhibit 3 also illustrates how aggregate classes contain one or more embedded class (e.g., analyzer, patient report, and test request). The number of allowable instances of an embedded class is documented by cardinality figures. For example, the diagram shows that each test request can have one or more tests and one or more samples. Some new entities also came out of the analysis. The lab technician can now specify what type of samples will be allowed. The notation used demonstrates how inheritance is documented.

The object model produced from documenting all the entities/classes, their relationships, and cardinalities is called the domain object model because it represents the entire domain in which the system operates. This does not necessarily represent the system to be created. Fusion uses a system object model to document which portion of the domain will actually be included in the system. This is documented by drawing a dashed line around the portion of the domain object model that will be delivered as the system.

The dashed line in Exhibit 3, for example, includes the patient report and inherited samples but excludes the analyzer, which is excluded because it will not be created as part of this system but will operate as an agent to the system. An agent is any entity in the system environment that invokes system operations or receives results. The analyzer therefore exists as part of the domain object model but is excluded from the system object model.

Interface Models. The interface models document how the system interacts with its environment. Three models are created: scenarios, operation schemata, and life-cycle expressions. These models document the system's interaction with its agents. They provide detailed descriptions of the interactions and document how they map to the requirements. The first step is to identify the agents and detail their interactions with the system. These interactions, also called events or system operations, are diagrammed in the scenarios. The operation schemata documents each system operation by inputs, outputs, system changes, assumptions, and results. The life-cycle expressions describe the constraints (temporal or otherwise) associated with system operations and events. The format for creating each of these models is well documented but again is flexible enough to allow customization within a given environment.

After the analysis models have been completed, Fusion provides techniques for determining consistency and completeness. The analysis phase should result in a detailed understanding of what the system should do in terms of how it interacts with its own internal components as well as external systems.

Design Phase

The design phase uses the object and interface models created in the analysis phase and determines how the work is to be accomplished through the interactions of the identified classes. Four models are created as part of the design phase: object interaction graphs, visibility graphs, class descriptions, and inheritance graphs.

Object interaction graphs show how the system-level capability specified by the operation schemata in the analysis phase is to be delivered. The first step is to identify the classes and agents (if any) that will be accessed during a system operation. A controller class is identified for each operation. This is the class primarily responsible for the operation to be described. A simple example of an object interaction graph is shown in Exhibit 4. A special controller object receives incoming messages. It creates new test-requests and tracks the current patient report. The beginnings of method documentation are illustrated by the create_tr(si,ti) statement between the report controller and test request objects. Also, the method sequence can be identified by use of sequence numbers as shown

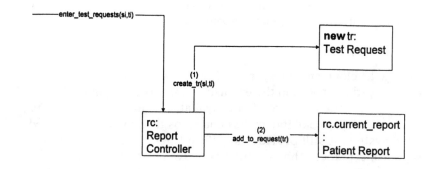

Exhibit 4. Object Interaction Graphs

in Exhibit 4. It is even possible to start documenting passed parameters and return values from methods.

Visibility graphs show the links between instances of a class and other objects. These links can be dynamic or permanent. A permanent link indicates that a reference to the linked object needs to persist beyond any given system operation (i.e., once when the report is run and once when it is called up for the technician). Permanent links are likely to translate to data attributes, whereas dynamic links are created at runtime and will not typically be placed in any type of persistent storage. The other main portion of documentation carried out by visibility graphs is the mutability of the references described by the links. Once a reference to another object is established, it is either constant (it persists while the object persists) or dynamic (it can be removed without removing the objects involved).

Many developers mistakenly begin their analysis and design work for an OO system using the last two models of the design phase: the class descriptions and inheritance graphs. The class description is a formatted textual description of each class identified during the analysis and design phases. Attributes, methods, parent classes, and embedded classes are all described in sufficient detail that this document could be translated into an actual piece of code in whatever language is to be used.

The inheritance graphs are as much a checkpoint at this stage as anything. By this time the developer will probably already have worked out all the appropriate inheritances, and the inheritance graph will just be a step to verify that the documentation of those inheritances is complete and accurate. It also provides a single, formalized document where all inheritance information can be found.

Implementation Phase

The implementation phase is language specific and thus no detailed description of it is necessary. Its purpose is to use the models and documentation created during the analysis and design phases to create actual code in some OO language. The result will be a testable product that meets the goals set in the requirements document.

CONCLUSION

A data development manager who is working with a small system may or may not need to engage in the extensive model building described in this article. A trimmed-down version is available, called lightweight Fusion, which removes some of the models and steps that could be bypassed in a simple system. It still provides significant benefit, however, by forcing design teams to focus their creativity in a systematic fashion.

Managers of large shops who want to invest in a full-blown computer-aided software engineering (CASE) tool for OO applications development will find that a number of them support Fusion, including Visual Thought by Hewlett-Packard, SELECT Enterprise by Select Tools, and Paradigm Plus by Platinum Software Corp. In addition, the inclusion of UML notation and techniques in the new release of Fusion will make many UML (unified modeling language)-compliant CASE tools practical options as well. Several books have been written about the Fusion method, and a growing number of educators are teaching it. HP has even provided Fusion-specific templates for Visio Corp., a supplier of business drawing and diagramming software, that are available at the Fusion Web site. In any case, the Internet provides a wealth of information about Fusion, other OO application development methodologies, and the CASE tools that support them.

Chapter II-2

ObjectDriver: A Method for Analysis, Design, and Implementation of Interactive Applications

Ilia Bider

OBJECT-ORIENTED, USER-FRIENDLY, DATA MODEL, PROTOTYPING — these terms are frequently used by developers in connection with the design and implementation of business software applications. There are almost as many interpretations of these terms as persons who use them.

Before discussing a new object-oriented methodology, let's review a few points about contemporary systems analysis. More often than not, "object-oriented" stands for an object-oriented implementation of a system; "user-friendly" stands for the use of menus, windows, and icons; "data model" stands for a static database schema; "prototyping" stands for the animation of a static database schema with the help of fourth-generation(4GL) tools.

When a system is implemented based on these interpretations of these concepts, the following consequences are likely to occur:

- A system is implemented in an object-oriented way (i.e., written in an object-oriented language such as C++ or Smalltalk), but it does not represent the application realities in an object-oriented manner and therefore is not object-oriented as far as the users are concerned.
- The user interface includes state-of-the-art pulldown and popup menus and windows, but it is still not object-oriented but rather functionally oriented (i.e., the user first chooses a required function in a multilevel menu and only then selects an object to which this function should be applied).
- Many static data models can be constructed for the same application. It is impossible to choose the most adequate one without taking into account the application system dynamics. Many existing tools for conceptual system design fail to express the dynamic behavior of a system. Thus, the use of these tools cannot itself guarantee the right choice.

- It may be too late to start prototyping after the data model has been built. The prototype is often the only means for dialogue between the designer and the future users of the system, because the language of data models is usually beyond the comprehension of an ordinary user. This dialogue cannot be of much use if the choice of the data model is not the optimal one.

These problems arise because the design concepts — object-oriented, data model, user-friendly, and prototyping — are applicable only to certain stages of the development process (e.g., implementation) or to specific parts of an application system (e.g., the user interface). Of course, different parts of the application can be designed separately, and different approaches and software tools may be used at different stages of the development. This strategy, however, can lead to application systems that will not have the desired properties.

For example, an object-oriented manner of implementation will not help to produce programs with a clear structure if the conceptual structure of the system is vague and does not adequately express the application field reality. Neither the use of icons nor the mouse can help to make such a system user-friendly.

A different strategy is to choose (or develop), at the first stage, a set of notions for expressing the application reality, and at the second stage to develop the ways of presenting these notions in a user interface and in program structures. Such a strategy supplies new meaning to the contemporary design terms.

AN ALTERNATIVE OBJECT-ORIENTED METHODOLOGY

The approach discussed in the chapter is aimed to support the design and implementation of interactive business applications. In it, the method of expressing application realities is based on four main concepts:

- **Objects.** Objects are used to represent the elements of the application realm (e.g., people, companies, projects). Objects possess properties and may have a complex structure (i.e., they can consist of subobjects).
- **Events.** Objects are not static; they undergo changes all the time. When an object changes, an event is registered. Event registration is performed by creating a special object — a registered event — at the time of the change. A registered event contains the information on the type of event (e.g., customer's call, invoicing), on the registration time, on the object that has been changed, and on the person who has introduced changes.
- **Activities.** As a unit of action, an activity is a function that can be applied to an object with a view to modifying it in a certain way. Activities can be planned for every object and executed later. Planning is

performed with the help of a special class of objects — planned activities. A planned activity contains the information on the type of activity (e.g., telephone call, invoice), on the planned date and time, on the deadline, and on the person who is responsible for performing the activity. When executed, a planned activity changes the object to which it belongs. This change may include adding new planned activities and deleting the old ones.

- **History.** When an object has changed its state, its former state is stored in the database. A sequence of the former object's states makes up a history of the object's evolution. The history may be used for planning and executing activities.

Redefinition of Key Terms

The design concepts of object-oriented, data model, user-friendly, and prototyping are reinterpreted and redefined in this approach as follows.

- Object-oriented stands primarily for an object-oriented way of presenting the application realities and an object-oriented user interface; object-oriented implementation is considered only subsequently.
- User-friendliness is achieved by means of a specially constructed navigation system. The navigation system helps a user to quickly and easily navigate to the required object or activity. Windows, menus, and the mouse are used as navigation controls. Users can browse not only through the current states of the objects, but also through their past (history) and future (planned activities). The activities are planned and executed partly by the application system, partly by the user. The registration of events makes the navigation system more flexible. For example, the user can get a list of all the latest events registered in the system, choose one of them, and quickly access the object that has been changed during this event.
- A data model is only one part of a system specification that describes all possible states of the objects selected to represent the application. The other part includes all possible transitions from one state to another. The latter can be expressed in terms of events, activities, and history. The task of the system design is to develop both parts as an integral entity.
- Prototyping is an integral part of the design process; prototyping starts before the data model is ready and is over only after the system is fully implemented. A prototype is a system specification written in a language that is fully comprehensible to the future users of the system. The navigation system with the database access switched off can be used as a prototyping tool at the very first stage of the system design. There is no need to have a database schema ready before starting on a prototype. Moreover, a database schema can be later derived from the prototype.

MANAGEMENT AUTOMATION USING OBJECTDRIVER

The method informally described in the following sections supports the development of interactive object- and time-oriented systems in the application field called management automation. The method is suitable for the design and implementation of systems used for sales management, marketing support, and medical patient records, or systems for which it is extremely important to have comprehensive information on everything that has happened and to be able to plan what is going to happen in the future.

This method was named ObjectDriver (OD) because it facilitates the development of systems whose purpose is to help a user "drive" certain objects through a number of predefined states to the successful conclusion. For example, a "sale" should be driven to receiving the payment, a "patient," to recovering and leaving the hospital.

The core of the OD approach consists of a small number of constructs that are used for expressing the variety of application environments. None of the basic constructs — object, event, activity, and history — are new; the novelty of the OD approach lies in the way these concepts are used to express various elements of application worlds, such as plans and calendars.

The OD approach also includes techniques for translating the basic constructs into:

- Elements of a user interface
- A database structure
- A structure of application programs

This chapter does not contain all the details of the OD approach; the primary goal is just to outline its main features. Familiar concepts from software design practice (e.g., windows, fields, menus, shortcuts, records, field entry, and exit programs) are used.

Objects

An object is a central notion in OD approach. Abstract objects serve to represent elements from a given application world. Objects can possess properties, be related to each other (e.g., a relation between a person and the company the person is working for), and may have a complex structure (i.e., objects can consist of subobjects).

The structure of objects in an application is defined by the database schema of this application. For the time being, the ObjectDriver deals only with formatted data — that is, the database schema of an application is fixed and cannot be changed by its users. The database schema is designed in terms of certain undirectional relationships:

- Object domains (classes)
- Attributes
- Links

Object-Subobject Relationships. An object domain defines a set of objects with the same main properties (i.e., same meaning). For example, in a sales management application, there will be such domains as COMPANY, PERSON, or SALE. Attributes express specific properties of objects from the same domain (e.g., the name of a company). A link connecting two object domains expresses the objects' relation. For example, the "employed-by" link from the PERSON domain to the COMPANY domain expresses the fact that an object from the PERSON domain may be connected to an object from the COMPANY domain. Such a connection has the meaning that the given person works for the given company.

To represent the object-subobject relationships between objects, a special kind of link called a "link to subobject" is employed. If in the database schema there is a link of this type directed from one object domain to another, then an object from the latter can exist only if it is connected according to this link to some "owner" — an object from the former domain.

A typical example of a subobject is an item of a sale, which describes what kind of goods have been ordered and how many. Such an item can be created only with a connection to some sale and should be removed from the database as soon as the sale is removed.

The connection between sales and items is represented in the database schema by the "ordered" link that is directed from the SALE domain to the ITEM domain; this link has the type of the "link to subobject."

Several object domains can be combined to produce a new object domain; attributes and links can be multivalued (in which case they are called soft attributes and multilinks, respectively).

These enhancements, along with the notion of the "link to subobject," give the static data model the same expressive power as that of advanced languages for conceptual design. It is possible to easily model the meaning of such concepts as generalization and aggregation with the help of combined domains and multilinks, respectively.

Object States. Objects in OD-based applications are not static; they change in time. The goal of an application is to control these changes. To express the idea of a change, a formal definition of an object state is required.

In ObjectDriver, the state of an object at a given time is represented by a marked directed graph. It includes attribute arcs that connect the object with the values of its attributes, and link arcs that connect the object with other objects in accordance with the links that were defined in the database schema. Arcs are marked with the names of the corresponding attributes and links. If a link arc ingoing to an object corresponds to a link of the "link to subobject" type, then all the arcs outgoing from this object are also included in the state of its "owner."

The formal definition of the state of an object is used to determine exactly what object(s) have been changed when something happens in the system. For example, if a person has left a job, it means a change in the state of the person, not in the state of the company the person was working for. This is true as long as the "employed-by" link is directed from the PERSON domain to the COMPANY domain. If the direction of the link is reversed, then it is the state of the company that has changed when somebody leaves a job. Which direction to choose for links depends on the goals of an application; such decisions should be made at the stage of conceptual design.

The state of an object cannot be changed arbitrarily. A description of the dynamic behavior of an application system should be built that distinguishes the valid transitions from one state to another from the invalid ones. In the OD approach this task is partly accomplished by user-interface programs that prevent users from modifying an object arbitrarily (see the section on "Conceptual Design vs. Prototyping" later in this chapter).

The greater part of the dynamic behavior of a system, however, is expressed in terms of activities — functions that transform one object state into another. Activities can be planned, thus defining the next desirable steps of the object modifications. Planned activities serve as a means to control the object evolution in time and to express the goals of an application system.

The validity of a transition from one object state to another may depend not only on the current state of the object in question but also on what changes it underwent in the past (e.g., the same goods cannot be invoiced twice). The required information about the past is obtained in OD-based systems by means of event registration and by storing the previous states of the objects.

The Object-Oriented User Interface

The most natural kind of user interface for applications in the management automation field is an object-oriented one. That implies that a user can view the objects, understand their complex structures, and easily navigate through the space of interrelated objects.

Navigation System. In OD-based systems, the user is aided by a navigation system that allows the user to move from one object to another along the link that connects these objects. For example, a user can view the list of all persons registered in the system, then filter it by a given street address, then choose one person from the resulting list and inspect all the information related to this person, including the company he or she is working for. This company represents the "employed-by" link, which goes from the PERSON domain to the COMPANY domain. Then the user can move to the other end of the "employed-by" link — the company — and view all the information related to it (e.g., all the persons employed in the company).

Users of an OD-based system can view objects in two main forms:

- The list form, in which objects of the same class are presented
- The object form, in which all the information related to a particular object is given

To be able to navigate, a user does not need any explicit knowledge of the object structure of the system. The user should just know what keys to press or what options of the menus to choose to go from the list form to the object form or vice versa, or from the head object of the object form to one of its subobjects, or to some other object linked to the head one. To make it easy to navigate through the object space for a novice, context-sensitive menus show the directions in which the user can move; an experienced user can use shortcuts to avoid these menus.

Comparison with Function-Oriented User Interface. An OD-based system introduces techniques that differ radically from those used in a traditional, functionally oriented administrative system. Users of traditional systems must first choose the function they want to perform, often in a multilevel menu; only then can they reach the object they want to apply this function to. Such a user interface has a great disadvantage when a user wants to apply several functions to the same object (e.g., update an address of some person, write a letter, and make a telephone call).

In the traditional system, a user is forced each time to return to the function menu (often by choosing ESC several times from the multilevel menu), choose another function, and then access the same object once more; the procedure is repeated as many times as there are different functions the user wants to apply to the same object.

With an OD-based system, users first choose the object they want to work with, then they perform all the necessary manipulations with it — modifying its attributes, installing and deleting link arcs, and executing activities, much like a state-of-the-art word processing system where users first select a text block and only then point to the function they want to perform (e.g., delete the block, copy it, or print it).

If a function-oriented interface is preferred, as it might be for users who usually execute only one type of activity (e.g., taking an order, invoicing), it is easy to introduce one. Such an interface can be expressed as a special way of navigating through the system's object space (an example is given in the section on "Dynamic Objects and Activities").

Registration of Events

If one or more objects have undergone some change at a given point in time, an event occurred at that time. Event registration is the process of saving certain information about each event that occurs in the application system — for example, the time when it happened, the event type (e.g., letter arrived, invoice printed), and the initiator of the changes (e.g., a user or the system itself).

Event registration in OD-based systems is accomplished with the help of a special class of objects — a registered event. The objects of this class are called r-events.

R-events. A new r-event is created each time a user or the application system changes some object, thus causing an event to occur. The structure of r-events (i.e., their attributes and links) depends on the application needs. Usually, however, there are such attributes as "registration-time" (the time when the event was registered in the system), "real-time" (the time when the event happened in real life), "type," "comment" (free text annotation), and such links as "modified-at" (a link to the object that has undergone changes during the event) and "initiator" (the link to the object representing a user who has introduced the changes).

Implementation. Event registration is implemented in the user interface in the following way: Each time a user tries to save the modifications he has introduced in some object, an "event window" appears where certain attributes of the new r-event (e.g., real time, type, comment) can be input. Only by pressing a transmit key in this window can the user save the changes along with the new r-event.

Once introduced, registered events can serve as a source of different kinds of information. For example, a list of all r-events constitutes the system chronicle. A list of all r-events with the same "modified-at" object gives the historic overview of the object evolution. A list of all r-events with the same "initiator" presents the full account of all activities of that person.

The registration of events can be used for increasing the flexibility of the navigation system. Suppose that an OD-based application registers an event of a "temporal interrupt" type each time a user interrupts work with a current object and moves to another object, for example, to register an

incoming phone call. Then a list of all r-events with the "temporal interrupt" type and the same "initiator" shows the jobs that have not been finished by the particular user. The user can choose one of these r-events and
easily move to the object that he started to modify earlier. Such a list can
be shown to a user every time he tries to log off the system.

In OD-based applications, it is possible to register an event even when
no objects have been explicitly changed inside the system. Such a need can
arise in case a particular application does not computerize all the activities
of the company or the organization. For example, incoming mail may not be
processed inside the system. But sometimes, it is useful to register a letter
arrival from a particular person along with a note on its contents. Such an
event is treated as a change in the external (not represented inside the
application) part of one or more objects.

R-events that correspond to external events have the same structure as
those corresponding to internal events (e.g., they have a link to the "modified-at" object). OD-based applications process both types of events in the
same way, so they can be presented to the users on the same list.

Dynamic Objects and Activities

Among all the objects chosen to represent an application environment,
there is always a class of objects that is central for the kind of application
in question. For sales management, it is sale objects that are important; for
marketing management, it is prospect objects that are important; for
project management, it is project objects that are important.

To discover such objects in a given application field is a task of conceptual design. Such objects are termed to be "dynamic," not because all other
objects are completely static (a company or a person can change a name,
an address, or a telephone number), but because the goal of the application system is to help its users to "drive" these objects through the given
number of states to the successful conclusion. For example, a sale should
be driven through shipping and invoicing to getting money; a prospect to
complete a sale; a project to produce a ready product.

A particular application system can be named by substituting the word
object with the name of the central dynamic object of the application (e.g.,
SaleDriver, ProspectDriver, ProjectDriver, or DealDriver). The drive is performed by using activities.

An activity is a function that transforms one object state to another. To
execute an activity is to apply the corresponding function to a particular
object. Activity execution may consist of three of the following actions (the
last action listed is the obligatory one):

89

- An internal action, such as changing the object state
- An external action, such as printing a document or sending data to an external database
- Event registration

For example, if the activity of "invoicing" is applied to an object from the SALE domain, the following results are achieved:

- The value of the "invoiced amount of money" attribute is changed.
- A printed invoice is produced.
- A new r-event is created that has the type of "invoicing" and refers to the given sale object.

Applicability of a particular activity to a given object may depend on the object's actual state or even on the object history and events that have been registered about this object. For example, invoicing activity cannot be applied to a sale on which an event of the "invoicing" type has been already registered.

Some activities can be performed without intervening of the user. Execution of others is impossible without the user's help. For example, "invoicing" can be done by the system, but in case of "shipping," the user should confirm that all the goods have been shipped or manually fill in how much of each type of goods has been shipped.

Activity execution can be directly started by the user. However, in management automation applications, it is often necessary to plan an activity first and execute it afterward. In the OD approach, the idea of planning is realized with the help of a special class of objects called planned activities. Objects of this class are called p-activities.

P-activities. These objects have a special attribute called "type" that defines the name of activity being planned. The presence of additional attributes and links in p-activities depends on the particular application, but there are some natural attributes and links that can be applied to all kinds of applications — "planned date and time," "deadline," and "responsible" (a link to the user who is responsible for execution of the planned activity, or more precisely, to the object that represents this user in the system).

A p-activity can exist only if it is a subobject of some dynamic object (i.e., in the database schema of an application, there is a link of the "link to subobject" type) that connects the domain of dynamic objects with the PLANNED ACTIVITY domain. All planned activities included in the state of a given dynamic object at a given time compose a PLAN of the object evolution.

P-activities are ordinary objects, which means that they can be created, modified, and deleted like all other objects. But they possess an additional property: when a user comes to a p-activity, he can execute it. In this case, the function defined by the "type" attribute of the p-activity is applied to the "owner" of the p-activity.

Replanning. Among all the modifications introduced in the owner's state during p-activity execution, a special group can be distinguished that changes only the owner's plan. This group is called replanning and it includes, at minimum, the deletion of the executed p-activity, since it is no longer needed. The replanning group may also include more complex modifications, such as the introduction of one or more new p-activities that show the next steps in the object evolution. A "shipping" p-activity may plan "invoicing" (if all the goods have been shipped) or a new "shipping" (if only a part of all goods has been shipped). Such replanning can be done automatically or with the user's help.

Calendar. A list of all p-activities connected to the same user according to the "responsible" link makes up a calendar of this particular user. A calendar is not an object, because all the p-activities on the list are already subobjects of different dynamic objects. A calendar is made of dynamic objects that are planned in the first place. People serve as a resource for activity execution. This resource is "limited," so care should be taken not to assign too many activities to the same person on the same day.

The users of an OD-based system are not forced to execute p-activities one by one. A user can take a list of all p-activities that the user is responsible for, filter it by a particular activity type, and then issue a special command that is called "execute all." If activities of the given type can be executed without human intervention, then all such p-activities that are ready for execution will be performed automatically. If the activity type needs the user's help, the system will execute the p-activities one by one asking the user to confirm or fill in some information.

The "execute all" command may serve as a means of adding a functionally oriented user interface to OD-base applications. For example, the main menu can include an option "functions" with a submenu of choices — for example, "invoicing" or "shipping." As soon as a user chooses one of these functions, the system presents a list of all ready-for-execution p-activities of the chosen type. Issuing the command "execute all" starts execution of these p-activities.

Saving the History

In certain circumstances, a user needs to know that an event of the particular type took place, but also needs to see the difference between the states of some object before and after this event. For example, suppose that during a sale there were several "shipments," and during one of them the shipped goods disappeared on the way to the customer. To manage this situation it is not enough to know when the goods were shipped; the user should also know how much of each type of goods were shipped at the time of the shipping in question. The latter can be calculated as a difference between the values of the "amount of shipped items" attribute before and after the shipping event.

Such information may also be needed for execution of certain kinds of activities. For example, credit invoicing needs to know how much money has been invoiced and what for. One way to walk around such problems is to store all needed information in the current object states or in the r-events. But this approach has the following drawbacks:

- Dynamic objects and r-events would become more and more complexly structured.
- It becomes difficult to expand the application with new activities that may need another kind of comparing of object stats (not saved in the r-events).

A more general approach requires that a system is able to reconstruct the states of its dynamic objects before and after any event. That means saving the whole history for at least dynamic objects. In the OD approach, this problem is solved in a special way.

All information is stored in the database in small basic units — records — each of which contains the values of one or more attributes or links of an object. Some records belong to the current state of the system; they are called *current*. Others describes the previous states of the system; they are said to be historic.

Both kind of records are stored in the same physical database structure. To distinguish the current records from historic ones and to point to the interval of time when a historic record was current, event numbering and event stamping of records are the techniques used.

Event Numbering and Stamping. All events are sequentially numbered. These numbers make up the time axis of the internal system time. Each record is supplied with two event stamps — opening stamp and closing stamp.

One is the number of the event when the record was created; the other is the number of the event after which the record became historic. The closing stamp of a current record contains a special code called "far future." This code is represented by a very large integer number that is always greater than the number of the last event that occurred in the system.

"Far future" expresses the meaning that the current record may be closed only in the future. If a new event occurs and some attributes or links that were stored in a given current record have been changed, then the following actions are undertaken: The closing stamp of the record changes its value from the "far future" to the number of the new event, thus making the record a historic one. A new record is created to store the modified values of the attributes or links; it stores the values of all the attributes or links that were represented in the former record, even those that were not touched during the event. This new record automatically becomes current, which means that its closing stamp gets the value of the "far future." Its opening stamp becomes equal to the event number of the new event.

All the current records related to a particular object compose the current state of this object; these records can be easily retrieved because they have the "far future" as a value of the closing stamp. All that is needed to reconstruct a state of the object at the time of the event with a given number is to collect all the records related to the object with the opening stamp greater than or equal to the given event number and the closing stamp less than it.

A query against a database with the described structure accepts an additional argument, which provides the query with the event number of interest. Such a database can also retrieve information such as the event number of the given object's birth, last modification, or demise. The event number of the object's birth is the smallest number among the opening stamps of all the records related to the given object. The event number of the object's last modification is the largest number among the opening stamps of all the current records related to the given object. The event number of the object's demise is the largest number among the closing stamps of all the records related to the given object. If this number is equal to the "far future," then the object is still active or alive.

An event number is tied to the real time only by the "registered time" attribute of the r-event that was born during this event. This means that if you want to find out what a particular object looked like at a given time, first find the r-event with the "registered time" immediately preceding the time of interest. Then find the event number of this r-event's birth and only afterward make a query about the object state at the calculated event number. All this manipulation can be made by the system automatically.

In OD-based systems, r-events serve as a record of a journey in the past. A user can take a list of all the r-events related to a particular object (a written history of the object), choose one of them, and view or move to the object's state that was current before or after the corresponding event. After moving to such a state, the user can continue navigating in the past by moving along the link arcs that existed at the chosen time. The user navigates in the past state of the system in the same way as he does in the current state, except the user cannot introduce changes in the database or execute activities.

In fact, saved history along with registered events (written history) gives an OD system an outstanding ability. In layman's terms, it works as a time machine.

Conceptual Design vs. Prototyping

In the ObjectDriver approach, there is a set of rules for mapping the elements of a database schema into the elements of the screen forms that show objects to users. For example, an attribute is represented by a field plus a leading text — the name of this attribute. A link is represented by the most important attributes of the "linked" objects. For example, on the form that shows a user an object from the PERSON domain, the "employed-by" link, which connects the PERSON domain to the COMPANY domain, may be represented by such attributes as "company name" and "company phone number." Multivalued attribute and multilinks are represented by scroll areas. An inverse link (i.e., a link ingoing into the given domain) is represented by a pop-up list that consists of objects from the domain for which this link is outgoing.

Because of these rules, the OD approach can suggest to a developer two opposite ways of conceptual design:

- **A database schema is created first, followed by the development of all the forms for the user interface.** This is the traditional method that appeals to those used to data modeling. When this approach is used, the fact that the chosen database schema is the right one assumes great importance.
- **The system designer first draws screen forms and ties them together with the help of function keys and menus.** The resulting prototype is then shown to the potential users. Only after the users are satisfied with the prototype does the designer proceed to derive the database schema from the forms that have been drawn in the prototyping process.

The navigation system of the object-oriented user interface, with the database access switched off, can serve as a perfect object-oriented prototyping tool. With its help, one can quickly paint object forms and insert them in the ObjectDriver's navigation system. There is no underlying database in such a prototype, but a user can navigate through the object space in the same way as he does it in the completed application; the user can modify attribute values, install and delete link arcs, create new objects, and see how to start different activities. The user cannot, however, save the information or see the results of application of some functions (e.g., the user cannot see the results of the list filtering).

In practice, the designer may use some combination of these two approaches. For example, if a new application is very much like the old one, a designer can first create a preliminary version of the database schema, then convert it into the interface forms and continue to develop it modifying the prototype. After the prototype is ready, the final database schema can easily be derived from it.

For a completely new application, it is easier to start directly with the form design. The database schema and the corresponding interface forms can be modified even after the prototype is ready and the database access has been added to the future application. That means that prototyping does not end with the ready "prototype"; the process continues until the whole application is ready for delivery.

RECOMMENDED COURSE OF ACTION

The approach detailed in this chapter has several advantages:

- **It is consistent.** Because this object-oriented methodology is based on parts of basic concepts, it supports all the stages of the design and implementation of management automation systems. A designer does not need to use one method or design tool for conceptual design (e.g., entity-relationship model) and another for system implementation (e.g., relational database with some 4GL).
- **It supplies applications with a consistent object-oriented user interface.** Once instructed how to navigate in one part of an OD-based system, a user can easily move to another part of it or to another OD-based application without any additional education.
- **An OD-based system has a well-defined implementation structure.** All general programs are included in the high-level tools; the system can be expanded by adding new activities and new objects, without any restructuring of the existing part of the system or the user interface.

A designer who wants to follow the ObjectDriver approach does not need to use all four constructs — object, event, activity, and history — at once. Using only the object concept and an object-oriented user interface, a developer can create a system for information maintenance.

By adding event registering, at least for some objects and some events, the developer can also store the details on when and who has changed the information and what was the source of information. The addition of directly executed activities gives possibilities to create simple management automation systems. Adding planned activities allows the developer to build fairly complex administrative systems. All four constructs give the designer possibilities to easily expand and modify the system.

This approach may also be used for systems design only. Implementation in this case should be done with the help of conventional means. A designer, for example, is not forced to use the object-oriented database, but can instead use a relational one and code all the object-oriented interface against the database by means of structured query language (SQL) or some other query language, though the designer can still use the navigation approach described in this chapter.

Acknowledgments

The ObjectDriver approach was developed by the author in cooperation with Maxim Khomyakov from Magnificent Seven (Moscow). A number of people took part in the implementation of the software tools (used for the user interface and for prototyping during conceptual design) and in the development of the end system, DealDriver. The author is very grateful to all of them, especially to A. Borkovsky, R. Sj[ouml]borg, and R. Svensson.

Chapter II-3
Creating GUIs Users Can Use: Usability Analysis

Luke Hohmann

INFORMATION SYSTEMS ARE SUPPOSED TO HELP, but very often end users regard a new system as a hindrance rather than a help. There are many explanations why users would find an information systems an obstacle in getting their work done. One is that the system does not perform the tasks users must do to accomplish their work. Another common reason is that the systems are just too difficult to use. Usability is the answer for such end-user complaints.

GUIs are the part of an information system that users work with. Often, when users refer to a system, they are actually referring to the GUI. Because of its importance to users, users may reject a system if they object to its GUI. Thus, creating a usable GUI is key to the success of any information system. This chapter gives systems development managers a firm understanding of what is usability, how to manage interface development when usability is a goal, and how to perform usability analysis so that developers know what users look for in an interface they can actually use.

WHAT IS USABILITY?

Usability refers to the quality of the user interface as perceived by the user. Unfortunately, both "usability" and "quality" can be nebulous terms, so human-computer interaction (HCI) professionals have used the following to more completely describe usability:

- A highly usable GUI allows the user to accomplish one or more specific tasks easily, efficiently, and with a minimum number of errors. Extremely usable interfaces fade over time and enable the user to concentrate completely on the task at hand. This is referred to as *transparency*. An extreme example of transparency in action is a child playing a video game.
- A highly usable GUI is easy to learn, and once learned is easy to remember.

0-8493-9979-3/99/$0.00+$.50
© 1999 by CRC Press LLC

- The use and arrangement of controls, the colors and layout of both large and small details, and the ability to customize the user interface all contribute to a sense of satisfaction, enjoyment, and accomplishment.

Usability cannot be determined without an understanding of users and the context in which they work. For example, a highly usable GUI for a chemical engineer performing experiments is quite different than a highly usable interface for an airlines reservations clerk. Developing a clear understanding of the users for each domain is a central aspect of the design process and will be discussed in greater detail later in this chapter.

The term *usability* addresses both quantitative and qualitative dimensions of the user interface. Depending on the specific user population, a development effort should focus its efforts on maximizing appropriate variables. For example, a data entry application should place more emphasis on such things as lowering error rates and efficiency of data entry, while a decision support system for senior executives might place more emphasis on learnability. Sometimes such goals are explicitly stated in requirements documents. Other times these goals must be inferred from an understanding of the development environment. In both cases the specific performance requirements with respect to usability should be discussed and agreed to by relevant groups.

Benefits of Usability

The importance of usability in a product can be described in economic terms. A large amount of compelling economic data indicates that usability is an investment that pays for itself quickly over the life of the product. Whereas a detailed summary of the economic impact of usability is beyond the scope of this chapter, imagine the impact of reducing the number of calls to the technical support organization by 20% to 50% because the application is easier to use. Or, imagine the impact of increasing customer satisfaction. Other benefits that commonly results in projects emphasizing usability include the following:

- Reduced training costs
- Reduced support and service costs
- Reduced error costs
- Increased productivity of users
- Increased customer satisfaction
- Increased maintainability

It is generally not possible to simultaneously achieve every possible benefit of usability. A system that is easy to learn for novices is likely to be far too slow for experts. Because of this, it is best to review the project requirements and determine the most important usability goals that will guide the development process. A subsequent section will provide greater detail on establishing usability goals.

Usability in Large Corporations

When you go to the store to purchase a piece of software for your personal use, you have the right to refuse any application that does not appear to meet your needs — including your subjective preferences. This effect of market forces continues to drive the designers of shrink-wrapped software to create projects that are truly easy to use.

Unfortunately, designers of software applications in large corporations are usually not driven by market forces. Instead, they attend to other forces — typically the needs of senior management. As a result, the usability of most applications in large corporations is abysmal. If you are a manager working on an internal application in a large application, concentrate on those ways you can introduce the usability-enhancing activities described below. While you may not be driven by the same market forces as managers creating shrink-wrapped applications, the benefits of usability are as applicable within the corporation as they are in the external marketplace.

COMPONENTS OF A USABILITY DEVELOPMENT PROCESS

Building highly usable software systems centers around four key components, which are detailed in the following sections.

Understanding Users. The cornerstone of building highly usable GUIs is based on an intimate understanding of the users, their needs, and the tasks that must be accomplished. The outcome of this understanding results in a description of the users' *mental model*. A *mental model* is the internal representation of the problem users have formed as they accomplish tasks. Understanding this internal representation enables designers to create a *system model* that supplements and supports users. Understanding the users and involving them in the design process is such an important part of building highly usable systems that it is often referred to *user-centered design.*

Progression from Lo-Fidelity to Hi-Fidelity Systems. Building usable systems is based on a gradual progression from "lo-fidelity" paper-and-pencil–based prototypes to "hi-fidelity" working systems. Such an approach encourages exploration through low-cost tools and efficient processes until the basic structure of the user interface has been established. This basic structure can then be validated through working systems. This approach is most effective when users are actively involved throughout the entire process from the earliest phases of the project.

Adherence to Proven Design Principles. Through extensive empirical studies HCI professionals have published several principles to guide the decisions made by designers. These simple and effective principles transcend any single platform and dramatically contribute to usability. The use of design principles are strengthened through the use of *usability specifications*, quantifiable statements used to formally test the usability of the system. Usability specifications (e.g., the application must load within 40 seconds) are the quantifiable expressions of the usability benefits desired from the project.

Usability Testing. Each outcome produced during development is tested — and retested — with users and iteratively refined. Testing provides the critical feedback necessary to ensure designers are meeting user needs. An added benefit of testing is that it involves users throughout the development effort. When testing is properly integrated, it encourages users to think of the system as something they own, increasing system acceptance.

Following sections of this chapter focus on the first component of the usability development process, understanding users. The following components will be examined in upcoming chapters.

Development Process Roadmap

The components of usability described above can be incorporated into an overall roadmap that describes the development processes along with the outcomes associated with each process. In Exhibit 1, traditional activities associated with the project are shown to the left, while the activities associated with usability are displayed to the right.

Traditional activities associated with systems development include product specification, system analysis including data and process modeling, system design, system architecture, detailed module design, and implementation. It is important to note that these activities are shown in a simplistic, waterfall inspired development process. I do not advocate the use of a waterfall process and instead prefer that systems be constructed iteratively.

The usability activities, depicted on the right-hand side of Exhibit 1, constitute the main activities associated with the usability aspects of the project. These include establishing usability specifications, user and task analysis, two distinct design phases, and the implementation of the design.

Importance of Prototyping

Prototyping seems to be getting a bad name. Developers are often scared to show naïve managers a prototype, fearful that their manager will do one of two hideous acts. First, the manager will prevent the development staff from making the inevitable modifications that are needed for the

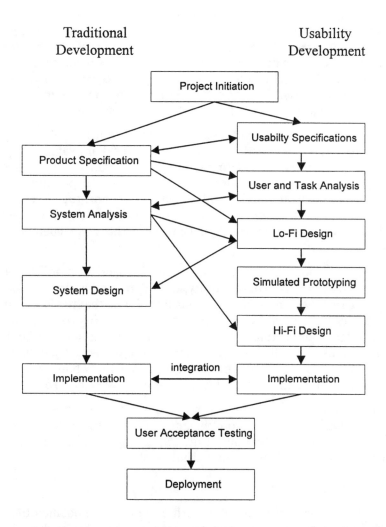

Traditional Development

Usability Development

Project Initiation

Usabilty Specifications

Product Specification

User and Task Analysis

System Analysis

Lo-Fi Design

Simulated Prototyping

System Design

Hi-Fi Design

integration

Implementation

Implementation

User Acceptance Testing

Deployment

Exhibit 1.   A Comparison of Activities in Traditional Systems Development and Usability-Based Development

final version of any system before it moves into production. The second reason, which is unfortunately both more common and more damaging, is that developers fear their managers will expect a fully functioning system after being shown just a prototype. Users are also highly susceptible to this second problem and can easily expect delivery of a system far too quickly. Because of this, prototyping is sometimes avoided altogether. Refusing to prototype at all is not the solution. Prototyping, in the form of lo-fi and hi-fi window design, is absolutely essential in any GUI development effort.

Users are quite poor at defining *exactly* what they want the system to do in advance. In other words, it is far easier to demonstrate what is *wrong* with a proposed user interface than to sit down and describe the ideal solution. This is why the first step of the design process is the creation of simple, paper and pencil, lo-fi window prototypes. I *expect* my users to make changes to my initial proposals. I *want* them to propose such changes, for unless *they* own the process I am not likely to be successful.

A prototype can be used to answer a difficult question without putting the project at risk or wasting valuable resources. For example, suppose I want to try a different report format. Instead of writing a complex query, I'd simply just write down the information on a piece of paper and show it to a user. Then, we would extend the design of the report together. Following this, I'd mock-up the report using my word processor to make certain it provided the required information. Only when this was signed off would I write any code.

Now, what about the first two problems: the need for modifications and the need to avoid mistaking a prototype for a production system? As a manager, you are indeed responsible for making certain that the final system as created by your development staff closely adheres to the prototype approved by your customer. Thus, you need to manage changes to the prototype just like any other set of changes to the project. Depending on the scope and complexity of the project, this means that changes to the user interface may be under the control of a formal change control board.

The second issue is just a matter of plain common sense: Don't expect your developers to turn a prototype, no matter how slick, into a working, production quality system overnight. Expecting this will produce ulcers, divorces, and burnout, not highly usable systems.

USABILITY SPECIFICATIONS

A software project is initiated with one or more specific objectives. Embedded in these objectives are both quantitative and qualitative aspects of usability. By writing such specifications in a concrete manner, the project can ensure these objectives are realized. A *usability specification* consists of specific attributes, ways to measure attributes, and a description of acceptable ranges.

Common usability attributes that impact the development of the system include the following:

- Ease of installation
- Learnability
- Ability to locate specific (advanced) features
- Overall acceptability
- Degree of internationalization

Exhibit 2.   A Way for Documenting Formal Specifications

Attribute	Measuring Concept	Unacceptable	Planned	Best Case
Overall Satisfaction	User selects a rating from 1 to 7 where 1 means "extremely dissatisfied" and 7 means "extremely satisfied"	<3	5	7

Measuring techniques include:

- Time to complete task
- Number or percentage of errors
- Percentage of tasks completed in a given time
- Time spent in errors and recovery
- Number of commands/actions to perform task(s)
- Frequency of help and documentation use
- Number of times users expressed frustration or happiness

Examples of acceptable ranges include:

- The system must boot in less than 90 seconds. More than 120 seconds requires a redesign.
- A user with 3 weeks constant use of the system must retain 85% of core skills (as measured by the standard competency test) after 3–5 weeks of disuse. Less than 85% retention indicates a need for reducing the conceptual load.

Be careful of the degree of detail in the usability specification. Many authors advocate establishing extremely formal usability specifications. The problem is that such specifications must be tested. Extremely formal approaches substantially increase the duration and effort of the testing effort. Of course, extremely precise specifications are appropriate if there is an economic or moral justification (e.g., a chemotherapy dispensing unit must be designed to be used with an absolute minimum number of errors), but most shrink-wrapped and corporate development efforts can produce quite acceptable levels of usability without such precise specifications. A common way of documenting formal specifications is shown in Exhibit 2.

An alternative, and less formal, way to think about usability specifications is to think of usability in terms of well-documented priorities. By sharing these priorities with the development staff, design decisions and future test plans can be made according to a shared set of priorities.

USER AND TASK ANALYSIS

The purpose of *user* and *task analysis* is to develop an understanding of the users, their tasks, and the context in which they conduct their required

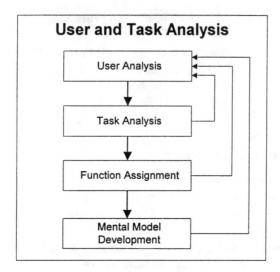

Exhibit 3. Activities in User and Task Analysis

work. Once these are complete a *function assignment* can be performed to clearly identify the distribution of tasks between the user and the system. These activities are displayed in Exhibit 3.

User Analysis

The purpose of a user analysis is to clearly define who the intended user of the system really is through a series of context-free, open-ended questions. Such questions explore users' experience, context, and expectations. They might include:

- Experience
  - What are your ideas about computers and GUIs?
  - When do they perform the task?
  - How do they perform the task?
  - How frequently do they perform the task?
  - What can you tell me about good ways of communicating with the user?
  - Does the user use any special language?
- Context
  - What is the working environment?
  - Tell me about the different groups of people who perform the work. Is work done alone or in a group? Is work shared?
  - Who interacts with the system in other ways?
  - For example, who installs/maintains/administers the system?
  - Tell me about the culture in which this system will be used — the places, the people, anything else?

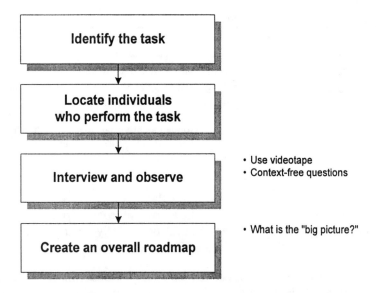

Exhibit 4. Initial Steps in Task Analysis

- Expectations
  - Can I talk with some users about what they'd like to have happen?
  - What features do they want? (If users have difficulty answering this question, propose specific features and ask if the user would like or dislike the specific feature).
  - How will the current work environment change when the system is introduced? How will it remain the same? (Designers may have to propose specific changes and ask if these changes would be considered desirable.)

Asking these questions usually takes no more than a few hours, but the data the answers provide is invaluable to the success of the project.

Task Analysis

Task analysis seeks to answer two very simple questions. First, what tasks are the users doing now that the system will augment, change, enhance, modify, or replace? Second, what tasks will the user perform in the new system?

The first part of task analysis is developing a clear understanding of how the system is currently being used. It proceeds as shown in Exhibit 4. The fourth step shown in Exhibit 4, creating an overall roadmap, is especially important for projects involved with replacing an existing user interface with a redesigned user interface. One common example of this is the decision to upgrade an older, 3270-style mainframe system with a state-of-the-art GUI. Navigating older systems to accomplish even simple tasks can be

Exhibit 5.   Sample Use Case

Use case:	Searching a patent database to find all patents invented by a given person.	
	Actors:	Human Resource Associate.
	Context/Motivation:	Identify key employees within the organization.
	Description:	This use case begins when a human resource associate searches a patent database to find all patents invented by a given person. The associate enters the name of the person into the patent management system, which returns all patents in the current database that match the name of that person. The system will optionally print a report of all such patents as requested by the user.

extraordinarily complex, and without an overall roadmap of how the system currently works developers cannot be entirely certain that the new system provides all the capabilities of the old system.

Use Cases. The second aspect of task analysis, describing how the new system will work, is often done through use cases. A *use case* is a structured prose document that describes the sequence of events between one or more *actors* and the system as one of the actors (typically, the user) attempts to accomplish some task.

Use cases come in several flavors, some appropriate for the initial stages of task analysis and some appropriate for later stages. A *high-level* use case is preferred in the early stages of the project, for it allows the interactions between the user and the system to be described in a manner that is *completely independent* of any specific user interface. This point is especially important: It is a mistake to settle on a given user interface when the basic tasks being undertaken by the user are not well known. An example of a high-level use case is given in Exhibit 5.

It is a mistake to get hung up on the specific format of a use case. Instead, concentrate on describing tasks in a format suitable for the development organization. A use case can be expanded into a more detailed format as needed later in the development process. For example, the use case above does not illustrate the specific format and contents of the report, nor does it show the content and format of the results of the query. Both of these items can be expanded during later stages of development. More importantly, use cases are not generated once and then placed on the shelf. Rather, they are used in conjunction with specific design techniques over the life of the project and are augmented with even more detail prior to implementation.

Function Assignment

As users and tasks are identified, the specific functions detailed in the requirements spring to life. At this stage it is often appropriate to ask if the identified tasks should be performed by the user, performed by the system automatically on behalf of the user, or initiated by the user but performed by the system. This step is called *function assignment* and can be absolutely essential in systems whose goals are to automate existing business processes.

To illustrate, consider an electronic mail system. Most automatically place incoming mail into a specific location, often an "in-box." As a user of the system, did you explicitly *tell* the mail system to place mail there? No. It did this on your behalf, usually as part of its default configuration. Placing mail automatically in an in-box is an example of a required task that is performed automatically by the user.

While most systems can benefit from a function assignment, it is an optional step in the overall development effort.

Mental Model Development

The final step of user and task analysis is to propose various mental models of how the users think about and approach their tasks. Mental models are not documented in any formal manner. Instead, they are informal observations about how designers think users approach their tasks. For example, a designer creating a new project planning tool discovered after several interviews that managers think of dependencies within the project as a web or maze instead of a GANTT or PERT chart. This provided insight into creative new ways of organizing tasks, displaying information, or providing notification of critical path dependencies.

User and Task Analysis in the Real World

In practice, user analysis, task analysis, and function assignment proceed in an iterative manner, as decisions made activity can affect prior decisions made in another. For example, the real user of the system is not always the user identified in the requirements.

In one project, a group of designers were asked to design a GUI for a new bookstore management system. The primary user identified in the requirements was the clerk, who would be using the bookstore to perform such tasks as searching the online catalog for books and placing special orders for books not currently within the inventory.

In attempting to understand the tasks performed by the clerk, the designers realized that one important user not explicitly listed in the requirement was the customer, who would much prefer to search for books on their own without the assistance of the clerk. Perhaps even more importantly, the clerks were glad to assist in the design of a system that would offload what they considered to be a mundane task.

In the long run, the system was able to effectively serve both classes of users. Customers could perform simple searches on their own, while clerks used more sophisticated searching techniques to help customers track down hard-to-find or ill-defined items. Such results are not surprising when designers are given a chance to interact with the intended users of the system during task analysis.

RECOMMENDED COURSE OF ACTION

A highly usable GUI is simply a GUI that lets end users work more efficiently and effectively with a system. To create a usable GUI, systems developers must understand their users, the context in which users work, and what users need to get their work done. The two major steps to arriving at an understanding of users is to gather usability specifications and user and task analysis. Following are checklist systems developers can use to ensure they have completed these to steps.

Usability Specifications Checklist

- No more than two primary usability benefits have been identified for the development effort and published throughout the development organization.
- A competent usability professional has been identified to assist with economic calculations should management require cost justification of this new approach to systems development.
- Each desired benefit has been associated with an appropriate user group as defined below.
- The usability specifications have been shared with the designers. The designers agree that the specifications are achievable.

User and Task Analysis Checklist

- A target population of representative users has been identified.
- An overall roadmap of the *tasks* of current users has been identified.
    - If redesigning a current system, developers have made screen snapshots of *every* screen and have annotated each screen with a description of the task(s) it supports.
    - If redesigning a current system, each task has a set of screen snapshots that describe, in detail, how the user engages the system to accomplish the task.
- A set of high-level use cases documents the current understanding of the system. These are specified without regard to any specific user interface that might be developed over the life of the project.
- A list of users has been reviewed.
- Users have reviewed the list of use cases.
- All requirements are covered by the use cases.

- No use case introduces a new requirement.
- A description of the mental model of the users summarizes findings.
- A functional assignment has been performed. (Optional)

Recommended Reading

The field of GUI design, and books that purport to tell managers and developers how to do it better, is growing every day. Fortunately, the following few timeless classics provide real value if you wish to find more information about a specific topic.

Gause G., And G. Weinberg. *Exploring Requirements Quality Before Design.* New York: Dorset House, 1989.

Managing requirements is at the heart of effective software development. Unfortunately, most projects do a surprisingly poor job of this! This book is appropriate for all levels of managers and developers, and is arguably *the single* most *practical* and *effective* book ever written on how to improve your software development practices.

Gould, J. D. "How to Design Usable Systems." in *Handbook of Human-Computer Interaction,* M. Helander (ed.) Elsevier Science Publishers B.V., New York, 1988.

This chapter is one of the most important ever written on the topic of designing usable systems. Gould provides his own set of checklists and numerous examples to support his claims.

Nielsen, J. *Usability Engineering.* New York: Harcourt Brace & Company, Publishers, 1993.

This book provides a more in-depth view of usability engineering. It includes a concise executive overview and a detailed list of testing techniques. This book is suitable for technical leads and senior architects who want to be aware of the issues without expending the energy to create an in-depth understanding of design.

Collins, Dave. *Designing Object-Oriented User Interfaces,* Redwood City, CA: The Benjamin/Cummings Publishing Company, Inc. 1995.

This book should be required reading for any developer given primary responsibility for the design of the user interface. Collins addresses the proper construction of the system model and shows how they should be implemented.

Microsoft Press, *he Windows Guidelines for GUI Design.*

Chances are good your applications will have to run on Microsoft Windows platforms. Why not make certain it adheres to the standard?

Chapter II-4
Designing Usable User Interfaces

Luke Hohmann

WHAT GOOD IS A SOFTWARE SYSTEM IF NO ONE CAN OR WANTS TO USE IT? To make sure end users actually can work with a system, software developers must ensure that its user interfaces are usable. Creating usable interfaces has become a specialty in systems development known as usability. Usability has been defined to cover three basic areas:

- A highly usable GUI allows the user to accomplish one or more specific tasks easily, efficiently, and with a minimum number of errors. Extremely usable interfaces fade over time and enable the user to concentrate completely on the task at hand. This is referred to as *transparency*. An extreme example of transparency in action is a child playing a video game.
- A highly usable GUI is easy to learn, and once learned is easy to remember.
- The use and arrangement of controls, the colors and layout of both large and small details, and the ability to customize the user interface all contribute to a sense of satisfaction, enjoyment, and accomplishment.

To create usable interfaces, developers must understand users and their requirements. This phase in developing interfaces was covered in Chapter II-3, "Creating GUIs Users Can Use: Usability Analysis." One of the greatest challenges of software development is translating the output of one phase into the input of the next phase. This chapter takes on this challenge and explains how to successfully translate the requirements established by usability analysis into a design that can be used to create a highly usable interface.

LO-FI DESIGN

With an understanding of the user, their tasks, and (possibly) a function assignment, the development effort is ready to begin the first design phase, the development of a lo-fidelity prototype. This step is critically important, as it is the first time the designer will make the transition from an understanding of the users mental model to the creation of a system model.

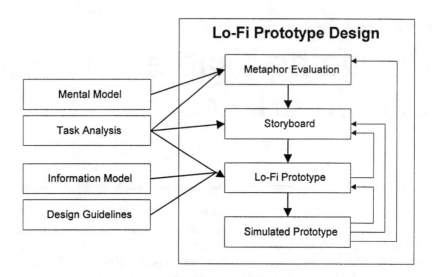

Exhibit 1.   The Basic Activities of Lo-Fi Design

Ideally, the system model will match the mental model in form and action. The only way to determine if this objective is achieved is through the iterative development of the lo-fidelity (lo-fi) prototype.

The specific objectives of this phase is to clarify the overall flow of the application, make certain the content, layout, and interaction of each window is appropriate, and ensure that each use case and/or function identified in the requirements is explicitly supported in the user interface. The basic activities, as outlined in Exhibit 1, consist of developing a storyboard, creating a lo-fidelity prototype, and beginning the testing process by testing the prototype with representative users. Among the inputs to this activity are the information model (an Entity-Relationship model for traditional systems or a Class Diagram for object-oriented systems) and design guidelines.

Capturing the System Model: The Role of Metaphor

The *system model* is the model the designer creates to represent the capabilities of the system under development. The system model is analogous to the mental model of the user. As the user uses the system to perform tasks, he or she will modify their current mental model or form a new one based on the terminology and operations the user encounters when using the system. Usability is significantly enhanced when the system model supports existing mental models.

To illustrate: your mental model of an airport enables you to predict where to find ticket counters and baggage claim areas when you arrive at a new airport. If you were building a system to support flight operations, you would want to organize the system model around such concepts as baggage handling and claim areas.

A metaphor is a communication device that helps us understand one thing in terms of another. Usability is enhanced when the system model is communicated through a metaphor that matches the users mental model. For example, the familiar desktop metaphor popularized by the Macintosh and copied in the Windows '95 user interface organizes our operations with files and folders as a metaphorical desktop. The system model of files and folders meshes with our mental model through the use of the interface. Another example is data entry dialogs based on their paper counterparts.

In the design process, the designer should use the concept of a metaphor as a way of exploring effective ways to communicate the system model and as a means of effectively supporting the user's mental model. Resist blindly adhering to a metaphor, as this can impede the user's ability to complete important tasks. For example, although the desktop metaphor enables me to manage my files and folders effectively, there is no effective metaphorical counterpart that supports running critical utility software such as disk defragmentation or hard disk partitioning. A paper form may provide inspiration as a metaphor in a data entry system, but it is inappropriate to restrict the designer of a computer application to the inherent limitations of paper.

Storyboarding

A storyboard is a way of showing the overall navigation logic and functional purpose of each window in the GUI. It shows how each task identified in the task analysis and described in the use cases can be accomplished in the system. It also shows primary and secondary window dependencies, and makes explicit the interaction between different dialogs in the user. (A primary window is a main application window. A secondary window is a window such as a dialog.) The storyboard often expands on the system model through the metaphor and clarifies the designer's understanding of the user's mental model.

An example of a simple storyboard for a mail system is shown in Exhibit 2. The example shows the name of each window along with a brief description of the window contents. A solid line means the user's selection will open a primary window, while a dashed line indicates the opening of a modal dialog. The notation used for storyboards should be as simple as possible. For example, the earliest phases of system design using a simple sheet of paper with Post-It™ notes representing each window is an effective way to organize the system.

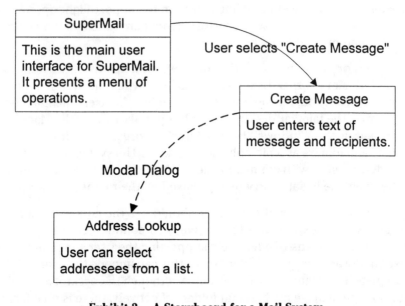

Exhibit 2.   A Storyboard for a Mail System

Storyboards have an additional benefit in that they can show the overall "gestalt" of the system. I've seen storyboards as large as 3'x6', packed with information, yet entirely understandable. This storyboard provided the development staff with a powerful means of making certain the overall application was consistent. The storyboard also enabled the project manager to distribute the detailed window design to specific developers in a sensible way, as the common relationships between windows were easy to identify.

The development of the storyboard should be guided by the use cases. Specifically, it should be possible to map each operation described in a use case to one or more of the windows displayed in the storyboard. The mapping of specific actions to user interface widgets will come at a later step in the development process.

Lo-Fi Window Design

Following the storyboard the design process proceeds to the development of the initial lo-fi window designs. During this phase the designer takes paper, pencil, and many erasers and prepares preliminary versions of the most important windows described in the storyboard. Which windows are these? Certainly the "main" window displayed to the user, as well as any dialogs that control critically important information. More importantly, the windows that *must* be designed are those associated with the most important use cases, those use cases that represent the most important functions of the system. Don't waste time drawing common windows. If the system is going to run on Windows '95™, and the designers need to portray the opening of a file, just grab a snapshot of the common dialog that supports this task and draw by hand what must be changed.

One critical decision point in lo-fi window design is determining the information that should be displayed to the user. The basic rule of thumb is to only display the information that is needed to complete the task. Although designers often think that adding more information contributes to usability, several studies have shown that any information not directly related to the task the user is trying to accomplish decreases usability. But, how does the designer know what information this is? There are two basic approaches, each of which is appropriate in a given context. The most common and effective approach is to perform an analysis of the requirements and problem domain to create a preliminary entity-relationship (or object) model. (It is beyond the scope of this chapter to describe how to do this in detail.) Use this approach when the problem domain is fairly well known, if the development is redesigning an existing system, or if the system must interface with legacy databases.

The second approach is to simply storyboard some high-level screens and see what information the users really need by iteratively refining these storyboards based on their feedback. Once the storyboards have been approved developers can create the necessary data models as appropriate. This approach is most appropriate when the needs of the user aren't all that well known as a way of reducing the overall risk associated with the development effort. By confirming the basic structure of the system with the user *before* costly prototyping or development begins, storyboarding ensures that when the system is actually constructed it will meet with much greater success.

Creating a lo-fi window design is arguably the most fun a designer can have in systems development. Instead of being constrained by the contents of a palette or being slowed down by a poorly performing drawing tool, the designer is free to explore whatever aspect of system interaction they feel will most benefit their user.

When I am engaged in lo-fi window design I find that pencils with enormous erasers and lots of paper are simply not enough. In addition, I like to have the following items easily accessible:

- Scissors
- Glue
- Clear and colored overhead transparencies
- White correction paper
- A computer with a screen capture program and a printer
- Clear tape

- Bagels, pizza, and diet Pepsi
- Whiteout
- A photocopier

Why is a computer and printer on this list? The answer is simple. Instead of drawing buttons and list boxes (and other common widgets by hand) it is more efficient to take screen snapshots of the desired widget, print it, and then glue or tape it into the lo-fi design. Does this mean that lo-fi designs represent a mishmash of hand-drawn and computer-generated graphics? Sure. It also means that the designer is working with the maximum amount of freedom, unencumbered by arbitrary constraints of what might represent good or bad design.

What *is* important, and what should be vigilantly searched for, is any sign the development staff is creating their designs on the computer. Pencil and paper are far faster than any CASE tool. This point is worth repeating. Designers should be actively discouraged from creating their initial designs in a CASE tool. Unless designers have extraordinary discipline or extensive experience, they are likely to be inextricably drawn into making the details of the creation correct (e.g., making buttons the same size, making input fields line up exactly, and the like). While these details must ultimately be finalized, worrying about them at this stage of the game is unimportant.

There are two additional reasons why designers should avoid using a computer in the development of a lo-fi prototype. This first concerns the psychological attachment all designers share with their creation. The greater the effort spent in creating the design, the greater the attachment. This can be particularly problematic as it is expected the initial design will undergo (possibly) substantial transformation during testing. The goal is to create a means whereby the designer will be sufficiently attached to produce high-quality work, but amenable to make the changes motivated by testing. Fortunately, this is an easy goal to achieve.

The second reason why designers should avoid using a computer in the development of lo-fi prototypes concerns the speed with which designs can be created. As stated earlier, most designers are far more efficient with paper and pencil than with a CASE tool. In the early stages of GUI development, obtaining feedback early is absolutely essential to ensure usability. Using a paper-and-pencil approach enables designers to complete their designs faster, substantially decreasing the amount of time they must wait before obtaining feedback.

DEVELOPMENT IN THE REAL WORLD

In practice, storyboarding, lo-fi window design, and even the generation of analysis entity-relationship (or object) models tend to coevolve in the development of the system. This is OK, as sometimes the only way to determine if you need certain information is to see what impact it has on the user interface. For example, I was once involved in the creation of an application for data entry personnel that reached the final stage of development before the designers realized that a critical piece of information would greatly enhance usability. Unfortunately, this information could not be added to the system without an extensive redesign of the database schema. This expensive oversight could have been avoided through the use of lo-fi prototyping.

It is also common to see a storyboard where one or two of the windows are drawn in a fairly detailed manner or where the interaction among a group of windows is outlined more explicitly than others. Like any modeling effort, developing storyboards, lo-fi prototypes, and data (or object) models should always add or retain information that is important to your development team for their specific environment. If they need more information, let them add it. If they need less, that is OK — they'll remove it. Avoid, at all costs, forcing the team to follow some arbitrary standard for creating models in the user interface, including storyboards. This does you and them little good.

SIMULATED PROTOTYPING

There are many kinds of testing systems in software development: performance, stress, user acceptance, and so forth. *Usability testing* refers to testing activities conducted to ensure the usability of the entire system. This includes the user interface and supporting documentation, and in advanced applications can include the help system and even the technical support operation. A specific goal of lo-fi prototyping is to enable the designer to begin usability testing as early as possible in the overall design process through a technique called *simulated prototyping*.

Simulated prototyping means the operation of the lo-fi system is *simulated*. Quite literally, a representative user attempts to complete assigned tasks using the prototype with a human playing the role of the computer. Before I describe how to conduct a simulated prototype test of the user interface, it is appropriate to describe its expected outcome.

The outcome of a simulated prototyping session is a report that details the results of the test. This report must include the following three items. First, it must be clearly identified for tracking purposes. Second, it must identify all individuals associated with the test. (Participants are not identified by name, but by an anonymous tracking number. Referring to the users involved with the test as participants rather than subjects encourages an open and friendly atmosphere and a free-flowing exchange of ideas. The goal is to keep participants as comfortable as possible.) Third, it must clearly summarize the results of the test.

Exhibit 3.   Roles and Responsibilities of Developers in Simulated Prototyping

Role	Responsibilities
Leader	• Organizes and coordinates the entire testing effort. • Responsible for the overall quality of the review (i.e., a *good* review of a poor user interface produces a report detailing exactly what is wrong). • Ensures that the review report is prepared in a timely manner.
Greeter	• Greets people, explains test, handles any forms associated with test.
Facilitator	• Runs test – only person allowed to speak. • Performs three essential functions: 1. Gives the user instructions. 2. Encourages users to "think-aloud" during the test so observers can record user's reactions to the user interface. 3. Makes certain test is finished on time.
Computer	• Simulates the operation of the interface by physically manipulating the objects representing the interface. Thus, the "computer" rearranges windows, presents dialogs, simulates typing, and so forth. • *Must* know application logic.
Observer	• Takes notes on 5x8 cards, one note per card.

It is common to see test results concentrating on the negative responses associated with the prototype, but designers should also be looking for the positive responses exhibited by the user. This will enable them to retain the good ideas as the prototype undergoes revision. Unlike a source code review report, the results of the simulated prototype can provide solutions to problems identified during testing the negative

Conducting the Test

A simulated prototype is most effective when conducted by a structured team of between three and five developers. The roles and responsibilities of each developer associated with a simulated prototype are described in Exhibit 3 (developers should rotate roles between successive tests, as playing any single role for too long can be overly demanding).

Selecting users for the simulated prototype must be done rather carefully. It may be easy to simply grab the next developer down the hall, or bribe the security guard with a bagel to come and look at the user interface. However, unless the development effort is focused on building a CASE tool or a security monitoring system the development team has got the wrong person. More specifically, *users selected for the test must be representative of the target population.*

If the system is for nurses, test with nurses. If the system is for data entry personnel, test with data entry personnel. Avoid testing with friends or co-workers unless developers are practicing "playing" computer. (It is critically important that designers be given the opportunity to practice playing computer. At first, developers try to simulate the operation of the

118

user interface at the same speed as the computer. Once they realize this is impossible, they become skilled at smoothly simulating the operation of the user interface, and provide a quite realistic experience for the participant.)

During the simulated prototype, make certain developers have all of their lo-fi prototyping tools easily available. A lot of clear transparency is necessary, as they will place this over screens to simulate input from the user. Moreover, having the tools available means they will be able to make the *slightest* on-the-fly modifications that can dramatically improve the quality of the user interface, even while the "computer" is running.

How should the test be run? The basic idea is quite straightforward: Explain the goals of the test to the participants, sit them down, and have them attempt to accomplish one or more tasks identified in the task analysis. While this is happening, the observer(s) carefully watch the participant for *any* sign of confusion, misunderstandings, or inability to complete the requested task. Each such problem is noted on a 3x5 card for further discussion once the test is completed. During the simulated prototype designers will often want to "help" the user by giving them hints or making suggestions. *Do not do this*, as it will make the results of the test meaningless.

Some authors recommend videotaping the entire process for a more extended analysis. While this can be helpful, I have found that few companies can afford the time to carefully review the videotapes. This is not to say that videotapes are not effective, and indeed, if creating a highly usable system is absolutely essential then videotaping should be used. Most systems, however, can derive substantial benefit from this simple approach.

The entire test, from preparing to run the test, greeting the users and running the test, and discussing the results should take about two hours. Thus, with discipline and practice, an experienced team can actually run up to four tests per day. In practice, I have found it better to plan on running two tests per day so that the development team can make critical modifications to the user interface between tests. In general, three to eight tests give enough data to know if the development effort is ready to proceed to the next phase in the overall development process.

One final word on selecting and managing participants. Remember they are helping create a better system. The system is being tested, not them. Participants must feel completely free to stop the test at any time should they feel any discomfort.

HI-FI DESIGN

Once simulated prototyping has validated the lo-fi prototype, the design process moves into the last stage before implementation: the creation of the hi-fi prototype. This is an optional step in the overall process and can be skipped if the project is experiencing extreme scheduling pressures.

Alternatively, this phase is essential if the project has produced detailed usability specifications, as such specifications can be validated only through a hi-fi prototype.

The focus of work in the development of the hi-fi prototype moves to the realization of the ideas validated in the lo-fi design. Data entry fields are drawn in a precise manner, complete with field and edit masks. Iconic buttons that were merely sketched in the lo-fi prototype must be rendered according to the constraints and requirements of the delivery platform. This means drawing the icons, making certain the proper states for each button exist, and testing the actual working of the button in source code.

A more difficult form of development comes when the team must craft a customized representation of a domain object. One of the reasons we find graphical user interfaces more appealing than their textual counterparts is that humans perceive and act on the world through the identification of objects. Thus, if the GUI shows a picture of a light switch in the "off" position, the user can infer that the state of the domain object represented by the switch is "off." Suppose the user can change this state by metaphorically flicking the switch with a click of the mouse. Making certain all of these interactions work properly takes attention to detail, substantial coding skills, and quite often a background in graphic arts.

Finally, this is the stage where developers enhance the presentation and aesthetics through the use of fonts, color, grouping, and white space. Doing this most effectively requires experience with graphic design, and the details are beyond the scope of this article. However, these details contribute substantially to the overall feelings of aesthetic enjoyment and satisfaction with the user interface and should be considered an essential activity in the overall development effort. Unless the development team has this experience, I recommend keeping the choice of fonts simple, using predominantly black on white text, and avoiding the use of graphics as adornments.

With all of this work going on, why do I refer to this as "hi-fi" window design and not the development of the final application? Mainly because the application at this stage of development is not considered truly complete. For example, even though the user interface is translated into a visible (and maybe even slightly working) system, the focus of the development is still on the creation of a highly usable interface. At this stage the system may not contain all error handling, connect to external databases, work over a network, and perform whatever other operations must be done before shipping the final product.

Tools for Hi-Fi Design

In general, the most effective tool for hi-fi window design is the development environment used to prepare the final system. The benefits of this approach include minimizing the number of tools that developers must learn, limiting overall development costs, and making certain the designs work as created. Tools such the Microsoft Visual C++ or IBM VisualAge for Smalltalk are examples of these environments.

In some cases it is more appropriate to use one tool for hi-fi design and other for the underlying implementation. An example of this approach is using Microsoft Visual Basic to construct the basic user interface and a combination of Visual Basic and Visual C++ to implement the functionality of the system. This approach requires a bit more sophistication within the development organization, but can be quite effective if the hi-fi window designers use a different tool set than the implementation developers.

Testing Hi-Fi Prototypes

The primary purpose of creating and testing a lo-fi prototype is to make certain the system model effectively supports the mental model and to lay the foundation of a highly usable system. It also helps the designer clarify the behavior of the system. For example, crafting a detailed lo-fi prototype will force the designer to identify potential error situations. Once identified, the designer can respond in several ways that contribute to usability. The designer may be able to design the error situation out of the interface. An example of this would be disabling a button when the button cannot be pressed instead of displaying a dialog indicating the user selected an illegal operation. Alternatively, the designer may identify a way to automatically "fix" the error, as when a system accepts illegal input but is able to convert this output to a legal value.

While lo-fi design and simulated prototyping help to answer most issues associated with the user interface, there are certain kinds of tests that simply cannot be done properly using a lo-fi prototype. Making certain response times are acceptable, determining error rates, and making certain the sketches of graphics and their interactions that make good sense on paper actually work for the user simply cannot be tested using a lo-fi prototype. Testing hi-fi prototypes is also essential if usability specifications were developed and contained detailed performance measures.

Although the results of a hi-fi prototype test are the same as a lo-fi test, the process is substantially different. First, the test environment is different. It is typically more formal, with tests conducted within a usability lab. A *usability lab* is a specially equipped room with video cameras, target test equipment, and other devices to record and monitor participants as they use the system. Usability labs are constructed similar to rooms that are used by market researchers to obtain feedback on products through focus groups, and include one-way mirrors that allow the users to be observed by usability professionals.

Second, the role of the computer is eliminated.

Third, the nature of the tasks being tested means the structure of the test is different. For example, lo-fi prototypes are most effective at determining if the overall design created by the development team will be effective. Specifically, the lo-fi test *should* have helped determine the overall structure of the user interface: the arrangement and content of menus, windows, and the core interactions between them. When the lo-fi testing is complete, the conceptual structure of the interface should be well understood and agreed upon with the users. The hi-fi test, on the other hand, should be organized around testing one or more concrete performance variables.

Finally, the overall functionality of the hi-fi prototype must reflect the needs of the test. If the test centers on the rate of errors in a data entry application, the hi-fi prototype must be functionally complete with respect to field and error management. Alternatively, if the effectiveness of on-line help is being evaluated, the on-line help system must be complete. All of these requirements mean that generating a hi-fi prototype will involve a substantial amount of real coding.

The *real* managerial impact of hi-fi testing is twofold. First, there is question of finding the right individuals to conduct the test. Does the team have access to individuals who can properly conduct a hi-fi test? Most development teams do not. While most developers can quickly and easily learn how to run an effective lo-fi test, conducting a properly structured hi-fi test requires significantly more training.

The second, and far more important question, is this: What is going to do be done with the results of the test? Like lo-fi test results, the results of a hi-fi test must be evaluated to determine what, if any, modifications are needed in the user interface. The problem is that modifying a hi-fi prototype takes a substantial amount of design *and* coding.

A Recipe for Disaster

The development team has successfully released the first version of the application. User feedback is generally positive, although some minor usability problems have been identified. The development team is asked to improve the user interface while significantly extending the functionality of the system.

Because the development team is confident in their knowledge of the application and the user, they design an entirely new user interface that they think will more effectively provide the required functionality without involving the users. Specifically, they draw a few sketches of the proposed user interface and proceed to build it without involving any users.

The first problem arises when the schedule slips by three weeks because the new user interface took considerably longer to develop than originally planned. The second problem arises when the beta version of the new system is released to a select group of users for customer acceptance testing. The results of the tests demonstrate that the new interface, which is based on a different metaphor, has serious usability problems. Fixing the problem requires a redesign of the entire user interface.

The developers, who are already demoralized from the feedback of the test, estimate that performing the necessary redesign will add approximately four months to the development schedule. Of course, sales and marketing have made several promises to large customers who need the new features provided by the product.

Each alternative is undesirable. If the product is shipped based solely on the deadline, developer morale will continue to plummet. And even if the product manages to ship on time it may ultimately fail in the marketplace because of usability problems. Redesigning the user interface and missing the deadline risks customer defection. What is the best solution?

This scenario, which is all too common in most development organizations, clearly demonstrates why I have structured the development process as described above. The use of lo-fi design techniques and simulated prototype testing *is simply the fastest way to develop highly usable systems!* In three weeks the developers described above spent crafting a single hi-fi prototype they could have developed *numerous* lo-fi prototypes, and tested *every single one of them* with users! At the end of the three weeks they would have a very clear understanding of exactly how the system should look and operate with the user. Moreover, they would have been certain that the radical new changes they proposed would enhance the overall usability of the system.

DESIGN PRINCIPLES

While usability testing is the only way to be certain the user interface is usable, there are several well-known and validated principles of user interface design that guide the decisions made by good designers. These principles are platform and operating system independent, and are applicable in almost any environment. Adherence to these principles is becoming increasingly important in the error of Web development, as there are no universal standards for designing web-based applications.

Apple Macintosh Design Principles

The first set of important design principles was published by Apple Computer Corporation for Macintosh developers. The principles are based on the idea that the designer is creating a "world" that supports the user in the achievement of well-defined tasks. (In this article, the world created by the designer is referred to as the system model). These principles are summarized in Exhibit 4.

Exhibit 4. Apple Macintosh Interface Design Principles

World-Building	The overarching goal is to design a "world" that is natural and comfortable for users.
Use of Metaphors	Use concrete metaphors and make them clear and understandable so that users have set of expectations to apply to computer environments. Whenever appropriate, use audio and visual effects that support the metaphor, but use these carefully. Gratuitous sounds, no matter how realistic, are annoying.
Aesthetic Integrity	Visually confusing or unattractive displays detract from the effectiveness of human-computer interactions. Users should be able to control the superficial appearance of their computer workplaces — to display their own style and individuality. Messes are acceptable only if the user makes them — applications are not allowed this freedom.
Consistency	Effective applications are consistent within themselves and with one another.
Perceived Stability	Users feel comfortable in a computer environment that remains understandable and familiar rather than one that changes randomly. A perfect example of what not to do can be found in the America Online user interface, which often automatically repositions Windows. The net effect is to severely disrupt the user's sense of trust in the application, detracting from the overall usability of the application.
World-Controlling	How do the users control the world created by the designers?
Direct Manipulation	Every action has a concrete and logical effect. Each action results in the commonsense display of the new state of the object.
See and Point	Users select actions from alternatives presented on the screen. The general form of user actions is "Object⇒Action," or "Hey, you — do this." Users rely on recognition, not recall; they should not have to remember anything the computer already knows. For example, in a word processing application a user selects some text ("Hey, you") and then chooses to apply formatting changes such as making the font boldface or underlined ("do this").
WYSIWYG (What you see is what you get)	There should be no secrets from the user, no abstract commands that only promise future results.
Feedback	Keep the user informed. User activities should be simple at any moment, though they may be complex taken together.
Forgiveness	Users make mistakes; forgive them. The user's actions are generally reversible — let users know about any that are not.
User Control	The user, not the computer, initiates and controls all actions. The user decides what is done, and in what order, *period*. If a designer feels that a certain action might be risky, they should by all means alert the user to this possibility. *But do not prevent them from doing it.* The design philosophy of the Macintosh assumes that users are intelligent and can decide for themselves what they need the program to do.

Neilsen and Molich Design Principles

Another important set of design principles was created by Neilsen and Molich, which are summarized in the following list:

- **Use a simple and natural dialog.** Simple means no irrelevant or rarely used information. Natural means an order that matches the task.

- **Speak the user's language.** Use words and concepts that match in meaning and intent the user's mental model. Do not use system-specific engineering terms. When presenting information, use an appropriate tone and style. For example, a dialog written for a children's game would not use the same style as a dialog written for a assembly line worker.

- **Minimize user memory load.** Do not make the user remember things from one action to the next by making certain each screen retains enough information to support the task of the user. I refer to this as the "scrap of paper" test. If the user ever needs to write a critical piece of information on a piece of paper while completing a task, the system has exceeded memory capacity.

- **Be consistent.** Users should be able to learn an action sequence in one part of the system and apply it again to get similar results in other places.

- **Provide feedback.** Let users know what effect their actions have on the system. Common forms of feedback include changing the cursor, displaying a percent-done progress indicator, and dialogs indicating when the system changes state in a significant manner.

- **Provide clearly marked exits.** If users get into a part of the system that does not interest them, they should always be able to get out quickly without damaging anything. Examples of clearly marked exits include the consistent and correct use of Cancel buttons and an "undo" feature.

- **Provide shortcuts.** Shortcuts can help experienced users avoid lengthy dialogs and informational messages that they do not need. Examples of shortcuts include keyboard accelerators in menus and dialogs. More sophisticated examples include command-based searching languages. Novice users can use a simple interface, while experienced users can use the more advanced features afforded by the query language.

- **Prevent errors.** Whenever a designer begins to write an error message they should ask: Can this error be prevented, detected, and fixed, or avoided altogether? If the answer to any of these questions is yes, additional engineering effort should be expended to prevent the error.

- **Good error messages.** There are many times the system cannot prevent an error (e.g., a printer runs out of paper). Good error messages let the user know what the problem is and how to correct it ("The printer is out of paper. Add paper to continue printing.").

The Importance of Consistency. The principle of *being consistent* means two distinct forms of consistency. The first is platform consistency, which means the application should adhere to the platform standards on which it was developed. For example, Windows '95 specifies the example distance between dialog buttons and the edge of the window, and designs should adhere to these standards. Each developer associated with the design of the user interface should be given a copy of the relevant platform standards published by each vendor. This will ensure that the application is platform compliant from the earliest stages of development.

The second is application consistency, which means that all of the applications developed within a company should follow the same general model of interaction. This second form of consistency can be harder to achieve as it requires the interaction and communication between all of the development organizations within a company.

I once worked with a large telecommunications firm that had created a significant usability problem in the process of migrating from the mainframe world to GUI-centric client-server applications. Some applications were designed using a drag-and-drop metaphor, while others took a more traditional approach of paper-inspired dialogs. Some applications were developed using the techniques described in the chapters; most were not. The net result? Instead of creating a consistent set of new applications that improved usability by orders of magnitude, the development teams produced a set of applications that were largely inconsistent with each other, requiring the user to learn the specific intricacies of each application. Fixing this problem required the creation of a common standard and substantial rework in many applications.

USABILITY INSPECTIONS

It is possible to formally incorporate the use of these design principles in the development of the user interface. A *usability inspection* is an evaluation of the user interface by a usability professional with respect to design principles and relevant platform standards. A usability inspection can be conducted at any time during the design process.

After lo-fi design, a usability inspection can help uncover obvious usability flaws before simulated prototyping. After hi-fi design, an inspection can identify any areas where the application fails to adhere to platform standards.

RECOMMENDED COURSE OF ACTION

This article has detailed the steps of designing user interfaces that incorporate the principles of usability. Such interfaces have the following characteristics:

- They allow users to accomplish tasks easily.
- They are easy to learn to use and remember how to use.
- Their overall arrangement and use give users satisfaction, enjoyment, and a sense of accomplishment.

If developers are to create such interfaces, they must understand the interfaces' users and how these users work. Developers then must translate this understanding into a design. This article has explained this design process, consists of the following phases:

- *Lo-fi design.* In this initial phase, developers clarify the overall flow of an application, make sure content, layout, and interaction of each window is appropriate, and ensure the interface's support of each use case or function identified in requirements.
- *Simulated prototyping.* This phase tests a lo-fi design by simulating the operation of the design.
- *Hi-fi design.* This phase is essential if detailed usability specifications have been worked up, but it can be skipped if schedules are running short. The focus of this phase is to realize ideas validated in lo-fi design.
- *Usability inspections.* These can be conducted after each design phase. It is an evaluation of the user interface by a usability professional.

The following checklists will help developers through each of these phases.

Lo-Fi Design Checklist

- We have created a storyboard that details the overall navigation logic of the application.
- We have traced each use case through the storyboard.
- We have created a data (or object) model that describes the primary sources of information to be displayed to the users and the relationships among these items.
- We have transformed our storyboards into a set of lo-fi prototypes.
- The first set of lo-fi prototypes were created using paper and pencil.

All information displayed in the lo-fi prototype can be obtained from the entity-relationship or object model or from some other well-known source

Simulated Prototyping Checklist

- We have prepared a set of tasks for simulated prototype testing.
- A set of participants who match the target user population have been identified.
- Any required legal paperwork has been signed by the participants.
- Our lo-fi prototype has been reviewed — we think it supports these tasks.

- The simulated prototyping team has practiced their roles.
- The "computer" has simulated the operation of the system.
- We have responded to the review report and made the necessary corrections to the user interface. We have scheduled a subsequent test of these modifications.

Testing Hi-Fi Design Checklist

- Our hi-fi test is measuring a specific performance variable.
- We have identified a qualified human factors specialist for hi-fi testing.
- We have prepared precise definitions of test requirements.
- We have secured the use of an appropriately equipped usability lab.

Usability Inspection Checklist

- Each developer has been given a copy of the design principles.
- Each developer has easy access to a copy of the platform standards. Ideally, each developer is given a copy of the platform standards and time to learn them.
- Each error situation has been carefully examined to determine if the error can be removed from the system with more effective engineering.
- A usability inspection form and a process for acting on its results were created before conducting a usability inspection.
- Management is prepared to properly collect and manage the results of the usability inspection.

Recommended Reading

Nielsen, Jackob. *Usability Engineering.* Boston: Academic Press, 1993.

Chapter II-5
Building GUIs Users Can Use: Usability Development

Luke Hohmann

BEGINNING WITH CHAPTER II-3, "Creating GUIs Users Can Use: Usability Analysis," and Chapter II-4, "Designing Usable User Interfaces," which examined how usability affects the front-end stages of development, this series of chapters on usability and graphical user interfaces (GUIs) concludes by explaining how usability is incorporated into the actual development of GUIs. Usability stresses the importance of end users' experience with an interface, which is a goal different from that of other development approaches. To reach that goal developers must change their attitudes toward developing GUIs and how the performance of this work is also different from other types of development.

The World Wide Web's reach has even affected GUI development. Web-based interfaces (i.e., browsers) have certain limitations and characteristics that affect usability development. This chapter ends by explaining how to adapt usability techniques for developing browser interfaces.

USABILITY DEVELOPMENT PROCESS

It is impossible to engage in a detailed discussion of development system planning in a chapter of this size — the variables, constraints, and forces are too complex. Disclaimers aside, it is important to understand just how a focus on usability affects development plans.

Exhibit 1 shows that many but not all of the activities associated with developing highly usable systems can be conducted in parallel with traditional development activities. Here are specific planning considerations for each activity.

Usability Specifications. Usability specifications are most effective when developed in concert with the product specification. They should be considered a part of the product specification. The usability specification

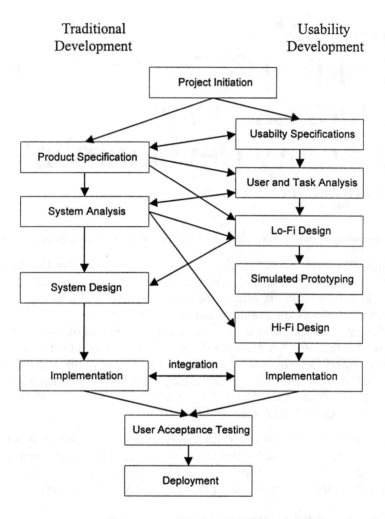

Exhibit 1. Activities in Traditional Systems Development and Usability-Based Development

often affects system analysis by sensitizing the development team to aspects of the system that require special attention.

User and Task Analysis. While the product specification (or associated marketing literature) should identify broad classes of target users, the information contained in these documents are not detailed enough for the development of a highly usable system. Thus, the product specification feeds the user and task analysis. Once the broad classes of users have been identified, user and task analysis can be conducted in parallel with other system development and analysis activities. Finally, the user and task analysis will coevolve with the system analysis.

Lo-Fi Design. Once systems development management has made the commitment to the usability approach articles, developers are often eager to begin lo-fi design as quickly as possible. Allowing developers to begin lo-fi design until product specification is complete is a mistake, as they are likely to waste effort in designing a user interface that fails to match the true needs of the user. However, lo-fi design can be initiated immediately upon completion of user and task analysis, even if the rest of the traditional analysis is not yet complete. If the plan calls for the development of a lo-fi prototype in parallel with traditional analysis, remember to conduct periodic reviews of both the lo-fi prototype and the data or class models to make certain the system can support the lo-fi design.

Simulated Prototyping and Hi-Fi Design. The motivation for simulated prototyping is to ensure that the basic structure of the system as specified in the lo-fi prototype meets the needs of users. It is in the transition of lo-fi design to simulated prototyping that the development plan can begin to exhibit high degrees of parallelism. Specifically, while the user interface design team is testing and enhancing the lo-fi prototype the remainder of the development team can be engaged in the design and implementation of the system.

Implementation. What specific implementation activities can be done at this time? Several. First, the development team should concentrate on building the core set of functions that must be provided independently of the user interface. Second, the development should focus on the creation of appropriate test plans to ensure the correct operation of the system. Third, the development team must make certain the database model of the system is correct. All of these core activities, and several additional ones, can be conducted in parallel with the final design of the user interface.

The final stage of development is the integration of the user interface with the remainder of the system. It is best to perform integration in a series of cycles that incrementally increase the functionality of the system. For example, the first cycle might consist of integrating the sign-on screen and one or two of the features provided in the main menu. Subsequent cycles would increase overall functionality by interconnecting additional screens with the underlying implementation guided by the most important use cases.

CHANGING DEVELOPERS' ATTITUDE

The degree to which a development organization changes its traditional planning practices to incorporate usability sends a strong signal to the development team as to how important the organization considers usable systems. Quite literally, if there is no time devoted to the creation of lo-fi prototypes, there will be no passion in the team for usability.

DEVELOPMENT STRATEGIES

The previous paragraph was written with the subtle implication that management does not want to practice usability engineering. While this can be true, most managers enthusiastically support the development of highly usable systems once they realize the clear and direct financial benefits of this approach. Specifically, developing usable systems is good for the bottom line.

But what happens when developers are reluctant to try this approach? For example, developers of a successful shrink-wrapped software application are asked to redesign their system to support new features. Problems occur when the user interface must undergo radical transformation to support these new features.

Because these developers have been successful without a usability approach, they may feel that they do not need to use the techniques described in this chapter for the redesign. This is a serious mistake for at least three reasons. First, changing an existing system can alienate users unless they are certain that learning the new system will provide the necessary benefits. Second, the business goals almost always include expanding the application into new market domains. Thus, while the development team may have obtained a great deal of knowledge about their current users, it is usually the case that very little is known about new users. More dangerously, unless the team takes the time to learn about these new users, they are likely to make design decisions on incorrect knowledge, seriously detracting from overall usability for *all* users. Third, it is usually the case that the development team has an overly inflated view of the true usability of their application. There are very few applications that cannot be substantially improved through the application of usability principles.

What is the appropriate managerial response in this case? First, developers should know that the development plan specifically includes the activities described in this article. Second, require the appropriate deliverables associated with each activity and do not let the development effort continue until these have been completed. If the development team knows management is serious about this approach, they will quickly adopt the same attitude.

DEVELOPERS AND ROLES

Complex systems are created by multifaceted teams: developers work in conjunction with technical writers, marketers, salespeople, and a host of others with specialized skills. This section addresses the roles and personnel needed in the development of highly usable systems. This section assumes the development effort is focused on creating a system for a corporate environment. Such systems range from decision support systems to financial accounting systems as well as a host of internal corporate systems such as human resource systems. Excluded from this category are such application categories as games, virtual reality systems, and web sites devoted to entertainment content.

Senior Architect. The senior architect is the person (or small team of up to three people) responsible for the creation of the system architecture. The system architecture defines the basic "structure" of the system (e.g., the high-level modules comprising the major functions of the system, the management and distribution of data, the kind and style of its user interface, what platform(s) will it run on, and so forth). A well-defined system architecture is absolutely essential if any of the discrete development activities are to be conducted in parallel.

Software Developers. Software developers perform the bulk of the work associated with the development of the system, ranging from requirements analysis to implementation and testing. Unfortunately, most development projects also ask their developers to design the user interface without giving them the necessary training. It is not that most developers cannot design adequate user interfaces. They can, given the proper training, such as a three- or five-day class in human factors or usability engineering.

Graphic Designers/Usability Engineers. Ideally, a project will have access to graphic designers to assist in the creation of the user interface and usability engineers to assist in the design and evaluation of the system. Can a development project succeed without individuals? Certainly. However, as the sophistication of the user interface increases (e.g., a greater emphasis on graphics or specialized interaction mechanisms such as drag-and-drop) the greater the risk to the project if the skills of such professionals are not retained.

The key point in selecting roles for the team is to ensure that the roles in the project efficiently and explicitly support the system architecture and overall usability goals of the project.

DEVELOPING USABLE INTERFACES FOR WEB SYSTEMS

While the basic principles of usability and the managerial approach for achieving it described in this chapter are the same for the Web as for any other application, there are some important usability considerations for Web-based applications. The first concerns the capabilities and limitations of Web browsers and Java. The second deals with important aspects of usability.

Capabilities and Limitations of HTML

As a mark-up language, HTML can perform a wide range of useful tasks. HTML can:

- Show a variety of fonts, embedded graphics, and tables.
- Present forms containing input fields, radio buttons, and check boxes.

HTML forms are used to gather input from the user, which is then sent to the server. Upon receiving the data, the server executes a program and returns the result.

Three essential aspects of usability, and several aspects of implementation, are affected by this approach. First, HTML forms have no "state." Thus, a designer cannot dynamically disable or enable a button based on a field value, a technique common in non-HTML GUI applications. Similarly, if an HTML input field requires a numeric value and the user enters a character string, only the server can detect and respond to the error. Second, there is no guarantee that what a designer creates is what the user sees because the user has ultimate control of the representation of the page. For example, if a designer uses graphics to enhance the usability of the application, the user may never see them! Third, HTML provides hyperlinking, which means one part of a page can directly access or "jump" to another page (or identified section of a page). The advantage is the ability to cross-reference vast amounts of information. This disadvantage is the ease with which a user can become lost in hyperspace.

From an implementation perspective, the server is responsible for processing forms and dynamically generating HTML-based responses. Based on the complexity of this response the programming required to do this can be fairly time consuming. Another common alternative is to use "helper" applications. A helper application is stored on the client and is used to process data coming from the server. For example, a company might place employee manuals in Adobe Acrobat format. When an employee wishes to learn more about a specific policy, the server would download the manual. The browser would then invoke the Abode Acrobat reader to display the information.

The most important aspect to remember is that HTML is *not* a programming language.

Java

Java is a full-featured object-oriented programming language designed to facilitate application development and deployment on the Internet. While an in-depth discussion of Java is beyond the scope of this chapter, here are the relevant aspects from the perspective of building highly usable Web-based applications.

Java is platform independent. Specifically, a Java application (usually referred to as an *applet*) is downloaded from the server to the client browser. The browser then executes this program, usually as a separate thread in the client. Because Java is a programming language, the appearance of the application is under control of the developer. Graphics can be dynamic, controls can enable or disable other controls, validate input, and so forth. New objects can be created on the fly.

One concern with Java and usability involves the potential for damage if a user downloads a potentially hostile applet. The designers of Java considered this undesirable affect and created a robust security model. The model is not perfect — a handful of researchers have been able to break it — but is steadily improving. By the time you read this chapter these problems should be fixed.

From an implementation perspective, Java is similar in syntax and structure to C++. Fortunately, Java is simpler and more robust, and many of the problems that plague C++ (such as templates and poor memory management) do not exist in Java.

CONCLUSION

Ultimately, creating highly usable systems is based on a more robust and healthy dialog between the development team and the users. The processes of user and task analysis, lo-fi design, simulated prototyping, and hi-fi design (with testing) all serve to increase the interaction between the development team and the user. This interaction is completely focused on the needs of the user as supported by the system in a manner that ensures all parties benefit: Users will enjoy their systems more, developers can take more pride in their work, and management can take the savings directly to the bottom line.

Chapter II-6
Effective Systems Development Management: The Experts Advise

Tom L. Roberts, Jr., Michael L. Gibson,
and William N. Ledbetter

THE EFFECTIVE MANAGEMENT OF SYSTEMS DEVELOPMENT PROJECTS IS AN ELUSIVE GOAL for all systems development professionals. The industry has a poor track record in bringing projects in on schedule, within budget, and with full performance characteristics and capabilities. Many factors contribute to the success or failure of a systems development project. A systems development project is often a complex interplay of project management tools, systems development methodology, and CASE tools.

Every system development project has individual characteristics and priority that makes management of the project unique. For every project, systems development managers must adapt their management skills to the unique aspects of the project to maintain quality and the project schedule. Because this task is complex, it is no surprise that effective systems development can be so elusive.

To help systems development mangers better understand the complexities of systems development project management, twelve leading systems development experts were interviewed to give insight to systems development management. They were interviewed to help systems development managers identify the project management skills and areas needed to bring a project to a successful conclusion. Among the topics discussed in these interviews were: roles and responsibilities, the development process, and the use of automated tools.

THE INTERVIEWS

The authors selected the twelve experts by using citation lists, leading consultants mentioned in IS literature, and consultants who were members of a large nonprofit organization of systems professionals. All the individuals selected are very knowledgeable in systems development methodologies. The mix of experts includes external consultants and practicing systems professionals, who may not be as well-known but have extensive experience in practical IS projects. The experts interviewed are:

- *Ed Yourdon.* Yourdon & Associates; Consultant, Author, Methodologist.
- *Garland Favorito.* Consultant.
- *Ken Orr.* Ken Orr & Associates; Consultant, Author, Methodologist.
- *Vaughan Merlyn.* Ernst & Young; Consulting Partner, Author.
- *Dr. Sami Albanna.* Yourdon & Associates; Consulting Manager.
- *Donna Wicks.* Consultant.
- *Mike Rice.* Coopers & Lybrand; Managing Associate.
- *Dennis Minnium.* Texas Instruments; IEF Developer.
- *John Riley.* Texas Instruments; National Consulting Practices Manager, IEF
- *Rick Bastidas.* Consultant.
- *Susan Ball.* IDE Director, Educational and Consulting Services.
- *Mariann Manzi.* Dun & Bradstreet Software; Software Development Manager.

The structured interview given to each expert was developed on the basis of reviewing system development methodologies, CASE, and IS projects in existing MIS and computer science literature concerning systems development methodologies. The structured interview questions were open-ended and intended to prompt the experts to freely and more completely offer insight on their perspectives and experience in developing and using methodologies, using CASE, and participating in IS projects.

The interviews were either conducted in person or by telephone and lasted one to two hours. Each interviewer followed the same structured interview guide with little variation. All interviews were taped and transcribed to assure complete reconstruction of answers to each question.

The content of each interview was analyzed. The interviewers separately identified and extracted items of importance from each expert's interview. They then combined the set of extracted items from each interview into a single set for that interview. A second content analysis was performed across the twelve different combined sets of extracted items to derive the final set of combined items across all expert interviews. The results of the second content analysis were compiled and collectively evaluated.

The rest of this chapter examines the most important points from the interviews.

THE IMPORTANCE OF UNDERSTANDING LIFE CYCLE PHASES

Valuable Points from Experts

- One must understand the phases to use a methodology.
- The methodology will guide you through the life cycle phases.
- Preceding phases build products for succeeding phases.
- Knowing the deliverables of each phase is crucial.
- You must understand the phases to assure proper utilization of the methodology not in terms of fixed deliverables.

Discussion

A vital point of the experts is that a methodology cannot be used unless its life cycle phases are defined and understood. The organization should have some individuals who understand all of the phases. However, many specialists involved in the process may not necessarily need to know all of the details. Many of these specialists may only need to know methodology phase deliverables (i.e., the output of each phase). Understanding a methodology's deliverables is crucial to its use.

Knowledge of the life cycle phases should be a major focus in training of personnel using the process. Training programs phase should possess segments that provide explanations of each life cycle phase to personnel involved with the phase. The use of experienced personnel and expert consultants can also help in making sure that the individuals involved in the process understand the methodology.

UNDERSTANDING WHEN SOME LIFE CYCLE PHASES MAY BE SHORTENED

Valuable Points from Experts

- Lay out the project plan at the beginning of the project.
- Recognize that there are a variety of different factors for particular projects.
- Realize that alternative life cycles enable you to customize the life cycle to a particular project.
- Train everyone on the overall life cycle and life cycle phases.
- Understand what happens if certain activities are deleted.
- Know the dangers of making everything optional.
- Realize that typically the entire universal set of a methodology is not used on every project.
- Make the life cycle phases flexible.

Discussion

The project plan should be laid out at the beginning. This plan should put together the schedule and identify and allocate the resources necessary to complete the project. The methodology provides the basis for carrying out a project. It can be customized to an environment for new system development, enhancements, maintenance, or packaged software acquisition. Adaptability of any life cycle-based methodology is critical at the project level. In training, everyone involved needs to know the overall life cycle and individual life cycle phases and must pay particular attention to what happens if certain activities are deleted. An inherent danger exists in making too many of these activities optional.

For efficient use of a methodology, a systems development manager plans each individual project and customizes the portions of the methodology to be used for the project. The realization that every project has its own characteristics should be taken into account. The key is coordination between methodology and project specifics.

UNDERSTANDING WHO SHOULD BE INVOLVED IN CERTAIN PHASES

Valuable Points from Experts

- Key players are needed for required activities.
- Roles and responsibilities are keys to phases.
- Specialists with particular skills are needed for each phase.
- Understanding who is involved in changes over the life cycle of a project.
- Identifying who should be involved in specific phases provides ownership of a particular deliverable and identifies roles and accountability.
- Not having the right people reduces system quality.

Discussion

Roles and responsibilities should be clearly defined for the project. Project success is based on having the right people with the proper skills at the appropriate time and place in the life cycle. Projects lacking people with the proper expertise are vulnerable to mistakes.

Coordination and efficient use of personnel by systems development managers is vital to successful project management. IS managers must decide upon the exact personnel needed to complete each phase of the project. These personnel decisions must be made before the start of the project during the project planning phase. Matching knowledge and expertise with methodology phases is essential to every project.

UNDERSTANDING THE REUSABILITY
BETWEEN LIFE CYCLE PHASES

Valuable Points from Experts

- Realize that the basis for any phase needs to be the deliverables from the previous phase.
- Make sure that one phase's deliverable is a clear communication document to the next phase.
- Understand the transition between phases.
- Identify reusable components.
- Make sure the life cycle used has full integration from phase to phase.
- Understand that a full life cycle methodology is cumulative.
- Realize that it is difficult to implement and control reusability.
- Have requirements traceable through the project to make sure original requirements are met.

Discussion

A full life cycle methodology should be integrated from stage to stage. The results of one stage should be used to start the next stage; without such integration some type of bridge must be built. The only real reason to have a full life cycle methodology is its cumulative nature.

The successful IS project manager will realize the capabilities of a methodology and use them as adeptly as possible. Virtually every methodology contains components that may be reused from one life cycle phase to the next. It is the challenge of systems development managers to reuse as many components as possible to streamline a project. However, systems development managers should exhibit some measure of caution to control reusability to ensure quality. Requirements traceability is a must for satisfying this need.

MANAGEMENT INVOLVEMENT IN LIFE CYCLE PHASE

Valuable Points from Experts

- Have project champions from the business.
- Project management and management involvement all the way through project and methodology implementation.
- Each management level understands their project roles.
- Upper management understands that their role is to force the use of the methodology.
- Management keeps track of the deliverables.
- Management knows what types of people from their organization are needed in the project.
- Create an overall plan, a schedule, and a resource plan for the project.
- Management knows what resources are needed from phase to phase.

- Management trains on the methodology.
- Provide feedback to managers on projects.

Discussion

Project management is the critical role. Project management and management involvement must begin at the outset and stay current all the way through the project. Management's role is to force the use of the methodology. Management must believe in the life cycle-based methodology; otherwise, people will abandon it.

Additionally, the project will need a champion from the business user group to sell the project to end users. The champion should know what types of people from their organization are needed as the project progresses through the life cycle.

Management must realize the importance of its role for successful projects. The only way for a manager to guarantee project success is to get directly involved with the project. IS managers should make an effort to understand the technology involved with the methodology being used and an effort to sell the benefits of this technology to IS personnel.

MANAGEMENT'S TIME COMMITMENT FOR IMPLEMENTING THE METHODOLOGY

Valuable Points from Experts

- Management allows enough time to implement the methodology.
- Management provides enough financial funding to implement the methodology.
- Management understands the learning curve, decreased productivity, and limited benefits before a methodology takes hold.
- Management commits time, resources, and money as well as the process changes.
- Realize that shortcuts will lead to lower quality.
- IS personnel realize that management cannot wait too long.
- Management commits to retraining personnel for the new methodology.

Discussion

Management must understand that they are tooling and retooling an IS factory. Commitment of learning curve time and resources is essential to implementing the methodology. Management must realize that the first few projects may increase in overall project completion time by several months. Adequate time to complete the project must be allowed, or shortcuts will be taken that cause problems for the whole process. The flip side is for management to not have to wait too long for project completion. If the methodology adds too much time to the process, the project will probably never be started. As a result, it is best to have the first projects that are completed with the new methodology to be important projects that have a relatively short duration time.

Patience is the key to using new technology and methodologies. Systems development managers must focus on the project process. They must understand that the benefits from using the new methodology will be realized once the learning curve concerning the technology has been reached by IS personnel.

DEVOTING ENOUGH TIME TO PERFORMING THE MODELING ACTIVITIES

Valuable Points from Experts

- Understand that enough time must be allocated or it is not worth attempting.
- Realize that modeling takes a lot of time.
- Know that enough time must be devoted to analyzing the area of study to determine what is necessary.
- Understand that methodologies emphasize where to spend time.

Discussion

A methodology should place emphasis on where systems personnel should spend time as opposed to where they would naturally spend the time. The process is going to take a lot of time, especially if staff members are going through classroom training. The learning curve on using the methodology for modeling will take a considerable amount of time.

Systems development managers should recognize that very few projects offer shortcuts to the systems development process. Business and systems modeling are vital components to system project success and performance. Many times project schedules attempt to circumvent modeling activities to simply get a system completed. Every effort should be made by systems development managers to resist any attempts to take shortcuts to just simply get the system out of the door.

MANAGEMENT'S RESOURCE COMMITMENT TO IMPLEMENTING THE METHODOLOGY

Valuable Points from Experts

- Have a methodology coordinator to develop in-house training.
- Have a champion for the methodology.
- Have management plan for the methodology implementation.
- Have management bring in consultants to help with the paradigm shift.
- Be sure management understands what resources are necessary.

Discussion

If IS does not commit time, people, and dollars, then it really does not have a commitment to the methodology. There must be a methodology coordinator, who among other activities will develop in-house training. If there is no champion in an organization, methodology implementation will not be successful.

Systems development managers should focus their efforts upon getting resources for the IS project. They should have an understanding of what resources are necessary for each particular project from the initial project planning phase. Once project specifics are known, managers should act as project champions in an attempt to sell it to senior management. This championing of a project is an essential part of getting the resources needed for a successful project.

MANAGEMENT FOLLOW THROUGH WITH THE PROCESSES

Valuable Points from Experts

- Upper management requires that the methodology be followed.
- Management provides a method of measurement to show some measurable observable benefits to the developers.
- Management commits to the methodology.
- Management follows through with the implementation process.
- Management creates an implementation plan.
- Management understands the need for investing in retraining and modernization.
- Project managers and IS personnel take operational responsibility.
- Management realizes that a cultural change is not completed unless it is mandated, enforced, watched, and measured.

Discussion

False starts kill business; if management does not assume the responsibility for the process of implementing the methodology, then it will not be done. A cultural change is not completed unless it is mandated, enforced, watched, and measured. It is important that managers measure across the implementation process just as they do elsewhere. You just do not take a methodology and dump it into an organization and expect it to grow by itself; you need an implementation plan. If management forgets about it, then people will also forget about it. Management must show commitment throughout the implementation and use of the methodology, not just at the beginning.

Following through with new technology is important. The key is involvement with the processes. Systems development managers must continually illustrate to their staff how important the process is to each project.

THE VALUE OF USING LIFE CYCLE SUPPORT TOOLS

Valuable Points from Experts

- Promote integration between different life cycle phases.
- Realize that if the tools are poorly integrated, the gains made during one phase may be dissipated in another phase.
- Use tools to implement techniques.
- Integrate code with models.
- Maintain diagrams from which the code gets generated.
- Automate the system development process.

Discussion

In the paper-based methodologies of the 1970s, problems were fixed directly in the code and not the specifications. Today, it is critical that a methodology be supported by automation and that the coding is eliminated. Diagrams from which the code is generated are maintained rather than the code itself.

Systems development managers should understand that automation supporting most information system development techniques exists in today's computing environment. Managers should make every effort to take advantage of these automated tools to assist with the development process.

THE VALUE OF SHARING FRONT AND BACK END CASE SPECIFICATIONS

Valuable Points from Experts

- Ensure accuracy of specifications.
- Make sure application systems reflect the business requirements.
- Allow models to help generate code.
- Create traceability.
- Reduce the need for documenting code and speeding up the maintenance process.

Discussion

Specifications should waterfall. The bottom line is that one should be able to take an attribute and not have to enter it again later in the physical design. Models should help generate the code. They should be tied together; otherwise, the whole reason for doing the modeling is lost.

THE VALUE OF USING OTHER WORKSTATION TOOLS

Valuable Points from Experts

- Measure a project's progress.
- Provide automated means for documenting work.

- Support presentations.
- Produce high-quality, better-looking documents.
- Provide error checking capabilities.
- Help to control the software development process.

Discussion

Online methodologies of the future will tie together workstation tools (project management, estimating tools, and CASE). The organization should have a project management-based methodology and graphics support. It is clear that some automated means of documenting the results of work is needed. Graphics on one life cycle phase should feed the next phase.

ACTUALLY USING TOOLS THE WAY THEY ARE DESIGNED TO BE USED

Valuable Points from Experts

- Understand which tools are flexible.
- Use tools the way your goals and objectives are set up.
- Find innovative ways to use tools within the process.
- Realize when innovations can impact the next phase of the life cycle.
- Realize that tools assist the methodology.
- Follow standards when using tools.

Discussion

In today's environment, the use of automated tools is essential. Many of the processes cannot be done by hand. Tools must be used the way they are designed to gain the greatest benefit from them. Some tools can be used to make the end deliverable look different than the original intent. These changes are not necessarily bad as long as they do not affect the next life cycle stage. Tools should be used consistent with the goals and objectives and every organization is going to be different. However, one should not get carried away with using the tools for special purposes for which they are not designed.

OTHER POINTS ABOUT PROJECT MANAGEMENT

The experts made supplementary statements that were not prompted by specific questions but are additional points of importance to project management.

Valuable Points from Experts

- Use estimating tools to estimate throughout the project.
- Provide greater productivity.

- Ensure quality and information integrity.
- Realize that initially there will not be productivity gains.
- Keep people on track with the methodology.
- Eliminate redundant activities.
- Realize that tools do not solve the problem.
- Guide the process.

Discussion

Project management tools are essential to successful projects. In general, project management tools keep people on track and guide the process. Estimating tools are important in producing guidelines for the life cycle. The combination of these tools provides a more complete set of workstation tools in support of using a methodology and completing IS projects on time, within budgets, and with a satisfactory final product.

CONCLUSION

The experts leave little doubt as to the need for managing the life cycle phases of the methodology. Knowing the phases and what goes into each phase is vital to successful projects. However, this knowledge does not guarantee success. The use of automated life cycle support tools is a necessary extension to the methodology in successfully completing IS projects. These tools should span the project management activities, project estimation, and actual performance of systems development tasks. Their integration is a prerequisite of a reliable project completion process.

The most important issues about systems development according to the panel of experts are

- The importance of understanding life cycle phases
- Understanding when some life cycle phases may be shortened
- Understanding who should be involved in certain phases
- Understanding the reusability between life cycle phases
- Management's involvement in life cycle phases
- Management's time commitment for implementing the methodology
- Devoting enough time to performing the modeling activities
- Management's resource commitment to implementing the methodology
- Management's follow through with the process
- The value of using life cycle support tools
- The value of sharing front and back-end CASE specifications
- The value of using other workstation tools
- Actually using tools the way they are designed to be used

Section II – Checklist
Development Strategies

1. What strategies does your organization promote in an effort to improve the application development process? Has this strategy been successful?
2. Does your IS organization embrace every new development methodology in an effort to find the perfect development process? If not, does it shy away from newer techniques altogether?
3. How would you compare your knowledge of new development techniques over those that have been successful for you in the past? Are new techniques worth studying?
4. Could your IS environment prove the use of newer development techniques as successful? If so, what means would it use (i.e., cost, time, staff, quality, etc.)?
5. Do you anticipate another paradigm change regarding application development? How will this affect decisions about changes to current practices in your organization?
6. What is your organizations position on embracing object-oriented development? Is it cautious?
7. Is object technology viewed as another trendy "panacea" or "silver bullet" within your organization? If so, is this opinion based on cursory evaluation or an in-depth analysis?
8. What steps have you taken to understand object-oriented development? Does this include programming techniques as well as analysis methodologies?
9. Do you have a development strategy for GUIs? If not, do you follow vendor recommended guidelines for GUI development?
10. In your opinion, should programmers or end users design GUIs? How is this done in your environment?
11. Do end users in your organization judge the value of an application based on the GUI or the entire functionality of the system?
12. What myths about software development still exist in your organization? Who holds them, users or developers?
13. How are development projects started in your organization? Is this based on business need or is it driven by the capabilities of new technology?
14. Do you hold meetings with your development staff to discuss new methods to improve development?

15. Based on your experience, is application development an art or science? What development strategy would be more suitable to your opinion. Could your develop your own strategy for developing quality applications?

Section III
Tools, Tips, and Practices

IDENTIFYING THE MOST EFFECTIVE TOOL OR METHODOLOGY for improving the application development process has been an evasive goal for many organizations. The multitude of products and techniques provide an unusual level of opportunity and, at the same time, can create confusion and uncertainty amid ongoing technical change. Caution should be exercised when struggling to find the single most important tool or the next "silver bullet" solution. It is doubtful that any one tool or procedure will satisfy the diverse demands of the development and support process.

For many organizations, the routine of selecting appropriate tools is often time consuming and difficult. Techniques that work in some organizations may not work in others. Furthermore, not every tool or technique will perform well in all development and support situations. Development managers must be aware that choosing the best suite of tools and/or techniques should be based on matching key factors that surround the unique characteristics of a given development environment. These factors may include organizational size, corporate culture, application development maturity, budget, and resource availability. As application tools and techniques continue to evolve, there will be an ongoing need to balance the use of tools and their overall contribution to development and support objectives.

Current appeal of object-oriented technology is founded on a long-standing idea of reusable software procedures. This concept has been implemented in early forms through functions, subroutines, and common code libraries. Despite the name, the premise of reusing code is often harder to exploit due to misunderstanding about the basic mechanics of the process. Chapter III-1, "Ten Steps to Realizing Application Code Reuse," offers a general overview for implementing and administering a workable reuse strategy. As a follow-up, Chapter III-2, "Managing Object Libraries," provides an excellent discussion on methods and practices to improve the success of software objects. The benefits of reusable software are often underachieved due to poor management of code libraries and the inventory mechanism to track existing modules, including appropriate identification of module functionality. By establishing early guidelines, reusable code or objects can be used by a greater number of software developers and thus improve development projects. Avoiding the effort to organize reusable code will eventual waste the promise of newer techniques such as object-oriented development.

Application software techniques provide important alternatives to the acquisition of packaged software tools. A more notable technique used for development has been Function Point Analysis. The benefit of function points has particular value with traditional system architectures. Chapter III-3, "Fundamentals of Function Point Analysis," and Chapter III-4, "Function Points Step by Step," both describe the basic concepts of the technique. This discussion is pertinent to the development of new systems as well as the postdevelopment support of legacy applications. Function Point Analysis should not be considered a panacea. However, with the appropriate understanding, it can be a powerful technique along with other methods used to improve software productivity.

Software metrics have become an increasingly popular technique in recent years. Metrics can provide valuable information to IS organizations when analyzing software support tasks, and assessment of enterprise software portfolio management. There is also an added benefit to improve development by applying well-defined metric measures. However, establishing meaningful metric indicators is not an easy task. Chapter III-5, "Software Metrics: Quantifying and Analyzing Software for Total Quality Management," reviews the basics requirements of a comprehensive metric program. Once established, development managers can adjust and tune metric measurements to further improve software development productivity and quality.

Another viewpoint on business process management is offered in Chapter III-6, "Developing Tool Support for Process-Oriented Management." The author presents the idea of developing a system tool that can gather and organize important facts about a development project. This extension of project management is accomplished through an automation program designed to meet the needs of the organization. Building tools to better manage projects is not a new idea. Many organizations have implemented proprietary project systems that were built as a result of past experiences in development.

New methods for providing adequate computer security are unfolding more rapidly and with significant attention. As more organizations pursue e-commerce and e-business activities, the need to protect against security violations becomes more paramount. But even though awareness is high, some organizations have ignored basic techniques that could safeguard vital information, especially in the area of messaging. Chapter III-7, "Securing Electronic Messaging Systems," discusses several methods for achieving a secure environment as well as providing insight on various intrusion techniques. Some debate exists on whether computing security is a technology or a methodology. More likely, it is a combination of both. Development managers who understand the risks of security, are more likely to include protection mechanisms in environments that use Internet technology as the basis for developing application systems.

Chapter III-1
Ten Steps to Realizing Application Code Reuse

Richard T. Dué

THE OVERWHELMINGLY FAVORABLE ECONOMICS of software reuse have been apparent for over 30 years. Unfortunately, the systematic reuse of application software has been elusive. Most organizations have no planned approach to the identification, evaluation, storage, and dissemination of proven application code. Highly productive individual programmers do reuse their own code, but often just in a "cut and paste" manner within their own programs. Interestingly, however, most programmers willingly reuse operating system, compiler, telecommunication, database, and system utilities code.

EIGHT REASONS WHY REUSE FAILS

It is the reuse of application program code that has, for the most part, been a failure. Time after time application programmers start with a blank sheet of paper, or an empty computer screen, and write code that essentially has already been developed hundreds of thousands of times before. The following eight reasons are among the causes for the failure to reuse application code:

- *"I didn't know the modules existed."* Because there are no inventories of existing code, nor any easy way to access these inventories, reuse of code is only accidental. Programmers only informally exchange modules of code based on chance meetings in hallways or on computer bulletin boards.
- *"I cannot trust code developed by other people."* Certainly, a lot of substandard, poorly documented code exists. Complex systems designs can result in unforeseen results as programs interact with each other, or with new hardware and software environments. However, writing

more code that no one else can trust is obviously not an effective solution.

- *"This application calls for unique code."* Certainly, there are situations (applications with critical hardware or time constraints, for example) that sometimes justify heroic programming efforts. Most new application code, however, is just repetition of typical information processing functions that have been already produced hundreds of thousand of times.

- *"It will be faster for me to write the code myself."* Paradoxically, programmers who make this argument are only willing to spend a few minutes looking for existing code before starting to write new programs that they expect will take them up to several weeks to develop.

- *"I was never taught about reuse."* Software engineering textbooks and university and technical school courses teach new practitioners to build systems from first principles. Reuse is not promoted or even discussed. Students are evaluated on the basis of their individual effort. Few attempts are made to teach students teamwork or to demonstrate the benefits of specialization and component-based systems assembly.

- *"I'm not reusing software that was built in that way."* The intellectual challenge of solving an interesting software problem in one's own unique way mitigates against reusing someone else's software components. Reuse initiatives are often attacked by the majority of programmers as stifling their creativity.

- *"I've never heard of any good experiences with reuse."* Efforts at creating reusable application code libraries have failed since the 1960s. Since reuse seems to be unobtainable, few organizations are willing to spend more time and money pursuing it.

- *"Why should I reuse software if I do not see the pay back?"* Less than 5% of organizations in North America measure the productivity of their investment in information technology. In the few organizations that even bother to measure the productivity of their application development resources, productivity is only measured and rewarded in terms of lines of new code written. In my opinion, it is this lack of appropriate productivity measurement that allows the preceding seven, largely spurious, arguments against reuse to prevail. There can be no movement to large-scale application code reuse until organizations institute effective information technology productivity metrics programs.

THE CASE FOR REUSE

Capers Jones, at Software Productivity Research, suggests that organizations will see a 30:1 return for every dollar invested in an appropriate reuse approach. There is no other greater information technology investment opportunity today. He points out that while the average cost to build a function point (a language-independent measurement of the functions or services provided by a computer program) in the United States is $1,000, an equivalent commercial package can be obtained for about $0.25 per function point. The equivalent shareware package would cost about $0.01 per function point.

Of course, despite their current popularity, commercial and shareware packages cannot always meet the unique needs of every organization. The effective reuse of packaged code will probably only occur at a much smaller level of granularity than an entire application. Unique systems can be assembled from well-tested and documented components and subsystems. Java and ActiveX components distributed on the Internet will certainly be a major step in the reuse of small, cost-effective packages of code that can be used to assemble systems.

The real benefits of reuse, however, are not to be found merely by the reuse of code. The cost of writing code is only about 15% to 20% of the total cost of developing and implementing a system. Even 100% code reuse is thus unlikely to have a major impact on the true costs and duration of an application development project.

EFFECTIVE STRATEGIES FOR REUSE

The significant difference, in my opinion, between the successful reuse of operating systems, compilers, telecommunication software, databases, and system utilities code and the failure to reuse application software is that system software is viewed as a given infrastructure that provides services that help develop applications. Most application programmers are happy to rely on this infrastructure.

The Application Code Infrastructure

In contrast, application development is viewed as an end in itself that always requires the development of unique code. It is time to stop viewing applications as unique projects. Instead, systems development managers must extend the scope of the concept of infrastructure to include the reuse of standard components and proven patterns of requirements specification, analysis, design, documentation, testing, training, and project management.

This infrastructure approach to reuse will require a fundamentally different systems development life cycle approach. Instead of analyzing (literally loosening up or pulling apart a thing into its constituent parts) and designing (arranging parts according to a plan), application developers are going to have to start focusing on the assembly of proven, reusable components. This component assembly, or object-oriented, approach requires developers to concentrate on "discovering" (observing and learning about) the application domain, assembling "real world" simulation models of the domain from proven components or objects, and then synthesizing the required information services from these collections of components. The benefits of this new "reuse-in-the-large" approach include:

- Proven solutions can be applied to similar problems.
- Less time need be spent on development.
- Existing documentation can be reused.
- People without theoretical systems engineering training and experience can follow patterns and guidelines to assemble applications from the existing infrastructure.
- Organizations can concentrate on the information services they require instead of worrying about how to implement systems.
- Management will be able to plan and control their organization's systems against standard frameworks.
- Auditors will be able to used established patterns to assess the economy, efficiency, and the effectiveness of the organization's information systems.

A TEN-STEP APPROACH TO CODE REUSE

The introduction of a successful code reuse initiative will require at least the following ten steps discussed in the following paragraphs.

Identify and Commit a Champion. A champion is the most senior manager who has the most to gain from the success of the reuse project. In most cases this will be a senior user department manager whose success will be directly attributable to the operation of competitive, flexible, and low-cost information systems.

Perform a Maturity Assessment. Paradoxically, reuse of application code is unlikely in organizations that consider information technology as a cost center rather than an investment center. As organizations move along the information technology management learning curve, they begin to identify, plan, control, document, measure, and manage their investments in information systems. Relatively immature companies that only consider the short-term costs of their information systems are unlikely to commit to the expense of the reuse-in-the-large approach. Companies that have successfully moved along the information technology management learning curve start to understand the long-term payoff of the reuse culture investment. There are several maturity assessment programs such as those offered by the Carnegie Mellon University's Software Engineering Institute, which can be used to measure an organization's information technology management maturity.

Establish and Use Productivity Metrics. A successful reuse program most be evaluated with an appropriate set of productivity metrics. Almost unbelievably, over 95% of North American organizations have no measures of the productivity of their investment in information technology. The following — rather unorthodox — set of productivity metrics should be used to measure the business success (as opposed to the technical success) of the reuse initiative:

- *Profitability.* What is the direct effect of the organization's investment in the reuse-in-the large approach and the organization's profitability?
- *Customer Satisfaction.* What is the effect of the organization's investment in the reuse-in-the-large approach on the satisfaction of the organization's ultimate customers? Ultimate customers are the final end users of the organization's products and services. They are not clients or users within the organization.
- *Time to Value.* How long does it take to turn Information Technology investments into profits?
- *IT Value Added.* How much value is added by Information Technology to the organization? Is this value increasing over time?
- *Business Alignment.* Are the organization's investments in Information Technology understood and supported by the managers in the main functional areas of the business?
- *Employee Satisfaction.* What are the cross-industry comparative rates of employee turnover and compensation? What is the rate of increase in the intellectual capital of the organization?
- *Productivity and Quality.* What is the actual level of productivity and quality of the organization's Information Technology personnel when compared to the best industry practices? Productivity measurement must be done using technology neutral measures such as function points.
- *Improvement Rate.* How quickly are all of the productivity metrics showing improvement?
- *SDLC Shape Change.* How is the organization changing the shape of its system development life cycle? Ideally the length of the cycle should be decreasing while an increasing percentage of the cycle is spent on planning and modeling compared to a decreasing percentage spent on coding, documentation, and testing.
- *Learning Rate.* How long does it take to introduce new technologies into the organization? What is the participation rate, how long does it take to reach a critical mass of users?
- *Rework Change Rate.* What is the rate of improvement in finding and fixing errors? Is there a shift in error identification and elimination of errors from the end of the system development life cycle to the beginning of the cycle?

Institute a Quality Assurance Function. The purpose of a quality assurance function is to ensure that the organization is adequately undertaking all of these ten steps.

Institute Project Management. The introduction of a reuse initiative is a project that will require effective project management. This means that a full-time project management expert will be required to plan, estimate, schedule, develop a risk analysis and contingency plan, and monitor the success of the reuse-in-the-large approach.

Select and Adhere to an Appropriate Reuse-Oriented Methodology. An appropriate methodology concentrates on identifying and employing proven component frameworks, design patterns, and best practices. In contrast, an inappropriate methodology is concerned with developing each individual application in isolation.

Institute Training. As with any new development technique, programmers needed to be trained in reuse. This is even true for beginning programmers, who have probably received no educational training on reuse.

Hiring Practices. A reuse-in-the-large program will require employees who are capable of working at high levels of abstraction, who feel comfortable with understanding and modeling the domain, who are able to work directly with users, and who are able to work in teams. There is no place for heroic "cowboy" coders in mainstream application development.

Acquire Tools. Appropriate reuse tools include groupware and repository-based CASE tools. These tools must be used to facilitate communication of proven frameworks, patterns, and best practices among all members of the organization.

Monitor Ongoing Benchmark Testing. The final step in the reuse program is to monitor the success of the reuse initiative against industry benchmarks and best practices.

CONCLUSION

Reuse-in-the-large requires that organizations establish and support a culture of reuse. This culture must include the use of appropriate systems development methodologies, the establishment of repositories of components, design patterns, and best practices, and the installation of rational productivity metrics. In the absence of a culture of reuse, the only alternative systems developers have to write their own code. The consequence is inefficient, uneconomical, and largely ineffective additions to the program maintenance headaches already facing most organizations.

The 10 steps toward establishing a culture of code reuse will help systems development managers to overcome the eight roadblocks to reuse in the following ways:

- By acquiring development tools and adopting a methodology that promotes reuse, application developers will be able to find code they can reuse. They will also better understand how the code was created and be more receptive to reusing it.
- By instituting a quality assurance function for reuse, developers will be able to better trust code's reliability and should have more confidence about reusing it.
- A code reuse champion will help dissuade developers' doubts about reuse raised by past negative experiences.
- By hiring developers who are capable of working with high levels of abstraction, systems development managers should find their developers will be less likely to find the need for creating unique code.
- A training program will also help developers to overcome the practices that were fostered by past education and training and that encouraged developers to write code instead of reuse it.
- Most important, the rewards of reuse have to be demonstrated to upper management as well as to developers. Benchmarking reuse, the companion step of performing a maturity assessment, and using productivity metrics as well as using project management techniques to roll out the reuse program will all help to buy the backing of the entire organization needed to realize the rewards of code reuse.

Chapter III-2
Managing Object Libraries

Polly Perryman

SOFTWARE REUSE IS A CONCEPT that has been bounced around in the industry for years and years, still information systems developers are searching for ways to master its implementation. The principles of object-oriented design and development have shown themselves to be a starting point for developing reusable software. Application of the principles, however, only offers a partial solution since compliance with the principles and the development of objects does not automatically result in reusability. It requires a great deal of planning and effective management of object libraries. This is because until the commonality of the object types is defined and effectively managed the value of software reuse cannot be realized.

Many companies miss out on valuable opportunities to streamline processes while improving product because they do not have a cohesive plan to implement object library management. Other companies lose out because they think object library management is a practice limited to documented object-oriented design methodologies. Still other companies use clumsy procedures intending to promote software reuse without ever realizing the importance of planning for software reuse, which is itself a form of object library management. When the essential components of object library management are understood and implemented, these missed opportunities can knock again.

One of the biggest mistakes companies make is "throwing" objects into a library without a scheme for making sure the team benefits from them. For example, a company had a practice of telling coders if they develop a routine that others can use to put it in Library X. This was so everyone could access and use the code. This had a major impact on one project. Several developers faithfully added routines to a common library that indeed saved development time for database access, output, and a number of other common functions. A young fellow we will refer to as Sam contributed a particularly well-used routine. The problem was that while Sam's common object executed beautifully, it was unfortunately a resource hog, and when it was used by other developers it created problems. The impact of modifying the object to correct and improve the performance issues and retest the

0-8493-9979-3/99/$0.00+$.50
© 1999 by CRC Press LLC

fifty-plus programs using the object was significant. The schedule delay was unacceptable to the customer. Funding for the project was withdrawn.

On another project where the "throw-it-in" approach to object library management was used without a master plan coders duplicated efforts by individually creating their own renditions of routines for common use. The object library became so convoluted with multiple objects for the similar types of functions that no one was able to use it. The benefits gained by the concept were preempted entirely by the approach.

So how can object library management be implemented effectively without impinging on the creativity of talented staff. It basically depends on three things to be successful. The first is appointment of a design authority. The designated design authority assumes full responsibility for establishing the highest classification for objects, the characteristics for base objects within the classification, and determining which objects possess commonality to the system for potential reuse within the application, upgrades, and related products. The person who takes on the role of the design authority must communicate beyond the structure of the objects, making certain that the development team understands the standards and methods used to structure, document, build, and subsequently maintain the object library.

The second area for success lies in the effective use of basic configuration management functions, such as version control and release management. The implementation of the configuration management functions may use any of the configuration management tools in the market today, such as Rational-Atria ClearCase or Intersolv's PVCS, that have been upgraded to work with large objects. The configuration management functions may also be implemented using internally developed tools and methods when purchase of these tools would strain the budget.

The third area for success is quality control and testing. The quality control and testing that must be performed covers more than the demonstration the coded object works to specifications. It also must ensure that development personnel are complying with the structure established for object management that allows for improvement in the processes used by development personnel using the object library.

Object library management can and should be practiced regardless of the development methodology being used because it offers direct benefits to developers and customers alike. The most direct benefit of object library management is better product at lower cost. While this may sound like a television commercial for every imaginable product on the market from baby diapers to automobiles, the positive effects of object library management can demonstrate improved productivity through team-focused procedures and higher quality through uniformity, consistency, and, most importantly, meaningful design controls.

With the components of success identified, it is important to note that as languages, systems, and user applications become increasingly complex to program, the need for object management takes on greater implications in the life of a product. As many companies are finding out, the effects of poor object library management impacts not only initial development of a product but results in spiraling chaos with the maintenance and upgrade of the product.

THE DESIGN AUTHORITY

The design authority is a role rather than a position. The role may be filled by a single individual, such as the engineering manager, the lead design engineer, the system architect, or by a group of people who work together to satisfy the goals of object library management. The critical point is to define the role and fill it. It is important not to confuse the design authority role with the responsibilities of a configuration control board whose function is quite different.

Once the design authority role has been assigned, the work of managing object libraries can begin in earnest. Using input from the users, a rudimentary framework for objects can be set up. It is here that the design authority may elect to use the Unified Modeling Language (UML). Whether UML or some other method is used, it is of particular importance that the system requirements are clearly defined, analyzed, and documented. They are the basis upon which all of the design and system testing are based and they must be clearly understood by all parties. The initial object framework can and probably will be a hodgepodge of objects and classifications both at the highest level and at base levels. The reason for this is that the users will be providing their input at different levels. For instance, one or two of the users may be listing specific types of reports they need to generate on a cyclical basis, while other users may be stating their desire to employ animation and sound without specifying what type of animation or sound. The result is that input will be provided on various levels and the design authority must be able to determine the value to place on the information.

This may be better explained by referring to some of the early discussions about object-oriented programming (see the **Recommended Reading** list at the end of this chapter) in which a classic shape example was used for clarification. In the example, shapes became the classification for managing objects that performed functions on a shape, such as changing the shape's size or moving it. The type of shapes, circles, squares, and triangles, inherit the capabilities of the objects. This allows functions to be performed on any type of shape, thus setting up the ability for reuse of the functions on shape types added to the system at later dates.

It is the design authority who begins to set up a framework for new and continuing development. Decisions will need to be made as to whether the input falls into the circle/square category, the perform-on category, or the shapes category. If it is a shape category it will hold objects. If it is an object it will do something. It is the objects then that need to be constructed. It is the classification and management of these objects that takes the design authority to the next critical work effort.

In order for an object to do it is something, it needs to possess both the data and function qualities necessary to perform. Peter Coad and Edward Yourdon expressed these qualities as an equation: Object-oriented = Objects + Classification + Inheritance + Communication with Messages.[1] The design authority, in maximizing the potential of solid object library management, must be able to cross reference and promote the use and reuse of these qualities in the development environment. For instance, objects in an edit classification may include copy, move, and delete. The construction of the object must permit these functions to be performed on any designateded text or graphic unit. As such, the design authority can, within the object library management structure, ensure the reuse of these objects from one product to another and from one upgrade to the next. In planning the object libraries, the design authority must also consider those types of objects that will more likely be upgraded in the short and long terms. While the quickness of advancing technology may make this step seem like crystal ball engineering, the design authority will have responsibility for working with management to minimize technological risks and keep development moving in a forward rather than circular direction.

It is not the role of the design authority to determine how the defined object structure is implemented within the configuration system. That function is performed by specialists in configuration management.

CONFIGURATION MANAGEMENT

Configuration management is a function best performed by a specialist who has three principal tasks. The first is making certain the version control mechanisms sustain the object classifications and hierarchy structure laid out by the design authority. The second is ensuring that the version control mechanisms put into place support the application development staff in easy retrieval and storage of objects. The third is tracking the correct object versions and building them into defined releases of the product. Whether your organization has a configuration management tool in place or not, when the decision to implement an object library management plan is made, a serious comparative capability evaluation of the existing tool and those available in today's market must be made.

Most of the recognized configuration management tools available today will at a minimum provide version control and support release builds.

Nearly all of the tools allow text, graphic, and multimedia object storage. The trick in selecting and using a tool for object library management is in evaluating the available tools in relationship to the scope of the efforts it will be supporting and the manpower investment the company is willing to make to ensure the successful implementation of the tool. It is critical that during this evaluation focus is maintained on the design structure and intended reuse capabilities desired. This means it needs to be evaluated not only for what it will do today, but whether it will meet the needs of your organization in terms of future growth. For example, current plans for your product over the next five year are to support both Windows and Macintosh users. The tool that best fits the design structure and size requirements for the projects only runs in a UNIX environment today. The question as to how the developers will effectively be able to take advantage of the version control features of the tool must be addressed, as does how clean the build feature of the tool really stays.

A similar dilemma presents itself when an organization uses off-site developers for various pieces of the system. One example can be taken from a company whose off-site animation staff developed their product, which was eventually embedded within the company's primary product. It turned out that the operating system used by the off-site developers was not compatible with the configuration management tool being evaluated. A number of work-arounds were drafted and discussed, but the bottom line was that each of them made the version control and build processes cumbersome and less reliable. A lesser known configuration management tool offered the necessary interface for this off-site work and provided all of the other features in a somewhat diminished capacity. The question that had to be asked and answered was which tool was going to best meet the goals of the organization now and in the future. If the organization was willing to fumble through for a while and gamble that the interface for off-site programming was going to constructed or the off-site programmers could be transitioned to a different compatible operating system, then perhaps the more well known tool would be a good choice. If the need for better object management was immediate and the organization was willing to gamble on the eventual expansion of the lesser known tool's capabilities, then the less sophisticated tool would be a good choice.

These examples are merely representative of the types of questions that must be part and parcel of a configuration management tool evaluation. Other important questions include, but are not limited to:

- What support does the vendor supply in configuring the tool in your organization's environment?
- If interfaces are going to be constructed by the tool vendor, will they become part of the configuration management tool product line or

stay a customized piece of software your organization will become responsible for maintaining?

- What training is required by your organization's staff to set up and operate the tool effectively?
- How many man-hours must be devoted to maintaining the tool in order to ensure successful use of it?

Even when the current in-house tool meets the technical specifications for object library management and object development, there are still set-up factors to be considered in assessing the planned design authority structure in relationship to the current configuration of the tool. New areas may need to be prepared and a different hierarchy may need to be defined to support the build features of the tool. This work cannot be overlooked during the evaluation process.

Another stumbling block to successful object library management is in the planning of releases. Here the design authority and configuration management specialists need to work closely to define the contents and status of each release. It is not sufficient for the design authority to send an e-mail that says include x, y, and z. Success is based on knowing not only that x, y, and z are in the release, but also knowing the problem state of x, y, and z within the overall scheme of the object library management plan. In other words, the plan for release A will include version 2.2 of x, version 2.3 of y, and version 4 of z, and we know that version 2.3 of y includes a few glitches that should be fixed before the release date but will not crash the software if they are not fixed. However, version 4 of z may cause some problems, in which case the fallback plan is to use version 2.8 of z because version 3 of z had to be recalled. This is the type of information that becomes part of the release plan composed by the design authority and the configuration management specialist. This, of course, brings us right to the third component needed for successful object library management, quality control and testing.

QUALITY CONTROL AND TESTING

How did the design authority and configuration management specialist make the decision on which version of z to use if the possible problems with z surfaced during the release build. The answer is that version 2.8 was a thoroughly tested and proven object within the system and it did not have a relationship with either x or y. It would not need to be retested. It could just be used because the quality control supporting solid object library management includes traceability, predictability, and uniformity, which are achieved by testing the design, the constructed objects, the object relationships, and the object system. Keep in mind that objects that have been tested can be used and used and used without having to test and test and test. New development will occur in a more orderly manner, because the structure laid out within the object library management plan will lend itself to a clearer and more logical next step. The quality controls are essential in taking the management of objects from basic reuse in the initial product to a viable expanded product vision.

Working with the design authority, quality control personnel complement the object library management plan while imposing and enforcing these controls, because the structure of the objects and the communication from the design authority to the development staff ensures that everyone is working toward the same goal. The quality group does the testing of the object and ensures that it meets the construction and use guidelines established. Quality control accomplishes this by being a part of the development rather than an appendage to development, validating the object structure and conducting walkthroughs where questions and issues can be raised and resolved. The quality group should work closely with the configuration management specialists to ensure the integrity of the released product by validating both the configuration of the tool being used for version control and release management and verification of the product release plan.

SUMMARY

The goal is to maximize an organization's competitive edge in the marketplace. The components for successful object library management presented in this chapter can be raised to whatever level of sophistication best fits your organization. The important thing is to plan and manage the objects constructed.

On a small project the biggest problem may appear to be people resources. Keep in mind that there are three roles that need to be played for success. This may mean that the lead designer is also the design authority and a developer and the configuration management specialist. The quality control and testing role, however, must be performed by someone other than this person. If necessary, even a nontechnical project manager can perform the quality control and testing role as long as the concepts and goals of the project are clearly stated and the basics of object library management are understood. The greatest benefit to the small project is that communication between the design authority and developers is stronger and the set-up of the configuration management tool generally much easier.

On a large project there are larger problems. There the design authority may be a team of people in which some protocol and tie-breaking mechanisms need to be laid out from the start in order to keep the design moving. Communication between the design authority and the developers is more difficult to maintain. The set-up of the configuration management tool may take several weeks and training sessions may need to be conducted to ensure that developers fully understand what is expected of them. And quality control and testing is more involved and necessary. The biggest benefit in a large project is the value of being able to gain a greater long-range vision for the application or product and in being able to cross-train personnel in many areas.

The point is to take action. Whether the project is the conversion of a legacy system to the new technology or the development of new systems with existing and future technology. Begin by committing in black and white what your organization needs to accomplish. Then establish an organization to assess and plan for that accomplishment. Once the plan is formulated, provide training whether it is vendor supplied, seminars, or in-house group sessions. Success can be repeated over and over again when there is a plan to implement and an understanding of the technology. Then appoint the design authority, start evaluating configuration management tools, and prepare a testing strategy that will meet your organization's goals for object management.

Notes

1. Coad, Peter, and Yourdon, Edward, *Object-oriented Analysis*, Englewood Cliffs, NJ: Prentice-Hall, Inc., 1990.

Recommended Reading

Jacobson, Ivar, Griss Martin, and Jonsson Patrik, *Software Reuse*, ACM Press, 1997, pp 60-61, 117, 356 and 436.

Entsminger, Gary, *The Tao of Objects, A Beginner's Guide To Object Oriented Programming.* M & T Publishing, Inc., 1990.

Chapter III-3
Fundamentals of Function Point Analysis

David H. Longstreet and Raffaela Ibba

HUMAN BEINGS SOLVE PROBLEMS by breaking them into smaller, more understandable pieces. Problems that may initially appear to be difficult are found to be simple when dissected into their components or classes. When the objects to be classified are the contents of software systems, a set of definitions and rules, or a scheme of classification, must be used to place these objects into their appropriate categories. Function point analysis is one such technique: a method to break systems into smaller components, so they can be better understood and analyzed. It also provides a structured technique for problem solving.

Function point analysis divides systems into five large classes and general system characteristics. The first three components are external inputs, external outputs, and external inquiries. Each of these components, called transactions, transact against files. The other two classes, internal logical files and external interface files, are the storage locations for data that is combined to form logical information. The general system characteristics assess the general functionality of the system.

BRIEF HISTORY

Function point analysis was developed first by Allan J. Albrecht in the mid-1970s. An attempt to overcome difficulties associated with lines of code as a measure of software size, function point analysis was designed to assist in developing a mechanism to predict effort associated with software development. The method was first published in 1979 and again in 1983 (Albrecht and Gaffeney, "Software Function, Source Lines of Code, and Development Effort Prediction: A Software Science Validation," IEEE Transactions on Software Engineering, November 1983). Since 1986, when the International Function Point User Group (IFPUG) was created, several versions of the *Function Point Counting Practices Manual* have been published by IFPUG (R. Ragland, ed., Westerville, OH: International Function Point User Group, 1994). (See Exhibit 1 for more information on the IFPUG.)

0-8493-9979-3/99/$0.00+$.50
© 1999 by CRC Press LLC

Exhibit 1.   The International Function Point User Group (IFPUG)

The primary mission of the IFPUG is to promote and encourage the effective management of application software development and maintenance activities through the use of function point analysis and other software measurement techniques. The IFPUG accomplishes this through conferences, preconference workshops, committees, and associated publications.

The IFPUG has two conferences per year, in the spring and fall. Their objective is to facilitate the exchange of knowledge and ideas for improved software measurement techniques. Additionally, the conferences provide an environment that stimulates the personal and professional development of attendees.

Since 1987, IFPUG membership has grown from 100 members to nearly 600 members in 1994. Clearly, the majority of IFPUG members are from North America, but function point analysis growth elsewhere is strong. There are eight affiliate organizations, in Australia, Quebec, Germany, Europe, France, Italy, Netherlands, and the UK.

In Italy, for example, the Gruppo Utenti Function Point Italia (GUFPI) was formed in 1990 with 20 business partners and today has 50. GUFPI and IFPUG are organizing a joint conference on software metrics, held in Rome in 1996.

There are several IFPUG committees that provide services to its members. The education committee (EC) organizes preconference workshops. The counting practices committee (CPC) works to enhance and keep the *IFPUG Function Point Counting Practices Manual,* version 4.0, current and up to date. The certification committee (CC) creates and administers certification exams.

OBJECTIVES OF FUNCTION POINT ANALYSIS

Function points measure software by quantifying its functionality provided to the user based primarily on the logical design. Frequently the term *end user* (or user) is used without specifying what is meant. For the purposes of this chapter, the user is a sophisticated user who understands the system from a functional perspective and could provide requirements or does acceptance testing. In other words, function points enable users to measure the size of the information systems according to what they see and interact with.

Because function points measure systems from a functional perspective, they are independent of technology, remaining constant for a system regardless of language, development method, or hardware platform used. The only variable is the amount of effort needed to deliver a given set of function points; therefore, function point analysis can be used to determine whether a tool, an environment, or a language is more productive compared with others within an organization or among organizations. This is a critical point and one of the greatest values of function point analysis.

Function point analysis provides a mechanism to track and monitor scope creep. Function point counts at the end of each phase, including the requirements, analysis, design, code, testing, and implementation phases, can be compared. The function point count at the end of requirements and designs, for example, can be compared to function points actually delivered. A larger number indicates that there has been scope creep. The amount of growth is an indication of how well requirements were gathered by and communicated to the project team. If the amount of growth of projects declines over time, the natural assumption is that communication with the user has improved.

CHARACTERISTICS OF QUALITY FUNCTION POINT ANALYSIS

Function point analysis should be performed by trained and experienced personnel. If conducted by untrained personnel, the reasonable assumption is that the analysis will be done incorrectly. The personnel counting function points should use the most current version of the *Function Point Counting Practices Manual.*

Current application documentation should be used to complete a function point count. For example, screen formats, report layouts, listing of interfaces with other systems and between systems, logical and preliminary physical data models will all assist in function point analysis.

Counting function points should be included as part of the overall project plan and, as such, should be scheduled and planned. The first function point count should be developed to provide sizing used for estimating.

THE FIVE MAJOR COMPONENTS

As computer systems commonly interact with other computer systems, a boundary must be drawn around each system to be measured before classifying components. This boundary must be drawn according to the user's point of view. In short, the boundary indicates the border between the project or application being measured and the external applications or user domain. Once the border has been established, components can be classified, ranked, and tallied. The five major components are as follows:

- **External Inputs (EIs).** EIs are an elementary process in which data crosses the boundary from outside to inside. This data may come from a data input screen or another application. The data is used to maintain one or more internal logical files.
- **External Outputs (EOs).** EOs are an elementary process in which data passes across the boundary from inside to outside. The data creates reports or output files sent to other applications. These reports and files are created from one or more internal logical files.
- **External Inquiries (EQs).** EQs are an elementary process with both input and output components that result in data retrieval from one or more internal logical files. The input process does not update any internal logical files, and the output side does not contain derived data.

173

Exhibit 2. External Inputs (EIs)

Number of FTRs	Number of Data Elements		
	1–4	5–15	Greater than 15
Less than 2	Low (3)	Low(3)	Average (4)
2	Low (3)	Average (4)	High (6)
Greater than 2	Average (4)	High (6)	High (6)

Exhibit 3. External Outputs (EOs)

Number of FTRs	Number of Data Elements		
	1–5	6–19	Greater than 19
Less than 2	Low (4)	Low(4)	Average (5)
2 or 3	Low (4)	Average (5)	High (7)
Greater than 3	Average (5)	High (7)	High (7)

- **Internal Logical Files (ILFs).** These files comprise a user-identifiable group of logically related data that reside entirely within the applications boundary and are maintained through external inputs.
- **External Interface Files (EIFs).** EIFs comprise a user-identifiable group of logically related data that are used for reference purposes only. The data reside entirely outside the application and are maintained by another application. The external interface file is an internal logical file for another application.

After a system's components have been classified according to these components, a ranking of low, average, or high is assigned. For transactions (i.e., EIs, EOs, or EQs), the ranking is based on the number of files updated or referenced and the number of data element types. For both ILFs and EIFs, the ranking is based on record element types and data element types. A record element type is a user-recognizable subgroup of data elements within an ILF or EIF. A data element type is a unique, user-recognizable, nonrecursive field.

Exhibit 2 and Exhibit 3 contain tables that assist in the ranking process. The numerical rating appears in parentheses. For example, in Exhibit 2, an EI that references or updates two file types referenced and has seven data elements would be assigned a ranking of average and associated rating of 4, when file types referenced are the combined number of ILFs referenced or updated and EIFs referenced.

For inquiries, both the input and output side of the transaction are considered when evaluating the ranking of low, average, or high. The higher of the output or the input side of the transaction is used to rank the external inquiry. Exhibit 4 can be used to assist in this evaluation. For example, if

Exhibit 4. External Inquiries (EQs)

External Input	External Output		
	Low	Average	High
Low	Low (3)	Average (4)	High (6)
Average	Average (4)	Average (4)	High (6)
High	High (6)	High (6)	High (6)

Exhibit 5. Internal Logical Files (ILFs)

Number of Record Element Types	Number of Data Elements		
	1–19	20–50	Greater than 50
1	Low (7)	Low (7)	Average (10)
2–5	Low (7)	Average (10)	High (15)
Greater than 5	Average (10)	High (15)	High (15)

Exhibit 6. External Interface Files (EIFs)

Number of Record Element Types	Number of Data Elements		
	1–19	20–50	Greater than 50
1	Low (5)	Low (5)	Average (7)
2–5	Low (5)	Average (7)	High (10)
Greater than 5	Average (7)	High (10)	High (10)

the input side of the transaction were rated low, but the output side were rated average, the inquiry would be rated average.

For both ILFs (see Exhibit 5) and EIFs (see Exhibit 6), the number of record element types and the number of data elements types are used to determine a ranking of low, average, or high. A record element type is a user-recognizable subgroup of data elements within an ILF or EIF. A data element type is a unique, user-recognizable, nonrecursive field on an ILF or EIF.

The counts for each level of complexity for each type of component can be entered into a table such as the one shown in Exhibit 7. Each count is multiplied by the numerical rating shown to determine the rated value. The rated values on each row are summed across the table, giving a total value for each type of component. These totals are then summed across the table, giving a total value for each type of component. These totals are then summed to arrive at the total number of unadjusted function points.

THE VALUE ADJUSTMENT FACTOR

The value adjustment factor (VAF) is based on 14 general system characteristics that rate the general functionality of the application being counted. Each characteristic has associated descriptions that help determine the characteristic's degrees of influence, which range on a scale of

Exhibit 7. Calculating Unadjusted Function Points

Type of Component	Complexity of Components			Total
	Low	Average	High	
External Inputs	____*3= ____	____*4= ____	____*6= ____	
External Outputs	____*4= ____	____*5= ____	____*7= ____	
External Inquiries	____*3= ____	____*4= ____	____*6= ____	
Internal Logical Files	____*7= ____	____*10= ____	____*15= ____	
External Interface Files	____*5= ____	____*7= ____	____*10= ____	
		Total Number of Unadjusted Function Points		_____

Exhibit 8. General System Characteristics Overview

General System Characteristic	Brief Description
1. Data communications	How many communication facilities are there to aid in the transfer or exchange of information with the application or system?
2. Distributed data processing	How are distributed data and processing functions handled?
3. Performance	Was response time or throughput required by the user?
4. Heavily used configuration	How heavily used is the current hardware platform where the application will be executed?
5. Transaction rate	How frequently are transactions executed daily, weekly, monthly, etc.?
6. Online Data Entry	What percentage of the information is entered online?
7. End-User Efficiency	Was the application designed for end-user efficiency?
8. Online Update	How many ILFs are updated by online transaction?
9. Complex Processing	Does the application have extensive logical or mathematical processing?
10. Reusability	Was the application developed to meet one user's or many users' needs?
11. Installation Ease	How difficult is conversion and installation?
12. Operational Ease	How effective or automated are start-up, backup, and recovery procedures?
13. Multiple Sites	Was the application specifically designed, developed, and supported to be installed at multiple sites for multiple organizations?
14. Facilitate Change	Was the application specifically designed, developed, and supported to facilitate change?

0 to 5, from no influence to strong influence. The IFPUG Counting Practices Manual provides detailed evaluation criteria for each of the general system characteristics; Exhibit 8 is intended to provide an overview of each general system characteristic.

Once all the 14 general system characteristics have been answered, they should be tabulated using the IFPUG value adjustment equation:

$$VAF = 0.65 + \left[(E\ Ci)/100\right]$$

where:

C = degree of influence for each general system characteristic
i = from 1 to 14, representing each general system characteristic
E = summation of all 14 general system characteristics

The final Function Point Count is obtained by multiplying the VAF by the unadjusted function point (UAF):

$$FP = VAF * UAF$$

CONCLUSION

Accurately predicting the size of software has plagued the software industry for more than 45 years. As indicated by the growth of IFPUG, function points are becoming widely accepted as the standard metric for measuring software size. Now that function points have made adequate sizing possible, the overall rate of progress in software productivity and software quality will improve. Understanding software size is the key to understanding both productivity and quality. Without a reliable sizing metric, relative changes in productivity (i.e., function points per work-month) or relative changes in quality (i.e., defects per function point) cannot be calculated. If relative changes in productivity and quality can be calculated and plotted over time, focus can be put on an organization's strengths and weaknesses. Most important, any attempt to correct weaknesses can be measured for effectiveness.

The following points sum up the benefits of function point analysis:

- Function points can be used to size software applications accurately. Sizing is an important component in determining productivity (i.e., outputs/inputs).
- They can be counted by different people, at different times, to obtain the same measure within a reasonable margin of error.
- Function points are easily understood by the nontechnical user. This helps communicate sizing information to a user or customer.
- Function points can be used to determine whether a tool, a language, or an environment is more productive when compared with others.

Due to space limitations, this chapter is a primer on — rather than a comprehensive guide to — counting function points. For more information, the authors recommend writing to the International Function Point User Group at IFPUG Executive Offices, Blendonview Office Park, 5008-28 Pine Creek Drive, Westerville, Ohio 43081-4899, or calling the organization at (614) 895-7130.

Chapter III-4

Function Points
Step by Step

David Longstreet and Raffaela Ibba

THE OBJECTIVE OF FUNCTION POINT ANALYSIS IS TO PROVIDE ACCURATE SIZING as early as possible, so that sizing can be used as an input into the estimating process. This type of analysis also serves as a mechanism to track and monitor scope creep.

Function point counts at the end of requirements, analysis, design, code, testing, and implementation can be compared; furthermore, the count at the end of the requirements phase or designs phase, or both, can be compared with the function points actually delivered, indicating whether the project has grown and there has been scope creep. The amount of growth is an indication of how well requirements were gathered by and communicated to the project team. If the amount of growth of projects declines over time, a natural assumption is that communications with the user have improved.

Key deliverables from a function point count are as follows:

- The total unadjusted function point count.
- The unadjusted function point count by each of five characteristics: external inputs (EIs), external outputs (EOs), external inquiries (EQs), internal logical files (ILFs), and external interface files (EIFs).
- The value adjustment factor (VAF).
- The total adjusted function point count.
- Validation reports, as prescribed in step 8 of this chapter.

Depending on the phase of the project the following documents will be needed:

- Documentation of the users' perceived objectives, problems, and needs
- Collected documentation regarding the current system, either automated or manual, of such a system
- Any refined objectives and constraints for the proposed system
- Any other requirement documentation completed to date
- Screen formats and dialogues

- Report layouts
- Layouts of input forms
- Interfaces with other systems and between systems
- Logical or preliminary physical data models, or both

Finally, the following assumptions are made:

- The International Function Point User Group's *Function Point Counting Practices Manual*, (R. Ragland, ed., Westerville, OH: International Function Point User Group, 1994) is used.
- The person completing the function point count has received training in function points before counting. Ideally, the application expert counts function points with the assistance of a function point counting expert.

INITIAL STEPS

Before counting function points, the users must determine the application boundaries, which should be drawn around the entire application rather than around individual project teams. The function point counting expert and the application functionality expert need to work together to determine the boundaries. The result of this initial step is a boundary diagram. Drawing of the application boundary is a critical step in counting function points, as it determines additional inputs into Checkpoint, a tool used for estimating.

Step 1: Planning the Function Point Count

The task of counting function points should be included in the overall project plan. That is, counting function points should be scheduled and planned. The first function point count should be developed to provide sizing used for estimating.

Function points can be counted before the completion of requirements but should be thoroughly documented so they can be easily maintained and updated. Of course, early estimates using function points — or any method — are subject to change as much as the requirements themselves. In short, if the scope and size of the project changes, the effort required to complete the project changes also. Function point analysis can be completed before having a complete set of requirements, but a function point count should be completed after the requirements have been finalized and again at implementation.

After the function point count has been completed, it should be compared to previous function point counts to verify any new or changed components, and the function point count should be updated accordingly. Each addition to the function point count should have a label attached, indicating if the new or changed component is the result of changed functionality or if it is the result of improved function point counting.

Step 2: Gathering the Documentation

The following recommended documentation assists in completing function point counts before the finalization of requirements:

- Documentation of the users' perceived objectives, problems, and needs
- Collected documentation regarding the current system, if such a system exists
- Any refined objectives and constraints for the proposed system
- A description of the overall system framework
- Any other requirement documentation completed to date

A more detailed function point can be completed after analysis and design. Recommended documentation includes:

- Screen formats and dialogues
- Report layouts
- Layouts of input forms
- Interfaces with other systems and between systems
- Logical or preliminary physical data models
- Filed sizes and formats
- Menu options

The function point counts completed before design should be compared with the function point counts after the completion design. This is an indicator of how much the application has grown since the requirements stage.

Recommended documentation at the conclusion or implementation of the project should include all the documentation mentioned in the list and any additional system documentation.

Step 3: Determining the Value Adjustment Factor (VAF)

The VAF should be reviewed during the initial stages of function point counting. As the count proceeds, the VAF can be updated as necessary and as more information is discovered. The VAF should be reviewed and updated at the completion of each subsequent step.

The VAF is based on 14 general system characteristics (GSCs) that rate the general functionality of the application being counted. Each characteristic has associated descriptions that help determine the degrees of influence of the characteristics. The degrees of influence range on a scale of 0 to 5, from no influence to strong influence. The International Function Point User Group (IFPUG) *Counting Practices Manual* provides detailed evaluation

Exhibit 1.   General System Characteristic Brief Description

General System Characteristic	Brief Description
1. Data Communications	How many communication facilities are there to aid in the transfer or exchange of information with the application or system?
2. Distributed Data Processing	How are distributed data and processing functions handled?
3. Performance	Was response time or throughput required by the user?
4. Heavily Used Configuration	How heavily used is the current hardware platform where the application will be executed?
5. Transaction Rate	How frequently are transactions executed — daily, weekly, or monthly?
6. Online Data Entry	What percentage of the information is entered online?
7. End-User Efficiency	Was the application designed for end-user efficiency?
8. Online Update	How many ILFs are updated by online transactions?
9. Complex Processing	Does the application have extensive logical or mathematical processing?
10. Reusability	Was the application developed to meet one or many user needs?
11. Installation Ease	How difficult is conversion and installation?
12. Operational Ease	How effective or automated are startup, backup, and recovery procedures?
13. Multiple Sites	Was the application specifically designed, developed, and supported to be installed at multiple sites for multiple organizations?
14. Facilitate Change	Was the application specifically designed, developed, and supported to facilitate change?

criteria for each of the GSCs. Exhibit 1 is intended to provide an overview of each GSC.

Step 4:   Taking Inventory of Transactions and Files

A complete inventory of all function point components (i.e., EIs, EOs, EQs, ILFs, and EIFs) should be completed before classifying the individual components. It is best to inventory all transactions — while maintaining a listing of files needed for the transactions — before taking an inventory of the files. After the inventory of transactions is complete, the file listing should be reviewed. Completing the file inventory this way helps to ensure files that are not ILFs or EIFs have not been included.

External Inputs (EI). EI is an elementary process in which data crosses the boundary from outside to inside. This data may come from a data input screen or another application and is used to maintain one or more internal logical files. A good source of information to determine EIs are screen layouts, screen formats and dialogs, and layouts of any input forms. Additional inputs from other applications should be inventoried here. Inputs from other applications must update ILFs of application being counted.

External Outputs (EOs). EOs are an elementary process in which data passes across the boundary from inside to outside. The data creates reports or output files sent to other applications. These reports and files are created from one or more internal logical files. A good source of information to determine the EOs are report layouts and electronic file formats that are being sent outside the application boundary.

External Inquiries (EQ). These are an elementary process with both input and output components that result in data retrieval from one or more internal logical files. The input process does not update any internal logical files, and the output side does not contain derived data. A good source of information to determine the external inputs are screen layouts, screen formats and dialogs, and layouts of any input forms.

Internal logical files (ILFs). These are a user-identifiable group of logically related data that resides entirely within the applications boundary and is maintained through external inputs. A good source of information to determine the ILFs are logical and preliminary physical data models, table layouts, and database descriptions.

External Interface Files (EIFs). These are a user-identifiable group of logically related data that are used for reference purposes only. The data reside entirely outside the application and are maintained by another application. The external interface file is an internal logical file for another application. A good source of information to determine EIFs are interface descriptions with other systems.

The completed inventory of components should be distributed among the project team to ensure that everything has been included. Once it is confirmed that all transactions and files have been included, classifying individual components can take place.

Step 5: Classifying Components

It is important to understand the matrixes associated with the transactions (EIs, EOs, EQs) and files (ILFs, EIFs). The counter should identify the appropriate row before determining the column. There is much less granularity in determining the appropriate row (i.e., the number of files referenced for transactions and the number of record types for files) than determining the appropriate column. This helps reduce the amount of effort required to complete a function point count.

Extending the above analysis, commonality should be considered before counting transactions and files. The function point counter should ask the following questions to help expedite the counting process.

- Do external inputs need more or less than three files to be processed? For all the EIs that reference more than three files, all the counter needs to know is whether the EI has more or less than four data element types referenced. If the EI has more than four data element types, the EI is rated high; if it has less than four data element types, the EI will be rated average. Any EIs that references less than three files should be singled out and counted separately.
- Do external outputs need more or less than four files to be processed? For all the EOs that reference more than four files, all the counter needs to know is whether the EO has more or less than five data element types. If the EO has more than five data element types, the EO is rated high; if less than five, the EO is rated average. Any EOs that reference less than four files should be singled out and counted separately. The same analysis can be conducted as outlined in EI and EO, but using the higher of the EI and EO as prescribed in the IFPUG *Counting Practices Manual.*
- Do all files contain one record type or more than one record type? If all or many of the files contain only one record type, all the counter needs to know is whether the file contains more or less than 50 data elements types. If the file contains more than 50 data elements, the file is rated average; if less than 50 data element types, the file is considered low. Any files that contain more than one record type can be singled out and counted separately.

Step 6: Reviewing 14 General System Characteristics (GSCs)

The 14 GSCs should be reviewed to ensure accuracy. Each GSC is rated on a scale from 0 (no influence) to 5 (strong influence). Once all the 14 GSCs have been answered, they should be tabulated using the IFPUG Value Adjustment Equation (VAF), as follows:

$$14$$

$$VAF = 0.65 + \left[(\Sigma \ Ci)/100 \right]$$

$$I = 1$$

where:

  Ci = each GSC
  .I = from 1 to 14, representing each GSC
  Σ = summation of all 14 GSCs

It is important to apply the GSCs and VAF accurately, because they can affect the overall function point count by ±35%.

Exhibit 2. Calculating Unadjusted Function Points

Type of Component	Classification of Components			Total
	Low	Average	High	
External Inputs	_____ *3= _____	_____ *4= _____	_____ *6= _____	
External Outputs	_____ *4= _____	_____ *5= _____	_____ *7= _____	
External Inquiries	_____ *3= _____	_____ *4= _____	_____ *6= _____	
Internal Logical Files	_____ *7= _____	_____ *10= _____	_____ *15= _____	
External Interface Files	_____ *5= _____	_____ *7= _____	_____ *10= _____	

Total Number of Unadjusted Function Points _____

VAF * Unadjusted FPs _____

Total Adjusted Function Points _____

Step 7: Tabulating Results

The counts for each level of complexity for each type of component can be entered into a table, as shown in Exhibit 2. Each count is multiplied by the numerical rating shown to determine the rated value. The rated values on each row are summed across the table, giving a total value for each type of component. These totals are then summed across the table, giving a total value for each type of component. These totals are then summed down to arrive at the total number of unadjusted function points.

The unadjusted function point count is multiplied by the value adjustment factor to obtain the adjusted function point count.

Step 8: Validating Results

The results of the function point count should be reviewed by the entire project team and validated by the metrics coordinator. The greatest sources of errors in function point analysis are errors of omission. Other errors arise when physical constructions are substituted for logical constructions and are counted as components. The project team therefore should review the function point analysis for completeness and should verify that all components (i.e., the EIs, EOs, EQs, ILFs, and EIFs) have been included. The metrics coordinator should work with the function point counter to ensure the process has been followed properly and that he or she followed the prescribed validation process.

CONCLUSION

Any key question that is asked during function point counting no needs a short explanation. The following key questions should be asked:

- Is the function point count a task in the overall project plan?
- Is the person performing the function point count trained in function point counting?

- Did the function point counter use current documentation to count function points?
- Were IFPUG 4.0 *Counting Practices Manual* guidelines followed?
- Were internally developed function point counting guidelines followed?
- Was the application counted from the user's point of view?
- Was the system counted from a logical and not a physical point of view?
- Does the established boundary for the FP count match the boundary of other metrics (time reporting, defect tracking)? If not, why?
- Do the individual FP components (ILFs, EIFs, EIs, EOs, and EQs) percentages conform to industry averages (40% for ILFs, 5% for EIFs, 20% for EIs, 25% for EOs, and 10% for EQs) and averages established for GTE? If not, is there a valid reason?
- Has an inventory of transactions (EIs, EOs, and EQs) and files (ILFs and EIFs) been reviewed by the project team?
- Do each of the 14 GSCs fall within the ranges of other projects counted within the organization?
- Has the count been logged into a Function Point repository?
- Are all the assumptions consistent with other projects counted?
- Have all the assumptions been thoroughly documented?
- Has the count been reviewed by an experienced FP counter?

Chapter III-5

Software Metrics: Quantifying and Analyzing Software for Total Quality Management

Bijoy Bordoloi and Joe Luchetski

ONCE AN IS DEPARTMENT HAS ESTABLISHED A SOFTWARE DEVELOPMENT PROCESS, it must quantitatively determine the parameters associated with that process and its products. A quantitative approach allows the organization to compare its performance with that of its competitors. Weaknesses and areas requiring management's attention are highlighted, and benchmarks are established to measure the organization's future improvement. These quantitative measurements are performed using software metrics.

Today, software metrics are enjoying widespread interest as mainstream IS organizations adopt the Total Quality Management (TQM) strategy and its emphasis on quantitative measurement. This renewed inquisitiveness is generating new and increasingly powerful metrics.

Software metrics are quantifiable measures used to determine various characteristics of a software system or a software development process. Software system characteristics are typically size, complexity, and reliability, whereas the software development process is characterized by cost and allocation of resources. The product versus process classification is the most common method of differentiating software metrics. However, other metric classifications have been suggested, including:

- Predictor versus result
- Direct versus indirect
- Subjective versus objective
- Quality versus productivity

0-8493-9979-3/99/$0.00+$.50
© 1999 by CRC Press LLC

None of these classifications are mutually exclusive. They serve to characterize the point of view of the metric user rather than the metric itself.

PROCESS METRICS

Process metrics are also known as resource or global metrics. Their objective is to quantify characteristics for the overall software development process, as opposed to the characteristics for a specific life cycle phase. Typically, process metrics predict overall cost, total development time, work effort, or the staffing levels and durations required to implement a software development project. Most process metrics are based on empirical data and employ a series of adjustments to tailor their predictions to the specific product and development process. They are designed to be used very early in the development process, usually by the end of the requirements analysis phase or early in the system design phase. Often, they are constructed to allow metric users to revise and refine their predictions as the software development process progresses.

FUNCTION POINT METRICS

The function-oriented approach allows the function points for a particular project to be calculated very early in the development process, usually in the requirements analysis phase and no later than the system design phase.

The number of function points for a particular project is calculated as follows. First, five product parameters are counted:

- Number of external inputs
- Number of external outputs
- Number of logical internal files (i.e., master files)
- Number of external interface files
- Number of external inquiries

Each parameter is assigned a complexity rating based on a three-level scale, simple (i.e., low complexity), average, or complex (i.e., high complexity), as shown in Exhibit 1. Each parameter count is multiplied by its

Exhibit 1. Complexity Rating

| Parameter | Count | Complexity Rating | | | Total |
		Low	Average	High	
Inputs	x3	x4	x6	=	
Outputs	x4	x5	x7	=	
Logical Internal Files	x7	x10	x15	=	
External Interface Files	x5	x7	x10	=	
External Inquiries	x3	x4	x6	=	
	Total Unadjusted Function Points (FC)				

assigned complexity rating, and the resulting values are summed to obtain the total unadjusted function points (FC).

Next, the Degree of Influence is determined for each of the project's 14 general characteristics. The Degree of Influence is based on the following six-level scale:

- Not present/no influence = 0
- Insignificant influence = 1
- Moderate influence = 2
- Average influence = 3
- Significant influence = 4
- Strong influence = 5

The 14 general characteristics are as follows:

- Data communications
- Distributed functions
- Performance
- Heavy use configuration
- Transaction rate
- On-line data entry
- End-user efficiency
- On-line update
- Complex processing
- Reusability
- Installation ease
- Operational ease
- Multiple sites
- Facilitated change

The degrees of influence for all 14 characteristics are summed together to yield the total degree of influence (DI). The Processing Complexity Adjustment (PCA) is calculated using the formula PCA = 0.65 * 0.01 DI. Finally, the number of function points for the project is calculated by the formula:

$$\text{Function points} = \text{FC(PCA)}$$

To determine the size, cost, or work effort required for a particular project, its calculated function point value is compared to historical data for projects with the same or relatively similar values.

With the size and availability of historical data increasing rapidly, the function point method is probably the most widely used metric; however, it is not without its critics. The popularity and widespread use of function points has spurred the development of a number of variations.[1] These alternate methods and the subjectivity required to determine complexity ratings and degree of influence have caused a number of experts to question function point reliability. The International Function Point User Group (IFPUG) has attempted to address these concerns by publishing the *IFPUG Function Point Counting Practices Manual,* offering training and certification in function point methodology and by funding a study with the Massachusetts Institute of Technology to evaluate function point reliability.

This study, by Chris F. Kemerer, examined interrater and intermethod reliabilities using more than 100 different function point totals from 27 actual commercial systems. Interrater reliability attempted to determine whether evaluation of the same system by two different individuals would result in the same value. Intermethod reliability attempted to determine whether evaluation of the same system using the IFPUG methodology versus one of the variations would result in significantly different function point values. The study's findings indicate that function point raters and methods are robust and reliable. The median interrater variation was approximately 12%, whereas the correlation across two methods was as high as 95%.[2]

THE CONSTRUCTIVE COST MODEL

Barry Boehm developed the Constructive Cost Model (CoCoMo) to predict the work effort and development time required for the management and technical staffs in a software development project. The formulas do not include support staff, such as secretaries. In addition, CoCoMo covers only the development phases, not the full software life cycle. CoCoMo estimates begin with the system design phase (i.e., after the system requirements have been analyzed) and conclude with the integration and system test phase. CoCoMo does not include installation of the product or maintenance. However, the model can be used for maintenance predictions by adjusting the parameters and drivers to reflect the maintenance task, environment, and reuse of design and code.

CoCoMo is size-oriented. Its estimates are based on the number of lines of source code delivered in thousands. The model is designed to provide predictions at three levels, basic, intermediate, or detailed, depending on the information known about the product. The model is also constructed to allow the user to adjust the prediction to compensate for the project's complexity and the development environment. This is accomplished using three modes (i.e., organic, semidetached, or embedded), 15 cost drivers, phase-sensitive effort multipliers, and a three-level product hierarchy.

The basic CoCoMo formulas take the general form:

$$\text{Effort (in person months)} = K_d = a(KDSI)^b \text{ and}$$

$$\text{Development Time (in months)} = t_d = a(K_d)^b$$

where:

KDSI = thousands of delivered source instructions.

The values of the parameters a and b are determined by the project mode and the model's prediction level. For effort (K_d), a equals:

Prediction Level Mode	Basic	Intermediate	Detailed
Organic	2.4	3.2	3.2
Semidetached	3.0	3.0	3.0
Embedded	3.6	2.8	2.8

Also, b varies with mode only:

Mode	For All Prediction Levels
Organic	1.05
Semidetached	1.12
Embedded	1.20

For development time (t_d), a equals 2.5 for all three modes and prediction levels, and b varies with the mode only:

Mode	For All Prediction Levels
Organic	0.38
Semidetached	0.35
Embedded	0.32

Mode is used to categorize the project type. Organic mode projects are typically developed by a small team, highly experienced with this type of application and the language used for implementation. Organic projects have fairly loose requirements.

Embedded projects exist at the other end of the spectrum. They are unique and technologically challenging, with stringent requirements. The project team is large and has very little experience with this type of application and language.

The semidetached mode falls somewhere between the easy organic and the difficult embedded projects. Semidetached projects are moderately complex, and the development team has a degree of familiarity with this type of project and the language.

The basic prediction level is used to obtain a quick-and-dirty estimate of the overall project's effort (i.e., K_d) and development time (i.e., t_d). This level is intended for use early in the development process, either at the end of the requirements analysis phase, or as soon as a reasonable estimate of the lines of source code is available. The predictions at this level can be adjusted for mode only.

Intermediate CoCoMo

This is the most commonly used prediction model. To the mode adjustment, intermediate CoCoMo adds 15 cost drivers to tailor the effort estimate to the complexity and development environment for the specific project. The data required to use intermediate CoCoMo should be available in the system design phase and definitely by the detailed design phase. This allows the metric user to refine and to update the estimates calculated using basic CoCoMo. In fact, CoCoMo estimates can be modified whenever development parameters change, the estimate of the KDSI improves, or new information becomes available.

The intermediate CoCoMo cost drivers are grouped into four attributes, as follows:

- Product attributes:
  - Required software reliability (RELY)
  - Database size (DATA)
  - Product complexity (CPLX)
- Computer attributes:
  - Execution time constraints (TIME)
  - Main storage constraints (STOR)
  - Virtual machine volatility (VIRT)
  - Computer turnaround time (TURN)
- Personnel attributes:
  - Analyst capability (ACAP)
  - Applications experience (AEXP)
  - Programmer capability (PCAP)
  - Machine familiarity and experience (VEXP)
  - Programming language experience (LEXP)
- Project attributes:
  - Modern programming practices (MODP)
  - Use of software (CASE) tools (TOOL)
  - Development schedule (SCED)

The effect of each cost driver is rated on a six-level scale: very low, low, normal, high, very high, or extra high. For most cost drivers, a numerical value is given for each rating level, with nominal always corresponding to a rating of 1.00. The appropriate rating for each driver is selected, and all selected values are multiplied together to yield the effort adjustment factor (EAF). The EAF adjusts the effort estimate as follows:

$$K_{dADJ} = EAF(K_d)$$

Intermediate CoCoMo also allows the total effort estimate to be partitioned into several life cycle phases, including product design (i.e., analogous to system design), detailed design, code and unit test, and integration and test. The partitioning is accomplished by project size (e.g., small [2 KD-SI], intermediate [8 KDSI], or medium [32 KDSI]) using a series of tables that provides an estimate of the total effort (by percentage) expended in each life cycle phase. Separate tables are provided for each project mode.

Detailed CoCoMo

This model adds two more enhancements to intermediate CoCoMo. The first enhancement provides separate cost driver ratings for each of the four life cycle phases covered by the model. The other enhancement allows the metric user to track the product through a three-level development hierarchy. These levels are module, subsystem, and system. Most authors agree that the increased complexity of the detailed level does not significantly improve the accuracy of CoCoMo estimates.

The effort and development time estimates are used to calculate productivity in KDSI/per month, full-time staffing levels (FSP), and peak FSP. These values can be obtained for the overall project and for individual phases, depending on the CoCoMo level used. Most other authors find the accuracy of CoCoMo estimates to be highly dependent on the selection of the cost driver ratings, which is a fairly subjective selection process. It is recommended that IS departments develop a database of CoCoMo estimates and the corresponding actual project data to allow future CoCoMo estimates to be calibrated to the organizations' specific development processes.

THE PUTNAM CURVE

Lawrence H. Putnam, in his characterization of the software development process, took a theoretical approach and validated it with empirical data. Putnam's theoretical approach is based on the work of Norden, who based his work on Lord Rayleigh's.[3]

Lord Rayleigh developed Rayleigh curves to explain the behavior of surface disturbances or waves. He observed that these waves are governed by two forces: one force acts on the rising edge of the disturbance, and the other acts on the decaying edge. He postulated that the overall shape of the wave could be modeled as a function of the relative changes in the magnitudes of the two forces over time. Exhibit 2 illustrates Rayleigh curves.

Norden postulated that the effort and time duration for research and development projects could be characterized using Rayleigh curves. Norden hypothesized that Rayleigh curves also describe the way people

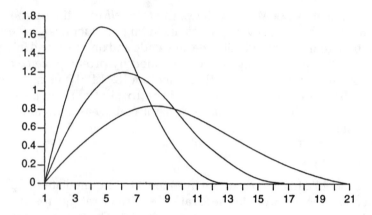

SOURCE: T.G. Lewis, *CASE: Computer-Aided Software Engineering* (New York: Van Nostrand Reinhold, 1991)

Exhibit 2.   Rayleigh Curves

approach and solve problems, and R&D projects are just a series of problem-solving opportunities. The rising force of the Rayleigh curve models the increasing knowledge (i.e., the learning curve) associated with continued problem solving. The decaying-force models the decreasing amount of work or problems remaining to be solved over time. Therefore, each phase in the development of a new product would conform to the shape of a Rayleigh curve, as shown in Exhibit 3, and the sum of all the individual curves would also follow a Rayleigh distribution.

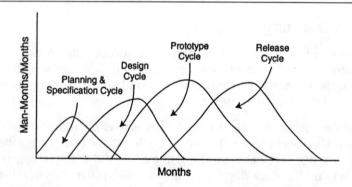

SOURCE: Victor R. Basili, "Resource Models," *Tutorial on Models and Metrics for Software Management and Engineering.* (New York: Computer Society Press, 1980)

Exhibit 3.   Norden Characterization of an R&D Project Using Rayleigh Curves

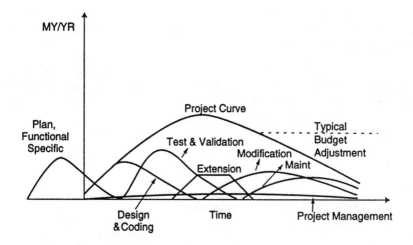

SOURCE: Lawrence H. Putnam, "A General Empirical Solution to the Macro Software Sizing and Estimating Problem," *IEEE Transactions on Software Engineering* SE-4 (1978)

Exhibit 4. Putnam Characterization of a Software Development Project Using Norden/Rayleigh Model

Putnam extended Norden's work to the description of the phases in the software development cycle, as shown in Exhibit 4, and the cycle itself. He validated this extension using data from approximately 200 large systems developed for the U.S. Army's Computer Systems Command. For most of these systems, the software development process followed the Norden/Rayleigh model well.

The general form of the Putnam curve to describe the software development process is $y = K(1 - e^{-at^2})$,

where:

    y = the cumulative effort expended through time t
    K = total effort required for the entire life cycle
    a = shape parameter
    t = number of time periods since the beginning of the project

The shape parameter a is calculated by taking the first derivative of the general form and solving for a when y' is at a maximum. The first derivative y' represents the peak staffing level for the project and is expressed as $y' = 2Kate^{-at^2}$.

For large systems, Putnam's empirical analysis determined that y'_{max} occurs when t is approximately equal to the system development time (t_d), which is at the end of the design and coding phase. Based on the shape of the total project curve, Putnam concluded that 39.35% of the total life cycle effort is expended developing the system and 60% expended testing, maintaining, and modifying it.

Putnam used the Norden/Rayleigh model and his empirical data to determine several other mathematical relationships to explain the software development process. Two of the most interesting relationships are the project difficulty and the time-effort conservation law. Putnam observed that project difficulty (D) could be expressed as:

$$D = K/t_d^2$$

where:

K = total effort required for the entire life cycle
t_d = development time

A small value of D indicates a relatively easy system to develop; a large D value corresponds to a hard system.

The time-effort conservation law is based on Putnam's observation that Kt_d^4 is a constant. This indicates that effort (K) and development time (t_d) are inversely related, an intuitively obvious relationship, but as a function of the fourth power of t_d^4. The practical use of this relationship becomes apparent when evaluating the effect of reducing td to compress the project schedule. The total effort required (K) increases as a function of t_d, yielding a very large increase in effort (ΔK) for even relatively small development time reductions (Δt_d).

Putnam's curve and its various mathematical relationships are used to predict costs, development, and total schedules, and work effort required to support the software life cycle. The relationships are also employed to evaluate the effects of various resource constraints and to perform what-if scenario analyses. The few basic assumptions required to use the curve can be made during the requirements analysis phase and later refined and updated as the project progresses.

Analysts have found Putnam curve predictions to consistently overstate the effort and development time required, especially for small- and medium-sized systems. Nevertheless, it provides viable estimates that can be used in worst-case scenarios or with other process metrics.

The Putnam curve is sometimes referred to as Putnam's Software Life Cycle Model (SLIM). However, SLIM is a proprietary CASE tool offered by Quantitative Software Management, Inc. that uses Putnam's concepts.

PRODUCT METRICS

Process metrics concentrate on how the overall software development process performs (i.e., costs, schedule, and resource allocations); product metrics, on the other hand, concentrate on what the process produces. Product metrics focus on the quantitative evaluation of the output of individual phases in the development process. The majority of the product metrics focus on code-related attributes, such as size, complexity, and reliability, but the trend is moving toward the evaluation of the output of the system design and detailed design phases. These product metrics attempt to measure design structure.

SOFTWARE SCIENCE

Software science metrics are size-oriented code metrics, but they are not lines of code counts. Instead, all of Maurice Halstead's metrics are theoretically derived and focus on a count of the operands and the operators in a program or module. Operands are all the variables and constants used in the program (e.g., x, y, Π, 57; whereas operators are all the symbols used to affect or to order an operands (e.g., +, −, *, <, >, GO TO). The operands and operator counts for a program are defined as follows:

n_1 = number of unique or distinct operators
n_2 = number of unique or distinct operands
N_1 = total number of occurrences for all operators
N_2 = total number of occurrences for all operands

From these counts, two basic program attributes are calculated. One is program vocabulary (n) where:

$$N = N_1 + N_2$$

The other is observed program length (N), where:

$$N = N_1 + N_2$$

All software science metrics are calculated from these counts and totals and are summarized as follows. For the mathematical details of each metric, interested readers are referred to Halstead's monograph.

- Estimated Program Length (N) is calculated from the number of unique operators (n_1) and operands (n_2).
- Program Volume (V) is the size of the program in bits of information. This value is dependent on the programming language used; the more powerful the language, the lower the V value.
- Program Volume (V*) is the minimum theoretical volume in bits of information. This value is programming-language independent.
- Program Level (L) indicates how well a given algorithm has been implemented in a specific language. It is the ratio of V* and V. Values of L vary between 0 (i.e., poor) and 1 (i.e., perfect).
- Intelligence Content (I) is the language-independent information content of a given algorithm. The value of I should remain constant for

197

implementations of a given algorithm in different programming languages.

- Programming Effort (E) is the total number of elementary mental discriminations required to generate a program.
- Estimated Programming Time (T) is the estimate of time required to generate a program. Calculated using programming effort (E) and the Stroud Number, typically 18 mental discriminations per second.
- Language Level (γ) is the relative power of a programming language. The higher the γ value, the more powerful the language.

To use software science metrics, source code must be available. Therefore, the application of these metrics is limited to the coding and unit test phase and the operation and maintenance phase. In these phases, the metrics measure the relative size of the program or module. A large-size measurement may indicate high complexity, poor or inefficient programming, and a large number of faults. In this way, software science metrics identify code that is a likely candidate for rework or additional testing. In the operation and maintenance phase, the metrics are also used to estimate the effort, time, and difficulty required to modify a particular program or module.

Experts have criticized Halstead's metrics for the since-discredited psychological theory on which some of them are based and for ambiguities and variations in the determination of operators and operands. In spite of this, however, conclusive evidence of their validity remains elusive. For almost every book and journal article that uses or supports them, there are just as many that do not. Still, Halstead's software science metrics remain the benchmark against which most other metrics are evaluated.

CYCLOMATIC COMPLEXITY

Whereas Halstead's software science metrics employ a size-oriented approach to analyze programs, Thomas McCabe based his metric on program complexity. He reasoned that complexity is directly related to the paths created by control and decision statements. As the number of paths increases, the complexity of the program or module increases. As complexity increases, the testability and maintainability of the program decreases.

McCabe's cyclomatic complexity metric uses graph theory to illustrate the number of linearly independent paths in the program or module. From the source code, a control graph is created. This is a directed graph with a distinct entry node and a distinct exit node. In the graph, nodes represent blocks of sequentially executable code, and the arcs connecting the nodes represent the flow or paths through the program. For McCabe's metric to function correctly, the program control graph must be strongly connected; that is, every node must be reachable from every other node. To meet this requirement, most programs require the addition of a dummy arc from the

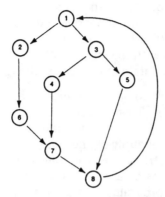

SOURCE: Thomas J. McCabe, "A Complexity Measurement," *IEEE Transactions on Software Engineering* SE-2 (1976)

Exhibit 5.   Program Control Graph

exit node back to the entry node. A representative program control graph is presented in Exhibit 5.

McCabe's cyclomatic complexity metric V(G)is taken directly from the cyclomatic number C(G) in graph theory, and it is expressed as:

$$V(G) = e - n + p$$

where:

e = number of edges (arcs)
n = number of vertices (nodes)
p = number of components (for a single program or module, p = 1)

According to the example in Exhibit 5, the number of arcs (e) equals 10; the number of nodes equals 8, and there is only one component, p equals 1. Substituting into the equation for V(G) yields:

$$V(G) = 10 - 8 + 1$$

$$= 3$$

This value represents the number of linearly independent paths in the graph, and by extension, the program. There are three unique paths in Exhibit 5. These are 1-2-6-7-8,1-3-4-7-8, and 1-3-5-8.

McCabe, based on his working experience with Fortran programs, proposed 10 as the ideal upper limit for a program's cyclomatic complexity number. Below this level, McCabe reasoned that a program was easy to test (i.e., there were a manageable number of paths to validate) and to maintain (i.e., with a reasonable number of paths, the program was easier to understand and modify). If a program had a V(G) value greater than 10, McCabe recommended that it be rewritten or partitioned into less complex modules. The consensus opinion appears to be that there is nothing particularly special about a V(G) of 10 or less, but it is a sensible value. In general, programs or modules with low cyclomatic complexity metric values are easier to test and to maintain than those with high values.

At first, McCabe's cyclomatic complexity metric was used to analyze code after it was written. This approach confined the metric to the coding and unit test phases, and the operation and maintenance phase. In keeping with the current trend of applying metrics as early as possible in the software life cycle, this metric is now routinely employed to analyze the control and data flow charts created in the detailed design phase. The early detection of complex programs or modules significantly lowers the time and effort expended to code, test, and maintain them in subsequent life cycle phases. This reduces the cost of the entire software development process and improves quality.

Integration Complexity

In 1989, McCabe proposed an extension to his cyclomatic complexity metric that enables it to be used in the system design phase. This extension, integration complexity employs similar graph theory concepts, but it applies them to structure charts or hierarchy trees, rather than code or control flow graphs. Integration complexity is a function of design complexity and the number of modules in the software system. From an intuitive standpoint, the metric is sound, but as yet there is little or no empirical evidence to support it. However, this work represents another serious effort to focus software metrics on the early stages of the software development process.

INFORMATION FLOW

In conjunction with a metrics program, a Total Quality Management–oriented IS department should adopt structured design techniques. These techniques reduce the complexity of the design, allowing coding, debugging, and modification to be performed easier, faster, and cheaper. One of the design characteristics that structured design attempts to minimize is coupling, a measure of the interconnectivity between modules. If a module exhibits a large number of interfaces and interconnections with other modules, it is strongly coupled and therefore difficult to understand, test, and modify by itself, because it is highly interrelated with other modules.

One of the most popular metrics to quantitatively measure coupling is Henry and Kafura's Information Flow Metric. The metric is based on the flow of information between a procedure and its environment. A procedure can be a module or a group of modules (i.e., a subsystem). Information flow is defined in terms of fan-in and fan-out. Fan-in is the number of local flows into a procedure plus the global data structures from which a procedure retrieves information. Fan-out is the number of local flows from a procedure plus the global data structures that the procedure updates.[4] The information flow metric is expressed as:

$$C_p = (\text{Fan-In} * \text{Fan-Out})^2$$

The information flow metric is also classified as a structure metric. Structure metrics, like structured design, focus on the system design rather than its physical implementation (i.e., code).

Structure metrics are intended for use early in the software development process. As soon as control and data flows are identified for a module, the information flow metric is also classified as a structure metric. Structure metrics, like structured design, focus on the design of the system, not its physical implementation (i.e., code). Structure metrics are intended for use early in the software development process. As soon as control and data flows are identified for a module, the information flow metric is available to analyze its complexity. This usually occurs in the system design phase and no later than the detailed design phase. The metric may also be used in the integration and system-test phase, and the operation and maintenance phase. It highlights overly complex modules that are likely candidates for additional testing or maintenance modifications. In addition, when a module is identified for maintenance, it can assess the relative complexity of that module and how many other modules are affected.

Hybrid Metrics

There is also a hybrid metric form of the Henry and Kafura Information Flow Metric. Hybrid metrics usually combine a structural complexity metric with a code complexity metric to provide a complete picture of the module's complexity. The structure metric measures the module's external complexity, whereas the code complexity metric measures the internal complexity. The hybrid form of the information flow metric is:

$$C_p = C_{ip} * (\text{Fan-In} * \text{Fan-Out})^2$$

Fan-in and fan-out have the same definition as the structure metric form; and C_{ip} is any code complexity metric, such as McCabe's Cyclomatic Complexity Number [V(G)] or Halstead's Length (N). Hybrid metrics are used primarily in the detailed design phase, but they may also be employed in the integration and system test phase and the operation and maintenance phase.

RELIABILITY METRICS

One of the major objectives of the TQM approach is the early prevention and detection of errors and faults. As an example, the cost per fault to correct problems in the field has been shown to be from 20 to over 300 times greater than correcting problems in the design phase for a particular Siemens software product. Therefore, the importance of early fault elimination cannot be overemphasized, and the key to fault elimination lies in product metrics.

The goal of all the previously discussed product metrics is to reduce a program or module's size or complexity, or both, so the number of errors and faults is reduced correspondingly; but their primary focus is not on faults, per se. Reliability metrics' sole objective is to predict, find, and measure faults. Reliability metrics are applicable to every life cycle phase, but not every reliability metrics is appropriate for every phase. According to Goel, reliability models can be divided into four classifications:

- Times between failures models
- Failure count models
- Fault seeding models
- Input domain based models

These classifications are based on the approach taken by the model to predict remaining faults. The first three models are measurement-oriented techniques that can be categorized as product metrics. The input domain–based model is more of a test strategy, providing a methodology for selection of test data for black- or white-box tests, and therefore this chapter does not discuss it. In addition to his classifications, Goel also suggests the appropriate life cycle phases in which to employ each model.

Time Between Failure Models

These metrics predict the time interval between the ith and the ith +1 failure using a statistically derived hazard function. These hazard functions are determined by statistically analyzing the actual time intervals between previous failures and fitting them to a known distribution, such as the exponential or gamma distributions. Examples of time between failure models are the Jelinski and Moranda De-Eutrophication Model, the Schick and Wolverton Model, and the Goel and Okumoto Imperfect Debugging Model. The most appropriate life cycle phase for using these metrics depends on the definition of failure. If failures are defined as module, subsystem, or system crashes, these metrics are appropriate for all phases between coding and unit test and operation and maintenance, inclusive. When a broader view of failure is taken to include human errors in the preparation of design requirements, specifications, or other documentation, then the metrics are also appropriate for the system design and detailed design phases.

Time between failure models are concerned with the time interval between successive failures, whereas fault count models are concerned with the number of faults occurring in a specified time interval. Several simple fault count metrics can be employed in every phase of the software development life cycle. An example is a fault rate metric calculated from the number of faults detected per unit time. When this rate is constant or increasing, the software product requires additional review or testing before release to the next life cycle phase.

Fault count metrics use stochastic methods to analyze and predict the number of faults remaining in a module. Typically, a nonhomogeneous Poisson distribution is used. Examples of the stochastic fault count metrics are the Goel-Okumoto Nonhomogeneous Poisson Process Model, the Musa Execution Time Model, and the Shooman Exponential Model. The statistically derived metrics are appropriate for both test phases and the operation and maintenance phase. During unit or system testing, the metrics provide an indication of the status or relative success of the testing process. In the operations and maintenance phase, they identify modules requiring corrective maintenance.

The premise underlying fault-seeding models appears to be counterintuitive to the elmination of faults and errors. In fault seeding, known faults are intentionally but randomly inserted into the software product. The theory behind this model is that if all or a large portion of the known faults are detected by the testing process, all or a large portion or the indigenous faults are also detected. At the end of each testing phase, the number of seeded faults detected is compared to the total number of seeded faults. If the detected number is significantly below the total number, additional testing is required. Mills and Dyson's Hypergeometric Model is an example of this type of metric. It is appropriate for use in the unit and integration test phases but not for final system acceptance tests. The objective of final acceptance testing is to demonstrate conformance to specifications and performance requirements, not to detect faults. Therefore, fault seeding is inappropriate for this type of test.

CONCLUSION

To become or to remain competitive, IS departments must embrace the Total Quality Management strategy and adopt a process-oriented approach toward the development and maintenance of software. Instituting a metrics program quantitatively measures and controls that process. Emphasizing this need for total software quality management, this article and its companion, "Software Metrics: Developing Software for TQM" (33-30-71), present a concise yet comprehensive review of the software development and maintenance process and recommend a few appropriate software metrics to quantitatively measure and control the overall process and each phase of the software life cycle.

TOOLS, TIPS, AND PRACTICES

In addition to the improvement of existing metrics and the application of metrics to earlier phases in the life cycle, research must be conducted to develop appropriate metrics for fourth-generation languages and for object-oriented environments. Virtually all the existing process and product metrics were developed and evaluated using third-generation, or earlier, languages. Several authors have said that these metrics are inappropriate for software developed in a fourth-generation language environment, but no one has presented empirical evidence to substantiate that assertion.

The object-oriented environment is emerging as the development process of the near future. This approach is radically different from the approaches used to develop current software metrics. Research must be conducted to establish whether current metrics are able to function in an object-oriented environment, and if not, to develop metrics that are. A first step in this direction has been taken with Chidamber and Kemerer's six object-oriented design metrics. However, much more work remains to be done in this area.

1. Jessica Keyes, "Peeling Back Layers of Quality Equation," *Software Magazine* (May 1991), pp. 42-61.
2. Chris F. Kemerer, Chris F. Kemerer, "Reliability of Function Points Measurement. A Field Experiment," *Communications of the ACM* 36, no. 2 (1993), pp. 85-97.
3. Lawrence H. Putnam, "Trends in Measurement, Estimation, and Control," *IEEE Software* (March 1991),pp. 105-107.
4. Sallie Henry and Roger Goff, "Comparison of a Graphical and a Textual Design Language Using Software Quality Metrics," *Journal of Systems and Software* 14, no. 3 (1991), pp. 133-146.

Chapter III-6

Developing Tool Support for Process-Oriented Management

Ilia Bider

COMPUTERS CAN INCREASE PRODUCTIVITY in many ways, such as by assisting workers in completing their everyday activities and providing management with information needed for decision making. Decision making requires two types of information: external (e.g., on potential customers and competitors) and internal about the company itself. External information can be purchased, but it may prove to be of little use without internal information. Often, the latter may be obtained only if it is collected daily.

To cope with the task of collecting reliable internal information, an integrated computer system is required that embraces all aspects of an individual's routine work. Routine work includes such operations as:

- The execution of simple activities, like writing a letter, taking an order, or giving a medicine to a patient
- Registration of the activities performed
- Planning of new activities
- Communication with colleagues concerning the above activities

A system supporting all these routine operations can automatically gather internal information that supports decision making. Such a system also helps to organize the bulk of individuals' everyday routines, which is why it is referred to in this chapter as an organizing system — or, for short, an org system.

Org systems do not as yet have widespread use; however, if a company begins any new system (or reengineered system) project by building an org system, at the later stages, statistical analysis and other types of information processing necessary for decision making (e.g., expert system support) can be added. (The reversed order of the development would lead, for example, to an expert system design, but with no access to reliable internal information.)

0-8493-9979-3/99/$0.00+$.50
© 1999 by CRC Press LLC

GROUPWARE ASPECTS

One of the main problems that enterprises face is to organize the efforts of people working on common goals. As such, org systems development belongs to the application field of groupware.

Most of the solutions to this problem of coordinating the efforts of many people working together originate from the time before computers became available. It is a general practice even now that systems developers follow the old management scheme. Modern computers, however, offer unique opportunities for implementing new, far more effective approaches to management of group-oriented work.

Limitations of Existing Management Schemes

The limitations of existing management schemes became apparent while computerizing the sales and marketing activities of a small trading company. The objective was to develop a system to assist office workers in all aspects of their routine work.

One of the tasks was a conventional one — to support such activities as taking orders, delivering goods, and making phone calls. The other one was more ambitious — to register all completed activities and to help plan new activities based on the completed ones.

This second objective could not be achieved within the functional management scheme adopted in the company. To cope with the task, it was necessary to view the company's activity as a number of processes (e.g., "processing an order" or "closing a deal") without regard to the way these processes were being managed. As a result a new approach to management was used — process-oriented management.

Definition of Process-Oriented Management. Process-oriented management can be described as project management without project managers. Instead, the project manager's functions (e.g., planning and controlling the execution of activities) are distributed among the workers involved in a particular process.

Process-oriented management permits a company to gain full control over all the processes within the framework of the existing, often functionally oriented, organizational structure. Process-oriented management facilitates also the communication between workers involved in the same process, and it provides them with actual information on the state of the process, as well as on all activities performed and planned.

MANAGEMENT OF ROUTINE WORK

The main objective of management is to ensure a successful achievement of a company's goals at minimal costs. A company has several different long-term and short-term goals to achieve at any given moment.

Operational Goals

Management of routine work includes conventional, everyday goals — referred to as operational goals. A typical operational goal for a trading company is to drive an incoming order through delivery to receiving payment within certain time limits. A typical operational goal for a hospital is to administer appropriate treatment to patients so they can be discharged from the hospital. A typical operational goal for a software development company is to build a software system according to the specifications; for its technical support department, a typical operational goal is to process a bug report so that the bug is fixed or a workaround solution is found.

Though operational goals may be unsophisticated, they nevertheless constitute the backbone of any business, because they have to be achieved daily to ensure the proper functioning of the company. Although the character of operational goals depends on the type of business, they have a number of common features:

- Operational goals pop up more or less regularly.
- There is usually a standard procedure for achieving the operational goals of a given kind (even though a particular goal can be approached in a different way, if needed).
- There is often a set time limit for achieving an operational goal. If the goal is impossible to achieve within the time limit, it is discarded in a standard way.

To achieve an operational goal, a series of activities needs to be completed. A series of activities aimed at getting payment for an incoming order includes delivery of goods and sending an invoice to the customer but may include more items in certain circumstances. For example, if the ordered goods are out of stock, they should be produced or ordered from the suppliers.

The activities aimed at achieving an operational goal are not usually executed immediately one after another (e.g., if the ordered goods are out of stock, it takes some time to get them from the suppliers). The execution of these activities is a process that continues over some period of time.

Different activities concerning the same goal can be completed by different workers from different divisions. Another objective of management is, therefore, to coordinate the work of all workers participating in the process of achieving an operational goal.

Function-Oriented vs. Project-Oriented Management

Approaches to management of operational goals may be divided in two types — function-oriented and project-oriented.

Function-oriented management is usually used in environments where many relatively simple operational goals occur very frequently. Function-oriented management implies that operational goals are handled in a routine manner by the staff, where each member has his or her own function in achieving operational goals. A manager does not coordinate the execution of activities for each goal; workers just react to incoming work (e.g., documents or phone calls) by completing the activities they are assigned and forwarding the received or newly composed documents on to their colleagues.

Project-oriented management is usually used with more sophisticated goals, such as construction or software projects. Project-oriented management implies that a process for a new goal is planned in detail before the work on it starts, and there is someone (e.g., a project manager) who supervises all the work being done.

Function-oriented management is most cost-effective, but it works poorly when a process of achieving an operational goal deviates from a standard pattern, as it lacks control over individual processes. Project-oriented management gives full control over an individual process, but it is inefficient when many coexisting processes are involved.

There are working environments where one or the other type of management fits well. But in most environments a combination of these two approaches would be the way to obtain both full control over all processes and efficiency.

COMPONENTS OF PROCESS-ORIENTED MANAGEMENT

Process-oriented management integrates function-oriented and project-oriented management schemes. The main objective is to control the processes; this is in contrast to function-oriented management, which places the emphasis on the execution of activities, and project-oriented management, which emphasizes plans.

The process-oriented management approach is based on the notions of "org objects," "histories," and "dynamic and distributed planning." To explain how process-oriented management works, a real work environment — the trading company — is used as an example.

Org Objects

Project-oriented management involves developing a detailed plan for achieving a project's goal before the work on the project can start. This plan is premised on certain assumptions that may turn out wrong after the project is under way. The plan should then be adapted to the changed conditions. For this purpose, a clear picture of the current state of the project is required to figure out what should be done to complete the project.

A project often involves developing some product that is a physical object (e.g., a software system or a building). This product comes into existence in some form at the earlier stages of the project (e.g., a half-ready software system or a building under construction). This half-ready product serves as a good representation of the current state of the project. Because the half-ready product can be studied without regard to how it has been produced, the plan can be revised without going into details of the project's history.

In cases where function-oriented management is involved, there is no half-ready product to represent the current state of achieving an operational goal. An abstract object that contains all information on the current state of the process would be helpful here, because it would serve as an organizing device for achieving the goal. This object is termed an org object.

Examples. An org object representing a process such as "Get payment for an incoming order" may be a record that contains information about:

- The name and address of the buyer
- A description of each kind of goods ordered
- The quantity and price per unit of each kind
- The quantities of goods already delivered
- The amount of money invoiced
- The amount of money received

Having this org object, the conditions for the successful achievement of the "Get payment" goal could be formulated as follows:

- Have the numbers representing the quantities of "goods ordered" and "goods delivered" equal for each kind of goods.
- Have "money invoiced" equal to the sum of "ordered" multiplied by "price per unit" for all kind of goods.
- Have "money received" equal to "money invoiced."

As the process develops, the corresponding org object should change so that it reflects the current state of the process. As soon as some activity is completed, the org object representing the process is modified. Thus, in this example, after full or partial delivery, the quantities of the goods delivered are modified; if the customer has changed the order, the types and quantities of the goods ordered are modified.

To ensure that the org objects are always up-to-date, the routines for every type of activity should list not only the operations required for completing the activity (e.g., packing and shipping for delivery), but also instructions for the appropriate modifications of the relevant org objects.

Thus, the current state of an org object reflects the overall result of all activities completed earlier and shows what actions should be taken to achieve the goal.

To return to the example, if the quantity of the goods ordered is greater than the quantity of the goods delivered, the missing goods are to be delivered. If, on the other hand, the quantity of the goods ordered is less than the quantity of the goods delivered, then the customer should be asked to return some of the goods. Other examples: if the amount of money invoiced exceeds the payment received, then the customer should pay the difference. If the amount of the money received exceeds that invoiced, then a credit note should be issued.

Histories

The current state of an org object contains only the result of the completed activities, but not a list of them (e.g., the quantity of the goods delivered, but not the number of separate deliveries; the amount of money invoiced, but not the number of separate invoices). This is fine provided all goes as it should. But if something goes wrong — for example, some goods sent off did not arrive — then the information on all activities performed is vital when figuring out what actions should be taken. This information can be collected through logging all the activities completed in the frame of the given process.

Importance of a Logging Scheme. Every time a worker executes an activity, the worker does not physically change the previous state of the relevant org object. The worker makes a new record instead that contains the new state of the org object and leaves the former one unchanged. For example, after a delivery, a new record is made containing the same information as the previous one except for the information on the quantities of the goods delivered. The latter is updated according to the packing list.

The record on the previous state of an org object is placed in a special file containing the history of the given org object. The worker who completes an activity composes a report as well to record the kind of activity completed, the name of a person who completed it, the date, time, and comments. This report is saved together with the previous state of the org object in the history file.

Given two consequent states of an org object and an activity report, it is possible to reconstruct exactly what happened during the activity execution. In case of delivery, the worker would know exactly by whom and when the goods were delivered, and in what quantities. Thus, the log provides easy access to information on both the activity performed and the state of events before and after it was performed.

Dynamic and Distributed Planning

Project-oriented management involves designing a detailed plan for each new process. Try to apply the same type of detailed planning to a function-oriented management environment and two problems would arise:

- Since function-oriented processes are often trivial, their plans would be trivial too. It would be meaningless to record plans for every process.
- Unpredictable external events that often occur in function-oriented management environments would demand revising the whole plan (e.g., if a customer changes an order, additional delivery may be required or an invoice has to be sent later than was initially planned).

Dynamic planning is an answer to these problems. Dynamic planning involves planning only the first few activities at the first stage. As soon as one or several of these are completed, new activities are planned with regard to the emerging state of the relevant org object. For example, after a delivery, another delivery is planned if not all ordered goods have been delivered, or invoicing is planned if all goods have been delivered.

The use of dynamic planning is fully beneficial in the case of processes that follow a standard pattern. If it is difficult to foresee whether a process is standard or deviates from a standard pattern, dynamic planning can be used at first, followed by conventional planning if necessary.

Another problem when trying to introduce project-oriented management in a function-oriented environment is how to supervise a process. In cases where the project-oriented management is involved, there is usually a project manager who supervises the execution of planned activities and corrects the plan if needed. In an environment typical for function-oriented management, a project manager supervising each process would result in significant overhead.

The solution can be described as "distributed planning." Distributed planning implies that the worker who has completed a planned activity plans the subsequent activities. Moreover, workers can assign these new activities not only to themselves, but to other people too. For example, a worker who completes a delivery plans invoicing to be completed by another worker.

Distributed planning does not exclude the possibility of a centralized supervision of a process. In fact, a supervisor may intervene at any time and correct the plan if needed. Moreover, any member of staff can consult the supervisor in case problems are encountered on a particular process. The worker can do it by planning a special activity (e.g., asking for help) and assigning his or her supervisor to complete it.

Integrating Plans into Org Objects. Org objects and plans are separate entities. However, by putting a plan inside the org object representing the corresponding process, the org object will contain information on the current state of the process (e.g., on the customer, goods, delivery, and payment) as well as a list of planned activities(e.g., delivery, invoicing), each containing information on what should be done, who is to do it, and when.

Thus, a plan becomes part of an org object. Consequently, correction of the plan becomes one of the operations of changing the org object in the course of completing an activity. Instructions for modifying org objects should be included in the working procedures for each type of activity. To ensure proper dynamic planning, these instructions should embrace modification of the process's plan.

In a simple case, a worker who has completed an activity modifies the relevant org object by removing this activity from the list of planned activities. In more complex cases, the worker adds new activities to the list or removes some other activities from it.

By being an integral part of the org object representing a process, a plan is subjected to the logging described previously. As a result, all acts of replanning are registered in the same way as other modifications of org objects. Thus, for example, the name of a person who modified the plan is recorded, which may prove to be useful in case of resolving conflicts.

ADVANTAGES OF PROCESS-ORIENTED MANAGEMENT

The main advantage of the process-oriented management is its flexibility, for it makes it possible to choose the optimum approach to coping with each process, and within the same management scheme. Simple processes that follow a standard pattern are dealt with in a completely decentralized manner, whereas some more sophisticated cases will be dealt with by centralized individual planning and supervising.

Moreover, the same process may be treated differently at different stages. For example, it may be started as a standard process, but later it can be planned and supervised individually. As a result, full control over all kinds of processes is gained and efficiency is not sacrificed.

Process-oriented management is not bound to any particular type of organizational structure. It can be used both in cases where the same member of staff completes all the activities required for achieving an operational goal and in cases where each activity type is assigned to a particular worker. This preserves the same management scheme when the organizational structure is changed, as in the case of a company's expansion.

Other advantages of process-oriented management are as follows:

- **Org objects provide insight into the company's state of affairs.** The information stored in the org objects can help management staff quickly evaluate the state of a process (without going into its history). It also helps to give prompt answers to customers' questions. This kind of information is not easily obtainable when traditional management schemes are used. When function-oriented management is used, only the information on the executed activities of a given type is easily accessible, and when the project-oriented management is used, only the information on the state of the plan's execution is easily accessible.
- **Histories make it easy to trace all activities completed on a given process, which helps to devise plans for complicated cases.** Histories are also an important source of data for all kinds of statistical analysis and other types of information processing required for decision making.
- **The company's staff becomes goal- and process-conscious.** It is easy for any person to overview all the activities (one's own and those of others) completed in a process they are involved in. Histories are useful for "learning by example," which may help a worker find solutions in difficult cases. By comparison, under function-oriented management, the worker does not see how a process is accomplished. Workers' personal goals become to complete as efficiently as possible the activities they are responsible for. Thus a seller may concentrate on making telephone calls, most of which do not close a deal. Project-oriented management emphasizes following the schedule, which becomes the main goal of the workers engaged in a project. There is a danger that the workers do not keep their eyes open for changes in the surrounding world — which is the main reason why large software projects often produce out-of-date systems.
- **Conflict resolution is aided.** Because all the information on the past is being stored, the management staff can better anticipate various kinds of conflicts — internal conflicts among workers engaged in the same process and external conflicts with customers or suppliers.
- **Distributed planning helps coordinate work and alleviates excessive communication among workers engaged in the same processes.** Workers get the required information from the current states of org objects and their histories instead of having to exchange too many documents and phone calls.

DEVELOPING THE SUPPORTING COMPUTER SYSTEM

When process-oriented management is supported by an org system, org objects do not circulate between various members of the staff who are to work with them; they stay in the same place together with their history and plans and are easily accessible to all workers involved. All planned activities assigned to given individuals appear immediately in their personal calendar, so every worker knows exactly what activities to complete and when.

A supporting computer system provides the means to increase efficiency by:

- Assisting workers in executing each activity
- Offering an extremely user-friendly interface

These two features are a key to successful implementation. Without them, people would not be motivated to use the system; consequently process-oriented management would not work.

Level of Help

All operations needed for executing an activity under the process-oriented management approach belong to one of the two groups:

- External operations (i.e., operations that affect the outside world)
- Maintaining operations (i.e., operations aimed at maintaining org objects)

The character of external operation depends on the type of activity, (e.g., packing and shipping for delivery, programming and testing for developing a software module). Maintaining operations are the same for all activities. They include:

- Updating the information contained in the relevant org object
- Correcting the plan
- Logging the preceding state of the org object

An org system assists a worker to complete both the external operations and the maintaining ones.

External Operations. The level of help that is possible for completing external operations depends on the type of activity. For example, programming and testing of a software module are usually performed inside the computer and are already fully computerized. Here, an org system should just integrate the existing tools for software development (e.g., editors, debuggers) so that a proper tool is invoked when a user chooses to execute these operations.

Packing and shipping are not that easily computerized, but even then an org system can be helpful to some extent by making up a packing list. Some level of help in completing the external operations for each kind of activity is needed. There is a risk otherwise. If some activity is left without system assistance, a worker who completes it can easily forget to make the appropriate changes in the org object concerned. In that case, the completed activity will still remain on the list of planned activities and the org system

214

will keep reminding the worker to complete it. There is also a danger that the same activity will be completed several times.

Updating. Modification of an org object can often be done on the basis of the information collected in the process of executing the external operations. For example, an "order" object contains information on the quantities of the goods already delivered. This information should be updated after each separate delivery. The new quantities can be easily calculated based on the packing list that was made at the previous step, which permits an org system to update the object without assistance from the users.

Correcting a Plan. When correcting a plan, a worker is prompted by the system on the appropriate activities to plan next; in simple cases the plan is corrected by the system itself. This is possible because an org system possesses knowledge about:

- The working procedures used in the company, which helps to plan new activities
- The division of responsibilities between different business sections and workers, which helps to correctly assign new activities

Logging. Logging includes two operations: saving the old state of the org object and making a report on the activity completed.

Saving the old state of an org object is done by the system without any user assistance, but an activity report needs a human participant. Even then, an org system helps by automatically supplying the information on what activity has been executed, by whom, and when. The rest of the report (e.g., comments) is the responsibility of the worker.

Object-Oriented User Interface

Conventional computer systems are designed as a set of functions operating on a common database, the main facility of the user interface being multilevel menus. This type of user interface provides users with quick access to the functions they want to complete. It reflects the objective of a conventional computer system, which is to help workers to cope with single activities, such as updating information or printing a report.

Because an org system's objectives are much wider, a completely different kind of user interface is required. The user interface permits end users to freely choose between the object-oriented and activity-oriented way of working with org objects, as well as easily switch from one to the other.

The object-oriented approach is applied when a user wants to work with a particular org object for a longer time. In this case, the user may need to look at the object's current state and its history, as well as to plan and execute various activities involving the org object.

The activity-oriented approach is applied when a user wants to complete the same activity for a number of org objects. In this case, the dialogue designed for a given activity is repeated for all relevant org objects.

The object-oriented way is particularly useful when one worker is responsible for many activities or when management staff needs to evaluate the state of a particular process and devise a plan for a difficult case. The activity-oriented approach is preferable if a worker is responsible for only one type of activity. It is also the right approach for completing simple activities that do not require much human assistance (e.g., printing an invoice).

Personal Calendars. Another distinguishing feature of an org system's user interface is that it maintains personal calendars. A personal calendar is a list of activities assigned to a particular worker. These activities are included in different org objects and the calendar permits a perfect overview of a person's many tasks. Users can browse through their calendar or parts of it to see all activities planned for a particular day or all activities of a certain type.

To maintain its user-friendly character, the user interface should satisfy the following two requirements:

- **Easy access to all information required for working with org objects.** For example, when working with an org object representing an order, a user should have access to all information related to the customer who ordered goods (e.g., the customer's address, previous contacts with the customer).
- **Consistency.** There should be standard procedures for navigating to an org object for getting information (e.g., a company's address), for planning, and for starting the execution of activities. These standard procedures should be the same for all types of org objects and activities.

JOYS AND HARDSHIPS OF AN ORG SYSTEMS DEVELOPER

There are, naturally, technical problems to solve in the development of an org system. The system requirements discussed in the previous section must be met. However, the systems designer's greatest problem is that development usually occurs in an environment initially not based on process-oriented management.

Design

The systems designer should begin by:

- Identifying the company's operational goals
- Determining what processes are used to achieve them
- Designing org objects to represent these processes

The designer's next task is to review all the working procedures and tailor them to fit the process-oriented management scheme (by adding and maintaining operations to each activity). This is often a difficult job because there are seldom written descriptions of such working procedures and, if they do exist, they are far from complete. The only way to cope with the job is to get the missing information from the company's workers.

The workers would, naturally, know nothing about org objects, but they know their job. The conditions in which the systems designer works are similar to those of a linguist who studies a language that exists only in the spoken form. Linguists have special methods permitting them to get the necessary information from the native speakers without teaching them any linguistic notions.

A Role for Rapid Prototyping. The systems designer needs similar methods in order to redesign the company's working procedures without introducing the workers into the world of org objects and distributed planning. Rapid prototyping is the right method in these cases.

As soon as a designer has identified the company's operational goals and processes and designed the org objects to represent them, the designer should make a prototype of the system and let the future users test it.

To be able to use prototyping, an org system designer needs appropriate applications development tools to quickly produce a sketch of the system that has the look and feel of a real system, but lacks processing routines and database access.

Working with this prototype of the system, users can navigate among org objects in the same way they will when the org system is ready. The user can modify existing org objects, create new ones, and see how to start different activities. However, with the prototype, the user cannot save the information or see the results of the completed activities.

After the future users have accepted the prototype, the designer can stepwise add database access and processing routines, which would be done also with the help of applications development tools.

Implementation

Implementing an org system means introducing process-oriented management in a non-process-oriented management environment. This may be achieved in one of two ways:

- By substituting all the old working procedures in the company at once
- By gradual introduction of the new working procedures

The first approach may suit small companies whose workers often switch from one activity type to another. An org system would support workers who usually have many different jobs to do and preserve order in their affairs. Staff members find it easy to understand the advantages of using all facilities provided by an org system, especially object- and activity-oriented ways of working, personal calendars, and easy access to the history.

In the case of large companies, the second approach of gradual introduction of new working procedures may be the best choice. Large companies usually have many workers involved in only one or several activities for each process. These workers may believe that an org system is too complex for their simple tasks. It may be difficult for them to see the advantages of the object-oriented user interface, and their earlier experience of traditional computer systems may only make things worse.

Because the user interface provides a means for working in the activity-oriented manner, workers can, however, complete simple activities with ease. Even if most office workers continue to use the activity-oriented approach, some key people on the management staff can benefit from the object-oriented approach.

PRACTICAL APPLICATION: THE DEALDRIVER SYSTEM

Process-oriented management and the concepts described in this chapter were used by the author, together with several colleagues, when developing an application for supporting sales and marketing activities of a trading company. The system is called DealDriver because it helps workers to drive the deals to the desired end, which is receiving payment. Deals were thus the first type of org objects designed.

The work on the project started in spring 1989, and the first version of DealDriver was ready in summer 1990. Since then, DealDriver has been successfully used at the home office of IbisSoft, a small consulting firm in Sweden, to support one of its business activities — reselling professional software.

The DealDriver project provided valuable insights into the problems of org systems development. An experimental version of applications development tools to support org systems development was also developed. These tools have been used for building both prototypes and functioning systems in other application fields such as hospital administration. The methodology and the toolkit is being used with systems under production in 10 or more sites in Moscow.

Related Research

As described previously, org systems development belongs to an application field called groupware. Other related research fields are:

- The behavior of dynamic objects, which is being formalized by the theory of object-oriented systems
- Methods of storing and accessing structured information, which are the subject of the database theory, especially semantic databases, object-oriented databases, and temporal databases
- Artificial intelligence research, which encompasses methods of planning for robots. The results obtained there may in some cases be directly applied to the management field. For example, the difference between classical and reactive planning corresponds to the difference between the pure project-oriented and function-oriented management

Why This Approach Works

The main ideas of process-oriented management originate from previous research work on the Concurrent Human-Assisted Object Systems (CHAOS) project. The project's objective was to work out a formal model for describing distributed interactive systems. This model is based on the notions of objects and connectors.

Objects and Connectors. Objects are used to represent elements of the real world (e.g., people, companies, projects), whereas connectors are the active elements of the system whose task is to make changes in the objects. A connector may be thought of as a little computer connected to one or several objects. As soon as some of these objects change, the connector changes all the other objects to restore the consistency of the system.

Thus defined, a model has a purely reactive nature — that is, changes in objects are made as a reaction to changes in other objects. However, objects in a model can be complex (i.e., they can contain connectors, which means that a reaction can result in adjusting the system configuration to changes in the environment).

The CHAOS model fits the management field so well that all the developers of DealDriver had to do was to use another set of terms. Thus, complex objects became org objects, connectors became planned activities, and the principle of reactive reconfiguration of the system was called dynamic and distributed planning.

The CHAOS model is abstract, but the approach taken in the DealDriver project was very pragmatic. The objective of the project was to create a working system, not to speculate on the management automation issues.

This project differs in many significant ways from similar research projects.

Computer Environment. The developers worked with PCs under MS-DOS in standalone and network versions, whereas research projects are often completed on UNIX-based workstations. Text-based terminals were used because they were affordable for the average company, such as the trading company, which did not have a graphics-based windowing computer environment.

Development Tools. Research workers often choose programming languages popular among computer scientists, such as Lisp, Prolog, or Smalltalk. These languages have a sound theoretical basis (e.g., function theory, logic), but they require a lot of programming when they are used for the development of an application. The developers of DealDriver made a point of getting the maximum available help with programming by employing commercially available applications development tools. JAM from JYACC was used as a front-end tool, and Btrieve from Novell was used as a record manager. These tools were important because the developers had limited resources (in terms of time and manpower) for completing the project.

Design Principles. Researchers are often far too interested in the technical issues, such as methods of software design and programming. The developers of DealDriver concentrated on user-interface issues instead and required a program that could easily make necessary changes. All programming was done in the C language, and although the system was object-oriented to a very high degree, no object-oriented extension to C was employed.

CONCLUSION

Two factors contributed to the successful completion of the DealDriver project:

- The use of a powerful abstract model
- A pragmatic approach to systems development

The experience of developing DealDriver proves that the management of routine work can often become substantially more automated than originally thought. This chapter has outlined an approach to accomplish this mission. In addition, this experience illustrates that there is no need to wait 10 or more years, which is how long it usually takes for new research ideas to be implemented in applications systems. New ideas can be implemented today and with the means available now.

ACKNOWLEDGMENTS

Because the main ideas of the process-oriented management came from the CHAOS and DealDriver projects, the author is very grateful to all who participated in them, especially: A. Borkovsky, M. Khomyakov, E. Pushchinsky, R. Sjb[ouml]rg and R. Svensson. I'm also very much indebted to Claudia Dobrina for her comments and help with editing and correcting this text.

BIBLIOGRAPHY

Ariav, G. "Temporally Oriented Data Definitions: Managing Schema Evolution in Temporally Oriented Databases." *Data & Knowledge Engineering*, no. 6 (1991).

Bertino, E. and Martino, L. "Object-Oriented Database Management Systems: Concepts and Issues." *Computer* (April 1991).

Downs, J. and Reichgelt, H. "Integrating Classical and Reactive Planning Within an Architecture for Autonomous Agents." ed. J. Hertzberg. *Proceedings: European Workshop on Planning* (1991).

Ehrich, H.D., Goguen, J.A., and Sernadas, A. "A Categorical Theory of Objects as Observed Processes." ed. J.W. deBakher, et al. *Proceedings: Foundation of Object-Oriented Languages. REX School/Workshop* (Noordwijkerhout, The Netherlands, May/June 1990).

Ellis, C.A., Gibbs, S.I., Rein, G.L. "Groupware–Some Issues and Experience." *Communications of the ACM* 34, no.1 (January 1991).

Hayes, F. "The Groupware Dilemma." Presented at UnixWorld (February 1992).

IbisSoft ab. "IS-Maker–Software Tools for Building Interactive Object- and Time-oriented Systems." Internal report. Stockholm, Sweden (1991).

Chapter III-7
Securing Electronic Messaging Systems

Duane E. Sharp

THE SECURITY OF MESSAGES IN ELECTRONIC MESSAGE HANDLING SYSTEMS IS A FUNDAMENTAL REQUIREMENT, to ensure that these systems are used for their intended purpose. Wherever information is transmitted, the communication partners expect the information transmitted to arrive unaltered and not to be diverted or used for illegal or unintended purposes.

Security features are important in any messaging system where both transmitting and receiving authority are present. For example, they are prerequisites for a message handling system that is intended to transmit contracts, documents, or electronic bank transfer orders.

In the communications-oriented world of electronic commerce, verification of message traffic allows organizations to communicate with each other and to perform business transactions in a way in which they could not be performed before, resulting in significant benefits to these organizations. These benefits are to be found in the automating and streamlining of numerous day-to-day operational functions, which can now be performed much more quickly and accurately than previously. Security forces individuals to take responsibility for their actions, adding an official, authoritative tone to electronic messages.

ACHIEVING A SECURE SYSTEM

To achieve security has been defined as "defending a system against threat," and while security systems are not necessarily easy to deploy, they provide specific benefits to the commercial sector and are mandatory components in many government environments, such as the military and intergovernmental affairs, where secure transmission of information is a requirement.

There are several different types of security services that can be used by system designers to ensure the overall security of message handling systems. They are

0-8493-9979-3/99/$0.00+$.50
© 1999 by CRC Press LLC

- Confidentiality
- Non-repudiation of delivery
- Content integrity
- Prevention of replay
- Authentication of originator
- Access control
- Accountability

Each of these services has been developed to counter different types of threats to the security of a message handling system and to ensure that the benefits of these systems are not jeopardized by intrusion.

ANALYZING THE THREATS

To make a system secure, the potential threat or threats to security must be analyzed. There are a number of reasons why attempts may be made to attack an electronic messaging system, ranging from simple curiosity, through espionage and theft, to deliberate interruption of company-internal communications or alteration of electronically transmitted instructions. Even regular users of the system may violate some security procedures and protocols, by denying having sent or received a message, to avoid the legal or social implications of that message.

Intrusion of a messaging system may occur at any level, against components of the system, for example, computer systems and application programs running on them, as well as against connections between computers. These intrusions may be initiated by anyone from a systems administrator to an outsider (a "hacker," for example). No system is immune to efforts to penetrate its structure, to intercept and manipulate data, and otherwise disrupt legitimate business communications, for nefarious purposes. Exhibit 1 shows some of the possible points at which a message handling system might be attacked.

Attacks against a connection involve reading or modification of data packets on the link or interruption of the link. Efforts to penetrate a system typically involve reading or alteration of stored messages or management information. For example, an intruder can "masquerade," setting up a connection from his system to the message transfer agent (MTA) of the host company, announcing himself as another MTA, in order to steal or introduce messages. Even end users may attempt to send or receive messages under false names.

METHODS OF INTRUSION

There are various methods open to an intruder, once a message handling system has been penetrated: individual systems or connections may be disrupted to restrict or totally halt the operation; messages may be

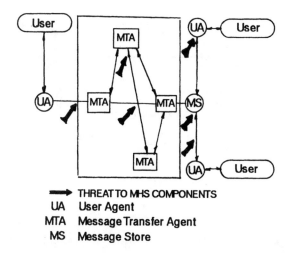

THREAT TO MHS COMPONENTS
UA   User Agent
MTA   Message Transfer Agent
MS   Message Store

Exhibit 1.   Points of Intrusion in a Message Handling System

forwarded illegally; messages may be read, altered, or deleted, or the intruder may introduce his own messages, delete, duplicate, or alternate the sequence of messages; or "preplay" messages marked for deferred delivery.

The experience of the past several years has taught us that these threats must be taken seriously by designers of security systems. There are numerous documented examples of successful attacks on security systems. In 1988, the computer operations of numerous computers connected to the U.S. Internet were disrupted for days by the injection into the network of an "Internet worm," a program that copies itself independently over a network into another computer, where it starts up in the same way. Among other things, the program used weak points in the implementation of a message handling system to penetrate previously unaffected computers.

In another well-known example, USENET, the worldwide UNIX bulletin board system, which is not unlike a very large electronic message handling system, is plagued by a large number of joke messages every year on April 1. Most of these messages are fed in under illegal originator names and, therefore, it is difficult to determine their origin.

Business has been seriously affected by network intrusion and there are many recorded instances, some public, some not so public, in which computer theft has moved funds illegally, sometimes of significant value. In one well-known case, a group of hackers succeeded in smuggling an electronic banker's order worth several millions into the network of an English bank. Fortunately, the false instruction was discovered, since the bank's internal guidelines required telephone confirmation for orders involving large

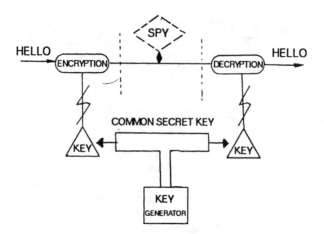

Exhibit 2.   Typical Symmetric Encryption System

amounts of money — an automated security system whose ultimate check was a manual one requiring human intervention.

CRYPTOGRAPHIC TECHNIQUES

To protect messages and parts of messages against intrusion, a number of techniques are available to system designers. The security elements of X.400, for example, are all based on the use of cryptographic techniques, which protect sensitive components against illegal reading or alteration, by encrypting them. These techniques enable only legitimate recipients who know the secret key to decrypt these components.

Symmetric Encryption Systems

Symmetric coding systems use the same secret key to encrypt and decrypt messages among partners in the messaging system (see Exhibit 2). These coding systems have been known for some time, and though they are relatively simple to initiate in practice, one of their main disadvantages is that both sender and receiver must know the secret key. This requirement leads to a problem of key distribution, since the keys must be distributed over secure channels. Of course, communication partners must have confidence that no one will reveal or misuse the key.

In this system, electronic signatures are not possible, because a recipient receiving an encrypted message knows the sender, since only the sender and recipient know the key. The drawback is that the recipient cannot prove this to third parties, since he can generate and encrypt any message himself.

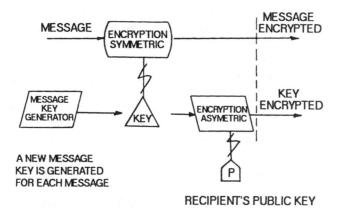

Exhibit 3.   Asymmetric Coding

Asymmetric Public Key Systems

To correct some of the deficiencies in symmetric cryptosystems, asymmetric coding systems have been developed that use different keys for encryption and decryption (see Exhibit 3). The two keys are generated at the same time — one of the keys (the "public" key), is made accessible to all interested parties, while the other key (the "secret" key), is known only to a single communication partner, the key holder. Once the two keys have been separated, it is extremely difficult to deduce the secret key from the public key, a process that has been estimated to take several weeks or months of computing time on a series of supercomputers working in parallel — a sufficiently arduous and time-consuming task to deter the most persistent of intruders.

There are two types of asymmetric cryptosystems used in data communications:

- Encryption
- Electronic signature

For encryption, the encoding key is made publicly accessible, while the decoding key becomes the secret key. Any partner may encode messages to prevent illegal use; however, only the key holder can decode and read them.

The use of electronic signatures involves the reverse process to encryption, publishing the decoding key, while the encoding key is kept secret. Any partner may decode an encoded message, which will have to come from the key holder, since only this individual is able to encode messages with the private key. This encryption is effectively an electronic signature.

TOOLS, TIPS, AND PRACTICES

Of the numerous asymmetric cryptosystems developed to date, the RSA cryptosystem, developed about 1978, is the most popular. RSA Laboratories is a California-based company that reviews, designs, and implements secure and efficient cryptosystems. The RSA cryptosystem is based on calculations in modular arithmetic, where certain operations are only possible when mathematical conditions are present and met. Breaking the RSA cryptosystem can only be accomplished at excessive computational cost — several months or years of computing time, depending on the computing resources available. In addition, the RSA cryptosystem has the advantage that a single public and private key may be used both for encryption and for electronic signatures.

Disadvantages of Asymmetric Correcting Coding. All asymmetric coding procedures have a severe disadvantage: they are computationally very expensive in comparison with symmetric procedures. To minimize this problem, fast symmetric coding systems are usually combined with slower asymmetric ones. The message is itself encoded using an efficient symmetric procedure. The encoding key for each message is transmitted to the message recipient in asymmetrically encrypted form. In this process, the message key is encrypted with the recipient's public key and is thus readable only by the latter. Only the legitimate recipient can recover the message key by decoding with his private key and can decrypt the message itself.

Another advantage of this method is apparent when a message is sent to several recipients simultaneously, where the encoded message and the corresponding message key are the same for all recipients; only the message key itself must be encrypted separately for each recipient.

There are also efficient procedures for generating and verifying electronic signatures, which combine asymmetric encoding with efficiently implementable checksum algorithms.

INTEGRITY OF PUBLIC KEYS

Users are the central focus of every electronic message handing system. In a secure message handling system based on asymmetric coding schemes, each user is assigned a user name together with a public and private key. The public key is "published," that is, made available to all interested parties, together with the user name; the private key is known only to its key holder.

An interested partner can now authenticate the key holder through the capability to add an electronic signature to data elements. However, this only ensures that the partner corresponds to that key; authentication of the partner by name requires a mechanism to guarantee that names and public keys belong together. The problem is comparable to that of personal identity card, in that a match between the partner and the photo on the identity card does not mean that the partner's name is actually that given on the identity card.

The idea of the identity card can be carried over to the electronic form. The corresponding "identity cards" are called certificates. It is also possible to distribute pairs of names and keys to the partners via secure channels and store them with write protection. If there are few subscribers, the names and public keys of all possible communication partners may be stored in a table in the electronic message handling system. It is necessary to ensure that the names and public keys actually belong together. In practice, this means that the pairs of names and keys must be distributed via secure channels and stored in the systems with write protection.

For a large number of subscribers, this procedure rapidly becomes impractical, and in this case, the public keys may be distributed by electronic message transfer, while at the same time an electronic signature is used to protect the keys against alteration during distribution. The combination of names and public keys is electronically signed by a third party, the *Certificate Authority* (CA). Knowledge of the public key of the CA is in itself sufficient to test the authenticity of a certificate at any time.

By analogy with identity cards, the CA corresponds to the place of issue of the identity card, where all the partners covered are issued with identity cards including their names and addresses. To prevent forgery, the identity cards incorporate authentication features (special patterns, watermarks, stamps) that can be generated only by the place of issue itself. Whoever knows the authentication features used is able to authenticate the name of the partner from such an identity card.

SECURE MESSAGE TRANSFER: TRUSTED COMPONENTS

Every message transfer system contains numerous trusted components with specific tasks, the correct operation of which is crucial to the security of the system as a whole. CAs, for example, if they were to issue current certificates under false names or make known their private keys, could jeopardize the electronic message transfer system as a whole. It is apparent that nearly all components, both human and systems elements in a message transfer application, must be trusted in some respect and must adhere to the defined criteria for the Certification Authority.

ROLE OF THE DIRECTORY SERVICE

Some of the services discussed in this profile inherently depend on the availability of a Directory Service. The CCITT X.500 Recommendations [X.500] describe such a Directory Service, including an authentication framework that can be used as the basis for distributing certificate and token information associated with asymmetric-based encryption and key management.

USING SECURITY TECHNIQUES AGAINST SPECIFIC THREATS

The techniques described for achieving the objectives of the various security mechanisms can be applied to counter a number of typical security threats, such as: eavesdropping, traffic analysis, masquerading, and duplication of messages. All of these techniques are essential to ensuring secure message handling in the commercial environment.

Secure messaging adds a commitment to commercial applications — contracts, financial transactions, legal transactions — and a secure E-mail system can ensure the confidentiality and authority of all message traffic. These features provide a new dimension to the business world and its capability to meet demands for faster and more efficient business communications.

Appendix
Electronic Messaging Security Attributes and Enabling Techniques

Content Integrity

Objective: To allow recipient of a message to check whether the message has been altered during transmission

Technique: Electronic signature

Content Confidentiality

Objective: To let only the legitimate recipient read the contents of a message

Technique: Encrypting the message content using the recipient's public key. Because the encryption is time consuming, a combination of asymmetric and symmetric encryption is used.

Message-Security Labeling

Objective: To provide a message with a machine-readable classification. This is important for systems where this classification is used to control access rights and the separation of data into security classes.

Technique: Setting either the message-security label field or the corresponding field in the token. It is also possible to protect the security label against (illegal) reading by implementing it in the encrypted part so that the classification of the message is not shown on the outside.

Message-Sequence Integrity

Objective: To preserve the sequence in which messages are sent and ensure that messages are neither lost nor duplicated

Technique: Introducing a message-sequence number in the message token and having the user agent maintain a per sender/per recipient message-sequence register

231

Proof of Delivery

Objective: To provide an electronic acknowledgment confirming that the recipient has received the message in readable form

Technique: The recipient's user agent signs the (decrypted) message electronically and sends the signature to the originator when requested.

Nonrepudiation of Origin

Objective: To provide the recipient with a more secure form of message authentication that verifies the origin of the message both to the recipient and to third parties

Technique: Electronic signature

Nonrepudiation of Delivery

Objective: A more secure form of proof of delivery that lets the sender prove to third parties that the message has been correctly received

Technique: Electronic signature of the (decrypted) message by the recipient using an appropriate asymmetric encryption system

Nonrepudiation of Submission

Objective: A more secure form of proof of submission involving third parties

Technique: Electronic signature of the message transfer agent adjacent to the user agent employing a suitable asymmetric cipher system

Message-Flow Confidentiality

Objective: To prevent an outsider from obtaining information on message traffic, based on number and size of encrypted messages

Technique: Deliberately routing messages around relatively insecure connections or introducing empty messages

Section III — Checklist
Tools, Tips, and Practices

1. What is your definition of a software tool? Is it a tangible entity or methodology.
2. How would you categorize the tools, techniques, and practices used in your organization?
3. Is your definition or understanding of software tools consistent with the manner in which tools are used in your organization?
4. From your experiences, what is more valuable: tools that are powerful but require long learning periods or tools that are limited in scope but can be mastered and implemented quickly?
5. Do your experiences in tool use influence the decision on which tools your organization acquires? If not, why?
6. In your opinion, when are software tools inappropriate? Should this be acknowledged by tool providers?
7. Does your organization favor broad-based tool products or are narrowly focused tools more commonplace? What is the affect of this on your development and support efforts?
8. Have you observed differences between tools aimed at the mainframe and those for micro platforms? If so, are these differences related to platform technology or the nature of the application system?
9. Do you think that tools used for development can also be used for support? Does your organization have such tools?
10. How are software tools or new methodologies evaluated in your organization? Does this seem reasonable to you?
11. What techniques have you learned and then passed onto other members in your organization? Do these techniques still hold value in current technology environments?
12. Does your organization document or provide guidelines on the tools and techniques used in your organization. If not, how does a new staff member gain knowledge?
13. Does your organization have a procedure to measure the success or failure of development and support projects?
14. Have you ever tried to measure programming productivity? If so, have the results been accurate?
15. Can productivity measurement of tools, methods, and practices be accurately performed in your environment? If not, how do you determine return on investment?

Section IV
Programming Techniques

OBJECT-ORIENTED PROGRAMMING (OOP) HAS BECOME AN ESTABLISHED ALTERNATIVE to the nature of aging third-generation programming languages. The justification for OOP has been well documented. Based on numerous studies of object-oriented development; there have been significant gains over traditional programming practices. However, there remains considerable debate over "true" OOP languages vs. those that implement OOP-like features and functionality. Furthermore, the software industry has been struggling with both proprietary and standard OOP language implementations. This impacts the choice of programming language and also influences associated tools, methodologies, and middleware technologies. Development managers should be encouraged by potential gains that object-oriented technology offers to the creation of new application systems. But, as with all new technology, caution should be exercised in selecting the appropriate products and services.

One of the more prevalent OOP languages is C++ and its popularity stems from the widespread use of the C language used over the last 20 years. Although C++ advocates praise the strengths of the language, there is evidence that may suggest performance issues when compared to C. Many OOP languages suffer performance problems because of the embedded logic of object-oriented functionality. And accurate methods for performance measurement of object languages has been difficult. In Chapter IV-1 "Benchmarking C++ Performance," and Chapter IV-2, "Performance of Object-Oriented Programs: C++," the authors examine several experiments where the speed of C++ is compared to that of C. These tests were limited in size and scope; nevertheless the results provide important information about the performance characteristics of C++. This can be very beneficial in environments that have an invested base of C programs and desire migration to C++.

Java has entered the object-oriented programming arena as the next evolution of application development languages. The tremendous interest in this programming tool is based on the cross platform strengths and portability. Despite the competition between vendors regarding the standardization of Java, the language continues to gain popularity against C++ implementations. Chapter IV-3, "Java and C++: Similarities, Differences, and Performance," offers valuable insight to the internal operations between the two language environments. This information is extremely useful in determining the appropriate deployment strategy for Java-based applications.

Technical advancements in software used for Internet/Intranet applications have generated interest over earlier implementations of client-server technology. In particular, Java is recognized as a significant step for enabling more practical improvements. In Chapter IV-4, "Using Java to Improve Client/Server Applications," an interesting discussion is given on the benefits of Java technology to the overall development process. Some critics argue that Java may not employ an exhaustive command set when compared to other languages. But the simplistic, yet powerful functions of Java are proving extremely productive to both older legacy systems and newer client-server systems.

Applications portability is being promoted as one of the major benefits of the two leading (and competing) object middleware standards, CORBA and COM. Chapter IV-5, "Programming Components: COM and CORBA," examines how to develop components that enable applications portability. Like the preceding chapter, it focuses on applications development for a client/server environment. As Internet-based and object-oriented technologies continue to converge, the distinction between client/server systems and Internet-based systems will blur as these two systems architectures begin to meld into one.

Software reuse is yet another benefit offered through object-oriented languages. Unlike traditional methods of code reuse, object-based languages and subsequent developed systems are firmly built on the premise of reusability. As such, keeping track of object entities is similar to the difficulties of managing legacy subroutine libraries, only more critically. Chapter IV-6 "Secure and Managed Object-Oriented Programming," offers an explanation of control techniques for object libraries. Development managers should factor this information as part of the overall decision in migrating to object-oriented language development.

Structured Query Language (SQL) has been one of most widely used languages for accessing database information. Originally designed as a simple reporting tool, SQL is often used to facilitate complex queries against large-scale relational databases. More often, SQL is invoked through on-line interfaces that have been useful to end-user departments. But SQL also has powerful batch capabilities. Chapter IV-7, "Creating Effective Batch SQL Jobs," explores the vast power of the SQL language in the batch execution environment. For organizations that process and manipulate large quantities of database data, understanding the strengths of batch SQL can be an effective agent in maximizing computing resources.

Chapter IV-8, "Building Database-Enabled Web Applications with IDC," examines another aspect of SQL. IDC (Internet Database Connector) is a technology developed by Microsoft that enables an SQL statement to execute against a database and to return results in HTML page format. This technology works only with another Microsoft offering, Internet Information Server (IIS), but any browser that interprets HTML pages can be used to access database information with IDC. As the Internet and World-Wide Web are used as a standard platform, Web-based programming technologies will become more commonplace.

Many organizations are reviewing existing legacy systems as part of an overall initiative to upgrade application systems. In conjunction with program upgrades, organizations face considerable challenges addressing the vast amount of information stored in proprietary data files. Chapter IV-9, "Automatically Migrating COBOL Indexed Files: A Case Study," reviews how to leverage the power of new technology by exporting data into newer file structures. This represents an important issue for many organizations that must eventually migrate legacy systems. Development managers should weigh the advantages of new application implementation through careful assessment of program logic and repository architecture.

Chapter IV-1

Benchmarking C++ Performance

Paul J. Jalics and Ben A. Blake

THERE ARE MANY ASPECTS TO PROGRAM PERFORMANCE; for the purposes of this chapter, the authors limit the meaning to the execution performance of C++ programs (i.e., the amount of time it takes to execute specific C++ statements and programs).

Jalics and Heines developed a set of performance tests to measure the performance of C programs and the C statement level, including central processing units, I/O statements, some routine-level modules, and some C Library routines. These tests were augmented by a number of statement-level C++ tests and a few whole program C and C++ benchmarks. Execution times throughout are shown in microseconds, unless otherwise specified.

These experiments were run on various C and C++ compilers: Borland C and C++ (3.1) on a 386-20 machine, Gnu C and C++ on a DEC 5000 workstation, and Gnu, AT&T C and C++, and Gnu C++ on a SUN SLC Sparc workstation. Thus, the observations encompass not just a single C++ implementation but a broader picture of C++ performance.

THE DHRYSTONE C++ BENCHMARKS

There is a C++ version of the Dhrystone Benchmark that was used to look at C++ performance. The two classes Int and Char were implemented to replace the standard built-in data types int and char. This test accurately measures the worst-case performance cost of introducing new data types that are used throughout an application. Exhibit 1 shows the results of executing several versions of the C++ Dhrystone on various systems.

The results show the performance of the tested system in Dhrystones (i.e., a bigger number is faster). The following observations can be made:

- Replacing int and char by inline (dr2 versus dr1) implementations of Int and Char in the entire benchmark degrades performance by 43% on the two Sun C++ compilers, by 84% on the DEC5000, and by 72% on the 386. Perhaps the DEC5000 and the 386 do less inline work than the Suns.

0-8493-9979-3/99/$0.00+$.50
© 1999 by CRC Press LLC

PROGRAMMING TECHNIQUES

Exhibit 1.   Int and Char Classes Used in Dhrystone Benchmark (in Microseconds)

Test	Sun4SLC AT&T	Sun4SL C G++	DEC5000 G++	Intel 386-20 Borland	Test Description
dr1	6437	7481	16574	5000	Using int and char
dr2	3717	4160	2695	1388	Using Int and Char inline
dr3	1243	1832	2633	373	Using Int and Char (not inline)
dr4	1006	1541	2013	306	Using Int and Char (not inline) return by value
dr5		1221	1794	301	Using Int and Char (no inline)
dr6	5780	6493	7194	1612	Using Int only inline
dr7	4016	4958	3405	3333	Using char only inline

Note: Results are in Dhrystones when high implies fast.

- If the implementations are changed to use procedure calls for member functions (i.e., noninline, dr3 versus dr1), the degradation factors go up to 81% for the Sun AT&T, to 76% for the Sun g++, to 85% for the DEC, and to 93% for the 386.
- Using by-value return of results instead of by-reference (dr4 versus dr3) reduces performance further by about 25%.
- Making the member functions virtual (dr5versus dr4) further reduces performance by 1% to 26%.
- Tests dr6 and dr7separate out the performance differences due to Int and Char and indicate that performance degradation due to the introduction of just inline Char is only about 12% for the two Sun systems, 57% for DEC, and 68% for the 386.
- Performance degradation due to the introduction of just inline Int (see test dr6) is 34% for the two Sun systems and the 386, and 80% for the Digital Equipment Corporation.

THE GPERF BENCHMARK

Gperf is a program that generates a perfect hashing function for a known set of keys; it was designed in C++, and a separate version exists in C (Cperf). This Gperf benchmark consists of 3906 lines of code and is a reasonable object-oriented design whose performance might be compared to the C version. Whether this is a fair comparison might be debated, but any performance samples are of interest. The results of running this benchmark are illustrated in Exhibit 2.

Exhibit 2.   The Gperf Benchmark

	SUN_SLC_AT&T_C++		386_20_Borland_C++
	(CPU Sec)	(Elapsed Sec)	(Elapsed Sec)
Cperf (C)	1.8	2.3	1.21
Gperf (C++)	2.1	2.4	0.88

Exhibit 3. The Xref Benchmark

| | SUN_SLC_AT&T_C++ | | 386_20_Borland_C++ |
	(CPU Sec)	(Elapsed Sec)	(Elapsed Sec)
Cperf (C)	8.8	9.2	37
Gperf (C++)	6.9	7.4	34

The results show a 16% increase in CPU time for the C++ version on the Sun; the same program, however, shows only a 4% increase in elapsed time on the Sun and a 28% decrease in elapsed time on the PC. Again, there is not a clear trend that is identifiable in C versus C++.

THE XREF BENCHMARK

This benchmark inputs a list of files, lists them (including file name and line number), and then provides a cross-reference listing of all symbols. The original xref0.c program (375 lines) is of poor design, as it was transported originally from COBOL and has seen many modifications. It has, however, been in widespread use by one of the authors for over a decade. Cxref.cc (303 lines), on the other hand, is a completely new object-oriented design that was undertaken as part of learning about object-oriented programming and C++.

Results of running the xref benchmark are illustrated in Exhibit 3.

Even though the algorithms are not identical in these two programs, the inputs, outputs, and the work done are meant to be the same. The results show a 20% improvement for the C++ version on the Sun and an 8% improvement on the PC. The results may be explained as follows. The potential loss of performance in a C++ program (when compared to a C program) can be more than overcome in some cases by improving the design and paying attention to performance.

OBJECT LIBRARIES: THE CLASS TEST BENCHMARK

One of the most compelling reasons for choosing object-oriented programming and C++ is the availability of object libraries and application frameworks that have hopes of fulfilling the dream of producing reusable software objects, much in the way integrated circuit chips are used in hardware. The I/O stream library is an example of such a library that exists in every C++ implementation. Others include the Borland Container Class Library and the Turbovision Application Framework, which supports the use of multiple windows. The authors have performed a number of experiments on the use of the Container Class Library in Borland C++ and want to look at the performance of those library objects vs. building proprietary code to do the same.

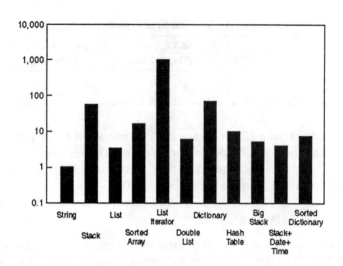

Exhibit 4.   Timing Ratio of Straight C Code to C++ Code Using Container Classes.

Exhibit 4 shows the result of running comparison benchmarks on the Borland C++ Container Class Library. For each of the containers (e.g., String, Stack, List, Sorted Array, ListIterator, DoubleLList, Dictionary, Hash Table, Stack with Date and Time, and a Dictionary with alphabetically sorted associations), a timed measurement was made using the class object, and then compared to a manually written piece of code that attempts to perform the same function. Observations are as follows:

- The container class objects are slower in 10 of the 11 measurements by a factor that ranges from 3 to 930.
- The performance of the class implementation is typically three to five times as slow as the C code.

The performance of the object library functions was expected to be less than the specifically targeted code that an organization might write. Because of the simplicity of the object library functions, however, the size of the performance degradation was surprising.

USE OF APPLICATION FRAMEWORKS: THE TVEDITX BENCHMARK

The authors started with an interactive file editor TVEdit, which is written using the Turbovision Application Framework and is provided by Borland as a demonstration program. It is a full-function file editor with mouse support, using multiple windows, scroll bars, cut-and-paste, window movement, and management. TVEdit consists of 562 lines of C++.

The authors extended this program to list all occurrences of a specified symbol in a collection of source files in a new window; the program then allows the user to move quickly between multiple windows, showing the

242

context of each of the symbol references using mouse points and clicks. The code to do the above required a total of 260 new lines of C++ code.

The performance of the new functions may be slower, but it would have taken thousands of lines of code and many hours to implement. Actually, performance does not play a role in this case, because the code performs much faster than the human eye and hand can interact with the application. The real performance issue here is development time and debugging time. This benchmark is perhaps the best of all the ones above because it delivers the promise of object-oriented programming and class libraries, which serve as reusable modules. Looking at the 260 lines of modifications and additions, the idea of reusability and adaptation is everywhere: a number of existing menu-related classes are instantiated, and new member functions are added to two different classes, which inherit most of their functionality from classes defined and implemented by Turbovision.

CONCLUSION

Use of object libraries is still in the early stages, and certainly performance is just one of the issues to be considered. The Borland C++ Container Class Library is not very impressive in execution performance. Because the objects supplied are so simple and do not give functionality that cannot be written simply in a few lines of code, it is hard to understand why the performance should be so low, so for now users might be best advised to stay away from such objects in favor of using their own techniques when execution performance is essential. Also, these class libraries will become more attractive once they are standardized across compilers and platforms. Again, the best approach for performance critical code is to compare use of the object libraries provided with code written by the developer.

Application Frameworks, such as Turbovision, has impressive functionality to which users gain access using only a few lines of code. This is coming close to the software chips idea, which is analogous to hardware microchips that have revolutionized computer hardware design. Performance measurements here are not practical, but development time and debugging time might be considered. The major negative impression is that it takes a lot of time for a novice to use the classes in Turbovision. The programs are very hard to compile, but debugging time was quite short. Perhaps better documentation with many complete examples for Turbovision objects would help to shorten the learning curve. Subsequent experiments with Windows-oriented GUI application frameworks, such as the Microsoft Foundation Classes, gave even more impressive results to the difficult task of windows programming.

PROGRAMMING TECHNIQUES

The developer interested in performance must measure that performance, run experiments with different options, and compare the performance to best select the one with the best performance.

Developers interested in C++ program performance must become very familiar with their compiler's performance-related options.

Chapter IV-2
Performance of Object-Oriented Programs: C++

Paul J. Jalics
Ben A. Blake

BJARNE STROUSTROP, the creator of C++, said he wanted "something that ran like greased lightning and allowed easy interfacing with the rest of the world." The authors examine this performance aspect of C++ and compare it with C, which has a fine reputation in the performance area.

There are many aspects to program performance; for the purposes of this chapter, the authors limit the meaning to the execution performance of C++ programs (i.e., the amount of time required to execute specific C++ statements and programs).

THE SPECIFICATIONS OF THE EXPERIMENTS

Jalics and Heines developed a set of performance tests to measure the performance of C programs and the C statement level, including CPU, I/O statements, some routine-level modules, and some C library routines. These tests were augmented by a number of statement-level C++ tests and a few whole program C and C++ benchmarks. Execution times throughout are shown in microseconds, unless otherwise specified. These experiments were run on various C and C++ compilers: Borland C and C++ (3.1) on a 386-20 machine, Gnu C and C++ on a Digital Equipment Corp. (DEC) 5000 workstation, and Gnu, AT&T C and C++, and Gnu C++ on a SUN SLC Sparc workstation. Thus, the observations encompass not just a single C++ implementation but a broader picture of C++ performance.

Sun4SLC AT&T		Sun4SLC Gnu		DEC5000 Gnu		Intel 386-20 Borland		
C	C++	C	C++	C	C++	C	C++	Description
0.74	0.74	0.74	0.74	0.32	0.32	1.63	1.63	if(a==b) true
0.70	0.72	0.70	0.70	0.32	0.32	1.40	1.76	if(...&&...)first true
1.04	1.21	1.21	1.21	0.57	0.55	1.76	1.76	if(...LL...)false both
1.15	1.15	1.10	1.15	0.53	0.49	2.28	2.18	nested if false,true
0.75	0.80	0.80	0.80	0.35	0.40	0.78	0.77	for(a=1;a<32;a+=1){;}
0.60	0.85	0.75	0.85	0.45	0.45	0.78	0.79	do{a+=1;while(a<32);
0.75	0.80	0.75	0.70	0.45	0.45	0.95	0.92	x:a+=1;if(a<32)goto x
2.77	2.79	2.68	2.66	1.23	1.30	3.83	3.80	switch(a)0,1,...:d=1
3.34	2.58	2.60	2.58	1.08	1.10	15.48	15.56	switch(a)0,1000,...:d=1
0.42	0.42	0.42	0.40	0.19	0.14	0.67	0.65	a=a + b;
0.38	0.42	0.40	0.40	0.19	0.17	0.71	0.72	a=a - b;
3.60	3.45	3.47	3.49	0.61	0.61	1.07	1.05	a=a * b;
1.34	1.21	1.21	1.23	1.47	1.51	1.73	1.73	a=a/b;
1.36	1.23	1.21	1.23	1.42	1.45	1.75	1.74	a=a & b;
0.46	0.40	0.42	0.44	0.17	0.14	0.88	0.87	a=b + c;
1.70	1.53	1.53	1.51	0.66	0.66	4.62	4.62	a=addm(b,c);
0.27	0.23	0.25	0.25	0.06	0.06	0.17	0.18	d=1
49.72	48.83	48.30	48.46	23.11	23.01	83.72	84.18	total

Exhibit 1.   C Versus C+ + CPU Tests (in Microseconds)

C LANGUAGE SUBSET PERFORMANCE

C++ is approximately a superset of C, so one area of interest is the subset of features contained in the C language. Exhibit 1 shows a small subset of results from the earlier C experiments. These and other results of the experiments show that there is little difference between the C and the equivalent C++ program performance when only the C features of the language are used. This was an expected result and worth the effort to observe on the various systems, especially because performance measurements often deliver surprising results. The sum of times on two of the four systems are actually faster for C++ than for C, although the difference is probably not significant statistically.

C+ + Procedure Call Overhead: The Ctax Benchmark

An object is a collection of data, like a C struct mechanism, that also has a collection of procedures to manipulate that data. These procedures are called member functions. The key word class defines objects in C++. One observation from looking at object-oriented programming (OOP) programs in general and C++ in particular is that the OOP discipline tends to create many objects, each with several relatively small member functions (i.e., 30 to 100 lines). If most procedures are smaller in comparison to non-OOP programs, it seems logical that OOP programs cross substantially more procedures boundaries than non-OOP programs in accomplishing the same task. This factor increases the importance of procedure call overhead in OOP programs.

The following list contains features of C++ that are likely to influence the function call overhead:

1. An inline attribute can be specified for any member function of a C++ class in the class declaration. When code is generated to call such a member function, the executable code in the member function is actually inserted instead of code to put the parameters on the stack followed by a subroutine call instruction. This means that if there are 10 calls to this member function in a program, the machine instructions that implement the procedure are actually generated 10 times instead of 10 procedure call instructions to a single procedure implementation. Thus, when inline is used, the procedure call and return overhead are eliminated altogether, and the implementation code is simply inserted into the calling procedure in each instance that member function is called.

2. A simple procedure call, as in C, that is unrelated to a C++ class needs to be distinguished from a member function of some class. One would expect some performance difference between these two because when calling a member function, a hidden parameter (i.e., the address of the C++ object instance the function is to work on) must also be passed by the compiled code.

3. In a program with inheritance, the inherited class may override some member functions of the base class. For example, the base class has a member function SumIt(), and the inherited class also implements SumIt(). Thus, the second SumIt() will be called for the inherited class, and the question becomes, Does this overridden member function execute as quickly as the base class function?

4. Finally, virtual versus nonvirtual functions must be considered. Virtual functions, or polymorphism, create the ability to decide at execution time which exact member function is to be called. (Usually the function to be called is decided on at program compilation time.)

   Whereas the inline feature of C++ is intended to reduce this procedure call overhead, experience shows that C++ compilers often give up or abort inlining because of procedure length or complexity. An effective optimizing compiler should, as a standard feature, do the same inlining as the Unisys 2200 C compiler or the IBM VS/COBOL II, which does inlining for up to two levels of nested PERFORMs.

Test	Sun4SLC AT&T	Sun4SLC Gnu	DEC500 Gnu	Intel 386-20 Borland	Test Description
1	0.61	0.7	0.46	3.5	call normal function
2	0.38	0.39	0.13	0.85	call inline member function
3	0.69	0.73	0.49	4.74	call non-inline member function
4	0.39	0.39	0.12	0.9	call virtual inline function
5	0.7	0.73	0.5	4.65	call virtual non-inline function
6	0.4	0.39	0.12	0.91	call overridden inline member function
7	0.69	0.72	0.5	4.74	call overridden non-inline member function
8	0.38	0.39	0.12	0.86	call overridden virtual inline function
9	0.7	0.74	0.5	4.63	call overridden virtual non-inline function
10	0.68	0.78	0.5	4.84	polymorphism base (ptr to member function)
11	1.2	1.42	0.7	5.63	polymorphism of non-inline virtual classes
12	1.2	1.4	0.7	5.75	polymorphism of in-line virtual classes
13	0.69	0.82	0.46	3.85	call normal function with 1 param
14	0.33	0.39	0.22	4.04	call normal function with 2 param
15	0.42	0.44	0.26	3.97	call normal function with 3 param
16	0.43	0.48	0.3	4.28	call normal function with 4 param
17	1.17	1.12	0.61	6.03	call normal function with 8 param

Exhibit 2.   Measuring C++ Procedure Call Overhead (in Microseconds)

The authors developed a procedure call overhead measurement program and named it Ctax.cc. The rest of this section looks at the results of running Ctax on the three platforms using four compilers. Exhibit 2 shows the results to be as follows.

A comparison of tests 1, 3, and 13 shows that in most cases the additional overhead of calling a member function is the same as adding an extra parameter to a normal function. One would expect this, because in calling member functions, C++ adds one hidden extra parameter, namely the pointer to the object being referenced. The actual increase in overhead for the four systems ranges from 4% to 35%.

Making a member function inline, as shown in a comparison of tests 2 and 3, often reduces the calling overhead by 45% to 82%. The best reduction, of 82%, is on Borland C++; this reduction may also be indicative of a relatively high procedure call overhead on the Intel 386 when compared to DEC and Sun workstations, which are especially fast in procedure calls. The smallest reductions are on the two Sun systems, on which the role of the procedure call overhead may be even lower.

Also noteworthy is the extra overhead of adding parameters one at a time, as in tests 1 and 13 through 17. Whereas the additional overhead is fairly constant on the Borland C++, at about 10% for adding one parameter, the workstations do much worse in this regard. The overall increase going from

248

two to nine parameters on workstations is 214% to 361%, as compared to 59% for the PC. Virtual member functions and overridden member functions do not have any performance penalties over other member functions when the compiler can figure out at compile time which function is to be called. This is shown in tests 2 through 9.

When member function access is through a pointer, as in tests 10 through 12, the performance slows down to a normal member function that is not inline. Specifying inline has no effect in these cases.

When polymorphism is involved, as in tests 11 through 12, the member function is accessed by pointers, when the appropriate possibly inherited function needs to be decided on at execution time by a virtual array. The execution time for polymorphism goes up further from that mentioned previously by 20%, in Borland C++, to 82%, on the two Sun Sparc systems.

There is a substantial difference between the two compilers on the same SUN SLC Sparc system. For example, the increase for the Gnu C++ for polymorphism is 40%, whereas for the AT&T, it is around 80%. So as usual, performance is a function of the compiler, the language, and the hardware.

C++ I/O Streams Performance: the X18S Series Benchmarks

C++ does include the standard C I/O facilities, such as printf, fprintf, getc, and putc. There is, however, a new Stream I/O library that can replace most of the C I/O library. A set of benchmark programs was constructed that attempts to look at the relative performance of the C versus C++ I/O mechanisms. The tests are based on benchmarks and are augmented by testing equivalent I/O mechanisms from the C++ Stream libraries. For example, one test measures the speed of execution of

```
printf("the answer is %d ",dx).
```

The corresponding test for C++ is

```
cout << "the answer is" << dx << ' '.
```

Even though Exhibit 3 compares the C I/O facilities with the new C++ I/O stream facilities just for one C++ implementation (i.e., Borland C++), it can still give some insights into the performance implications of using the new C++ mechanisms. The Borland C++ tests measure elapsed time on a standalone MS-DOS system, which does not have a concept of CPU execution time.

Exhibit 3 summarizes the results of running these benchmarks on the Borland C++ on a 20 megahertz 386 PC system without a floating-point processor. The following observations can be made from the benchmarks.

The C++I/O stream output to the screen is about 21% slower than the

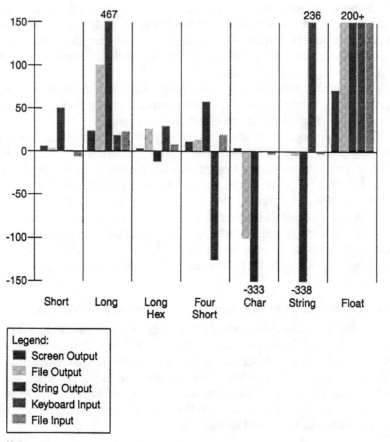

Notes:
Positive Values Indicate Percent Speed-Up Using C Versus C++; Negative Values Indicate
Percent Speed-Up Using C++ Versus C.

Exhibit 3. Comparing C and C+ + I/O

printf overall; the handling of longs is about 30% slower; and float is over 80%
slower.

The C++ stream output to a disk file is, overall, twice as slow as fprintf to
a disk file, with great variations on individual data types. It is the same as
fprintf for a third of the tests; it is almost twice as slow for longs; and it is three
to five times as slow for gloat (off the chart). Surprisingly, char and string are
faster in C++ streams.

For in-memory output conversions, the C++ streams are four times
slower than sprintf overall, with longs and floats being five times as slow, but
chars and strings are again about four times as fast as the C sprintf.

For in-memory input conversions, using C++ mechanisms are overall three times slower than sscanf. C++ is about the same for the majority of tests, except for floats, which are again five times slower.

For input conversions of data read from a disk file, the C++ mechanisms are overall twice as slow but seem to be only slightly slower—by about 10%—in most cases except longs, which are 70% slower, and float and double, which are about three times slower. Char and string are again 20% faster than for fscanf.

Overall, the C++ I/O streams on Borland C++ seem to be somewhat slower than the corresponding C mechanisms on the same compiler, but they certainly are of the same order of magnitude. Some of the slowness may simply be a lack of tuning on a relatively new class library. Surely the floating-point results show a lack of tuning and would be dramatically different with hardware floating point support on the test system.

The same experiments were rerun on the Sun SLC AT&T C++ system, with quite different results. The overall figures show I/O streams to be faster by about 33% in CPU execution time and 4% slower in elapsed time, indicating that C++ I/O stream performance need not be worse than C I/O and very much a function of software implementation and tuning. The experiments could not be run on the Gnu C++ compilers because they do not yet implement the C++ Release 2 I/O streams.

It is not really clear that the I/O streams provide a significant new dimension to programming. Well-practiced C programmers may find them harder and more inconvenient to use, especially when using manipulators instead of clear and concise format strings in C. Also, the I/O stream libraries are not described well enough in C++ books and compiler manuals, and there is a scarcity of detailed examples of the many ways that they can be used. One thing certainly favors C++ I/O streams: the whole methodology of I/O streams is in better harmony with C++'s philosophy of complete type-checking each data item being input or output.

SCREEN EMULATOR PERFORMANCE

A problem is posed: how to model a screen object for a terminal emulation system. Normally, the screen was modeled as a two-dimensional array in which each entry contained a data byte and an attribute byte specifying color. Thus, several solutions were implemented using C++ objects and normal C one- and two-dimensional arrays. The function measured by the benchmarks was to add together all the byte values on the screen. The results for the three systems are shown in Exhibit 4.

The simplest implementation is as a one-dimensional array of char [4000], as shown in test 1. This was the fastest on the Borland C++, but surprisingly

Test	Sun4SLC AT&T	Sun4SLC G++	DEC5000 Gnu	Intel 386-20 Borland	Test Description
1	1110	1240	820	11680	sum char[4000] array
2	750	1030	560	16720	sum char[25][160] array
3	940	1180	720	17370	sum [25][80] array of classes
4	3060			21800	sum [][] oper overload array inline
5	3310			21880	sum [][] oper overload dynamic array inline
6	4930			56970	sum [][] oper overload dynamic array not inline
7	1940	1310	780	16070	sum (r,c) with rowindex inline

Exhibit 4.   Screen Emulator Object Performance (in Microseconds)

the two-dimensional array char, as in test 2, was the fastest on the three workstation systems.

The next attempt, test 3, was to use an array of structures with two char items in each class but no member functions. This was slower than the two-dimensional array on all systems but was still faster than the one-dimensional array on the three workstation systems.

The next three attempts, tests 4 through 6, used real classes with member functions that implemented double subscripting by using inheritance with one object to specify the row subscript and the other to specify the column. There is no [][] operator. These three tests use operator overloading, which is a C++ feature that allows programmers to ascribe new meanings to the standard operators, such as +, -, *, =,>, and []. Unfortunately, the Gnu C++ compiler was not able to compile these tests, so the results are only for the Sun AT&T system and Borland C++.

The results show the huge impact of inline member functions for solving real problems. On Borland C++, the inline solution (see tests 4 and 5) are about three times faster than the on-inline test 6. On AT&T Sun, the inline solutions are one-third faster than the on-inline one. The final version is a simple class with a member function ref(row, column), which selects the appropriate screen position and returns a reference to it. This inline solution proved to be the most efficient of all the real class solutions (see tests 4 through 7) on both Borland C++ and the AT&T Sun, showing above all that simple object solutions such as test 7 may perform better when compared to complex schemes such as double subscripting using two classes and inheritance. In any case, the obvious solution yields a more readable and easier-to-understand implementation.

The best object solutions (see test 7) were still much slower than the best original nonobjects solutions (see tests 1 through 3). On the AT&T Sun the object solution is 158% slower than char[25][160]. On the SUN Gnu C++

Test	Sun4SLC AT&T	Sun4SL C G++	DEC5000 G++	Intel 386-20 Borland	Test Description
dr1	6437	7481	16574	5000	using Int and char
dr2	3717	4160	2695	1388	Using Int and Char inline
dr3	1243	1832	2633	373	Using Int and Char (not inline)
dr4	1006	1541	2013	306	Using Int and Char (not inline) return by value
dr5		1221	1794	301	Using Int and Char (no inline)
dr6	5780	6493	7194	1612	Using Int only inline
dr7	4016	4958	3405	3333	Using char only inline

Exhibit 5.   Int and Char Classes Used in Dhrystone Benchmark (in Microseconds)

the object solution is 27% slower than char[25][160]. On DEC Gnu C++ the object solution is 39% slower than char[25][160]. On Borland C++ the object solution is 39% slower than the char[4000] solution. These increases in execution time are large, and the question is, Where is the additional time spent? Procedure call overhead is eliminated, because the member function ref is inline. In the generated code for Borland C++ (with all optimizations turned on), there are about one-third more machine instructions in the inner loop, having to do with generating a reference to an object and then dereferencing it to get at the table entries.

THE DHRYSTONE C++ BENCHMARKS

There is a C++ version of the Dhrystone Benchmark that was used to look at C++ performance. The two classes Int and Char were implemented to replace the standard built-in data-types int and char. This test accurately measures the worst-case performance cost of introducing new data types that are used throughout an application. Exhibit 5 shows the results of executing several versions of the C++ Dhrystone on various systems.

The results show the performance of the tested system in Dhrystones (i.e., a bigger number is faster). The following observations can be made:

- Replacing int and char by inline (dr2 versus dr1) implementations of Int and Char in the entire benchmark degrades performance by 43% on the two Sun C++ compilers, by 84% on the DEC5000, and by 72% on the 386. Perhaps the DEC5000 and the 386 do less inline work than the Suns.

	SUN_SLC_AT&T_C++ (CPU Sec) (Elapsed Sec)		386_20_Borland_C++ (Elapsed Sec)
Cperf (C)	1.8	2.3	1.21
Gperf (C++)	2.1	2.4	0.88

Exhibit 6.   The Gperf Benchmark

- If the implementations are changed to use procedure calls for member functions (i.e., noninline, dr3 versus dr1), the degradation factors go up to 81% for the Sun AT&T, to 76% for the Sun g++, to 85% for the DEC, and to 93% for the 386.
- Using by-value return of results instead of by-reference (dr4 versus dr3) reduces performance further by about 25%.
- Making the member functions virtual (dr5 versus dr4) further reduces performance by 1% to 26%.
- Tests dr6 and dr7 separate out the performance differences due to Int and Char and indicate that performance degradation due to the introduction of just inline Char is only about 12% for the two Sun systems, 57% for DEC, and 68% for the 386.
- Performance degradation due to the introduction of just inline Int (see test dr6) is 34% for the two Sun systems and the 386, and 80% for the DEC.

THE GPERF BENCHMARK

Gperf is a program that generates a perfect hashing function for a known set of keys; it was designed in C++, and a separate version exists in C (Cperf). This Gperf benchmark consists of 3,906 lines of code and is a reasonable object-oriented design whose performance might be compared to the C version. Whether this is a fair comparison might be debated, but any performance samples are of interest. The results of running this benchmark are illustrated in Exhibit 6.

The results show a 16% increase in CPU time for the C++ version on the Sun; the same program, however, shows only a 4% increase in elapsed time on the Sun and a 28% decrease in elapsed time on the PC. Again, there is not a clear trend that is identifiable in C versus C++.

THE XREF BENCHMARK

This benchmark inputs a list of files, lists them (including file name and line number), and then provides a cross-reference listing of all symbols. The

	SUN_SLC_AT&T_C++		386_20_Borland_C++
	(CPU sec)	(elapsed sec)	(elapsed sec)
Cperf (C)	8.8	9.2	37
Gperf (C++)	6.9	7.4	34

The Xref Benchmark

Exhibit 7. The Xref Benchmark

original xref0.c program (375 lines) is of poor design, as it was transported originally from COBOL and has seen many modifications. It has, however, been in widespread use by one of the authors for over a decade. Cxref.cc (303 lines), on the other hand, is a completely new object-oriented design that was undertaken as part of learning about object-oriented programming and C++.

Results of running the xref benchmark are illustrated in Exhibit IX-2-7.

Even though the algorithms are not identical in these two programs, the inputs, outputs, and the work done are meant to be the same. The results show a 20% improvement for the C++ version on the Sun and an 8% improvement on the PC. The results may be explained as follows. The potential loss of performance in a C++ program (when compared to a C program) can be more than overcome in some cases by improving the design and paying attention to performance.

OBJECT LIBRARIES: THE CLASS TEST BENCHMARK

One of the most compelling reasons for choosing OOP and C++ is the availability of object libraries and application frameworks that have hopes of fulfilling the dream of producing reusable software objects, much in the way integrated circuit chips are used in hardware. The I/O stream library is an example of such a library that exists in every C++ implementation. Others include the Borland Container Class Library and the Turbovision Application Framework, which supports the use of multiple windows. The authors have performed a number of experiments on the use of the Container Class Library in Borland C++ and want to look at the performance of those library objects versus building proprietary code to do the same.

Exhibit 8 shows the result of running comparison benchmarks on the Borland C++ Container Class Library. For each of the containers (e.g., String, Stack, List, Sorted Array, ListIterator, DoubleLList, Dictionary, Hash Table, Stack with Date and Time, and a Dictionary with alphabetically sorted associations), a timed measurement was made using the class object, and then compared to a manually written piece of code that attempts to perform the same function. Observations are as follows:

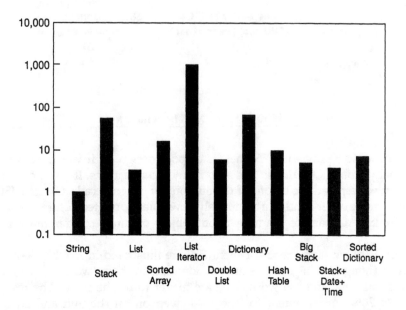

Exhibit 8. Timing Ratio of Straight C Code to C++ Code Using Container Classes

- The container class objects are slower in 10 of the 11 measurements by a factor that ranges from 3 to 930.
- The performance of the class implementation is typically three to five times as slow as the C code.

The performance of the object library functions was expected to be less than the specifically targeted code that an organization might write. Because of the simplicity of the object library functions, however, the size of the performance degradation was surprising.

USE OF APPLICATION FRAMEWORKS: THE TVEDITX BENCHMARK

The authors started with an interactive file editor TVEdit, which is written using the Turbovision Application Framework and is provided by Borland as a demonstration program. It is a full-function file editor with mouse support, using multiple windows, scroll bars, cut-and-paste, window movement, and management. TVEdit consists of 562 lines of C++.

The authors extended this program to list all occurrences of a specified symbol in a collection of source files in a new window; the program then allows the user to move quickly between multiple windows, showing the context of each of the symbol references using mouse points and clicks. The code to do the above required a total 260 new lines of C++ code.

The performance of the new functions may be slower, but it would have taken thousands of lines of code and many hours to implement. Actually, performance does not play a role in this case, because the code performs much faster than the human eye and hand can interact with the application. The real performance issue here is development time and debugging time. This benchmark is perhaps the best of all the ones above because it delivers the promise of OOP and class libraries, which serve as reusable modules. Looking at the 260 lines of modifications and additions, the idea of reusability and adaptation is everywhere: a number of existing menu-related classes are instantiated, and new member functions are added to two different classes, which inherit most of their functionality from classes defined and implemented by Turbovision.

SUMMARY

C++ performance can be made as good as C performance because C++ is close to a superset of C, and most C++ compilers give an identical performance when using only features available in C. Thus, C++ is as good as C from a performance standpoint, given the same C code.

C++ I/O Stream library performance can be as fast as C I/O, but much depends on the details of the implementation. Developers are able to affect this performance by a few compiler options but cannot easily otherwise change this performance. Developers are able to have a big impact on I/O performance by their choice of a C++ Compiler system, when that is possible. For example, Intel 80x86 systems have several very fine compiler systems from which to choose.

Procedure call overhead on a given hardware plays a substantial role in performance. This is especially important in C++, in which member functions tend to be small. Compiler optimizations can play a big role in reducing this overhead. The inline attribute for a member function can also greatly enhance performance, but often compilers may ignore this attribute. In some cases, developers may choose a particular computer platform just because it has a low procedure call overhead.

The use of new data types via C++ objects is one of the outstanding features of C++ but should be used with some care when performance is a critical issue. Developers should prototype the new data type and compare its performance to that of comparable built-in types, as the authors did for the screen emulator benchmark.

The performance of C++ implementations varies widely, and users should run experiments on their target system to help make design decisions that ensure that performance goals can be met.

Use of object libraries is still in the early stages, and certainly performance is just one of the issues to be considered. The Borland C++ Container Class Library is not very impressive in execution performance. Because the objects supplies are so simple and do not give functionality that cannot be written simply in a few lines of code, it is hard to understand why the performance should be so low, so for now users might be best advised to stay away from such objects in favor of using their own techniques when execution performance is essential. Also, these class libraries will become more attractive once they are standardized across compilers and platforms. Again, the best approach for performance critical code is to compare use of the object libraries provided with code written by the developer.

Application Frameworks, such as Turbovision, has impressive functionality to which users gain access using only a few lines of code. This is coming close to the software chips idea, which is analogous to hardware microchips that have revolutionized computer hardware design. Performance measurements here are not practical, but development time and debugging time might be considered. The major negative impression is that it takes a lot of time for a novice to use the classes in Turbovision. The programs are very hard to compile, but debugging time was quite short. Perhaps better documentation with many complete examples for Turbovision objects would help to shorten the learning curve. Subsequent experiments with Windows-oriented graphical user interface application frameworks, such as the Microsoft Foundation Classes, gave even more impressive results to the difficult task of windows programming.

The developer interested in performance must measure that performance, run experiments with different options, and compare the performance to best select the one with the best performance.

Developers interested in C++ program performance must become very familiar with their compiler's performance-related options.

Chapter IV-3

Java and C++: Similarities, Differences, and Performance

Adam Fadlalla, Paul J. Jalics,
and Victor Matos

OBJECT-ORIENTED PROGRAMMING (OOP) IS AN IMPROVEMENT IN PRO-
GRAMMING TECHNOLOGY and C++ is the most visible and commonly used
OOP dissemination vehicle. However, C++ drags with it a lot of the "history" of C, which includes assumptions from the 1960s that a system implementation language needs to be completely "open" and (consequently)
"sloppy" so that programmers can implement, inside the confines of an
operating system, all the artifices and "magic" that might be desired. [1]

While this position for "total openness" could be arguably justified, it
clearly brings an undesirable amount of language inconsistencies, ambiguities, exceptions, and clumsiness. On the opposite side, an experience [2]
from Xerox's Mesa language indicates that a strongly type-checked language can go a long way in avoiding or eliminating execution-time errors.
C++ was intended to go in this direction, but backward compatibility to the
very important C language had the side effect of leaving a great deal of the
"slop" that was in C to remain in C++.

To make matters worse, the architecture of the initial C++ implementations was geared to converting the C++ source programs to C code, so that
existing C compilers could be used for compilation. As a result a number of
unwanted side-effect anomalies can occur. For example, it is possible in
C++ to cast any variable or pointer to anything else; functions without a
return type may still return an integer; pointers are most often used without any checking as to whether they were initialized; subscripts for arrays
are not checked; # preprocessor commands and variables can generate a
multitude of erroneous code.

Adding to all these problems, there is one more disturbing factor: C++ is
a compiled language that interacts with "real" computers. For each real
computer there is an OS interface to C++, and unfortunately it is different

0-8493-9979-3/99/$0.00+$.50
© 1999 by CRC Press LLC

for each operating environment! Try to convert a Borland C++ GUI application to Microsoft C++. It is akin to starting over, in one sense, especially if the original author did not design his application to be portable [3]. Bear in mind that all this portability conflicts we refer to are, at the moment, confined to the same Intel machine architecture and the same Windows 95 operating system.

This is much more so than in newer programming environments like the two mentioned above because the integrated debugging environments (IDE) and their "wizards" often generate a good deal of C++ source code. The programmer than inserts his application code in the midst of all the automatically generated code.

In summary, C++ is an extraordinary programming language that is unfortunately too complex, too error-prone, difficult to teach or learn because of its wealth of features. We believe the intent of the Java developers [4] was to retain the important features of C++ while eliminating unnecessary complexity and error-prone language features. At the same time, Java introduces some new techniques that are superior to their C++ counterparts. For instance, all pointers are eliminated, all objects are always passed by reference, and address arithmetic is forbidden.

DIFFERENCES BETWEEN C++ AND JAVA

Java is different from its predecessor programming languages (C, C++, Modula, Ada) in several ways, for instance [8]:

- Java is a small language; however it provides support for object-oriented programming.
- Arrays are the only predefined data structure type offered by Java, yet it provides access to classes that could be used to support any user-defined data structure.
- Java includes a rich Graphical User Interface (GUI) and multimedia facilities (sound, images, animation). Java is intrinsically GUI oriented. Its applications — called applets — are displayed by a web browser rather than directly delivered to the computer's monitor.
- Java provides a self-contained environment for concurrency control, as well as a set of primitive programming facilities to support networking operations.

Exhibit 1 takes a piecemeal approach in our comparison of the two languages. Concepts from a C++ standpoint are mapped into their equivalent versions in Java. Even though the list is not exhaustive, it contains many of the building blocks needed for a good perspective of the differences between C/C++ and Java. Exhibit 2 summarizes the table in Exhibit 1.

Exhibit 1. A Comparison of C/C++ and Java	
C and C++	**Java**
Program Organization C and C++ programs normally consist of two parts, a header file (.h) containing the class definition and a (.cpp) file containing the implementation of the class. However, one can write very unobvious C++ programs using the preprocessor commands: *#define, #ifdef,* and *typedef* constructions.	Each complete logical unit of Java code is placed alone into one single piece of code (.Java file). This creates a single source for a class, which sometimes has the disadvantage that one is not able to get a good overview of the class declaration as it often spans many pages. Projects are made by combining several independent Java files together. There is no preprocessor activity. There are no header files. #ifdef, #include, #define, macros, and other preprocessor commands are not available.

Constants
C/C++ constants have no explicit type, they could be defined in a global mode.
 	
#define MILETOKMS 1602
#define PI 3.141592
class circle {
  double radius;
  circle(double r) {radius = r; };
  double area() { return (2*PI*radius); }
};
Note: 1- Semicolon at the end of the class is needed.
      2- #define variables are global.
	The data type of Java constants must be explicitly defined. Constants must be made *public* and placed inside a class.
	class circle {
	  //constants
	  static final double MILESTOKMS = 1602;
	  public static final PI = 3.141592;
	  //variable
	  double radius;
	  //method
	  circle(double r) {radius = r; };
	  double area () {return (2*PI*radius);};
	}
	Note: 1- Semicolon at the end of class is not needed.
	      2- Public constant *circle.PI* is global.

Global Variables Variables, constants, and data types could be made *global* by positioning them outside of a class definition or the implementation of a class's methods.	Java has no global variables and so all variables must be defined in some class. This implements more fully the object-oriented nature of the language. There are **static** variables just like in C++ and if they have a **public** access they can be used like global variables with a class prefix. For example,: myCompany.phoneNumber; myCompany is the class, and phoneNumber a public static variable).

Structures
C++ structures offer a rude method of providing *Data Encapsulation*.
struct EnglishDistance {
    int feet;
    double inches;
 	
};
 	
an instance is defined as
struct EnglishDistance myboat;
	In Java there are no structures. Therefore C++ structures must be converted into Java classes:
	class englishDistance {
	    int feet;
	    double inches;
	}
	an instance is defined:
	englishDistance myBoat = new myBoat();

Exhibit 1 (Continued). A Comparison of C/C++ and Java	
C and C++	**Java**

Functions and Methods C/C++ programs are collections of functions. There is a distinguished function called *main* that is the first to be executed. C++ supports a heterogeneous mix of both methods inside classes and C-like functions.
 	
double calculateCircleArea (double radius)
  {
  return (2 * PI * radius);
  }
 	
Used in the context:
  Double r1 = 5.4;
  Area1 = calculateCircleArea (r1);
e
	Java has no functions. All the activity provided by functions must be written as methods inside a class.
	Methods in a function need to receive a fixed number of parameters. Java functions that return no value must be declared as returning void.
	Class circle {
	    double radius;
	    circle(double r) {radius = r; };
	    double calculateArea()
	      {return (2*myConst.PI * radius);};
	}
	Used in the context
	    circle circle1 = new circle(r1);
	    Area1 = circle1.calculateArea();
	here circle1 is defined as an instance of the circle class, with an original radius r1.
	All Java methods are *virtual* so that the actual function called is determined at execution time. Also, the final modifier declares that a method may not be overridden by subclasses.

Access Modifiers Visibility (*Hiding*) of data and member functions inside a class is controlled using access specifiers: **Private:** Can be accessed only *within* the class. **Public:** Visible outside of the class as class.part. **Protected:** Similar to private but accessible to the methods of any derived class.	Java uses the concept of *packages*. A package is a container for classes and other packages. A class is a container of data and code. Java uses combinations of the access modifiers: public, private, and protected, but it adds more control in visibility by ruling how classes and packages interact with one another. Table 1 summarizes the scoping of variables and functions. [9]

Automatic Typecasting C++ allows coercion in which loss of precision could occur. For instance, assigning a double to an integer (loosing decimals) is a valid C operation
  int age = 20;
  double dogAge = age/7.0;
  //next is a valid assignment in C++
  //however it may produce a warning msg
  age = dogAge;
	Java forces the programmer to *explicitly* typecast assignments operations in which a loss of representation may occur
	  int age = 20;
	  double dogAge = age/7.0;
	  //explicit coercion is needed below
	  age = (int) dogAge;

Operator Overloading C++ offers operator overloading, which in many cases offers a great degree of elegance in dealing with data objects. Consider the C++ example.	Java does not support operator overloading. Overloading is implemented with normal methods, which are functionally equivalent to the action of the operator.

Exhibit 1 (Continued). A Comparison of C/C++ and Java	
C and C++	**Java**

class eDistance {//English Distance
private: int   feet;
    double inches;
public:
eDistance (int f, double I)
    {feet= f; inches= i;};
eDistance operator + (eDistance d2) {
inches+=d2.inches;
        feet+=d2.feet;
        if (inches >12) {
           feet++;
           inches-=12.0;
        };
        return eDistance(feet, inches);
    };
};
which could be used in the context
    d3 = d1 + d2;
where d1, d2, d3 are instances of eDistance.
	Class eDistance {//English Distance
	    int feet;
	    double inches;
	eDistance add (eDistance d2)
	{
	    double sumInches = inches + d2.inches;
	    double sumFeet = feet + d2.feet;
	    if (sumInches >12) {
	      sumFeet++;
	      sumInches-=12.0;
	    }
	    return new eDistance(sumFeet, sumInches);
	    };
	}
	
	Used in the context
	    d3 = d1.add (d2);
	where d1, d2, d3 are instances of
	englishDistance.

Strings
C/C++ does not include support for strings.
Those must be either treated as a user-defined
object or a zero-terminated array of
characters. For example,:
    #include <string.h>
    char Name[20];
    strcpy(Name, "Don Quixote");
    size = strlen(Name);
	Java offers strings as *primitive* objects. Strings
	are part of the Java language specification;
	therefore their behavior is rigorously well
	defined across programs.
	    String Name = new String();
	    Name = "Don Quixote";
	    size = Name.length();

Input-Output Streams C++ offers three standard streams: in, out, error, as well as the overloaded operators << and >> int age; cout << "Enter your age: "; cin >> age; cout << "you said " << age << " years";	Java applications also support the concept of *streams.* However there is no << or >> operators int age; System.out.println ("Enter your age: "); System.out.flush(); age = System.in.read(); System.out.println("You said " +age+" years");

Command-Line Arguments
C/C++ passes an integer argc indicating the
total number of arguments present in the
command line, and argv[] which is an array of
pointers to chars
 int main (int argc, char* argv[]) {
  for (int i = 0; i<argc; i++)
    cout << argv[i];
};
	Java applications use a *String* collection to
	pass parameters. Path/Prog name are not
	displayed.
	public class test2 {
	  public static void main (String[] arg) {
	    for (int j = 0; j<arg.length;j++)
	      System.out.println (arg[j]); }; }

Exhibit 1 (Continued). A Comparison of C/C++ and Java

C and C++	Java
Friends and Packages C++ classes use *friend* functions to act as a bridge between two unrelated classes, or to improve readability by providing a more obvious syntax. When another class declares your class as a friend, you have access to all data and methods in that class.	Java has no *friend* functions. This issue has been controversial in the design of C++. The Java designers decided to drop it. However, Java variables, which are (1) in a class that is part of a package, and (2) introduced without an access modifier, acquire the *friendly* access type of the package. Those variables could be called without *get* and *set* functions from other classes in the same package

Inheritance
C++ provides multiple inheritance. An object has access to all the data and methods of its ancestors.
class student: public person,
public athlete,
public intellectual
{
//derived class definition
...
};
the student class is derived from the three ancestor classes: person, athlete, and intellectual. Any data and methods defined in the upper classes are reachable from the subclass.
	Java implements single inheritance. Each object has only one ancestor, however *interfaces* could be used to support dynamic method resolution at runtime. Java *interfaces* are like classes, but lack instance variables and their methods contain only a signature but no body. An interface is similar to a C++ abstract class which specifies the behavior of an object without specifying an implementation. A class may include any number of interfaces. The body of referenced methods must be provided in the subclass.
	class student **implements** person, athlete, intellectual
	{
	//subclass definition
	...
	}
	keyword *implements* is used to introduce the names of *interfaces* other than the primary ancestor

Basic Data Types C++ offers the following primitive data types (given with their field widths in bits): char:8, int: 16, long:32, float:4, double:64, long double:80, unsigned char:8, unsigned int:16, unsigned long:32 C++ also has bitfields, enumerated types, unions, structs, and typedef to enrich the possibilities.	The following built-in data types with field widths in bits are available: boolean:1, byte:8, char:16, short:16, int:32, long:64, float:32, double:64. Please note that char is 16 bits wide and supports the international Unicode standard for all foreign alphabets including Japanese and Chinese. Java has no *enumerated type*, no *bitfields*, no variable number of arguments for functions, no *struct*, no *unions*, no *typedef.*
Strings C++ has no direct support for strings. Programmers must use zero-terminated arrays of characters or include add-in libraries (MFC, OWL, STL) to provide additional facilities to handle strings	Java uses the built-in class *String* to replace most uses of null terminated character strings as used in C++. class Greetings { public static void main(String args[])

| Exhibit 1 (Continued). A Comparison of C/C++ and Java ||
C and C++	Java

#include <string.h>
...
char myStr [80];
strcpy(myStr, "Hello");
strcat(myStr, " World");
This example uses an array of null-terminated chars, and the <string.h> library to support strings.
	{
	String myStr;//a reference to the string
	myStr = new String("Hello World");
	myStr = "Hello" + " World";//assign concat
	  }
	}

Arrays
An array definition defines a starting address and reserves storage for allocation
  int deptNumber[4];
  int dNumb[] = {10, 20, 30, 40 };
	Arrays are defined in two steps. First a reference to the repeating group is made, then new is used to allocate storage and define the array's size.
	  int deptNumber[];
	  deptNumber = new int[4];
	  int deptNumb[] = new int[4];
	  int dNum[] = {10, 20,30,40};
	Arrays that have no claimed space using the new command are set to *null*. Since array subscripts are always checked, the most common form of program failure in Java is trying to use a null reference type which is caught by the Java virtual machine.

Pointers
C and C++ make extensive use of pointers. The addressing and dereferencing operators are used to signal a pointer to data and the value of such address
  int Number = 10;
  int *ptrNumber = &Number;
This example has no equivalent translation in Java.
	Java has no pointers and thus no pointer arithmetic. Referencing and dereferencing operators (*,&) do not exist. There are, however, *references,* which is a safe kind of pointer.
	  BTreeType mytree;//reference
	  mytree = new BTreeType();//initialization
	Both arrays and objects are passed by *reference.* When one creates an instance variable of a class (BTreeType mytree;), it is just a reference variable to an instance of that class. The instance variable *must be initialized* with a **new** operator (mytree = **new** BTreeType();) to create an actual instance of that class. The default value of all objects and arrays (i.e., reference types) is *null* (which means an absence of a reference).

Operators There is a large number of arithmetical and logical, operators such as: ++, --, +, -, *,/, %, &&, !, I I, etc.	Java supports almost all of the C++ operators, including bit-wise logical operators, and has minimal extensions .
Flow Control Typical flow control structures are: if [else], for, while, switch, break, continue, goto.	Same as C/C++ with the exception of the **goto** statement which is not implemented. Java also includes a **synchronized** statement to protect critical sections of multi-threaded applications.

| Exhibit 1 (Continued).   A Comparison of C/C++ and Java ||
C and C++	Java
OS Utilities Input-output operations are not intrinsically defined in the language, but they are rather acquired by using the standard C libraries (stdio.h, stdlib.h, etc.). Another alternative is to use the more powerful set of classes or class libraries provided by the Microsoft MFC, and the Borland OWL. However, those libraries are different and incompatable [3] for every compiler.	Java has designed into it a set of predefined and standardized classes for *I/O, Graphical User Interface (GUI)* access at a high-level, *networking, multiprogramming* with threads, and other operating system services.
Linking In C++ one typically links the application into an executable (myBtreeApp.exe), which is all loaded into memory when the program is started.	Uses a built-in *dynamic linker* and it is common to load new .class files in the middle of execution. Java has no .exe form but is instead a *collection* of .class object files. Thus Java .class 'es are often downloaded from the Internet and executed with subsequent parts (.class modules) downloaded as needed.
Executing C++ is compiled into highly efficient machine language.	Java is typically *interpreted,* thus Java has (for the present) compromised performance to get portability. We will discuss performance in a later section.
Security C++ has an infinite number of ways in which its integrity and security can be defeated.	Java has a *Code Verifier* that checks each .class module before it is loaded to verify that it is well-behaved and obeys the basic rules of the Java language. The *Class Loader* maintains a list of classes it has loaded, as well as the locations from which they came. When a class references another class, the request is served by its original class loader. This means that classes loaded from a specific source can be restricted to interact only with other classes retrieved from the same location. Finally, the *Security Manager* can restrict access to computer resources like the file system, network ports, external processes, memory regions outside of the virtual machine, etc.
Internet C++ was not designed with the Internet in mind; therefore, there is nothing directly connecting them.	Java provides a GUI "interpretable" code-type called an Applet. Applets are applications that can be *run in a standardized environment,* which happens to be provided by a browser such as Netscape or MS-Internet Explorer. Therefore, one can develop a GUI application which can run on the Internet browser of any computer.

Exhibit 1 (Continued). A Comparison of C/C++ and Java
Miscellaneous
• Debugging code can be included in your source directly and conditioned on constant variables: thus the Java compiler will remove the code if these variables are not set.
• We do not need a *destructor* member function very often in Java because returning new and other heap storage is done automatically by Java when it is no longer pointed to by any reference types.
• Java exception handling is similar to C++ but not exactly the same. The try block is followed by potentially several catch functions, and a clean-up function finally which is executed in any case. The throw statement generates an exception, and a throws clause in a function declaration indicates that a specific exception might occur in that function. This policy promotes error information to the same level of importance as argument and return typing.
• C++ classes sometimes have a "fragile base class" problem which makes it difficult to modify a class which has many derived classes: changing the base class may require recompilation of the derived classes. Java avoids this problem by dynamically locating fields within classes.

Exhibit 2. Summary of Differences between C/C++ and Java

Data Hiding Object	Access Modifiers applied on a variable or member function				
	Private	No Modifier	Private Protected	Protected	Public
Same class	Yes	Yes	Yes	Yes	Yes
Same package subclass	No	Yes	Yes	Yes	Yes
Same package nonsubclass	No	Yes	No	Yes	Yes
Different package subclass	No	No	Yes	Yes	Yes
Different package nonsubclass	No	No	No	No	Yes

IMPACT OF THE MISSING C++ FEATURES IN JAVA

With about 10,000 lines of Java programming behind us and 7+ years of C++ programming, we wish to hazard a guess as to the impact on Java's potential of some of the features of C++ that are missing in Java:

• *Multiple Inheritance*: While one can give many examples of cases where multiple inheritance might be the "best" solution, the concept is not totally clear, and it is at least bothersome. In our experience we find that we have not used it in C++ much at all, so the impact of losing it should be minimal. Nonetheless, there is the possibility of implementing multiple inheritance in Java using *interfaces*.

• *The C++ preprocessor* is certainly the source of many possible errors, but it is also a powerful tool for managing different versions such as the performance tests described below. For example, the timing code in the benchmarks was inserted into each benchmark using #include. In Java these were simply manually copied into each benchmark (when a bug was discovered in the timing code, it was time to hand-edit

267

19 different versions of the same code). Also in the C++ timing code we used an array of structures where the test procedure address was stored along with the repetition count, etc. In Java this could not be accomplished and so another procedure layer needed to be inserted that used a switch statement to call any of the tests in the current group with appropriate parameters.

- *Pointers.* While it is true that traditionally C/C++ have relied heavily on "pointer logic" to access data, and manipulate parameters, it is also clear that a significant portion of the program development effort is related to cleaning-up that type of logic. Dangling pointers and long chains of indirect addressing are by far the most perturbing and error-prone elements of C/C++ programming. Certain retraining might be needed by the C programmer to adjust to a pointer-free environment. Notice, however, that the concept of *reference* to an object is somehow similar to the pointer notion, just simpler. [10]

We do not feel too many other limitations will imperil the C programmer from making a smooth transition to Java.

JAVA PERFORMANCE CHARACTERISTICS

Among the greatest concerns in Java is execution performance: Java is designed to be *interpreted* — rather than executed. Java .class "executable" programs are pieces of machine code for a non-physically-existent computer. This hypothetical computer is totally implemented in software, and is called the *Java Virtual Machine*. In order to execute .class programs we use a computer program (a Java enabled browser such as Netscape, or an emulator such as Jview.exe), which interpretatively executes the machine instructions in the .class files.

The industry rule of thumb for the execution speed of interpreted code is that it is slower by an *order of magnitude*. While it is true that computer hardware speeds are getting ever faster, our appetite for solving larger and more complex problems means the execution speed is still very much crucial.

We started looking at the issue of execution evaluation with the Sun Microsystems White Paper. [5] Later on, we found a number of Java benchmarks, most of those studies are meant to compare the following:

- The speed of one Java implementation vs. another
- The relative merits of different Internet browsers when executing Applets
- The rating of different hardware platforms when executing the same code. However just a few of those benchmarks made some comparison between C++ vs. Java. [6a-6f]

We decided to do an exhaustive analysis of the two languages on a feature-by-feature basis. The focus was to obtain a gross evaluation of how far

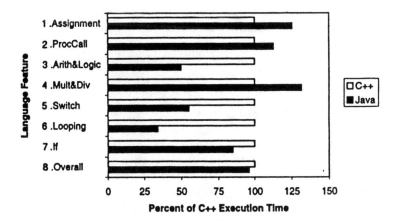

Exhibit 3. CPU Language Features: Java vs. C++

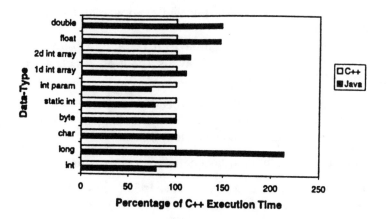

Exhibit 4. Java Data-Type Performance vs. C++

apart is one tool (C++) from the other (J++). We converted to Java a number of C++ benchmarks programs that were written earlier to study C++ performance. [7] We then ran all of them first in C++ and then again in Java to study the relative performance of C++ vs. Java.

The performance tests were executed on the same computer, a Pentium 133 megahertz laptop with 32 megabytes of memory, running Windows-95. The software systems were: Visual C++ 4.0 compiler from Microsoft and Microsoft Visual J++ version 1.1.

A battery of tests called the *X tests* measures CPU execution speeds of different language features (see Exhibits 3 and 4). Both the Java and the C++ test programs were executed using a non-GUI interface. C++ code in the form of .exe files targeted a plain DOS platform, while the Java programs were produced as "applications" to be executed by the JVIEW emulator.

As summarized in Exhibit 3, we found that in a test of CPU language features, Java vs. C++,

- A simple assignment is 25% slower in java as compared to C++.
- Procedure call overhead in actual time is 13% slower in Java when compared to C++. However, in C++ a procedure to add two integers executes 8.1 times as long as the "in-line" assignment c = a+b; in Java this factor is 2.1. Thus the additional overhead for the procedure call in this case in Java is one fourth as much when compared to C++.
- Arithmetic, logical, and shift statements overall appear to be about 50% faster in Java.
- Multiply and Division statements (*,/,%) appear to be about 32% slower in Java as compared to C++.
- The switch statement performance in Java is 45% faster than in C++.
- Looping statements (for,do while,while) appears to be 3 times as fast in Java as in C++.
- If statement execution times in Java are faster by 15%.
- The overall execution time of Java is about 4% less than the corresponding C++ measurement.

The only surprise here is the low procedure-call overhead in Java, and just the insight that the performance of the main language facilities in Java is comparable to the known-to-be-efficient C++.

As summarized in Exhibit 4, Java data-type performance testing found:

- Double precision floating point in Java is 52% slower than in C++.
- Java single precision floating point is 53% slower than in C++.
- Two-dimensional array access in Java takes 14% longer than in C.
- Accessing elements of a one-dimensional array in Java takes 10% longer than in C++.
- Int parameters in Java take 27% less execution time than in C++.
- Statements involving Java static variables perform 22% faster than in C++.
- The Java byte data-type (8-bits) takes about the same execution time as the 8-bit char types do in C++.
- The Java char data-type (16-bits) takes about the same time as the C++ char (but the C++ 16-bit short takes 6.5% more execution time than the Java char).
- Java statements involving longs take 113% more execution time than C++ longs. Note that Java ints are 32-bit and Java longs are 64 bits, whereas C++ ints and longs are each 32-bits on the Pentium chip.
- Java ints perform 21% faster than ints in C++.

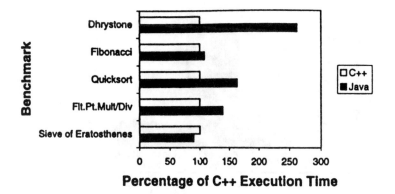

Percentage of C++ Execution Time

Exhibit 5.   Routine-Level CPU Benchmarks

All-in-all, paying attention to the choice of data-types can have a significant impact on performance. The single most striking example is the use of longs, which has no performance penalty in C++ on the Pentium, but is over twice as slow in Java, where it is a 64-bit "super long."

As summarized in Exhibit 5, routine-level CPU Benchmarks found:

- The Dhrystone benchmark, which is designed to be typical of the CPU part of what programs do (no I/O), takes 2.61 times as much time as in C++.
- The highly recursive Fibonacci number calculation performs 8% slower in Java when compared to C++.
- The QuickSort sorting algorithm performs takes 63% more time in Java when compared to C++.
- A floating point multiply and divide sequence takes 39% more time in Java when compared to C++.
- The Sieve of Eratosthenes code takes 10% less time in Java when compared to C++.

These measurements simply confirm that the measurements in the first two sections above can be reaped in a routine that does some specific useful task.

What is clear from the above tests is that unless one pays extraordinary attention to I/O performance, there is little hope of getting a reasonable whole program execution time when compared with what is possible in C++.

As summarized in Exhibit 6, routine level I/O test discovered the following:

- Writing 23-character records to a disk file takes 12.2 times as long in Java as in C++.
- Copying a file using readByte/writeByte of a Random AccessFile takes 505 times as long in Java as the corresponding getc/putc commands in C++.

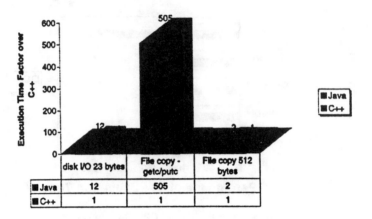

	disk I/O 23 bytes	File copy - getc/putc	File copy 512 bytes
■ Java	12	505	2
■ C++	1	1	1

Exhibit 6. Routine-Level I/O Test

- Copying the same file by using 512-byte write statements in Java takes only 56% more time than in C++.

What is clear from the above tests is that unless a programmer pays extraordinary attention to I/O performance, there is little hope of getting a reasonable whole program execution time when compared with what is possible in C++.

As summarized in Exhibit 7, a simple whole-program benchmark found that

- An electric bill processing benchmark takes 56 times as much time in Java as in C++.
- A string search of a file benchmark takes 63 times as long in Java as the C++ version.
- A bowling scores calculation program takes 224 times as long in Java as the C++ version.
- A TreeSort benchmark takes 15 times as long in Java as in C++.

The actual performance factors here probably have a great deal to do with the I/O usage in the above benchmarks, which we will try to improve below.

The Ctax benchmark found the following:

- A Java procedure call of a static function takes only 60% of the time of a global function in C++.
- A normal Java member function takes 8% less than in C++. Also, the normal member function in Java takes 45% more time than a static function.
- Since all Java member functions are virtual (i.e., exact function is decided at execution time), performance is identical to the above even if using polymorphism, overridden or final.

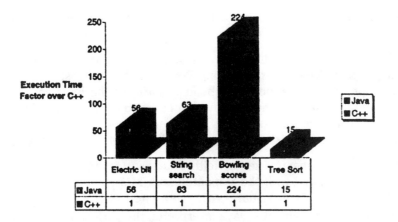

Exhibit 7. Simple Whole-Program Benchmarks

- The performance of passing parameters to a procedure is about 4% extra for each parameter used. (In C++ the factor is about 3.5% extra.)
- The performance of a new of a 4-byte class without member functions is identical to the corresponding C++ new.

The Screen Emulator Benchmark discovered the following:

- Summing up the contents of a CGA 4000 char screen buffer in Java takes 16% more time than in C++.
- Summing up a char[25][160] in Java takes 56% more time than above in Java (the increase in C++ is 27%).
- Summing up a Java class aspot {char a,b;} in an array of classes [25][80] takes113% more than item 1 (in C++ this takes 24% extra time).
- Summing up a Java class cga that has a member function caref(row,col), which returns a reference to an aspot class instance, takes 263% more than the item 1 above (in C++ this takes 216% extra).
- Accessing class variables of another class instance in Java is 33% slower than a local variable (in C++ it is 3% slower).

IMPROVING THE PERFORMANCE OF JAVA PROGRAMS

The purpose of the section above is to give an idea of the overall performance of the Java language using C++ as a framework of reference. The results were mixed; however, they seem to indicate that Java can be as fast as C++ thanks to the intervention of Just-In-Time (JIT) compilation, which does a "mini-compile" into native code as the program is being executed. Looking at the results we questioned our methods a great deal since *so many of the tests showed Java to be as fast or even faster than C++*. However, we were relieved to find that other experimenters have found similar results. [6.f]

To compound this evaluation we must add the obvious issue that not all Java compilers/Viewers are the same. We speculate that most of the relative gains in performance appear to depend primarily on the combination of the Java compiler used to generate the bytecode, and the Java Virtual Machine interpreter utilized for execution. To prove this point we tried a combination of compiles and viewers. Let us consider the following findings:

- One of the measurements yields an execution time of .155 seconds when compiled with the Symantec Java 1.0d compiler and executed with the Microsoft Visual J++ 1.1 Jview interpreter.
- If we use the Symantec Java interpreter, the performance doubles to .327 seconds.
- If we use the Microsoft Visual J++ compiler instead to compile and execute, the execution time doubles again to .675 seconds.
- If, on the other hand, we compile with the Microsoft Visual J++ compiler but run on the Symantec Java interpreter, the execution time is highest at .793 seconds.

A dramatic factor of the above measurements is that while Java "looks good" in most of the measurements, it also provides a disconcerting wide range of variability. We found the execution factor of Java/C++ to be 2, 5, 10, 100, or even 500 in our small number of measurements. To shed some light on this issue we attempted a few performance improvements on some of the benchmarks programs. For instance:

- The electric bill calculation benchmark started with an execution time of 23.79 seconds. Suspecting that the I/O time was causing the problem, we replaced the input file of 8000 integers with a table in memory. This had little effect. The only thing left was to put a *buffering into the print output file: this reduced the execution time by 53.5%* down to 11 seconds.
- The string search benchmark originally took 52 seconds (*a factor of 63 times* the C++ version), and was basically searching for a word in an input file and writing the matching line with some trivial formatting. We were already using Java's substring match facility, so there was not much obvious to improve. We again put the maximum file buffering into both the input data file and the output report. This had the dramatic effect of reducing execution time to 4.5 seconds (*a factor of 11.9 times* the C++ version).
- The bowling scores program took 47 seconds to execute (*a factor 191 times* the C++ version). For this program there is no input file and the output report is only a dozen lines. Yet when we put in maximum buffering for the report file the execution time went down to 43.5 seconds

(*a factor of 177 times* the C++ version). The rest of the program does some calculations on two-dimensional arrays.

- The Java program profiler was used to assess where the time is spent in individual applications. In a large medical application with many screens, the time to bring up a given screen for the first time was excessive and the profiler indicated that most of the time was spent in class initialization for the various classes involved. The reason for this was a great mystery and a workaround was attempted: create the classes involved right as the program starts when we do not even know the identity of the patient. Sure enough this reduced the excessive screen switching times substantially. We speculate that the Just-In-Time compiler might be generating native code for member functions for the class as it is being constructed (under VisualCafe).

I/O PERFORMANCE SUMMARY

So just from these few experiences one can see that I/O performance can be improved in a big way by simply using Buffered streams for both file input, file output, and report output. Also, Java has a readFully method that reads in an entire file in one I/O call. Now that virtual and actual memories are so large, this can be a dramatic way of achieving performance improvement, of course at some cost! In one medical data application, bringing up a patient screen *took 20 seconds*, an "eternity" if you're staring at the screen. When the reading of the patient file was changed to readFully, the time *was reduced to 0.4 seconds* (an improvement factor of 50). Obviously, those applications deemed to be real-time critical will benefit tremendously from this "read-ahead" protocol; on the other hand, not all applications need such a solution.

CPU PERFORMANCE SUMMARY

The CPU-bound portions of a program can also be improved with the knowledge derived from the measurements of the different data types described above. But one should always be aware of the relative performance of different compilers, and Java interpreters, which are changing fast as the Java development platforms come of age. It is important to point out that *Java applications are nearly 100% portable between any platform, operating system, and development system*. We took turns using the Sun development kit, Symantec VisualCafe, and Microsoft Visual J++ with no compatibility problems so far.

CONCLUSION

Java is probably a very important software development language for the present and the future. The combination of practical choices made in terms of language features for an Object-Oriented Programming Language, a standardized set of system interfaces for input/output, Graphical User Interfaces, networking, Operating System facilities, and a platform independent executable code will likely make it an important tool for some time to come.

While performance is a serious issue, our measurements show that Java bytecode behavior can approach executable C++ code in a very impressive way. However, we also witness cases in which much work is needed to make the gap between both languages shrink to a reasonable value. The authors have seen some production-level software developed that generally meets the performance requirements of an interactive Windows application. Also, the technology is still emerging so there will likely be more optimization of the JVM code generated, compilers that generate native code, a steady improvement in the performance of Java Virtual Machine emulators and Just-In-Time optimization, and even the possibility of auxiliary hardware CPU's that implement the Java Virtual Machine.

Recommended Reading

[1] Brian Kernigham, Dennis Ritchie, *The C Programming Language*, Prentice-Hall, 1978.

[2] P. Jalics was a researcher at the Xerox-Parc Palo Alto Research Center in Palo Alto California where the super strongly typed Mesa language was developed and used to implement an Operating System and applications.

[3] A. Fadlalla, P. Jalics, Victor Matos, "Portability of GUI based Object-Oriented Applications," *Systems Development Management*, Auerbach Publishers, accepted January 1997.

[4] James Gosling, "The Java Language: A White Paper," Sun Microsystems, 1993.

[5] "The Java Language Environment: A White Paper," Sun Microsystems, October 1995.

[6a] "The CaffeineMark Java Benchmark" from Pendragon Software.

[6b] "Jmark 1.0 Java Benchmark", *PC Magazine,* January 7, 1997, vol. 16, No. 1, p.182.

[6c] Doug Bell, "Make Java Fast: Optimize!," *JavaWorld,* http://www.java-world.com/javaworld.

[6d] Jonathan Hardwick, Java Optimization site: http://www.cs.cmu.edu/~jcl/java/optimization.html.

[6e] The Fhourstones 2.0 Benchmark (ANSI C,Java), tromp@cwi.nl.

[6f] f. "Jstones" by Sky Coyote, (Java, C++), sky@inergalact.com.

[7] P. Jalics, B. Blake, "Performance of Object-Oriented Programs: C++," *Systems Development Management,* Auerbach Publishers, 1992.

[8] Judith Bishop, *Java Gently,* Ed. Addison-Wesley, 1997.

[9] Patrick Naughton, *The Java Handbook,* Osborne – McGraw-Hill, 1997.

[10] Deitel and Deitel, *Java — How to Program*, Prentice Hall, 1997.

Chapter IV-4
Using Java to Improve Client/Server Applications

Nathan J. Muller

DESPITE THE INITIAL PROMISES held out for client/server solutions, today many are still dissatisfied with their implementation. Client/server solutions are too complex, desktops are too expensive to administer and upgrade, and the applications are not secure and reliable enough. Furthermore, client/server applications take too long to develop and deploy, and incompatible desktops prevent universal access. However, all this is about to change radically, as companies discover the benefits of the Internet and such new development tools as Java.

The Internet is fundamentally changing the way people in large organizations work and communicate with each other. Companies are looking to the TCP/IP-based Internet, as well as private intranets, for a variety of applications. In addition to electronic commerce, these networks are being used for interactive applications that involve customer access to corporate data bases, collaborative business applications among corporate staff, and the distribution of multimedia training courses.

The Internet is a large, packet-based client/server network held together by links that run the industry-standard suite of TCP/IP protocols, which offer the advantages of stability, reliability, and openness. The servers and the clients can be located anywhere in the world. The Internet's appeal is its platform independence, which means that virtually any client can have instant access, whether it is based on Windows, OS/2, Macintosh, UNIX, or any other type of operating environment. The same platform independence and ease of use makes this client/server network readily adaptable for use as a private intranet.

In fact, through the use of TCP/IP, client/server applications can be extended throughout the enterprise very economically. With tools such as Java, client/server applications can be developed faster, perform better, and even operate more reliably and securely than other enterprise computing solutions. With new protocols, such as the resource reservation protocol (RSVP), levels of bandwidth and delay can be assigned to bandwidth-intensive applications to improve their performance over packet-based intranets and the public Internet. New software development kits make it easy to integrate RSVP into multimedia applications.

THE INFLUENCE OF JAVA

Java is a relatively new language that originated with Sun Microsystems. Java is similar to C++, at least superficially, but it is really both a simplified version of C++ and an improvement on it. The language has been built to take full advantage of current software technologies. For example, it was designed to be completely object oriented. This is unlike C++, Object Pascal, and Visual Basic, which add object-oriented extensions to their languages but still retain the procedural orientation they had originally. Another way Java takes advantage of current technology is its support for multiprocessing via threads. Threads make it easy to create background processes in Java.

Java's approach enforces a way of thinking about problems that helps the programmer to be consistent. To give programmers a head start, Java includes a standard set of objects for performing many tasks, such as socket-based network communication and graphical windowing.

All of these features makes Java better suited to the development of distributed applications than other tools, especially the popular scripting languages. These languages, which include PERL and TCL, can also trace their lineage to the C language. The advantages Java brings to applications development include:

- *Performance.* Applications are fast because today's processors can provide efficient, virtual machine execution. The performance of graphical user interface (GUI) functions and graphical applications are enhanced through Java's integral multi-threading capability. Just-in-time (JIT) compilation and direct Java execution in silicon can deliver even higher performance.

- *Reliability.* Because the Java runtime system actively manages memory, management errors that plague traditional software development are eliminated.

- *Security.* Applications are more secure than those running native code because the Java runtime system (part of the Java Virtual Machine) checks all code for viruses and tampering before running it.

- *Portability.* Applications are able to run across computing platforms because the Java Virtual Machine is available on all systems.

- *Rapid Development.* Development is facilitated through code reuse, making it easier to test and faster to deploy applications via the Internet or corporate intranet.

JAVA ADVANTAGES

Java applications can run anywhere the Java Virtual Machine software is installed, including any Java-enabled browser, such as Microsoft's Internet Explorer and Netscape Communications' Netscape Navigator. The Virtual Machine functions exactly the same way on any "real" machine that hosts it. Java compilers generate code for the Java Virtual Machine, rather than for any specific computer or operating system. This automatically makes all Java programs into cross-platform applications. In being able to download and run any Java application, companies can free themselves of the complexity and client administration needs of traditional PCs.

Cost Savings

Sun estimates that the annual cost of operating Java-based "thin" clients in an enterprise environment is less than $2,500 per seat. In comparison, the typical expenses of managing heterogeneous desktop-centric clients or "fat clients," such as Windows 95, Windows NT, UNIX, OS/2, and Macintosh, are in the $10,0000-to-$15,000 range. According to The Gartner Group, located in Stamford CT, the annual cost of running fat clients is about $11,900 per seat. If only 10 percent of users needed to continue with a fat client for highly intense applications, tremendous savings could be realized for as many as 90% of an enterprise's clients. Thus, the savings from moving from a fat-client to a thin-client architecture could be as much as $84.6 million annually for a company with 10,000 clients (calculated as follows: $11,900 per fat client, minus $2,500 per thin client, multiplied by 10,000 = $94 million. Since approximately 90 percent of desktops can be converted to thin clients, the total annual cost savings is $84.6 million).

Aside from cost savings, Java can ensure that necessary features and functions are available to all enterprise users, with application front ends accessed through a common environment. This may be either a Java-enabled browser on an existing desktop platform or a more economical Java-based "network appliance." There is no need to discard current technology investments: Java applications can be enabled on currently installed computing platforms, followed by a phased migration to the most economic platforms. In the same way, Java-based client front ends can be added to existing legacy back ends in a phased, incremental approach.

SECURITY

Today's enterprise computing environments have a number of security vulnerabilities that are addressed by various Java features, including:

- *Strong Memory Protection.* Java eliminates the possibility that memory locations outside a program's boundaries can be maliciously or inadvertently read or corrupted, or both. This means Java applications, otherwise known as applets, cannot gain unauthorized memory access to read or change contents.
- *Encryption and Signatures.* Java supports the use of encryption technology to protect information from unauthorized users and verify through a signature that an applet came from an authorized source.
- *Rules Enforcement.* When Java objects and classes are used to represent corporate information entities, the rules governing the use of such objects can be explicitly stated. With these rules embedded within the objects themselves, the introduction of ad hoc access and manipulation methods can be closely controlled.

In addition, because Java devices get all of their programs and data over the network, they can be configured without local removable storage, thus enhancing security. This may be desirable to keep viruses out of the network or to keep data within the network, where it can be controlled.

Reliability

The scale and complexity of enterprise computing today results in an inherent degradation of reliability. This is because a failure at any point in the network can cause a failure in the application. Java, on the other hand, provides a seamless environment spanning the network, from server to client. The same Java applications run on all platforms and networks, and the simplicity of building the client and server software using the same Java programming platform significantly improves client/server reliability.

The Java language itself encourages the production of reliable, simple code. Because the language is object oriented, it promotes reuse, which, in turn, increases reliability. Once tested, objects can be used any number of times with the assurance of error-free code. Java also promotes sound software engineering practices with clear separation of interfaces and implementations and easy exception handling. Furthermore, Java's automatic memory management and lack of pointers remove one of the leading causes of programming errors.

Platform Independence

Traditional enterprise environments require the porting of applications to each separate client environment. This raises the cost of implementation on all clients to an extent that cannot be justified for many applications. In addition, certain application features or functions may not be available on particular platforms because of inherent limitations of the platform. The result is the deployment of incompatible applications, often platform dependent, to meet specific needs in various parts of the enterprise. Java eliminates this situation through the deployment of consistent Virtual Machine platforms, which can run any Java-compliant application program, across the enterprise. Consequently, the entire concept of porting an application to different client platforms becomes a thing of the past.

COMPARISON WITH INTERPRETATIVE LANGUAGES

Before Java, many developers used PERL (Practical Extension and Report Language) and other interpretative languages, such as TCL, to create common gateway interfaces (CGI) between servers and clients on the Internet. A CGI defines how information, collected from a user by means of a form in a Web browser, is passed through the Web server to an executable program and how the results are passed back and displayed to the user by the Web browser. In most cases, the CGI script converts the results into a HyperText Markup Language (HTML) document, which is sent back to the client.

With interpretive languages, the script must be compiled and run each time it is called. Ttime and memoryare required to start up and tear down the interpreter every time a script runs, which degrades performance. For complex tasks such as interactive multimedia and collaborative applications, performance bottlenecks can build up very quickly, especially when many users access the server at once.

When a CGI program is implemented in PERL, for example, two sources of bottlenecks exist. First, a process in which to run the PERL interpreter must be launched, which in turn runs the PERL program. Creating such a process once a minute is not a problem, but creating it several times a second is a major problem. Second, the PERL program takes time to send back the information it generates as output. Waiting for a small PERL script that does something simple like send the contents of an HTML form over e-mail is not a problem, but waiting for a large script that does something more complicated, such as allowing customers to access account information stored on a mainframe and execute financial transactions, definitely is a problem.

Netscape's Javascript is another interpretive language. Javascript is not really related to Java and is incapable of implementing true applications. Javascript is useful in adding items of interest to Web pages, such as scrolling text, digital clocks, prompts, windows, and other such features. To implement these and other features, Javascript code is embedded within the HTML page itself.

Java application code, in the form of applets, is dynamically downloaded from server to client, on demand. Java differs from the HTML and CGI approach in that the applets, once downloaded, can link directly with a data base server on the Internet. The applets do not need a Web server as an intermediary and, consequently, do not degrade performance. In some cases, the applications are stored in cache on a hard disk at the client location and in others, they are stored in DRAM. Because applications are delivered to the client only as needed, administration is done at the server, ensuring that users have access to the latest application release level.

IMPROVING NETWORK PERFORMANCE

TCP/IP-based intranets and the Internet use packet technology to move information between source and destination computers. However, some types of data, such as digitized voice and video, which are key components of multimedia applications, are time-sensitive, and packet technology cannot guarantee that the traffic will get to its destination without the quality undergoing severe degradation. Building a dedicated net or making the jump to ATM to improve performance are not realistic options for most companies because of their high cost.

Several protocols from the IETF (Internet Engineering Task Force) make it possible for packet networks to carry voice and video in addition to the bursty traffic that is already coming off the LAN to the wide-area intranet. The protocols can be implemented in routers and host software.

The resource reservation protocol (RSVP), for instance, works by permitting an application transmitting data over a routed network to request and receive a given level of bandwidth. Two classes of reservation are defined: A controlled load reservation provides service approximating "best effort" service under unloaded conditions; a guaranteed service reservation provides service that guarantees both bandwidth and minimal delay.

A key advantage of RSVP is that it works with any physical network architecture. In addition to Ethernet, it runs over other popular networks, such as token ring and FDDI, as long as IP is the underlying network protocol. This makes RSVP suitable for companywide intranets as well as the Internet, providing end-to-end service between them.

RSVP is implemented by the routers on the network. Cisco Systems, for example, not only supports RSVP but also two other quality of service mechanisms as well: priority output queuing and weighted fair queuing. With priority output queuing, network managers can classify traffic into four priorities and provide the available bandwidth to the queues in the order of their priority. The highest priority queue gets as much bandwidth as it needs before lower priority queues get serviced.

A variation of these schemes—custom output queuing—enables multiple queues to be defined, with each assigned a portion of the total bandwidth. For example, custom queuing gives mission-critical network application running over Novell's Internetwork Packet Exchange/Sequenced Packet Exchange (IPX/SPX) the ability to receive 40% of available bandwidth at all times; a video conference session on TCP/IP can be assigned 30% of capacity to ensure smooth reception, while other network applications can share the remaining 30%. When the video conference terminates, that amount of bandwidth goes back into the pool, ready to be reallocated to other network tasks.

Another technique used by Cisco routers is weighted fair queuing, which ensures that the queues do not starve for bandwidth and that the traffic gets guaranteed service. This is accomplished by classifying data into low-latency traffic and high-volume traffic and serving it fairly. This is similar in concept to the way supermarkets service customers with only a few items through express lanes and other customers through regular lanes.

The request is passed on to an upstream router and then to the next router until eventually a path is established that meets the bandwidth and latency requirements of the application. However, if the bandwidth is not available, the request is returned to the application as undeliverable. The application is then responsible for the reissuing the request at set intervals until the required bandwidth becomes available.

Several vendors, including Precept Software, Inc. and Microsoft Corp., offer various means to let programmers integrate RSVP into their applications. An RSVP Software Development Kit (SDK) from Precept is designed for creators of multimedia applications (e.g., videoconferencing, video broadcasting, Internet telephone) who want to ensure that these typically bandwidth-intensive applications are allocated sufficient network capacity for transmission over the public Internet or private IP-based networks.

Precept's RSVP SDK runs on Windows 95 and Windows NT systems. It includes a 32-bit RSVP service application that runs on top of the Winsock 1.1 or 2.0 interface, an Application Programming Interface (API) library consisting of a set of C++ language functions that are linked into the end-user application and provide an interface to the RSVP application, and a sample application that illustrates the use of the APIs.

Precept's modular approach to RSVP implementation (i.e., a standalone RSVP application running over Winsock 1.1 or 2.0) contrasts with that of Microsoft, which has announced plans to integrate RSVP directly into the stack, but only for Winsock 2.0.

Stack-integrated RSVP may be appropriate in several years, when Winsock 2.0 is ubiquitous. As yet, however, the specification for interfacing between RSVP and Winsock 2.0 is still evolving. More than 95% of users still have Winsock 1.1. Precept's approach can work for these users today; and later, as they upgrade to Winsock 2.0., Precept's API library will provide an easy migration path.

IP MULTICAST

The IETF has enhanced the basic IP communication protocol to support multicast delivery, a technique critical to conserving valuable network bandwidth as the Internet grows in use and as new data types such as audio and video multimedia transmissions proliferate. The deployment of these multicast enhancements will enable enterprise IP networks and the global Internet to dramatically increase the efficiency with which they use existing bandwidth.

One of these protocols, Protocol Independent Multicast (PIM), enables this multicast setup information to be communicated between the various routers so that only segments with clients wishing to receive the multimedia data stream actually get it. PIM allows data streams to be broadcast to multiple receivers using as little network bandwidth as possible. Instead of sending duplicate packets all over the network to reach the various receiving stations, PIM enables packet replication at the last possible router in the network. PIM communicates multicast setup information between routers so that only segments with clients wishing to receive the multimedia data stream actually get it, thus consuming as little network bandwidth as possible. The result is substantial savings in bandwidth and less processing burden on the sending host.

Although several specifications and implementations of multicast for routers, switches, end-node adapters and protocol stacks already exist, movement to full deployment has been slow, primarily because the infrastructure vendors (i.e., product suppliers and Internet service providers) have waited for application demand before investing in the necessary software upgrades. Meanwhile, applications continue to overload the network by saturating it with less efficient unicast (i.e., point-to-point) communication to multiple destinations because the infrastructure is not yet supporting multicast on a wide basis. The promising news is that several industry efforts currently are underway to address this situation.

SUMMARY

Java and other Internet technologies can offer a major improvement in simplicity, expense, security and reliability versus many of the enterprise computing environments in place today. Java reduces the time spent in application development, testing, and rollout, leaving more time and money for creating new added-value applications. Instant rollout of applications on an intranet Web site allows much shorter, more iterative application development cycles and the ability to react quickly to bugs, which results in happier users. Java builder tools from a number of vendors enable programmers to improve productivity even more. Developers are seeing productivity increases of as much as five times over traditional languages such as C or C++.

Network performance can be improved by assigning a class of service to each application through RSVP and by deploying multicast enhancements that enable enterprise IP intranets and the global Internet to dramatically increase the efficiency with which they use existing bandwidth.

As more corporations migrate to the more economic net-centric model of client/server computing, with most of the applications written in Java, there will be a corresponding need for developers to add in support for network protocols, such as RSVP and PIM, to ensure that their applications achieve optimal performance over the net.

Chapter IV-5
Programming Components: COM and CORBA

T.M. Rajkumar and David K. Holthaus

DATABASE TECHNOLOGIES HAVE EVOLVED from the 1970s' hierarchical databases to relational database management systems in the 1980s and to object databases and client/server systems in the 1990s. While the shift from central processing to client/server did not fully leverage object technology, Internet-based technologies promise to provide the infrastructure for objects. Web-based browsers are poised to become the universal clients for all types of applications. These applications increasingly depend on components, automation, and object layers linking systems.

During the same period, it became less and less possible for software developers to quickly, efficiently, and inexpensively develop all of the functions and modules demanded by customers. Therefore, software development methodologies for Internet and Web applications are increasingly focused on component technologies. Component technology breaks the application into intrinsic components and then glues them to create an application. Using components, an application is easier to build, make robust, and deliver quicker.

WHAT IS A COMPONENT?

A component is an independently delivered package of software services. A component is language independent and allows reuse in different language settings. Software components can be either bought from outside or developed in-house. Implementation requires that it must be possible to integrate them with other applications using standardized interfaces. They must implement the functionality specified in the interface efficiently. Components may be upgraded with new interfaces.

A component encapsulates methods (i.e., behavior) and data (i.e., attributes). Component must provide encapsulation, but inheritance is not as rigid a requirement. Components may include other components. Components do not necessarily have to be object-oriented, though a large majority of them are because it provides mechanisms to hide the data structure (i.e., encapsulation). Using objects makes components easier to understand and easier to create.

Components may be classified in many different ways. One such classification is based on their function within applications: business or technical components.

Business components usually include the logic that supports a business function or area. These must be developed in-house because it forms part of the core knowledge of an organization. In addition, business knowledge required to create them generally do not exist outside. They are also difficult to develop because organizations must standardize in some manner. There must be a common vision for the organization, and a common architecture must be present to develop business components.

Technical components are represented by elements that are generic and that can be used in a wide variety of business areas. These typically come in the form of GUI components, charting, or interapplication communication components.

A second classification is based on granularity of components. Fine-grained components such as class libraries and encapsulated components are typically small in size and are applicable in a wide range of applications. Although they have large reuse across multiple applications, they are close to code and provide limited productivity to a developer in large-scale applications.

Large-grained components provide broader functionality, but they have to be customized for use. A framework is an example of a large-grained component. Frameworks provide two benefits: flow of control and object-orientation. A framework can be thought of as groupings of components packages or components that belong to a logically related set and together provide a service. They provide a substrate or lattice for other functional components, and a framework can be composed of other frameworks. They also provide the flow of control within components. This helps in the scale of the solution developed.

Object orientation of frameworks helps with the granularity of the components. Ideally, during the assembly stage one wants a small number of large components. However, to increase generality of the solution created, one wants a large number of small components. Large components must be customized prior to delivering needed functionality. Frameworks allow developers to modify and reuse components at various levels of granularity. Frameworks are examples of "white-box" components (i.e., you can look inside the components to reuse it). With inheritance, the internals of parent classes are visible to subclasses in a framework. This provides a developer with flexibility to modify the behavior of a component. Thus,

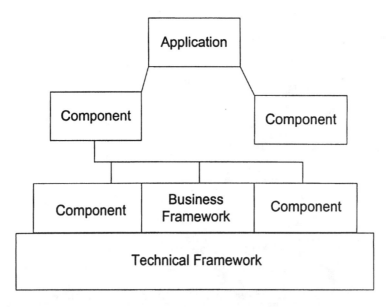

Exhibit 1.   Application Integration with Components

frameworks enable customization, allowing developers to build systems quickly using specialized routines.

Frameworks come in two categories: technical and business. Technical frameworks encapsulate software infrastructure such as operating system, graphical user interface (GUI), object request broker (ORB), and transaction processing (TP) monitor. Microsoft Foundation Class (MFC) is an example of such a framework. Business frameworks contain the knowledge of the objects in a business model and the relationships between objects. Typically, they are used to build many different components or applications for a single industry. Technically, while not based on components, Enterprise Resource Planning (ERP) such software as SAP are examples of business frameworks. An application is generally built with both technical and business frameworks (see Exhibit 1).

CLIENT/SERVER COMPONENTS

Client/server systems typically use three tiers — presentation layer, business layer, and data or server layer (see Exhibit 2). The objective behind the three tiers is to separate the business layer from the presentation and data layers. Changes in one layer are isolated within that layer and do not affect others. Within component technologies, the business layer communicates to the presentation layer and the data layer through an object bus, which is typically an object request broker (ORB). This layering makes the system very scalable.

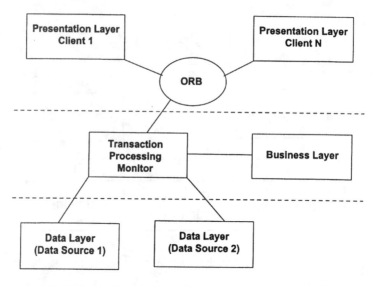

Exhibit 2.   Three-Layer Client/Server Architecture

An ORB is a standard mechanism through which distributed software objects and their clients may interact. Using an ORB, an object and its clients can reside on the same process or in a different process, which they can execute on different hosts connected by a network. The ORB provides the software necessary to convey the requests from clients to objects and responses from object to client. Since the ORB mechanism hides the details of specific locations, hosts, and conversion of data representation, and hides the underlying communication mechanism, objects and clients can interact freely without having to worry about many details. Thus, distributed applications can incorporate components written in different languages and are executable on different host and operating system platforms. This flexibility allows the data layer to be composed of both legacy software, and relational, object databases.

Business logic may reside on multiple server computers and data may reside on multiple servers. A TP monitor must be used to manage the business logic to provide centralized control. A TP monitor also manages the logic on the serves by providing an array of mission critical services such as concurrency, transactions and security, load balancing, transactional queues, and nested transactions. A TP monitor can prestart components, manage their persistent state, and coordinate their interactions across networks. TP monitors thus become the tool to manage smart components in a client/server system with components.

The real benefit of components in client/server applications is the ability to use the divide-and-conquer approach, which enables clients to scale through distribution. In this approach, an application is built as a series of ORBs. Since an ORB is accessible by any application running on a network, logic is centrally located. Developers can change the ORB to change the functionality of the application. If an ORB runs remotely, it can truly reflect a thin client. ORBs are portable and can be moved from platform to platform without adverse side effects to interoperability and provide for load balancing.

COMPONENT STANDARDS

Object models such as ActiveX, which is based on COM, CORBA, and Java Beans define binary standards so that each individual component can be assembled independently. All component standards share the following common characteristics:

- A component interface publishing and directory system
- Methods or actions invocable at run time by a program
- Events or notifications to a program in response to a change of state in an object
- Support for object persistence (to store such information as the state of a component)
- Support for linking components into an application

The following paragraphs describe each standard.

ActiveX, COM, and DCOM

ActiveX is based on COM technology, which formally separates interfaces and implementation. COM clients and objects speak through predefined interfaces. COM interfaces define a contract between a COM and its client. It defines the behavior or capabilities of a software component as a set of methods or properties. Each COM object may offer several different interfaces but must support at least one Iunknown. COM classes contain the bodies of code that implement interfaces. Each interface and COM class have unique IDs, IID, and CLSID, which are used by a client to instantiate an object in a COM server. There two types of object invocations:

- In process memory (DLLs), where a client and object share the same process space
- Out-of-process model, where a client and object live in different processes

Clients can call either easily. A remoting layer makes the actual call invisible to a client. An ActiveX component is typically an in-process server. An actual object is downloaded to a client's machine. DCOM is COM extended for supporting objects across a network. DCOM allows objects to be freely distributed over several machines and allows a client to instantiate objects on remote machines.

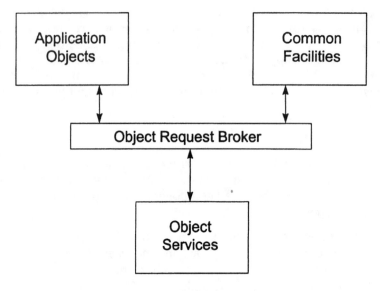

Exhibit 3.   CORBA Architecture

CORBA

The Common Object Request Broker Architecture (CORBA) is a set of distributed system standards promoted by an industry standards organization, the Object Management Group. It defines the ORB, a standard mechanism through which distributed software and their clients may interact. It specifies an extensive set of bus-related services for creating and deleting objects, accessing them by name, storing them in a persistent store, externalizing their states, and defining ad hoc relationships between them.

As illustrated in Exhibit 3, the four main elements of CORBA are the following:

- *ORBs*. This defines the object bus.
- *Services*. These define the system-level object frameworks that extend the bus. Some services are security, transaction management, and data exchange.
- *Facilities*. These define horizontal and vertical application frameworks that are used directly by business objects.
- *Application objects*. Also known as business objects or applications, these objects are created by software developers to solve business problems.

A Comparison of CORBA and DCOM

Both CORBA and DCOM use an interface mechanism to expose object functionalities. Interfaces contain methods and attributes as a common means of placing request to an object. CORBA uses standard models of inheritance from object-oriented languages. DCOM/ActiveX uses the concept of multiple interfaces supported by a single object. DCOM requires that multiple inheritance be emulated through aggregation and containment of interfaces.

Another difference is the notion of object identity. CORBA defines the identity of an object in an object reference, which is unique and persistent. If the object is not in memory, it can be reconstructed based on the reference. DCOM in contrast defines the identity in the interface, the reference to the object itself is transient. This can lead to problems when reconnecting because the previously used object cannot be directly accessed.

Reference counting is also different in both. A DCOM object maintains a reference count of all connected clients. It uses pinging of clients to ensure that all clients are alive. CORBA does not need to do remote reference because its object reference model allows the re-creation of an object if it had been prematurely deleted.

CORBA uses two application program interfaces (APIs) and one protocol for object requests. It provides the generated stubs for both static and dynamic invocation. In addition, dynamic skeleton interface allows changes during runtime.

DCOM provides two APIs and two protocols. The standard interface is based on a binary interface that uses method pointer tables called *vtables*. The second API, object linking and embedding (OLE) automation, is used to support dynamic requests through scripting languages. OLE automation uses the IDispatch method to call the server.

CORBA is typically viewed as the middleware of choice for encapsulating legacy systems with new object-oriented interfaces, since it provides support for languages such as COBOL and mainframe systems. DCOM has its roots in desktop computing and is well supported there.

Java Beans

Java Beans enables the creation of portable Java objects that can interoperate with non-Java object systems. Unlike ActiveX, which predominately operates in Windows environments, Java Beans is intended to run in diverse environments as long as there exists a Java Virtual Machine that supports the Java Bean API. Java Beans provides the standard mechanisms present in all the component technologies. This standard is still continuing to evolve.

Comparison of Java and ActiveX

A trusted Java Bean has all the capabilities of a Java application. However, if you run a Java Bean that has not been signed by a digital source, its capabilities are limited like any other applet. Java also has limited multimedia support. In contrast, ActiveX objects cannot run from the Web unless they are trusted and have access to all of Windows's capabilities. Hence, ActiveX supports multimedia.

ActiveX and Java both use digitally signed certificates to protect against malicious attacks. In addition, Java Beans is available for a large number of machines and has cross-platform capability. ActiveX is most widely available on the Windows desktop.

Irrespective of the technology standard, bridges, available from different vendors, can translate between standards. Hence, organizations should choose a standard in which they have the greatest expertise for analysis, design, and development.

HOW TO DESIGN AND USE COMPONENTS

As shown in Exhibit 1, applications are built from the composition and aggregation of other, simpler components, which may build on frameworks. Application design is broken into component and application development. Component development is divided into component design and implementation. A good knowledge of an application's domain is necessary to develop frameworks and components. In general, the steps of domain definition, specification, design, verification, implementation, and validation must be done prior to application. The following sections explain these steps.

Domain Definition. This defines the scope, extent, feasibility, and cost justification for a domain. An organization must define the product it plans to build as well as define the different business and technical areas that must be satisfied through the use of software.

Domain Specification. This defines the product family (i.e., framework) used for application engineering. It includes a decision model, framework requirements, and a hierarchy of component requirements. The decision model specifies how components will be selected, adapted, and reused to create complete application systems. Product requirements are arrived at by analyzing similarities in functions, capabilities, and characteristics as well as variances among them. The component part of the product family is represented hierarchically. When an organization considers components, it must consider not only what the component will do for the domain now but also in the future.

Domain Design. A domain expert must work with component designer to use a modeling methodology and extract the design patterns that occur in that domain. Design patterns are repeatable designs used in the construction of an application. The architecture, component design, and generation design are specified here. Architecture depicts a set of relationships among the components such as hierarchical, communication, and database. Component design describes the internal logic flow, data flows, and dependencies. Generation design is a procedure that describes how to select, adapt, and compose application systems using the decision model and architecture.

Domain Verification. This process evaluates the consistency of a domain's requirements, specification, and design.

Domain Implementation. During this procedure, components are either developed or acquired off the shelf to fit the architecture. Each component must be tested within the common architecture it supports as well as any potential architecture. Certification of components must be acquired when necessary. It must also decide how to store it in repositories, the implementation of application generation procedures, and how to transition to an assembly mode.

Domain Validation. This evaluates the quality and effectiveness of the application engineering support. Application engineering consists of the following:

- *Defining requirements.* In this process, an application model that defines a customer's requirements is defined. This model uses the notation specified in the domain engineering steps. Typically, a use case model can be used to identify requirements. Use cases are behaviorally related sequences of transactions, that a user of a system will perform in a dialogue
- *Selecting components and design.* Using rules in the decision model, reusable components are selected based on the component specification (capabilities and interfaces) and design (component logic and parameters).
- *Generating software.* The application is then generated by aggregating components and writing any custom software.
- *Testing.* Testing involves the testing of use cases, components, integration testing, and load testing.
- *Generating documentation.* The application documentation is created.

MANAGING THE COMPONENT LIFE CYCLE PROCESS

Developing with components means an organization must move from doing one-of-a-kind development to a reuse-driven approach. The aim is to reorganize the resources to meet users' needs with greater efficiency. The steps in this process are discussed in the following sections.

Establishing a Sponsor. This involves identifying component reuse opportunities and shows how their exploitation can contribute to an organization's IS goals. Sponsors must be identified and sold on the various ideas.

Exhibit 4. Assessment of Component Potential for Reuse

Concern	What to Ask
Domain potential	In the given domain, are there applications that could benefit from reuse?
Existing domain components	Are expertise and components available?
Commonalities and variables	Is there a sufficient fit between need and available components? Can they be customized?
Domain stability	Is the technology stable? Do the components meet stable standards? Are the components portable across environments?

Exhibit 5. Assessment of an Organization's Capability to Reuse Components Columns

Application Development	Component Development	Management	Process and Technology
Component identification for use in application	Needs identification, interface, and architecture definition	Organizational commitment, planning	Process definition and integration
Component evaluation and verification	Components needs and solutions	Managing security of components	Measurement and continuous process improvement
Application integrity	Component quality, value, security, and reusability determination	Intergroup (component and application) coordination	Repository tool support and training

Developing a Plan. This plan should guide the management of the component development process. The plan includes the following:

1. *Reuse assessment.* This assessment should evaluate the potential opportunity for reuse, identify where the organization stands with respect to reuse, and evaluate the organization's reuse capability Exhibits 4, 5, and 6 can be used to conduct the assessment.
2. *Development of alternative strategies.* On the basis of the assessment, an organization can develop a strategy to implement and align the process as well as choose the appropriate methodologies and tools.
3. *Development of metrics.* In the planning stage for implementation, metrics must be used to measure success.

Implementation. The organization finally implements the plan. Incentives can be used to promote reuse by individuals and the organization.

296

Exhibit 6. Organizational Reuse Capability Model

Stage	Key Characteristics

Opportunistic	• Projects individually develop reuse plan
	  – Existing components are reused
	  – Throughout project life cycle reuse of components is identified
	  – Components under configuration and repository control

Integrated	• Reuse activities integrated into standard development process
	  – Components are designed for current and anticipated needs
	  – Common architectures and frameworks used for applications
	  – Tools tailored for components and reuse

Leveraged	• An application-line reuse strategy is developed to maximize component reuse over a set of related applications
	  – Components are developed to allow reuse early in the life cycle
	  – Process performance is measured and analyzed
	  – Tools supporting reuse are integrated with the organization's software development efforts

Anticipating	• New opportunities for reuse of components build on the organization's reuse capability
	  – Effectiveness of reuse is measured
	  – Organizations reuse method is flexible and can adapt to new process and product environment

CONCLUSION

Component technology is changing the way client/server applications are being developed. Supporting tools for this software environment are rapidly emerging to make the transition from regular application development to a component-based development. With proper training of staff, planning, and implementation, organizations can smoothly transfer to this new mode of development and rapidly develop and efficiently deliver client/server applications.

Chapter IV-6
Secure and Managed Object-Oriented Programming
Louis B. Fried

SOFTWARE DEVELOPMENT HAS always been expensive. Those who pay the bill dream of obtaining results for lower cost and in less time. The search for tools to realize this dream has produced data base management systems (DBMSs), query systems, screen development tools, fourth-generation languages, graphic programming aids, and code generators. The ultimate tools, however, will free developers from programming altogether, and the best way to do this is to reuse existing code.

The various tools that developers already use are effective because they reuse code in some sense. For example, using DBMSs, programmers need not develop their own access routines as they were forced to do many years ago.

The developers of object-oriented programming (OOP) languages and tools promise to take the reuse of code to new levels, but there are ongoing debates about the benefits and the potential problems associated with object-oriented programming. For each argument there are various responses.

THE OVERRIDING BENEFIT: REUSABLE SOFTWARE

One concern is that objects require continuous maintenance and enhancement to keep up with the changing needs of the business. However, software has always required maintenance.

Another concern is that the analysis task required to identify and define appropriate objects is formidable. Advocates of object-oriented programming respond that the best software development efforts result from spending more time in the definition and specification phases; in addition, developers can reuse objects for long-term savings.

0-8493-9979-3/99/$0.00+$.50
© 1999 by CRC Press LLC

In fact, proponents of object-oriented programming point out that the need to define class and subclasses of objects, the objects themselves, and the attributes, messages, methods, and interrelationships of objects forces a better model of the system to be developed. Many objects developed in OOP code will not be reused; however, the real benefit is that OOP code is usually more lucid and well organized than are traditional coding methods. The process that forces analysts to define the object hierarchies makes the analysis more familiar with the business in which the application will be used.

When these problems and objections are analyzed, many of them can be discounted; however, some remain. Viewed in isolation, object-oriented programming is simply an attractive way to facilitate structured, self-documenting, highly maintainable, and reusable code. In the context of enterprisewide application building, object-oriented programming does present unique challenges whose solutions require additional tools and management methods.

THE OOP ENVIRONMENT

As object-oriented techniques gradually find a place in corporate programming departments, there will be attempts to expand the use of this technology from single applications to broad suites of applications and from the sharing of objects among a limited group of applications developers to use by developers and users throughout the organization. To accomplish this expansion of use, object-oriented programming will need to be used within a development framework that is composed of computer-aided software engineering (CASE) tools implemented in a distributed, cooperative processing environment.

A likely scenario of the way in which organizations will want to use object-oriented programming in the future is as follows:

- Objects will be used by decentralized development groups to create applications that are logically related to one another and for which common definitions (i.e., standards) are imposed by various levels of the organization.

- Users will employ objects to develop limited extensions of basic applications or to build local applications, in much the same way spreadsheets and query systems are currently used. Users may access corporate data bases in this environment through objects that encapsulate permitted user views of information.

- Object-oriented programming will become integrated with CASE platforms not only through the inclusion of object-capable languages but through repositories of objects that contain both the objects themselves and the definitions of the objects and their permitted use. Improved

CASE tools that can manage and control versions and releases of objects as well as programs will be needed.

This scenario envisions optimum use and benefit from object-oriented programming through extensive reuse of proven code with a framework that allows authorized access to objects.

The current status of object-oriented programming is far from this scenario. The effective use of object-oriented programming depends on the ability to solve problems related to two major areas of concern: the management of the object inventory and the preparation of information security in an object-oriented development environment.

MANAGING THE OBJECT INVENTORY

Objects in the inventory must reside in a repository that uses an object-oriented DBMS. Objects are identified by classes and subclasses. (Object class definitions are themselves objects.) This identification provides a means of inventory management. For example, retrieving an object within a class called Accounts Payable would help to narrow the domain being searched for the object. A further narrowing can be done by finding a subclass called Vendor's Invoice, and so forth. Polymorphism allows the same object named to be used in different contexts, so the object Unit Price could be used within the context of the Vendor's Invoice subclass and the Purchase Order subclass. Some relational DBMSs also allow polymorphism.

Several problems arise as a result of this organizational method. To take advantage of the reusability of objects, the user must be able to find the object with as little effort as possible. Within the classification scheme for a relatively straightforward application, this does not appear to present a substantial problem.

Most organizations undertake the development of applications on an incremental basis. That is, they do not attempt to develop all applications at once. Furthermore, retroactively analyzing and describing the data and process flows of the entire organization has failed repeatedly. By the time all the analysis is completed, the users have lost patience with the IS department.

It is feasible to limit objects to an application domain. However, limiting objects to use within the narrow domain of a single application may substantially reduce the opportunities for reuse. This means that developers will have to predict, to the extent possible, the potential use of an object to ensure its maximum utility.

Cross-Application Issues

It is possible to establish a class of objects that may be called cross-application objects. Such objects would be the same regardless of the context within which they were designed to be used. For example, the treatment of data related to a specific account in the corporate chart of accounts may always be the same. The word *account* appears in many contexts and uses throughout a business. Therefore, another approach to this problem is that some objects may be assigned an attribute of cross-application usability.

As more object-oriented applications are created, the typical data dictionary or repository will not be able to serve the needs of users for retrieving objects. Analysts and programmers who are required to move from one application to another to perform their work may find the proliferation of objects to be overwhelming. The IS department will need to develop taxonomies of names and definitions to permit effective retrieval.

Developing and maintaining a taxonomy is in itself a massive effort. For example, a large nuclear engineering company realized that the nuclear power plants it had designed would be decommissioned and dismantled in 50 years. The personnel responsible for dismantling a plant needed to know all about the plant's 50 years of maintenance in order to avoid potential contamination of the environment and injury to themselves.

The company discovered that various names were used for identical parts, materials, and processes (all of which are objects) in the average plant. Furthermore, because the plants were built throughout the world, these objects had names in many different languages. If personnel could not name an object, they could not find the engineering drawings or documents that described the object. If they searched for only the most likely names, they would overlook information that was stored under an unusual name.

A taxonomy project was initiated to adopt and use standard terminology for all components of the plant and all information relating to those components. Within two years, a massive volume was assembled. Still, several problems surfaced. It was impossible to know when the taxonomy would be complete. New terms had to be created to avoid duplication. The taxonomy manual was so large that engineers and other employees refused to use it.

This example can provide some obvious guidelines. A comprehensive, detailed data model will never be completed because the organization constantly changes while the model is being created. Instead, a high-level process and information model of the organization should be designed to indicate potential or existing relationships between data. This model will also be used to identify data and objects that can be reused in future applications development projects. Limited domains or business processes should be chosen for the creation of objects within an application. Also, object-naming conventions and an object-inventory system should be established before any object-oriented application is developed. Most important, defining objects, as well as developing applications, is an incremental process and objects will not be reused if they cannot be easily found.

One dimension of the problem of naming and defining objects has been examined. In a world of increasingly distributed processing and decentralized use of computing, IS must also consider the following:

- Analysts and programmers will not be under centralized control in all instances.
- Other personnel, such as engineers, clerical staff, and knowledge workers, will use objects to create their own programs.

Retrieval Methods to Facilitate Reuse

The ability of users to develop their own programs and applications is one of the greatest benefits that can be obtained from object-oriented programming and should not be ignored. Nor can the demands of an increasingly computer-literate clientele be refused. This means that the methods for retrieving objects must be available to all users for a relatively small amount of effort. If not, objects will not be reused.

With users as a recognized component of the management problem, another concern emerges. Not only must objects cross application domains, they must exist at various levels of the organization. For example, an object may be defined as applicable throughout the organization in a given context (i.e., a Standard object). Such an object may be called a Corporate object either through being in a class of corporate objects or by having a standard attribute as a corporate object. Another object may be applicable only within a specific strategic business unit and may be called, for example, an Engine Manufacturing Company object. At the next level, an object may be called a Casting Division object. Objects can be described in this manner down to the level of the desktop or the computer-controlled machine tool.

Two types of tools may come to partial rescue in resolving this problem. Text search and retrieval systems allow users to search for objects within various contexts. The result, however, could be the retrieval of many possible objects from a repository, compelling the user to evaluate them before a selection is possible.

An approach is needed that allows the user to obtain a limited number of possible objects to solve a problem and yet does not force the organization to develop a taxonomy or limit the use of terms. Self-indexing files for nonhierarchical search may prove helpful, but this may mean using the object-oriented DBMS repository in a manner not compatible with its structure.

Regardless of the method used, there is a clear need to establish and conform to documentation standards for objects so that searches for objects will return meaningful results. One possible solution is to use an expert system in conjunction with a text search and retrieval system. Expert systems can accomplish classification and are capable of supporting natural language interfaces. Ideally, the user could describe to the system the nature of the object needed and the system could find the most appropriate object. The user could then describe the application at a high level and the system would find and assemble all appropriate objects that fit the system context.

Object Maintenance

When objects are used throughout a large organization it must be assumed that they will reside in repositories on a variety of machines in many locations. Each of these repositories must be maintained in synchronization with the master repository of approved objects for the organization and its divisions. Distributed environments imply additional problems that must be solved before object-oriented techniques can work successfully.

For example, if objects are automatically replaced with new versions, there must be a mechanism for scheduling the compilation or relinking of programs that use the affected objects. If objects are used in an interpretive mode (rather than being compiled into machine code), replacements will automatically affect their use in existing procedures, perhaps to the detriment of the application. Some methods currently used to maintain distributed data base concurrency and to control the distribution of microcomputer programs throughout a network may be adapted to solve part of this problem. Another approach may adapt the messaging capabilities of objects to send notification of a potential change to any subobject within the hierarchy of the object being replaced.

Another problem is that identical objects may need to be developed in different languages to meet the needs of users of different hardware systems. Even if objects are developed in the same language, the options are to use either a restricted subset of the language compatible with all potential environments or a language that allows compiler flags to be placed on code and alternative versions of the code embedded in the object. Neither of these choices is attractive, and the first may require other classes of objects to differentiate between identical objects used on different machines (though polymorphism can help in this respect). As a result, the testing process for new or replacement objects becomes more complex.

Organizations will also need to assign someone the job of deciding which objects should be distributed to which of the distributed repositories. Standard corporate objects may have wide distribution, whereas others may require more circumscribed distribution. Object and object-class management become major administrative tasks.

OBJECT SECURITY

To use objects in developing programs or applications, users, analysts, and programmers need access to these objects. Such indiscriminate access provides a real threat to the security of objects.

Information security has been defined as consisting of three primary properties: availability, confidentiality, and integrity. As applied to the object inventory, these may be defined as follows:

- Making objects available to those who need to use them, when they need to use them.
- Ensuring the integrity of objects by preventing unauthorized changes.
- Ensuring the confidentiality of objects by preventing unauthorized access.

Current repositories and directories generally assume that all personnel authorized to access the directory are authorized to access any item in the directory. This line of thinking does not do for an object inventory.

Access Control

An object inventory requires an extended set of security controls to make its use safe for the organization. Such controls, required to preserve integrity, must be implemented at the object attribute level. For example, in a payroll file the individual salary rate (an attribute) may be restricted to certain users. The attribute must therefore have an attached attribute (sometimes called a facet) that specifies which programs are allowed to read the attribute Salary Rate. Alternatively, the salary rate attribute could have a facet that is a function that returns an empty field or no data to nonauthorized callers. In essence, each object defined in the inventory may need to be individually controlled as well as controlled within a set or class of objects.

A solution is to ensure that each object in the inventory can be separately locked to prevent change. When an object is accepted into inventory, the lock is activated. A system that truly intends to protect the integrity of the objects would not permit any change to a locked object. If an object needed to be changed, it would have to be deleted and replaced by an approved, tested replacement. Furthermore, a limited group of authorized inventory managers would be the only personnel able to delete an object. Finally, a safeguard system would automatically file all deleted objects in a locked, backup repository file so that they may be retrieved in the event of incorrect removal.

Locking logic itself is a problem. In current DBMSs, the problem referred to as a deadly embrace—that is, two parties concurrently attempting to update a record by different logical paths—has been solved. When the locking mechanism must deal with atomic objects rather than transactions or records, the solution may be more difficult.

Ownership

In current security practice, the levels of security assigned to information are designated by the application owner. Each application owner has the duty to specify who may access application information and under what conditions. When objects are in common use, new ways of designating ownership become necessary and certain questions must be addressed: Who owns an object that is used across many applications? Who owns a corporate object?

When the ownership decision is made, the next issue is how to assign access permission. Some access permissions may be assigned by sets or classes of workers. (In the new alliance model of business operations, it is not only employees who work with an organization's systems but also its suppliers and customers.) Permissions may be granted by levels in the management hierarchy, by sets of people in specific functional areas, by organization unit, and by individual. Permissions need to include (as they do today) the authorization to perform certain functions with an object. Functions for which authorization may need to be defined include read only, delete, add, copy, use, and lock.

Integrity

Integrity may also be addressed by attaching rule-based logic to classes, subclasses, and objects to describe the conditions under which they may be used. The marriage of artificial intelligence techniques and object data base structure may be necessary to prevent misuse of objects.

Availability of objects partially depends on systems availability and network availability, for example. Another concern is that the object is appropriately distributed throughout the organization's processing resources so that it can be conveniently accessed by authorized personnel regardless of the time or location. In large organizations, objects may be distributed in repositories on a variety of machines in various locations, so the potential for erroneous use is multiplied.

Confidentiality

Confidentiality may require that two levels of information access are designated for objects. One level of access may be to permit a user to determine whether a desired object or reasonable facsimile exists in the inventory. This level may permit authorized personnel only to learn of the existence of objects and to obtain a brief description. A second level of access control may be needed to permit users to actually read the object content itself.

Confidentiality can be breached in another way. The aggregation of intelligence through repeated access to selected data bases of information is a threat to current systems. When the atomic level of applications is downsized to objects, a significant change occurs. The aggregation of objects into new relationships may permit combinations of information that would not usually be available to users, thereby enabling unauthorized users to assemble intelligence to which they are not entitled.

The property of inheritance—in which an object subclass contains information about the methods and structure of the superclass it is related to—presents special concerns. A classification mechanism may be needed that defines permitted relationships among objects and establishes authorization for object relationships, perhaps as a facet or attribute. Alternatively, it is possible to maintain independence between data and code that permits access controls to be placed on the data at the user view or field levels within a data base.

ACTION PLAN

Many potential problems faced by object-oriented programming are similar to those that have plagued other systems development tools. However, to satisfy customer demands, these problems have been addressed by development tool vendors.

The potential benefits of object-oriented programming appear to be substantial. However, until this technology enables users and managers to manage and protect their information assets, object-oriented programming should be used under strictly controlled circumstances. As such, the following guidelines are recommended:

- The current lack of methods to manage inventories of objects poses a potential problem to effective widespread reuse. The inventory management capabilities of proposed OOP development systems should be examined and only those tools with which management methods will work should be used.
- Without solving the problems related to object security, it may not be possible to protect information that is widely used throughout the organization.
- Corporations are real-world entities that change according to changes in business needs and strategies. A comprehensive, detailed data model will never be completed because the organization will always undergo changes. Building an enterprise data model should not be attempted. Instead, a high-level process and information model should be designed to indicate potential or existing relationships between data. Then, a limited domain or business process should be chosen for object-oriented development.
- Object-naming conventions and an object-inventory system should be established before any object-oriented application is developed. For subsequent development projects, the high-level process model should be used to identify potentially reusable data and objects.
- Vendors should be urged to develop appropriate inventory management and security control tools. As soon as such tools are available and proven, they should be acquired.

Chapter IV-7
Creating Effective Batch SQL Jobs

Len Dvorkin

IN RECENT YEARS, THE ARRIVAL OF MATURE RELATIONAL DATABASES powerful enough to handle mission-critical functions has provided systems developers with the ability to perform complex processing much more simply than was possible using traditional data repositories and languages.

This power, however, has represented a double-edged sword when combined with traditional programming approaches and styles. When complex business requirements are combined with the power of SQL, the result can be code that is syntactically correct, but that runs poorly or not at all at production-level data volumes.

This problem commonly occurs during the creation of online transaction processing (OLTP) systems, when a frequently encountered scenario has developers coding and testing an application in a test environment, certifying it as ready for production, and watching it fail with a higher number of users, more data, and so on. Fortunately (or unfortunately), this type of failure generally manifests itself directly and clearly in the form of an online function that stops working or only performs slowly.

A more subtle trap relates to batch processing in SQL. Most significant DBMS-based systems have batch components to support them. These components include:

- *Internal processing:* Using data from tables in the system to update other tables within the system
- *Data loading:* Updating the system's database with data from other systems
- *Data extraction:* Creation of tables or flat files for use by an outside system
- *Reporting:* Collection of data from within the system in order to present it for user review

These components are not as "flashy" as their online cousins; however, they have the potential to seriously impact a system if they are not created and managed correctly. And batch routines are here to stay — the power represented by relational databases does not exempt mature systems from requiring tasks to run automatically and unattended, separately from any online components.

Most of the recurring problems in batch SQL are also frequently encountered when creating SQL for online purposes — after all, the language is the same. However, given the usual purposes of batch SQL, certain traps tend to manifest themselves with annoying frequency, even when coded by experienced developers. This chapter describes principles and techniques that represent good practice when designing any SQL job, but seem to be forgotten or left out more often when the batch environment is concerned (see Exhibit 1).

SQL CODING PRINCIPLES

Joins

A common operation in batch SQL involves combining data from multiple tables that have a relationship to each other. These may be a series of transaction tables coming from different sources or a single transaction table with several foreign keys that need to be referenced.

In these cases, it can be hard to resist the power of SQL's ability to join database lookups across multiple tables. While careful design of queries can result in a tightly tuned, fast-performing join, most databases use rules coded in an internal optimizer to examine a query and develop the plan that will guide the database engine in processing the query. In complicated joins, it is not uncommon for the database optimizer to make an unexpected decision on the join order and turn what should be a simple query into a large, slow-running database killer.

For example, assume that a report extract is needed for a table with four foreign keys to code tables. As a join, this could be coded as follows:

```
INSERT INTO report_table
SELECT t.column1,
       t.column2,
       a.description,
       b.description,
       c.description,
       d.description,
       <other columns>
FROM transaction_table t,
       code_table1 a,
```

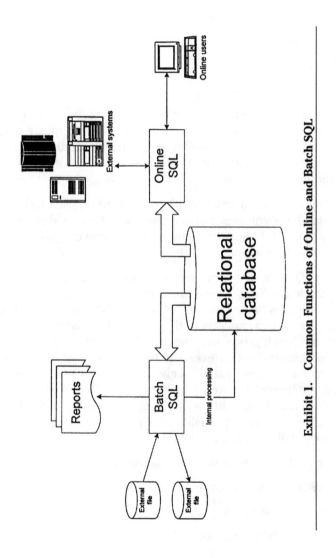

Exhibit 1. Common Functions of Online and Batch SQL

```
        code_table2 b,

        code_table3 c,

        code_table4 d

    WHERE t.code_a = a.code

    AND t.code_b = b.code

    AND t.code_c = c.code

    AND t.code_d = d.code

    AND <other conditions>
```

Under low-volume conditions, or under high-volume conditions when the database statistics are current and the database's query optimizer is working effectively, this query will run well. The first table to be examined will be *transaction_table*, and code values found there will be used to reference the required code tables.

Sometimes, though, a large number of *where* clauses or a significant change in database volumes can confuse the optimizer, resulting in disastrous query plans (building the result set in the above example from one of the code tables, for instance).

In a batch SQL job, we are generally not worried about shaving seconds off of transactions. What we are much more interested in is predictable, arithmetic increases in performance time directly related to database table volumes. (There are exceptions to this statement — some systems have a very restricted batch processing time window within which their processing must be completed. However, the techniques in this chapter can be used to reduce the server load of a given batch job, or to permit multiple jobs to run concurrently, potentially fixing these "batch window squeeze" situations.) To that end, splitting the single multitable join into separate queries involves a relatively small performance penalty in exchange for a predictable overall run time. For instance:

```
    loop for each qualified record in transaction_table:

        SELECT:col1 = t.column1,

            :col2 = t.column2,

            :code_a = t.code_a,

            :code_b = t.code_b,

            :code_c = t.code_c,

            :code_d = t.code_d,

            <other columns>
```

```
FROM transaction_table t
WHERE <other conditions>

SELECT:description_a
FROM code_table1
WHERE code = :code_a


SELECT:description_b
FROM code_table1
WHERE code = :code_b

SELECT:description_c
FROM code_table1
WHERE code = :code_c

SELECT:description_d
FROM code_table1
WHERE code = :code_d

INSERT INTO report_table
VALUES (:col1,
        :col2,
        :description_a,
        :description_b,
        :description_c,
        :description_d,
        <other columns>)
end loop
```

At the cost of a few extra lines of code, the 5-table join in the first example becomes a bullet-proof routine with predictable performance under virtually all conditions of data volume or database statistics.

Note that the number of required database lookups in the code above has not changed from the more complicated example, leaving only a small net extra cost in separate processing of the SQL statements. If these statements are running inside the database engine (in a stored procedure, for instance), the overhead becomes even smaller.

DECLARATIONS AND INITIALIZATIONS

The top section of any routine should contain declarations of any variables that will be used in the job. If a data value is likely to be changed during testing or after the job is running in production, consider changing it to a "constant" variable. This makes it easier to read and maintain the code. Similarly, table columns containing code values are easier to deal with if their code values are stored in constants. Consider the example below:

```
declare:MIN_DOLLAR_VALUE float = 10.0

declare:SALE char(1) = "S"

declare:RETURN char(1) = "R"


<other processing>


SELECT sum (trans_value)

FROM trans_table

WHERE trans_value >:MIN_DOLLAR_VALUE

AND trans_type = :SALE
```

Read Once, Write Once

Depending on the specific driver program type and database implementation being used, the cost of an SQL table hit is easily 10 times or more expensive than processing a simple logic statement. However, many batch programs are profligate in their use of table access statements. In the example below, a single row in a source table is read once for its index value, a second time for a lookup value, and a third time for other information needed to write to an output table:

```
loop for each qualified record in transaction_table:

    SELECT:index_field = t.index_field

    FROM transaction_table t

    WHERE t.transaction_date = <today>


    < processing of the record >


    SELECT:transaction_type = a.type_description

    FROM transaction_table t,

        code_table1 a

    WHERE t.index_field = :index_field

    AND t.type_code_a = a.type_code_a
```

```
< other processing of the record >

INSERT INTO report_table
SELECT t.column1,
       t.column2,
       :transaction_type,
       <other columns>
FROM transaction_table t
WHERE t.index_field = :index_field
end loop
```

When examining this program structure, developers often explain that this is a straightforward approach to satisfying the program's requirements — what's wrong with it? They may be influenced by the method in which one reads a traditional/hierarchical data store, where the first access to a record brings all of its data directly into a program cache, and subsequent access to fields on the record are virtually "free" reads of local memory.

However, this is certainly not the case when we are discussing database access. Each time that the (same) row in a table is referenced in a select statement, a nontrivial amount of database work must take place. Most database implementations will cache the affected data row in its local memory pages after the first read, preventing hard disk access in subsequent reads. However, the overhead cost of parsing the statement, determining a query path, supporting a join, identifying the desired row, determining that it is resident in memory, etc. is still significantly higher than that of a simple reference to a local variable in the program's memory space.

The routine above can be rewritten with a minimum of effort to access each table only once, retrieving all columns that will be required in this select statement and saving them locally for use later in the process:

```
loop for each qualified record in transaction_table:

SELECT:index_field = t.index_field,
       :type_code_a = type_code_a,
       :column1 = column1,
       :column2 = column2,
       <other columns>
FROM transaction_table t
```

```
        WHERE <conditions>

        < other processing of the record >

        SELECT:transaction_type = a.type_description
        FROM code_table1 a
        WHERE a.type_code_a = :type_code_a

        < other processing of the record >

        INSERT INTO report_table
        VALUES (:column1,
              :column2,
              :transaction_type,
              <other columns>

    end loop
```

An analogous situation can occur when writing an output record. Rather than adopting a simple structure that first inserts a skeleton of a new output row, and then updating elements of the same row during processing, the column data to be inserted can be saved in local variables and inserted in a single SQL statement.

Indexes

The optimizers in today's database engines have matured tremendously compared to those of several years ago. For ad hoc, complex queries, it is now often possible to rely on the optimizer to determine the optimum query path that should be taken to minimize a query's run time.

However, even the best optimizers cannot be used as a safety net for all queries. If a database's internal table statistics are not up to date, for instance, many optimizers will choose poor query plans or even switch to table scans with sometimes disastrous results. This problem can be avoided, to some extent, by regularly running an "update statistics" routine that re-creates internal table data volume and distribution statistics. However, in cases where the volume or type of data is changing frequently in a table, even daily or weekly updates of table statistics may be not be adequate to guarantee the use of a desired index.

For that reason, good defensive coding practices take the approach that "It is nice to have a database optimizer, but let's not leave anything to chance." Every query on a table of nontrivial size should be examined, with particular attention to ensuring that its where clauses correspond to an existing index. If an appropriate index does not already exist in the database, it should either be added to the table or, if this is not practical, consideration should be given to redesigning the query.

An extremely common development scenario has normally careful developers designing batch jobs without consideration of indexes ("After all, we won't have any users sitting at their desks waiting for this job to finish tonight"), testing the jobs under low-data-volume conditions and verifying their correctness, and then watching in horror as the batch job run time grows steadily under regular data volume conditions.

There can be some exceptions to this principle — for instance, when an entire table is being read and processed using a cursor, direct sequential access can be faster than involving any indices. But, in general, every database access in the routine should be explicitly designed to use a predefined index. If this is done, then overall job performance may grow geometrically in proportion to the volume of data being processed, but the time should be manageable and predictable from the start.

Transaction Commitments

One of the common design tradeoffs in batch routines involves decisions around committing transactions. As in other aspects of the batch routines, developer approaches adopted in the construction of online routines do not always correspond well to the design requirements of a batch routine.

Within a transaction block, either all updates are applied to the database, or none of the updates are applied. This makes the approach to determining whether a transaction is required for an online SQL routine (and, if so, what its scope should be) a relatively simple exercise. The programmer simply identifies the logical unit of work, in terms of database changes, which may not be left partially complete in case of data or database problems.

The logical extension of this concept to batch routines would be to place a transaction block around every set of inserts and updates that comprised a single block of work. The problem with this straightforward approach is that the impact of processing individual transactions blocks in a routine reading an input table of, say, 20,000 rows can seriously affect the database's performance and logging.

A compromise approach to transaction design in batch routines involves grouping together a larger number of individual input records into a single transaction, and repeatedly beginning and committing transactions when that number of input records has been processed. The example below groups input records into batches of 500 for the purpose of transaction processing:

317

```
declare:counter int = 0

declare:MAX_RECORDS_IN_COMMIT int = 500

BEGIN TRANSACTION

loop for each qualified record in transaction_table:
        SET:counter = :counter+1
        if:counter = :MAX_RECORDS_IN_COMMIT
                COMMIT TRANSACTION
                BEGIN TRANSACTION
        end if
        <process record>
end loop

COMMIT TRANSACTION
```

Some experience is necessary to determine the best number of rows to include in a single commit block, as this decision depends on the specific database implementation and environment. Establishing this number as a local constant or parameter to the routine (as in the example above) is an effective way to make it easily tunable based on actual experience.

Note that if the batch routine will be running while online users are working on the system, the MAX_RECORDS_IN_COMMIT value should be kept relatively low to avoid locking an excessive number of rows or pages needed by other processes.

If the input records are not being deleted or flagged in a specific way when they are processed, transaction parameters can be used in conjunction with transaction diagnostic messages to facilitate restartability of the routine. They allow a person responding to a problem encountered when running the routine to determine quickly and accurately how much data had been processed successfully before a problem occurred. In this way, steps can be taken to reset the input source and restart the job without incurring the risk of missing or double-processing input data.

Data All in a Row

Most batch routines, either as part of a recurring loop or as a one-time operation, must read data and conduct processing based on that data. The "read-once, write-once" approach discussed elsewhere in this paper applies hereData All in a Rowthe aim is to select data from tables as few times as possible. This may mean storing data in local variables, or organizing the

318

routine in order to defer executing the select statement until all required selection criteria have been established.

If the source data is read in a loop, there are several useful techniques available to "walk through" the qualifying rows.

Cursors. Cursors support a single selection of input data, and one-by-one processing of the results. Depending on the database implementation, it may not be practical to use cursors when the number of input rows is large.

Ascending Key Read. This method stores a starting key position and repeatedly reads additional records with larger key values. This method is simplest when the routine can count on the existence of a sequential key in the source table. If that key is indexed properly, this can also be a very efficient way to read the table rows:

```
declare:current_key int

SET:current_key = <appropriate starting value>

loop:
        SELECT <columns>
        FROM trans_table
        WHERE trans_key = :current_key

        if <no rows found>
                exit loop
        else
                SET:current_key = :current_key + 1

        <process the selected row>
    end loop
```

Read and Delete. This is appropriate for cases when the data in the input table does not need to be saved after the routine is complete. This is implemented simply by deleting the rows from the source table as they are processed.

This approach is most suitable for cases where a flat file needs to be processed in a database. The batch jobstream can first transfer the flat file data into a temporary table, and then invoke the batch routine to process the records one by one. If a problem halts the batch routine in midstream, it should be automatically restartable with the (presumably) smaller input table, which would contain all unprocessed rows.

Reading a table in this approach can be highly efficient, especially in database implementations that allow the programmer to specify a row retrieval limit in its syntax (for instance, the "*set rowcount 1*" statement in SQL Server). With this restriction in place, the read can be a simple, nonindexed select statement that permits the database to retrieve the first physical record encountered with no need to refer to indices or complicated query plans.

The program structure for this approach is somewhat similar to the example above:

> *loop:*
>
> > *<restrict selection to 1 row>*
> >
> > *SELECT:key_field = key_field,*
> >
> > > *<other columns>*
> >
> > *FROM trans_table*
> >
> > *<remove the single-row restriction>*
> >
> > *if <no rows found>*
> >
> > > *exit loop*
> >
> > *<process the selected row>*
> >
> > *DELETE trans_table*
> >
> > *WHERE key_field = :key_field*
>
> *end loop*

Read and Flag. This is very similar to read and delete, but it is used when the input table must be kept intact after being processed. Rather than deleting each input row as it is processed, a status flag is set in one of its columns, indicating that it has been used and should therefore not be picked up on the next loop iteration:

> *declare:PROCESSED char(1) = "P"*
>
> *loop:*
>
> > *<restrict selection to 1 row>*
> >
> > *SELECT:key_field = key_field,*
> >
> > > *<other columns>*
> >
> > *FROM trans_table*

```
WHERE processing_status ! = :PROCESSED

<remove the single-row restriction>

if <no rows found>

    exit loop

<process the selected row>

UPDATE trans_table

SET processing_status = :PROCESSED

WHERE key_field = :key_field

end loop
```

GENERAL PRINCIPLES

Consistency

In many development environments, database routines seem to suffer often from a lack of structure, design, and clean formatting. This is perhaps due to the ease with which they can be coded and the relatively relaxed formatting restrictions of most SQL implementations. When compared to regular 3GL or 4GL processing code, many database routines are characterized by few (or nonstandard) comments, inconsistent indentation, and capitalization of keywords, resulting in an erratic look and feel. Batch routines, because they tend to be longer and more complex, are particularly impacted by this lack of consistency.

While there are many standards that could be described as clear, and this chapter does not attempt to define a single "best" one, the important thing is to choose a standard and stick with it for all SQL routines in a system. This coding discipline generally pays for itself many times in reduced overall maintenance time in the long term.

In addition to these cosmetic issues, an objective of clarity can lead a structured development shop to convert complex batch routine syntax into simpler statements, even if this involves a small cost in terms of performance. For instance, even if a complex table join has been tested and verified to be correct in all circumstances (including tests under high-volume conditions), it can be worthwhile to review the performance and coding cost involved in splitting it into separate but more simple queries. If this cost is not excessive, it will almost certainly be recovered with interest when the routine needs to be modified due to system problems or new business requirements.

Diagnostics

If a batch routine is running without a user sitting at a screen waiting for its completion, it is very tempting to build it with a minimum of inline diagnostics. Sometimes a small set of control totals may be generated and saved as part of the job run, but batch routines are commonly built without even that level of output.

While it is true that there is little need for detailed diagnostics when a job is working correctly, their lack is felt most deeply in the most stressful situations — when problems manifest themselves. In a typical real-life scenario, the complex batch job runs for several months without problems and then, due to some unforeseen data input scenario, starts producing incorrect results. The support staff designated to investigate the problem are faced with a sometimes daunting task of diagnosis and repair, often complicated by less-sophisticated debugging tools for the database environment.

To speed up diagnosis and resolution of these problems, a relatively small amount of developer time and batch job run time can be applied to producing diagnostic messages directly from the batch routine. A simple, but comprehensive approach involves issuing two types of diagnostic messages:

Control Diagnostic Messages. These act as milestones along the road of a batch routine. If one section becomes slow or fails to work, then the offending section should be immediately obvious by referencing the control diagnostics. These could read, for instance, as follows:

ddMMMyyyy hh:mm:ss Routine "process_transactions" started

ddMMMyyyy hh:mm:ss Beginning to process input rows from trans_table

ddMMMyyyy hh:mm:ss Processed 1000 input rows

ddMMMyyyy hh:mm:ss Processed 2000 input rows

ddMMMyyyy hh:mm:ss Processed 3000 input rows

ddMMMyyyy hh:mm:ss Processed 4000 input rows

ddMMMyyyy hh:mm:ss 4692 input rows processed

ddMMMyyyy hh:mm:ss Beginning generation of report_table

ddMMMyyyy hh:mm:ss Generation of report_table complete, with 2456 adds and 1205 changes

The level of detail and wording can depend entirely on development shop standards, as long as they satisfy their primary purpose — to facilitate quick identification of the likely location of problems.

Transaction Diagnostic Messages. These support a more detailed look at the data being processed by the batch routine. Their existence acts as a record of the data processed and can be used to quickly answer questions like "Why didn't product #5682 get reset last night?" or "Why do the sales to customer #7531 appear twice on this morning's reports?"

Transaction diagnostics can represent quite a large quantity of data and, for that reason, they are generally overwritten on a daily or, at least, weekly basis. Using the same example as above, they could look like this:

ddMMMyyyy hh:mm:ss Routine "process_transactions" started

ddMMMyyyy hh:mm:ss Beginning to process input rows from trans_table

ddMMMyyyy hh:mm:ss Processing product #14, status "A"

ddMMMyyyy hh:mm:ss ... Sales record: Sold 50 units to customer #5532 at $45

ddMMMyyyy hh:mm:ss ... Sales record: Sold 14 units to customer #5532 at $48

ddMMMyyyy hh:mm:ss ... Returns record: Returned 12 units from customer #5532 at $43

ddMMMyyyy hh:mm:ss Processing product #18, status "A"

ddMMMyyyy hh:mm:ss ... No sales records found

ddMMMyyyy hh:mm:ss ... No returns records found

ddMMMyyyy hh:mm:ss Processing product #22, status "D"

ddMMMyyyy hh:mm:ss ... Skipping discontinued product

ddMMMyyyy hh:mm:ss Processing product #23, status "A"

ddMMMyyyy hh:mm:ss ... Sales record: Sold 10 units to customer #5532 at $2.50

ddMMMyyyy hh:mm:ss ... Sales record: Sold 12 units to customer #18006 at $2.75

ddMMMyyyy hh:mm:ss ... Sales record: Sold 985 units to customer #34925 at $2.60

... and so on

If applicable (or necessary), control diagnostics and transaction diagnostics can be combined into a single output file. The emphasis here is not on a cosmetically fancy report layout — rather, the point should be to produce useful diagnostic information that can be referenced when results of the batch process are in question and details of its processing are needed.

If disk space is not adequate to generate transaction diagnostics on a regular basis, the routine can be coded to issue them only when an input "debug" parameter is set. In normal situations, the debug parameter would be turned off. When specific problems arise and there is a need to trace the routine's running more carefully, the parameter would be turned on. By coding the parameter into the routine from the start, production diagnostics can be turned on and off months or years later without changing a single line of code.

Affecting Other Batch Jobs

In many cases, batch processes will be scheduled for times when there are no online users accessing the database. In these cases, using the power of SQL to access many rows in a single statement can have the dual advantages of simplicity and speed. For instance, to copy details from today's transactions to a reporting table, the statement

```
INSERT INTO report_table

SELECT t.column1,

        t.column2,

        <other columns>

FROM transaction_table t,

WHERE t.transaction_date = <today>
```

can certainly be very effective (assuming an appropriate index on the transaction date field).

However, it is very important to realize that, in most database implementations, even a single statement like this one places an implicit transaction on all data accessed in its select statement. This lock ensures that either the entire selection is made and inserted into the destination table, or none of it is.

This means that all rows selected by the query are locked for its duration. If the table and/or number of rows being affected is large, this has the potential to freeze any online users or other batch jobs attempting to access the locked records (or pages, depending on the database implementation of locking).

Running this type of query during the day — to create an ad hoc report, for instance — is often responsible for frustrating calls to the help desk where online users report intermittent freezing of their systems in no discernible or reproducible pattern.

The same phenomenon can occur if multiple batch jobs are scheduled concurrently by system administrators. In the worst case, two batch jobs can fall into a deadlock situation where each is holding resources needed by the other.

To avoid this trap, the most important point is to remember that "you're not alone." If query speed and simplicity is paramount, then designers and database/system administrators must be very conscious of the database access contained in these routines and consciously schedule them in such a way to preclude conflicts.

If robustness of the system is important enough to accept a small speed penalty in running the routine, then a walkthrough approach can produce the same ultimate results as the single query, but without locking tables or inflicting performance penalties on other users or processes sharing the database:

```
loop for each qualified record in transaction_table:

    SELECT:col1 = t.column1,

        :col2 = t.column2,

        <other columns>

    FROM transaction_table t

    WHERE t.transaction_date = <today>

    INSERT INTO report_table

    VALUES (:col1,

        :col2,

        <other columns>)

end loop
```

CONCLUSION

Many problems in batch SQL jobs can be avoided by developing and applying a good set of SQL programming instincts. These instincts comprise rules of thumb that sometimes represent simple common sense, but in other cases are not in the natural toolkit of a developer coming from other technology platforms.

However, applying an ounce of prevention in the design and construction phases of a project's batch SQL components can easily pay back several "pounds" of savings in future maintenance effort.

Chapter IV-8
Building Database-Enabled Web Applications with IDC
Ido Gileadi

THE WORLD WIDE WEB (THE WEB) HAS BEEN PRIMARILY CONSTRUCTED from static HTML pages. These pages generally contain text, graphics, and hyperlinks that give net users the ability to search and view information easily with the click of a mouse. The static page always displays the same information regardless of individual user selections or personal preferences. Furthermore, the static page displays the whole range of information available to it without consideration of the specific requirements of unique, busy individual users accessing the web site.

In recent years, there has been a strong movement toward a more dynamic approach for web page design. Web pages can now be created on the fly, customized to an individual viewer's requirements, and linked with database servers to provide accurate, up-to-the-minute data. There are many techniques for creating dynamic web pages. Some of the technologies available involve creation of a web page on the fly based on selections a viewer makes in previous pages. Active pages and CGI scripting can easily achieve these tasks.

In many cases we would like to create dynamic web pages that contain subsets of data based on the viewer's selection of a query. A simple example of this type of application is a telephone directory publication on the web. Such an application requires the ability to select and display one or more entries from the database, based on a selection (query) the user makes on the screen. Most likely the selection will involve a last name and/or first name combination.

The traditional way of creating a database-enabled web application, such as the telephone directory, is to use CGI scripting. The CGI script is a program that is referenced by the selection screen. It is invoked by the submission of the selection criteria (last name and first name) and receives the selections as input parameters. Once invoked, the CGI script works like any other program on the server and can access a database server to retrieve the information that is required. It then builds the dynamic web page based on the retrieved data and presents it back to the user on the web page.

0-8493-9979-3/99/$0.00+$.50

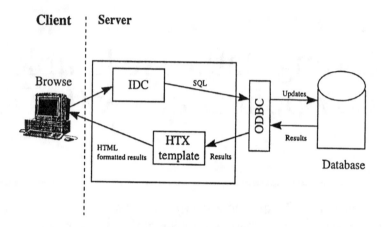

Exhibit 1. IDC Operation

This approach is lacking in execution speed and requires programming knowledge in Perl or some other computer language that is used to construct the CGI script. In this chapter, we will write a database-enabled application using the Internet Database Connector (IDC) technology. Building this application will require no traditional programming skills and relies only on minimal coding statements.

INTERNET DATABASE CONNECTOR (IDC)

IDC is a technology developed by Microsoft to allow the execution of an SQL statement against a database and represent the results in an HTML page format. This technology works only with an Internet Information Server (IIS) that is a Microsoft web server offering. Any browser can be used to access database information using IDC because the only requirement is that the browser be able to interpret HTML pages. Exhibit 1 depicts the way in which IDC operates.

In this example, a client machine (e.g., your PC) is running a web browser. The browser requests an IDC page, which happens to be a text-based page. The server intercepts the request and sends the SQL statement included in the IDC file to the ODBC data source defined in the IDC file. The database returns a result set or performs the insert/update operation. The data returned is formatted using the format specified in the HTX template into a valid HTML stream that is in turn sent back to the requesting client to be displayed by the browser.

In the following sections of this chapter, this functionality will be demonstrated by building a simple telephone directory application.

Exhibit 2.   Example Database Structure

Field Name	Description	Type	Comments
id	The directory entry unique id	Counter	This is an automated counter that will be incremented every time a new record is inserted into the database
LastName	Last name	Text	
FirstName	First name	Text	
tel	Telephone number	Text	

DEVELOPING THE TELEPHONE DIRECTORY APPLICATION

Requirements

This is a small sample application designed for the sole purpose of demonstrating some principles of database access over the web. The requirements are identified in terms of the required functionality and access. The functionality required is as follows:

- Store first name, last name, and telephone number of multiple individuals.
- Allow the user to search for a specific directory entry using a part or the whole of the last name and first name.
- Display a list of all matching entries as the results of a search.
- Allow the users to add a new entry to the directory.
- Allow users to access the telephone directory through a web browser and their Internet connection.

The preceding requirements are sufficient to begin developing the application. The following sections provide a guide that can be used on a step-by-step basis to develop the application.

The Database

An Access database will be used to support this sample application. Any database with an ODBC-compliant driver can be used. A new database that contains only one table will be created to contain the directory entries. The structure of the table is shown in Exhibit 2.

IDC requires an ODBC datasource to communicate with the database. We will create an ODBC datasource for the access database we have just created using the 32bit ODBC manager in the control panel.

Programming Tip. The datasource must be defined as a system datasource for the web server to be able to access it.

The datasource will be named Tel_Directory and pointed to the newly created access database. Security will not be added to the database for the purpose of this example. In a real-life application you will most likely want to create a user id and a password for the users accessing the database over the network and have them key it in at run time. Another alternative is to create a user id and a password with very limited permissions and include the login parameters in the IDC file to avoid the extra step of logging in.

Warning. The IDC file is a plain text file and can be viewed easily by anyone with access to the web. When storing the login parameters in this file, you must execute great caution to restrict the user access to the very minimum required.

The Application Directory

Any directory that will be accessed by the web server (IIS) has to be defined in the administration section of the web server. This allows the web server to know about the directory and allows the developer to set some parameters for each directory. The parameters of interest in this discussion include the access rights. There are two access parameters:

- **Read** access allows the server to read the files in the directory and send their contents to the requesting browser. This is sufficient for regular HTML files.
- **Execute** access allows the server to execute the program stored in the files in the directory. This is required for CGI scripts as well as IDC files.

For our application we will create one directory that will contain all the files we need to run the application with the exception of the database file. We will grant both read and execute permissions to this directory.

Programming Tip. Create the directory under the web server's home directory (typically .../wwwroot) and make sure you grant read and execute permissions to the home directory. The home directory is marked in the directory property window of the web administration section.

The Search Screen

As defined in the requirements we must allow a search by a combination of first and last name. We will define the search screen as an HTML form, which will allow us to pass the user's selection as parameters to the IDC script. Exhibit 3 shows the search screen as it will display on the browser.

The HTML code for the preceding screen was created using Microsoft Front Page and it consists of the following:

```
<!DOCTYPE HTML PUBLIC "-//IETF//DTD HTML//EN">

<html>

<head>
```

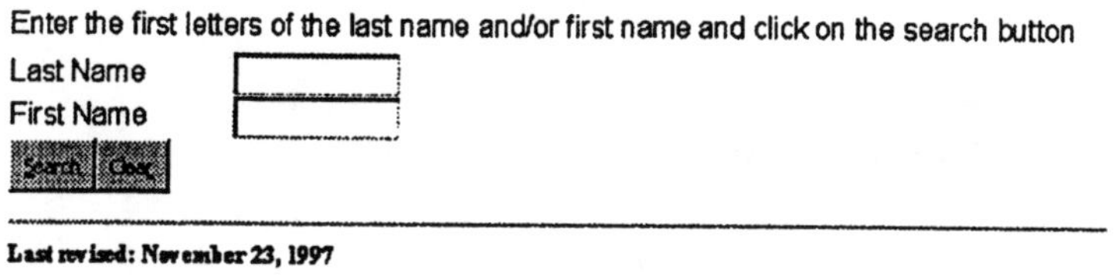

Enter the first letters of the last name and/or first name and click on the search button

Last Name

First Name

Exhibit 3. Search Screen

```
<meta http-equiv = "Content-Type"
content = "text/html; charset = iso-8859-1">
<meta name = "GENERATOR" content = "Microsoft FrontPage 2.0">
<title>Search Directory</title>
</head>
<body>
<h1>Search Directory</h1>
<hr>
<p>Enter the first letters of the last name and/or first name and click on the
search button</p>
<form action = "Search.idc" method = "POST">
    <table border = "0">
        <tr>
            <td>Last Name</td>
            <td><input type = "text" size = "20" maxlength = "20"
            name = "lname"></td>
        </tr>
        <tr>
            <td>First Name</td>
            <td><input type = "text" size = "20" maxlength = "20"
            name = "fname"></td>
        </tr>
    </table>
    <p><input type = "submit" value = "Search"> <input type = "reset"
    value = "Clear"> </p>
```

```
</form>

<hr>

<h5>Last revised: November 23, 1997</h5>

</body>

</html>
```

The HTML code is a standard form with fields that are arranged into a table for cosmetic reasons. Highlighted are the names of the input fields that will be passed as parameters to the IDC script.

The Search IDC Script

The general format of an IDC script is as follows:

```
Datasource: <Name of a system ODBC datasource>

Username: <User id for accessing the database>

Password: <Password for the user>

Template: <A URL of the HTML template file *.HTX>

SQLStatement:

+<Lines of the SQL statement>

+<Lines of the SQL statement>
```

There may be more than one SQL statement in the file. This feature will be revisited in the following sections.

The IDC script used with the search screen is as follows:

```
Datasource:Tel_Directory

Username:

Password:

Template:Directory.htx

SQLStatement:

+SELECT id,FirstName,LastName,Tel from Directory

+WHERE LastName like '%lname%%' and FirstName like '%fname%%'
```

A username or password has not been included for this sample. In a production environment you would definitely include a user id and password or prompt the user for one using a login screen.

The SQL statement containing the SELECT statement will typically return a result set. The result set may be empty or contain one or more rows. The HTML template file will have to handle the display of multiple

332

rows. We also observe that the field names in the SELECT section reflect the names of the columns in the database, and the parameter names in the WHERE clause reflect the field names on the search HTML form. The parameters coming from the HTML form are enclosed in a percent sign (%). In our case, we also enclose the percent signs (%) in single quotes so that the WHERE clause will contain the correct syntax for a text field. In addition we want to allow the user the flexibility of keying only the first few letters of the name. We include an additional percent sign (%) that acts as a wild card character indicating that any string of characters can replace it. The final SQL statement may look like:

SELECT id,FirstName,LastName,Tel from Directory

WHERE LastName like 'Smi%' and FirstName like '%'

This will return all the entries where the last name starts with 'Smi' regardless of the first name.

The Search Result Screen

The search results are displayed using the HTX template. The HTX file is a regular HTML file and can contain any codes included in an HTML file. In addition to the standard HTML codes it contains the following construct:

<%BeginDetail%>

Any valid HTML code <%FieldName1%><%FieldName2%>

Any valid HTML code <%FieldName3%><%FieldName4%>

<%EndDetail%>

Anything contained between the <%BeginDetail%> and the <%EndDetail%> will be repeated in the constructed HTML file for each row of results coming from the database. The <%FieldName%> parameters are the field-names as they appear in the database and will be substituted with the values returned from the database.

Following is the listing for the Search results HTX file. The name of this file is stated in the IDC script, it is 'Directory.htx'. This template was created using Microsoft Front Page. Highlighted in the following example are the important construct elements, including begindetail, id, Last-Name,FirstName, Tel, enddetail, if CurrentRecord EQ 0, action = "AddEntry.idc", and endif:

<!DOCTYPE HTML PUBLIC "-//IETF//DTD HTML//EN">

<html>

<head>

<meta http-equiv = "Content-Type"

```
content = "text/html; charset = iso-8859-1">
<meta name = "GENERATOR" content = "Microsoft FrontPage 2.0">
<title>Directory Listing</title>
</head>
<body bgcolor = "#FFFFFF">
<p><font color = "#0000FF" size = "5"><em><strong>Telephone Directory
Listing</strong></em></font></p>
<table border = "2" cellpadding = "2" cellspacing = "3">
    <tr>
        <td><font color = "#0000FF"><em><strong>Entry
        ID</strong></em></font></td>
        <td><font color = "#0000FF"><em><strong>Last
        Name</strong></em></font></td>
        <td><font color = "#0000FF"><em><strong>First
        Name</strong></em></font></td>
        <td><font color = "#0000FF"><em><strong>Tel
        Mumber</strong></em></font></td>
    </tr>
<%begindetail%>
    <tr>
        <td><%id%></td>
        <td><%LastName%></td>
        <td><%FirstName%></td>
        <td><%Tel%></td>
    </tr>
<%enddetail%></table>
<p> </p>
<%if CurrentRecord EQ 0%>
<table border = "0" cellpadding = "0" cellspacing = "4">
    <tr>
        <td><form action = "AddEntry.idc" method = "POST">
            <p><input type = "submit" name = "B1" value = "Add
Entry"></p>
        </form>
        </td>
```

```
    </tr>
  </table>
<%endif%></body>
  </html>
```

In the preceding listing we notice that there is an additional conditional construct that looks like

<%if CurrentRecord EQ 0%> any HTML code <%endif%>

This conditional construct allows for better control over the creation of the HTML code. In our example, we use the construct to add an AddEntry button that will activate the add entry screen.

Tip. The conditional construct can also contain the element <%else%> that will allow the creation of a completely different HTML code based on the result set.

Warning. The conditional construct will not work if used before the <%BeginDetail%>

The CurrentRecord is one of the built-in variables that can be used in the template. It indicates the current record being processed. If used after the <%BeginDetail%> <%EndDetail%> construct will hold the last record number. The record number relates to the sequential number within the result set.

The Add Entry Screen

The Add Entry button will appear on the search results screen only when there are no records in the result set. Having no records in the result set will indicate that the entry was not found and therefore may be entered into the database. The Add Entry button is a submit button within an HTML form that points to the AddEntry.idc script.

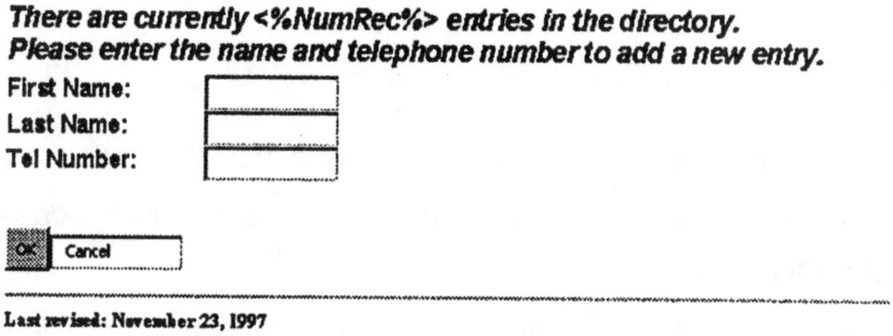

There are currently <%NumRec%> entries in the directory.
Please enter the name and telephone number to add a new entry.

First Name:
Last Name:
Tel Number:

| OK | Cancel |

Last revised: November 23, 1997

Exhibit 4.   Add Entry Screen

The AddEntry.idc script will fetch the total number of entries in the database and invoke the HTML template named AddEntry.htx. Following is the listing for the AddEntry.idc script:

```
Datasource:Tel_Directory

Username:

Password:

Template:AddEntry.htx

SQLStatement:

+SELECT count(id) as NumRec from Directory
```

The AddEntry.htx template is different from the search result template we have seen previously. We only expect one record to be returned to this screen. That record will contain the total number of records in the database. The rest of the template is an HTML form that will allow the user to enter the details of the new directory entry and submit them to the database. Exhibit 4 shows the Add Entry screen.

The following example is the AddEntry.htx HTML listing supporting Exhibit 4: Add Directory Entry Screen:

```
<!DOCTYPE HTML PUBLIC "-//IETF//DTD HTML//EN">

<html>

<head>

<meta http-equiv = "Content-Type"

content = "text/html; charset = iso-8859-1">

<meta name = "GENERATOR" content = "Microsoft FrontPage 2.0">

<title>Add Entry</title>

</head>

<body>

<h1>Add Directory Entry</h1>

<hr>

<%BeginDetail%>

<p><font size = "4"><em><strong>There are currently

&lt;%NumRec%&gt; entries in the directory.</strong></em></font></p>

<%EndDetail%>

<p><font size = "4"><em><strong>Please enter the name and telephone

number to add a new entry.</strong></em></font></p>
```

```html
<form action = "Add2DB.idc" method = "POST">
    <table border = "0">
        <tr>
            <td><strong>First Name:</strong></td>
            <td><input type = "text" size = "20" maxlength = "20"
            name = "fname"></td>
        </tr>
        <tr>
            <td><strong>Last Name:</strong></td>
            <td><input type = "text" size = "20" maxlength = "20"
            name = "lname"></td>
        </tr>
        <tr>
            <td><strong>Tel Number:</strong></td>
            <td><input type = "text" size = "15" maxlength = "15"
            name = "tel"></td>
        </tr>
    </table>
    <blockquote>
        <p> </p>
    </blockquote>
    <p><input type = "submit" value = "OK"> <input type = "button"
    value = "Cancel"> </p>
</form>
<hr>
<h5>Last revised: November 23, 1997</h5>
</body>
</html>
```

In the above listing, note the <%BeginDetail%> and <%EndDetail%> around the <%NumRec%> variable without which the %NumeRec% variable will not be assigned a value. Also note the form action is referencing yet another IDC script named Add2DB.idc. The Add2DB.idc script contains the SQL INSERT statement that will insert the new record into the database. The listing for the Add2DB.idc script is as follows:

```
Datasource:Tel_Directory

Username:

Password:

Template:Directory.htx

SQLStatement:

+INSERT INTO Directory (FirstName, LastName, Tel)

+VALUES ('%fname%', '%lname%', '%tel%')

SQLStatement:

+SELECT id, FirstName, LastName, Tel FROM Directory
```

Let us examine this script carefully. It has an SQL INSERT statement that takes as parameters the values that had been entered in the HTML form. The INSERT statement is not the only statement in the script. There is a second SQL statement that selects all the records in the telephone directory. The second select statement will populate the Directory.htx template that we have seen before. This script performs the insert action and then displays all records in the directory including the newly inserted record.

Tip. Results returned from the database must match the template.

Each result set returned from the database will correspond with a single <%BeginDetail%> <%EndDetail%> in the template. There may be more then one <%BeginDetail%> <%EndDetail%> in the template. If one SQL statement does not return a result set, it will be skipped and the next result set will be matched to the <%BeginDetail%> <%EndDetail%> in the template. In our example, the INSERT statement does not return a result set. The second SQL statement does return a result set and will therefore be used by the <%BeginDetail%> <%EndDetail%> in the template.

Organizing the Application

The application directory was created previously. All the HTML, IDC and HTX files should now reside in the same directory. They are all built to reference each other in a cyclic fashion. Exhibit 5 depicts the relationships between the various screens and scripts.

CONCLUSION

The sample application created in this chapter demonstrates the principles of accessing a database through a web server. The task is accomplished without the need for traditional programming. All the developer

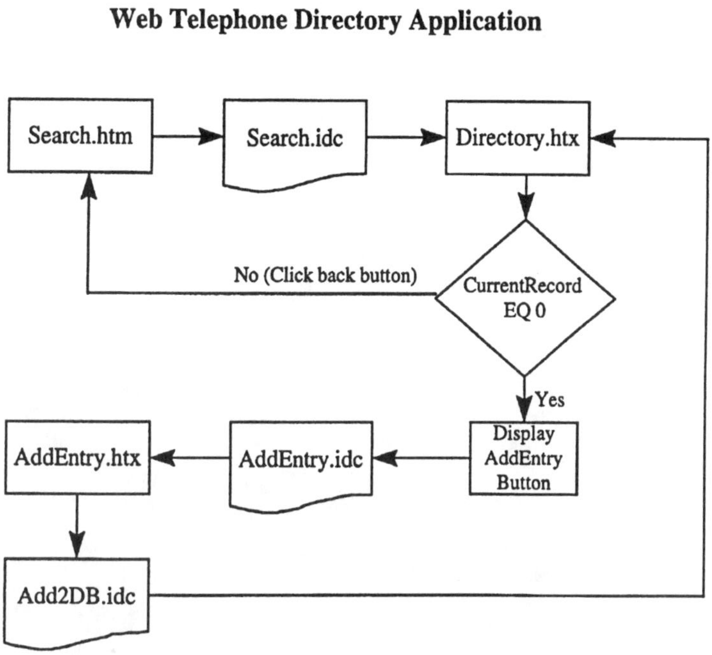

Web Telephone Directory Application

Exhibit 5.   Web Telephone Directory Application

needs to know are basic SQL statements and some HTML coding. With this basic knowledge we have managed to create an application that can be useful and provide value.

The IDC technology is compatible with a Microsoft Internet Information Server. The personal web server version was used to test this application. Users accessing the telephone directory can do so with any browser that can read and interpret HTML code (e.g., Netscape or Microsoft).

There are many ways to access data through the web, IDC is the simplest and quickest way of doing so. If the requirements for your applications can be met with this method, it will be a convenient and low maintenance solution.

Chapter IV-9
Automatically Migrating COBOL Indexed Files: A Case Study

Andrew J. Swadener and Lee Janke

MANY ORGANIZATIONS ARE FACED with addressing the modernization of what has come to be known as their "legacy systems." Unfortunately, the definition of a legacy application has become obscured in the industry. A negative connotation has sometimes been assigned to the term for purposes of selling an agenda of reengineering applications that have been developed in presumably mature (a.k.a. old) software environments — COBOL programming environments are a case in point. Scrutiny toward the goal of identifying such tactics should be undertaken, as an organization may be swayed into buying technology for the sake of the technology, with the primary benefactors being the technology's providers.

It is important *always* to remember the lay-person's fundamental rule of software development, as we all learned it: "Let the requirements drive the technology … not the other way around." An organization's software environment may be mature, but it may also have been appropriately developed, for the most part, in that environment. A major reengineering effort is not always automatically warranted.

In choosing how to evolve an organization's application into its capitalizing on modern technologies, automation services providers must orient themselves toward identifying where the changes need to take place — in the short, intermediate, and longer terms. It is important to provide a strategy that is cost-effective and dynamic by design, and that maximizes the organization's previous software investment. For many application stewards, the definition of the correct direction along these lines may appear daunting or ellusive.

As is the case in most projects, dissecting this problem into component parts provides for more manageable, tangible solutions. When attempting to strategize the efforts described above, business rules can be analyzed separately from data stores. The solutions for each may be surprisingly more diverse and, in some cases, easier than originally imagined. The paradigm shift is in mentally separating *how* an application and its users generate data (the programs/processes) and *what* the data is (data stores). Both programs and data can be considered product lines, and are, at a minimum for all organizations, valuable assets. The important fact is that the programs and the data *can* be managed differently.

For the most part, the following discussion focuses on the data assets of an organization. The business rules, or software programs, of the original application are assumed to be already functionally rich — at least enough so that existing short-term mission-critical business requirements are met with them. Even if there are areas where the existing functionality of the application is lacking, there are strategies that can be employed that have proven to work in conjunction with the solutions outlined here for the evolution of the application's data stores. In the discussion provided here, the application's programs are assumed to have been written in ANSI-85 Standard COBOL. From the data store perspective, COBOL programs are intimately tied to proprietary file-handling systems, due to the equally proprietary nature of COBOL compilers and "run-time" components.

When focusing on the data component assets within an application, the above-mentioned paradigm shift opens exciting possibilities for access to and reuse of data stores inside and outside of the original application (see Exhibit 1).

CHOOSING AN OPEN ARCHITECTURE

There is no doubt that we are in the midst of rapidly changing technologies and faced with needing environments that can no longer be thought of as exclusively proprietary or that are held up behind our organizations' closed doors. With the burgeoning Intra/Internet and World Wide Web marketplaces, advances in personal computer "desktop" technologies, and widespread easier standard accessibility options for our automated applications (especially for the data associated with them), there are very few organizations that are not faced with needing to open their applications' doors — while, at the same time, controlling the process with intelligent future-sighted decisions.

After serious evaluation, a decision on the "open architecture" question needs to be formulated. This is especially the case for legacy applications, since they were usually designed without the advantages or requirements of today's open features. Not all applications, or not all the components of an application, *need* to be changed. Candidates for open architecture deployment must be evaluated on the basis of:

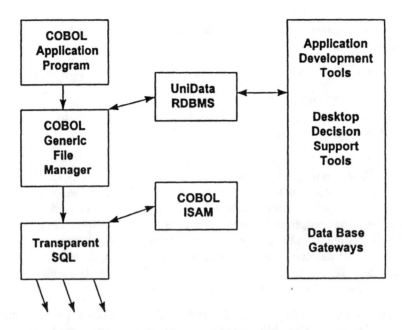

Exhibit 1.   COBOL Reuse through Open Systems

- Data access requirements (from the desktop or from tools not necessarily developed by your organization)
- Ease of use and end-user exposure to newer technologies (for consistently providing nearly the same methods for application usage or access)
- Functionality
- Future development requirements

Potential rehosting and/or component-based modifications may be the identified route to be taken. It is important to evaluate the best approach for accomplishing your open architecture goals from the onset of the feasibility analysis phase of the project. Targeting the right mix of required changes, based on your organization's needs is critical to control the scope (and expense) of the transitions ahead.

This discussion is based on an identified need for an application to be in an open environment — for reasons coming out of the above-mentioned analysis activities.

Case-Study

A case study examined in this and subsequent sections outlines the previously discussed activities for Banctec, Inc., a Dallas-based provider of electronic and document-based transaction-processing systems, applications software, and support services. The company is responsible for maintaining and managing systems software for more than 4000 document processing systems that Banctec has manufactured and for maintaining network software.

Banctec was interested in open architecture for the following reasons:

- Data querying capabilities
- Desktop data access capabilities in a client/server mode
- Post-implementation follow-on development

Banctec's application was initially implemented in a DG-INFOS COBOL DG-MV/AOS environment. After evaluating various options for deploying their application into a new open environment for the reasons above, it was determined that a multidimensional database was needed, in order to avoid a major reengineering effort. Banctec needed a way to map indexed data structures in COBOL to a relational database, which posed important questions for Banctec regarding a relational database that could maintain and accept OCCURing data and data REDEFINEs. (See the following sections for detailed discussions on these topics.)

Banctec chose Unidata, Inc.'s Nested RDBMS and COBOL Direct Connect for these reasons. The ability to migrate the data and to accommodate data access requirements in an open environment with no significant data structure changes was critical to a feasible application transition.

Beyond initial migration, Banctec needed options available in order to be able to also get to the data. They wanted to be able to access the data in a "native" fashion, directly taking into account the multiple dimensions of their database — Unidata's UniQuery and wIntegrate QueryBuilder satisfied these needs. These mechanisms allow the ability to retrieve the COBOL-oriented data in a predictable fashion, automatically formatted for the original OCCURs and REDEFINEs.

In addition to native access, though, Banctec realized the need to access their application's data in an industry-standard open fashion (e.g., ODBC), which presently does not directly accommodate multidimensional databases. Unidata's product set allowed for this type of access as well. These technologies allow them to access their application's data from popular desktop applications offered by Microsoft or Lotus Development Corporation.

Lastly, with the above access capabilities, Banctec was presented with a large number of options for future development, and possibly reengineering with other state-of-the-art open environment tools.

The major effort for Banctec's transition to this ideal environment for them was focused on the transition from the original COBOL environment to a COBOL environment that Unidata supports (DG-INFOS was not one of the environments supported). Banctec chose to migrate their application to Acucobol-85 (Acucobol, Inc., San Diego CA) on a Data General AViiON-9500 computer, under the DG-UX operating system.

The remaining discussion provides some insight into Banctec's experiences in the overall migration process. It is important to note that Banctec chose to migrate their application in two phases:

- Phase-1 migrated the COBOL environment to Acucobol-85 and implemented that environment into production first.
- Phase-2 migrated the Aucocobol-85 Vision indexed files into a UniData RDBMS using COBOL Direct Connect

SELECTING TARGET FILES FOR MIGRATION

Depending on the goals of the organization in moving their data to an open environment's RDBMS, the purposes for choosing targeted application files may differ. It is important to ensure that the strategy for migration focuses on providing options. A migration strategy that, by default, places all of an application's data into relational format will usually not serve most organizations' needs. If it is important to provide customers with open access to their application's data for ad hoc querying, for example, internally used transient data files can be excluded from the database. The option should be available to *not* migrate selected data files (i.e., to retain their native/proprietary structure).

In addition to selecting files for migration based on eventual usage requirements, some data may not lend itself easily to migrating to a RDBMS structure, by their intrinsic characteristics. COBOL Indexed Files usually fall into three categories:

- Indexed (primary and alternate keys)
- Relative (dynamic keys)
- Sequential (no keys)

Indexed files are those that should be analyzed for RDBMS deployment. Each indexed file should be reviewed for deployment applicability for the reasons just mentioned.

Case Study

The BancTec application is a corporate mission-critical solution that requires high reliability and availability. Named BancTec Automated Service Executive (BASE), the application helps BancTec's cusotmer service representatives mange nearly 10,000 calls about customer contracts per month.

When project management initially reviewed the migration requirements, it was obvious that these requirements must be met for the migration to be a success. Only then could the added benefits of the relational database be employed. To achieve that goal the decision was made to migrate all indexed data to a RDBMS, which supported full system back up and recovery. Although some of the new tables may never be used in a manner to maximize their existence in the relational model, by moving all data the customer can take advantage of any of the standard recovery products, which were offered by Unidata. Also this will allow them to move to a desired future solution involving data replication on a second server that can be deployed in event of a significant system hardware failure.

Another issue that was considered here — and should be for all migrations — was the idea of ongoing access to the application data by IS and user staff members. By migrating all indexed tables, the customer is assured that any desired ad hoc reporting or desktop access can be supported either through query to the migrated indexed structures or by constructing views that can span multiple tables. This decision at BancTec has ultimately allowed the customer to open up the data to the end users without concern over data availability in multiple database structures.

REDIFINED AND MULTIPLY DEFINED COBOL DATA

Data that occurs, is redefined, or is in multiple COBOL file definitions can be very complex in its design. At first glance, it may appear that logical modeling of the data into a relational database requires an entirely new file/table design. Capturing these file definitions and constructing a relational table that complies with program I/O logic can greatly reduce the data migration and program testing windows. Creation of this model must allow for a variable data store that can relate to the COBOL specific variable data fields allowed under redefine, occurs, and multiple record type logic. A normalized relational representation will not easily lend itself to the flexibility inherent in these features and can require significant "background" table manipulation activity when driven out of COBOL with standard relational SQL logic. Techniques used to leverage these COBOL characteristics become the driving force in the estimation of migration time frames and ultimately project success or failure.

Case Study

Using the UniData RDBMS data model, accessed through the COBOL Direct Connection Interface, BancTec was able to redirect its file I/O into the relational environment without affecting the existing business logic of the COBOL application. COBOL data structures involving multiple record definitions in the same file were translated into a relational table containing attributes for all possible data fields. Using a mapping constructed during the COBOL Direct Connect migration phase, attributes are populated only when the logic of the application dictate and the data is reflected in the manner in which it is populated by the COBOL program rules. This allows

346

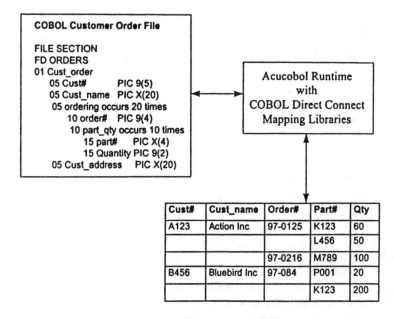

COBOL Customer Order File

FILE SECTION
FD ORDERS
01 Cust_order
 05 Cust#   PIC 9(5)
 05 Cust_name PIC X(20)
 05 ordering occurs 20 times
  10 order# PIC 9(4)
  10 part_qty occurs 10 times
   15 part#   PIC X(4)
   15 Quantity PIC 9(2)
 05 Cust_address PIC X(20)

Acucobol Runtime
with
COBOL Direct Connect
Mapping Libraries

Cust#	Cust_name	Order#	Part#	Qty
A123	Action Inc	97-0125	K123	60
			L456	50
		97-0216	M789	100
B456	Bluebird Inc	97-084	P001	20
			K123	200

Exhibit 2. File I/O Reduction

for multiple record types in a single relational table and allows for a one-to-one correlation between existing file/record structure and the new table/row storage implementation (see Exhibit 2).

This same logic supported the integrity of the existing group redefine logic and allowed for database access under naming conventions familiar to the BancTec programming staff. Table data implemented under the COBOL occurs clause logic was easily mapped to the UniData RDBMS multivalued and multisubvalued storage repository. This allowed the existing application to continue to retrieve records with a single I/O request, while supporting the query requirements of multiple tuples native to the non-first-normal-fort (i.e., nested or NF2) database.

DATA INTEGRITY

In any migration, regardless of the platform and the data structures, the issue of data integrity must be addressed. To migrate COBOL-indexed data structures into a relational model, one must first understand the inherent systems allowance for data fields to be populated in a manner that is contradictory to its definition. COBOL-indexed structures by nature allow for this by putting the emphasis for data validation in the hands of the programmer. Block movement of data and the use of working storage redefine structures allows for fields to contain values and structures that will not necessarily match the record definitions described in the file definition

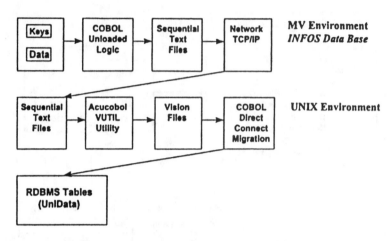

Exhibit 3. A Two-Phase Migration of Application Data

layouts. Field and record initialization techniques are also optional procedure in many COBOL environments and have been left to the individual programmer to develop when systems standards are not apparent or actively enforced.

Along with these issues, certainly there is the need to evaluate and resolve issues relating to date field integrity in both structure and ability to support larger Year 2000 compliance issues. Any migration not examining these issues will fall short in scope and will require a follow-up project covering data functionality. For these reasons care must be taken in a migration to examine data as it is migrated and not to rely on the file definitions as the final word on data-filed integrity.

Case Study

The nature of the BancTec migration involved a two-phase migration of application data (see Exhibit 3). Initially, it was "flattened" and unloaded from the INFOS database into sequential files for importing into the UNIX Acucobol VISION-indexed structure. From there it was moved into the UniData RDBMS using the COBOLO Direct Connect product. Because of the two-phase approach. Care was taken at each phase to validate data integrity. "Unload" programs included field validation and initialization as application testing revealed issues with data consistency. Some clean up was accomplished with C language programs to perform specific field manipulation when issues dictated modifications to the extracted data. During the UniData load phase, the COBOL Direct Connect product provided record-by-record verification of the data as it was loaded into the relational database. Data inconsistencies appearing at this phase were addressed through modifications to load programs.

A known issue was the problem of dates that were not correctly validated and in some cases incorrectly defined in structure (e.g., a field defined as YYMMDD contained MMDDYY data). BancTec chose to move data fields over as pure numeric data and to address the correction of this data in conjunction with a later project to open for desktop access. With the scope of the problem fully defined during the migration, a project was begun to implement the UniData elapsed day/date formats to allow for proper date-sequence query capabilities and to export back into COBOL programs a value that will support date logic into the next century.

PROVIDING OPEN ACCESS MECHANISMS

Opening data to ad hoc query and desktop access is where the relational database shows its most outstanding values within the goals of the migration. Having a repository of data defined by structure data dictionaries and accessible to any attribute, can rapidly change an organization's ability to understand and manipulate its legacy data. User reliance on IS as the only means of solution delivery can be redirected into self-sufficiency in many of the ongoing day-to-day requirements. These features are often delivered as standard products in a relational environment and can be integrated into the enterprise solution either during the migration or as postmigration enhancements.

Case Study

Upon the completion of migration, BancTec chose to go forward with a number of UniData query and reporting tools. IS staff are using native UniData UniQuery command line capabilities to support ad hoc reporting, application data review issues and database maintenance activity. This product has allowed for the viewing of data structures in a COBOL look and feel that has supported the staff's understanding of the relational model. From this, development of more sophisticated interface logic in SQL and ODBC access tools has progressed.

The BancTec user community is in the process of expanding its access to the BASE application through the implementation of solutions based in the wintegrate GUI modernization product. This product along with supporting terminal emulation needs provides a desktop access interface to relational data allowing for point-and-click query building and downloading into desktop spreadsheets and data stores. BancTec IS staff is building data access views that are concatenations of the COBOL data to support the more involved access requests. The database administrator is in charge of refining the existing data dictionaries to support greater access and understudying of all application data, driving the organization to greater user independence from IS staff requests to information.

PRODUCTION ENVIRONMENTS

During the migration of a COBOL application to a RDBMS, it is necessary to understand the underlying rules under which each data model has been constructed. Indexed files are designed to provide both rapid random access on-keyed inquiries and sequential access through a data file on a record-orientated basis. Access is typically driven through a COBOL application program and all data grouping and reporting is done within the record-level access of the program I/O.

As applications are moved to an RDBMS, it is important to note that the capabilities now exist to go beyond the record processing paradigm. It is these features that will supplement the standard process and allow for the introduction of replacement or new logic to processing requirements. For example, it certainly will be more efficient in the relational model to use table-orientated processes for requirements such as data purging, as opposed to writing a COBOL application that will sequentially read through an entire table examining each record for compliance to purging criteria.

While sequential record access through an entire table may be efficient within the constraints of the COBOL language, a strong argument can be made for the flexibility and speed of new development under the relation native tool solution. This idea can also be expanded in the area of data sorting and reporting, which, while effective once completed in COBOL, is often overshadowed by the need for application modification and "one time" usage. By employing these and other relational processing techniques, any performance or functionality issues that arise during the migration process can be addressed in a manner that will provide comparable results.

Case Study

To fulfill existing processing window requirements, certain tasks have been modified to include native Unidata relational table processing activity. Using functionality based around "select list" processing these applications now take better advantage of the power of the relational environment. Data extractions that previously read entire data files are now driven by smaller subsets of data that contain only table data pertinent to the task at hand. Whenever possible, ad hoc reporting has been moved to the requesting department level, and through the use of the Unidata tools these requests are being formalized for access by all personnel involved in similar activity.

Data cleanup and purging activity is now accomplished outside the application when requirements allow. This activity is coordinated with global database administration tasks done under command line activity, which was previously confined to solution development in COBOL programs. Training and pilot projects have followed for moving existing solutions from the COBOL file extract mentality to an ODBC compliant data access solution, which will serve as a model for all future access processes.

FOLLOW-ON DEVELOPMENT

Open system functionality either at the RDBMS vendor tool level or through standards ODBC interface levels is one of the strongest value propositions of migration to the relational data structure. This feature brings to the forefront the many options for future development outside the COBOL environment, which, if properly structured, can lead to higher programmer productivity and increased application functionality. The merging of the COBOL-based legacy business rules with the newer visual and rapid application development tools on the market is an effective deployment solution in most open systems environments. It is at this point in the migration life cycle that the decision to migrate the application as opposed to rewriting becomes fully validated in both cost and time categories.

Case Study

Although BancTec has continued to develop in Acucobol as requests for maintenance and new development surface, the emphasis has moved to review and selection of supplemental development environment for future requests. Because of previous staff experience with Visual Foxpro, some pilot project activity is proceeding with that product. Unidata's Unibasic language has been used for utility application development, as it allows for rapid database manipulation at the base attribute level, fully understanding the Unidata data structure and the native storage formats.

CONCLUSION

BancTec's conversion took approximately one year and cost approximately $300,000. BancTec's BASE application is now running on series AViiON server hardware running the DG/UX operating system, both from Data General.

The three most measureable benefits to BancTec from its COBOL migration solution are

- Time savings due to stronger system performance
- More open data access by the systems users themselves
- Increased efficiency of staff serving customers

Section IV – Checklist
Programming Techniques

1. Have you concluded that object-based technology is superior to traditional programming techniques? If not, what concepts of object technology would you improve on?
2. Assuming your support of object technology, would you endorse a rapid conversion of your organization's development efforts to object-oriented programming? If not, how would you implement this technology?
3. How would you prepare your programming staff for migration to object-based system development? Is this a skill that traditional programmers can adapt to easily?
4. Which object-oriented programming languages has your organization researched or used? Are these languages fundamentally the same?
5. Would you choose a development language based on strict inherent compliance to object principles or are object-supported languages acceptable? What pros or cons are there in your reasoning?
6. How should development managers determine the selection of an object-based language? Does your organization have guidelines?
7. Is language performance more important than language functionality when selecting an object-oriented language? Would this change based on the application?
8. Does the struggle between vendors for proprietary control over newer languages such as Java cause your organization to take a wait-and-see approach before committing to an object programming adoption?
9. Do you think that your organization should adopt several OOP languages standards in order to "rightsize" development projects?
10. When was the last time that your organization evaluated the success of object technology, including the value of reusable code?
11. Is reusable code practical in your environment? If not, is this due to security and administrative issues with object libraries?
12. Do you envision a vast change in using Internet technology to develop application systems? In particular, is Java better suited for this, or are other tools available for programming Web-based applications?

13. What if your perception of SQL has a reporting/query tool for online and batch execution? Does SQL have any merits for application programming or do you view it as an extension of the database utility environment?
14. Has there been a serious endeavor to migrate legacy applications in your environment to new technology? If so, is there a fixed time frame for this conversion?
15. How should your organization evaluate the existing worth of information stored in legacy data files? Would you support migration or new deployment of such data?

Section V
Database Functionality and Design

ENTERPRISE DATA MANAGEMENT HAS BECOME A CRUCIAL CONCEPT in the overall strategy of leveraging information as a corporate asset. Isolated, autonomous, and proprietary data structures used in the past are no longer acceptable repositories for most organizations. Instead, there is a mandatory requirement for accessing all corporate data via simple, expedient, and comprehensive techniques. The ongoing pursuit of "distributed databases" and "data warehousing" can be attributed to the increased need for accessing such organizational information. This need has also triggered a growth in communicating and linking data structures worldwide. While database development was important in past computing environments, it is now perceived as critical to those who understand the power of information.

Even though the goals of uniform data access are easily justifiable, they can be complicated, if not difficult, to achieve. Disparate file structures and inconsistent database designs are some of the impediments associated with an enterprise wide data architecture. Client/server, cooperative processing and distributed computing add further complexities by raising questions about the overall data access philosophy that is needed.

The spectacular growth of information databases, in terms of size and scope, has occurred very rapidly in many organizations. Maintaining an accurate index of accumulated data items is often laborious, and ineffective. As a result, there is a tendency to lose meaningfulness in stored data. Chapter V-1, "Knowledge Discovery, Data Mining, and Database Management," explains the process used to extract value from large data repositories. The trend toward data mining has received considerable attention in recent years. Much of the interest is focused on the potential for discovering vital business information to be used for competitive advantage. To date, no single method for data discovery has yielded the greatest result. However, it is expected that further research into this form of database technology will continue with much anticipation.

Numerous Data Warehousing systems have become virtual extensions to existing database structures rather than a redundant collection of data. On the other hand, some argue that very nature of data warehousing requires a unique structure to enable better use of information when compared to traditional databases. In order to accomplish this task, modeling is frequently used as a basis for the new storage paradigm. Chapter V-2, "Enterprise Data Modeling Practices," provides a strong rationale for the existence of central data warehousing and the corresponding modeling techniques. Some critics argue that a centralized approach does not meet current departmental needs. The information in this chapter addresses this argument and offers supportive advice for development managers.

Another viewpoint to modeling is presented in Chapter V-3, "Data Warehouse Design: Issues in Dimensional Data Modeling." This chapter provides detailed information about the techniques used to create accurate and efficient models, including star schemas matrix for data warehouse design. Additional information on schema architecture and its impact on database functionality is also discussed. The complexity of current and future database structures should not be taken lightly. Early design analysis can save precious time and help ensure the necessary functionality that is required in the development project.

Alternative methods for retrieving information across multiple database platforms have posed serious challenges to the development of client-server applications. Various approaches to solving this dilemma would enable interoperability with different database management systems and allow application programs universal data access. Chapter V-4, "Using CORBA to Integrate Database Systems," provides an overview on the Common Object Request Broker Architecture, one of the more popular approaches used to integrate heterogeneous databases. The advantages of CORBA are founded in the principles of object technology. Although this has tremendous merit, CORBA is not a panacea. Development managers should carefully study the details of database integration before embarking on broad implementation.

Future database designs should take advantage of newer computing technology advancements. In many cases, database usage, especially in the area of transaction processing, has taxed the performance of hardware and operating systems. The result is often an upgrade to the processing hardware, or implementation to an operating environment that favors database processing. Chapter V-5, "Data Warehousing and Parallel Databases," describes the next generation in database technology. Similar to parallel-based application programming, parallel databases can offer increased throughput and quicker retrieval, and can handle complex queries from various data repositories.

Chapter V-1
Knowledge Discovery, Data Mining, and Database Management

Patricia L. Carbone

BOTH THE NUMBER AND SIZE OF DATABASES in many organizations are growing at a staggering rate. Terabyte and even petabyte databases, once unthinkable, are now becoming a reality in a variety of domains, including marketing, sales, finance, healthcare, earth science, and various government applications. As their databases grow, organizations have realized that there is valuable knowledge buried in the data that, if discovered, could provide competitive advantage.

Data mining and knowledge discovery are the processes that organizations are using to extract knowledge from their databases. Knowledge discovery is the overall process, in which data mining is used to extract or identify knowledge in large data sets. Examples of data mining applications include:

- *Customer segmentation.* Retailers, credit card companies, banks, and other such organizations are very interested in determining if there are groups or clusters of people who exhibit certain similar characteristics. For example, banks and credit card companies use classification for credit scoring to create segments of those customers that are better credit risks than others. Factors that are analyzed include income, current debt, past payment history, and potentially even geographic area and other demographics.

- *Relationship management.* Retailers and advertisers are interested in the buying patterns of customers. Such attributes that are analyzed include items purchased, dates of purchase, and the type of payment. These attributes can perhaps be used in combination with the customer segments described above. Based on certain buying patterns, such as seasonal purchases of camping equipment by upper-middle-class people in the northeast U.S., retailers and advertisers can better target their advertising dollars toward specific media,

357

items, or geographic areas to capture the customers they want to attract. Relationship management is becoming of particular interest in electronic commerce.

Knowledge discovery and data mining rely on many underlying technologies, which include:

- Data warehousing and online analytical processing (OLAP)
- Human computer interaction and data visualization
- Machine learning (especially inductive learning techniques)
- Knowledge representation
- Pattern recognition
- Intelligent agents

This chapter looks at how these supporting technologies enable data mining and how knowledge discovery can be applied in several different domains.

THE PROCESS OF KNOWLEDGE DISCOVERY IN DATABASES (KDD)

Data mining is actually a step in a larger *KDD process*. The KDD process uses data mining methods or algorithms to extract or identify knowledge according to some criteria or measure of interest, but it also includes steps that prepare the data, such as preprocessing, subsampling, and transformations of the database. To follow one particular example, consider the application of credit card fraud, or determining when credit card users are purchasing items with a stolen credit card.

Targeting Data

To begin the KDD process, the application or analysis must first have an overall purpose or set of goals. For the credit card fraud example, the purpose of the analysis would be to identify those customers with credit card usage patterns that differ from previously established usage patterns. Databases must be identified that contain the desired data to be analyzed. In this example, incoming credit card transactions must be analyzed to halt fraud immediately. In addition, to identify the fraud trends, historical data should be examined.

The first step in the KDD process is to select data to be analyzed from the set of all available data. In many cases, the data is stored in transaction databases, such as those databases that process all incoming credit card transactions. These databases are quite large and extremely dynamic. In addition, there may be several different transaction databases running simultaneously at various sites. Again, with the credit card example, large credit card companies typically have several processing sites to handle specific geographic areas. Therefore, a subset of data must be selected from those databases, since it is unnecessary in early stages to attempt to analyze all data.

Preprocessing Data

Target data is then moved to a cache or another database for further preprocessing. Preprocessing is an extremely important step in the KDD process. Often, data has errors introduced during the input process, either from a data entry clerk entering data incorrectly or from a faulty data collection device. If target data are being extracted from several source databases, the databases can often be inconsistent with each other in terms of their data models, the semantics of the attributes, or in the way the data is represented in the database.

As an example of the data models being inconsistent, a credit card company may have two different sites handling transactions. If the two databases were built at different times and following different guidelines, it is entirely possible that they may be two different data models (relational and object-oriented) and two different representations of the entities or objects and their relationships to each other (e.g., a customer-centric view versus an account-centric view).

As an example of the differences in the way the data may be entered into the database, it is possible for the same customer to be represented in the two databases in different ways. In one database, the name field may contain the last name of the customer only. In another database, the name field may contain the first name followed by the last name. The preprocessing step should identify these differences and make the data consistent and clean.

Transforming Data

The data can often be transformed for use with different analysis techniques. A number of separate tables can be joined into one table, or vice versa. An attribute that may be represented in two different forms (i.e., date written as 3/15/97 versus 15-3-1997) should be transformed into a common format. If the data is represented as text, but it is intended to use a data mining technique that requires the data to be in numerical form, the data must be transformed accordingly.

Mining the Data

At this point, data mining algorithms can be used to discover knowledge (e.g., trends, patterns, characteristics, or anomalies). The appropriate discovery or data mining algorithms should be identified, as they should be pertinent to the purpose of the analysis and to the type of data to be analyzed. In the example, an algorithm could be chosen that would automatically look for clusters of behavior in the data.

This type of algorithm might find, for example, a set of customers that make relatively low numbers of purchases over time, a set of customers that make large numbers of purchases over time, and a set of customers that make large numbers of purchases in very short periods of time. These behaviors could be examined further to determine whether any of the patterns is representative of credit card fraud behavior. If subsets of data have been established that represent fraud behavior versus normal usage, algorithms can be used that would automatically identify differences between the sets for discrimination purposes. Again, in the example, in looking at two sets of data, the algorithm might characterize fraud behavior as numerous purchases over a short period of time and often in a different geographic area than the user typically shops, as opposed to credit card usage that is relatively consistent for that user over time.

Role of Domain Information. Often, the data mining algorithms work more effectively if they have some amount of domain information available containing information on attributes that have higher priority than others, attributes that are not important at all, or established relationships that are already known. In the credit card fraud example, domain information might include a known relationship between the number of purchases and a period of time. Domain information is often collected in a *knowledge base*, a storage mechanism similar to a database but used to store domain information and other knowledge.

Patterns and Knowledge. When a pattern is identified, it should be examined to determine whether it is new, relevant, and "correct" by some standard of measure. The interpretation and evaluation step may involve more interaction with a user or with some agent of the user who can make relevancy determinations. When the pattern is deemed relevant and useful, it can be deemed *knowledge*. The knowledge should be placed in the knowledge base for use in subsequent iterations. Note that the entire KDD process is iterative; at many of the steps, there may be a need to go back to a previous step, since no patterns may be discovered, new data should be selected for additional analyses, or the patterns that are discovered may not be relevant.

Visualization. In many steps of the KDD process, it is essential to provide good visualization support to the user. This is important for two reasons. First, without such visualizations, it may be difficult for users to determine the usefulness of discovered knowledge — often a picture *is* worth a thousand words. Second, given good visualization tools, the user can discover things that automated data mining tools may be unable to discover. Working as a team, the user and automated discovery tools provide far more powerful data mining capabilities than either can provide alone.

TECHNOLOGIES ENABLING DATA MINING AND KDD

Data mining and KDD are supported by an array of technologies. This section examines how database management, data warehousing, statistics, and artificial intelligence enable data mining and KDD.

Database Management

One of the basic differences between machine learning and data mining or knowledge discovery in databases is the fact that analysis or learning (i.e., the induction of patterns) is being done on database systems, rather than on specifically formatted file structures of the data for use with one algorithm. Database management systems (DBMSs) provide a number of essential capabilities to data mining, including persistent storage; a data model (e.g., relational or object-oriented), that permits data to be managed using a *logical* rather than physical view; and a high-level query language (e.g., SQL), that allows users to request *what* data they want without having to write complex programs specifying *how* to access it. In addition, database management systems provide transaction management and constraint enforcement to help preserve the integrity of the data. Database technology also provides efficient access to large quantities of data.

As discussed in the previous section, the KDD process implies that one is performing knowledge discovery against data that resides in one or more large databases. Typical properties of databases that complicate knowledge discovery include:

- *Large volume.* Databases are capable of storing terabytes, and now petabytes, of data, therefore requiring a need to focus or preprocess the data.
- *Noise and uncertainty.* As discussed in the previous section, noise can be introduced by faulty data collection devices. This causes uncertainty as to the consistency of the data.
- *Redundant information.* For a variety of reasons, data can be stored multiple times, causing redundant information. This is especially a problem if there are multiple source databases.
- *Dynamic data.* Transaction databases are specifically set up to process millions of transactions per hour, thus causing difficulty for data mining tools which are oriented to look at static sets of data.
- *Sparse data.* The information in the database is often sparse in terms of the density of actual records over the potential instance space.
- *Multimedia data.* DBMSs are increasingly capable of storing more than just structured data. For example, text documents, images, spatial data, video, and audio can now be stored as objects in databases, and these databases are used to handle World Wide Web sites. It is becoming extremely desirable to mine this data in addition to the traditional structured data.

Recent advances in data warehousing, parallel databases, and online analytical processing tools have greatly increased the efficiency with which databases can support the large numbers of extremely complex queries that are typical of data mining applications. Databases provide a metadata description that can be used to help understand the data that is to be mined and can also aid in determining how the database should potentially change (e.g., its schema, indices, the location of data, etc.), based on what has been learned.

Data Warehouses

Data warehousing is a technology that is currently being employed at a growing number of large firms. Data warehouses are extremely large DBMSs that are designed to hold historical data. The data model for the data warehouse is oriented to support the processing of analyses and potentially complex queries (known as online analytical processing, or OLAP), as opposed to handling large numbers of updates (which is the purpose of traditional online transaction processing, or OLTP, databases). Because the data is stored over time, the data warehouse must support temporal queries.

An example of a data warehouse is one created for a company with transaction processing dispersed to numerous sites. The process for creating and maintaining the warehouse involves selecting the data from the source databases that will be stored in the warehouse. The selection process involves replicating the new data in the transaction databases at some regular interval for further processing. Once selected, the data is passed through applications that scrub the data to ensure the warehouse is clean (i.e., error-free) and consistent. The fusion applications draw the data from the separate databases together into one model for storage in the warehouse. The extraction, scrubbing, and fusion parts of the data warehousing process match the selection, preprocessing, and transformation parts of the KDD process.

Once a data warehouse has been created, an organization can create smaller views of the warehouse that are oriented toward a particular function. These more focused views are called data marts.

It is important to note that data warehouses are increasingly being used to store not only structured data that is collected from transaction databases, but also textual data. Several vendors have constructed large DBMSs that can be used for data warehousing and also to perform data management for an Internet web site. In addition, online analysis processing tools are being extended to handle not only temporal and spatial queries as part of the complex query and analysis process, but also to perform textual queries.

Metadata Repositories. An important technology associated with data warehousing that could potentially be better utilized in data mining is the metadata repository. The metadata repository is essentially a database that contains information about the data models of the transaction databases, the data warehouse, and any data marts. The information can include the meanings of the attributes, agreed-upon conventions for attribute representation, and relationships among attributes, tables, and databases. Metadata can also contain information regarding the rankings of attributes (e.g., attribute "X" from the western U.S. database is often more current than the same attribute "X" from the north/central American database), or even the validity of the sources of the data.

The goal of the metadata repository is to aid in maintaining consistency among the data warehouse, data marts, source databases, and any analysis applications. Applications performing the selection and scrubbing, and fusion functions rely on input from the metadata repository for criteria on the extent to which the data must be cleaned and transformed.

As discussed earlier, many data mining algorithms can employ domain information when it is available to aid in the analysis of the data. The information in the metadata repository is similar to the domain information and should be used by the data mining algorithms. Some research on data mining techniques includes the use of metadata.

Contributions of Statistics

The area of statistics is an important one to data mining. For many years, statistical methods have been the primary means for analyzing data. Statistical analysis methods are still the standard means of analysis for determining credit scores for loan or credit card companies, for analyzing clinical trials data when determining whether a drug should or should not be approved by the Food and Drug Administration, and for performing other types of market basket analysis and customer segmentation.

Statistical methods differ from machine learning techniques (discussed in the next section) in that the user must typically have a hypothesis of the attributes that are in relationship to each other, then search the data for the mathematical expression the describes the relationship. In some data mining systems, this is called "top-down" learning.

There are three basic classes of statistical techniques with implementations used in data mining today: linear, nonlinear, and decision trees. Linear models describe samples of data, or the relationship among the attributes or predictors, in terms of a plane so that the model becomes a global consensus of the pattern of the data. Linear modeling techniques include linear regression (for prediction) and linear discriminant analysis (for classification). Recent advances in this area allow a model to adapt to data that involve multiple attributes (multivariable linear regression) or that are not described easily by only one linear function and may need several functions (e.g., a different function for each time period).

Nonlinear or nonparametric methods characterize data by referring to existing data when a new point is received in order to estimate the response of that point. An example of this is a higher-order regression curve; another example is the nearest neighbor. In the nearest neighbor technique, a new point is matched against existing data. Based on proximity to already characterized data, the new point is classified as being fraudulent usage or normal usage.

A variation on nonlinear techniques is the creation of decision trees. Decision trees describe a set of data in terms of a set of decision points. Based on the response to the decision point, the data are subdivided into regions. In the statistical community, Classification and Regression Tree (CART) algorithms are used to build decision trees.

Very popular commercial tools used for statistical analysis include

- SAS
- SPSS
- S/S-Plus
- MATlab
- DataDesk

Artificial Intelligence

Artificial intelligence (AI) technology provides many capabilities that support the KDD process. Principally, these contributions are in the more specific fields of machine learning and visualization.

Machine Learning. As opposed to statistical techniques that perform a "top-down" analysis approach, machine learning techniques do not need a priori knowledge of possible attribute relationships, thus providing a "bottom-up" analysis approach. Machine learning techniques are automated systems that use artificial intelligence search techniques to look for patterns and relationships in the data. These search techniques should be flexible and employ adaptive or heuristic control strategies to determine what subset of the data to focus on or what hypothesis to test next.

Machine learning techniques are able to perform several types of discoveries. They can generalize, or produce a more generalized set of rules or patterns to describe a specific set of data. A more specialized case of generalization would be to be able to predict. Generalization is typically an inductive process. Deduction occurs when there is a pattern such that if A implies B, and B implies C, then one can deduce that the existence of A will imply the existence of C. However, if C exists, one can only induce that A exists also. For example, given a set of data that describes a series of events in time, the system induces that an event at a later time may be correlated to the original pattern. As an example of generalization, a set of data may describe valid credit card usage, and an algorithm could learn that purchases are generally spread over a longer period of time in a regional area near where the customer resides.

The algorithms can also cluster data. Given data that describe specific instances, the system can identify groups of instances that are more similar to each other than to instances in other groups.

Models that are discovered are represented in a knowledge representation language that is sufficient to allow description of the model. These representations include symbolic ones (e.g., rules, decision trees, semantic networks), neural networks, and mathematical models. If the representation language is too limited, then the model will not be accurate enough to describe the data. Finally, the machine learning technique must evaluate how well a discovered pattern actually describes the data. The evaluation can include how accurately the model is able to perform prediction, utility of the model, and understandability.

Systems that employ symbolic representation of the data such as rules or decision trees are quite easy to understand by a user, particularly if the variables being tested have threshold splits (i.e., a threshold split applied to the number of purchases variable). Of course, the larger the number of attributes represented in the rules or trees, or the more complex the split descriptions, then the more complicated the rule or decision tree representation will actually be.

Commercial tools that provide a rule-based output include:

- WizSoft's WizWhy
- REDUCT
- Lobbe Technologies' Datalogic
- Information Discovery's IDIS

Commercial tools that employ the use of decision trees include

- Isoft S.A.'s AC2
- Angoss Software's KnowledgeSeeker
- NASA COSMIC's IND

Commercial tools that cluster data include:

- NASA Ames Research Center's Autoclass III
- COSMIC's COBWEB/3

Neural Networks. Neural networks are quite popular in the field of credit card fraud detection, as they are easily trainable and quite fast at processing incoming data. Neural networks can be trained to perform classification and other such tasks. The problem in the past, however, has been that one cannot see inside a neural network in the same way as with rules or trees to understand how the algorithm is classifying and where it may fail. However, recently neural networks have been expanded to output a rule representation of the learned model.

Some popular commercial neural network packages include:

- Right Information System's 4Thought
- NeuralWare Inc.'s NeuralWorks Professional II/Plus
- California Scientific Software's BrainMaker

There are also neural network components for SPSS and MATLAB.

Multistrategy Learning. Because each type of machine learning technique has positive and negative aspects, depending on the type of data being analyzed and the goal for the learning, it is increasingly desirable to employ more than one technique during a data mining session. *Multistrategy learning* allows a high-level controller to choose two or more machine learning algorithms to be applied to the data, based on characteristics of the data, the available algorithms, and the goals for the learning. Although there is no fully automated tool that will perform multistrategy learning without user intervention, more commercial tools are including multiple techniques in the overall package.

Some of these tools include:

- Thinking Machine Corporation's Darwin
- Integral Solutions' Clementine
- IBM's Intelligent Miner
- Information Discovery Inc.'s Data Mining Suite

Limitations of Machine Learning. Having pointed out the benefits of machine learning to data mining, it is important to note that these techniques have limitations also. Machine learning can only learn or discover general categories of things for which they are programmed to look. The representation language, as pointed out earlier, can limit the effectiveness or expressiveness of the model of learned behavior. Also, learning algorithms have a learning bias, so they are not always effective on all problems.

Visualization

A picture is worth a thousand words, as the old saying goes. This is particularly true in the area of data mining. Many tools are currently being developed that allow a user to interact with the data and the way that data is portrayed on the screen. One such method that has been employed for a number of years is link analysis. Link analysis portrays relationships

366

among data in terms of links connecting nodes. For example, if an analyst wanted to look at telephone call records using link analysis, the number from which the calls were made would be displayed in the center of the screen with links to all numbers that were called. Depending on the number of times a number was called, the link between the two numbers might be heavier or lighter or color-coded in some manner. This method of portraying the data would allow an analyst to make connections that are not readily visible by simply looking at tables of numbers.

Increasing research is being done to find more effective ways to portray data. Interactive visualization allows a user to change the attributes shown on a screen, or the scale of the attributes. Users can change the scales on the axes of a chart or zoom in on particular portions of the data in order to get a better understanding.

Virtual Reality. Virtual reality is increasingly being touted as the future way to perform visual analysis of the data. The idea is to allow users to "fly through," touch, and manipulate the data to see relationships that were not previously visible from a two- or three-dimensional representation. Virtual reality may be a method that is used in the future to perform data mining against large amounts of textual documents such as those available on the Internet. The visualization technique would group documents according to some criteria, then allow the data to move through those groupings in order to better choose the desired publication, similar to looking through a library in order to select a book.

Commercial tools are becoming more mature in their capability to provide more effective mechanisms for data display. Some of the tools include:

- ALTA Analytics' NetMap
- IBM's DX: Visualization Data Explorer
- Artificial Intelligence Software's VisualMine
- Data Desk
- Belmont Research's CrossGraphs
- Information Technology Institute's WinViz

PRACTICAL APPLICATIONS OF DATA MINING AND KDD

Many successful systems have been constructed and are now in daily use in a variety of domains. For example, A. C. Nielson has a system called OpportunityExplorer that analyzes retail point-of-sale information to help formulate marketing strategies. Customers for such systems include retailers, advertisers, and product producers, to name a few. IBM's Intelligent Miner is being used by retail stores to better analyze customer buying trends and product popularity. NCR has also been doing research in this area and has developed tools to aid their retail customers.

Another interesting application is the use of data mining by the Traveler's Insurance Company to determine the cost of hurricane insurance to various coastal locations, based on analyses of historical hurricane tracks and the amount of damage caused to coastal areas.

There has been a great deal of activity in the area of analyzing dynamic financial markets, but little of it has been publicized (because of the huge financial gains that can result from even a slight competitive advantage). The Lockheed Artificial Intelligence Center has a system called Recon that has recently been moved from the research lab to become a commercial product. Recon has been used in a number of applications, including one to select a stock portfolio. Currently, that application analyzes both historical and current dynamic data on thousands of stocks and makes recommendations for stocks to purchase by predicting stocks that may do well based on certain predictors. Typically, this area has been dominated by the use of statistical analysis, although neural networks and are also being explored for this domain.

In the area of credit cards and loans, there is the application involving credit scoring and credit card fraud detection. In these areas, statistical analysis and neural networks are quite popular. Neural networks have proven quite efficient at being able to distinguish between good and bad credit risks, and between valid and illegal credit card purchases. The neural network is trained based on collected data that characterizes the types of credit risks or the types of credit card purchases. HNC has a popular neural network application being used by credit card companies for both credit scoring and fraud detection that has proven quite accurate and very able to handle the immense numbers of transactions that are being processed.

Many organizations have become extremely interested in the reduction, analysis, and classification of data in large scientific databases. For example, the SKICAT at NASA's Jet Propulsion Laboratory was developed to catalog sky objects from the second Palomar Sky Survey. The input to the system is a digitized photographic plate, and the output is a set of catalog entries for all objects in the image (e.g., stars, galaxies, or other artifacts). SKICAT has been used successfully with a 3 terabyte astronomical data set and has generated catalogs on billions of objects, including 2×10^7 galaxies, 2×10^8 stars, and 10^5 quasars.

In addition to these and other specific applications, there are general-purpose toolkits for building KDD applications. Many of the tools discussed in the previous section are applicable for use in a variety of domains, including financial and banking applications, the petroleum industry, and in marketing analyses, among others. The limiting factor on any use of a data mining tool is to ensure that the appropriate tool is being used with the given data and goals for the analysis.

Information Retrieval and Text Processing

Information retrieval has typically been concerned with finding better techniques to query for and retrieve textual documents based on their content. Data mining is being applied to this area so that the vast amounts of electronic publications currently available may be brought to users' attention in a more efficient manner.

Data mining and information retrieval are being merged to provide a more intelligent "push" of information to a user. Information retrieval techniques have included the use of a user profile to help focus a search for pertinent documents. The addition of data mining techniques to the creation of a profile is currently being researched to improve the documents that are retrieved or brought to the user's attention. For example, if a user's profile shows that a user is interested in reading articles with the topics of "football," "baseball," and "soccer," a data mining algorithm could generalize these specific topics to "organized outdoor team sports." This type of generalization is increasingly necessary when one considers that topics of interest can change over time (i.e., the three above-mentioned sports are typically run during specific seasons), so the data mining can allow the profile to be more proactive.

CONCLUSION

Knowledge discovery has been defined as the extraction of explicit, previously unknown, and potentially useful information from data. Data mining combines artificial intelligence, statistical analysis, and database management systems to attempt to pull knowledge from stored data. A number of terms have been used in place of data mining, including *information harvesting, data archaeology, knowledge mining,* and *knowledge extraction.* In fact, all the terms imply the process of sifting through potentially vast quantities of raw material (i.e., the data) and extracting the "gems" or useful knowledge that can drive an executive's decision making.

Data mining continues to receive enormous attention by both commercial and scientific communities for three reasons. First, both the number and size of databases in many organizations are growing at a staggering rate. Terabyte and even petabyte databases, once unthinkable, are now becoming a reality in a variety of domains, including marketing, sales, finance, healthcare, earth science, molecular biology (e.g., the human genome project), and various government applications. Second, organizations have realized that there is valuable knowledge buried in the data that, if discovered, could provide those organizations with a competitive advantage. Third, some of the enabling technologies have only recently become mature enough to make data mining possible on large data sets.

Data mining is actually a step in a larger *KDD process*. The KDD process uses data mining methods or algorithms to extract or identify knowledge according to some criteria or measure of interest, but it also includes steps that prepare data, such as preprocessing, subsampling, and transformations of the database.

Data mining and KDD are hot technologies. They will continue to be so because they give organizations such great advantages that most companies find they need data mining and KDD. As the supporting technologies and applications examined in this article are refined, the need for these technologies will continue to grow.

Acknowledgments

The author thanks David Duff and Eric Bloedorn for their helpful comments. The author also thanks Len Seligman for his work on the previous version of this paper.

Recommended Resources

There are a number of resources available to readers who would like to remain current on the latest developments in this fast-evolving area. Those with access to the Internet can explore the Knowledge Discovery Mine, a World Wide Web home page maintained by Gregory Piatetsky-Shapiro of GTE Labs. This page has a great deal of information on both research projects and commercial products, and it has links to many other Internet resources related to data mining: http://info.gte.com/~kdd.

Chapter V-2
Enterprise Data Modeling Practices

Wolfgang Keller

ENTERPRISE DATA MODELING HAS RECENTLY BEEN IN THE CROSSFIRE of attacks asserting that it is completely useless. Most critics say that such an inflexible, top-down, and centralist approach is not equipped to deal with problems like changing environments, pressure from global markets, and decentralization. A central data model is said to be a contradiction to a decentralized organization. Critics say that the rapid change will make the data model outdated before the data analysts can bring it to the market.

If analyzed, most of the arguments against data modeling have their roots in existing problems and frequent errors in practice. But this does not mean that enterprise data modeling in general is faulty or useless. Many of the arguments can be attributed to improper use of data modeling equipment.

Data modeling was invented to avoid the problems associated with isolated, nonintegrated systems. This chapter is designed to help users avoid some typical errors by focusing on correct data modeling practices.

ARGUMENTS AGAINST ENTERPRISEWIDE DATA MODELS

The following is a list of common arguments against data modeling. Many financial institutions and other organizations are reconsidering their data modeling practices in light of the bad press it has been receiving. A financial application is used as an example throughout this chapter because information processing is one of the core activities of the banking business.

Critics of data modeling assert that:

- It is not able to keep pace with new developments. Information processing systems of financial institutions must be adapted to change rapidly because of the globalization of markets and new requirements for customer service.

0-8493-9979-3/99/$0.00+$.50
© 1999 by CRC Press LLC

- It cannot provide a bank with information systems that adapt with the speed of innovation. New financial instruments require fast adaption of IS capabilities.
- It acts as a brake and not a booster for rapid systems development.
- It promotes structures that should not be changed. Change is the norm in systems development. This adds to the characterization of data modeling as a brake.
- It creates additional complexity in the process of software development. Applications development is impaired by the use of top-down data modeling practices.
- It can lead to the violation of normalization rules, with the consequent need to adapt the integrated systems.
- It has to incorporate all possible future options of a system, which slows operation down to a standstill. The level of abstraction tends to increase indefinitely until no one is able to understand the results of the process.
- It is useless, if purchased off the shelf as prefabricated data models.

STARTING POINTS FOR BETTER DATA MODELING

The following four requirements should be the starting points for data modeling. These goals are essential to a reasonable process of software development. Despite the criticism, these basic requirements are often acknowledged as essentials of any software development process:

- Integrated systems are a prerequisite for the survival of a financial institution, to manage complexity, and to master interdependencies. Data modeling was invented to integrate systems and important terminology. The goals of this effort are reuse and data integration.
- The separate systems of an enterprise must use consistent terms to provide a consistent processing of data across the boundaries of several systems.
- Integration of old and new systems is necessary for routine systems development. As system integration is the norm in systems development, bottom-up strategies and reengineering of old systems must be supported. Good data modeling practice will provide support for this process.
- Fundamental structures or invariants of a business are the basis for all systems development.

Is Enterprise Data Modeling Really That Bad?

The rebuttals to the arguments will show that most of the problems with data modeling can be fixed by a data modeling process that is oriented toward goals.

Data Modeling Does Not Accommodate Rapid Change. Rebuttal: No attempt should be made to model transitory facts in a data model. Hardwired organization schemes are not subject to data modeling. The core of business activities and business rules is subject, however, to data modeling. A bank account will stay the same for years. Such an object is not subject to rapid change. Data modeling should concentrate on such core entities.

Data Modeling Is Inefficient for Financial Instruments. Rebuttal: There are data models for financial instruments that use factorization to describe them. A new instrument is a combination of known elements — a pattern of thinking that is well known from linear or polynomial functions or from industrial part list problems. No developer will try to model each new function or product; instead, it is sufficient to find the set of parameters that fully describe the function. This decomposition is often called a "high level of abstraction." Some argue that it is too high to understand. This depends on the granularity of the basic elements used to describe a product or instrument.

Data Modeling Slows Down Projects. Rebuttal: Data modeling can accelerate projects by acting as a service function. Data administration groups can report on entities that already exist and about how other groups solved problems in a reference model. A data administration group that does reviews only after project completion is indeed a slowdown. A data administration group that helps projects by reporting on current problem-solving efforts is a very important step toward reuse and reusable objects.

Data Modeling Promotes Inflexible Structures. Rebuttal: The basic structure of a bank account is an entity that does not change.

Applications Development Is Slowed by Top-Down Methods. Rebuttal: There is no law that says developers have to work from the top down when practicing data modeling. There should be a framework, called a top-level data model, (e.g., level A or B of an enterprise data model). But no developer will seriously try to go all the way down to level C before starting his or her first project. Instead, most developers recommend a process that creates a top-down frame of about 50 entities on a B level. This frame is then filled from the bottom up by projects with their project data models.

Normal Forms Are Violated. Rebuttal: There is also no law saying there must be a fifth normal form. Models, such as reference models, are often highly normalized. This should not lead to the conclusion that denormalization at the logical level is forbidden in every case. In a level C logical data model, there is no need to stick with the highest normal form available on the market at the time of creation.

Data Modeling Is Inflexible for Future Change. Rebuttal: The problem of having to model all future options in a certain problem can be discussed using the example of financial instruments. The same approach is valid for the abstraction level of several reference data models — it has to fit the needs of many corporations. To adapt a reference model to individual needs, it should not be made more abstract, but it should be simplified to adapt it to the needs of the organization that uses it.

Reference Data Models Are Useless. Rebuttal: Reference data models, also called application platforms, are often mistaken for off-the-shelf, prefabricated data models intended for use in every financial institution. However, they are very useful and can be tailored to specific organizations.

Alternatives to Data Modeling

The question most of the critics leave unanswered is what happens if data modeling is not performed? The first alternative is to build island solutions, as in the pioneering days of data processing. These islands are connected via interfaces. The lack of common terminology leads to problems and considerable effort. The negative experiences with these solutions resulted in a data modeling approach to fix those problems.

Another approach is to take business processes as the fixed point of analysis. Processes can be analyzed, and in most cases elementary processes will be found that will be grouped in entities. This approach is a purely dogmatic, bottom-up, object-oriented approach.

A practical approach is somewhere between bottom-up and top-down. A healthy mixture of a top-down approach, manifested in level A and B enterprise object models and bottom-up methods represented by project-driven level C logical models, should be much better than any pure, dogmatic approach.

ORGANIZATIONAL ASPECTS–DEFINING GOALS

A formal definition of goals and objectives for data modeling may seem bureaucratic. But a short statement defining the goals of data modeling in a company can be helpful for new employees in the data administration department or for the more experienced employees as a reminder of their goals.

When looking at an organization's data modeling procedures, quality and technical issues pertaining to the integration of data modeling should be checked in the software development organization. The following list of questions is derived from the criticisms and rebuttals of data modeling and should help organizations identify weak spots in their data modeling practice:

- Is there a written definition of the objectives for the data administration group?
- Are the goals consistent with goals stated in this chapter?
- What are the project goals of systems development projects in aspects of data modeling?
- Is there a top-level data model that is publicized and available?

Data Administration as a Service Provider

A Data Administration group can be of enormous use to project teams, or it can be an enormous source of frustration. If a data administration group comes up with some sound solutions or possible designs before a project starts with specification of details, it can be of great assistance. The data administration department is a service and not a control function. Management may want to ask:

- Is the data administration a service provider or only a review institution?
- Do they have a written statement that they are a service provider?
- What do the project managers think about the service provided by data administration?
- What is the ratio between services and control functions in the data administration department?

Integration of Data Modeling Activities into the Process of Specification

Data modeling should be an integral part of the specification process right from the beginning. This practice will promote reuse and avoid revisiting old arguments. To ensure that data modeling is properly integrated, managers should ask themselves:

- When do the project teams usually meet the data administration group — at the start of a project or at the end in the review?
- Are there separated project data models?
- Are there people who do data modeling on a C level for their own sake without a project needing it?
- Is there a mechanism that allows projects to borrow parts of the data model for rework and new developments?
- How do projects integrate their results into the global master enterprise data model? Is there any assistance or tool for integration?
- Who supervises the process of integration?

Separated Levels of a Data Model

Reference models separate clearly between different levels of abstraction in a data model. This is required because different levels are different blueprints for different groups of people (A, B levels for business administration,

C for data systems professionals). The Data administration group should ask:

- Do we have level A and B data models that are more than just a pure copy of a reference mode?
- What do the users think about data modeling?
- Is there a repository that strictly separates levels of the data model?
- Will users working on projects see at once which level they are currently looking at when dealing with the dictionary?

Quality of Data Model Contents

The quality of the contents of a data model is often intangible. Typical errors can be seen in existing data models — for example, an account number is the number of an account. Definitions such as this often occur when old pools of data have been reengineered in a sloppy manner. Data administration groups should make sure that data models are of high quality, and if not, examine the reasons why. Sometimes projects lack the budget to do a proper job, or employees may lack the motivation.

Rate of Change

A low rate of change, combined with efficient software development and systems integration, is an indicator of high-quality data modeling. If data modeling describes the core of the business rather than listing simple organizational facts, the indicator will show a decrease in change.

Managers of data administration should ask themselves:

- Does data administration monitor the change rate? If so, is it an automatic function?
- Is the change rate seen as a problem? If so, why? What are the reasons for frequent change?
- Is the data administration department clogged with change requests?

Is the Data Model Up to Date?

A data model should reflect the current state of the business for which it is designed. The terminology must reflect the corporate facts and the meaning of certain terms. The data administration department should ensure that the data model is fully up to date and carefully monitor the time it takes to process a change request — the shorter the better.

Quality of Upper Model Levels

The upper level (i.e., levels A and B) of a data model should be understood and approved by the users, because they are the people who run the business and generate the profits that pay for Data Administration. Data administration should make every effort to find out what users think about modeling efforts. It is also wise for data administration to find out how project teams perceive the quality of the data model.

Data Types as Entities

Data administration should know whether:

- There are data types that are being modeled as entities (e.g., records that have no natural key, but a key that consists of all attributes).
- There are enumeration types coded as attributes that occur in several entities.

DATA ADMINISTRATION: QUALITY ASSURANCE AND SELF-CONTROL

Quality cannot be reached simply by defining formal objectives for quality assurance. In some cases explicit goals for quality assurance will help lead activities down the right path. This is also true for data modeling activities. In the absence of other goals, some data administration departments adhere to normal forms and similar theoretical approaches as indicators of quality — but this is not the essential goal. It is better to use business — driven objectives such as integration, reuse, and modeling of the core business.

Quality Objectives

There should be a documented statement of the data administration department's quality goals. The goals will be either business driven or theory driven — the order of goals will imply which.

Reuse. Reuse is an explicit goal of many IS organizations and should be measured. The reuse quota is an indicator for the quality of data modeling activities.

Typical reuse quotas from projects are about 50%. Some are less and some are more, depending on the project and previous activities. Projects retrieve information about known entities from a variety of sources. For example, information can be retrieved from a host-based repository only (an adequate method) or from discussions with the data administration group during the design process (a better method) as well as from a repository.

Data Integration at the Physical Level. Physical data integration across several applications is an indicator for good data modeling practice. Another good sign is the presence of logical objects that are implemented over and over again.

Reference models are not off-the-shelf production data models. They have to be fitted to fulfill the individual needs of the organization using them. They should best be separated physically or logically from the production data model.

The data administration group may want to analyze its data integration attempts by posing the following questions:

- Is there a physical border between logical, physical, and reference data models?
- Is there a clear logical border? Is it possible to see at first glance whether an entity is in production or an entity from a reference model?
- Is the reference model subject to a version concept?
- Is the production model subject to a version concept? If so, is this separated from the versions of the reference model?
- How is the reference model acquired — paper, or files for a computer-aided software engineering (CASE) tool?

Level of Abstraction. Reference models often have a level of abstraction that is too high for the needs of a single company. The other case, a production model with a higher level of abstraction, should occur only as a rare exception. In most cases, it is useless to raise the production data model to an even higher level of abstraction than a reference model. If there are examples of production models having a higher level of abstraction than reference models in an organization, the reasoning for this should be investigated thoroughly.

Transforming the Logical to a Physical Data Model. A one-to-one implementation of a logical data model can be successful, but in many cases it leads to slow implementations. The transformation process from logical to physical data models requires a great deal of knowledge and experience. It is not economical, and also not very probable, that every analyst has the know-how required for this delicate task. Before attempting this task, data administration should find out the following:

- Do projects teams document their decisions? Can those decisions be retrieved by data administration or other projects?
- Are there reviews of the physical data model? If so, who does them?
- Is there a set of design rules somewhere in the company? If not, is there capable help for documenting them?

Dialogs and Data Modeling. The acceptance of data modeling — especially of physical data modeling — will rise when data models and check routines are directly coupled. Automation is crucial for the development of large, consistent systems. Before automation is undertaken, the data administration group should ask:

- Is there an automatic link between the data model or another repository, screen elements, and their captions?
- Is there an automatic reference between screen elements, check routines, and data type definitions?
- Are screen element tables in specifications generated automatically?

Database Access Layers. Database access layers for logical views on a physical model should be generated automatically from relation descriptions. Many companies use either no access layers at all or code frames for access layers. The generation of access layers is not possible without a rigid data modeling practice. The effort saved by not performing access layer programming is a very tangible effect of data modeling. It should be determined whether the software development department uses access layers, and if so, whether they are generated or at least standardized.

Data Types. Most COBOL or PL/I shops do not have a concept of data types. This leads to enumeration types being redundantly described in textual attribute descriptions, structures being described as entities, and other design flaws. It is helpful if an organization has a data type concept that is supported by code-generation facilities and a repository that allows a data type concept.

Data Dictionary Product Properties. It is important for data dictionary software to support requirements concerning the separation of model layers, version concepts, and data types. It is a good sign if the software developers and project teams like the look and feel of the data dictionary. A data dictionary should:

- Support data types such as enumeration types, records, range types, and a code generation facility.
- Be adaptable to changes in its metamodel. Improvement of the software development process can be slowed or made impossible by an inflexible dictionary.
- Have a version concept.
- Support integration of project data models. This is best done using check tools that support the Data Administration group.
- Support separation of levels, documentation of transformations between levels, and separated production and reference models.

CONCLUSION

A broad range of criticism has been brought against data modeling. This chapter focused on the criticism to derive several lists of critical questions concerning organizational, technical, and quality success factors for a good data modeling practice. These questions were used to check the data modeling practice of a large financial institution. Exploring the issues covered and considering the questions posed should help data administration groups avoid some of the problems common to data modeling.

Chapter V-3

Data Warehouse Design: Issues in Dimensional Data Modeling

Jack McElreath

BEFORE BEGINNING A DISCUSSION of the methods of modeling information in a data warehouse, it is important to agree on the type of data to be stored in the warehouse and how the data differ from traditional operational data.

OPERATIONAL VERSUS DATA WAREHOUSE APPLICATIONS

Operational applications track business events (e.g., orders and payments) and the entities associated with those events (e.g., customers and products) from creation to completion. The status of each event is constantly updated, and the general objective of OLTP (online transaction processing) systems is to get the event processed and completed as soon as practical; processing usually means cost, and completion usually means revenue. Data is typically accessed at the detail level; individual records are read, updated, and replaced. Entities associated with the in-process events are constantly updated to reflect current attributes, and, generally, no history of an entity's prior status is maintained. Entities are usually retained while there is an open business event or likelihood of an incoming event.

Data warehouse applications capture completed business events and all associated information necessary for strategic analysis. Events are static (i.e., history cannot be changed) and held as long as they provide some historical significance. Data is typically accessed at aggregate levels; detail events are summarized across selected entities or categories. In general, the information retained for the entities related to completed events is limited to that needed for aggregation or filtering of analytical queries; snapshots of entities may be needed to reflect the entity at the time of any associated events.

The operational model is process oriented and, often, application oriented; records and relationships support the flow of data from creation to

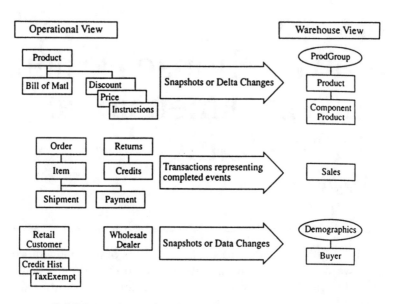

Exhibit 1. Operational and Warehouse Data Models

completion. Warehouse models are analysis oriented and, ideally, subject oriented; records and relationships support the desired query aggregations. Data moves from the operational application to the warehouse but the data view — the model — should be quite different (see Exhibit 1).

Ideally, there should be little redundancy between the operational and warehouse databases. The completed events are purged from the operational database and moved to the warehouse on completion. The entities associated with the events have some necessary redundancy — the same product may be referenced on both active and historical events. However, redundancy should be limited to those entity attributes needed for both processing in the operational system and strategic analysis in the warehouse.

In practice, closed events must often be retained for some period in the operational system, and sometimes in-process events must be recorded by the warehouse. For example, it may be impractical, inefficient, or undesirable to move the data real-time to the warehouse; it is often more efficient and less intrusive to extract and move the data periodically. It is also common to access recent history in the processing of active events (e.g., prior payment is shown on a new bill), and it may not be practical to cross over to a warehouse on a separate platform to retrieve this data. The goal, however, should be to avoid both of these cases to reduce the data inconsistency problems that accompany redundancy. The fastest way to destroy confidence in systems is to provide different answers to the same data questions because of redundant sources.

EXAMPLE OF EXPENDITURE ANALYSIS

To explore dimensional modeling issues, consider the example of a personal application for strategically analyzing expenditures. Most people certainly have an operational system to buy and pay for items, but many (including me) do not know where their money went, whether outgo matches income, or what their expenses should or will be in the future.

A data warehouse would certainly facilitate analysis. This simple personal application essentially has the same functional issues and analytical challenges as those encountered in any corporate warehouse; it is smaller in volume of data and users but no less complex. The technical issues increase with volume, but the business issues and user views are just as difficult as they are in most large corporations.

An example assumes that the individual (me in this case) has an automated system for all cash outlays: purchases, payments, donations, and all other family expenses. This software can be used for all purchases and payments made by check, credit card, or cash to provide a monthly file (more likely a shoe box of illegible receipts) containing completed purchase and payment events. Information about each entity (e.g., stores, people, banks, and credit card issuers) associated with purchases and payments must also be made available to the warehouse. This includes snapshots of the relevant family members, products, and vendors.

Because the transaction volumes or usage patterns to be supported in the warehouse are unclear, I first select my hardware and software platforms. My spouse is currently controlling the operational systems using Quicken Version 1.0 running on a Compaq 286 portable. I think I will probably need a 200-MHz multimedia client hooked to a 64-bit UNIX server with a fiber Internet connection. I will also need software from Cognos, SAS, Oracle, Arbor, and ActiVision, which is easily obtainable from a local retailer. Spending too much time on infrastructure decisions is not worthwhile because the technology becomes obsolete in a few months anyway.

The advantage designers of smaller (in terms of data volume and number of users) warehouses enjoy is that there is probably no need to compromise functional requirements because of technical performance or capacity constraints. The line separating small from large data collections is constantly being raised; 20 years ago, we would become concerned at hundreds of thousands of records; 10 years ago, our concerns started at 1 million records; and today, concern is piqued at tens of millions of records and panic sets in at hundreds of millions. I would have predicted that billions of records would be routinely handled by the year 2000, but the date problems will implode the industry and make all else academic.

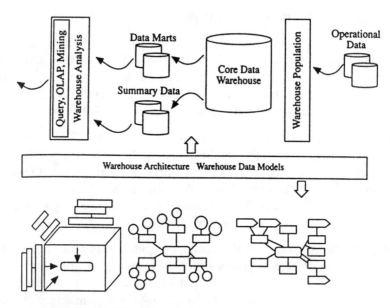

Exhibit 2. Warehouse Architecture and Data Models

ADVANTAGES AND DISADVANTAGES
OF DIMENSIONAL MODELING

The general conclusion evolving from the experts and tool vendors of data warehouse solutions is that for the purpose of schematically defining and analyzing historical information, dimensional modeling is preferable to the techniques used to model operational data (usually some form of entity-relationship or network diagram). Dimensional models are, in theory, simpler for users to understand and manipulate. Simplicity is both the benefit and the problem. It is difficult to model complex information with a simple technique. If the model is too complex, it will not serve users' needs; if it is too simple, it cannot answer tough questions.

Dimensional models are logical, not physical, constructs; the underlying database for dimensional models is either relational or a multidimensional cube. It may also be necessary, based on the complexity of warehouse data, to employ different modeling techniques in the progression from the user view back to the data source, such as cube for the user, star model for the analyst, and entity relationship for the database administrator (see Exhibit 2). The ideal solution is to have the mapping capability to transparently transform the simpler user view to the complex physical data view, efficiently and correctly. Unfortunately, data warehouse tools have not fully evolved to meet this need.

This shortcoming is the driving force behind the popularity of data marts — a mechanism to create a simple and focused subset of the more complex core warehouse. Their place in the warehouse architecture is also shown in Exhibit 2. If most user access can be satisfied from the custom view, then the complexities of the base warehouse are masked from the user. The problem with this approach is, of course, that as new requirements evolve, the party responsible for creating custom warehouse views (and this is seldom the user) must get involved in fulfilling new queries, potentially delaying information delivery.

Once the data warehouse is populated, the strategic user forms complex aggregate views of this data to isolate trends and establish profound changes in the management or direction of the enterprise, which, in the case of our example, is the family. Individual events (e.g., a given purchase) are seldom of interest; more often, it is the aggregation of facts across selected dimensions (e.g., total spent on mail-order children's clothing in late summer). In general, individual events are provided only when some highlighted aggregate event must be exploded (i.e., drilled-down) to provide supporting detail. For example, once I have determined that I am spending excessively on sporting equipment, I might drill-down and discover that the purchase of the $500 titanium golf club was the major culprit.

DATA MODELS

In dimensional modeling, the numeric attributes of the event represent facts, such as quantity, cost, discount, and tax. People, places, times, things, and categories associated with the fact are shown as dimensions.

The Star Model

The star model (as shown in Exhibit 3) gets its name from the dimensions that radiate from central facts. An alternative explanation for the name could be that stars shed little light and even that light takes a long time to arrive; actually, stars, like data warehouses, emit a lot of light — it is just that so little ever reaches us.

The Snowflake Model

A snowflake model is an extended star model in which each dimension radiates aggregate categories (see Exhibit 4). These categories (sometimes called outboards) are what provide the richness of analysis within the data model. For example, we might ask how much is being spent by certain family members for clothing products to be used on family pets during the Christmas season. I believe these models are called snowflakes because they crystallize with infinite variety. However, in sufficient quantity, their beauty may be masked by the need to plow through them to make progress.

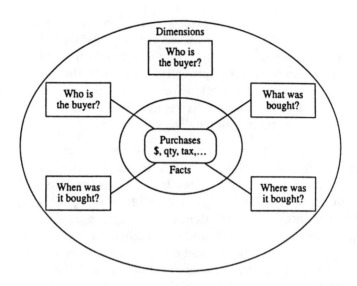

Exhibit 3. The Star Model

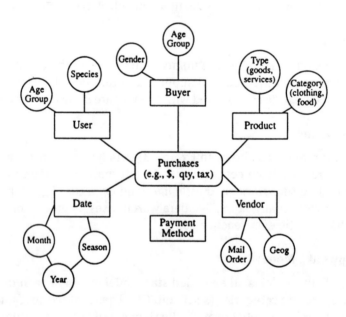

Exhibit 4. The Snowflake Model

The Cube Model

Some vendors prefer to visualize the data as a cube — dimensions form the axes of the cube of facts; outboards are shown as hierarchies of each dimension. These multidimensional cube or hypercube models can be

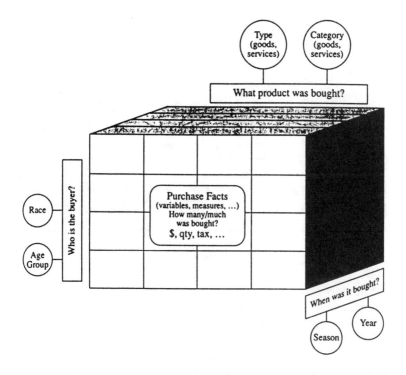

Exhibit 5. The Cube Model

effective, but complex aggregations become difficult to envision, draw, or display on a two-dimensional surface. In Exhibit 5, purchases are analyzed at the intersection of three base dimensions (i.e., buyer, month, product); multiple purchases by the same buyer of the same product in the same month are conceptually summarized.

Dimensions may be rotated or eliminated in any requested view, such as drop product from the analysis and show purchases by buyer/month with month on the vertical axis. Hierarchical groupings may be incorporated above each base dimension as outboards or snowflakes. These result in a large number of additional aggregation possibilities, such as age group/month/product and year/product class/gender. It is clear that a relatively small number of dimensions and categories can result in many potential aggregations. The eight types across three dimensions in the exhibit provide more than 100 different permutations (approximately $2^8 - 1$). If we were to construct a six-dimensional cube with 13 outboards from the snowflake model in Exhibit 4, the possible aggregate permutations would exceed 100,000. Some of these aggregations are surely nonsensical or unnecessary; the trick is to match current and future user requirements to permissible aggregations and further determine which of these aggregations are to materialize statically (i.e., during the data load) versus dynamically (i.e., during the query).

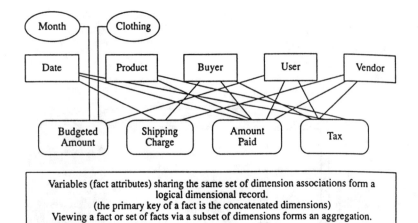

Exhibit 6. Purist View of Dimensional Data

A purist view of dimensional data would define each fact or variable separately and associate that variable with 1 to n dimensions (see Exhibit 6). A logical record would then consist of any variables sharing the same set of dimensions (including categories). An aggregated view would occur whenever a variable is viewed through a subset of existing dimensions. For example, tax and amount paid are part of a logical fact record because they have identical dimension associations. Budgeted amount is associated with user, month, and product group. A view of tax and amount paid through month/date, product group/product, and user would be a conceptual aggregation of all facts associated with only those dimensions. Budgeted amount could then be compared to actual expenditures at that level.

Database Management Systems

There is an evolving debate about whether online analytical processing (OLAP) modeling and implementation should be based on relational base management system (DBMS) products, multidimensional DBMSs, or both (e.g., relational for atomic data, multidimensional for aggregations). Although valid arguments can be posed for both, the final outcome is based more on the success of individual DBMS products in providing aggregation capabilities that are flexible (in terms of ease of adding new facts and dimensions), efficient (in terms of acceptable response time), manageable (in terms of data quality), and easy to use (in terms of providing the user with understandable views of complex data).

Another major factor involves the dynamic versus static aggregation decisions and the ability to alter these choices as data usage evolves. Static aggregation would occur as data are loaded; dynamic aggregation would occur as the query is executed. Currently, relational products seem to have the lead in flexibility and efficiency for high volumes and multidimensional products in ease of use.

To meet the needs of complex data warehouses, dimensional models and the associated software tools must evolve to incorporate the following:

- Complex facts where a network of related events can be combined to form a single fact view
- Complex dimensions containing subsets (including repeating groups) and supersets of data
- Dimension-to-category associations that include many-to-many relationships (i.e., networks in addition to hierarchies)
- Recursive associations within categories
- Temporal associations (i.e., point-in-time data)
- Business rules in data derivation
- Effective aggregate navigation, or the ability to recognize presummarized data

There are certainly other needs, but these directly affect the modeling of data.

DATA MODELING LEVELS

Data modeling should occur at four levels: conceptual, logical, physical, and technical.

The Conceptual Data Model

The conceptual data model is a high-level definition of the major entities, events, and associations required for the application being defined; it contains few, if any, attributes of the conceptual entities. For a data warehouse, the conceptual model should be subject oriented rather than application oriented, and use dimensions, facts, and categorizations rather than entities, events, and tables. Subject orientation means that data from separate operational applications (e.g., business expenses, donations, rentals, purchases, and budgets) should be consolidated into a single analytical subject (i.e., expenditures).

The Logical Data Model

The logical data model should define all entities/roles, events, categorizations, and relationships necessary to deliver the warehouse user requirements. The model is fully attributed and somewhat normalized. We have been taught that OLTP logical models are defined in third normal form, but the clarity of warehouse data is often improved by denormalizing some information (e.g., derived attributes, business rules, summary data, and I model should not be dictated or affected by the data marts). The logical model should not be dictated or affected by the DBMS type (e.g., network, relational, multidimensional, and object) or product (e.g., Oracle, IMS, DB2, and Redbrick) chosen for implementation. In theory, one could convert from any DBMS to any other and use the logical model as a starting point for conversion.

The Physical Data Model

The physical data model is the phase in which the logical model is adapted to the major software and performance constraints of the DBMS, data and usage statistics, and intended processing platform. Physical design decisions are not usually transparent to the applications using the database. Ideally, the physical model mirrors the logical model.

It is more difficult to define the precise line between logical and physical design with warehouse models. Some examples of physical modeling steps include conversion of the dimensional model to a relational or multidimensional structure, data distribution or logical partitioning, entity and referential integrity methods, obvious denormalization needed for performance, and temporal data management options. In many cases, data summarization and creation of distributed custom warehouses are better handled in the logical modeling phase. The major question is whether these decisions involve the clarity of the user view of data (i.e., the realm of the logical model) or are dictated by performance issues or query/DBMS product shortcomings (i.e., the realm of the physical model).

The Technical Data Model

The technical data model incorporates the initial and ongoing tuning of the database, transparent to the applications using it. Indexing, bit maps, physical partitioning, and DASD space management are examples of technical modeling. This is the domain of the database administrator (a complete grasp of the subject usually occurs concurrent with the inability to function as a member of society at large).

Model Expansion

If a dimensional model for the logical model is chosen, it is necessary to simplify the data (and perhaps the user requirements) or explode complex components to incorporate essential network or hierarchical subsets of information. The warehouse in the family expenditures application is intended to track all expenditures, not just those for real products. What happens when the simple model must be expanded to incorporate payments for such items as services, health care, charity, and tolls? And, if one decides to include budgeted amounts for some dimensions, should returns and reimbursements be included? The model needed to fulfill the user requirements may begin to resemble Exhibit 6's depiction of the explosions

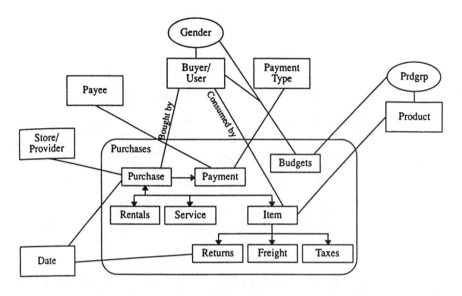

Exhibit 7. Expanded Model of Expenditure Facts

of the individual components of the simple dimensional model. Many of these modeling decisions are subjective.

The star model may classify as expenditures a complex collection of components, depending on the type of purchase, method of payment, and the relationships to surrounding dimensions. In defining my family expenditures warehouse, I decided to incorporate all expenditures in a single fact set. I could have created separate fact tables for each class of expenditure — charity contributions, tax payments, highway tolls, and rentals — but any analysis across classes would have become impractical.

The extended model of expenditure facts in Exhibit 7 was created for several reasons, including the following:

- A single purchase can consist of multiple items (e.g., a VCR and a maintenance contract).
- The fact attributes can vary significantly between different expenditures (e.g., goods have quantities, services have hours, not all are taxed, and returns apply only to goods).
- A single purchase could involve multiple payments (e.g., part cash and part credit card, and installment payments).
- Relationships to dimensions may vary based on the type of component (e.g., buyers are associated with all purchases; users are optional and relate to the individual items).

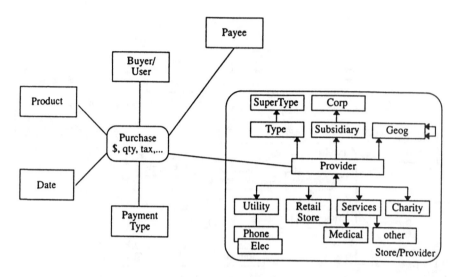

Exhibit 8. Expansion of Data for Store/Provider Associated with Purchases

- A single analysis may use many of the fact components (e.g., is the rate of returned purchases by female buyers of mail-order goods resulting in increasing freight costs?).
- Budgeted amounts will be created for some dimensions and categories.
- All the preceding are important for strategic analysis.

It may be possible to jam all this information into a single purchase fact by imbedding repeating groups and defining lots of attributes that are exclusive to a subset of records. In fact, this may have to been done during physical modeling if the software constraints or performance constraints leave no option. This model pollution should not be done, however, during logical design. The ideal is to provide software (i.e., query and DBMS) that can deal with complex data and transparently present that data in a simple customized view. Today, one is usually forced to simplify by restricting the core warehouse or by providing customized local repositories (i.e., data marts).

Dimensions can also become complex. Exhibit 8 shows a similar expansion of data for the producer associated with purchases. Provider types have both similarities and differences; stores selling goods may not have the same attributes or higher-level categorizations as other business or private entities providing charity, service, mortgage, or energy. The provider or payee associated with an expenditure could be a person (the plumber), a distributor (Wal-Mart), a manufacturer (Nike), a church or synagogue, a municipal government, and on and on. One could increase the number of dimensions to include all distinct provider types as separate, mutually exclusive entities, but this usually results in even more complexity and constraints. In general, it is better to consolidate into a dimension role, because it is easier to add a new type to an existing dimension than to add a new dimension to the model.

The following assumptions should be made about our strategic information needs for the provider dimension:

- The base provider describes all attributes common to every provider and serves as the focal point for most fact relationships: the supertypes (i.e., categorizations) above and subtypes (i.e., attributes exclusive to only some provider types) below. Subtypes may be squashed into the base component during physical design, but it is more informative to segregate them during logical modeling. Repeating groups, or arrays, of subtype data are especially messy and restrictive to embed in the base entity (i.e., the utility company provides both gas and electricity).
- Some fact relationships may be linked firmly or optionally to a subtype or supertype rather than the base producer: for example, I donated to United Funds and not to individual member charitable organizations. Dimension categorizations must be established, each identifying subjective and objective criteria.
  - Are the categorization levels fixed or recursive? (For example, only permit two levels of corporate affiliations but permit variable levels of geography, such as city, state, country, and planet.)
  - Can a single producer concurrently belong to more than one member of a given category? (For example, producer is both Fortune 500 and pharmaceutical, each subjectively defined as a separate type in my model.)
  - Are the categorizations temporal? (For example, the producer has moved and, therefore, changed geographical affiliations. Do I have to remember the history to analyze older facts?)
  - These dimension categorizations are implemented as metadata in many of the OLAP tools; not only the schema (i.e., type to class), which is truly metadata, but the actual member values (e.g., meat and beverage records aggregate to food).

The ideal model, whether entity-relationship or dimensional, permits a simplistic view of dimensions and facts, transparently consolidating the complex underlying data as needed. For example, if I ask for the total spent on housing last year, it would be most effective if the request could be satisfied from presummarized data marts or from a myriad of detail composing that summary with no effect on the user view. The difficulties, of course, are that the consolidation can result in wrong or misunderstood results, and the DBMS and query software tools are somewhat limited in translating logical models to the supporting physical models.

Chapter V-4
Using CORBA to Integrate Database Systems

Bhavani Thuraisingham and Daniel L. Spar

INFORMATION HAS BECOME THE MOST CRITICAL RESOURCE in many organizations, and the rapid growth of networking and database technologies has had a major impact on information processing requirements. Efficient access to information, as well as sharing it, have become urgent needs. As a result, an increasing number of databases in different sites are being interconnected. In order to reconcile the contrasting requirements of the different database management systems (DBMSs), tools that enable users of one system to use another system's data are being developed. Efficient solutions for interconnecting and administering different database systems are also being investigated.

There are two aspects to the object-oriented approach to integrating heterogeneous database systems. In one approach, an object-oriented data model could be used as a generic representation scheme so that the schema transformations between the different database systems could be facilitated. In the other approach, a distributed object management system could be used to interconnect heterogeneous database systems. This chapter explores the distributed object management system approach by focusing on a specific distributed object management system: the object management group's (OMG) Common Object Request Broker Architecture (CORBA).

INTEROPERABILITY ISSUES

Although research on interconnecting different DBMSs has been under way for over a decade, only recently have many of the difficult problems been addressed. Through the evolution of the three-tier approach to client/server, the capability of integrating DBMS's has improved significantly. The traditional two-tier client/server approach included the layers of

1. Client
2. Server

For small systems, the two-tier approach works reasonably well. For larger systems with greater numbers of connected clients and servers, and greater levels of complexity and requirements for security, there is a substantial need for three-tier architectures. Two-tier systems are notorious for their development of the "fat client," where excessive amounts of code running business logic is required to be loaded on to the client machine.

The three-tier approach breaks client/server components into the layers of

1. Client (presentation layer)
2. Middleware (business logic)
3. Server (data and resource management)

The result is much more efficient use of resources, and greater "plug and play" capabilities for both clients and servers. Clients can be superthin browsers running JAVA applets, and servers can be efficiently integrated and load-balanced.

With the advent of web servers, the three-tier model becomes "n-tier," since a web server is often placed between the client and middleware layers.

Schema Heterogeneity. Not all of the databases in a heterogeneous architecture are represented by the same schema (data model). Therefore, the different conceptual schemas have to be integrated. In order to do this, translators that transform the constructs of one schema into those of another are being developed. Integration remains most difficult with the older legacy databases that are prerelational.

Transaction Processing Heterogeneity. Different DBMSs may use different algorithms for transaction processing. Work is being directed toward integrating the various transaction processing mechanisms. Techniques that integrate locking, timestamping, and validation mechanisms are being developed. However, strict serializability may have to be sacrificed in order to create a heterogeneous environment. Independent transaction processing monitor (TP monitor) software is now readily available in the distributed systems marketplace. TP monitor software has been used for years on mainframes, and is now of great assistance in high-volume systems such as Internet commerce. Examples include web-based stock brokerage trading sites.

Query Processing Heterogeneity. Different DBMSs may also use different query processing and optimization strategies. Research is being conducted to develop a global cost model for distributed query optimization.

Query Language Heterogeneity. Query language heterogeneity should also be addressed. Even if the DBMSs are based on the relational model. Structured query language (SQL) and relational calculus could be used to achieve heterogeneity. Standardization efforts are under way to develop a uniform interface language.

Constraint Heterogeneity. Different DBMSs enforce different integrity constraints, which are often inconsistent. For example, one DBMS could enforce a constraint that all employees must work at least 40 hours, even though another DBMS may not enforce such a constraint. Moving these business rules over to the application servers on the middle tier and away from the DBMSs on the third tier will also help isolate and correct business rule inconsistencies.

Semantic Heterogeneity. Data may be interpreted differently by different components. For example, the entity address could represent just the country for one component, or it could represent the number, street, city, and country for another component. This problem will be difficult to resolve in older systems that combined multiple domains in a single database field and often assigned cryptic names to tables and fields that do not reveal their content.

THE COMMON OBJECT REQUEST BROKER ARCHITECTURE (CORBA)

CORBA was created to provide an object-based central layer to enable the objectives of three-tier distributed systems, especially in the area of interoperability.

The three major components of CORBA are the object model, the object request broker (ORB) and object adapters, and the interface definition language (-IDL).

The Object Model

The object model describes object semantics and object implementation. Object semantics describe the semantics of an object, type, requests, object creation and destruction, interfaces, operations, and attributes. Object implementation describes the execution model and the construction model. In general, the object model of CORBA has the essential constructs of most object models.

The Object Request Broker (ORB)

The ORB essentially enables communication between a client and a server object. A client invokes an operation on the object, and the object implementation provides the code and data needed to implement the object. The ORB provides the necessary mechanisms to find the object implementation for a particular request and enables the object implementation to receive the request. The communication mechanisms necessary to deliver the request are also provided by the ORB.

In addition, the ORB supports the activation and deactivation of objects and their implementation as well as generating and interpreting object

397

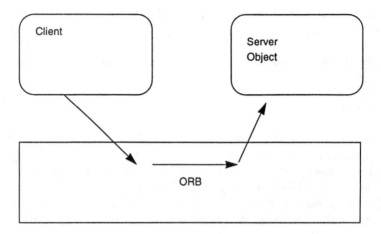

Exhibit 1. Communication through an Object Request Broker (ORB)

references. Although the ORB provides the mechanisms to locate the object and communicate the client's request to the object, the exact location of the object, as well as the details of its implementation, are transparent to the client. Objects use object adapters to access the services provided by the ORB. Communication between a client and a server object using the ORB is illustrated in Exhibit 1.

INTERFACE DEFINITION LANGUAGE (IDL)

IDL is the language used to describe the interfaces that are called by client objects and provided by object implementations. IDL is a declarative language; client and object implementations are not written in IDL. IDL grammar is a subset of ANSI C++ with additional constructs to support the operation invocation mechanism. An IDL binding to the C language has been specified, and other language bindings are being processed. Exhibit 2 illustrates how IDL is used for communication between a client and a server. The client's request is passed to the ORB using an IDL stub. An IDL skeleton delivers the request to the server object.

INTEGRATING HETEROGENEOUS DATABASE SYSTEMS

Migrating legacy databases to new generation architectures is difficult. Although it is desirable to migrate such databases and applications to client/server architectures, the costs involved in many cases are enormous. Therefore, the alternative approach is to keep the legacy databases and applications and develop mechanisms to integrate them with new systems. The distributed object management system approach in general, and the CORBA approach in particular, are examples of such mechanisms.

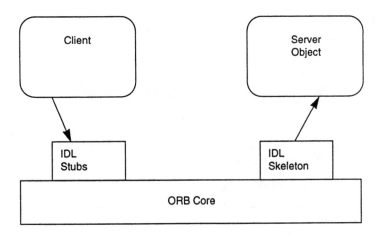

Exhibit 2. Interface Definition Language (IDL) Interface to Object Request Broker (ORB)

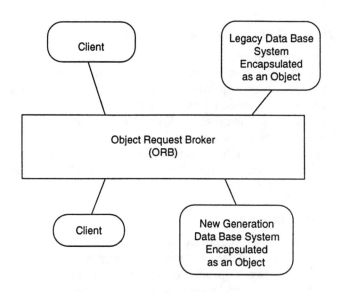

Exhibit 3.   Encapsulating Legacy Databases

Although the major advantage of the CORBA approach is the ability to encapsulate legacy database systems and databases as objects without having to make any major modifications (see Exhibit 3), techniques for handling the various types of heterogeneity are still necessary. The CORBA approach does not handle problems such as transaction heterogeneity and semantic heterogeneity. However, the procedures used to handle the types

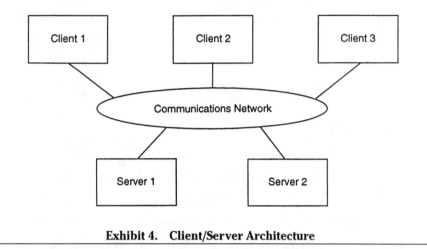

Exhibit 4.   Client/Server Architecture

of heterogeneity can be encapsulated in the CORBA environment and invoked appropriately.

Handling Client Communications with the Server

A client will need to communicate with the database servers, as shown in Exhibit 4. One method is to encapsulate the database servers as objects. The clients can issue appropriate requests and access the servers through an ORB. If the servers are SQL-based, the entire SQL query/update request could be embedded in the message. When the method associated with the server object gets the message, it can extract the SQL request and pass it to the server. The results from the server objects are then encoded as a message and passed back to the client through the ORB. This approach is illustrated in Exhibit 5.

Handling Heterogeneity

Different types of heterogeneity must be handled in different ways. For example, if the client is SQL-based and the server is a legacy database system based on the network model, then the SQL query by the client must be transformed into a language understood by the server. One representation scheme must be transformed into another. The client's request must first be sent to the module that is responsible for performing the transformations. This module the transformer could be encapsulated as an object. As illustrated in Exhibit 6, the client's SQL request is sent to the transformer, which transforms the request into a request understood by the server. The transformed request is then sent to the server object. The transformer could directly transform the SQL representation into a network representation, or it could use an intermediate representation to carry out the transformation.

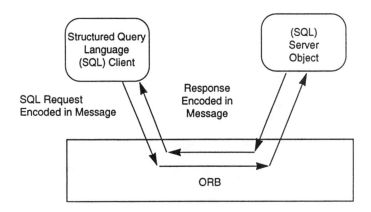

Exhibit 5. Common Object Request Broker Architecture (CORBA) for Interoperability

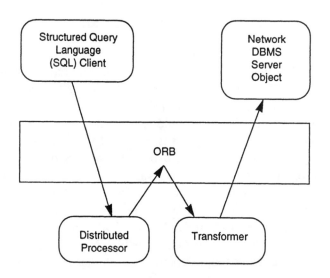

Exhibit 6. Handling Transformations

Handling Transformations

The distributed processor could also be used to perform distributed data management functions. The distributed processor is responsible for handling functions such as global query optimization and global transaction management. This module is also encapsulated as an object and handles the global requests and responses. The response assembled by the server is also sent to the transformer to transform into a representation understood by the client. Response delivery is illustrated in Exhibit 7.

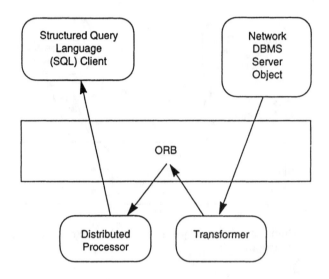

Exhibit 7. Delivering Responses

Semantic Heterogeneity. If semantic heterogeneity has to be handled, a repository should be maintained to store the different names given to a single object or the different objects represented by a single name. The repository could be encapsulated as an object that would resolve semantic heterogeneity. For example, a client could request that an object be retrieved from multiple servers. The request is first sent to the repository, which issues multiple requests to the appropriate servers depending on the names used to denote the object. This approach is illustrated in Exhibit 8. The response may also be sent to the repository so that it can be presented to the client in an appropriate manner. The repository could be an extension of the transformer illustrated in Exhibit 6. All the communications are carried out through the ORB. This example highlights some of the benefits of separating the business logic from the actual data stored in the DBMS servers.

CONCLUSION

The rapid growth in distributed systems has placed two key demands on IT managers:

1. How can the most efficient and effective design — the three-tier model — best be implemented to manage a very heterogeneous environment?
2. How can the semantic meaning of the legacy data elements be best understood so they can be shared across systems?

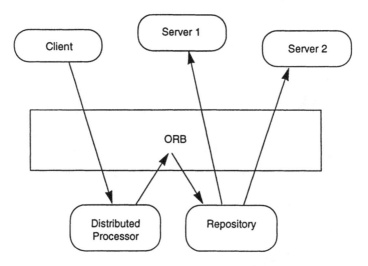

Exhibit 8. Handling Semantic Heterogeneity

The CORBA approach is an excellent means of addressing heterogeneity, especially with respect to queries, languages, transactions, schemas, constraints, and semantics. However, although CORBA is useful for integrating heterogeneous database systems, there are still several issues that need further consideration. For example, should a server be encapsulated as an object? How can databases be encapsulated? Should an entire database be encapsulated as an object or should it consist of multiple objects? Should stored procedures be encapsulated also?

Although there is still much work to be done, the various approaches proposed to handle these issues show a lot of promise. Furthermore, until efficient approaches are developed to migrate the legacy databases and applications to client/server-based architectures, approaches like CORBA and other distributed object management systems for integrating heterogeneous databases and systems are needed.

Chapter V-5
Data Warehousing and Parallel Databases

T.M. Rajkumar and David K. Holthaus

THE SUBJECT OF PARALLEL PROCESSING BRINGS TO MIND an interesting analogy from a *Byte* magazine article: "…when farmers wanted to pull heavier loads, they did not breed larger horses, they simply used more than one. Aside from providing extra pulling power, a team of horses provided flexibility, because the farmer could harness them in whatever arrangement suited the task at hand." In a similar fashion, when hardware vendors wanted to give computers more powerful processing capabilities, they did so by using more than one processor. Multiple CPUs not only offer a boost in performance, but allow increased scalability in applications.

Today, parallel processing is beginning to establish itself in the marketplace. Companies such as IBM Corp., Tandem Computers, Inc., and Pyramid Technology Corp. offer hardware that uses multiple processors. Likewise, organizations, specifically those specializing in database technology, such as Oracle Corp., IBM Corp., Informix Software Inc., and Sybase Inc., are developing software to take advantage of a parallel processing platform. With information needs and database sizes approaching multiple terabytes, the demand for powerful and scaleable parallel processing platforms has arrived.

PARALLEL PROCESSING TECHNIQUES

The two most common processing techniques incorporated into parallel processing systems are symmetric multiprocessing (SMP) and massively parallel processing (MPP).

Symmetric Multiprocessing (Shared Memory)

SMP is an example of a tightly coupled system. In a tightly coupled system, multiple processors share memory through a common bus in a single node.

"Symmetric" in SMP means that no processor has preferential access to any of the system resources such as memory or I/O devices. Each processor has full access to the entire shared memory region. It is this access to

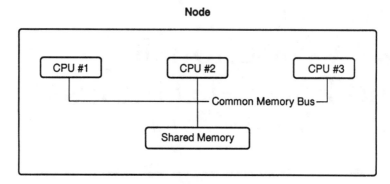

Exhibit 1. Tightly Coupled System

shared memory that limits scalability in a tightly coupled system. As traffic on the memory bus increases, bandwidth of the bus approaches the maximum capacity. Thus, SMP designs with larger bandwidths on the memory bus can support more processors.

Memory management is also a factor. In an SMP system, each CPU has its own memory cache that stores the data associated with the processes it is executing. When these processes migrate from one processor to the next, the data it needs does not travel with it. The new processor must then update its cache, which blocks the CPU from doing any other reads or writes. Consequently, overhead increases in an SMP system. The advantage of SMP is its openness and programming versatility in addition to its ability to multithread tasks. Exhibit 1 shows the architecture of a node in a tightly coupled system.

Massively Parallel Processing (Shared-Nothing Systems)

A slightly different approach is used in a loosely coupled system. In this type of system, each node can be comprised of one or more CPUs, each with associated memory. Each node has access to other shared resources such as disk drives. Memory is not shared between nodes, thereby avoiding the potential constraint of a memory bus. However, there are limitations elsewhere. Communication between nodes occurs through a high-speed bus. It is the bandwidth of this bus, as contention for resources increases, that limits the number of nodes that can exist in a loosely coupled system. Exhibit 2 shows the architecture of a loosely coupled system.

MPP does not have the constraints of a tightly or loosely coupled system, because the nodes in a massively parallel system are arranged in a hypercube. In a hypercube, the processors are arranged so that each one is connected to log2n other processors, where n is the number of processors in the MPP system. For example, in a 16-processor hypercube,

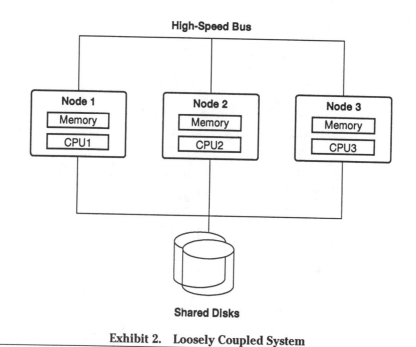

Exhibit 2. Loosely Coupled System

$\log_2 16 = 4$, so each processor is connected to four other processors and can easily communicate with all other processors as a result. Exhibit 3 shows an example of a hypercube with eight processors.

MPP systems are more stable, because there are multiple paths to communicate with shared resources and other nodes. If one processor goes down, other communication paths are still available. On many hardware platforms, processors and other resources can be hot-swapped or replaced in case of failure without bringing the entire system down.

MPP systems are also called shared-nothing systems because memory is not shared between nodes and each node has its own bus-to-I/O devices. In an MPP system, thousands of processors can be supported because each processor has multiple communication paths to other nodes and no bottleneck to resources such as I/O devices. Consequently, MPP systems are extremely scalable for applications development or very complex queries. A disadvantage of MPP is the level of difficulty in managing these large, complex systems.

Hybrid Parallel Systems. In addition, hybrid parallel systems are available that improve on the drawbacks of each approach. Clustered SMP is a method in which separate SMP systems are connected via some type of high-speed interface, network, or switch, which allows SMP to erase the constraints associated with shared memory. Hardware manufacturers are

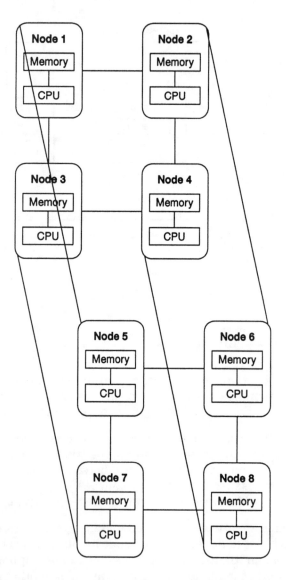

Exhibit 3. Massively Parallel System with Eight Nodes

also starting to integrate symmetric multiprocessing into individual MPP nodes.

PARALLEL QUERY PROCESSING

Once parallel systems became available, DBMS vendors were among the first to take advantage of this highly scalable architecture. Commercial organizations have always generated large amounts of data, and although they may have been willing to pay high prices for secondary storage devices, it was still nearly impossible to get performance from the DBMS with very large volumes of data. Once database vendors released parallel versions of their database software for the various parallel platforms, it was possible to store and process terabytes of information in a timely fashion.

Database vendors had the challenge of inventing ways to parallelize the various tasks involved in managing and effectively using the DBMS in a parallel environment, including finding a way to maintain a logical view of the DBMS over several nodes. Parallel query processing (PQP) is the process of optimizing large, complex, time-consuming queries by dividing the workload into smaller tasks to achieve performance improvements on parallel systems. Tasks such as queries, index creations, data loads, and recovery are all candidates for parallelization.

Query Servers. Parallel query processing is accomplished by dividing up units of work into separate, more manageable units. The separated units are distributed among the nodes of the parallel system and are called query slaves or query servers. The degree of parallelism refers to the number of query servers used to process an SQL query.

Each query server is allocated some piece of the query and performs the processing on it. In the case of a full-table scan, each server would receive the parsed structured query language (SQL) statement and a piece of the data in the table to perform the processing. Upon completion of its processing, the server returns the result set to a query coordinator, which in turn organizes the result sets from all query servers. The query coordinator delegates the work to the query servers. It then organizes and returns the full result set to the process that originated the query.

Interquery and Intraquery Parallelism. Common metrics used in databases are throughput (i.e., transactions per second) and response time. Interquery parallelism occurs when several queries are processed simultaneously (one query to each processor) and increases the global throughput. Intraquery parallelism occurs when several processors cooperate to process the same query and decrease the response time. However, intraquery parallelism involves some overhead such as initialization, synchronization, and communication. This overhead reduces the throughput, but improves the response time. Hence, interquery and intraquery parallelism have to be balanced and cannot be tuned independently of each other.

One of the challenges of effectively implementing parallel query processing is ensuring that all query servers obtain proportional parallelism so that each performs an equal amount of work. Early PQP techniques consisted of interquery parallelism, where the system assigns one processor to each query (see Exhibit 4). This method creates major problems with processing queries of varying complexity. A relatively simple query is performed

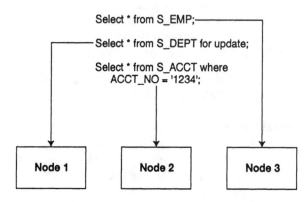

Exhibit 4.   Interquery Parallelism

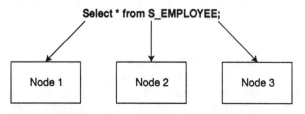

Exhibit 5.   Intraquery Parallelism

very quickly, whereas one with several joins takes much longer, giving the perception of separate physical systems accessing one logical database. However, intraquery parallelism is available in most DBMSs today and is used to perform individual queries in parallel across multiple processors (see Exhibit 5).

Candidates for Parallelism

SQL queries that are best candidates for being performed in parallel are those that involve full-table scans in the database. Whether a full-table scan is used in a given query depends on the SQL optimizer. In general, if an index existing on a table query references the index key, then the index will be used. However, there are times when a full-table scan is more efficient than using an index, as is the case in the following example.

A query is submitted that ultimately returns 70% of the rows in the table and an index is referenced to select the rows. For each row, the index is accessed to find the database block where the row resides. In a nonparallel world, an index is probably optimal to a full-table scan. However, if enough query servers can be employed so that each part of the full-table scan is more efficient than one server using an index, then a parallel full-table scan would be best. Future challenges to parallel query processing will be to integrate interquery and intraquery parallelism to maximize overall efficiency of the DBMS. Other query operations that are prime candidates for parallelism (and consequently involve full-table scans) include:

- The DISTINCT qualifier
- Sort, merge, and nested loop joins
- Union all, minus, intersect, and union operators
- "Order by" and "group by" subqueries of insert, update, delete, and create table statements

Parallel Joins

The join procedure is possibly the most computationally difficult operation in a database. Therefore, it should make perfect sense that parallelizing joins is very important to overall performance in a parallel database.

Pipeline Parallelism. There are two types of parallelism to maximize the performance of the database during join operations. The first is pipeline parallelism, which can be likened to a UNIX pipe procedure, where output is passed on for subsequent processing.

For example, consider a query that requires four join operations. Pipeline parallelism assigns each join operation to a processor. The result set of the first join is then passed to the second processor and its result set is passed, and so on. However, this is an inefficient process. First, processors that have been assigned joins down the line remain idle while waiting for the result sets to be passed. Second, there is no balancing; some joins could be very complex and large and others simple and smaller, leading to skewing. Third, result sets from some joins can be significantly larger than others. In Exhibit 6, several Scan processes run in parallel on the Scan node and each is passed to the Report node.

Partition Parallelism. Pipeline parallelism is not the only answer for join operations. The need for a better means of parallelizing joins resulted in a second type of parallelism — partition parallelism. In the example shown in Exhibit 7, each thread within the model is performing pipeline parallelism with the result sets eventually combined into a Merge operator.

There are two approaches to using partition parallelism and both use query servers to split up the join process. The first approach is the fragment-and-replicate join (see Exhibit 8). This technique splits the contents of the first table in the join and distributes it to the query servers and also sends the second (i.e., broadcast) table in its entirety to each query server. Each query server determines if any rows in the partitioned table match the broadcast table.

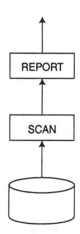

Exhibit 6. Pipeline Parallelism

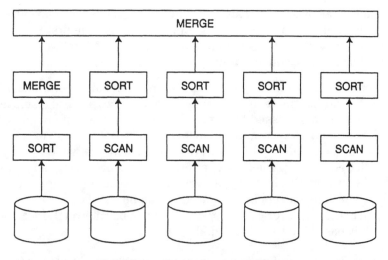

Exhibit 7. Partitioned Parallelism

The second approach is called symmetric partitioning. This method performs the join along the join key. An example of a join key using this method might be the days in a week. In this case, each query server might receive a different day of the week (i.e., seven query servers total). Each query server would then receive the rows from both tables where the join key contained the specific day of the week and determine whether any rows from the first table could be joined with the second for that specific day of the week. Exhibit 9 illustrates this symmetric partitioning concept.

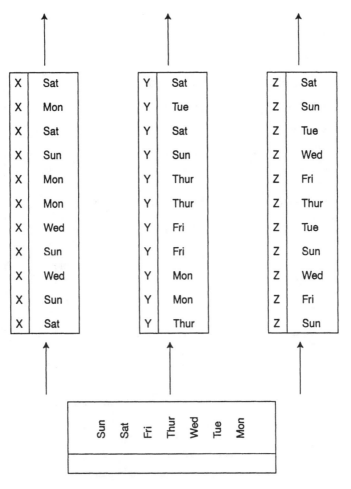

Exhibit 8.   Fragment-and-Replicate Join

Choosing an SQL Optimizer

When using the parallel query option, there are several additional parallel database issues that should be considered. First is the SQL optimizer used by the DBMS.

The two most common types of optimizers are rule-based and cost-based. The rule-based optimizer determines the execution plan of an SQL statement based on rules for maximum performance. The cost-based optimizer uses collected statistics on past activity in the database to determine the most efficient execution.

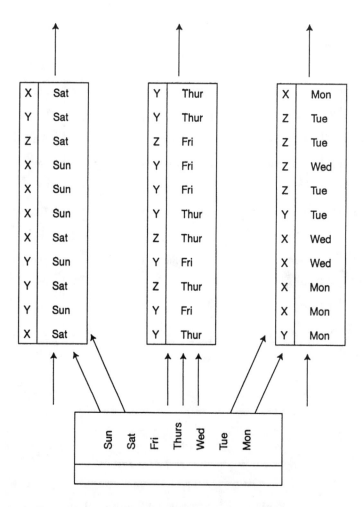

Exhibit 9.   Symmetric Partitioning of a Join

There are cases in which each type of optimizer makes mistakes when determining the execution plan. Generally, database systems allow users to modify the parallel features of queries at different levels in the database. Users and developers typically know much more about the data that is stored in the database than the DBMS. For example, information about how the data is partitioned, the frequency of matches in a table (i.e., number of rows that will be retrieved or computed), and even the number of I/Os required may give the user better information than the DBMS. At the query level, the degree of parallelism can be set by the user using hints in most database systems, giving the user coding the SQL statement ultimate control over the execution of the query.

Function Shipping Versus Data Shipping

Another issue important to parallel query processing is how query servers are distributed among the nodes of a parallel system. It comes down to whether or not any intelligence is given to the query coordinator when distributing query servers to the nodes. The more popular term for this is "function shipping versus data shipping."

In data shipping, a query server is assigned to a node regardless of where the data actually resides. When the query servers process their piece of the information, the data is shipped from the various disks across the communications subsystem and back to the query server that requested the data. Function shipping takes into account where the data actually resides.

For example, if the data in a table actually resides on disk across three nodes, the query servers would be assigned to those three nodes where the data reside. This avoids the data transfer across the communications subsystem, which decreases performance time on a parallel query.

Shared Disk Versus Shared Nothing

Another consideration for parallel query processing is the architecture used by parallel database systems. This is more commonly known as the shared-disk vs. shared-nothing debate.

When discussing MPP systems, shared-nothing is viewed as each node having access to its own memory and I/O devices. A similar concept exists in database terms. In a shared-disk database, each node on the system has access to the entire database, regardless of the physical disk where the data may reside. Even though data are stored on individual disks that belong to only one node, the database instance sees the aggregation of data.

The database instance is able to see the aggregation of data because of a software layer known as virtual shared disk (VSD) that is used on the IBM SP2. This layer allows any node on the parallel machine to transparently access any disk as if it were locally attached to that node. The VSD traps a request for a remote shared disk at the disk driver level and ships the requests directly to the corresponding node. This allows the database to totally ignore the concept of a node "owning" certain disks. Instead, all disks are accessible by all nodes to provide a single logical view of the database.

In a shared-nothing architecture, each node is granted exclusive access to a portion of the database (called a partition). Each node has its own set of disks on which the node's database partition is stored. Each node can access only its partition of data and does not have direct access to other nodes' disks.

Additional Parallel Operations

Other database operations can be performed in parallel within a DBMS, such as data loads, index creation, and backup and recovery operations. A large data load is a good candidate for parallelization. As databases scale in size to multiple terabytes of data, effective parallel methods for loading and reorganizing data will increase in importance.

In a single processor model, data are loaded using one process to load a single table from a single file to a single database file. With parallel methods, it is possible to load multiple data files into a single table and multiple database file at a certain point in time. However, it is necessary that the data be organized efficiently to parallelize the load process. The data should be striped (i.e., partitioned) across the disks of the parallel system so that multiple load processes can be engaged. In addition, the physical database files should also be striped across multiple disks. This allows data files to be arranged so that they are capable of being loaded into a database file that resides on the same node. In essence, several single processor models are all simultaneously accessing one logical database.

Index creation can also be performed in parallel. Some DBMSs use a producer-consumer relationship that is quite common for sorting procedures. The producer-side carries out a full-table scan and performs the I/O to retrieve the database blocks and the consumer takes the blocks and performs the sort. There may be several producer and consumer tasks engaged in a single index procedure.

Scalability and Performance Issues

The two major parallel database architectures are SMP and MPP. Two factors that should be considered when selecting a parallel system are the system's scalability to the user's requirements during the application's expected life, and the system's maximum potential performance. SMP systems have been around longer and are very cost-effective. They are rich in application simplicity, availability, and openness.

However, SMPs are not scalable beyond a few dozen processors. Also, applications that are larger than the CPU cache do not run very efficiently. The shared-memory approach creates bottlenecks on the memory bus. Scalability is also limited in SMP systems with very large databases. SMP database sizes are usually 100GB and less because of these scalability limitations.

MPP systems achieve scalability at the expense of application development. MPP systems are scaleable up to thousands of processors, but are much more difficult to manage. Applications on MPP systems differ in application efficiency depending on how the software is designed. The software must be designed to take advantage of parallel processing benefits, where applications using SMP can generally run as is. In the future, these issues will likely have less impact as architectures are integrated into one another.

IMPROVEMENTS IN PARALLEL QUERY PROCESSING

Parallel query processing has greatly enhanced performance in databases. However, there is room for improvement, especially in regard to the database optimizer.

Many optimizers in parallel databases determine the execution plan of an SQL query in a nonparallel fashion. The query coordinator then determines how the query can be parallelized at runtime. The optimizer should be able to determine the best path based on both parallel and nonparallel execution paths. Parallel queries will improve with the integration of pipeline parallelism and symmetric partitioning. In some cases these two types of parallelism are already working together to increase overall performance.

The real goal of parallel systems and parallel databases is to eliminate bottlenecks so that system and application performance can truly blossom and stabilize. There will always be bottlenecks in performance no matter how efficiently parallel systems are designed and configured. There will always be room for improved performance at four basic levels: processing power, memory, communications, and physical I/O.

THE ADVENT OF THE DATA WAREHOUSE

Data warehousing is a way for businesses to organize their data so that it can become a strategic aid in the decision-making process. A data warehouse is nothing more than a single logical store for company data, which is subject to interpretation. Depending on the size of the company, the finance department alone may have its own warehouse where complex financial analysis results are stored — usually termed a data mart.

The data warehouse is a collection of data used throughout the life of the company for performing complex and accurate analyses. By the time the data are loaded into the data warehouse they are void of any inaccuracies and generally are read-only data. Because the data are collected over several years, information about the time the data are collected is an important piece of each record or transaction in the warehouse.

Why Build a Data Warehouse?

A data warehouse allows a single view of the data in an organization, eliminating the need for systems to pass data to several other systems. A simple analogy is the path of an interesting rumor in an office environment that flows through several individuals, each one applying their own interpretations. By the time it reaches the last person, the rumor barely resembles the story from the first individual.

The same thing happens with data that are passed to different systems. Each system applies its own terminology for the data fields as relevant to the area of the business, and by the time it reaches the last system, the data have lost their true identity. There is confusion among different functional areas as to what the data are and where they really come from. In a warehouse environment, the systems are built to "pull" data from the data warehouse.

Another reason to build a warehouse is operating efficiencies. A single organized data store should reduce the costs of maintaining the systems the data warehouse feeds or increase the serviceability to new and existing systems. When there is no centralized warehouse, existing systems feed data to other systems, which feed others, and so forth. It quickly becomes difficult to track the path of data in an organization because it is a cluttered mess. Adding more processing to an application now takes even more time and resources to track through all the different systems to find what is really needed.

DESIGNING THE DATA WAREHOUSE: WHAT IS THE OPTIMAL METHOD?

The two most popular data warehouse architectures are the relational model and the multidimensional model. The relational model uses a time-tested approach to database design, but not necessarily an optimal approach to data warehouse design. The relational model focuses on ensuring data consistency by reducing data redundancy. By reducing the number of places the data reside in the database, the DBMS becomes easier to manage.

Easier management alone does not make one design method an optimal choice for a data warehouse. In contrast, the multidimensional model focuses on the power of analysis. The data are stored and retrieved so that they can be viewed from a number of different perspectives (or dimensions) to enhance the decision-making process.

The Relational Model

The relational model is an extremely valuable architecture for operational databases, generally referred to as OTLP systems. The relation model's value in decision support systems, termed OLAP, is often challenged. Briefly, the process for designing a database using the relational model consists of the evolution from a high-level conceptual data model to a logical design showing entities and relationships for specific business processes.

The next step in database design is the physical design that documents the specific transactions and the organization of the relations within the database. Within the logical design phase, normalization techniques are applied to minimize any anomalies that may compromise data consistency. This is also the process in which data redundancy is minimized. The only redundancy should be in the keys of each relation needed to maintain relationships within the database.

This is not to say that multidimensional views are not part of the relational model with OLAP (ROLAP) processes. The architecture is three-tiered — a layered approach. The database layer provides data storage, access, and retrieval processes. The application logic is provided by a separate ROLAP engine, which provides multidimensional views of the data to end users.

Pros and Cons of the Relational Model. The advantages of using the relational model for data warehousing are its:

- Established standards
- Efficiency for transaction processing
- Better performance for very large databases
- Flexibility in the tradeoff between query response time and the amount of aggregation

The disadvantages of using the relational model for data warehousing are that it:

- Provides poor support of the end user's conceptual view.
- Is inefficient for complex queries and analyses.
- Is limited by the query language standard.

The question becomes whether this model is still feasible for data warehouses and OLAP. With data warehouses, OLAP queries can span literally millions of rows of data. The relational model performed poorly in the early years, but its overwhelming popularity and sound design has led many RDBMS vendors to spend considerable research and development to optimize their software. The biggest issue has to do with the relational SQL join. It is easy to imagine a join over three 50-million-row tables using OLAP. Such queries require enormous amounts of processing power that challenge the most powerful computers. In OLTP applications, it is unheard of to find a query this large.

How Query Processing Is Performed in OLAP and OLTP. Transaction processing systems generally issue static queries repetitively. In an order processing system, an order entry transaction is performed when the customer places the order (i.e., a record is inserted into the database), the record is modified when the order is shipped (i.e., an update transaction), and the order is deleted when the products have been delivered to the customer (i.e., a delete transaction). A database can be highly optimized in this environment with very little overhead. In most cases, the record resides in RAM during the entire insert-update-delete process. OLAP systems are very dynamic, often summarizing several years' worth of information to complete a trend analysis. In this case, records are likely funneled in and out of memory as they are retrieved and used for running calculations.

Proponents of the relational model in data warehousing argue that OLAP capabilities are best provided directly against the data warehouse. There are valid reasons for this thinking. When using the relational model, atomic-level information is stored in the database. The designer can choose to aggregate any percentage of the warehouse, which gives the designer options related to optimal performance in the warehouse. Data warehouses can grow to anywhere from several hundred gigabytes to multiple terabytes. Conventional database optimization techniques will likely be inadequate, so designers must precalculate some of the values.

Although storage requirements increase when aggregation occurs, the benefits outweigh the costs (especially with dropping prices in disk storage). There are varying degrees of aggregation available to a designer. Using very little aggregation improves performance in situations where resources and response times are very high. Fully aggregated databases imply that query performance takes absolute priority, while a choice somewhere in the middle may be used to accommodate the most frequently accessed warehouse objects.

For all of the inefficiencies of relational joins in a data warehouse, it is still considered a better choice for very large databases, particularly those over 100G bytes in size. The introduction of parallelism within the database software greatly improves the performance of complex queries. In addition, relational data warehouses are highly scalable. As the data warehouse grows in size, the addition of more processors is fairly linear to offset increased processing requirements. Flexibility and stability are vitally important in a data warehouse solution. Standards for the relational model have been established and tested in the software arenas. With all atomic data in the warehouse, all options are available.

Multidimensional Databases

While no one can argue with the value of the relational model for OLTP processing, there are limitations in using the relational model for OLAP, as outlined previously. The multidimensional database model serves as a possible solution to those limitations.

The disadvantages of the relational model become advantages under a multidimensional DBMS (MD-DBMS). The foundation of the multidimensional model is that true analytical capabilities cannot be served by a two-dimensional view of the data; rather, data need to be viewed in multiple dimensions — 3, 5, 10, 20, or even 100 dimensions — because of the complexity of the analysis being performed.

Very rarely are two-dimensional analyses performed with OLAP queries (e.g., the sales of product X, Y, and Z over the past year). A more common query might be the comparison in sales of product X, Y, and Z over the past year by month in division #1 in the northwest region for colors red and blue vs. the previous year's numbers. This type of analysis is usually termed "business intelligence," because the answer provides decision-making value. The query requires five dimensions, and no relational table can support it.

Pros and Cons of Multidimensional Analysis. Data is organized in a multidimensional database by dimensions, which are commonly referred to as keys in the relational world. Values in dimensions are unique just as primary keys are unique. The values that make up each dimension are called positions. The actual data values are stored in arrays. Arrays are multiple occurrences of the data item and are calculated by the dimensions that define them. The arrays of data show the relationships between dimensions.

The biggest advantage of multidimensional databases is performance of complex queries. A multidimensional query is much faster than the join of relational tables to accomplish a five-dimensional view. This is because the data in a multidimensional database is calculated over the dimensions that define it.

However, there is a price to pay for the increased query performance, and that is the level of aggregation in multidimensional databases. The relational model provides a choice based on the needs of the end user. In multidimensional views used in decision support, there is no choice. A high degree of aggregation is required for sufficient performance. Multidimensional databases characteristically are not efficient with very large amounts of data, typically with databases totaling 100G bytes or more. High aggregation means that overall database size can increase by two to three times the original amount of data.

The Total Warehouse Solution

The relational database model continues to be the predominant choice as a warehouse repository. The combination of stability, scalability, and maturity make it optimal for storing atomic-level data. Although multidimensional databases offer more intuitive analysis, there are scalability questions when considering it to build a data warehouse. Because performance suffers in very large warehouses, it is not a total solution. However, there is no question that multidimensional databases belong in an organization's warehouse solution. At this time, its place is firm as the front end to the data warehouse, allowing users to query the multidimensional database for analysis.

In the future, once reasonable performance is attained and both atomic data and aggregation can reside in the same database, multidimensional databases may become the optimal solution. Some companies are already integrating multidimensional and relational structures, offering a best-of-both-worlds scenario that combines the benefits of each approach.

As it stands today, the architecture used to support a data warehouse can take several forms, from a total relational solution to a combination approach to a total multidimensional solution. In the case of using one of the two total solutions, atomic-level detailed transactions must be stored together with aggregated (i.e., summarized) information in the same logical database. This does not mean that the same physical database has to be used. One physical database can store the detail or several functional databases (each containing a piece of the detail) can be used, which then feeds the databases containing the summary data. However, because of the performance implications of messages passing between databases, performance will suffer.

Using a combination approach, transaction detail should be stored in a RDBMS and summary data in a multidimensional structure. Relational databases are good at handling detail transactions, whereas multidimensional databases are good at performing complex queries.

USING PARALLEL COMPUTING TO SUPPORT DATA WAREHOUSES

Data warehouses will have to use parallel computing resources to achieve reasonable performance, but it is not obvious how parallel resources need to be configured. Although multidimensional databases are becoming more common. However, this article addresses parallel computing issues from a relational database standpoint only. At the time of this writing, statistics on the performance of multidimensional databases on parallel architectures are not readily available.

Just sticking a data warehouse on a parallel machine does not produce acceptable performance. There are some techniques that can be applied to improve database performance on a parallel architecture.

SQL Tuning. By far, the most important technique that can be applied in any data warehouse application is proper tuning of SQL going against the data warehouse. Queries that take more than three hours to run can be trimmed down to the five-minute range by examining the SQL execution plan and properly using indexes. Eliminating full-table scans where only a small percentage of the rows are queried is absolutely necessary for any data warehouse query.

Improved Performance in Full-Table Scans. Database vendors are continually improving the performance of full-table scans. In Oracle databases, for example, it is generally agreed that if 70% of the rows are scanned, a full-table scan is optimal. Related to this issue, execution plans are not always optimal. There may be times when hints are needed to force a read on a certain index or when it is necessary to spread the query over a specific number of processors to yield optimal performance.

Data Partitioning. Beyond SQL application tuning, data partitioning is required to achieve optimal performance in a data warehouse and it is one of the major benefits of the parallel computing architecture. Data partitioning is the practice of splitting data in the database among the nodes of a parallel system. The goal is to split the data among the node of the parallel system so that work can be spread among the nodes and the query can be processed faster. Depending on what type of parallel computer (i.e., SMP or MPP) and database is installed, different partitioning paths may be chosen.

The goal of partitioning is to give each processor an equal amount of work; beyond that, the real goal should be to ensure that each processor finishes its part of the query at the same time. Complexity increases if nodes have varying amounts of memory, processing power, and disk space. Shared-nothing versus shared-everything also impacts partitioning. Physical database reorganizations are much more difficult under shared-nothing architecture, because data are only accessible by the node that owns them.

Three partitioning methods are used at the database level to assist in parallel operations:

- Range partitioning
- Round-robin partitioning
- Hashing

In range partitioning, a key of a relation is split so that tuples with similar characteristics reside on the same disk or node. This may be preferred when sequential access to a table is required. However, it is very likely that skewing will occur — that is, the distribution of data across disks can vary in favor of a few nodes, which can lead to variances in query server processing time in a parallel query.

Round-robin partitioning reduces skewing because data values play no role when the rows of a relation are assigned to a disk. One row is assigned to the first disk, the next row is assigned to the next disk, and so on. Hashing also minimizes skewing by assigning the rows to disks based on a hashing function against a specific attribute of the row.

If these methods sound familiar, it is because they can also be used when creating indexes in a database. Each of these methods may be used at the application level to force a particular partitioning alternative. The advantage to keeping partitioning techniques in the database is that programming logic does not have to be spent and maintained. Conversely, these methods may not perform optimally for all warehouse applications.

Beneficiaries of Partitioning. The primary beneficiaries of data partitioning are parallel database operations:

- Data loads
- Index creation
- Backup and recovery

The performance of these operations improves dramatically when using parallel processing. However, the data must be partitioned into separate files on each node. In the database load process, both the local input file and local database file are specified to insert against a specific table and tablespace.

Index creation is more of a parallel query statement, where the number of query servers is specified. Parallel backups are made easy when database files are striped across nodes. Each node can be connected to a high-speed tape device, and its data files can be backed up independently of other nodes. In the database recovery process, the tape backups can then be used. This is especially handy when a single node crashes because of media failure.

CONCLUSION

Data warehouses supported by parallel processing computers are high-value components in an organization's systems inventory, provided the business is able to overcome the hurdles. A sizable investment in infrastructure (i.e., hardware and resources) is required. The hardware can easily be a multimillion-dollar purchase. Because most parallel systems run on high-end UNIX platforms, it is difficult to find people with both the operating system and parallel database experience.

Applications development is anything but trivial, and there is still a lack of data warehouse design tools available. Besides database software makers, few vendors produce versions of their software to run on parallel machines. Few programming languages adapt well to parallelization of tasks.

Entry costs are high, but the potential return on investment is also high. Parallelization offers the ability to analyze data in new ways that can lead to a more complete picture of a company's business and industry and, ultimately, better decision making. Early adopters are the winners and laggards may eventually succumb to stay competitive.

Section V — Checklist
Database Functionality and Design

1. Does your organization have a dedicated staff for data administration? If not, does this present difficulties for data integration?
2. Is your organization considering either implementation of distributed database or data warehousing? If so, would this work?
3. What factors would need to change in your organization in order to implement a new database concept such as data warehousing?
4. In your opinion, are most database configurations fundamentally the same? Has this been demonstrated in your environment?
5. How is database information managed in your environment? Is there a dedicated group for data administration? If not, should there be one created?
6. Does your organization suffer from multiple database repositories that do not communicate or share data dictionary information? How will this be resolved?
7. Is the lack of Enterprise Data Management contributing to the difficulties of system development and support in your IS environment? If so, can this be measured in a quantifiable manner?
8. Is data modeling used effectively in your organization? If so, what guidelines are used to help the modeling process?
9. Could data modeling techniques be used to analyze your organization's production data requirements?
10. How complicated is the production data flow in your environment? What tools and/or techniques are used to document or identify data processes?
11. Has data analysis become more important to your application development efforts? If so, how much emphasis is placed on accurately assessing data processes.
12. Based on your perception of data maturity, how would you assess the state of your organization's database stability and organization? What steps would you take to improve this?
13. Has your organization attempted a portfolio analysis of the various data repositories in your organization? If not, would this be worthwhile to improve consolidation of enterprise data?
14. Does your organization struggle from proprietary data structures that cannot communicate with each other? If so, how is data shared

between environments? Has this caused more redundant data to exist?

15. What are the processing demands of most data transactions in your environment? Does this force frequent upgrades of hardware, or is it increased demand handles through performance tuning?

Section VI
Operating Platforms

ADVANCEMENTS IN HARDWARE PLATFORMS and corresponding operating systems have brought about new opportunities for building new systems. Development managers now have numerous technical options in which to create and deploy enterprise level business applications. However, selecting the most appropriate combination of platform and system environment has become critical to the overall success of application development efforts. In addition, many operating platforms have been proprietary in nature, which potentially limits true portability of some applications. Although vendors are striving toward common operating system standards, industry competition will continue to challenge those who seek uniformity in building operating-neutral software applications.

One of the most significant differences between vendor operating environments exists in the object middleware arena. The two strongest standards have been the Common Object Request Broker Architecture (CORBA) and the Component Object Model. However, each proposes different mechanisms that affect the development of object based systems. Chapter VI-1, "Evaluating Object Middleware: DCOM and CORBA," furnishes an important discussion about these two technologies and the impact on application development efforts. Microsoft's COM vs. Object Management Group's CORBA has been the topic of much debate. Neither technology has emerged as the single standard, and it is expected that application managers will need to understand both technologies before choosing one over the other.

Migration of host-based systems to desktop computing has been a strong rationale for implementing new operating platforms. It has also created various paradigms for interconnecting and executing application processes. Chapter VI-2, "Client/Server vs. Cooperative Processing," reviews and compares two of the contemporary architectures used in desktop application development. The characteristics of these techniques is often misunderstood and sometimes confused with each other. This chapter helps differentiate the unique attributes of each method and also provides useful information in choosing hardware platforms and operating environments.

Windows NT has steadily gained popularity and has a Network Operating Environment as well as a Desktop Operating System. The benefits of Windows NT have been lauded by those who seek stronger functionality in

427

operating platforms. Many organizations are making a transition to Windows NT, and Chapter VI-3, "Windows NT Project Planning," gives pointers on making the switch. An important concern for networks and desktops operating environments has been the need for improved security. Chapter VI-4, "Access Security in a Windows NT Environment," provides an overview of the security features available from the Microsoft product. Development managers have historically shied away from security issues. But complex multi-tiered application systems must be more sensitive to an organization's security requirements. This should be part of the application design process and an early decision on the appropriate operating environment can be critical to project goals.

Future desktop operating environments will start employing parallel execution capabilities as part of the standard environment. Although parallel systems have been around for some time, the migration toward business environments is becoming increasingly important. Chapter VI-5, "Massively Parallel Processing: Architecture and Technologies," offers a glimpse into the powerful world of concurrent program techniques. This chapter is offered as an opportunity for application managers to prepare for changes in program development. Similar to object oriented technology, parallel-based development will require a shift in programming procedures that have been previously based on a sequential paradigm.

Chapter VI-1
Evaluating Object Middleware: DCOM and CORBA

T.M. Rajkumar and Richard J. Lewis, Jr.

OBJECTS IN THE FORM OF SOFTWARE COMPONENTS ARE CHANGING the way applications are developed and delivered. Component technology breaks the application into intrinsic components and then glues them to create the application. Using components, the application is easier to build, robust, and delivered quicker. A middleware is used as the object communication bus to enable distribution of these components across heterogeneous networks and operating systems.

The need for reliable distributed computing middleware environments is becoming pressing as three-tier client-server networks become commonplace. While much of the industry backs the Common Object Request Broker Architecture (CORBA) as the standard object bus, Microsoft is pushing its own Distributed Component Object Model (DCOM). Managers and system architects have to determine what object bus to use in their companies. This chapter reviews the two primary forces in distributed object technology, CORBA and DCOM. It discusses their individual strengths and weaknesses across a wide spectrum of categories, and gives some sensible advice on what technologies might be best applicable to current projects. Finally, it takes a look into what the future has in store for these architectures.

WHAT IS CORBA?

CORBA is a set of distributed system standards promoted by an industry standards group called the Object Management Group (OMG). The idea behind CORBA is to allow applications to communicate with one another no matter where they are located or who has designed them. The CORBA standard defines the ORB, a mechanism through which distributed software and their clients may interact. It specifies an extensive set of bus-related services for creating and deleting objects, accessing them by name, storing them in persistent store, externalizing their states, and defining ad hoc relationships between them.

History

OMG has more than 700 member companies who have been working on the CORBA standard for eight years. CORBA 1.1 was introduced in 1991 by OMG and defined the Interface Definition Language (IDL) and the Application Programming Interfaces (API) that enable client/server object interaction within a specific implementation of an Object Request Broker (ORB). CORBA 2.0, adopted in December 1994, defines true interoperability by specifying how ORBs from different vendors can interoperate.

Since 1989, the Object Management Group has been working to create standards for object-based component software within the framework of its Object Management Architecture. The key component is the Common Object Request Broker Architecture (CORBA), whose specification was adopted in 1991. In 1994 CORBA 2.0 defined interoperability between objects in heterogeneous systems. Since then the world has seen a growing list of CORBA implementations come to market. Dozens of vendors have recently announced support for the CORBA Internet Inter ORB Protocol (IIOP), which guarantees CORBA interoperability over the Internet. Specifications of several generally useful support services now populate the Object Services segment of the architecture, and work is proceeding rapidly in specifying domain specific technologies in many areas, including finance, healthcare, and telecommunications.

CORBA Architecture

The four main elements of the object management architecture are shown in Exhibit 1 and are the following:

- **ORBs:** The ORB defines the object bus and is the middleware that establishes the client/server relationships between objects. The ORB provides interoperability between applications on different machines in heterogeneous distributed environments and seamlessly interconnects multiple-object systems.
- **Object Services:** These define the system-level object frameworks that extend the bus. They include services such as security, transaction management, and data exchange.
- **Common facilities:** These define horizontal and vertical application frameworks that are used directly by business objects. They deal more with the client than a server.

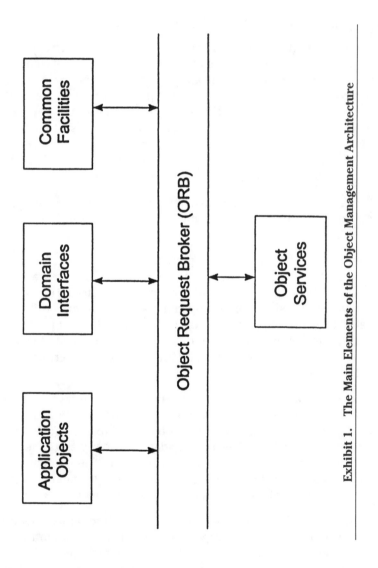

Exhibit 1. The Main Elements of the Object Management Architecture

- **Domain interfaces:** These are interfaces like common facilities but are specific to a certain domain, such as manufacturing, medical, telecommunications, etc.
- **Application interfaces:** These objects are defined by the developer to solve the business problem. These interfaces are not standardized.

ORB Component and CORBA Structure

Interface definition language (IDL) stubs provide static interfaces to object services. These define how clients invoke corresponding services on the servers. The ORB intercepts the call and is responsible for finding an object that can implement the request, pass it to the parameters, invoke its method, and return the results. The client does not have to be aware of where the object is located, its programming language, its operating system, the communication protocol that is used, or any other system aspects that are not part of an object's interface. The CORBA structure as shown in Exhibit 2 specifies the workings of the ORB component of the OMG specification.

While IDL stubs are static, dynamic invocations enable the client to find (discover) at run time a service that it wants to invoke, obtain a definition, issue a call, and return a result.

On the server side, the object implementation does not differentiate between a static or dynamic invocation. The ORB locates an object adapter, transmits the parameter, and transfers control to the object implementation via an IDL skeleton or a dynamic skeleton interface (DSI). The IDL skeleton provides support for the IDL-defined methods of a particular object class. The DSI provides a run-time binding mechanism for servers by inspecting the parameters passed by the message to determine the target object and method.

The object adapter accepts the requests for service on behalf of the server objects. If necessary, it starts up server processes, instantiates or activates the server objects, assigns an object id (object reference), and passes the requests to them. The object adapter also registers the classes it supports and their run-time object instances with the implementation repository. Object adapters are specific to each programming language, and there can be multiple object adapter for every object.

Inter-ORB protocols allow CORBA products to interoperate. CORBA 2.0 specifies direct ORB-to-ORB interoperability mechanisms when the ORBs are resident in the same domain (i.e., they understand the object references, IDL type system, etc.). Bridge-based interoperability is used otherwise. The bridge then maps the ORB-specific information across domains. General Inter-ORB protocol specifies the transfer syntax and a set of standard message formats for ORB interoperation. Internet Inter-ORB Protocol is the implementation of this specification over a TCP/IP network. These

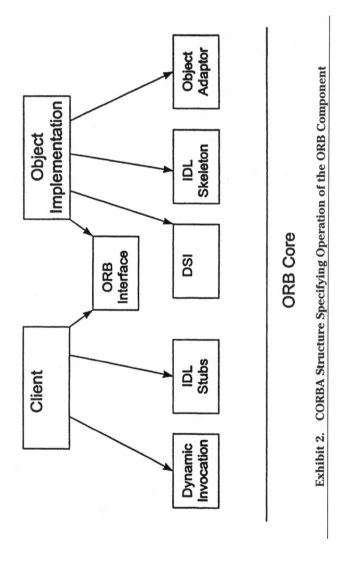

Exhibit 2. CORBA Structure Specifying Operation of the ORB Component

systems also support interobject references to locate and identify an object over the TCP/IP network.

CORBA IN THE REAL WORLD

CORBA has been around for a long time, but differences in early CORBA implementations made application portability and interoperability between implementations difficult. Different CORBA implementations fragmented an already small market, thereby rendering CORBA ineffective. Only recently have issues such as interoperability been addressed.

Other recent events have given rise to the hope that the industry can overcome these early missteps. First, the World Wide Web has created an incentive for a mainstream component architecture. Second, Netscape, Novell, and Oracle have licensed the Visigenic Software ORB, targeting one CORBA implementation. And Netscape has the potential to propagate large numbers of that implementation in its browser, which could create critical mass. Third, IBM, Netscape, Oracle, and Sun have agreed to ensure interoperability between their CORBA and IIOP implementations. Still, these vendors are fighting an uphill battle, and significant interoperability problems remain.

WHAT IS DCOM?

Microsoft's Distributed Component Object Model (DCOM) is object-oriented middleware technology that allows clients and servers in a distributed system to communicate with one another. It extends Microsoft's Component Object Model (COM) technology to work on the network. As is the case with Windows, Microsoft owns DCOM and controls its development. There will be no differing DCOM implementations to fragment the market, and Microsoft has begun shipping DCOM on both Windows NT and Windows 95. In other words, critical mass is quickly building.

COM Architecture

COM is an object-based framework for developing and deploying software components. COM lets developers capture abstractions as component interfaces and then provide binary classes that implement those interfaces. Encapsulation is enforced by COM such that client applications can only invoke functions that are defined on an object's interface.

COM interfaces define a contract between a COM object and client. It defines the behavior or capabilities of the software component as a set of methods and properties. COM interfaces are implemented by COM classes. COM classes are bodies of code that implement at least one COM interface. All COM classes implement two functionalities: lifetime management and interface management. COM classes may implement several interfaces. COM clients must explicitly request the interface they need. It also lets clients

434

widen their interface requirement at run-time or query whether a component supports an interface. Lifetime management is accomplished by reference counting.

COM classes reside in a server either as DLLs or EXEs. COM classes implemented as DLLs share the same address space (in-process) as their clients. COM classes implemented within EXEs live in different processes (out-of-process) than their client. Such out-of-process clients are supported via remote procedure calls.

COM classes are like meta classes. They create instances of COM classes, and also store static data for a class interface. For example, if a COM server has four different COM classes inside, that COM server will also have four class objects — one for each kind of COM class within the server.

OLE is a set of system services built on top of COM for constructing compound documents that is also used for supporting components. OLE Automation allows a component object to expose its methods through the Idispatch interface, allowing late binding of method calls. OLE Controls (OCXs) provide exposure to the interface of an object using method pointer tables called vtables.

COM's binary interoperability standard facilitates independent development of software components and supports deployment of those components in binary form. The result is that software vendors can develop and package reusable building blocks without shipping source code. Corporate application developers can use COM to create new solutions that combine in-house business objects, off-the-shelf objects, and their own custom components.

DCOM Architecture

DCOM, or Distributed Component Object Model, extends COM to the network with remote method calls, security, scalability, and location transparency. With COM objects may be loaded into the client's process or launched in a separate process on the the same machine. DCOM extends this transparency to include location transparency, allowing objects to exist anywhere on the network. When the client and the object server are on different machines (see Exhibit 3), the remoting layer adds a proxy object in the client's process space and a stub process on the server's process space. The proxy object is then responsible for marshalling the parameters and makes the function call. The stub unmarshals the parameters and makes the actual function call on the component object. The results are then marshalled and sent back to the proxy object where it is unmarshalled and given to the client. The entire process of creating the

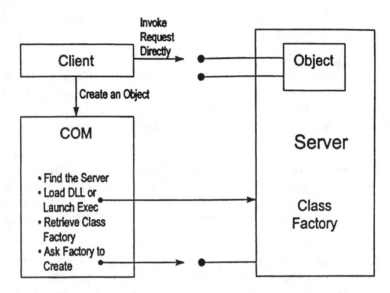

Exhibit 3. A COM Object and an Invocation by a Client

proxy and stub is invisible to either the client or the server, and they use remote procedure call as the interprocess communication mechanism.

ARCHITECTURE: CORBA VS. DCOM

The member companies of the Object Management Group have shared one consistent vision of an architecture for distributed, component-based object computing since OMG's inception in 1989. The architecture is described in the Object Management Architecture Guide, first published in 1990, and has been incrementally populated with the specifications of the core interobject communication component (CORBA), and with common services for handling transactions, security, concurrency control, and other vital support functions for object-based applications. Both the architecture and the individual specifications are vendor-neutral, and control of their technical direction and definition is via a public process that ensures broad cross-industry consensus. The specifications are available to all (OMG members or not), and free rights to implement software using the specifications are guaranteed by the terms of the OMG's constitution.

DCOM, being a version of Microsoft's COM, has deep roots in the client desktop GUI side as well as the server side. However, CORBA's main focus has always been on the server side. ORB vendors were in the past expecting the now defunct OpenDoc to compete with Microsoft's COM on the client side. Today CORBA has no model specification to compete with desktop COM components for heterogeneous client GUIs. However, Java Beans, a component technology from SUN, is being integrated to support client components with CORBA. This technology is still evolving. Until COM is ported to other platforms, however, Microsoft's client side advantage exists only on 32-bit Windows platforms.

The CORBA Object Reference differs from DCOM's Interface Reference in several ways. CORBA supports multiple inheritance of object interfaces, whereas DCOM has a mechanism allowing multiple independent interfaces per object.

Interfaces. Both use the interface mechanism to expose object functionalities. Interfaces contain methods and attributes as a common means of placing requests on an object. CORBA uses standard models of inheritance from object-oriented languages. DCOM/ActiveX uses the concept of multiple interfaces supported by a single object. DCOM requires that multiple inheritance be emulated through aggregation and containment of interfaces.

Identity. Another difference is the notion of object identity. CORBA defines the identity of an object in an object reference that is unique and consistent. If the object is not in memory, the reference is used to reconstruct the object. DCOM in contrast defines the identity in the interface, but the reference to the object itself is transient. This may lead to problems when reconnecting because the previously used object may not be directly accessible.

Reference Counting. Reference counting is also different in both. A DCOM object maintains a reference count of all connected clients. It uses pinging of the clients to ensure that the clients are alive. CORBA does not need to do remote reference, because its object-reference model allows the re-creation of the object if it had been prematurely deleted. CORBA does not attempt to track the number of clients communicating with a particular object. If a client releases the object on the server while another is using it, the object will be destroyed and an error will return to the other client on the next method call. Thus, it is up to the object implementation to provide life-cycle management if such behavior is unacceptable. Without a transaction manager integrated into the distributed system, it is very difficult to implement a reliable life-cycle management system.

APIs. CORBA uses two application protocol interfaces (APIs) and one protocol for object requests. It provides the generated stubs for both static and dynamic invocation. In addition, dynamic skeleton interface allows changes during runtime. DCOM provides two APIs and two protocols. The standard interface is based on a binary interface that uses method pointer tables called vtables. The second API OLE Automation is used to support dynamic requests through scripting languages.

PROGRAMMING DCOM AND CORBA

CORBA defines a finite set of primitive data types used for argument passing and structure definitions. CORBA interface definition language (IDL) files are similar in syntax to the C language, but deals only with interface-related details.

Two of the primary differences between COM and CORBA are structure and naming. A COM object consists of one or more categories of interfaces, where each one is named and has its own derivation hierarchy. A CORBA object follows a standard object model in that its interface is defined by its class and all the ancestors of that class. In the COM interface definition, the developer provides a universal identifier (UUID) that uniquely identifies the interface and class definitions. The UUID identifies classes instead of a class name so that you can have multiple classes with the same name but different vendors and functionality. CORBA, on the other hand, uses a naming system that includes the class name and an optional module name. Module names are equivalent to the C++ namespace concept, where class names can be scoped (assigned) to a particular module. The COM approach ensures that a collision will not occur. The CORBA version would allow a program to use two or more classes of the same name if their module scopes are different.

Error conditions and the amount of information they return is another difference. CORBA implementations provide an exception mechanism that returns errors as a structure embedded within another object called the Environment. A standard System Exception structure is defined for system-level and communications errors that can occur during a remote method call. Since CORBA is generally implemented with an object-oriented language, the exception systems of CORBA and the language can be tied together. Thus in C++, an error that occurs on the server will result in an exception being thrown on the client. In contrast, all methods in COM return an HRESULT integer value that indicates the success or failure of the call. This integer value is split up into a number of bit fields that allow the programmer to specify context, facility, severity, and error codes, making error handling more laborious.

The error-handling example is an area that CORBA is better at supporting than DCOM. Though both promote the aspect of location transparency, the reality that object implementations exist in other processes and the complications that can result from this are exposed in the way errors are handled. Developers like to know where an object exists when an error occurs. CORBA seems better, with its support for reporting system errors separate from application-level errors, which makes it easier for the developer to build appropriate exception-handling code.

438

Existing Services. To quickly implement distributed object technologies, it is important to have a built-in core set of components that applications can use. While DCOM comes bundled with a few more than CORBA, both suffer from a lack of existing components.

SECURITY

DCOM has a more flexible security implementation than does CORBA. DCOM provides multiple levels of security that can be selected by the administrator. DCOM uses access control lists (ACLs) on COM components. Administrators can use ACLs to determine who has access to the objects. DCOM methods can also programmatically control authorization of individual method invocations. By combining NT APIs and registry keys, a method can implement custom security. DCOM's security managers are platform-dependent. However, they employ readily available authenticators from third parties.

CORBA object services specify three levels of security. Level 0 specifies the authentication and session encryption using technology similar to that of the secure sockets layer (SSL) on web servers. This requires that the IIOP be secure, and object servers have to register themselves with the ORB as secure. Levels 1 and 2 are differentiated based on whether the CORBA clients and server objects are aware of the security layer. In Level 1, they are not aware, and in Level 2 they are aware of the security layer. Because CORBA's security specification has only recently been completed, ORB vendors have in the past had to come up with their own security implementations, which were incompatible with each other. Most vendors are currently only supporting SSL and Level 0 security.

SCALABILITY

Transaction Processing (TP) monitors help with scalability of any application by providing two critical services:

- Process management — starting server processes, filtering work to them, monitoring their execution, and balancing their workloads.
- Transaction management — ensures atomicity, consistency, isolation, and durability (ACID) properties for all processes and resources under its control.

Both DCOM and CORBA leverage TP monitors to provide for scalability and robustness.

DCOM is designed to work with the Microsoft Transaction Server, which began shipping in early 1997. Transaction Server is a transaction processing system that enables development, deployment, and management of multi-tier applications composed of COM and DCOM objects. DCOM is used for all object communication among machines. Transaction Server transparently provides transaction support to objects; manages threads, processes, ODBC database connections, and sharing data among concurrently executing objects. Transaction Server has a tight integration with SQL Server, and it can be used with a wide range of databases. Transaction Server currently does not support failover and load balancing, though it is expected to in future releases. In addition, DCOM is scheduled to work with a next-generation Directory Services, scheduled to ship with Windows NT 5.0. These services will provide a highly scalable store for object references and security information for DCOM.

CORBA has a specification called Object Transaction Services (OTS) that is designed to interoperate with X/Open-compliant transaction monitors. Hence, CORBA OTS is designed to work both with ORB-based and traditional TP transaction processing services. OTS offers the capability of supporting recoverable nested transactions that supports ACID and two-phase commit protocols. IDL interfaces can be used to provide a way to access the TP monitor application remotely. Integrating TP monitors within an ORB allows the CORBA components to be wrappers of existing business functionality, and to support legacy data.

PLATFORM SUPPORT

DCOM will currently only run on 32-bit Windows platforms. It is currently integrated into Windows NT 4.0, both Server and Workstation, and is available free for Windows 95.

However, cross-platform support for DCOM is coming, with third-party ports coming for UNIX, including one for Linux, Digital UNIX, HP/UX, and Sun's Solaris, as well as IBM's MVS and DEC's OpenVMS. Microsoft is actively seeking partners to port DCOM to other platforms, although some are concerned that Microsoft will favor its Windows-based implementations over the published DCOM standards. Applications using DCOM running on non-Windows platforms are only able to invoke the services on the Windows platforms, as opposed to allowing applications to be built anywhere.

Among UNIX users, there is a driving need to have an easy means to connect application on the desktop and the server. Software AG, a developer of three DCOM-on-UNIX ports, estimates that of the 600,000 UNIX servers in production systems worldwide, about 80% need an easier way to bridge the worlds of UNIX and Windows.

Critics of DCOM point out that the DCOM component model isn't inherently distributed. It has to be ported to every platform where it is to be used in order to get portability, which is clumsier than CORBA, which was built from the ground up to be distributed.

In order for DCOM to be widely used for creating enterprise applications, cross-platform services such as Transactions Server and Message Queue Server must be in place. Although Microsoft is expected to provide versions of its COM-based messaging and transaction services on other platforms, directly or through a third party, no formal commitment has been made.

LANGUAGE SUPPORT

CORBA is well suited for use by object-oriented languages. The code is much cleaner, because the bindings fully exploit the features of the host language. DCOM, on the other hand, has done nothing to provide management classes for the method arguments or a way to link error conditions to the C++ exception mechanism. CORBA also has a superior mechanism for handling arrays and sequences and provides an "any" data type for marshaling arguments whose type you do not know in advance. For object-oriented languages such as C++, the DCOM interface is cumbersome and requires more low-level code.

On the other hand, since DCOM supports OLE automation, applications can be developed with popular, nonobject-oriented languages such as Visual Basic or Delphi. If you are developing a PC-based application within these environments DCOM is definitely easier. For those dealing with object-oriented languages and significant object models, the CORBA model is more of a natural fit, because of COM's inability to support polymorphism and framework development.

INDUSTRY SUPPORT

Although many key companies such as Netscape, Oracle, and Sun Microsystems have agreed to support the emerging CORBA standards, there is some doubt whether they are fully committed to the standard, or if they will shift to DCOM if it gains considerable market share. DEC has announced it will use more than one technology, and HP has indicated interest in supporting COM on their versions of UNIX, but remains uncommitted to DCOM.

Others, such as IBM, seem to be firmly backing CORBA. IBM has introduced a CORBA-based development suite of middleware products, including Component Broker Connector and Component Broker Toolkit, which it plans to offer free with many of its products.

Tools vendors such as Oracle are hoping to find a middle ground in the battle for market share between DCOM and CORBA. Oracle has released a development environment that supports both native COM and CORBA components.

MATURITY

CORBA and DCOM have great potential for creating seamless distributed computing environments, despite the fact that today CORBA is struggling to establish its standards and DCOM has yet to prove it can operate as a cross-platform solution.

A Complete Tool?

While both architectures can create the structure for enterprise-level applications, neither is capable of generating an actual enterprise-ready application, which requires other services such as transactions, event notification, concurrency control and naming. While neither CORBA nor DCOM is a complete solution for network programming, CORBA offers good code for object-oriented languages. DCOM is easy to use with non-object-oriented languages such as Visual Basic.

PERFORMANCE

The network performance of DCOM is comparable to that of CORBA's IIOP, with each accomplishing reasonable request-reply response times. However, a standard method of communicating over an asynchronous transport is needed for both DCOM and CORBA. Currently, because of their highly synchronous operation, these technologies are limited to operating over LANs and server backbones. Internet use, or use over a company WAN, is not practical with the current technologies because of the high rate of synchronous request-reply activity required.

The OMG is in the midst of finalizing the Asynchronous Messaging service. This service extends CORBA's synchronous processes and provides a notion of "store-and-forward" processing with a variety of quality of service guarantees for messaging, reporting, and similar functions.

SUPPORT FOR THE WORLD WIDE WEB

Netscape has declared the Internet Inter-ORB Protocol (IIOP) as its standard for communicating between distributed objects and has included object broker technology in Communicator and SuiteSpot. Microsoft continues to position its Windows, DCOM, and ActiveX as its distributed object solution, and Explorer is the only browser to support ActiveX.

Notification services are being provided in conjunction with the asynchronous messaging services in CORBA to enable an object to subscribe and receive notification of changes. This is essential to support the various push technologies emerging on the Web. Along with Event services, this provides support for publish and subscribe to be effectively supported. Many CORBA vendors have provided support for this technology. However,

442

they are not very scalable, since by their very nature the Event-services uses a point-to-point connection oriented approach.

PROTOCOLS SUPPORTED

DCOM supports several protocols, such as TCP/IP, IPX/SPX, and Named Pipes. Though not limited to IIOP, CORBA ORBs only support the TCP/IP-based Internet Inter-Orb Protocol (IIOP) or proprietary inter-ORB protocols. DCOM's core network protocol is called Object Remote Procedure Call (ORPC). It is based upon DCE RPCs (Distributed Computing Environment Remote Procedure Calls), with extensions such as the addition of a primitive data type to support object references.

EASE OF USE

DCOM has just a few key management tools and has based the transport and security mechanisms on familiar Distributed Computing Environment (DCE) standards. This has made managing distributed components much less of a challenge.

INTEROPERABILITY BETWEEN CORBA AND DCOM

Currently, the Internet Inter-ORB Protocol (IIOP) is the OMG-approved method of linking distributed CORBA objects. Microsoft says it has no plans to support IIOP in DCOM, and there is currently no built-in COM support in CORBA. This battle of standards is making the implementation of both CORBA and COM services difficult.

As most enterprises will have both COM and CORBA environments, it is necessary that the objects in each be able to communicate with each other. OMG published a specification two years ago called "COM/CORBA Interworking" (now part of the CORBA 2.0 specification), which defines standardized mappings between COM and CORBA objects. There are several companies shipping implementations of this specification, including IONA, HP, Digital, and Expersoft. Basically, one of two approaches are used: encapsulation or converter. In the encapsulation approach, a call to the server object system is wrapped in an implementation of the object from the client system. ORB vendors provide generators to create such a bridge from the interface description of the object. In the converter approach, conversation proxies are generated during runtime based on the interface description of the object it represents. Both support bidirectional calls to and from either object systems.

THE FUTURE

Microsoft is about to release a new version of COM called COM+, which is designed to simplify the creation and use of software components. COM+ will provide a runtime and services that are readily usable from any programming language or tool. It is intended to enable extensive interoperability between components regardless of how they were implemented.

Where COM+ really shines, and where it most affects DCOM, is how COM+ will address the difficulties inherent in writing component-based distributed applications. COM+ will introduce an extensibility mechanism called interception, which will receive and process events related to instance creation, calls, returns, errors, and instance deletion. Services that the Microsoft Transaction Server provides today will become a part of COM+, and thus will be a core part of future Microsoft operating systems.

Similarly, OMG is defining and filling in the services required for most of the service layers, such as directory service, transactions, and security. Vendor implementations of these are starting to appear. Others such as persistence, concurrency, time, query, trader, collection, and versioning will slowly trickle in over the next couple of years. In addition, Java Beans technology is being pushed as the client component technology, and Java support for CORBA is emerging. This may help provide additional support for CORBA on the desktop.

CONCLUSION

DCOM is more accessible than CORBA at this stage of the technologies, because of Microsoft's experience and focus on the included DCOM management tools. For Microsoft-centric companies, DCOM is a solution that is tightly integrated with the Windows operating system. Customers have the most to lose in the object wars, and interoperability between CORBA and DCOM will likely be an important issue for many years. Where cross-platform capability or access to legacy objects is required, CORBA is currently the clear winner. CORBA provides companies with the highest degree of middleware flexibility through its extensive third-party support. More likely, all enterprises will use a mix of the two technologies, with DCOM at the desktop, and CORBA at the enterprise level.

In essence, DCOM and CORBA provide similar enough services that debates on minor technical issues ought to be dismissed in favor of more practical concerns, such as scalability, openness, availability, and maturity. Other important issues to be considered are the operating systems and programming languages used in the current project. Availability of CORBA and DCOM bridges may render the choice moot, and users will not be aware nor care whether it is DCOM or CORBA under the covers, because what they will use will be higher services (such as business facilities) built on top of either architecture.

Notes

[1] Object Management Group, 1997, "CORBA vs. ActiveX," http://www.omg.org/activex.htm..

[2] Object Management Group, 1997, "What is CORBA?," http://www.omg.org/omg00/wicorba.htm.

[3] T.M. Rajkumar, 1997, Client Server Development with Components.

[4] *InfoWorld*, August 4, 1997, v19 n31 p6(1), HP to push DCOM as part of CORBA, McKay, Niall.

[5] *Network Computing*, July 15, 1997, v8 n13 p98(5), Is DCOM truly the object of middleware's desire?, Frey, Anthony.

[6] *Network Computing*, July 1, 1997, v8 n12 p101(1), Three's a crowd with object lessons, Gall, Nick.

[7] *InformationWeek*, May 26, 1997, n632 p122(1), Component software war, Harzog, Bernd.

[8] *InfoWorld*, May 19, 1997, v19 n20 p51(2), Microsoft's cross-platform DCOM plans raise questions, Bowen, Ted Smalley.

[9] *PC Week*, May 12, 1997, v14 n19 p8(1), DCOM-to-Unix ports on the way, Leach, Norvin.

[10] *PC Week*, May 12, 1997, v14 n19 p93(1), Single victor unlikely in object protocol war, Lewis, Jamie.

[11] *Byte*, April 1997, v22 n4 p103(3), Programming with CORBA and DCOM, Pompeii, John.

[12] DBMS, April 1997, v10 n4 p26(6), Inside DCOM, Roy, Mark and Ewald, Alan.

[13] Object Management Group, 1997, IIOP, http://www.omg.org/corba/corbi-iop.htm.

[14] Microsoft Corporation, 1997, "COM and DCOM," http://www.microsoft.com/cominfo/.

[15] *Byte*, April 1997, v22 n4 p93, Distributing Components, Montgomery, John.

[16] *Microsoft Systems Journal*, 1997, v12 n11, Object-Oriented Software Development Made Simple with COM+ Runtime Services, Kirtland, Mary.

[17] *Object Magazine*, July 1997, p. 68-77. CORBA/DCOM interoperability, Kotopoulis, Alexander and Miller, Julia.

[18] BMS, March 1997. p. 43-50 CORBA Masterminds Object Management, Kueffel, Warren.

[19] *Application Development Trends*, October 97, p. 41-46. Deeper Inside CORBA, Dolgicer, Max.

Chapter VI-2
Client/Server vs. Cooperative Processing
David Friend

BECAUSE THE COOPERATIVE PROCESSING model offers more centralized control than the distributed client/server architecture, it is highly useful for widespread enterprise applications or applications in which data base replication is impractical. By keeping data and applications in one central repository, cooperative processing overcomes certain problems associated with application and data integrity, maintenance of enterprisewide applications, and data security—problems that are difficult to solve with distributed client/server products.

These advantages, however, come at a certain price. The purpose of this chapter is to help systems managers compare the characteristics of cooperative processing with those of distributed client/server computing and to identify the application and hardware environments that work best with these solutions. Each has its advantages and limitations.

DEPARTMENTAL VERSUS ENTERPRISEWIDE APPLICATIONS

Client/server computing and its cooperative processing variant are the two most important technologies for realizing the potential benefits of downsizing and distributed computing. These distributed computing topologies can provide superior performance at a lower price than traditional host-based solutions.

Distributed client/server computing distributes the processing work load somewhat more efficiently than does cooperative processing. Because distributed client/server applications can be built and supported at the departmental level, they have proliferated work group by work group, often haphazardly.

Although mainframe performance has been surpassed by distributed client/server systems, no amount of speed or performance can overcome the lack of security inherent in such distributed systems, nor can they make such systems a good fit for hierarchically organized businesses in which central-ized control is important. The peer-to-peer topology of pure client/server solutions makes them ideal for local and departmental solutions. The more hierarchical topology of cooperative processing makes it more appropriate for enterprisewide applications in which users are geographically dispersed and data is constantly changing.

Some information systems have a greater need for centralized control and sophisticated security. By their nature, mainframe operating systems are de-signed for enterprisewide solutions, serving everyone in the organization from top to bottom. Cooperative processing takes advantage of the security and centralized control of a mainframe system while offloading as much processing as possible to the workstation. This centralized control, however, requires that more of the processing take place on the host than would be the case in distributed client/server computing.

A FURTHER COMPARISON

Superficial similarities exist between cooperative processing and distrib-uted client/server systems. In both cases, computing is distributed between personal computers (PCs) and back-end processors. In the case of cooperative processing, these are generally referred to as the workstation and host. In distributed client/server computing, they are referred to as the client and server. Physically, they are really the same things: a PC on the desktop hooked up to a larger processor that is shared by all the users of the appli-cation. The network that connects the PC and the host/server may be dif-ferent, however, because as a general rule, distributed client/server applica-tions require much greater bandwidth than cooperative processing applications (the bandwidth issue is discussed in more detail later).

The most important difference between distributed client/server and co-operative processing is where control of the application resides. In the case of a distributed client/server application, control resides at the workstation. The application runs on the workstation and the client application is in charge. The client application tells the server what to do and the server, as its name implies, provides back-end services. In a client/server application, the client is in charge and sends requests for data and computing services to the server.

Just the opposite is true with cooperative processing: the application re-sides on the host. The host is in charge and tells the workstation what to do, and the workstation provides various front-end services (e.g., laying out a screen or creating a graph). Not only does the data base reside on the host but so does the application. The workstation executes machine-intensive tasks under the command of the host-based application (see Exhibit 1).

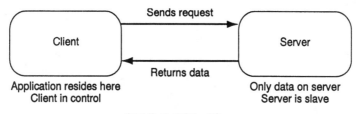

a. Distributed Client/Server

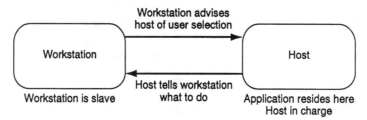

b. Cooperative Processing

Exhibit 1. Distributed Client/ Server Versus Cooperative Processing Model

---

Architectural Differences

A distributed client/server application really has two completely separate pieces of software. The client software and server software are completely independent, interconnected through an industry standard, open systems protocol. For example, the user might have a spreadsheet application running on the client machine, talking to a data base on the server. In fact, one client machine can talk to multiple servers and one server can talk to multiple clients by using an open protocol that all the different clients and servers understand.

In a cooperative processing application, the software running on the host and the software running on the PC are two pieces of one integrated system. One cannot be used without the other. The data that flows over the network is encoded in a special proprietary language (see Exhibit 2).

Even though the connection between the host and workstation is closed (i.e., the workstation can talk only to its associated host, and vice versa), the user can still attach other host products (e.g., SQL data bases) through an application program interface (API) on the host. Similarly, the workstation portion of a cooperative processing application can talk to other workstation programs (e.g., spreadsheets) through a workstation interface such as Windows' Dynamic Data Exchange (DDE).

The advantage of having a closed architecture between the host and the workstation is that the application has complete control of everything that

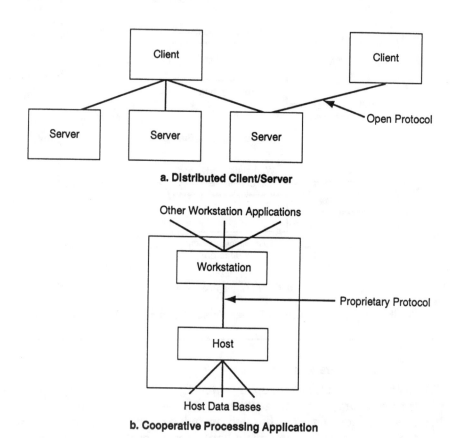

a. Distributed Client/Server

b. Cooperative Processing Application

Exhibit 2. Open Versus Proprietary Protocol

---

goes across the network. It is this closed architecture and the intelligence built into the software at both ends of the wire that allow such highly interactive programs as Pilot's Command Center, the Sears/IBM Prodigy system, or CompuServe to operate over low-bandwidth phone lines.

CENTRALIZED VERSUS DISTRIBUTED APPLICATIONS AND DATA

One of the advantages of distributed client/server computing is that applications can be developed by users without IS involvement. If the server with its data bases is maintained by IS, users can still hook up whatever client software they want and build their own applications.

The server becomes, in effect, a library, and IS becomes the librarian, helping users find the data they need, though not necessarily helping them use it. Data and applications are distributed to the user's PC or local area network (LAN) server.

The advantages of openness can become a disadvantage when IS is held accountable for the user's applications. If the applications developer cannot control the application running on the user's PC, the developer cannot ensure that what the user sees on the screen is correct.

In addition, security cannot be enforced once the data is out of the control of IS. Data security and data integrity are two of the most vexing problems associated with distributed client/server applications.

Cooperative processing applications are more like traditional host-based applications because both applications and data reside on the host, where, presumably, they are under IS control. Users are guaranteed to see exactly the same data and applications at any time. IS can have total control regardless of whether users are local or around the world. The trade-off is that somewhat less processing is offloaded to the workstation and the interface between the host and workstation is closed, which makes it harder to snap in other pieces of software.

WORKSTATION CACHING

Those who have used a cooperative processing system have probably noticed that the system seems to get faster the more they use it. That is because a workstation caching scheme ensures that the user never has to send any screen templates or data to the workstation more than once.

A cooperative processing screen consists of a template, which is sent from the host to the PC. The template includes predefined areas for data, text, pictures, icon, and hot spots. Once this template has been received by the workstation, it is cached—that is, saved on the workstation's disk, along with a unique version stamp. Any time the template is needed for a data display, it is recalled from disk and merged with data coming from the host (see Exhibit 3). The complete screen (template plus data) is cached temporarily in case it is needed again during the session. Anytime a cached template is used, the PC checks with the host to make sure the version has not been updated on the host.

The two benefits of the caching scheme are speed and terse communications. Recalling a cached template from disk takes only a fraction of a second (compared with perhaps 5 to 10 seconds to transmit the template in the first place). After a while, most of the screens the user sees will have been accessed previously and cached. So the system gets faster the more it is used. In addition, only the bare minimum of information needs to be transmitted across the network. This reduces network costs and, more important, further

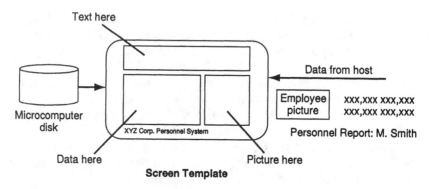

Screen Template

Note:
The template is retrieved from the microcomputer's cache and merged with data transmitted from the host.

Exhibit 3. A Cooperative Processing Screen Template

---

contributes to fast response time. The sample cooperative session, illustrated in Exhibit 4, shows how the host and PC interact and use caching to speed up response and minimize communications. In the example, the user fires up a PC to access financial reports. The important thing to recognize about this sample session is that communication between the host and the PC is minimized because the PC caches everything that comes down to it for possible future use.

COOPERATIVE PROCESSING AS A WAY TO SIMPLIFY DOWNSIZING

The centralized control and unique communications characteristics of cooperative processing can simplify downsizing. Cooperative processing combines the advantages of a high-quality graphical user interface (GUI), much of the cost efficiencies of distributed client/server computing, and most of the desirable security and integrity features of a mainframe application.

The biggest complaints about traditional host-based applications concern cost, speed, and quality of human interface. PC software has set the market's level of expectations for ease of use and attractiveness. Both these characteristics are made possible by the inexpensive processing power of a PC. GUIs (e.g., Windows), however, require a significant amount of computing power if they are to run fast.

A traditional mainframe and dumb terminal cannot give the user the kind of graphical interface that exists on a basic PC; there is no point-and-click mouse capability and no high-quality color graphics, and response times are

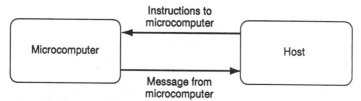

• AUTOEXEC starts microcomputer software Log-on script connects microcomputer to host.	• Host identifies user and looks up user's first screen.
	• Host asks microcomputer if it has screen on disk already.
• Microcomputer responds "yes" and sends version stamp.	• Host recognizes version as obsolete and sends latest version.
• Microcomputer displays screen and stores it for future use.	• Host awaits instructions from microcomputer.
• User clicks on icon for "Finance Report." Microcomputer sends notification to host.	• Host looks up what it is supposed to do when user clicks this icon.
	• Host tells microcomputer it needs screen template XYZ.
• Microcomputer responds "I have version xxx."	• Host says, "Display it."
	• Host accesses data base, does computations and ships data to fill in template.
• Microcomputer displays template and data, then saves it for reuse during session.	• Host awaits instructions from microcomputer.
• User clicks on a number on the screen in order to see trend bar graph.	• Host accesses historical data from data base and sends it to microcomputer with instructions to turn numbers into a bar chart.
• Microcomputer captures incoming numbers, creates bar chart.	• Host awaits instructions from microcomputer.

Exhibit 4. Sample Cooperative Processing Session

---

unpredictable. The whole business is expensive because all the computing must be done on the host, where the MIPS (millions of instructions per second) are most expensive.

Downsizing typically involves rewriting applications to run in a distributed environment, as shown in Exhibit 5. Instead of each remote location having a live connection to the mainframe, each location has its own

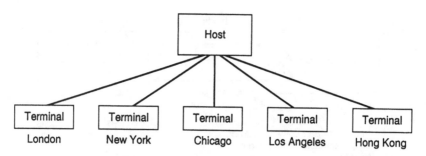

a. Central Host Links to Terminals by Phone Lines or Packet Switching Networks

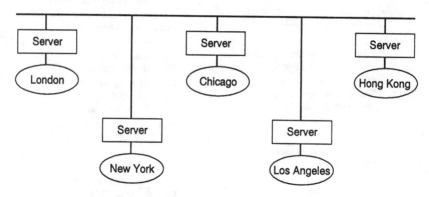

b. Remote Locations Have Live Connection to the Mainframe

Exhibit 5. Mainframe-Based Versus Distributed Application

LAN with its own server and local data bases. The LANs are linked together in a wide area network (WAN). It is important to remember that the bandwidth of a LAN is usually several orders of magnitude greater than the bandwidth of the WAN (which may be as simple as a 9,600-baud line). Although large amounts of data can be moved cheaply from server to workstation, moving data from one server to another is considerably slower and more costly. This means that distributed client/server applications (which typically depend on the high bandwidth of a LAN) will not operate effectively across different LANs. In other words, a client on the LAN in London cannot use the server in Chicago and get reasonable response time because the bandwidth across the WAN is much lower than the bandwidth of one of the LANs.

Because it is usually not practical to run an application across the WAN, the application must be replicated on each LAN server to make it accessible

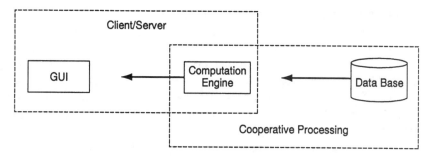

Exhibit 6. Computation Engine

to everyone in the organization. This creates another problem: Centralized control over the application is lost. There is no longer just one copy of the data and application on a mainframe that everyone shares.

Organizations that are trying to downsize traditional host-based applications frequently discover this the hard way. They wind up with different versions of data and applications on different servers and PCs, and IS has no easy way to ensure the accuracy or integrity of what users see on the screen. This is one of the reasons IS people refer to such applications as fragile. And it is one of the reasons that distributed client/server applications require significantly more manual labor to maintain than host-based applications. Cooperative processing applications require much less bandwidth than do distributed client/server applications, so they can operate across a WAN to a centralized host. At the same time, much of the processing is offloaded to the users' workstations, thereby affording some of the economies inherent in distributed client/server applications. In addition, because the workstations can run popular GUIs, users get the same state-of-the-art interfaces as offered by distributed client/server applications.

COMPUTATION ENGINES

Why do distributed client/server applications require so much more network bandwidth? The answer lies partly in where on the network computation and data manipulation take place (see Exhibit 6). In either a distributed client/server or a cooperative processing application, data gets to the screen in three steps: from the data base to the computation engine to the GUI.

The amount of data that flows from the data base to the computation engine is much larger than the amount that flows from the computation to the GUI. For example, if there is a data base of daily sales of 1,000 products and the user wants to see total sales monthly for the year to date (and it is approximately three months into the year), about 90,000 numbers would have to be retrieved from the data base and passed to the computation engine, where they would be added up into three monthly year-to-date figures. The resulting totals would then be passed to the GUI. In this case, there would be only three numbers passed from the computation engine to the GUI, whereas there are 90,000 numbers passed from the data base to the computation engine.

If the computation engine resides on the PC, as is the case in most distributed client/server applications, much more bandwidth is needed to get all the data to the workstation quickly. If the computation engine is on the host, as it is in cooperative processing, very little bandwidth is needed because the user is sending only the summarized data. A well-designed cooperative processing application usually works acceptably even over phone lines, which would be far too slow for most distributed client/server applications.

FIVE CARDINAL RULES OF COOPERATIVE PROCESSING

There are five important rules for designing any cooperative processing system; these rules are at work in any commercial cooperative processing product or development environment.

Rule 1. Keeping Total Host Processing to an Absolute Minimum. The key is to make the PC work as hard as possible. Only those operations that must architecturally remain on the host should execute on the host. Usually this means data bases, consolidating computation (to reduce network traffic), and applications logic. The actual operations (e.g., formatting screens or creating graphs) should execute on the workstation.

Rule 2. Providing the Fastest Possible Access to Information and Using Caching for Instantaneous Access to Repeat Data. Low-bandwidth communications reduce information bandwidth to the logical minimum possible. Fast links should be provided between the computation engine and underlying data bases, especially fast access to relational data bases.

Rule 3. Never Forcing the Data Base to Access the Same Data More Than Once. Users should remember always to cache anything at the workstation that might be needed again, and always to use version stamps to make updating automatic.

Rule 4. Keeping Communications Between the PC and Mainframe to the Logical Minimum. Terse codes should be used to instruct the workstation and compress data transmission whenever possible.

Rule 5. Preserving All the Security and Integrity Features of the Host Operating System. Because control resides on the host, it is unnecessary to give up any of the security features usually found on the host.

SUMMARY

Systems managers want to take best advantage of their options when downsizing and distributed computing are concerned. This chapter has explained the characteristics, limitations, and advantages of two distributed topologies. The concepts reviewed help determine when to use cooperative processing and when to use a client/server solution for an organization's applications.

Chapter VI-3
Windows NT Project Planning

Bill Camarda

THIS CHAPTER, INTENDED FOR ORGANIZATIONS that are planning a migration to Windows NT, covers:

- Identifying the organization's goals for deploying NT
- Identifying resources that can assist in the migration process
- Evaluating the organization's installed base
- Choosing vendor partners to assist in the migration
- Planning a pilot rollout
- Running a full-scale rollout

ESTABLISHING BUSINESS AND TECHNICAL GOALS FOR NT DEPLOYMENT

Before beginning a migration to Windows NT, it is important to understand what the business and technical goals are.

Business Goals for NT Deployment

Exhibit 1 lists some possible business goals for an NT project, along with the deployment issues that will need to be addressed to reach those goals.

Technical Goals for NT Deployment

Exhibit 2 lists some possible technical goals for an NT project, along with deployment issues related to each of these goals.

Building the Migration Team

Once the goals have been established, the next step in planning a smooth migration to NT Workstation and/or NT Server is to divide the responsibilities. Most large organizations identify several teams, each with a leader and a specific role in planning and deploying Windows NT. These teams may include:

Exhibit 1. Business Goals and Deployment Issues

Goal	Deployment Issues
Improve internal communication to shorten product delivery cycles	Using Internet Information Server (IIS) to deploy an intranet; choosing the appropriate strategy for directory services (Windows NT Directory Services, Distributed File System, planning for Active Desktop, or integrating Novell Directory Services)
Improve communication with suppliers and customers to enhance organizational responsiveness	Using firewalls, Windows NT name resolution tools, and PPTP tunneling to build extranets that encompass business partners
More effectively leverage the corporation's data for decision-making	Architecting the NT network to support database mirroring and query-intensive OLAP network traffic
Reduce costs	Standardized hardware and software configurations, Zero Administration for Windows, NetPCs, support, training, and Help Desk issues

Exhibit 2. Technical Goals and Deployment Issues

Goal	Deployment Issues
Providing a standard user environment that simplifies maintenance and training	Zero Administration Windows; system profiles; standard hardware configurations
Centralizing security while giving users a single log-on to all network resources	Domain planning; user account planning; Distributed File System
Making all users accessible through a single enterprisewide network directory	Choosing between Windows NT Directory Services and the long-term Microsoft Active Directory strategic direction; or Novell's robust NetWare Directory Services (NDS)
Preparing for growth by maximizing scalability	Choosing multiprocessor hardware and considering new clustering options, such as Microsoft Cluster Server (formerly known as Wolfpack)
Reducing the risks of server and network failure	Choosing NTFS file systems, RAID disk solutions and server mirroring, and architecting your network with adequate backup domain controllers (BDCs)

- A planning and coordination team that includes the project leader and representatives of each other team.
- An executive team that includes the IT organization's leader (or project manager responsible for the NT deployment); others with authority over relevant IT procedures; finance management; and executives from lines of business that will be impacted by the NT deployment.

- An installation team consisting of technicians who will actually install NT, as well as technical experts who can evaluate and test configurations for performance and compatibility.
- Training and/or support team(s) that may include help desk representatives, internal trainers, those responsible for hiring external trainers, and decision-makers responsible for providing adequate resources to frontline support staff.

In organizing these teams, it is all too common to disregard the central role of users: the people who will ultimately have to be productive with NT on a day-to-day basis. Bringing user representatives into the process early improves the likelihood of achieving wholehearted buy-in, and substantially improves a company's chances for success.

IT Qualifications Needed for the Deployment Team

One way to identify the right internal and external resources for the NT deployment team is to work with Microsoft Certified Professionals (MCPs). In addition to hiring certified professionals, an organization may decide that certifying more of its existing IT staff as NT experts should be an important element of the deployment process. A company might consider providing training for installers, system administrators, support staff, and anyone else with day-to-day responsibilities for Windows NT systems.

There are currently four MCP certifications, and it is important to understand the differences among them:

- Microsoft Certified Systems Engineers (MCSEs) have passed four operating system exams, at least two of them related to Windows NT. There are currently two tracks: one for Windows NT 3.51 and another for Windows NT 4.0. The NT 4.0 core requirements contain deeper coverage of NT 4.0 Server deployment issues.
- Microsoft Certified Solutions Developers (MCSDs) have passed two core exams covering Windows 32-bit architecture, OLE, user interface design, and Windows Open Services Architecture components, along with two elective exams covering Microsoft development tools and/or SQL Server.
- Microsoft Certified Product Specialists (MCPSs) have passed one detailed operating system exam: either Windows NT Workstation, Windows NT Server, or 16-bit Windows.
- Microsoft Certified Trainers (MCTs) teach (or intend to teach) at Microsoft Authorized Technical Education Centers; Microsoft certifies both their subject matter expertise and exposure to some basic training techniques.

Exhibit 3. Selected Resources Available on Microsoft's Web site

Resource	Web Address
Windows NT Deployment Guide	www.microsoft.com/ntworkstation/aantdeplguide.htm
Windows NT Migration Planning Template (Microsoft Project format)	www.microsoft.com/ntworkstation/aantprojtemp.htm
Guide to Automating Windows NT Setup	www.microsoft.com/ntworkstation/Deployment-guide.htm
Windows NT Workstation 4.0 Deployment Strategy and Details	www.microsoft.com/organizations/corpeval/1322.htm
Windows NT Server Enterprise Planning Guide	www.microsoft.com/ntserver/info/entplan.htm
Windows NT Server Domain Planning Guide	www.microsoft.com/ntserver/info/domainplanwp.htm
Windows NT Server Interoperability Planning Guide	www.microsoft.com/ntserver/info/ntsnwkinterop.htm
Windows NT Server TCP/IP Implementation Guide	www.microsoft.com/ntserver/info/tcpimplement.htm

Gathering Information Resources

It is helpful to gather as many deployment resources as possible early in the planning process. Not surprisingly, Microsoft is a prime source of free and low-cost information on deploying Windows NT. In addition to the Windows NT Workstation 4.0 Resource Kit and Windows NT Server 4.0 Resource Kit, Exhibit 3 lists many of the free resources available on Microsoft's Web site.

EVALUATING THE INSTALLED BASE

Now that the teams are in place, it is important to thoroughly understand the computing environment into which Windows NT is being deployed. Consider these elements:

- Desktop PCs and servers that may be upgraded to, replaced with, or served by Windows NT systems
- Other equipment, especially mainframes, minicomputers, UNIX servers and workstations, and NetWare servers that Windows NT will need to coexist with

It is extremely helpful if a company has a detailed inventory of the desktop and server systems in use throughout the organization. If there is no detailed inventory, the company will need one before initiating a full-scale rollout. For the moment, however, the IS department can identify a representative sample of systems in order to begin creating standard configurations, testing them, and making "upgrade vs. replace" decisions.

Planning for New Workstations

If the organization is purchasing new workstations, IS should seriously consider standardizing on one brand of PC throughout the organization. This has several benefits, including:

- A single point of contact for technical support (both hardware and Windows NT), troubleshooting, upgrades, and accountability
- A single approach to manageability. While the new NetPC and Intel's proposed "Managed PC" may standardize hardware management, each leading vendor currently has its own approach — not necessarily compatible with anyone else's
- Pricing leverage associated with quantity purchasing

If at all possible, test proposed new workstation configurations on both Windows NT 4.0 and Windows NT 5.0. Preliminary NT 5.0 benchmarks can help an organization ensure that its systems will be useful well past the year 2000.

At this writing, a reasonable, minimum new system for NT Workstation 4.0 is a 200-MHz Pentium. Although better performance can be expected from higher-speed Pentium IIs, these microprocessors are only now being paired with chipsets that enable them to take full advantage of their inherent speed.

Upgrade Planning for Existing Workstations

The installed base and normal upgrade schedule will play an important role in determining which existing systems are worth upgrading. Within this context, IS should start by determining the lowest-performance PC worth upgrading to NT Workstation. While NT Workstation can theoretically run on a low-end 486, most companies restrict upgrades to systems with substantially more power.

For example, where processing requirements are modest, a company might use Pentium 75 or Pentium 90 systems as a preliminary cutoff point. Systems slower than this would rarely be considered for upgrades to Windows NT. Starting from this baseline, the IS department would then test borderline systems to determine whether they will deliver adequate performance.

In most cases, these systems will require memory upgrades — probably to at least 32 MB. To determine whether these systems are in fact worth upgrading, IS will need to price the time and cost of these upgrades, and consider the remaining useful life of the hardware.

Where processing requirements are more substantial, IS might want to start with Pentium 133, 150, or 166 systems as a cutoff point — effectively ruling out all systems more than 18 to 24 months old. Again, it is important to take memory upgrades into account, although it is possible that some of your Pentium 133 to 166 systems are already configured with adequate memory to run Windows NT Workstation.

Whatever level is selected, it is helpful to check whether the organization's representative systems appear on Microsoft's Windows NT Hardware Compatibility List. Many major vendor systems intended for business use do appear on the list, although not all. While many systems that have not been certified by Microsoft will run Windows NT successfully, Microsoft will not support these configurations. If a company owns systems that do not appear on the Hardware Compatibility List, IS will have to decide whether to take full responsibility for supporting these workstations running NT. If these systems cannot be replaced, the organization may wish to identify third-party or vendor resources that can assist in maintaining them.

Before beginning testing, make sure the version of Windows NT selected reflects the latest Service Packs introduced by Microsoft. To check for the latest Service Pack — and to download it — visit www.microsoft.com/ NTServerSupport/Content/ServicePacks/Default.htm.

It is not enough to test Windows NT on standalone systems. IS needs to set up a test network that is as representative of the planned network as is practical.

Evaluating and Testing Software

An organization does not need to test software carefully before deploying it widely on Windows NT systems. The following sections describe some of the issues to take into account.

Win16 (Windows 3.x) Applications. Older 16-bit Windows applications will run in the new Windows 4.0 16-bit subsystem; a Windows 3.x emulator sometimes called "Windows on Windows" or WOWEXEC. IS will be needed to test both the reliability and the performance of applications running on this emulator. IS may also have to determine whether to run these applications in their own memory space (the default setting) or in a shared memory space with other Win16 applications (potentially faster, but one failed Win16 application can crash all Win16 applications running at the same time).

DOS Applications. Many people have discovered that DOS programs will not run in Windows NT because they must address hardware directly. Many other DOS applications will work, via Windows NT Workstation's DOS emulator. If the company still depends on DOS applications, they should be tested carefully. IS may also have to experiment with settings in each DOS application's Properties dialog box to maximize performance — especially settings in the Memory tab that control the amount of conventional, expanded, extended, and MS-DOS protected mode memory available to an application.

Windows 95 Applications

Even if all the applications are 32-bit Windows applications that utilize the Win32 API, there are a few "gotchas," including:

- APIs specific to Windows 95 that are not available in Windows NT Workstation 4.0, such as Direct3D, Independent Color Matching, Plug-and-Play, "Flat Thunks," and the Pen API, as well as these Windows 95 OSR 2-specific APIs: FAT32 File System, DirectX 2, ActiveMovie, and Windows Internet Extensions API
- APIs that are common to both operating systems but may work differently, including Unicode and some security attributes

Upgrading Custom Applications

Many companies depend on custom applications originally written for 16-bit Windows 3.x environments. For performance and compatibility reasons, organizations will usually want to port these applications to the Win32 API rather than running them in the "Windows on Windows" emulator.

This is, as programmers say, a nontrivial task. There are significant differences between Win16 and Win32 applications. In the Visual Basic environment, these include differences in naming, treatment of integers, and string routines; deserialized input; changes due to preemptive multitasking; and changes to DLLs. The bottom line: if the company wants to roll out revised Win32 custom applications when it rolls out Windows NT, IS should start updating those programs now.

Identifying, Evaluating and Testing Peripherals

In addition to the PC hardware itself, IS will need to systematically identify all the peripherals and other devices the organization expects to use with NT Workstation or NT Server. Once this is done, IS should review Microsoft's Hardware Compatibility Web Page for Windows NT (http://www.microsoft.com/ntworkstation/hwtest.htm) to determine whether these devices have NT 4.0 compatible drivers. If in doubt, visit the vendor's Web site. IS should consider each of the following:

- Video cards
- Video capture cards
- Audio cards

465

- SCSI host adapters and devices, including CD-ROM drives, tape drives, removable media, and scanners
- Other (non-SCSI) CD-ROM drives and tape drives
- Network interface cards (Ethernet, Fast Ethernet, ATM)
- ISDN adapters
- Modems and multiport serial adapters
- Printers
- PCMCIA (PC Card) devices
- Uninterruptible power supplies
- Mice and other pointing devices

If IS is deploying NT throughout the entire organization, then the availability of final-release (not beta) NT drivers should be considered as a prerequisite for future purchases. NT drivers should be tested carefully — especially video drivers that now run in the Windows NT kernel, where they can potentially impact Windows NT's stability.

Integrating Macintosh Desktops

If an organization has an installed base of Macintoshes that it does not intend to replace with Wintel systems, its testing needs to encompass Windows NT Server Services for Macintosh. Services for Macintosh, a standard component of Windows NT Server, makes it possible to:

- Create Macintosh volumes on an NT Server system
- Support AppleShare, allowing NT disks and folders to appear on Macintosh client desktops
- Support AppleTalk networks, including AppleTalk Internet Routers — eliminating the need to purchase additional routers to support Macintoshes
- Provide file sharing and print services to Macintosh clients

Microsoft even provides a Web administration tool (available at www.microsoft.com/ntserver/webadmin/webadmindl.htm) that makes it possible to administer an NT Server system from a Macintosh (or any other) client, using a Web browser front-end.

There are some limitations to Windows NT Server's Macintosh support. Macintoshes cannot access other Windows clients, and neither the server nor other Windows clients can access files stored locally on a Macintosh. If these limitations will be a problem in an organization's environment, then IS might consider third-party products such as Dave (Thursby Software Systems, Inc., www.thursby.com, 1-817-478-5070) or MacLAN Connect (Miramar Systems, www.miramarsys.com, 1-800-862-2526).

UNIX Servers and Workstations

Windows NT is increasingly being introduced into UNIX environments. Windows NT can integrate with UNIX workstations and servers, but users will probably have to rely on third-party products to accomplish their goals. Most companies need one or more of the following elements of UNIX/NT interoperability:

- Network File System (NFS) file and printer sharing
- X terminal access from Windows NT workstations to run X applications hosted on UNIX systems
- X terminal access from UNIX hosts to Windows NT, so UNIX systems can display Windows applications

As part of the project planning and testing, IS will need to identify the company's needs for UNIX interoperability and compare the products available to provide it. Of course, this means that project teams will need individuals with significant UNIX experience.

Mainframes/Hosts

Some organizations may be planning to use Windows NT as a client/server platform that supplements mainframe-based legacy systems or helps to migrate away from them. If so, IS should consider SNA gateways and associated hardware designed to:

- Improve desktop workstation response time
- Support query-intensive and communications-intensive applications
- Add redundancy and load balancing
- Support advanced groupware and intranet solutions cost effectively

As traditional dumb terminals have been replaced by PCs running terminal emulation software, traditional cluster controllers are also being replaced by SNA gateway software and hardware. These solutions, such as Microsoft's SNA Server and IBM's Comm Server, are typically much less expensive to purchase, install, and support than controllers were. They typically offer better performance as well.

SNA Server offloads network traffic from mainframes and IBM AS/400 midrange systems, freeing up host resources for line-of-business applications. It serves as a TCP/IP-to-SNA gateway, helping companies migrate to TCP/IP while retaining the reliability and securities advantages of SNA.

SNA Server also extends NT Server's existing domain-based unified sign-on capabilities to mainframe and AS/400 systems, so users who have been authenticated by a Windows NT domain controller can gain access to files, printers, databases, messaging systems, and other applications running on hosts — consistent with security restrictions that IS establishes.

To take full advantage of SNA Server or products like it, an organization will need robust server hardware. It may be necessary to integrate third-party mainframe channel adapters as well. For example, companies such as General Signal (1-888-GSN-DATA, www.gsnetworks.com) and Polaris Communications (1-800-353-1533, www.polariscomm.com) deliver PCI-based boards that support IBM's Enterprise System Connection (ESCON) high-speed connectivity.

Before deploying SNA Server, IS should check with its Microsoft account representative to understand Microsoft's strategic direction for this product. It has been rumored that Microsoft may eventually fold SNA Server functions into NT Server and SQL Server.

Planning Issues to Handle Concurrently with Evaluation and Testing

As IS evaluates its installed base of hardware and software, the NT deployment teams can concurrently consider several other important issues. For example, they can:

- Create budgets and timetables for the deployment and rollout
- Determine which NT capabilities to deploy; which to disable; and which to deploy only on selected workstations
- Decide whether to deploy NT using Microsoft System Management Server (SMS) or third-party software delivery tools
- Plan for training installers, Help Desk personnel, and trainers

CHOOSING AND MANAGING VENDORS

Among the most critical decisions IS will make is the choice of vendors to partner in the deployment of Windows NT. Many companies want the business; this is not surprising because services tend to deliver much higher margins than commodity hardware sales.

Given the rapid growth of Windows NT in the enterprise, many companies are focusing on delivering Windows NT services. These include major consultancies and system integrators such as EDS and Entex, as well as the services organizations of traditional hardware suppliers such as Digital and IBM. If NT is being deployed in a smaller company, that organization might choose a local or regional systems integrator or client/server developer to assist.

Vendors with Strategic Microsoft Relationships

Microsoft maintains especially close relationships with some suppliers of PC and server hardware. These relationships certainly do not preclude users from choosing other suppliers, but they may be worth considering when making vendor decisions. At minimum, IS may want to question

Microsoft's strategic partners on how they are delivering the benefits their alliances are supposed to provide — and question competitors on how they can deliver comparable benefits.

On the server side, Microsoft has announced especially close partnerships with Digital (DEC) and Hewlett-Packard. To varying degrees, these relationships have led these vendors to deliver more fully integrated solutions for NT deployment. For example, Digital already has 1400 engineers with NT certification from Microsoft. Digital's service offerings for NT include:

- Legacy NOS Migration to Windows NT services, including methodologies for migrating user files, access privileges, print services, and other features of legacy NOS environments, including NetWare, Banyan VINES, DEC PATHWORKS, IBM LAN Server
- Building NT Applications for the Enterprise, services to plan, design, and implement client/server computing built on Windows NT
- Software Support for Windows NT, services to provide support for Windows NT environments, with a selection of response times and problem-resolution capabilities
- Installation and Startup for Windows NT and Windows NT Clusters, services to rapidly install, configure, and implement NT servers and clusters

Hewlett-Packard's recent partnership with Microsoft has thus far led to improvements in scalability on Intel-based servers, as well as a new family of Business Recovery Services intended to help companies prevent and recover from failures associated with NT servers.

It is important to note that while Microsoft's NT partnerships with Digital and Hewlett-Packard have been the most prominent to date, other leading vendors now offer extensive support for Windows NT. To cite just two examples, Unisys recently established the Enterprise NT Services organization, intended to offer a full suite of services for deploying mission-critical applications on NT systems; NCR also offers substantial Windows NT consulting services.

On the workstation side, Microsoft and Intel lead the NetPC effort intended to lower the cost of administration; partners in this effort include Compaq, Dell, Digital, Gateway 2000, Hewlett-Packard, Packard Bell NEC, and Texas Instruments.

As already mentioned, standardizing on a single provider of PCs, a single provider of servers, and a single provider of network interface cards can simplify management tasks for years to come. Whether preparing a formal RFP, or requesting proposals on a less formal basis, above all it is important to be explicit about what is expected from the vendor. In addition to cost, the following items should be considered when making choices:

- A track record with your company or companies like yours
- Availability of a trustworthy single point of contact
- Ability to deliver an end-to-end solution
- Support commitments, both for hardware and for Windows NT
- Availability of specific technical resources where and when you need them
- Product delivery dates and a vendor's track record in meeting them — especially if notebook PCs are involved
- Contract flexibility (e.g., the ability to substitute more advanced technologies for those covered in the contract)

Testing Standard Configurations

Once IS has established standard configurations of both existing and new equipment, they should run detailed tests of:

- The NT installation process and automated batch scripts
- Network connectivity
- Applications software
- The uninstall process (restoring previous operating systems on upgraded computers)
- Disk space variables (both for installation and swap files)
- Local and server-based administration tools

IS may find that it needs to make adjustments to the standard client configuration to improve performance, compatibility, stability, or user convenience.

PLANNING AND MANAGING A PILOT ROLLOUT

In most organizations, the next step is to perform a pilot rollout in a small department or division. Ideally, choose an organization that is open to new technology and not stressed by a major project deadline or recent downsizing. (Obviously, some organizations may not have this luxury.) A typical pilot rollout may include the following steps:

- Prepare a detailed logistical plan for the pilot rollout, including tested scripts for automated installation from distribution servers.
- Prepare and implement a support plan, so users have immediate access to assistance when they need it.
- Plan a schedule (e.g., how many systems can be upgraded per day, and how long the pilot rollout will take).
- Notify users well in advance of the installation.
- Develop training materials that reflect both the performance of standard NT tasks and concerns unique to your company (e.g., logons, file locations, custom applications, etc.).
- Schedule training.

- Perform a verified backup, a virus-check, and disk defragmentation on all pilot machines that will be upgraded to Windows NT.
- Virus check all pilot machines prior to installation.
- If necessary, upgrade BIOSes, memory, or other hardware prior to installation.
- Make sure NT driver software is available for installation wherever needed.
- Run the installation at a time least likely to interfere with deadlines.

Once the pilot installation has taken place, IS should:

- Follow up to ensure all systems are working properly.
- Stay in close contact with all members of the pilot group to identify problems, questions, and other issues.
- Respond to user concerns and carefully track the changes that users request or require.
- Assign technicians to check real-world performance against expectations, so adjustments can be made, if needed, before a full-scale rollout.
- Compare schedules and costs against expectations, so budgets and timeframes can be adjusted for the full-scale rollout later.

PREPARING FOR FULL-SCALE DEPLOYMENT

Now that the pilot rollout has been conducted, IS can begin to prepare for the organizationwide rollout by:

- Creating budgets and schedules that reflect the actual experience
- Revising the company's IT procedures to reflect the changes that NT will require, and notifying users where necessary
- Performing a complete systems inventory and storing the information in a centralized database that can be updated to reflect changes to individual systems
- Hiring or reassigning any additional staff needed for the full-fledged rollout
- Rolling out Windows NT using the procedures used in the pilot rollout — adapted, of course, to reflect any necessary changes

CONCLUSION

This chapter has discussed many of the issues involved in successfully rolling out Windows NT Workstation. But Windows NT is inherently a networked operating system, designed for use in highly distributed environments. It is important to review the critical networking issues associated with planning an NT deployment — including what is needed to architect Windows NT domains that will serve your company well for years to come.

Chapter VI-4
Access Security in a Windows NT Environment

Gilbert Held

ACCESS SECURITY IN A WINDOWS NT ENVIRONMENT is controlled through the use of the User Manager for Domains program. That program can be directly accessed from the Windows NT 4.0 Start menu button by selecting "programs" from that menu, selecting the "Administrative Tools (Common)" entry in the program pop-up bar, and then selecting the "User Manager for Domain" entry from the next pop-up menu displayed in response to selecting the "Administrative Tools (Common)" program entry. Exhibit 1 illustrates the sequence of previously discussed pop-up menus invoked from the Start button to select the "User Manager for Domains" entry. The latter is shown selected by the highlighted bar in the right pop-up menu.

The User Manager for Domains is the Windows NT program through which the administrator and authorized users can control access to the server. Exhibit 2 illustrates the initial display of the User Manager program for the computer used by this author. In examining Exhibit 2, note that the screen is subdivided into two horizontal portions. The upper portion of the screen lists the currently configured users' authorized access to the computer while the lower portion of the screen lists in alphabetical order predefined groups and a description of each group. Note that the Administrator's group has the highest level of privileges. Members of that group can add and delete user accounts and group accounts as well as control access to the computer and individual files on the computer. In comparison, the default Guest group contains the least amount of privileges and is normally associated with the predefined username Guest, which is included in each version of Windows NT to allow users without an account a limited degree of computer access.

In examining Exhibit 2 it should also be noted that the Administrator and Guest usernames represent default names established when the server software is installed. The username *gxheld* was added when the

0-8493-9979-3/99/$0.00+$.50
© 1999 by CRC Press LLC

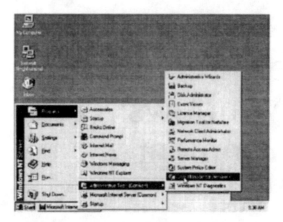

Exhibit 1. Accessing the User Manager for Domains Program from Windows NT 4.0 Start Button

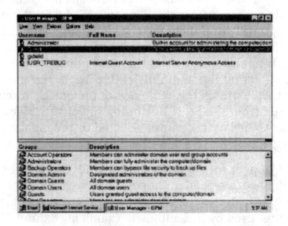

Exhibit 2. Initial Display of the Windows NT User Manager Program

server software was originally configured, while the username *IUSR_TREBLIG* represents a guest Internet account. That account is automatically created by the Windows NT 4.0 Server when you install Microsoft's Internet Information Server (ITS) software, and the account provides anonymous access to the Windows NT 4.0 Server's World Wide Web server program. If you wish to restrict access to valid predefined server user accounts, the first thing you should do is to remove the Internet Guest account. In addition, from a security standpoint, it is a good idea to disable the general Guest username to preclude unauthorized users from attempting to use that predefined account as a mechanism to try to breech server security. Since the best way to obtain an appreciation of

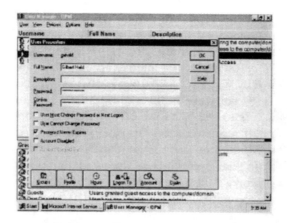

Exhibit 3. User Properties Dialog Box

Windows NT's access security is by working with a user account. In doing so we will also note how easy it is to disable a predefined Guest account.

ACCOUNT MANIPULATION

Through the use of the User menu at the top of Exhibit 2 you can add, delete, or modify a user account. In addition, by double clicking on a specific username you can generate a dialog box labeled "User Properties," which provides the basic mechanism for associating different levels of access control to a specific user.

Exhibit 3 illustrates the User Properties dialog box for the username *gxheld* used by this author. After you enter an optional full name and description for the user, you must enter a password twice, with the second entry used to confirm the password. Windows NT is similar to many other operating systems in that it does not provide restrictions on the composition of a password other than its length. Although you could use "rabbit," "bigbill," "termite," or a phrase such as "abadabado," it is suggested that if you do so you should also add some numerics to the word or phrase. Otherwise an unscrupulous person could write a program to use each entry in an electronic dictionary in an attempt to gain unauthorized access to a user account.

Under the second password entry box you will find a series of five small square boxes and labels associated with each box that define its use. By clicking on an appropriate box, a check mark will appear that sets or enables the option. For example, a check mark is shown in the box labeled "Password Never Expires," which allows this author's account to remain active with the same password. Note the entry below the "Password Never Expires" entry. That entry, which is labeled "Account Disabled," provides

475

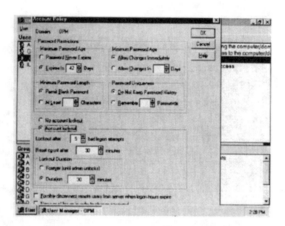

Exhibit 4.   Account Policy Dialog Box

you with the ability to temporarily disable a previously created account. It is highly recommended that you do this to the Guest account until such time as you determine there is sufficient reason to have this type of account. At that time you would select the Guest account and again click on the square associated with the label "Account Disabled" to remove the check mark, which then enables the use of the account. The fifth box whose label is light gray and barely visible is "Account Lockout," set by Windows NT if a predefined number of access attempts fail. You can only deselect or remove a lockout from the User Properties screen.

POLICIES

To provide a degree of control over password composition and account lockout, Windows NT includes an Account Policy dialog box. This box is displayed by selecting the Account entry from the Policy menu located at the top of Exhibit 3. Exhibit 4 illustrates the Account Policy dialog box in which this author added a few entries. In examining the available password options, note that Windows NT simply allows an administrator to specify a minimum character length, the use of a blank password (which is NOT recommended), an expiration date, and password history that can force the next password to be different from the previously selected password. Unfortunately, Windows NT is similar to other operating systems in that it does not check the composition of the password to prevent the use of common words or phrases susceptible to a dictionary attack.

The lower portion of Exhibit 4 shows the settings for an account lockout. In this example the account will be locked out after five bad attempts and the user will have to wait 30 minutes prior to attempting to reconnect; however, the user can always call the Administrator and ask the person to remove the lockout.

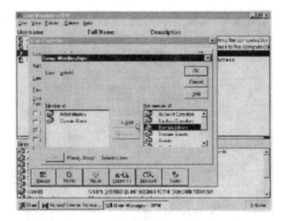

Exhibit 5.   Group Memberships Dialog Box

GROUP ASSOCIATION

If we return to the User Properties display previously shown in Exhibit 3 we will note a series of six buttons in the lower portion of the display. Those buttons can be used to change the group membership of a user, their environment profile, login hours during which they can use the computer, basic account information, and their ability to access the server via a modem dial-in communications connection.

Exhibit 5 illustrates the resulting display generated by selecting the Groups button. The resulting dialog box, labeled "Group Membership," indicates the groups the user is currently a member of in the left portion of the display, while the right portion of the display lists those groups the user is not a member of. In Exhibit 5 the entry "Domain Administrator" is shown selected in the list of groups the user is not a member of. To make the user a member of the group you would then click on the button labeled "Add." Similarly, to remove a group you would first select the group you wish to remove, which would result in the highlighting of the button under the Add button labeled "Remove." Clicking on that button would remove the selected group from the box labeled "Member of" located on the left side of Exhibit 5. By controlling the membership of a user in different groups, you can control their ability to perform server backups, administer the server, set up accounts, and perform other functions.

ENVIRONMENT PROFILE

The User Environment Profile dialog box shown in Exhibit 6 is displayed when you click on the button labeled profile. This dialog box is primarily used to associate desktop settings with a user's logon by specifying a path to a profile file. You can also configure this dialog box to invoke a script file

477

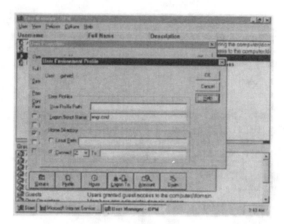

Exhibit 6.   User Environment Profile Dialog Box

when a user logs onto the system. That script, which is shown in Exhibit 6 entered as engr.cmd, can be a .cmd, .bat, or executable program. However, care should be taken to ensure that an executable program by itself or included in a .cmd or .bat logon script file does not perform any operations the user is not to be provided with. Otherwise, the use of a script file would override certain Windows NT settings and could produce an unintended capability that you might not want the user to have.

LOGON RESTRICTIONS

You can restrict the ability of a user or group of users to log onto an NT Server during portions of the day or week. To do so, you would select the "Logon to" button shown in the lower portion of Exhibit 6. This action will result in the display of a dialog box labeled "Logon Hours" similar to the display shown in Exhibit 7.

In examining the Logon Hours display shown in Exhibit 7 the default of all hours allowed was changed by blocking out the hours from 3:00 a.m. to 7:00 p.m. on Monday and Tuesday. To accomplish this task that block of hours is first selected by highlighting them with a drag cursor operation. Once those hours are selected, clicking on the button labeled "Disallow" blackens each hour box.

The use of logon hour restrictions should be considered if you require the use of guest accounts yet wish to prevent such accounts from being used anytime. Another potential use for logon hour restrictions is to add an additional level of access control to users that only have a server account to perform a predefined operation, such as running a tape backup of the contents of the server. By carefully considering logon hour restrictions in

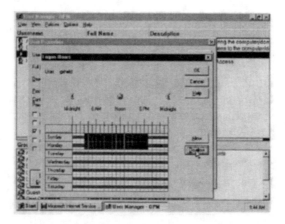

Exhibit 7.   Windows NT Logon Hours Dialog Box

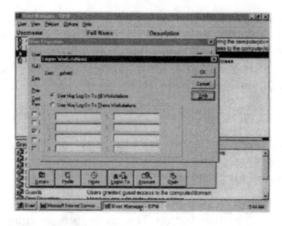

Exhibit 8.   Windows NT Account Information Dialog Box

conjunction with other access control features, you should be able to add an additional level of security to your Windows NT computer system.

ACCOUNT INFORMATION

Through the strip of six buttons shown in most previously displayed Windows NT screens you can select the display of the Account Information dialog box. This is accomplished by clicking on the button labeled "Account." Exhibit 8 illustrates the resulting display.

In examining Exhibit 8, note that through this dialog box you can control the expiration date of a user account as well as the type of account. Concerning the former, you can specify an indefinite account period by selecting the button associated with the label "Never" or you can select a date on

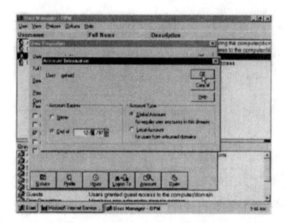

Exhibit 9.   Windows NT Dialin Information Dialog Box

which the account terminates. Concerning account type, if your server is a domain controller it becomes possible for accounts established on the server to become global in the domain. As an alternative you can restrict the account to the local computer. Thus, the Account Information dialog box provides you with the ability to control the length and breadth of access.

DIALIN INFORMATION

The last access control feature we will focus our attention on is dialin access. Dialin access governs the ability of a remote user to initiate a modem connection to the server.

Exhibit 9 illustrates the Dialin Information dialog box that is displayed when you click on the Dialin button. This dialog box provides you with the ability to enable or disable dialin access for a particular user as well as to add an additional level of security by requiring the server to perform a callback.

The use of a callback represents a very important security verification mechanism, since it results in the server first disconnecting the incoming telephone call and then originating a call to the person requesting dialin access. You can use the Dialin Information dialog box to set a no callback option, set the callback based on a telephone number submitted by the caller or present the callback to a fixed number. Concerning the last two options, using the set by caller option should only be considered for traveling executives and sales personnel. Other personnel, such as technicians working at home, should have a present telephone number since a callback to an employee's home is usually the best method to verify the identity of the person requesting a remote dialing session.

Callback provides a supplement to the user of the UserID-password pair and should be used to provide an additional level of security for dial-in access to a Windows NT server.

RECOMMENDED COURSE OF ACTION

In this chapter we examined the use of a number of Windows NT 4.0 Server access control features that can be used in addition to a UserID-password sequence to control access to the server. By carefully examining each feature against your specific organizational security requirements you can note those features you should consider for implementation on an existing platform or a platform you anticipate acquiring.

Chapter VI-5
Massively Parallel Processing: Architecture and Technologies

Prem N. Mehra

ORGANIZATIONS TODAY REQUIRE a great deal more processing power to accommodate new kinds of applications, such as an information delivery facility, data mining, and electronic commerce. This need for large computing cycles may be met relatively inexpensively through massively parallel processing.

Although massively parallel processors have been around for some time, their use has been limited primarily to scientific and technical applications, and to applications in the defense industry. Today, parallel processing is moving out to organizations in other industries, which find their own data volumes growing exponentially. The growth is not only from traditional transaction systems but also from new data types, such as text, images, audio, and video. Massively parallel processing is enabling companies to exploit vast amounts of data for both strategic and operational purposes.

Parallel processing technology is potentially very powerful, capable of providing a performance boost two to three orders of magnitude greater than sequential uniprocessing and of scaling up gracefully with database sizes. However, parallel processing is also easy to misuse. Database management system (DBMS) and hardware vendors offer a wide variety of products, and the technical features of parallel processing are complex. Therefore, organizations must work from a well-considered vantage point, in terms of application, information, and technical architectures.

This chapter reviews parallel processing concepts, current and potential applications, and the architectures needed to exploit parallel processing — especially massively parallel processing — in the commercial marketplace.

0-8493-9979-3/99/$0.00+$.50
© 1999 by CRC Press LLC

PARALLEL PROCESSING CONCEPTS

Massively parallel computing should be placed within the context of a more general arena of parallelism, which has been in use in the commercial marketplace for some time. Many variations and algorithms for parallelism are possible; some of the more common ones are listed here:

- *OLTP.* Concurrent execution of multiple copies of a transaction program under the management of an online terminal monitor processing (OLTP) manager is one example. A program written to execute serially is enabled to execute in parallel by the facilities provided and managed by the OLTP manager.
- *Batch.* For many long-running batch processes, it is common to execute multiple streams in parallel against distinct key ranges of files and merge the output to reduce the total elapsed time. Operating systems or DBMS facilities enable the multiple streams to serialize the use of common resources to ensure data integrity.
- *Information delivery facility (data warehouse).* The use of nonblocking, asynchronous, or prefetch input/output (I/O) reduces the elapsed time in batch and information delivery facility environments by overlapping I/O and CPU processing. The overlap, parallelism in a loose sense, is enabled by the DBMS and OS without user program coding specifically to invoke such overlap.

Recent enhancements in DBMS technologies are now enabling user programs, still written in a sequential fashion, to exploit parallelism even further in a transparent way. The DBMS enables the user structured query language (SQL) requests to exploit facilities offered by the new massively parallel processors by concurrently executing components of a single SQL. This is known as intra-SQL parallelism. Large and well-known data warehouse implementations at retail and telecommunications organizations (such as Sears, Roebuck and Co. and MCI Corp., respectively) are based on exploiting this form of parallelism. The various architectures and techniques used to enable this style of parallelism are covered in this chapter.

Facets of Parallelism

From a hardware perspective, this chapter focuses on a style of parallelism that is enabled when multiple processors are arranged in different configurations to permit parallelism for a single request. Examples of such configurations include symmetric multiprocessors (SMP), shared-disk clusters (SDC), and massively parallel processors (MPPs).

From an external, high-level perspective, multiple processors in a computer are not necessary to enable parallel processing. Several other techniques can enable parallelism, or at least give the appearance of parallelism, regardless of the processor environment. These styles of parallelism have been in use for some time:

- *Multitasking or programming.* This enables several OLTP or batch jobs to concurrently share a uniprocessor, giving the appearance of parallelism.
- *Specialized processing.* Such functions as I/O managers can be executed on specialized processors to permit the CPU's main processor to work in parallel on some other task.
- *Distributed processing.* Similarly, peer-to-peer or client/server style of distributed processing permits different components of a transaction to execute in parallel on different computers, displaying yet another facet of parallelism.

Multiprocessors, important as they are, are only one component in enabling commercial application program parallelism. Currently, the key component for exploiting parallelism in most commercial applications is the DBMS, whose newly introduced intraSQL parallelism facility has propelled it to this key role. This facility permits users to exploit multiprocessor hardware without explicitly coding for such configurations in their programs.

System Components

In general, from the perspective of commercial application programs, such facilities as parallelism are characteristics of the entire system, not merely of its components, which include the hardware, operating system, infrastructure, and DBMS. However, each of the components plays an important role in determining the system characteristics.

Exhibit 1 shows one way to depict a system in a layered fashion. The hardware layer, which consists of a multiple processor configuration, offers the base component. Operating system (OS) and the function and I/O shipping facilities, called infrastructure, influence the programming model that the DBMS layer uses to exhibit the system characteristics, which is exploited by the application program.

This part of the chapter first discusses the hardware configurations and their characteristics, including scalability. It then discuss the DBMS architectures, namely shared data and buffer, shared data, and partitioned data. The chapter focuses on the DBMS layer, because it is generally recognized that the DBMS has become the key enabler of parallelism in the commercial marketplace. The OS and infrastructure layer will not be explicitly discussed, but their characteristics are interwoven in the hardware and the DBMS discussion.

HARDWARE CONFIGURATIONS

Processors are coupled and offered to the commercial users in multiple-processor configurations for many reasons. These have to do with a number

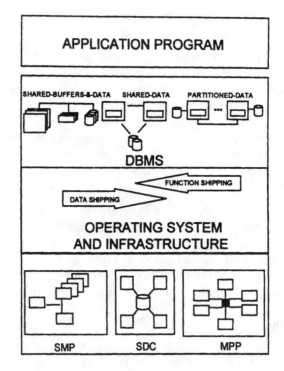

Exhibit 1. System Components

of factors — performance, availability, technology, and competition — and their complex interaction in the marketplace.

Multiprocessors provide enhanced performance and throughput because more computing resources can be brought to bear on the problem. In addition, they also provide higher data availability. Data can be accessed from another processor in the event of a processor failure. Historically, enhanced data availability has been a key motivation and driver for using multiple processors.

Multiprocessor Classification

A formal and technically precise multiprocessor classification scheme developed by Michael J. Flynn is widely used in technical journals and by research organizations. Flynn introduced a number of programming models, including the multiple instruction multiple data (MIMD) stream, the single instruction multiple data (SIMD) stream, the single instruction single data (SISD) stream, and the multiple instruction single data (MISD) stream. This taxonomy, based on the two key characteristics of processing and data, is still used. For the purposes of this chapter, however, multiprocessors can be classified into three simple types:

1. SMP (symmetric multiprocessors)
2. SDC (shared-disk clusters)
3. MPP (massively parallel processors)

Sometimes this simplification can lead to misunderstandings, it is; (for example, clusters may be variously interpreted. It is,); it is, therefore, advisable to clarify these terms early in any discussion to avoid the pitfalls of oversimplification.

How are multiprocessors distinguished from uniprocessors? The basic building block for other configurations, a uniprocessor is a single processor with a high-speed cache and a bus to access main memory and external I/O. Processors are very fast and need data at high speeds to avoid wasting valuable processing cycles. On the other hand, memory, the supplier of data, is made of slow-speed, inexpensive dynamic random access memory (DRAM) chips, which cannot keep up with the demands of these processors. Cache provides a small amount of buffered data at high speeds to the processor to balance the fast data requirements of the processor and the slow speed of DRAM memory. Cache is not as fast as a processor but much faster than main memory and is made from fast but expensive static random access memory (SRAM) chips.

Even though SMPs, clusters, and MPPs are being produced to provide for additional processing power, vendors are also continuing to enhance the uniprocessor technology. Intel's 386, 486, Pentium, and Pro-Pentium processors exemplify this trend. The enhancements in the PowerPC line from the alliance among Apple, IBM, and Motorola is another example. Although research and development costs for each generation of these processors require major capital investment, the competitive pressures and technological enhancements continue to drive the vendors to develop faster uniprocessors, which are also useful in reducing the overall elapsed time for those tasks that cannot be performed in parallel. This is a very significant consideration and was highlighted by Amdahl's law.

An SMP is a manifestation of a "shared-everything" configuration (see Exhibit 2). It is characterized by having multiple processors, each with its own cache, but all sharing memory and I/O devices. Here the processors are said to be tightly coupled.

SMP configuration is very popular and has been in use for over two decades. IBM Systems/370 158MP and 168MP were so configured. Currently several vendors, including Compaq, DEC, HP, IBM, NCR, Sequent, SGI, and Sun offer SMP configurations.

A very important consideration that favors the choice of SMP is the availability of a vast amount of already written software; for example, DBMSs, which is based on the programming model that SMP supports. Other

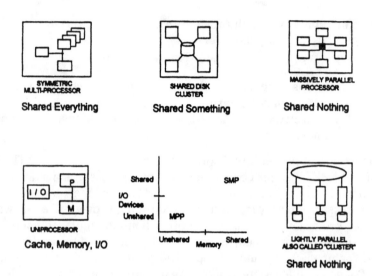

Exhibit 2.   The Symmetric Multiprocessor

alternative platforms, such as loosely coupled multiprocessors, currently do not have as rich a collection of enabling software.

The fact that multiple processors exist is generally transparent to a user-application program. The transparency is enabled by the OS software layer, which hides the complexity introduced by the multiple processors and their caches, and permits increased horsepower exploitation relatively easily. It is also efficient, because a task running on any processor can access all the main memory and can share data by pointer passing as opposed to messaging.

The subject of how many processors can be tightly coupled together to provide for growth (i.e., scalability) has been a topic of vast interest and research. One of the inhibitors for coupling too many processors is the contention for memory access. High-speed cache can reduce the contention, because main memory needs to be accessed less frequently; however, high-speed cache introduces another problem: cache coherence. Because each processor has its own cache, coherence among them has to be maintained to ensure that multiple processors are not working with stale copy of data from main memory.

Conventional wisdom has held that because of cache coherence and other technical considerations, the practical upper limit for the number of processors that could be tightly coupled in an SMP configuration is between 10 and 20. However, over the years, a number of new schemes, including Central Directory, Snoopy Bus, Snoopy Bus and Switch, Distributed Directories using Scalable Coherent Interconnect (SCI), and the

Directory Architecture for Shared memory (DASH), have been invented and implemented by SMP vendors to overcome the challenge of maintaining cache coherence. Even now, new innovations are being rolled out, so SMPs have not necessarily reached their scalability limits. These newer techniques have made it possible to scale well beyond the conventionally accepted limit, but at an increased cost of research and development. So, economics as well as technology now become important issues in SMP scalability. The question then is not whether SMP can scale, but whether it can scale economically, compared to other alternatives, such as loosely coupled processors (e.g., clusters and MPPs).

Clusters

A cluster is a collection of interconnected whole computers that are used as a single computing resource. Clusters can be configured using either the shared-something or shared-nothing concept. This section discusses the shared-something clusters, and the MPP section covers the shared-nothing clusters.

Shared-something clusters may share memory or I/O devices. Shared I/O clusters are very popular; various DEC clusters and IBM sysplex are examples. Because of their wide use, people colloquially use the word *cluster* to mean a shared-disk configuration. However, sharing disks is not a requirement of a cluster; for that matter, no sharing is necessary at all for clustering.

Digital Equipment Corporation has offered VAXCluster since the early 1980s (see Exhibit 3) and followed it with Open VMSCluster and, more recently, DEC TrueClusters.

IBM Parallel Sysplex configuration uses a shared electronic storage (i.e., a coupling facility) to communicate locking and other common data structures between the cluster members. This helps in system performance.

A shared-disk cluster (SDC) presents a single system image to a user application program. OS, DBMS, and load-balancing infrastructure can hide the presence and complexities of a multitude of processors. Nonetheless, a user application program can target a specific computer if it has an affinity to it for any reason, such as the need for a specialized I/O device.

Shared-disk clusters offer many benefits in the commercial marketplace, including high availability, incremental growth, and scalability. If one processor is down for either planned or unplanned outage, other processors in the complex can pick up its workload, thus increasing data availability. Additional processors can be added incrementally to the cluster to match the workload, as opposed to having to purchase a single large computer to meet the eventual workload. Also, the scalability challenge faced by the

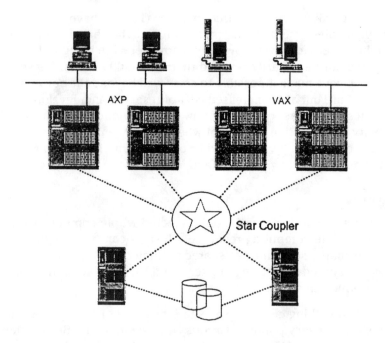

Exhibit 3.   The VAXCluster Configuration

SMP is not encountered here, because the independent processors do not share common memory.

Clusters face the challenge of additional overhead caused by interprocessor message passing, workload synchronization and balancing, and software pricing. Depending on the pricing model used by the software vendor, the sum of software license costs for equivalent computing power can be higher for a cluster as compared to an SMP, because multiple licenses are required.

The Massively Parallel Processor (MPP)

In an MPP configuration, each processor has its own memory, and accesses its own external I/O. This is a shared-nothing architecture, and the processors are said to be loosely coupled. An MPP permits the coupling of thousands of relatively inexpensive off-the-shelf processors to provide billions of computing instructions. Because an MPP implies coupling a large number of processors, an interconnection mechanism (e.g., buses, rings, hypercubes, and meshes) is required to provide for the processors to communicate with each other and coordinate their work. Currently, many vendors, including IBM, ICL, NCR, and nCUBE, offer MPP configurations.

From a simplistic I/O and memory sharing point of view, there is a distinction between MPP and SMP architectures. However, as will be discussed later in the chapter, operating systems (OSs) or other software layers can mask some of these differences, permitting some software written for other configurations, such as Shared-Disk, to be executed on an MPP. For example, the virtual shared disk feature of IBM's shared-nothing RS/6000 SP permits higher-level programs, for example, Oracle DBMS, to use this MPP as if it were a shared-disk configuration.

Before the mid-1980s, the use of MPPs was essentially limited to scientific and engineering work, which typically requires a large number of computing instructions but limited I/O. Such a task can often be split into many individual subtasks, each executing on a processor and performing minimal I/O. Computational fluid dynamics is an example of this. Subtask results are then combined to prepare the final response. The decomposition of tasks and combination of results required sophisticated programming tools and skills, which were found in the scientific and engineering community.

Traditional commercial work, on the other hand, requires relatively fewer computing cycles (though this is changing) but higher I/O bandwidth. In addition, typical programming tools and required skills for exploiting MPPs in commercial environments were not available. The combination of these factors resulted in minimal use of this technology in the commercial arena.

In the late 1980s, offerings introduced by NCR's DBC1012 Teradata database machine started to permit online analytical processing (OLAP) of commercial workloads to benefit from the MPP configurations. More recently, innovations introduced by several database vendors, such as Oracle and Informix, have further accelerated this trend.

An important point is that a key ingredient for the acceptance of MPP in the commercial marketplace is the ease with which parallelism can be exploited by a DBMS application programmer without the programmer needing to think in terms of parallel programs or needing to implement sophisticated and complex algorithms.

The technique used by the DBMSs to exploit parallelism is the same as mentioned above for the scientific work. A single task (i.e., an SQL request) is split into many individual subtasks, each executing on a processor. Subtask results are then combined to prepare the answer set for the SQL request. In addition, the packaging of processors in an MPP configuration offers several administrative benefits. The multitude of processors can be managed from a single console, and distribution and maintenance of software is simplified because only a single copy is maintained. The system makes the same copy available to the individual nodes in the MPP. This

Exhibit 4. Comparison between MPPs and Lightly Parallel Clusters

Characteristic	MPP	Lightly Parallel Cluster
Number of processors	Thousands	Hundreds
Node OS	Homogeneous	Can be different, but usually homogeneous
Internode security	None	Generally none
Performance metric	Turnaround time	Throughput and turnaround

administrative benefit is very attractive and at times used for justification of an MPP solution, even when no parallelism benefits exist.

At times, financial requests for additional hardware may also be less of an administrative concern, because the upgrade (i.e., the addition of processors and I/Os) is made to an existing installed "serial number" machine, and does not require the acquisition of a new one, which may involve more sign-offs and other administrative steps.

Currently, the DBMS vendors have focused on MPP technology to implement strategic information processing (e.g., data warehouse) style of applications. They have placed only a limited emphasis on operational applications. As more experience is gained and technology matures, it is likely that more operational applications, such as OLTP, may find a home on the MPP platform.

However, the current reduction in government grants to scientific and defense organizations, the slow development of the software, and fierce competition in the MPP marketplace have already started a shakedown in the industry. One analysis by the *Wall Street Journal* has suggested that by the time the commercial marketplace develops, quite a few suppliers will "sputter toward the abyss."

In addition to MPP, the shared-nothing configuration can also be implemented in a cluster of computers where the coupling is limited to a low number, as opposed to a high number, which is the case with an MPP. In general, this shared-nothing lightly (or modestly) parallel cluster exhibits characteristics similar to those of an MPP.

The distinction between MPP and a lightly parallel cluster is somewhat blurry. Exhibit 4 shows a comparison of some salient features for distinguishing the two configurations. The most noticeable feature appears to be the arbitrary number of connected processors, which is large for MPP and small for a lightly parallel cluster.

From a programming model perspective, given the right infrastructure, an MPP and shared-nothing cluster should be transparent to an application, such as a DBMS. As discussed in a later section, IBM's DB2 Common Universal Server DBMS can execute both on a shared-nothing lightly parallel cluster of RS/6000 computers and on IBM's massively parallel hardware, RS/6000 SP.

Lightly parallel shared-nothing clusters can potentially become the platform of choice in the future for several reasons, including low cost. However, software currently is not widely available to provide a single system image and tools for performance, capacity, and workload management.

It is expected that Microsoft Corporation's architecture for scaling Windows NT and SQL Server to meet the enterprise-wide needs may include this style of lightly parallel shared-nothing clustering. If this comes to pass, the shared-nothing clusters will become very popular and overshadow their "big cousin," MPP.

The various hardware configurations also offer varying levels of scalability (i.e., how much usable processing power is delivered to the users when such additional computing resources as processors, memory, and I/O are added to these configurations). This ability to scale is clearly one of the major consideration in evaluating and selecting a multiprocessor platform for use.

MULTIPROCESSORS: SCALABILITY AND THROUGHPUT

An installation has several hardware options when requiring additional computational power. The choice is made based on many technical, administrative, and financial considerations. From a technical perspective alone, there is considerable debate as to how scalable the various hardware configurations are.

One commonly held opinion is that the uniprocessors and massively parallel processors represent the two ends of the spectrum, with SMP and clusters providing the intermediate scalability design points. Exhibit 5 depicts this graphically.

As discussed in the previous section, a commonly held opinion is that an SMP can economically scale only to between 10 and 20 processors, beyond which alternative configurations, such as clusters and MPPs, become financially more attractive. Whether that is true depends on many considerations, such as hardware technology, software availability and pricing, and technical marketing and support from the vendors. Considering all the factors, one can observe that hardware technology, by itself, plays only a minor role.

SMPs currently enjoy the most software availability and perhaps a software price advantage. Shared-disk clusters, in general, suffer the penalty from higher software prices, because each machine is a separate computer requiring an additional license, although licenses are comparatively less expensive, as the individual machines are smaller than a corresponding

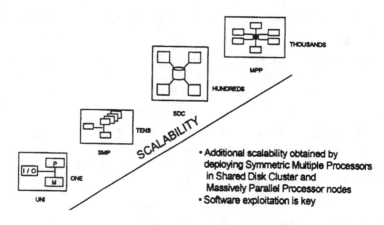

Exhibit 5. Scalability

equivalent single SMP. However, new pricing schemes based on total computing power, number of concurrent logged-on users, or other factors are slowly starting to alter the old pricing paradigm, which put clusters at a disadvantage.

Clusters and MPPs do not suffer from the cache coherence and memory contention that offer SMP design challenges in scaling beyond the 10-to-20 range. Here, each processor has its own cache, no coherence needs to be maintained, and each has its own memory, so no contention occurs. Therefore, from a hardware viewpoint, scaling is not as challenging. The challenge lies, however, in interconnecting the processors and enabling software so that the work on the separate processors can be coordinated and synchronized in an efficient and effective way.

To provide more computing resources, vendors are including SMP as individual nodes in cluster and MPP configurations. NCR's WorldMark 5100M is one example in which individual nodes are made of SMPs. Thus, the achievement of huge processing power is a multitiered phenomenon: increasing speeds of uniprocessors, combination of faster and larger number of processors in an SMP configuration, and inclusion of SMPs in cluster and MPP offerings.

SOFTWARE LAYERS

All the approaches to parallelism discussed to this point have touched on multiprocessing. All the approaches manifest and support parallelism in different ways; however, one underlying theme is common to all. It may not be very obvious, but it needs to be emphasized. In almost all cases, with few exceptions, a commercial application program is written in a sequential fashion, and parallelism is attained by using some external mechanism. Here are some examples to illustrate the point.

During execution, an OLTP manager spawns separate threads or processes, schedules clones of the user's sequential program, and manages storage and other resources on its behalf to manifest parallelism. In batch, multiple job streams executing an application program are often organized to processes different files or partitions of a table to support parallelism. In the client/server model, multiple clients execute the same sequential program in parallel; the mechanism that enables parallelism is the software distribution facility. Another way of looking at client/server parallelism is the execution of a client program in parallel with an asynchronous stored procedure on the server; the facility of remote procedure calls and stored procedures enables parallelism.

In the same way, a single SQL call from an application program can be enabled to execute in parallel by a DBMS. The application program is still written to execute sequentially, requiring neither new compilers nor programming techniques. This can be contrasted with building parallelism within a program using special constructs (e.g., doall and foreach), in which the FORTRAN compiler generates code to execute subtasks in parallel for the different elements of a vector or matrix. Such constructs, if they were to become widely available in the commercial languages, will still require significant retraining of the application programmers to think of a problem solution in terms of parallelism. Such facilities are not available. In addition, from an installations point of view, the approach of sequential program and DBMS-enabled parallelism is much easier and less expensive to implement. The required new learning can be limited to the designers and supporters of the databases: database and system administrators. Similarly, tools acquisition can also be focused toward the task performed by such personnel.

Now, SQL statements exhibit varying amounts of workload on a system. At one extreme, calls (generally associated with transaction-oriented work) that retrieve and update a few rows require little computational resource. At the other extreme, statements (generally associated with OLAP work) perform large amounts of work and require significant computational resources. Within this wide range lie the rest. By their very nature, those associated with OLAP work, performed within a data warehouse environment can benefit most from the intra-SQL parallelism, and those are the current primary target of the parallelism.

If the user-application code parallelism is attained only through the use of other techniques listed earlier (e.g., OLTP), it is questionable whether DBMS-enabled parallelism is limited to the OLAP data-warehouse-oriented SQL. This is really not valid. New enhancements to the relational database technology include extensions that permit user-defined functions and data types to be tightly integrated with the SQL language. User-developed application code can then be executed as part of the DBMS using these facilities.

In fact, Oracle7 allows execution of business logic in parallel using user-defined SQL functions.

DBMS ARCHITECTURE

As discussed earlier, from an application programming perspective, exploitation of hardware parallelism in the commercial marketplace was limited because of lack of tools and skills. It is now generally recognized that database management system (DBMS) vendors have recently stepped up their efforts in an attempt to address both of these challenges. They are starting to become the enablers of parallelism in the commercial arena. Additionally, more and more applications are migrating to DBMS for storage and retrieval of data. Therefore, it is worthwhile to understand how the DBMS enables parallelism.

This understanding will help in choosing an appropriate DBMS and, to some extent, the hardware configuration. Also, it will help in designing applications and databases that perform and scale well. Lack of understanding can lead to poorly performing systems and wasted resources.

In a manner similar to the three hardware configurations, DBMS architectures can also be classified into three corresponding categories:

- Shared-data and buffer
- Shared-data
- Partitioned-data

There is a match between these architectures and the characteristics of the respective hardware configuration, (namely SMP, shared-disk clusters, and MPP), but a DBMS does not have to execute only on its corresponding hardware counterpart. For example, a DBMS based on shared-data architecture can execute on a shared-nothing MPP hardware configuration.

When there is a match, the two build on each other's strengths and suffer from each other's weaknesses. However, the picture is much cloudier when a DBMS executes on a mismatched hardware configuration. On the one hand, in these cases, the DBMS is unable to build on and fully exploit the power of the hardware configuration. On the other hand, it can compensate for some of the challenges associated with using the underlying hardware configuration.

Shared-Data-and-Buffer

In this architecture, a single instance of the DBMS executes on a configuration that supports sharing of buffers and data. Multiple threads are initiated to provide an appropriate level of parallelism. As shown in Exhibit 6, all threads have complete visibility to all the data and buffers.

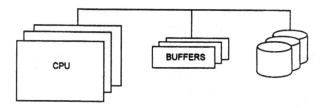

Characteristics:
- Data Partitioning not needed
- Systems management & load balancing easier
- Scalability concerns

Examples:
- Informix PDQ
- Oracle7 Parallel Query
- DB2 (MVS) CPU Parallelism

Exhibit 6.   Shared Data and Buffers

System administration and load balancing are comparatively easier with this architecture, because a single instance of the DBMS has full visibility to all the data. This architecture matches facilities offered by SMP configuration, in which this architecture is very frequently implemented. When executed on an SMP platform, the system inherits the scalability concerns associated with the underlying hardware platform. The maximum number of processors in an SMP, the cache coherence among processors, and the contention for memory access are some of the reasons that contribute to the scalability concerns.

Informix DSA, Oracle7, and DB2 for MVS are examples of DBMSs that have implemented the shared-data-and-buffer architecture. These DBMSs and their SQL parallelizing features permit intra-SQL parallelism; that is, they can concurrently apply multiple threads and processors to process a single SQL statement.

The algorithms used for intra-SQL parallelism are based on the notion of program and data parallelism. Program parallelism allows such SQL operations as scan, sort, and join to be performed in parallel by passing data from one operation to another. Data parallelism allows these SQL operations to process different pieces of data concurrently.

Shared Data

In this architecture, multiple instances of the DBMS execute on different processors. Each instance has visibility and access to all the data, but every instance maintains its own private buffers and updates rows within it.

Because the data is shared by multiple instances of the DBMSs, a mechanism is required to serialize the use of resources so that multiple instances do not concurrently update a value and corrupt the modifications made by another instance. This serialization is provided by the global locking facility of the DBMS and is essential for the shared data architecture. Global locking may be considered an extension of DBMS local locking facilities, which ensures serialization of resource modification within an instance, to the multiple instances that share data.

Another requirement, buffer coherence, is also introduced, because each instance of the DBMS maintains a private buffer pool. Without buffer coherence, a resource accessed by one DBMS from disk may not reflect the modification made by another system if the second system has not yet externalized the changes to the disk. Logically, the problem is similar to "cache coherence," discussed earlier for the SMP hardware configuration.

Combined, global locking and buffer coherence ensure data integrity. Oracle Parallel Server (OPS), DB2 for MVS Data Sharing, and Information Management System/Virtual Storage (IMS/VS) are examples of DBMSs that implement this architecture.

It must be emphasized that intraquery parallelism is not being exploited in any of these three product feature examples. The key motivation for the implementation of this architecture is the same as those discussed for the shared-disk hardware configuration, namely: data availability, incremental growth, and scalability. However, if one additionally chooses to use other features of these DBMSs in conjunction, the benefits of intraquery parallelism can also be realized.

As can be seen, there is a match between this software architecture and the facilities offered by shared-disk clusters, where this architecture is implemented. Thus, the performance of the DBMS is dependent not only on the software but also on the facilities provided by the hardware cluster to implement the two key components, global locking and buffer coherence.

In some implementations, maintenance of buffer coherence necessitates writing of data to the disks to permit reading by another DBMS instance. This writing and reading is called "pinging." Depending on the locking schemes used, pinging may take place even if the two instances are interested in distinct resources but represented by the same lock. This is known as false pinging. Heavy pinging, false or otherwise, has a negative effect on application performance, because it increases both the I/O and the lock management overhead.

System vendors use many techniques to minimize the impact of pinging. For example, IBM's DB2 for MVS on the Parallel Sysplex reduces the pinging I/O overhead by using the coupling facility, which couples all the nodes in the cluster via high-speed electronics. That is, disk I/Os are replaced by writes and reads from the coupling facility's electronic memory. In addition, hardware facilities are used to invalidate stale data buffers in another instances.

Even if the hardware and DBMS vendors have provided adequate facilities to minimize the adverse impact of pinging, it is still an Application Architect and Database Administrator's responsibility to design application and databases such that the need for sharing data is minimized to get the best performance.

It is interesting to note that Shared-Data software architecture can be implemented on hardware platforms other than shared-disk. For example, Oracle Parallel Server, which is based on shared-data software architecture, is quite common on IBM's RS 6000 SP, an implementation based on shared-shared-nothing hardware configuration. This is achieved by using the virtual shared disk feature of RS/6000 SP.

In this case, Oracle7's I/O request for data residing on another node is routed by RS/6000 SP device drivers to the appropriate node, an I/O is performed, if necessary, and data is returned to the requesting node. This is known as data shipping and contributes to added traffic on the node's interconnect hardware. The internode traffic is a consideration when architecting a solution and acquiring hardware.

In general, for the database administrators and application architects, it is necessary to understand such features in detail because the application performance depends on the architecture of the DBMS and the OS layers.

Partitioned Data

As the name implies, the database is partitioned among different instances of the DBMSs. In this option, each DBMS owns a portion of the database and only that portion may be directly accessed and modified by it.

Each DBMS has its private or local buffer pool, and as there is no sharing of data; the kind of synchronization protocols discussed above for shared-data (i.e., global locking and buffer coherence) are not required. However, a transaction or SQL modifying data in different DBMS instances residing on multiple nodes will need some form of two-phase commit protocol to ensure data integrity.

Each instance controls its own I/O, performs locking, applies the local predicates, extracts the rows of interest, and transfers them to the next stage of processing, which may reside on the same or some other node.

As can be seen, there is a match between the partitioned-data option and the MPP hardware configuration. Additionally, because MPP provides a large amount of processing power, and the partitioned-data architecture does not need the synchronization protocols, some argue that this combination offers the highest scalability. Thus, it has been the focus of recent development in the DBMS community. The partitioned-data architecture requires frequent communication among the DBMS instances to communicate messages and transfer results. Therefore, low latency and high bandwidth for the interconnect are required if the system is to scale up with the increased workload.

As mentioned earlier, NCR's Teradata system was one of the earliest successful commercial products based on this architecture. Recent new UNIX DBMSs offerings from other vendors are also based on this architecture. IBM DB2 Parallel Edition, Informix XPS, and Sybase MPP are examples.

In this architecture, requests for functions to be performed at other DBMS instances are shipped to them; the requesting DBMS instance receives only the results, not a block of data. This concept is called function shipping and is considered to offer better performance characteristics, compared to data shipping, because only the results are transferred to the requesting instance.

The partitioned-data architecture uses the notion of data parallelism to get the benefits of parallelism, and data partitioning algorithms play an important role in determining the performance characteristics of the systems. Various partitioning options are discussed in a later section.

The partitioned-data architecture also provides an additional flexibility in choosing the underlying hardware platform. As one can observe, partitioned-data matches well with the MPP hardware configuration. It also matches with the shared-nothing lightly parallel clusters. The distinction between these clusters and MPP is primarily based primarily on the number of nodes, which is somewhat arbitrary.

For illustration, DB2 Parallel Edition is considered a Partitioned-Data implementation. As shown in Exhibit 7, Parallel Edition can execute both

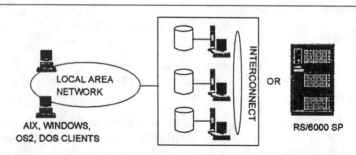

Exhibit 7.   DB2 Parallel Edition as a Partitioned-Data Implementation

on RS/6000 SP, an MPP offering, and on a cluster of RS/6000 computers, which are connected by a LAN. However, for a number of technical and financial reasons, the RS/6000 cluster solution is not marketed actively. On the other hand, there are conjectures in the market that similar system solutions are likely to become more prevalent when Microsoft becomes more active in marketing its cluster offerings.

THE THREE DBMS ARCHITECTURES: SUMMARY

A great deal of debate goes on as to which of the three software models — shared-buffer-and-data, shared-data, or partitioned-data — is best for the commercial marketplace. This debate is somewhat similar to the one that revolves around the choice of hardware configurations (i.e., SMP, clusters, or MPP). One might assume that making the choice of a software architecture would lead to a straightforward choice of a corresponding hardware configuration, or vice-versa; however, this is not the case.

OS and infrastructure layers permit cohabitation of a DBMS architecture with a nonmatching hardware configuration. Because of the mismatch, it is easy to observe that the mismatched components may not fully exploit the facilities of its partner. It is somewhat harder to appreciate, however, that the shortcomings of one may be compensated to some extent by the strengths of another. For example, a shared-data software architecture on an MPP platform avoids the management issues associated with repartitioning of data over time as the data or workload characteristics change.

This variety and flexibility in mix-and-match implementation presents trade-offs to both the DBMS and hardware vendors and to the application system developers. Even after an installation has made the choice of a DBMS and a hardware configuration, the application architects and the database and system administrators must still have a good understanding of the trade-offs involved with the system components to ensure scalability and good performance of the user applications.

CONCLUSION

The future seems extremely promising. Making faster and faster uniprocessors is not only technically difficult but is becoming economically prohibitive. Parallel processing is the answer. In the near future, all three hardware configurations are likely to find applicability:

- SMP on desktops and as departmental servers
- Shared-disk SMP clusters as enterprise servers
- MPP as servers of choice for strategic information processing, and as multimedia servers

Image and video servers, requiring large I/O capacity seem ideal for parallel processing. This need can be satisfied by a variety of current MPP,

501

which emphasizes scalability of I/O more than the scalability of processing power.

Lightly parallel shared-nothing clusters based on commodity hardware and ATM or Ethernet interconnect are likely to become very popular because of their low cost as soon as software for workload management becomes available.

Making long-range predictions in this business is unwise. However, one can be assured that parallel processing solutions in the commercial marketplace will be driven less by the hardware technology, and more by the software innovations, systems management offerings, pricing schemes, and most important by the marketing abilities of the vendors.

Section VI – Checklist
Operating Platforms

1. Would you characterize the operating environment of your computing environment as complex? What factors contribute to this?
2. How many different operating platforms does your organization use for application development? Does this create difficulty in developing enterprise-based applications?
3. Is it important for your organization to develop applications across platforms or between operating systems? Will this continue in the future?
4. What challenges does cross-platform application development pose in your environment? Have you found solutions to the problems or have you abandoned the effort?
5. Does the struggle between CORBA and COM standards affect your plans when developing application systems?
6. Assuming both CORBA and COM remain industry co-standards, would you favor one over the other to help simplify development practices or does it make more sense to use each for their own strengths?
7. How does your organization define and implement client/server and/or cooperative processing applications? Is there confusion on the implementation strategy?
8. Who governs the connectivity between host-based systems and micro-based systems? What controls or auditing procedures are used to ensure the reliability and integrity of the connection?
9. Could you identify the hardware connectivity options available in your environment? If not, what criteria are used for cross-platform development?
10. What changes would you recommend as a means of improving the execution of application systems in a client/server environment?
11. Can you identify the differences between n-tiered applications in your organization? Should these differences be a function of operating platform or application requirements.
12. How is security incorporated into application development in your environment?
13. Should security functions remain independent of an application design? If so, where should security issues be addressed in the development process?

14. Would you favor standard security components (as objects) to be used across all programming environments, or should organizations develop their own security mechanisms?
15. Is parallel processing an important consideration for future operating platforms in your organization? Can this technology improve complex application requirements that are currently part of your environment?

Section VII
Networking and Connectivity

NETWORKING AND CONNECTIVITY REMAIN SALIENT ISSUES in the future role of corporate computing. Continued growth of communication technologies has prompted many organizations to capitalize on the distributed power of multiplatform processors. This has been especially true for Internet and Intranet environments. While the benefits of connectivity are encouraging, there is significant effort in deciphering the various networking options and directions. Since communication is at the heart of computing architecture, it has a profound impact on an organization's technical prowess. Pursuing bleeding edge networking products too rapidly, or delaying implementation of stable technology, can have adverse affects on application development and support. Furthermore, the IS industry is debating the merits of Network Computers (NC) over the prevailing establishment of Desktop Computers. Arguments about the "computer being the network" and vice versa have only added more challenges to the effort for implementing network-centric applications.

One of the more interesting and lively debated topics of network computing has been the future of large-scale mainframe processors. Long regarded as dead, mainframes have surprised many in the IS community. In fact, just the opposite may be occurring through a resurgence in the role of these workhorse machines. Chapter VII-1, "The Mainframe as an Enterprise Server," looks at the trends for incorporating the mainframe as an integral part of the networking environment. As technology advancements increase in the network server arena, the line between mainframe and server computers has become less distinguishable. Given the deployed base of mainframes, organizations would be wise to exploit the vast power of large-scale processors for the sake of network servers.

Advancements in technology for e-commerce business applications have generated tremendous interest in the last year. And predictions for continued growth in cyber commerce have been meeting or exceeding many expectations. However, there is equal concern that security for e-commerce systems is still lacking and requires careful monitoring. Chapter VII-2, "Developing a Trusted Infrastructure for Electronic Commerce Services," discusses the diverse issues involved with securing commerce networks. This chapter also proposes ways of confirming sender and recipient identities, protecting confidentiality, and date stamping to ensure trustworthy applications.

Electronic Messaging Systems, in the form of e-mail, are some of the earliest examples of a network-centric application. Most organizations have some form of message system, and in numerous instances there can be several that are concurrently implemented in a given environment. Furthermore, it is not uncommon for organizations to migrate from one type of message system to another in order to improve overall communication efficiency. Chapter VII-3, "Integrating Electronic Messaging Systems and Infrastructures," gives an overview of the issues surrounding consolidation of disparate messaging systems. This information can be useful when developing applications that encompass e-mail as part of system functionality.

The explosive use of the Internet has also fueled considerable concern about the general security and safety of network environments. Incidents of security breaches seem to occur daily, and there is an expanding need to tighten control on network communications. At the center of Internet security lies the mechanism to encrypt and decrypt information. Chapter VII-4, "Understanding Public Key Cryptology," reviews the basic structure of cryptological systems. Although many crypotological systems are currently in use, there have been known weaknesses that allow for security violations. Development managers should maintain a close watch on the ongoing changes and advancements in Internet security as it pertains to the application development process.

Chapter VII-1

The Mainframe as Enterprise Server

Brian Jeffrey

AMONG COMPANIES THAT HAVE USED INFORMATION SYSTEMS (IS) to sustain competitiveness, a new kind of IS strategy is emerging. IS technology is being used not only to automate business tasks and processes, but also to turn information itself into a powerful competitive weapon. Simple, effective techniques enable the IS infrastructure to deliver continuous, accurate, and useful information to executives, line managers, sales professionals, and front-line workers throughout the organization.

At the same time, new integrated software systems increase the efficiency of all business operations. Products and services are delivered more rapidly. Sales and service become more responsive to customers. And organizational structures as well as business processes are streamlined to reduce operating costs and eliminate unnecessary administrative overheads.

ENTERPRISE SERVER ROLE

The basis of a new IS strategy is a modernized, upgraded mainframe system equipped with new database and application tools that enable it to function as an enterprise server. Mainframe-based computing retains its embedded strengths of economy of scale, robustness, and business-critical computing. The mainframe continues to run the core systems without which the business could not function, providing high levels of availability, data integrity, and security.

However, these systems also acquire powerful new client/server capabilities. Central databases play a new role, in concentrating, protecting, and providing access to all corporate data resources. Users employ PCs, workstations, and mobile computers to access this data, and to communicate via organizationwide network infrastructures.

New development tools deliver high-quality, flexible applications in a fraction of the time previously required. In most cases, legacy data, applications, and skills carry over to the new IS environment. More important, there is no significant business disruption.

The transition from conventional mainframe computing to an enterprise sever-based IS strategy uses simple techniques and proven solutions. In most growth companies, it can be realized within 12 to 18 months. Key applications can be brought on-line even more rapidly. In an organization that already uses mainframe systems efficiently, and employs modern hardware and software technologies, much of the infrastructure will already be in place.

BUSINESS BENEFITS

Costs will vary from company to company. But such an IS strategy, if properly applied, will yield business gains and improvements in efficiency that more than justify the investments. Within the IS infrastructure, data center operating costs are normally reduced by two to eight times. Application development productivity can be increased up to eight times. PC/LAN costs can be reduced 50% to 80%. Telecommunications costs can be reduced up to 50%. Savings can also be realized in other areas.

TECHNICAL IMPLEMENTATION

The technical infrastructure for a leadership IS strategy is based on upgrading a mainframe system with new capabilities that enable it to function as an enterprise server. The enterprise server is the cornerstone of this strategy. It concentrates key IS resources to better support distributed and remote users. It also increases the volume, quality, and accessibility of information for all users, improves availability of application, data, and network resources, and maximizes the cost-effectiveness with which all IS resources are used.

ENTERPRISE SERVER BASICS

An enterprise server combines the following distinct and, until recently, separate computing technology streams.

Mainframe Computing

In most growth companies, this focuses on business control systems, such as accounting, finance, asset management, personnel administration, and payroll, and the core business-critical systems without which the company could not function. The mainframe's key strengths are its robustness, its ability to handle large-scale, organizationwide workloads, its ability to provide high levels or availability and data integrity, and its capability to manage all system, data, and network resources effectively in performing these tasks. Mainframes also leverage economies of scale, benefits of concentrated resources, and consistencies of architecture that are inherent to the central IS environment. Few seriously question the superiority of mainframe systems in these areas.

Client/Server Computing

This refers to the use of PCs and workstations. Although industry debate often treats client/server computing as a single phenomenon, in practice it involves several different types of applications. A basic category includes text processing, electronic mail, and personal productivity tools. These are useful and fairly easy to implement in an end-user environment. The largest and, from a business standpoint, most valuable category involves "informational" client/server applications that access, manipulate, and process data. Applications include decision support, market research, financial analysis, human resources, and planning applications.

In most organizations, mainframe databases are the primary source of data used by such applications — over 95%, according to some estimates. The data is generated by the production business control and business-critical applications that run on mainframes. There is therefore an obvious synergy between mainframe and client/server computing. To realize business benefits from new types of applications, this synergy needs to be exploited to its full potential. By consolidating key databases and implementing reliable, organizationwide network infrastructures, all data can be made accessible at the workstation level.

In combining these technology streams, most growing companies are faced with the choice of upgrading a mainframe to act as a server or trying to equip a UNIX server to act as a mainframe. Upgrading the mainframe is normally both less expensive and less disruptive. Moreover, it is substantially less difficult to provide client/server capability to a mainframe than it is to provide mainframe-class robustness to a UNIX server. The strengths of the mainframe environment have developed over more than 30 years of handling high-volume, business-critical workloads with high levels of availability and data integrity. Few users have been prepared to entrust genuinely business-critical applications to UNIX servers. The experiences of those who have tried are not encouraging.

IMPLEMENTATION PLAN

Establishing an enterprise server involves several steps. A core database management system (DBMS) must be put in place. This should be capable of handling on-line transaction processing (OLTP) and batch workloads required for business control and business-critical applications, as well as the new, query-intensive workloads that will be generated by organizationwide client/server computing. Multiple databases, such as the common customer database and common operational database, are created within the core DBMS, which also ensures the accessibility, currency, integrity, security, and recoverability of all corporate data.

In some organizations, it may be necessary to replace older hierarchical database and file structures. This is, however, a relatively fast and easy process, particularly if automated tools are used. Legacy data and applications can be converted to run on the new core DBMS. Existing applications written in COBOL and leading fourth-generation languages (4GLs) can be ported in this manner without the necessity for major rewrites.

New applications must be delivered. Leadership applications require special types of tools. Conventional COBOL- and 4GL-based techniques are often too slow and do not provide adequate levels of integration and flexibility. Equally, light-duty client/server development tools for PCs and small servers may not be able to handle the size and functional requirements of new, high-value-added solutions.

Packaged software can be used. However, most independent software vendor offerings address only standardized accounting, human resources, and business-critical requirements. They do not usually provide a direct competitive edge for companies that use them, and they are difficult to customize.

The logical candidates to use to develop these new high-volume applications are latest-generation computer-aided software engineering (CASE), rapid application development (RAD), and object-oriented development tools for the mainframe environment. These deliver high-quality, large-scale applications that fully support client/server capabilities, including graphical user interfaces (GUIs). Moreover, they do so in a fraction of the time required with conventional techniques.

Where existing applications remain viable, a number of techniques can be used to make them more flexible and user-friendly. For example, PC-based GUIs can typically be added to legacy applications without the necessity for major changes in platforms or software architectures. Similarly, existing applications can be redeveloped and maintained using new PC-based COBOL visual programming tools.

Once the core DBMS is in place, considerable flexibility is possible. New systems can coexist with legacy applications, and light-duty database query, decision support, and related tools can also be employed.

Data center operations must be rebuilt around modern, efficient hardware and software technologies, automation tools, and improved management practices. High levels of capacity usage, increased performance, reduced operating costs, and minimal outages or production job failures will be the norm.

PC/LAN clusters must be integrated. To support distributed PC users more effectively, LANs are interconnected and managed from a central point. New tools are also put in place to regularly back up data on LAN servers to data center storage. This ensures that departmental data is properly managed and protected, and is accessible to other users within the organization.

These initiatives significantly improve the quality and availability of LAN infrastructures and reduce support costs.

Network infrastructures should be transparent and functional enough to allow information to flow freely throughout the organization. Increased use of client/server computing normally increases network loading, which may mean that more bandwidth is needed at both the local and wide area network levels. In addition, wireless technologies may be used to support mobile sales, logistics, and other applications. Networking for mobile computing is typically simpler and less expensive to implement than for client/server solutions built around traditional PCs and LANs.

RETURN ON INVESTMENT

If the process is properly managed, investment in the technical infrastructure will pay for itself in a relatively short period of time. First, there will be a direct impact on business performance. Sales, customer loyalty, and corporate profitability will increase. If the introduction of new systems is accompanied by business reengineering or other forms of organizational streamlining, major reductions in personnel and other costs will typically occur. Employee productivity will also increase in all areas of the business supported by new IS solutions.

Second, there will be significant savings in the IS operations. Costs will be reduced as efficiency improves. In many companies, the use of IS resources is highly inefficient. Old systems have low-capacity usage and high environmental costs. Aging application portfolios and low-productivity programming techniques mean that application maintenance overheads are too high. Old, inefficient code and poor tuning generate excessive consumption of processor and storage resources. Networks are poorly optimized. And both mainframe and PC/LAN installations are characterized by low value-added, manpower-intensive practices.

Efficiency improvements yield gains in for main areas: data center costs, application costs, PC/LAN costs, and network costs.

Data Center Costs

If the organization starts with low levels of mainframe efficiency, annual operating costs, including hardware acquisitions, software licenses, maintenance, and most categories of IS personnel, can routinely be reduced by two to five times and may be reduced as much as eight times. If the data center is efficient to begin with, reductions of 10% to 20% per annum in operating costs can still be expected.

Application Costs

Latest-generation mainframe development tools deliver radical increases in the speed of application development and in developer productivity, compared with conventional COBOL. Applications can therefore be developed more rapidly, with fewer analysts and programmers. They will also have substantially longer life cycles and require less maintenance.

PC/LAN Costs

Hardware, software, support, and other costs for PC/LAN installations are normally in the range of $6,000 to $10,000 per user per year. Consolidation, mainframe-based, remote LAN management and backup tools, and other techniques can routinely reduce these costs by 50% to 80%.

Network Costs

These can be reduced by improved capacity management, data compression, and new technologies, such as frame relay, which has been shown to reduce telecommunications costs for SNA networks by up to 50%, depending on network size and configuration.

The objective may not always be to lower IS costs per se. In organizations that are experiencing growth in applications and workloads, the result may be that new requirements are met without increasing IS costs, rather than through net reductions in IS budgets. In either case, initial investment to create a more efficient, functional IS infrastructure built around a mainframe-based enterprise server will yield major payoffs both in positive business benefits and in significantly higher yields from IS expenditures.

CONCLUSION

The leadership IS strategy described in this document is about using IS resources for maximum, organizationwide business impact. That means focusing IS strategy not on any single theme in business performance but on all of the variables that affect the market penetration, competitive success, and profitability of a growing company. And it means moving beyond using IS to automate business tasks and processes more effectively, to turn information itself into a dynamic new tool that can be employed throughout the organization, from the executive suite to the front-line worker.

More fundamentally, a leadership IS strategy is also about integration and coordination. A company does not succeed as a collection of individuals and departments. Similarly, the IS infrastructure must do more than empower individual users. It must provide a further level of value, by creating a new cohesiveness in the way in which all of the company's resources — human, material, financial, and technical — are focused and deployed for success. In a leadership company, the whole is always more than the sum of the parts.

Chapter VII-2
Developing a Trusted Infrastructure for Electronic Commerce Services

David Litwack

THE USE OF INTERNETWORKING APPLICATIONS FOR ELECTRONIC COM-MERCE has been limited by issues of security and trust and by the lack of universality of products and services supporting robust and trustworthy electronic commerce services. Specific service attributes must be addressed to overcome the hesitation of users and business owners to exploit open systems — such as the Internet — for commercial exchanges. These service attributes include:

- **Confirmation of identity (nonrepudiation).** This indicates proof that only intended participants (i.e., creators and recipients) are party to communications.
- **Confidentiality and content security.** Documents can be neither read nor modified by an uninvited third party.
- **Time certainty.** Proof of date and time of communication is provided through time stamps and return receipts.
- **Legal protection.** Electronic documents should be legally binding and protected by tort law and fraud statutes.

SERVICE ATTRIBUTE AUTHORITY

To support these service attributes, an organization or entity would need to provide:

- Certificate authority services, including the registration and issuance of certificates for public keys as well as the distribution of certificate revocation and compromised key lists to participating individuals and organizations.
- A repository for public key certificates that can provide such keys and certificates to authorized requesters on demand.

0-8493-9979-3/99/$0.00+$.50

- Electronic postmarking for date and time stamps, and for providing the digital signature of the issuer for added assurance.
- Return receipts that provide service confirmation.
- Storage and retrieval services, including a transaction archive log and an archive of bonded documents.

These service attributes could be offered singly or in various combinations. The service attribute provider would have to be recognized as a certificate and postmark authority. The following sections describe how a service attribute provider should work.

Certificate Authority

Although public key encryption technology provides confidentiality and confirmation of identity, a true trusted infrastructure requires that a trusted authority certify a person or organization as the owner of the key pair. Certificates are special data structures used to register and protectively encapsulate the public key users and prevent their forgery. A certificate contains the name of a user and its public key. An electronic certificate binds the identity of the person or organization to the key pair.

Certificates also contain the name of the issuer — a certificate authority(CA) — that vouches that the public key in a certificate belongs to the named user. This data, along with a time interval specifying the certificate's validity, is cryptography signed by the issuer using the issuer's private key. The subject and issuer names in certificates are distinguished names (DNs), as defined in the International Telecommunications Union-Telecommunications Standards Sector (ITU-TSS) recommendation X.500 directory services. Such certificates are also called X.509 certificates after the ITU-TSS recommendation in which they were defined.

The key certificate acts like a kind of electronic identity card. When a recipient uses a sender's public key to authenticate the sender's signature (or when the originator uses the recipient's PKS to encrypt a message or document), the recipient wants to be sure that the sender is who he or she claims to be. The certificate provides that assurance.

A certificate could be tied to one individual or represent an organizational authority that in turn represents the entire organization. Also, certificates could represent various levels of assurance — from those dispensed by a machine to those registered with a personally signed application. Additional assurance could be provided by the personal presentation of a signed application along with proof of identity or by the verification of a biometric test (e.g., fingerprint or retina scan) for each use of the private key.

Exhibit 1 shows a possible scenario for obtaining a certificate. The registration process might work as follows:

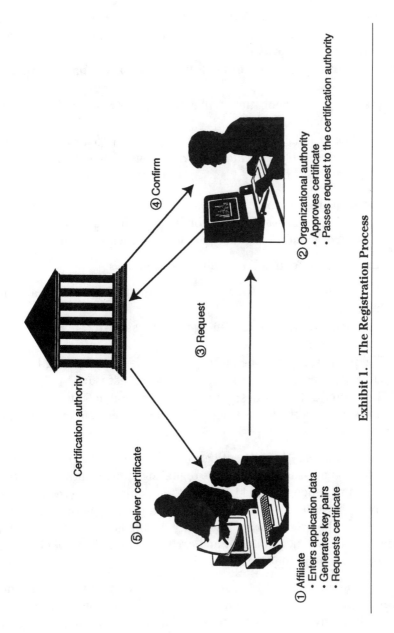

Exhibit 1. The Registration Process

- The affiliate (i.e., candidate for certificate) fills out the application, generates private-public key pairs, and sends for the certificate, enclosing his or her public key.
- The organizational authority approves the application.
- The organizational authority passes the certificate application to the certification authority.
- The certification authority sends back a message confirming receipt of the application.
- After proper proofing, the certification authority sends the certificate to the applicant-affiliate.
- The applicant-affiliate then loads the certificate to his or her workstation, verifies the certificate authority's digital signature, and saves a copy of the certificate.

Digital Signatures. Exhibit 2 illustrates how a digital signature ensures the identity of the message originator. It shows how a message recipient would use an originator's digital signature to authenticate that originator.

On the Web, authentication could work as follows:

- The originator creates a message and the software performs a hash on the document.
- The originator's software then signs the message by encrypting it with the originator's private key.
- The originator sends the message to the server attaching his or her public key and certificate to the message if necessary.
- The server either requests the originator's public key from a certificate/key repository or extracts the certification from the originator's message.

With this service, the authentication authority could either attach an authentication message verifying the digital signature's authenticity to the originator's message or provide that authentication to the recipient via a publicly accessible database. Upon receipt, the recipient would either acknowledge the originator's authenticity via the attached authentication message or access the public key and certificate from the publicly accessible database to read the signature.

To provide such levels of assurance, the certification authority must establish proofing stations where individuals and organizations can present themselves with appropriate identification and apply for certificates. The authority must also maintain or be part of a legal framework of protection and be in a position to mount an enforcement process to protect customers against fraud.

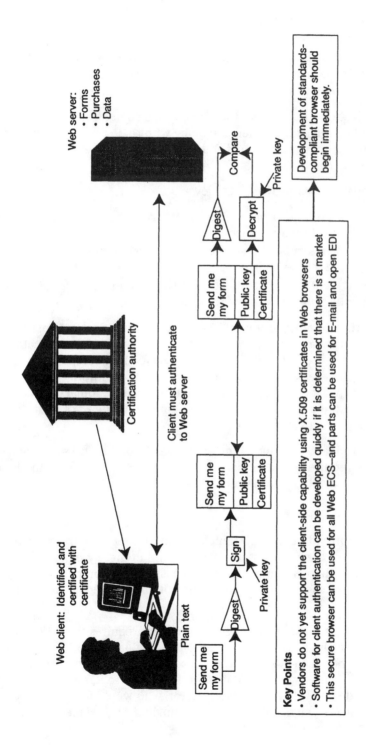

Exhibit 2.   Client Authentication

Certificate Repository

The certificate authority also provides the vehicle for the distribution of public keys. Thus the certificate authority would have to maintain the public key certificates in a directory server that can be accessed by authorized persons and computers.

Exhibit 3 shows how subscribers might use such a repository. Certificates could be retrieved on demand along with their current status. Additional information, such as e-mail addresses or fax numbers, could also be available on demand.

The repository would work as follows:

- The message originator creates a message, generates a digital signature, and sends the message.
- The recipient sends a signed message requesting the originator's public key from the certificate repository.
- The certificate repository verifies the requester's signature and returns the public key to the recipient.

The certificate authority could also use the certificate repository to maintain a certificate revocation list (CRL), which provides notification of certificates that are revoked pursuant to a suspected compromise of the private key. This service could also require that the authority report such compromises via a compromised key list to special customers — possibly those enrolled in a subscribed service — and that such notifications be made available to all customers.

Finally, transactions involving certificates issued by other certificate authorities require that a cross-certification record be maintained and made publicly available in the certificate repository.

Electronic Postmark

A service providing an electronic date and time postmark establishes the existence of a message at a specific point in time. By digitally signing the postmark, the postmarking authority assures the communicating parties that the message was sent, was in transit, or received at the indicated time.

This service is most useful when the recipient requires the originator to send a message by a specified deadline. The originator would request the postmark authority to postmark the message. The authority would receive a digest of the message, add a date and time token to it, digitally sign the package, and send it back to the originator, who would forward the complete package (i.e., signed digest, time stamp, and original message) to the recipient, as shown in Exhibit 4.

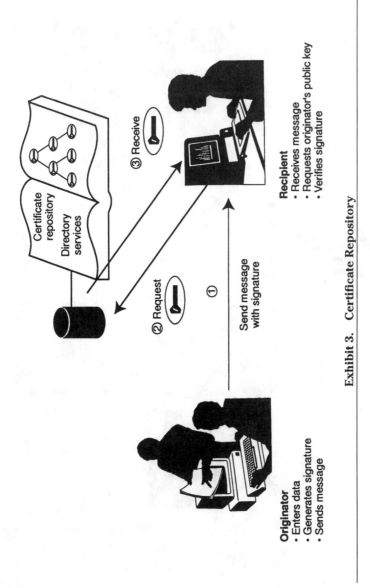

Exhibit 3. Certificate Repository

519

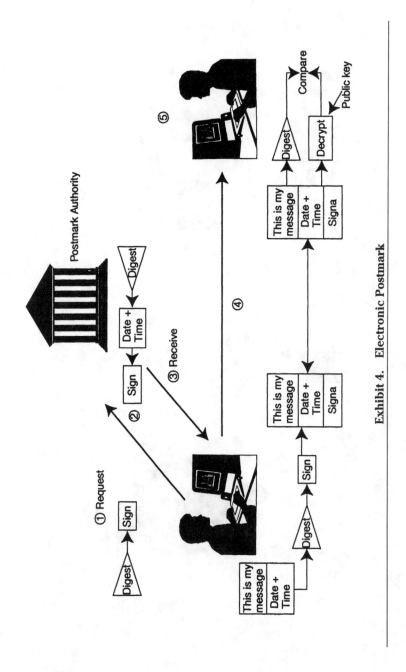

Exhibit 4. Electronic Postmark

Electronic postmarking functions as follows:

- The originator sends a request to the postmark authority to postmark a message or document (i.e., a digital digest of the message or document).
- The postmark authority adds date and time to the message received and affixes its digital signature to the entire package.
- The postmark authority sends the package back to the originator.
- The originator sends the original message or document plus the post-marked package to the recipient.
- The recipient verifies the postmark authority signature with the authority's public key and reads the message or document.

Return Receipts

This service reports one of three events: a message has transited the network, it has been received at the recipient's mailbox, or the recipient has actually decoded and opened the message at a specific date and time. In the latter instance, the transaction delivered to the recipient that has been encrypted might be set up only to be decrypted with a special one-time key, as shown in Exhibit 5. This one-time key could be provided by the postmark authority upon receipt of an acknowledgment from the recipient accompanied by the recipient's digital signature.

Here is how return receipt might work:

- The originator sends a message digest to the return receipt and post-mark authority (the authority) with a request for a postmark and return receipt.
- The authority receives the message digest, adds date and time, encrypts the result, attaches a message to the recipient to request the decryption key from the authority upon receipt of the message, and affixes its digital signature to the package.
- The authority returns the postmarked, receipted package to the orig-inator, who sends it to the recipient.
- The recipient receives the message package and makes a signed request for the decryption key from the authority.
- The authority receives the recipient's request, verifies the recipient's digital signature, and sends the decryption key to the recipient, who then decrypts and reads the message.
- The authority simultaneously forwards the return receipt to the origi-nator.

Storage and Retrieval Services

These services include transaction archiving where copies of transactions are held for specified periods of time, as illustrated in Exhibit 6. The service might also include information (i.e., documents, videos, or business transac-tions) that can be sealed, postmarked, and held in public storage to be

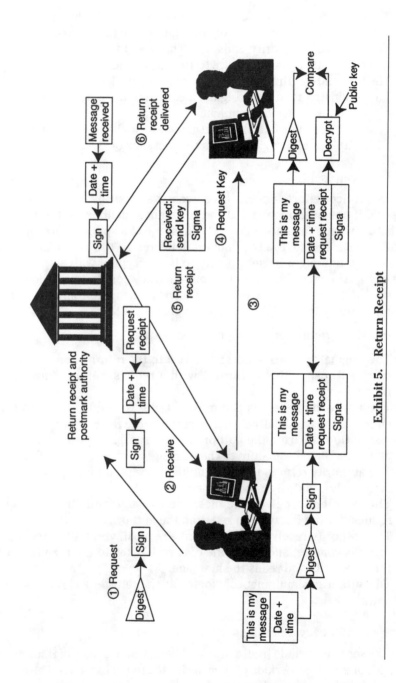

Exhibit 5. Return Receipt

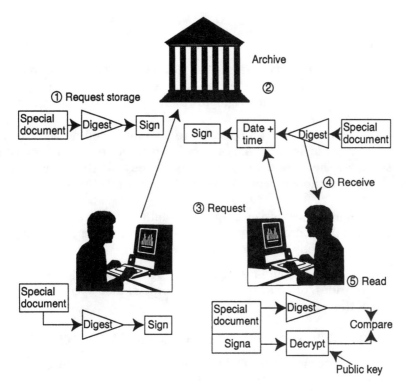

Exhibit 6.   Storage and Retrieval

retrieved via any authorized access. Likewise, encrypted information (i.e., documents, videos, or business transactions) can be sealed, postmarked, and further encrypted and held in sealed storage for indefinite periods of time. Each of these storage and retrieval capabilities must carry legal standing and the stamp of authenticity required for electronic correspondents.

Storage and retrieval works as follows:

- The originator sends a request to the archive to archive a document or message for a specified period of time and designates this information as publicly retrievable.
- The archive adds date and time to the message, verifies the identity of the originator, affixes a digital signature to the package, and archives the package.
- A customer requests the document from the archive.
- The archive retrieves the document, adds a date and time stamp to the package, affixes another digital signature to the new package, and sends it to the recipient.
- The recipient verifies the first and second archive signatures and reads the message.

USE OF THESE COMMERCIAL EXCHANGE SERVICES

Electronic Commerce services (ECS) may be used in one of three ways:

- The originator sends a message to the authority with a request for service, the authority provides the service and returns the message to the originator, and the originator then forwards the message to the recipient.
- The originator sends a message to a value added network (VAN), which then forwards the message to the authority with a request for services. The authority provides the service and returns the message to the value added network, which then forwards the message to the recipient.
- The originator sends a message to the authority with a request for service and the address of the recipient. The authority then forwards the message directly to the recipient.

All these services could be provided by a single authority, by a hierarchy of authorities, or by a network of authorities, each specializing in one or more of these services.

AVAILABLE TECHNOLOGIES FOR ELECTRONIC COMMERCE

Currently, three major technologies are capable of providing electronic commerce services — e-mail, the World Wide Web, and open EDI. Typical of advanced technologies, security elements are the last to be developed and yet are essential if these technologies are to be deemed trustworthy for electronic commerce.

The issues of confidentiality, confirmation of identity, time certainty, and legal protection apply to all these technologies. The solutions — certification, key repositories, postmarking, return receipts, and storage and retrieval — are equally applicable to each of these technologies. Although the state of universality and interoperability varies among these technologies, they are all in a relative state of immaturity.

Secure e-mail

Electronic messaging's most classic manifestation is e-mail. Because of its capacity for handling attachments, e-mail can be used to transfer official business, financial, technical, and a variety of multimedia forms.

DMS and PEM. Both the Department of Defense standard for e-mail, which is based on the ITU's X.400 standard for e-mail (called the Defense Message System or DMS), and the Internet e-mail standard, the simple mail transfer protocol (SMTP), have made provisions for security. The DMS uses encapsulation techniques at several security levels to encrypt and sign e-mail messages. The security standard for the Internet is called

Privacy Enhanced Mail (PEM). Both methods rely on a certificate hierarchy and known and trusted infrastructure. Neither method is fully developed.

Secure World Wide Web

The phenomenal growth of the Web makes it a prime candidate for the dissemination of forms and documents. Organizations see the Web as a prime tool for services such as delivery of applications and requests for information. However, Web technology has two competing types of security: one at the application layer that secures hypertext transfer protocol (HTTP) formatted data (known as SHTTP), and one at the socket layer that encrypts data in the format in which it is transported across the network.

In addition, vendors do not yet support either client-side authentication or the use of X.509 certificates. Although software for such activities as client authentication can be developed relatively quickly, vendors have to be convinced that there is a real market for such products. This technology is about to emerge, and although it will emerge first to support Web applications, it will also speed the development of e-mail and EDI security services.

Secure Open EDI

Until now, EDI has been used in closed, value-added networks where security and integrity can be closely controlled. Signing and encryption have been proprietary to the EDI product in use or to the value-added EDI network provider.

By contrast, open EDI, running across open networks, requires adherence to the standards that are still being developed and a yet-to-be developed infrastructure that can ensure trusted keys. To date, the various schemes to accelerate the use of open systems for EDI have not captured the imagination of EDI users and providers.

THE OVERRIDING ISSUE: A PUBLIC KEY CERTIFICATE INFRASTRUCTURE

The suite of services and technologies described in this article depend on trusted public keys and their bindings to users. Users could be completely assured of the integrity of keys and their bindings if they were exchanged manually. Because business is conducted on a national and international scale, users have to be assured of the integrity of the registration authority and the key repository in an inevitably complex, electronic way.

One as-yet-unresolved issue is whether such an authority or authorities should be centralized and hierarchical or distributed. The centralized, hierarchical scheme would mean that certification authorities (and purveyors of the accompanying services) would be certified by a higher authority that, in turn, might be certified by yet a higher authority — and so on to the root authority. This kind certification would create a known chain of trust from the highest to the closest certification authority. This scheme is often referred to as the Public Key Infrastructure (PKI).

The alternative assumes that the market will foster the creation of a variety of specialized certification authorities to serve communities of interest. A complicated method of cross-referencing and maintaining those cross-references in the certificate repository for each community of interest would then develop.

The outcome of this debate is likely to result in a combination of both methods, such as several hierarchies with some kind of managed cross-referencing to enable public key exchanges between disparate communities of interest when required. Following are some of the issues yet to be resolved:

- Agreement on the exact contents of certificates
- Definition of the size of prime numbers used in key generation
- Establishment of the qualifications required for obtaining a certificate
- Definition of the identification and authentication requirements for certificate registration
- Ruling on the frequency with which certificates are renewed
- Agreement on the legal standing and precedence for such technology

CONCLUSION

Groups such as the Internet Engineering Task Force (IETF), the federal government's Public Key Infrastructure (PKI) users group, and even the American Bar Association are tackling these knotty issues.

In fact, with toolkits now available that allow the user to become his or her own certificate authority, everyone can get into the act. Private companies such as VeriSign are establishing themselves as certification authorities so that users will give their public keys and certificates credence. The National Security Agency wants to become the certificate authority for the federal government. The U.S. Postal Service is intent on offering electronic commerce services to businesses and residences by acting as the certificate authority and provider.

An infrastructure will emerge, and it will probably work for users very similar to the way that it has been described in this chapter.

Chapter VII-3
Integrating Electronic Messaging Systems and Infrastructures

Dale Cohen

IMPLEMENTING A MESSAGING SYSTEM INFRASTRUCTURE requires taking small steps while keeping the big picture in mind. The complexity of the endeavor is directly affected by the scope of the project.

If implementing messaging for a single department or a small single enterprise, a vendor solution can probably be used. All users will have the same desktop application with one message server or post office from that same application vendor.

By contrast, integrating multiple departments may require proprietary software routers for connecting similar systems. When building an infrastructure for a single enterprise, the IT department may incorporate the multiple-department approach for similar systems. Dissimilar systems can be connected using software and hardware gateways.

If the goal is to implement an integrated system for a larger enterprise, multiple departments may need to communicate with their external customers and suppliers. The solution could implement a messaging backbone or central messaging switch. This approach allows the implementers to deploy common points to sort, disperse, and measure the flow of messages.

If an organization already has an infrastructure but needs to distribute it across multiple systems connected by common protocols, the goal may be to make the aggregate system more manageable and gain economies of scale. Implementations can vary widely, from getting something up and running to reducing the effort and expense of running the current system.

HOW TO ACCOMPLISH ROLLOUT AND MANAGE CONSTRAINTS

Messaging is a unique application, because it crosses all the networks, hardware platforms, network operating systems, and application environments in the organization. Plenty of cooperation will be necessary to accomplish a successful rollout. The traditional constraints are time,

0-8493-9979-3/99/$0.00+$.50
© 1999 by CRC Press LLC

functionality, and resources, though implementers must also manage user perceptions.

Resource Constraints: Financial

In an international organization of 5000 or more users, it is not unreasonable to spend $200,000 to $500,000 on the backbone services necessary to achieve a solution. The total cost — including network components, new desktop devices, ongoing administration, maintenance, and end-user support — can easily exceed $2,500 per user, with incremental costs for the e-mail add-on at $300 to $500 per year.

The initial appeal of offerings from Lotus Development Corp., Novell Inc., and Microsoft Corp. is that a component can be added at a low incremental cost. In reality, the aggregate incremental costs are huge, although most of the purchaser's costs are hidden. For a corporate PC to handle e-mail, the corporatewide and local area networks and support organizations must be industrial strength.

Although this investment may at first glance seem prohibitively high, it allows for add-ons such as Web browsers or client/server applications at a much lower startup cost. Vendors argue that they make it possible for the buyer to start small and grow. It is more likely that an organization will start small, grow significantly, and grow its application base incrementally. In the long run, the investment pays for itself repeatedly, not only for the benefits e-mail provides but for the opportunities the foray offers.

Resource Constraints: Expertise

It is easy to underestimate the expertise required to operate an efficient messaging infrastructure. Most IT departments are easily able to handle a single application in a single operating environment. Multiple applications in multiple operating environments are a different story.

Messaging systems must be able to deal with multiple network protocols, various operating systems, and different software applications — all from different vendors. Given these facts, it is difficult to understand why already overburdened LAN administrators would take on the significant systems integration responsibilities of a messaging system rollout.

When confronted with problems during a messaging system integration, the staff must be able to answer the following questions:

- Is it a network problem or an application issue?
- Is it an operating system-configured value or an application bug?
- Can the problem be handled by someone with general expertise, such as a front-line technician or a support desk staff member?

Skill Sets. Individuals performing the rollout must be technically adept, have strong diagnostic skills, and understand how to work in a team environment. They must be adept with multiple operating systems and understand the basics of multiple networks. Ideally they understand the difference between a technical answer and one that solves the business issue at large.

Many organizations make the mistake of assigning first-tier support staff to an e-mail project when systems integrators are called for. The leanest integration team consists of individuals with an understanding of networks and their underlying protocols, operating systems, and two or more e-mail applications. Database knowledge is very useful when dealing with directories and directory synchronization. A knowledge of tool development helps automate manual processes. Application monitoring should occur alongside network monitoring, because nothing signals a network error as well as an e-mail service interruption.

Cross-Functional Integration Teams. The most efficient way to coordinate a rollout is through cross-functional teams. It is important to incorporate e-mail implementation and support into the goals of the individuals and the teams from which they come. Many organizations do this informally, but this method is not always effective. A written goal or service level agreement is extremely helpful when conflicting priorities arise and management support is needed.

When creating the core messaging integration team, it is very helpful to include individuals from WAN and LAN networking, systems, operations, and support desk staff, in addition to the individual application experts from each e-mail environment.

Functionality and Scope

At any point in the project, network administrators may find themselves trying to implement an enterprisewide solution, a new departmental system, a corporatewide directory service, or a solution for mobile e-mail users. When building a house, it is commonly understood that the plumbing and waste systems must be installed before hooking up the bath fixtures. This is not the case with messaging.

A messaging system rollout should start with a basic infrastructure "plumbed" for future expansion, and be followed directly with reliable user functionality. Results should be monitored and measured, and original infrastructure issues should be revisited as appropriate. Project success comes with regular reports on what has been delivered and discussions of incremental improvements in reliability and services.

Supporting Internal and External Customers

No matter how good the features of any product or set of products, if the system is not reliable, people cannot depend on it. If the system is perceived as unreliable, people will use alternative forms of communication.

To satisfy user needs, the IT department should separate internal customers from external customers. Internal customers are those that help provide a service. They may be IT management, support personnel, or networking staff — they could be considered an internal supplier.

Because of the nature of most organizations, internal customers are both customer and supplier. They need to be provided with the means to supply a service. For example, IT management may need to create step-by-step procedures for the operations staff to carry them out. If the information technology group cannot satisfy the requirements of internal customers, it probably will not be able to satisfy the needs of external customers.

External customers are the end users. If they are in sales, for example, external customers may include the enterprise's customers from other companies. It is the job of the IT staff to provide external customers with messaging features, functionality, and reliability so they can do their job.

IMPLEMENTATION MODELS AND ARCHITECTURES

It is helpful for network managers to know how other enterprises have implemented messaging systems. The next few sections describe the various components of the infrastructure, common deployment architectures, and how to plan future deployments.

Infrastructure Versus Interface

Often messaging systems are sold with the emphasis on what the end user sees. Experienced network managers know that this is the least of their problems. The behind-the-scenes components, which make the individual systems in an organization work as a near-seamless whole, include:

- Network services
- Message transfer services
- Directory services
- Management and administration services

Network Services. The network services required for a messaging rollout involve connectivity between:

- Desktop and server
- Server to server
- Server to gateway
- Gateway to foreign environment

530

It is not unusual to have one network protocol between a desktop device and its server and a second protocol within the backbone server/gateway/router environment. Servers may communicate via WAN protocols such as TCP/IP, OSI, DECnet, or SNA, and the desktops may communicate over a LAN protocol such as IPX or NetBIOS. WAN connections may occur over continuous connections or over asynchronous dialup methods.

The network administrator's greatest concern is loss of network connectivity. It is important to understand how it happens, why it happens, how it is discovered, and what needs to be done on an application level once connectivity is restored.

If the network goes down, e-mail will be faulted. Weekly incident reports should be issued that cite direct incidents (e.g., an e-mail component failure) and indirect incidents (e.g., a network failure) as well as remote site issues (e.g., a remote site lost power). Such information can help to clarify the real problem.

Message Transfer Services. The message transfer service (also termed the message transport system) is the most visible part of the messaging infrastructure. The message transfer service is responsible for moving a message from point A to point B. This service consists of one or more message transport agents and may be extended to include gateways and routers. The most popular services are X.400 and SMTP international standards, and IBM's SNA Distributed Services (SNADS) and Novell's Message Handling Service (MHS) proprietary industry standards.

X.400. More widely used in Europe than in North America, X.400 is popular because it:

- Provides universal connectivity.
- Has a standard way of mapping features.
- Is usually run over commercial WANs so it does not have the security problems associated with the Internet.

SMTP. Simple Mail Transfer Protocol's allure is its simplicity. Addressing is easier and access to the Internet is relatively simple compared with establishing an X.400 connection. Because it is simple, there is not much that can go wrong. However, when something does go wrong, it is usually monumental.

Directory Services. The directory service is critical to a company's e-mail systems, but it is also problematic. The problems are a result of the difficulty in keeping directories up-to-date, resolving redundant or obsolete auto-registered entries, and failures of directory synchronization.

The directory serves both users and applications. End users choose potential recipients from a directory. The directory should list enough information for a user to distinguish between the George Smith in accounting and the George Smith in engineering. Some companies include in their directory individuals who are customers and suppliers. The ability to distinguish between internal users and external users is even more important in these cases.

Management and Administration Services. Management refers to scheduled maintenance and automated housekeeping procedures that involve system-related tasks such as reconfiguration and file maintenance. The constant I/O on messaging components leads to disk and sometimes memory fragmentation. Regular defragmentation procedures, including repro/reorg, tidy procedures, and checkstat and reclaim, are required. Whatever the environment, such procedures should be done more often than is recommended to prevent problems from occurring.

Alerts and Alarms. Alerts and alarms are extremely helpful, because the system can tell the user if there is a potential problem. Alerts generally refer to warnings such as "too many messages in queue awaiting delivery." Alarms are a sign of a more serious problem, such as a disk full condition.

Mail Monitoring. Mail monitoring is typically an administrative function. One way of monitoring a system is to send a probe addressed to an invalid user on a target system. On many systems, the target system will reject the message with a "no such addressee" nondelivery message. When the initiating system receives this message, it indicates that mail flow is active.

Timing the round-trip provides a window to overall system performance. A message that does not return in a preestablished timeframe is considered overdue and is cause for further investigation.

Reporting. Reporting is used for capacity planning, measuring throughput and performance, chargeback, and statistical gathering. At initial implementation, network administrators will generally want to report breadth of coverage to demonstrate the reach of the infrastructure. Breadth can be measured by counting users and the number of messaging systems within each messaging environment.

Performance can be measured by reporting the volume — the average number of messages delivered per hour, or messages in each hour over a 24-hour period. This measure can be divided further by indicating the type of message (i.e., text only, single/double attachments, read receipts). This information gives network managers a measurable indication of the kind of features the user community requires.

For network planning purposes, it may be useful to measure volume or "system pressure," ignoring the number of messages sent and focusing on the number of total gigabytes sent per day.

Exhibit 1. Implementation Scenarios

	Enterprise	
	Single	**Multiple**
Single Department	One-Tier Single System	Two-Tier Similar Systems
Multiple Departments	Two-Tier Dissimilar Systems	Three-Tier Cross-Enterprise Systems

IMPLEMENTATION SCENARIOS: A TIERED APPROACH

Manufacturing environments have long used a tiered approach to messaging for distributing the workload of factory floor applications. As environments become more complex, the tiered approach offers additional flexibility.

An entire enterprise can be considered a single department, indicating the need for a one-tier system where clients are tied into a single server or post office. Multiple departments in a single enterprise or a single department communicating with multiple enterprises require routers and gateways to communicate with the world outside. When multiple departments need to communicate with each other and with multiple enterprises, a messaging backbone or messaging switch is called for.

Exhibit 1 summarizes the implementation scenarios discussed in this chapter.

One-Tier Messaging Model

A single department in a single enterprise will most likely deploy a one-tier messaging model. This model consists of a single messaging server or post office that provides all services. It may be as large as an OfficeVision system on a mainframe or a Higgins PostOffice on a Compaq file server running NetWare. The department need only concern itself with following corporate guidelines for networking and any naming standards.

Caution should be observed when using corporate guidelines. It is often simple to apply mainframe conventions when standardizing PC LAN-based applications. Many large organizations tend to forget that the whole reason for deploying desktop computers is to move away from mainframe conventions (e.g., 8-character user IDs) that are nonintuitive for users. Exhibit 2 shows a typical one-tier model within a single department of an enterprise.

Two-Tier Model: Multiple Servers

As the number of e-mail users grow, or multiple departments need to be connected, an organization will probably deploy multiple servers. This two-tier model can consist of integrating similar messaging systems from the same vendor or from different vendors. Exhibit 3 illustrates a connection

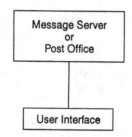

Exhibit 2. One-Tier Model

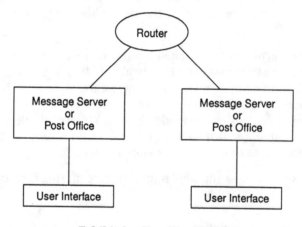

Exhibit 3. Two-Tier Model

between two departments using the same vendor software connected via application routers.

In a typical PC LAN environment using a shared-file system such as cc:Mail or Microsoft Mail, the router acts the same way as the PC. The post office is completely passive. When users send messages, their workstations simply copy the message to the file server as an individual file or as an insertion into a file server database. In either case the PC workstation actually does the work — the post office simply serves as a shared disk drive. The router is also an active component, but has no user moving messages. It periodically moves messages from one post office to another without user interaction.

Application Gateways for Integrating Dissimilar Systems

Many enterprises have different departments that have chosen their own e-mail systems without a common corporate standard. To integrate dissimilar systems, application gateways can bridge the technical incompatibilities between the various messaging servers (see Exhibit 4).

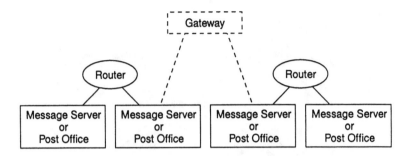

Exhibit 4.   Using Application Gateways

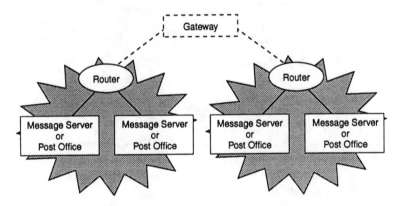

Exhibit 5.   Placing a Gateway Between Routers

A simple gateway can translate cc:Mail messages to GroupWise. A more complex gateway can bridge networks (e.g., Ethernet to Token Ring), network protocols (i.e., NetWare to TCP/IP), and the e-mail applications.

Converting one e-mail message to the format of another requires a lot of translation. Document formats (i.e., DCA RFT to ASCII), addressing formats (i.e., user@workgroup@domain to system::user), and message options (i.e., acknowledgments to read or deliver receipts) must all be translated.

Gateways can emulate routers native to each environment. They perform message translations internally. The alternative to this approach is to place the gateway between the routers as opposed to between the post office — this is not an end-user design, it is merely a function of the vendor software (see Exhibit 5).

If an enterprise is large, network administrators may want to make use of economies of scale to handle common administration, common gateways to X.400, and Internet networks. The network administration staff may simply need points in its network where it can measure progress.

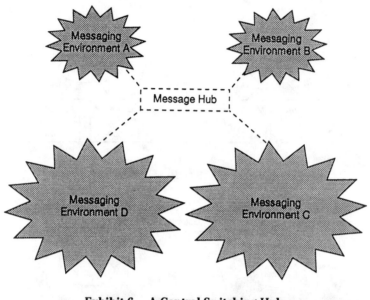

Exhibit 6.   A Central Switching Hub

Gateways from each environment to every other environment can be provided, but this solution becomes costly and difficult to maintain. A better approach would be to use a central switching hub or a distributed backbone, as shown in Exhibit 6.

Distributed Hubs. The central switch or hub allows for a single path for each messaging environment to communicate with all other messaging environments. The central hub, if it is relatively inexpensive, can be expanded into the distributed model. This is often done as the aggregate system grows and requires additional performance and capacity.

However, this implementation can be taken to an extreme, as seen by the number of companies that have grown PC LAN/shared file systems beyond their original design. It is inexpensive to grow these systems incrementally, but difficult to provide end-to-end reliability. Most organizations plug the technical gaps in these products with the additional permanent and contract personnel to keep the multitude of routers and shared-file system post offices up and running.

Some organizations have taken this distributed hub approach to the point where they have multiple connections to the Internet and the X.400 world (see Exhibit 7). Some organizations offer the single message switch for their global environment, and their messages are more well traveled than their administrators. A message sent from Brussels to Paris may stop in Los Angeles on the way because of the central switching mechanism. In addition to local switching, the distributed hub allows for redundancy.

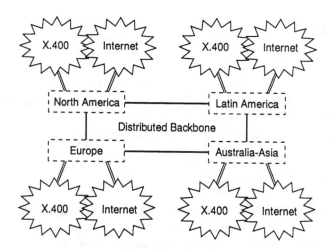

Exhibit 7. Worldwide Distributed Hubs

THREE DEPLOYMENT ARCHITECTURES AND OPTIONS

Most companies deploy e-mail systems using variations of three architectures: a common platform, where all e-mail systems are identical; a multiple backbone, where each e-mail environment has its own gateway; or a common backbone, where all systems share common resources. The following sections describe these architectures along with the advantages and disadvantages of each.

Common Platform Architecture

For years, a major automotive manufacturer delayed PC LAN e-mail deployment in deference to the purported needs of the traveling executive. Senior managers wanted to be able to walk up to any company computer terminal, workstation, or personal computer anywhere in the world and know that they would be able to access their e-mail in the same manner. This implies a common look and feel to the application across platforms as well as common network access to the e-mail server. In this company's case, PROFS (OfficeVision/VM) was accessible through 3270 terminal emulators on various platforms. As long as SNA network access remained available, e-mail appeared the same worldwide. This IBM mainframe shop had few problems implementing this model.

The common platform model is not unique to IBM mainframe environments. Another manufacturer used the same technique with its DEC ALL-IN-1 environment distributed across multiple VAX hosts. As long as a DECnet network or dialup access was available, users could reach their home systems. The upside of this approach is that an individual's e-mail files are

537

stored centrally, allowing for a single retrieval point. The downside was that the user had to be connected to process e-mail and was unable to work offline.

This strategy is not limited to mainframe and minicomputer models. A number of companies have standardized on Lotus Notes, Microsoft Mail, or Novell's GroupWise. None of these products are truly ready for large-scale deployment without IT and network staffs having to plug the technical gaps.

Multiple Backbone Model

The multiple backbone model assumes that an organization integrates its e-mail systems as though it were multiple smaller companies. The OfficeVision/VM system may connect via Advantis to reach the Internet and X.400 world. The cc:Mail WAN may have an SMTP gateway for access to the Internet and an ISOCOR MTA for access to the Message Router/X.400 gateway. All the various e-mail environments may have a proprietary Soft*Switch gateway for access to the IBM/MVS host so that everyone who needs to can access their OfficeVision/400systems (see Exhibit 8).

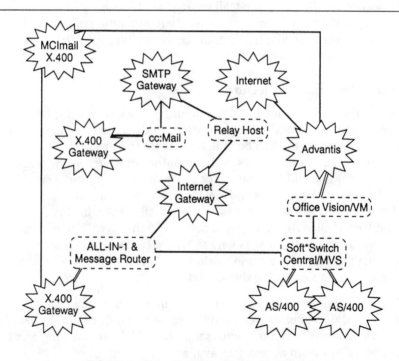

Exhibit 8.   The Multiple Backbone Model

On the surface, this hodgepodge of point-to-point connections may seem a bit unwieldy, but it does have advantages. Users of cc:Mail can address Internet e-mail users by filling out an SMTP template rather than waiting until the cc:Mail administrator adds recipients to the cc:Mail directory. OfficeVision/VM users can fill out a simple address block within the text of their message to reach an Internet user. AS/400 users can send mail to an application that forwards the message on their behalf. The trouble occurs when the recipients of the AS/400 users try to reply — they end up replying to the application that forwarded the message rather than the original sender, or originator, of the message.

This architecture may still work. If each e-mail environment had its own gateway, network administration could offer multiple connections to the Internet.

Common Backbone

The common backbone takes two forms:

- A central e-mail hub or message switch on a single system that serves as the common denominator among all e-mail environments.
- A distributed model where all backbone components run a common software protocol.

The common hub involves a single switch that serves the users' applications, thus serving their needs indirectly. Each e-mail environment has an application gateway that converts its environmental format to that of the common hub. Other systems are attached to this hub in a similar manner. Messages destined for dissimilar environments all pass through this central point to be sorted and delivered to their final destinations.

The distributed backbone takes the central hub and replaces it with two or more systems sharing a common application protocol. This solution offers the ability to deploy two or more less expensive systems rather than a single, more expensive system. Any system connected to any point in the backbone can use any other service (e.g., gateway) connected to that same backbone.

Network managers may decide to purchase a single hub and gradually add systems to form a distributed backbone. Should you decide to use a common backbone protocol like X.400 or SMTP, there is an advantage. Because these protocols are available from a number of vendors, the cc:Mail/X.400 gateway could connect to an X.400 system running in an HP9000, DEC/Alpha, or Intel/Pentium system — all running the same protocols. It is possible to change distributed servers without having to change the gateways to these servers. Exhibit 9 illustrates three-tier flexibility.

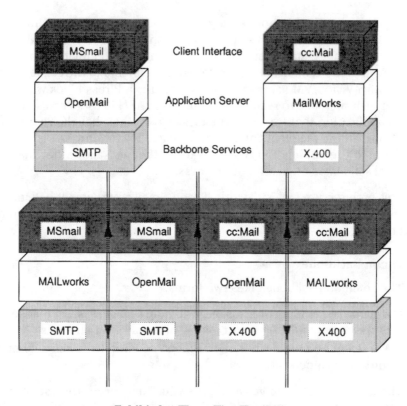

Exhibit 9.   Three-Tier Flexibility

A third approach is to use one central server or a distributed backbone of similar systems. In the central server/central hub approach, all e-mail environments use application gateways to connect to the central switch. There they are routed to their target environment.

Two-tier models may seem most convenient, because they can use the offerings of a single vendor. One problem is that the system must use that vendor's protocols for a long time. Three tiers allow the layers in the model to be changed, which allows for ease of transition.

Under most application scenarios, changing one component of the messaging environment entails changing all the pieces and parts with which it is associated. It may be necessary to provide adequate support staff and end-user training or hire consultants to handle the need for temporary staff during the transition — a significant business disruption.

For example, in one environment, users have Microsoft Mail on their desktops and a traditional MSmail post office is used, as well as message transfer agents (MTAs), to route mail between post offices. The engineering department uses OpenMail. The IT group would like to begin consolidating systems. With minor changes to the desktop, IT can retain the Microsoft Mail user interface, remove the back-end infrastructure, and use the same OpenMail system as the OpenMail desktop users by consolidating the second tier and simplifying the support environment. The client changes somewhat because it is using a different directory server and message store, but it appears as a minor upgrade to the users — no significant training is necessary.

Likewise, IT can change the back end and still allow the OpenMail systems to communicate with the MAILworks and ALL-IN-1 systems without locking into a single vendor solution. This is a feasible option. Today, users can plug an MSmail client into a MAILworks or OpenMail server. Novell recently announced the ability to plug a cc:Mail or MSmail client into its GroupWise XTD server. A Microsoft Exchange client plugs into various servers, and Lotus's cc:Mail can plug into anything.

ESTABLISHING MESSAGING POLICIES AND PROCEDURES

An organization can prevent misunderstandings, conflicts, and even litigation if it publishes its policies and procedures for messaging applications at the outset. Most important are privacy and confidentiality.

Privacy

A privacy policy serves two purposes: to properly inform employees that their messages may not be private and to protect the organization from legal liability. Most organizations create a policy that cautions users as follows: All electronic data is company property and may be viewed by designated personnel to diagnose problems, monitor performance, or for other purposes as the company deems necessary. While you normally type a password to access your e-mail and you may feel that your messages are private, this is not the case. The e-mail you create, read, or send is not your property nor is it protected from being seen by those other than you and your recipients.

Organizations can contact the Electronic Messaging Association (EMA) in Arlington, VA for a kit to aid in developing a privacy policy.

Proprietary and Confidential Information

E-mail appears to ease the process of intentional or inadvertent disclosure of company secrets. If this is a concern, an organization could try the following:

- Let users know that the IT department logs the messages that leave the company.
- Perform periodic audits.
- Apply rules or scripts that capture e-mail to or from fields, making it possible to search on competitor address strings.

Some systems insert a header on incoming e-mail that says: "WARNING: This message arrived from outside the company's e-mail system. Take care when replying so as not to divulge proprietary or confidential information."

A company may also specify that proprietary information should not be sent to Internet addresses if security measures on the Internet are inadequate for the company's needs. Users may be asked to confirm that only X.400 addresses are used. It is helpful to incorporate any such e-mail ground rules — for example, that the tranmission of proprietary information without a proper disclosure agreement is grounds for dismissal — as part of the new employee orientation process.

RECOMMENDED COURSE OF ACTION

One of the most important elements of a successful messaging system rollout is a staff that is well versed in the workings of the network, operating system, backup procedures, and applications.

Network Connections

An implementation needs individuals who can set up network connections efficiently. A messaging system needs procedures in place to notify users when a network link is unavailable. If the network goes down, often one of the first applications blamed is e-mail. It is the job of the network staff to diagnose the problem quickly and have the right people remedying the problem.

Operating Systems

Many e-mail groups have their own systems and servers and operate them as their own. Consequently, many successful organizations pair systems programmers or senior software specialists with systems engineers who can provide installation services and upgrade support.

Backup

Most messaging support organizations are not set up to provide 24-hour support. It is important to borrow methodologies from the mainframe support environment and staff an operations center that can answer phone calls, fix problems, and backup and archive applications regularly.

Applications Support

This function demands staff members with:

- Excellent diagnostic skills.
- Excellent communication skills.
- Database and business graphics experience.

- Cross-platform network experience.
- A basic understanding of the operating environment of each of the platforms.

E-mail integration by its nature involves cross-platform expertise. Most applications are fairly straightforward. In the case of an integrated infrastructure, an organization may need people familiar with NetWare, SNA, TCP/IP, and LAN Manager. They may also need to understand Mac/OS, UNIX, OS/2, and VMS.

When staffing an implementation, the key is to match expertise across the various groups within the company. The team should be application-centric with contributors from across the enterprise. If an implementation is properly staffed, and the implementers keep in mind the big picture as well as the daily objectives, the messaging system rollout is far more likely to be a success.

Chapter VII-4
Understanding Public Key Cryptology
Gilbert Held

THE GROWTH IN THE USE OF COMMUNICATIONS now provides end-users with the ability to perform a variety of functions that just a few years were unimaginable. Today, users can avail themselves of CompuServe, Prodigy, or the services of numerous Internet access providers, to order books, CDs, and even automobiles electronically. Although security has always been a limiting factor, holding end-users back from transmitting credit card information to on-line sales organizations, the use of public key cryptology represents a mechanism that can overcome that limitation.

The purpose of this chapter is to acquaint systems development managers with the operation and use of public key cryptology to include how this technology is being incorporated into World Wide Web (WWW) browsers, Web servers, and other computer-based software products. The systems development manager can apply knowledge about the operation of this technology to facilitate secure communications—and understanding the advantages over traditional methods used to secure communications. Because an understanding of the advantages of public key cryptology requires a comparison to traditional cryptology methods, this chapter first examines the general method by which traditional cryptological systems operate.

TRADITIONAL CRYPTOLOGICAL SYSTEMS

In a traditional cryptological system, both the person encrypting information and the person that will decrypt the received information use the same encrypting key. The encrypting device uses the key to perform an additive operation, usually a modular 2 (mod 2) operation. In comparison, the decrypting device uses the same key to perform a subtractive operation, which is normally based upon a mod 2 operation.

An example can best illustrate the operation of a traditional cryptological

0-8493-9979-3/99/$0.00+$.50
© 1999 by CRC Press LLC

system. A one-byte portion of the key sequence used to encrypt data is the binary sequence 10110010.

The mod 2 addition of the key and data results in a mod 2 sum is transmitted as encrypted data. At the receiver, the same key is used to perform a mod 2 subtraction from the mod 2 sum received, resulting in the reconstruction of the original data. Thus, decryption is performed by the mod 2 subtraction of the key from the received encrypted data.

Traditional Systems Limitations

Although traditional cryptological systems are in wide use and, depending upon the key length and method of key selection, are difficult to essentially impossible to break, they have a major limitation: The distribution of keys. When communications are limited to between two nodes or users, only one key is required. When three nodes or users require communications, the number of keys increases to three. Communications between four nodes requires the use of six distinct keys.

In general form, the equation to determine how many keys are required is:

$$k = n*(n-1)/2$$

where:

k = number of keys
n = number of users

This means that the use of a traditional cryptological system to secure communications for a large number of users can result in the expenditure of a considerable effort to distribute keys (e.g., for 15 users, 105 keys are required). In addition, each user requiring the ability to communicate with two or more nodes in a large network must be careful in his or her selection of keys, as the selection of the wrong key to encrypt or decrypt data will not produce the desired effect.

In a modern communications environment, such as the World Wide Web, with which the potential exists for tens of thousands of vendors marketing products to tens of millions of users, it becomes obvious that the use of a traditional cryptological system would not be practical for general purpose utilization. This is due to the massive number of keys that would be required to be distributed as well as the problem users would face in storing, retrieving, and using an appropriate key from an extremely large data base of keys. Clearly, an alternative method of key distribution and usage is required. A public key cryptological system is that alternative.

PUBLIC KEY CRYPTOLOGY OVERVIEW

A public key cryptological system is based on the use of a one-way function. Here the term *one-way function* represents a mathematical function whose inverse is extremely difficult, if not impossible, to compute. For example, for a given X, Y is easy to compute in the function:

$$Y = F(X)$$

However, in that same equation, for a given Y, X can be very difficult, if not impossible, to compute. The following relatively simple function is an example:

$$Y = X^5 - 2X^4 + 3X^3 - 2X^2 + X - 5$$

When X equals 2, for example, Y equals 13. However, given that $Y = 13$, solving for X would be a much more difficult task:

$$13 = X^5 - 2X^4 + 3X^3 - 2X^2 + X - 5$$

Computing X, which represents the inverse of a one-way function, is programatically much more difficult. In addition, without special information, the computation of the inverse of a one-way function can require a relatively long period of time. For example, without special information, such as at what point to start and what increment to use, the end user might employ a trial-and-error process, beginning with $X = 0$ and incrementing X by .00001, each time testing the equation to determine if the new value used for X results in balancing the equation.

Modern public key cryptological systems are based on the use of a large prime number in an exponential operation. The first public key system concept resulted from the work of Diffie and Hellman, professors at Stanford University, during the mid-1970s. In their seminal paper, they noted that exponentiation is a one-way function for a relatively large prime number. For example, if p is a prime number, given an X and N, it is easy to compute the equation:

$$Y = X^N \bmod p$$

However, for a given Y and X, it becomes difficult to compute N.

The basic computations published by Diffie and Hellman for their public key system are based on the use of large prime numbers and exponentiation, as follows:

$$\text{Encryption } Y = X^e \bmod p$$

$$\text{Decryption } X - y^d \bmod p$$

where:
X and Y = integers whose values are less than p
X = the plain-text

Y = the cipher-text
E = the secret encryption exponent
and D = the secret decryption exponent

One of the most interesting properties of an encryption and decryption function based on exponentiation is its commutative property. This can be demonstrated by the equation:

$$X^{E1} \bmod p^{E2} \bmod p = (X^{E2} \bmod p)^{E1} \bmod p$$

where:
$E1$ = one secret encryption exponent
$E2$ = a second secret encryption exponent

The commutative property permits two communications in a network to share a secret encryption exponent by only exchanging non-secret numbers. For example, assume Ted and Bob wish to communicate with each other and p represents any integer between 0 and p-1. For Ted and Bob to obtain a shared secret number, Ted would first generate a randomly selected secret number, X_T, and a corresponding public number, $Y_T = a^{XT} \bmod p$. Bob would also randomly generate a secret number, X_B, and a corresponding public number, $Y_B a^{XB} \bmod p$.

When a large prime number is used, it is for all practical purposes impossible to obtain the secret numbers from the public numbers. Thus, Tom and Bob can share a secret number that is unique to them and only need to exchange their non-secret public numbers. For example, Tom would send his public key Y_T to Bob, while Bob would send his public key Y_B to Tom. Based upon the commutative property of exponentiation, Tom can compute the equation:

$$C = Y_B{}^{XT} \bmod p$$

Bob can compute the same number by using the equation:

$$C = Y_T{}^{XB} \bmod p$$

Based upon the preceding, once public keys are exchanged, Tom and Bob can use their private keys to decrypt messages transmitted from one to the other. Similarly, either Bob or Tom can use his private key to encrypt a message that can be decrypted by any person that has the individual's public key. If this concept is expanded to include modern communications systems, such as the World Wide Web, the usefulness of a public key cryptological system becomes apparent. For example, a company wants to sell Widgets via the Internet and has installed a Web server to take credit card orders.

Without a public key system, the server operator would have to send a different traditional encryption key to every person who wishes to place credit card orders on the server in a secure environment. Thus, a person might first have to communicate with the server and request the server operator to him or her, via mail, a key to be used as a secure method to transmit the credit card number when ordering a Widget.

To avoid using the postal service, several server operators started using fax machines. A customer electronically places an order without the credit card number. The server then uses a dial-out fax system, which transmits an order form to the requester. The requester must then verify his or her order, enter his or her credit card number, sign the order form, and fax it back to the server operator. Obviously, this method requires the customer to have a fax machine, which can significantly limit the number of potential customers.

Through the use of a public key system, the server operator only has to identify his or her public key. This means that a person using a Web browser could access the server, retrieve the public key, and use that key to encrypt his or her credit card number. Because only the private key can be used to decrypt the message encrypted with the public key, only the server that has the private key can decrypt the secured information.

The method just described represents the technique used by Netscape Communications and other companies—with some slight modifications to provide secure communications for browser users when ordering information from World Wide Web server operators. For example, Netscape Communications markets secure server software which enables a server operator to generate a public key and a private key. If a Web user has a secure Netscape browser, once they access the Netscape secure server, the browser will automatically retrieve the public key from the server. This enables the browser operator to transmit credit card or other information to the server securely and without delay, avoiding the previously described problems associated with traditional cryptological systems.

OTHER APPLICATIONS

The use of public key cryptology can be used in a variety of ways to secure communications both inside and outside the organization. Concerning internal organizational use, different public keys could be provided to different departments that might require secure communications, and companywide public keys could be provided for secure communications between persons working in different departments within a company. For example, the sales department might wish to secure the transmission of sales forecasts as well as obtain the ability to transmit such information to corporate officers. Then, one public-private key set would be used for transmission of sales forecasts within or between members of the sales department, while a second public-private key set could be used to communicate sales forecasts to corporate officers.

ACTION PLAN

As indicated in this chapter, the use of public key cryptological systems considerably simplifies the management and transmission of keys. If an end-user requires secure communications, the systems manager should consider obtaining products that support the use of public key cryptology. For example, if users want to consider ordering information from Web servers, they should select a Web browser that supports public key encryption. Similarly, if users need to encrypt and transmit files in the form of diskettes or magnetic tapes, the systems manager should consider the use of file encryption software that supports public key encryption. Doing so can significantly reduce the time and effort required to manage keys which can provide an organization with an increase in your while maintaining a very high level of security.

Section VII – Checklist
Networking and Connectivity

1. Is your organization planning to use the mainframe computer as an integral part of network computing?
2. What considerations should be given to connect mainframe and local servers as a multitiered server environment?
3. How should mainframe networks be managed in comparison to local area networks? Are there more similarities or differences in your environment?
4. Are considerations given to the design of networks based on application development and support requirements?
5. Is your organization's network strategy evolving too rapidly? What impact has this created on development and support?
6. Would you consider your network environment as open and flexible or is it closed and restrictive? How has this altered development efforts?
7. How would you assess your organization's network security? Do you consider it vulnerable to breaches?
8. What steps are you taking to develop applications that have integrated network security functions within the developed application?
9. Should your organization be better prepared for security before e-commerce applications are implemented?
10. When does your organization plan to perform a security audit of its network and communication systems?
11. What is your interpretation of electronic message processing?
12. How many different e-mail systems does your organization have? Do these systems talk to each other?
13. Is your organization planning on integrating message systems and application systems together as part of a larger business system?
14. What unique challenges does multiplatform connectivity create when developing or supporting applications?

Section VIII
Testing Software Applications

SOFTWARE TESTING OF APPLICATION SYSTEMS IS A DEMANDING TASK for many IS professionals. The challenge of software testing has become even more rigorous due to the use of newer development technology that includes multiplatform, client/server processing and event-based systems. Other factors include lack of qualified testing staff and poorly practiced testing techniques. Despite acknowledgment of testing's importance, development managers are routinely faced with the dilemma of choosing between comprehensive testing and timely project delivery. More often than not, the requirement for punctual system implementation prevails and the test process is compromised.

Development managers can improve the value of software testing by reestablishing an understanding of testing principles and integrating the test process early in design and development phases. Chapter VIII-1, "Software Testing: Concepts, Tools, and Techniques," offers an important foundation for comprehending testing concepts and methods. A discussion on debugging techniques is also presented as a complement to the test cycle.

The tedious effort associated with testing has also contributed to weak software testing results. Numerous testing tasks are often manually processed and create hardships on those who perform the work. Chapter VIII-2, "Automating Applications Testing," reviews the challenges and benefits of testing automation. Although automated techniques cannot solve inadequately managed testing projects, it can boost productivity, alleviate repetitive functions, enhance quality, and improve development schedules.

Numerous testing initiatives are regaining more prominence as a critical phase of the application development process. Part of this acknowledgment is due to more complex application systems, such as client/server, which require extensive testing prior to implementation. Chapter VIII-3, "Building a Customized Testing Approach," provides recognition of software testing as it relates to the overall development effort. It also offers a detailed testing outline that can be used to customize a testing methodology within the framework of an organization's business environment. As a complement, Chapter VIII-4, "Software Testing to Meet Corporate Quality

Goals," offers additional insights and recommendations for improving the development process via a strong testing strategy. Both chapters emphasize the need for comprehensive application testing as a means to ensure more reliable business competitiveness.

Chapter VIII-1
Software Testing: Concepts, Tools, and Techniques

Steven Rabin

THE CREDIBILITY AND PROFITABILITY of a software organization are based on its ability to build and maintain defect-free systems. Practical and effective software testing techniques produce systems that are accurate and complete, although not necessarily practical and useful in the real world. That is the domain of the business system design and not a part of this discussion.

In the majority of data processing organizations, the testing function is undermanaged and mostly unstructured. Because of this, testing consumes nearly half of software development and maintenance expenditures. Given this situation, testing might be expected to have been refined into an exact science. This is not the case—in fact, less is known or written about software testing than about any other aspect of software development.

Many principles and concepts have been developed to enhance the art of software testing. These can be divided into two sections: system testing and unit or program testing. In addition, the Animator (Micro Focus, Inc.) is available to enhance the tester's ability to find and correct software problems (i.e., bugs).

This chapter concentrates on the principles of unit testing (i.e., debugging programs to remove all discrepancies as compared to the specifications). These principles can be enhanced through the careful use of interactive testing tools. Many of the concepts discussed are illustrated and applied to the facilities provided in most source-level, interactive testing tools.

The COBOL language and program examples are used as the basis for illustrations throughout this chapter. Similarly, the Animator, an interactive COBOL, source-level testing facility, is used to illustrate how the techniques described here can be applied. The principles described are, however, common to programs written in nearly any language.

0-8493-9979-3/99/$0.00+$.50
© 1999 by CRC Press LLC

TESTING AND DEBUGGING

Although the terms *testing* and *debugging* were previously used side by side, their meanings are actually quite different. Debugging is the process of correcting a known program error. This demands the use of intuition, hypotheses, experimentation, intelligence, and freedom. Debugging is one of the most original processes programmers experience in their profession. Testing, on the other hand, involves the systematic execution and examination of all portions of a program to ensure that the program performs as it was designed and, equally important, does not do things it was not intended to do. Testing is more predictable and constrained because it requires a systematic approach to reviewing all execution aspects of a program.

To summarize, testing is the destructive process of trying to find the errors (whose presence is assumed) in a program. A successful test is one that furthers progress in the direction of causing a program to fail. Eventually, testing establishes a degree of confidence that a program does only what it is supposed to do, but this purpose is best achieved by the process of thorough exploration for errors. Debugging looks at things on a much smaller scale. In other words, an error is known to exist and a method is established to isolate the cause of the error and then correct it. Although this sounds simple, a bug may appear intermittently, or multiple interrelated bugs may be present. The combinations are endless.

TESTING CONCEPTS AND PRINCIPLES

Individual methods have been devised for testing and debugging. Black box testing is a data-driven approach that allows the tester to be completely unconcerned about the internal behavior and structure of the program. The tester is concerned only with finding circumstances in which the program does not behave according to specifications.

Using this approach to find all the errors in a program would require testing every possible combination of input data and condition. Trying to imagine testing a COBOL compiler in this manner is daunting. This is not to say that black box testing is not useful, because it is. It does, however, point out that it is impossible to test a program of any complexity in such a way as to guarantee that it is error free, and some practical limitations must be used when testing.

The black box approach is useful for testing new programs as well as program modifications. Program modifications usually have a good deal of data available for testing. This data is generally a portion of the live data that has been through the program already. A carefully screened set of data, whose results are already known, can maximize the yield on the testing investment.

New programs must also have a carefully selected set of test data. In this case, however, the data must be more variable to test as many cases of the program as is feasible. Creating this data involves making certain reasonable assumptions about the program. The idea is to take an infinite number of possibilities and create a finite number of test cases.

White box testing is used to examine the internal structure of a program. This testing is more logic-driven and better suited to debugging. For this approach, test data is created on the basis of an examination of the program's logic. It is useful for pinpointing program error points that must be corrected. Program tracing and displaying data at different program points are examples of white box testing.

White box testing can be used to test every line of code in a program. This would be an exhaustive procedure, involving the creation of massive amounts of test data. Not only is it infeasible, but it may still leave the program with untested errors. The ideal is to create a set of test data that will lead the tester to the problem area and, with carefully planned data, offer some insight into its cause and possible correction.

In both methods, it is clear that one of the keys to successful testing is the test data. Because either approach by itself is insufficient or in many cases unreasonable (e.g., economically or in time), a combination of the two approaches is suggested. The best testing comes from a variety of approaches using a prepared test plan.

THE TEST CASE AND UNIT TESTING

A reliable set of test data, sometimes called the test case, must be created for both black and white box testing procedures. The test case defines the scope of each test by providing program data that is expected to yield a certain result or group of results. The better the test case, the greater the chances are of finding program problems. Well-planned tests and test cases result in fewer passes through the program and shorter time to validate a program.

Because testing can never guarantee the absence of all errors, a series of test cases must be devised. The design of a test case must ensure the highest probability of detecting the most errors. This is accomplished through a combination of reviewing program specifications and knowledge of the program code.

The test case must take into account the logic path or flow of the program. This identifies what things are expected to happen and in what order. Decision or branch coverage is the process of creating test examples that ensure that each decision (or as many decisions as is practical) had a true or false outcome at least once. PERFORM UNTIL, GO TO and IF statements fall into this category.

In addition, it would be better if each condition in a decision takes on all possible outcomes at least once. This decision-condition coverage does not guarantee that all conditions will be exercised because many complex programs contain conditional statements that mask other conditional statements. Multiple-condition coverage attempts to solve this problem by having the tester write sufficient test cases to cover all possible combinations of condition outcomes and all points of entry for each condition.

Another key element of the test case is boundary-value analysis. This is a data-driven process of checking that both input and resulting output data areas, including key intermediate working storage fields, are properly validated. This includes initialization and high-low ranges among alphanumeric and numeric fields. Items of particular importance are indicators, indexes, calculation fields, and any field that is required to have specific values. Many subtle boundary conditions exist and the test cases that cover these require much thought. If practiced correctly, data analysis can have a significant effect on final program product that goes into production.

Time must be spent considering what must be tested before any test cases are created. Although it is not likely or practical that all of the previously mentioned conditions will be tested—because of system deadline constraints and other priorities—these things must be considered. The test cases that are created can have a long productive life as long as the program is being executed and, as time goes by, modified. The initial test-case design effort is paid back many times in the future as additional modification and testing is performed.

Following are additional considerations when the test cases are being created:

- *A good test case is carefully planned and based on some reasonable assumptions about the program to be tested.* The assumptions involve how much of the program is to be tested and under what conditions.

- *A statement of the expected output or results of each test must be made.* Although this sounds obvious, it is a critical element of test-case development. Because many programs are very large and perform simultaneous functions that cannot be tested at the same time, each case must have a specific goal. This actually involves two things: a description of the input data and a precise description of the correct output for that set of data. Outside the scope of this discussion, such areas as range, boundary, and decision checking are accomplished as part of this statement.

- *The results of each test must be thoroughly inspected.* This is a corollary to the previous rule. The most well-planned test cases are not worth much if the resulting tests are not verified. One of the problems with testing is that the tester often tires of the task. In most cases, this is the programmer who has spent much time with the same program code and has trouble recognizing errors. Given enough time with the same program, all programs look good.

- *Test cases must be written for invalid and unexpected, as well as valid and expected, input conditions.* The natural tendency is to test expected conditions or results. A test case must also consider the unexpected. This allows the program to be checked for two important conditions: that it is doing what it is supposed to do, and that it is not doing what it is not supposed to do.

- *Throw-away test cases must be avoided.* A common practice, particularly for interactive programs, is to sit at a terminal and enter data haphazardly. This not only wastes time but wastes a valuable investment (i.e., test data that can be reused). When a program has to be tested again, it is much easier with a set of already verified data. The recreation of this data takes much time and often leads to a program being less rigorously tested the second time around. This is one of the reasons why small program modifications seem to have many bugs left undetected.

The use of these techniques does not guarantee that all errors will be found. No testing methodology yet devised offers that assurance. Following all these principles also represents a considerable amount of work. Testing is a compromise involving how much can be done in the time allotted. Because every program is different, all the techniques will not apply to every situation.

Testing tools contain a variety of facilities to help ease the task of test-case creation. Although the logic behind each test case must be carefully thought out, the data required to perform the test can be manipulated inside the testing facilities. Many different tests can be performed by manipulating a single test case through the proper use of the described testing environment.

Unit Testing

Once a good set of test cases has been developed and is available to the tester, unit testing can begin. Systematic testing, just as in programming, yields the best results. A method of incremental testing using a top-down or a bottom-up philosophy often provides reliable results in the shortest amount of time.

Top-down testing, as the name implies, is similar to the programming technique of the same name. The highest-level module is tested first, followed by each subsequent module. The only rule that need be applied to a subsequent module is that all of the module's parents (i.e., superordinate modules) must have been previously tested.

The bottom-up approach starts with the terminal modules (i.e., those modules that do not call other modules). After all these modules have been tested, modules at the next higher level are tested. The only rule that applies in this case is that a higher-level module cannot be tested until all its subordinate modules have been tested. When testing is performed bottom up, it is easier to create test cases. This is because the results of all modules except the lowest modules need not be considered. Modules at the bottom of a program structure usually perform very specific functions that can be readily tested and verified.

Both approaches require control over the program environment to be truly effective. The discussion of the Animator testing tool highlights facilities that are available to handle these functions. This means it is possible to control the flow and execution of a program to allow specific modules in a program to be viewed independently.

PRINCIPLES OF DEBUGGING

Debugging is a two-part process that uses the results of all the principles and techniques described thus far. Until now, the idea was to identify areas in the program that did not perform correctly or did not match the program's specifications. Now these problem areas must be identified in the code (i.e., the exact location found) and corrected.

Debugging is an exhaustive process because of the way some programs are designed or written. In addition, any location in the code is possibly the cause of the error. Finding the location of the error is almost always the hard part of the job. Once a bug has been identified and located, it is comparatively easy to make the correction. Estimates are that 85% of debugging time is spent finding the error and 15% is spent fixing it. The following methods are generally used to pinpoint the error:

- *The brute-force approach.* A brute-force approach involves debugging with dump or scattering print statements throughout the program. However, this method is haphazard in that it only uncovers certain problems. It is a popular technique because it is easy to perform and quick to get started. It is useful to get a general feel for the program's flow and its major bugs (i.e., those bugs that can cause an abnormal termination).

- *The induction approach.* The induction approach involves analyzing the data that is causing the problem in relation to where that data is used by the program. A relationship always exists between the data and the program problem that must be identified. Once the relationship is found, it is easy to determine where that relationship occurs in the code. Because bugs often occur in groups, it is important to prove that the problem is completely explained by the relationship. If this is not the case, multiple bugs may be causing the problem.

- *The deduction approach.* The deduction approach starts with general theories of the problem. The processes of elimination and refinement are then used to arrive at a conclusion (i.e., error location). Whereas induction determines the problem from the available clues, deduction starts with the possible problem areas and eliminates all but the guilty. The intelligent use of different data tests and refinement of the original hypothesis will track down the bug.

- *Backtracking.* In small programs, a backtracking technique can work well. This involves following the logic of the program until it goes astray. The tester starts at the problem point, reviews the available output, and reverses the program's logic. The problems are often easy to track.

These approaches offer different methods for debugging—finding the location of the error and making a correction. No one method is best—that depends on the type of error, the complexity and size of the program, and the tester's familiarity with the program. The Animator provides facilities to aid the tester for each of these debugging techniques.

INTEGRATED TOOLS FOR TESTING AND DEBUGGING

Although the purpose of this chapter is to describe the methods and means of testing, it is worthwhile to review some of the tools available to help automate this process. A wide variety of COBOL-oriented testing facilities are available to allow developers to take advantage of the techniques described in this article. Of special interest are those tools that provide cross-platform support and operate on the workstation.

The integrated toolset provided by Micro Focus is worthy of specific mention. Micro Focus produces COBOL compilers and programmer productivity tools for the development of business applications. They provide the facilities required to maintain a sophisticated testing environment for both host, workstation, and cross-platform development.

Workstation-based tools are available that support development for DOS, Windows, OS/2, and UNIX. In addition, many of these same tools support the development of mainframe-based code with host support services (e.g., CICS, DB2, and IMS).

The Animator

The Animator is a sophisticated testing tool that provides faculties to aid the tester in all phases of unit testing and debugging. It is not a substitute for the work that must be performed to determine the best testing approach and subsequent test-case design. This is an important point that cannot be overemphasized.

In the majority of cases people use testing tools as a substitute for careful planning. The easy way often involves using the brute-force method of debugging (i.e., using the tools as a testing driver). This technique should be avoided because it is not an efficient way of debugging. It will take longer to conclude the correction process, and it does not provide reliable test results. The best way to use testing tools is to supplement the approaches described in the preceding sections with applicable tool functions.

The Animator is best described as an interactive debugging environment for COBOL programs. It brings programs to life in that source code can be viewed, statement by statement, as it is executing. In other words, some debuggers require the understanding or translation of machine-level code, but this tool presents the program entirely in its source form. This enables the tester to follow the logic of the program as the machine does.

Program logic can also be viewed in a structured diagram or visual representation. This is particularly well suited for those situations requiring that the overall form of the program be understood. A good example is when a program requires repair by a programmer with little or no experience with the code. It is much easier to understand the flow and relationships of the program by viewing their interaction at a higher level (preferably pictorially). Once the basics of the program are understood, more detailed analysis and test planning can be performed.

Similarly, it is equally important to understand the data and program relationships in the code being tested. An integrated segment of this testing environment is COBOL Source Information (CSI). This facility provides extensive query facilities that allow the tester to quickly focus on key pieces of information. CSI includes where data is defined, used, and modified. A cross-reference is available detailing where procedures, paragraphs, and sections are called or executed, along with the data used within.

The Analyzer

The Analyzer is a complement to the Animator. It analyzes the frequency of execution of COBOL statements. Regardless of the testing methodology employed, it is useless if the code to be tested is not being properly executed. This is a function of the program's logic and the test data provided. This facility ensures that the portions of code requiring testing are actually being executed.

Data File Editor

Throughout the testing phase it is critical that workable test data be provided. This is often a difficult chore and one that causes an acceptable test plan to falter. The integrated Data File Editor solves this problem by providing a means to easily tailor data files for testing purposes. Data is displayed in a variety of formats (e.g., ASCII, HEX, or EBCDIC) to facilitate test data requirements in a native mode.

Session Recorder and Snapshot Analyzer

Regression testing is specifically supported by the Session Recorder and Snapshot Analyzer. The Session Recorder records a test session, capturing keystrokes and screen snapshots for later editing and playback. The Snapshot Analyzer compares two recorder sessions and reports all differences. These tools provide the means for faithfully validating, documenting, and demonstrating test results. On an ongoing basis, test scripts can be cataloged (along with their results) and used again, greatly reducing the time it takes to initiate a test case.

An important by-product of these integrated testing tools is their ability to teach a programmer the way around an unfamiliar program. Many times a program must be maintained by someone who has no previous experience with it. Even with adequate, up-to-date specifications it is hard to learn the relationships of the program. Attempting to modify a program in this situation is one of the most significant causes of introducing new program errors. Learning the program with the help of these tools allows a programmer to gain confidence with the program's logic.

USING TESTING TOOLS

All testing begins at a desk with the design of a test case or test cases. Testing tools are not intended and should not be used as a substitute for this function. Once the test script is designed, however, these faculties are ideally suited for quickly implementing the test.

Top-down and bottom-up testing are the two primary means of structured testing. Both of these techniques allow a program or a suite of programs to be thoroughly reviewed and tested as a whole before debugging. Current methods of testing often require small errors (and large errors) to be corrected before testing can continue. This is a problem because it distracts the tester and makes the testing process disjointed. It is more efficient to finish the processing of test cases and review the results before debugging. Corrections made haphazardly are often partial solutions or cause new problems.

Once the test script has been run through the program and each section of the program has been tested, a list of program problems should be available. This list must be carefully reviewed and categorized away from the computer. After this is done and potential problems, possible causes, and ways of proceeding have been determined, the testing environment can be used again.

If used properly, an integrated testing environment provides a variety of productivity enhancements. The common debugging session involves finding the error, editing the program to make a correction, compiling, and retesting. Under the best conditions this is a time-consuming cycle. The facilities previously described change this dramatically by allowing the test script to be implemented in its entirety.

Testing tools provide the facilities and control required to perform sophisticated, structured testing using the techniques and principles outlined in this chapter. Although not a substitute for a test plan, the test script can aid in the testing and debugging process. Like any powerful tool, it requires consideration to be used correctly. It can be misused if it is thought of as a replacement for test planning away from the computer. Successful testing requires proper management, an understanding of the concepts involved, and the right facilities.

SUMMARY

A variety of testing methods have been described in this chapter. Depending on the situation, it is important to select the method that provides the greatest payback. The use of these techniques does not, however, guarantee that all errors will be found. No testing methodology yet devised offers that assurance.

Following these principles also represents a considerable amount of work. Testing is a compromise that depends on how much can be done in the time allotted. Because every program is different, all the techniques will not apply to every situation. Sophisticated tools for implementing thess concepts and techniques are easily misused if a firm testing foundation is not in place. Random, brute-force, hit-or-miss testing with any tools is no substitute for a carefully prepared test plan. Once a test plan has been devised, an integrated test environment provides both an effective and productive means of carrying out the test.

Chapter VIII-2
Automating Applications Testing

Philip L. Arthur

TO MANY, the cost of applications testing seems too high. This impression is dispelled when they closely examine the applications testing process. Typically, testing includes such activities as creating test scenarios, identifying and creating input data, establishing test data bases, running test cases, evaluating test results, and debugging and resolving code deficiencies. At least one of these activities is repeated until the application is considered ready for production. Testing a sophisticated application requires planning, designing, validating, and examining for completeness; in many cases, separate groups each test the entire application. These activities are often repeated for enhancements or code fixes with little or no reuse of test data.

Application programmers control application code quality in many applications development organizations. Programmers receive requirements, write the code, create a few test cases, run some unit test cases, probably use a debugging tool to run test cases and identify defects, and put the code into production when they believe the code is ready. This process depends on subjective judgment, and it is repeated and reinvented for every enhancement or code fix; nothing is reused.

Programmers often test the same code they wrote, and this code may not meet the application requirements. To test the code that should have been written requires developing test cases from the requirements. Yet testing is seldom defined during the requirements phase. In addition, application function testing may not uncover defects that occur in a high-volume production environment.

The solution to these problems is a test environment in which testing is performed as a rigorous process and in which reuse is promoted. This chapter examines the activities involved in a rigorous test process. Testing tools have automated some of these activities and play a key role in promoting a rigorous test process and testing reuse. This chapter uses two testing tools from IBM, Corp., Workstation Interactive Test Tool (WITT) and Software Analysis Test Tool (SATT), to illustrate the role of tools in an automated testing environment.

APPLICATION DEVELOPMENT AND TESTING

The traditional software development process has one quality checkpoint; after the product has been built, the application code is tested. A more effective development process has quality checkpoints at each development phase. The software development life cycle then becomes a series of work products and releases, permitting continuous assessment of product quality and allowing changes to be introduced during the development process. The following sections examine the testing components of an effective development process.

Rigorous Requirements Definition

Rigorous requirements definition requires a rigorous mathematical definition and focuses on error prevention instead of code error removal. At each level of design, mathematical proofs of correctness are used to ensure the accuracy of the evolving design and the continued integrity of the product requirements. This design method introduces module and procedure primitives (e.g., sequences, branches, and loops) to handle the packaging of software designs into products. Such a definition provides a clear and concise set of programming specifications for the application programmer to write high-quality code. Rigorous requirements definition, which includes data domain, data type, and allowed-values information, allows application testers to build a rigorous set of test cases and validate the test results.

Thorough Inspections

Studies indicate that inspections can uncover about 60% of total product defects and that the errors are found through application testing. These inspections should be performed by a team whose members are from different areas in the project and include a moderator, developer, and inspectors. The diverse backgrounds of the inspection staff ensures continuity across work phases and work products, reflects multiple interests, and helps create varied scenarios of usage. For example, the requirements work product review should be inspected by a team of end users, analysts, and designers.

The cost of error removal dramatically increases the longer the error remains in the product. Therefore, requirements and design reviews are critical to developing quality software. Design inspections validate the interpretation of the requirements. Likewise, detailed design reviews verify the interpretation of high-level designs.

Unfortunately, inspections depend on qualified people having the time to perform thorough inspections, and the inspection process can become a bureaucratic checkpoint yielding limited results. Combining formal inspections and a rigorous testing methodology fosters the creation of software with fewer errors and with errors that are easier to find and fix. However, rigorous testing depends on thorough, high-quality requirements.

The thoroughness of test cases depends on the thoroughness of the requirements definition, which includes data domain values and application process descriptions. Most online applications test tools drive test cases from an end-user perspective through transaction screens. In addition, test coverage metrics are needed to evaluate the quality of both manual and automated testing.

Root Cause Analysis

A data base on software defects contains inspection and testing-identified errors. This data base is used for improving the development process by monitoring and controlling the development progress. Root cause analysis is performed on the entries in the data base to prevent further defects. The cause of the defect must be documented in the data base for future analysis. It is feasible to forecast the number of production defects at each development phase from historical data; statistical analysis can be used for analyzing error density and distribution.

APPLICATION TESTING THEORY

Application testing approaches are typically divided into black box and white box testing. Black box techniques test an application from a user perspective and focus on the user input and resulting output. The programmer or tester builds test cases and determines expected results from a combination of requirements, design, and user documentation. White box techniques test program logic rather than external specifications. Applications programmers often perform white box testing on the code they wrote. White box testing techniques focus on running enough test cases to ensure test coverage of the code.

Integration and Test Levels

Application developers typically perform structural or white box testing to verify that the code conforms to the design. This testing is usually performed in one or more steps, which are commonly defined as unit testing, string testing, and integration testing. These steps vary by development groups and differ primarily by the degree or scope of application integration. For example, unit testing may be performed on a single subroutine, paragraph, or module, and string testing may be performed on the entire transaction, which may consist of one or more modules.

Those who are not software developers perform functional or black box testing to verify that the function satisfies product requirements. This form of testing is also usually performed in one or more steps, which are commonly known as systems testing, acceptance testing, stress testing, and user-verification testing. The steps vary by development groups and are distinguished primarily by testing objectives. For example, systems testing tests the entire application for code quality; whereas stress testing tests the entire application for performance bottlenecks and stress-induced failures.

BLACK BOX TESTING TECHNIQUES

Common black box testing techniques include space partitioning, boundary analysis, cause-and-effect graphing, and error guessing. These data-driven techniques derive test data from the specifications and help the tester to define a subset of all possible input and output elements that have a high probability of detecting errors.

Space Partitioning. This technique partitions input so that input items in each partition are treated the same. As a result, the space partitioning technique is sometimes referred to as equivalence testing. The tester selects at least one data element from each partition, which is either a valid or invalid item. The goal of space partitioning is to define partitions so that each piece of data in the partition produces equivalent testing results. This allows testers to minimize the number of test cases but to invoke many distinct input conditions.

The space partitioning technique requires identifying the partitions and defining the test cases. Often, one partition is a data domain, which may be described by a range of values (e.g., minimum and maximum), a set of values (e.g., a table look-up), or a number of input values. Conversely, another partition can be data that is invalid and outside the data domain. Therefore, most data elements need two or more test cases. For example, the number of working hours in a regular work week can be described by the following range of values:

$$0 <= x <= 40$$

where:
x = the number of hours in a work week.

The valid data domain is 0 to 40 inclusive, and the invalid data domains are the values less than 0 and those greater than 40. Therefore, three or more test cases, one for each partition (e.g., -1, 30, 50) are desirable, especially for testing entries or updates to a data base or file.

Boundary Value Analysis. This technique is a special case of space partitioning. The tester selects one or more data elements that identify the boundary of a partition or data domain. If the partition represents a range of values, the minimum and maximum values are tested. If the partition represents a set of values as in a table look-up, the first and last table entries are tested. In the example using the number of hours in the regular work week, the testing data values -1, 0, 40, and 41 are four desirable test cases. It may be desirable to test the maximum and minimum values permitted by the transaction's screen input field, which may not be consistent with the data base definition. Experience indicates that boundary value analysis and space partitioning techniques apply equally well to output data by testing maximum output values and values higher than the maximum output ones, as well as minimum output values, and no output. Experience has also shown that boundary value analysis has a higher payoff than other techniques.

Cause-and-Effect Analysis. This technique transforms a natural language specification into a formal language specification and identifies the causes and effects using a Boolean graph or a decision matrix. It is a more sophisticated level of testing that considers the effects of one or more combinations of input values. This type of testing is highly productive and identifies incomplete and ambiguous points in the specification.

Error Guessing. This type of testing makes use of intuition and experience. It is often productive when technology or the application environment changes. Error guessing should not be used in place of the other types of black box testing but should be used to enhance their effectiveness.

WITT: A Tool for Black Box Testing. IBM's WITT tests applications from the end-user perspective. This automated test driver tool provides keystroke and mouse movement capture and playback. In other words, WITT plays back keystrokes instead of the application tester. WITT can also capture and compare screens and supports noncompare areas. When performing black box testing, the tester creates test scenarios from the specifications, and these test scenarios are executed by using WITT.

WHITE BOX TESTING

As stated in a previous section, white box techniques are used for testing program logic. These techniques include:

- *Statement Coverage.* An attempt is made to test every statement in a program at least once; this is considered the weakest of testing techniques.
- *Decision Coverage.* Enough test cases are developed so that each decision statement has at least one true and false outcome.
- *Condition Coverage.* Each condition for a decision is met so that all possible outcomes are made at least once.
- *Decision/Condition Coverage.* Each condition in a decision is tested for all possible outcomes at least once, and each decision is tested for all possible outcomes at least once.
- *Multiple Condition Coverage.* All possible combinations of conditional outcomes for each decision are invoked at least once.
- *Flowpath Combination Coverage.* All possible combinations of flowpaths are invoked for each outcome for each condition.

IBM's SATT provides four types of coverage metrics at four different levels—paragraph (i.e., subroutine), a module, component, and application. A component is an arbitrary division of an application (e.g., a batch component, online component, and an external interface component). SATT's four coverage types are the following:

- *Statement Coverage.* This metric is the percentage of statements executed within a paragraph, module, component, or application, and the number of times a statement was executed. This metric corresponds to the statement coverage technique.
- *Logical Paths Executed.* This metric measures the percentage of local paths executed within a paragraph, module, component, or application, and the number of times a statement was executed. This corresponds to the decision coverage, condition coverage, and decision/condition coverage techniques.
- *Internal Procedures.* This metric is the percentage of internal procedures (i.e., paragraphs) executed within a module, component, or application.
- *External Procedures.* This metric is the percentage of modules executed within a component or application.

White box testing alone cannot identify application code that does not meet specifications or is missing functional paths. In addition, it usually does not cover data-sensitive errors.

Using SATT: An Example

SATT is used to create a structure diagram of modules and their paragraphs. Exhibit 1 is a sample of such a diagram. As shown in the

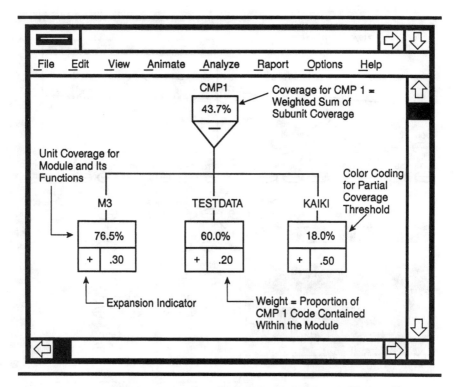

Exhibit 1. Sample SATT Structure Diagram

diagram, application component CMP1 has three modules: M3, TESTDATA, and KAIKI. Only 43.75% of the lines of code in component CMP1 were tested; 18% of the lines of code in the module KAIKI were tested, and KAIKI comprises 50% of the entire component CMP1. A plus sign is used in the diagram to indicate that the modules contain one or more paragraphs.

SATT computes the coverage metrics from execution histories (i.e., trace data), which were generated during testing of the programs. With SATT, coverage analysis reports can be produced and ad hoc queries can be performed on coverage data, which resides in the OS/2 Data Base Manager.

SATT helps the programmer understand programs and processes and therefore be better able to modify existing applications. Exhibit 2 shows a SATT display of call tree and call paths for a sample piece of application code. SATT can generate the structure diagram, call tree, and call paths by reading and processing the compiler listings. It is also capable of animating the application flow sequence, which is a static replay of the execution history, by highlighting the application flow through each module

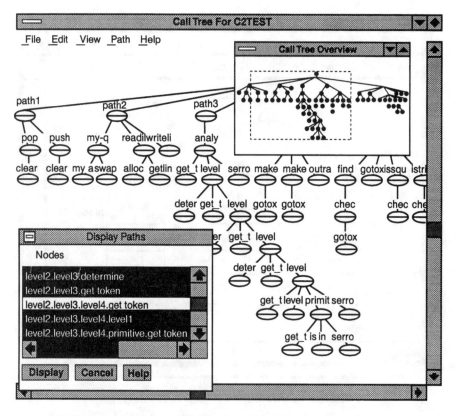

Exhibit 2. Sample SATT Display of Call Tree and Call Paths

and paragraph node in the structure diagram and the call tree. The tool displays the source code and animates the application flow through the source code by highlighting each line of code as it was executed during the test. SATT helps programmers identify and delete any unnecessary test cases and identify and create additional test cases to improve test coverage.

COMBINING BLACK BOX AND WHITE BOX TESTING

Black box testing techniques are sometimes capable of detecting and testing functions that are in an application but not in the specifications. White box testing techniques, however, can be used to discover three additional functions; such a discovery necessitates changes in the program or documentation. On the other hand, white box coverage analysis cannot be used to

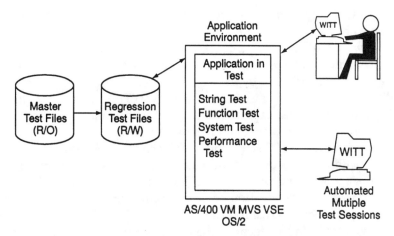

Exhibit 3. Components of a Definable and Repeatable Test Environment

---

find functions missing in the code but stated in the requirements specification. Nevertheless, white box coverage analysis can ensure the validity of the test case, and black box testing provides an efficient method for generating test cases.

Therefore, an effective testing method is to perform black box testing and white box coverage analysis. The following sections illustrate how such a method can be carried out with the automated testing tools, WITT and SATT.

Testing During Development

A definable test environment features a data base populated with test data. This test data is known by the programmers, and the programmers have defined the expected test results for this data from the application transactions. A repeatable test environment features data bases repopulated with the same definable test data to establish a regression test environment. A definable and repeatable test environment is critical to realizing the maximum potential of an automated test environment.

Exhibit 3 illustrates how a repeatable and definable test environment is enabled through updating files and tables for applications testing before running test cases. Once the test files have been initialized, a base script can be built and enhanced for further automation. Initialization can be performed by a WITT test case.

A WITT test case is a test script that consists of key strokes, mouse movements, WITT commands, editor (i.e., 2/REXX) statements, and test case comments. WITT scripts can be created with an editor or through recording a test session using WITT. Once a base script has been created, it can be parameterized with 2/REXX statements. Testers can thereby use space partitioning, boundary value analysis, cause-and-effect analysis, and error guessing techniques. The data generated by these techniques can reside in a file and can be read by 2/REXX statements. In this setup, WITT can perform unattended multiple test scenarios, capture the results for validation, and archive the results for future comparison and regression testing.

A parameterized WITT script can be further enhanced to test an application's function keys, provide error handling of unexpected events, and initialize the application data bases. WITT commands and 2/REXX logic statements enable the interrogation of screen data, complex data, and further processing through external routines.

Ideally, a tester independent of the development team should review the testing results. Once test results have been verified, the screens should be archived for future use. Often, changes to the application can still use all or most of the test scenarios, which may need only minimal changes. In addition, all or most of the archived screens serve as a baseline for comparing results produced by changed code.

WITT compares the screens and highlights mismatches. Testers review the mismatches between the archive screens and the current ones. WITT keeps application documentation current by printing the screens to a file that can be embedded in the application documentation.

During new code development, programmers often correct code, which must be subsequently fully regression tested. All test scenarios are rerun to ensure that previously tested scenarios still operate properly. WITT can be used to create more elaborate and comprehensive testware that corresponds to the complexity of the application. Parameterized WITT scripts serve as complete testware for functional verification of the code. The input file and WITT script represent the test plan documentation. This test testware should be reviewed and approved during the application design review, which occurs before writing the application code.

SATT Coverage Analysis Metrics. SATT's white box testing function complements WITT's black box testing functions by identifying any untested code or function. Subsequently, one would augment the test scenarios set to provide the test coverage where necessary. Using the execution history trace information, SATT animates the source code execution and thus allows the replay of test case execution. With SATT, programmers can replay failing test cases to determine the cause of the failure.

Network Stress Test. To ensure quality code for the production environment, stress testing the application is needed to identify storage violations, inconsistent results, and performance bottlenecks. WITT test scenarios can be used with IBM's Teleprocessing Network Simulator (TPNS) test drivers for testing across development test phases and groups. TPNS can simulate a large network with hundreds or thousands of concurrent users to stress test the application.

Maintenance Test Scenario

Maintenance programmers can use SATT to understand program logic before they make any changes to it. SATT can also be used to ensure test coverage of changes. SATT is used to display a program's structure diagram, call tree, and call paths. Once programmers have used SATT to understand application logic and have made the necessary changes, the new code must undergo regression testing.

Regression Testing. If necessary, the WITT test driver is edited to incorporate additional test scenarios and any changes to the transaction input screens and input data. The WITT test driver is run on the changed code and is used to compare the current screens file to the archive screens file. Results are validated, differences in the screens are certified, and the current screens file is archived and will serve as the new baseline. Applications documentation is updated as WITT is used to print the newly archived screens to a file that can be embedded in the documentation.

SUMMARY

The traditional application development life cycle focuses on writing code, unit testing with quickly-devised test cases, and unit testing with a debugging tool. Testing activities and data are repeatedly recreated as the application is fixed, enhanced, and maintained and little or no test cases and data are reused. This practice does not promote high-quality application code or lower testing costs.

Testing theory put into practice, data domains, and automated test drivers can improve productivity and quality as well as lower costs. A rigorous test process, test case reuse, and a definable, repeatable test environment can be used to implement what is needed to improve quality and lower costs. This chapter has examined the elements of a rigorous test process and a definable and repeatable test environment and has shown the role automated test drivers play in it.

Chapter VIII-3
Building a Customized Testing Approach

Polly Perryman

THE EFFECTS OF satellite communications and worldwide Internet use seen in the business world are among the driving forces in today's software community. The pressure is on to beat the leading technological standards currently available. These pressures come into the world of software development from three distinct areas: Business and industry demands, product quality, and world market competition. Each of these areas raises its own issues relative to testing. The result is that software developers and system integrators must alter their view of the work effort to ensure a more thorough and complete testing.

The perspective for a new view includes defining testing processes for the organization that not only overlap the development effort but also fully support the schedule and budgets of the project. These processes must address areas of testing that have traditionally been lumped into the part of the cycle where "a miracle occurs." Processes for planning, requirement mapping, change control, development tools, and testing tools are a few of the areas that are necessary to develop software and to integrate systems that satisfy the dimensions of twenty-first century technology. The development cycle may remain constant, but methods applied within the phases of the development cycle have become more sophisticated, and as a result, testing of these systems needs to be more thorough than when current systems were created.

Traditionally a problem area for containing costs and meeting schedules, testing processes are scrutinized in assessing the quality of a product and in selecting companies to develop software. More important, testing processes must meet the demands of business and industry for demonstrating that the software will meet the interoperability and reliability needed. Defining an approach to software testing that can be used on one or more software development projects can minimize problems previously prevalent throughout the software development community, but to accomplish this, it is necessary to start with a basic testing approach and to understand that there is a test cycle consistent with and complementary to the software development cycle. Once a basic approach for testing is developed, it can in turn be customized to meet the organization's quality goals.

As competition increases on the international front, business and industry continuously identify greater areas of need. To meet these needs, they are raising an outcry for technological solutions, which in turn translates into systems that are more complex and more secure. As a result, innovative systems of the late twentieth century, such as bank ATMs, home shopping telephones, and non-restricted scanners, are becoming substructures for twenty-first century technology. Routine, day-to-day tasks common to modern man are becoming automated, and the manual functions performed in corporations today are being reassessed for automation tomorrow. Even relatively simple systems for general business and financial applications must be integrated and perform at high speeds. To meet these technology-driven demands, software systems are becoming more complicated to design, construct, and test.

At every phase of the development effort, methods are needed for ensuring that new product specifications comply with the interface, interconnection, and interoperability requirements set for the software community, not only in the U.S. but the international marketplace. To test these systems adequately, testing processes must be well planned. Test objectives must be carefully defined. This is accomplished by accepting the changes that are already in process within the software community and in becoming knowledgeable about existing industry standards and those under development.

Whether the system to be developed is for corporate or home use, today's consumer expects the best. Corporate end-users have, at a minimum, a fundamental knowledge of computer technology on which to base their purchasing decisions. They do their homework to find out which products, software developers, and system integrators offer the best value. What they are looking for is the highest level of usefulness and quality relative to cost.

An important starting place is an assessment of the philosophy and the testing processes already in existence within the corporation. This article proposes and discusses the following testing philosophy.

ESTABLISHING A TESTING STRATEGY

For the purposes of this article, a philosophy for testing is proposed to be the process for finding and fixing the inconsistencies and problems present in software and the process of identifying and developing procedural work around for those that are not easily fixed. The testing process is intended to help attain perfection rather than proving perfection.

In building a testing strategy to support that philosophy, it is important to establish a familiarity with testing terminology among developers and managers responsible for testing, because as software is developed and tests are designed to ensure quality, decisions need to be made whether white box testing or black box testing, or both, will be performed.

The term *white box* test is generally used to describe a controlled test or a series of controlled internal system tests that demonstrate what happens within the system under certain circumstances. Individual modules and strings or threads of code are generally tested using white box techniques. The unit or thread is executed and stopped at various points in the processing to determine what happens when it is stopped and to determine whether the processing that was intended to occur in fact did occur.

The term *black box* test refers to a test that validates the use and operations of a system with the internal processes of the system transparent to the testers. Black box tests generally consider the input and the output without regard to what is going on within the system. Black box testing of a graphical user interface (GUI), for example, would be concerned with the human factors of the GUI, such as ease of use, correctness of the transportation through the system, and the response time of the displays.

Whereas these terms describe specific types of testing techniques, they do not represent or provide an overall strategy or approach for testing. A testing strategy is significant in being able to do one or more of the following:

- Show value (i.e., this product is better than the competition's product).
- Meet customer expectations (i.e., this product performs the functions needed with no failures).
- Contain costs (i.e., the problems are found as early as possible in the development cycle and fixed without exploding development budgets).
- Meet schedules (i.e., the defined processes used for development support better planning and execution).

In establishing a test strategy for single or multiple software development projects, five issues must be addressed: testing goals, pretest procedures, test methods and techniques, test cycle, and test activities.

TESTING GOALS

All organizations that are interested in finding ways to ensure the quality of their products through testing have a common goal, but the methods for achieving that goal employ many different testing methods and techniques. One way to determine if the methods and techniques meet the growing and changing technological advancements is to review what is being required in specific industries and for particular types of software. In the recently published book, *Software Engineering Standards and Specifications*, 46 national and international standards development organizations are identified. These organizations are making headway in projecting the needs of software within particular industries and in general. The standards they are developing are affecting the future of the software development in the areas of requirements definition, design, code, integration, project management, verification and validation, configuration management, quality assurance and others. Forty-five of these organizations deal specifically with standards for software testing in some form.

A review of these standards points to specific testing requirements at various levels and for particular types of software. The standards provide valuable guidelines in industries in which safety is foremost, as it is in nuclear and air transport. They are also useful to organizations whose software products require accuracy and integrity but that may not be mission critical. The usefulness is in reviewing the standards, editing them to meet explicit needs in the organization, and then using them to customize a testing approach for independent corporate use and to meet the expressed quality goals of the organization.

PRETEST PROCEDURES

Creating testing procedures is an intricate part of having a defined testing approach. It does not have to be a painful experience, but it does require decision makers to document the steps that will be taken as each new development effort is begun.

Acceptance Criteria

At a minimum, a procedure should exist to ensure that the software acceptance criteria are put into place while system requirements are being defined. Defining the acceptance criteria for the software to be developed before the design work begins is one of the first steps in containing costs. The acceptance criteria sets the baseline standard on which testing will be conducted, by giving the high-level measurements against which compliance with requirements will be evaluated. This measurement is used to judge the completeness and usability of the software by the end-user in deciding the acceptability of it for its intended purpose. For example, if a requirement states that the system must be available 99% of the time, the acceptance criteria must include those statements that explain precisely what constitutes 99% of the time. For example, does that mean 99% of a 40-hour work week or 99% of a 24-by-7 operation? If the requirement states that the system is to process four million documents annually, the acceptance criteria must clarify what constitutes a single document. For example, is a document a single sheet of paper, or is a document some number of related papers between 1 and 100?

Test Methods and Techniques

Defining the minimum types of tests to be run before the development cycle begins is also critical. This procedure ensures that the testing approach put into place will consistently review individual software projects. It will make certain that scheduled testing activities meet the minimum level of testing needed for specific types of software, including, for example, the mission-critical software included in weaponry, information-processing software, such as tax returns and bank statements, and automation-processing software for automated teller machines and robots. The types of tests to be considered include reliability, usability, interoperability, accuracy, safety, performance, and stress testing.

Compiling a written list of the minimum types of tests acceptable for the software to be developed provides a point of reference in analyzing software requirements during the requirements-definition phase of the development effort. A checklist may be included with the procedure. This procedure helps project managers understand the scope of testing needed for individual software projects, a key factor in ensuring that planned schedules and budgets are realistic from the beginning of the effort.

The Level of Testing Detail. Once the procedure specifying the types of tests is complete, guidelines are generated designating the level of detail that is needed for each type of test. The level of detail addresses both the technique and timing. The technique refers to method to be applied, and timing states when in the development cycle the test will be conducted. Determining the level of detail needed to perform thorough testing for each type of testing means that planned testing techniques for a given project are identified and recorded before the development work commences.

Defining both the testing techniques and the type of testing establishes a clear testing picture, and the intended approach to testing becomes more definitive. For example, the technique for usability testing might be a peer review of flowcharts and decision tables during the design phase or path testing by the programmer or team leader during the coding phase.

Establishing the correct level of detail for testing in relationship to the complexity of the system enforces a definitive level of testing and precludes subjective testing decisions from being based solely on schedule issues. In other words, the approach not only reduces the risk that the software will be more grandiose than necessary or not useable at all, it also ensures that realistic schedules and budgets can be established and met. Just as important, in defining the level of testing, the level of understanding needed to meet quality goals is demonstrated.

By identifying criteria, defining which tests to use, and establishing a level of testing detail, an organization shows a commitment to quality. It also establishes the foundation for a repeatable testing approach and can reasonably establish a testing tool kit that can be reused from one project to another, effectively improving productivity during the testing phase of the development cycle.

TEST MANAGEMENT AND TEST AUTHORITY

An organization should also define how it will control all testing efforts and should identify, by position, the authority structure for every testing effort. The value of having these procedures in place as part of the organization's overall testing approach is threefold. First, they provide consistency, and consistency is, in today's market, translated into quality. This is highlighted by the growing requirement to demonstrate quality both internationally, through the ISO 9000 series of standards for quality management, and nationally, at least for government projects, through the Capability Maturity Model (CMM), created by the Software Engineering Institute (SEI) at Carnegie Mellon University. (See Exhibit 1 for a more detailed discussion of ISO 9000 and SEI CMM.)

Second, consistency improves productivity by allowing personnel to do the job rather than trying to figure out how to do the job and how to get around personal agendas that can sabotage a project. These test management procedures also provide a baseline method from which process improvement can be attained and measured. Developers who work on one or more projects within an organization will find the snags in the process and be able to bring suggestions and recommendations for implementing day-to-day operations that support improvement of the procedure and ensure its smooth execution.

The third benefit is that an organization can correctly staff an upcoming development effort. Whether individuals are going to wear one hat or support multiple roles on a project, management must make several decisions before the project begins. It must define in advance how the testing effort is to be managed. Management must also determine what type of decision makers are going to be needed. By doing so, it minimizes the risk that the staffing process omits the skills necessary to complete the job on time and within budget. In other words, the planning can be more accurate and cost overruns can be minimized.

When establishing test management procedures, management must remember that the procedures will be the guidelines not only for managing staff, test environments, and schedules, but also for determining the test readiness of software. Consideration must be given to configuration man-

The SEI CMM, initially developed and implemented in the United States for use by the Department of Defense, is now a feature of the commercial world, as the technology of today's businesses expand for greater and greater personal access and use in areas of finance and security. The SEI CMM quality guidelines were created specifically to measure and validate software development processes, and compliance results in a level rating somewhere between one and five, with a rating of five being the highest. The SEI CMM rating is established though an assessment process and defined and structured as part of the model. The SEI CMM is finding its way into the international software community via United States representatives working in international communities.

ISO 9000 is composed of a series of standards and guidelines initially prepared to ensure that the processes used in the manufacturing of products met minimum criteria that could then be translated to assured quality of the product. Compliance with ISO 9000 is certified by registered ISO certification auditors. There are continuing efforts by representatives of ISO's subcommittee on software engineering and system documentation and by SEI CMM representatives to broaden the ISO 9000 quality-management guidelines in a manner that addresses software development quality issues.

SEI CMM and ISO 9000 are similar in that they both relate quality to process, both provide methods for validating the processes of an organization, and both result in recognized and accepted ratings or certification. Both the CMM and ISO 9000 seek to ensure consistency in the processes of an organization as part of the rating and certification assessments.

Exhibit 1. The Software Engineering Institute's Capability Maturity Model (CMM) and ISO 9000 Guidelines

---

agement in terms of version control, problem reporting and tracking, and the overall integrity of the test environment.

THE TEST CYCLE-DEVELOPMENT CYCLE RELATIONSHIP

The classic software development cycle is divided into five phases: requirements definition, system design, system development, testing, and implementation. The test cycle parallels the development cycle, and each phase requires certain testing activities. For example, product evaluations take place during the requirements definition phase of the development cycle. Selection of testing techniques occurs during the system design phase; test-case development and test-data definition both begin during system design and continue through the early development phase. The system development phase—and coding, in particular—coincide with particular testing activities, such as gathering and preparing test data and establishing the test environment. When the system design is complete, integration testing and system testing begin. Each phase of the system development cycle has a corresponding testing phase, and they are closely interrelated.

Some of the tools available for developers to generate code and refine designs are helpful to testers when they are used as part of an overall development methodology. Even though such tools are not designed specifically to support testing activities, these tools produce results that can be helpful to the professionals responsible for testing. For example, automated design products document transaction flows, inputs/outputs, and interfaces; the output of the product and the documentation produced both become useful tools for system testers. Therefore, testers must take responsibility for familiarizing themselves with the methodologies adopted for development efforts. In the process, testers also learn how to define the relationship between development, testing, and quality.

THE REQUIREMENTS DEFINITION PHASE OF THE DEVELOPMENT AND TEST CYCLES

Product Evaluations

Developers plan on using vendor-supplied products in either of two ways: For use during the development and testing of the end system under development, or in the end system itself. Product evaluations are performed during the requirement definition phase. When a proposed system includes vendor-supplied hardware and software products, however, evaluations are performed at two points during the development cycle: When the determination of platforms is made for the software development effort, and when the commercial off-the-shelf (COTS) integration occurs, alone or with software developed in-house to provide specific types of functionality.

A product evaluation must include an examination of the product specifications, testing of the product, and comparison of the individual COTS products. The results of the evaluation need to be distributed to the system architects and designers and to the business operations personnel responsible for budgets. These staff members must then work together to make the final selection of products for the system and for the development environment.

Testability Rules

General testability rules also are prepared well in advance of the start of development efforts, during the requirements definition phase. Rules include, for example, a definition applied for testing user friendliness and a recommended or typical percentage data base for testing. When these types of general rules are used as guidelines, they are helpful in defining a system's requirements by providing system analysts points to consider and discuss when working with the customer.

Testability rules, however, are not defined in isolation. Three parameters—requirements and acceptance criteria, as well as testability rules—need to be established during the system requirements phase of the development cycle. They are very closely related, and testers need to understand the role each of these sets of parameters plays and how they all work together.

System requirements itemize the functions and performance needs for the system to be developed and the minimal acceptable functions for the system; acceptance criteria interpret and clarify requirements; testability rules establish guidelines that are used to determine the testability of each software development requirement. As the development cycle proceeds and additional requirements are defined, measurements are identified that can demonstrate system compliance with the requirement. In this manner, the general test rules are expanded to ensure that each specific system requirement is testable. In some efforts, only some sort of data comparison will be necessary. Other projects may require the use of function point analysis, and still others may beg for throughput metrics to be applied. In any case, the goal of establishing testability rules that state how acceptance criteria are met is to have guidelines for assessing the testability of each requirement. Each requirement must be testable as to whether it satisfies acceptance criteria.

Requirements Analysis

During the requirements definition phase (and often into the design phase) of the development and test cycles, each requirement of a project should be decomposed to its simplest state. Much like reduction to the lowest common denominator in basic arithmetic fractions, decomposition of requirements speeds understanding of customer needs and supports better productivity in subsequent phases of the development cycle, from design to testing.

Once the requirements are decomposed, the analysis of them should continue. On most projects, the requirements include both functional and system needs to be met by the software. The functional requirements are statements that express what types of transactions the system must be able to process and where data must be routed once it is processed. The transaction information provided as part of the requirements may or may not include a breakout of inputs and outputs by data entity. If the information is not provided up-front, the types of data, at minimum, must be identified and gathered, as knowing the types is critical in determining how the requirement will be tested.

The system requirements state how quickly and in what order these transactions must be processed to permit end-users to perform day-to-day tasks. For example, a requirement is to make the system available 99% of the time, and the acceptance criteria says that 99% availability means a 24-by-7 operation. If the requirement also says that the system must process four million documents annually, the acceptance criteria clarifies whether "a single document" is a single sheet of paper or some number of related papers between 1 and 100.

THE DESIGN PHASE OF THE DEVELOPMENT AND TEST CYCLES

Testing Techniques Selection

At the beginning of the design phase, a decomposition and analysis of the requirements is undertaken and a high-level design for the system emerges. At the same time, staff responsible for testing consolidates a general idea of which techniques they will apply to test the system during each phase of the development cycle. Because using the appropriate technique during each phase of the effort significantly reduces risk, the techniques selected need to provide measurable return on the investment. Decisions, therefore, must be made in terms of how much and how little testing is going to be conducted during the development of the system. They need to be well thought out, documented, and implemented.

In general, the more critical the nature of the software, the higher the number of testing techniques applied. This correlation is important for three reasons:

- Ensure that all the requirements are being met adequately.
- Reduce risks associated with the identification of problems late in the development cycle.
- Reduce the risk of requirement creeping.

By examining each of these reasons to increase testing on large (or even small, but complex) systems, the value of this exercise becomes clearer.

All the requirements are being met adequately. As the architecture for the system is put into place, requirements for performance and reliability, human factors, and transaction processing need to be addressed. A requirement, for example, for the system to be able to print labels at some point in the processing may be a simple task for one type of system and a very tricky process for another system. A simple system would be a mail system that allows the input of names, addresses, and labels to be printed from a list, it can be considered a simple system and, as such, it probably does not warrant peer reviews and critical design reviews at the highest level.

A more complex problem would be to print labels and have the system handle the processing of tax forms or medical data from millions of people. In addition, the label needs to include specific system-produced information to ensure that the data of individuals can be retrieved and tracked for years into the future. In this case, the multiplicity of factors that must be addressed during the high-level design increases dramatically. Such factors as when the label can be generated, what type of printer will handle the volumes of labels that must be produced, and who in the customer organization has responsibility for ensuring the label information is correct must be considered.

In this case, the complexity of the system demands that reviews are conducted early in the process to ensure that the system will allow the system to print labels with the correct amount of information on them. The review is a test process that does more than just pass the print label requirement if a printer is shown in the architecture. Instead, the test process ensures that the printer shown in the architecture is compatible with the other pieces of proposed hardware, that it will handle the volume of work projected, that the size and shape of the printer fit into the space proposed for the printer, and that the printer will, in fact, print the types of labels (e.g., sheets or single roll) that are needed to fit in the physical environment. When the review shows that the printer meets the customer needs, the second reason for increasing test techniques becomes easier.

Risks associated with the identification of problems late in the development cycle are reduced. A situation to be avoided is one in which all project members reach the end of the development phase feeling really successful because the project is within budget and on schedule. They only at that point discover that the printer selected for printing labels does not handle the size labels needed by the customer. That late in the project, only two choices are available. Either the staff convinces the customer to use what the system will produce, thereby risking customer dissatisfaction, or fix the problem.

For argument's sake, the customer cannot modify the label size, and the problem needs to be addressed head on. The solution could be simple, maybe; however, the risk here is in whether the market has another printer available that is compatible with all the other components in the system, and whether the only printer on the market that meets the customer's requirements is three times more expensive than the one currently in the system. The risk also includes the possibility that the correct printer is incompatible with other system components, and new interfaces need to be designed and developed. The cost of the system and schedule for delivery begin to wobble. In this case, the developers could have mitigated the risk by using testing techniques early in the life cycle.

The risk of requirement creeping is reduced. Both the customer and the developer need to beware, because requirement creeping may be one of the most serious problems in the development of systems. The bigger and more complex the system, the bigger the risk is that requirement creeping will occur. Implementing testing techniques to reduce this risk becomes essential to maintaining schedules and budgets. For example, in the case mentioned in the previous section, the requirement initially states that the system must produce a label that includes a certain range of information. Reviews have confirmed that the printer selected will do this and that the software under development will capture the information needed for printing the information. Six months into the project, however, the customer explains that there are exceptions to the information that needs to be handled, labels must be produced with different information on them. This might arise because the customer has just begun offering a new service, has been affected by the industry they service, or has just now remembered to mention it. If the design and development have not made provisions for capturing and printing this new information, the requirement has just creeped.

Test techniques for handling this requirement creeping are progress reviews and code walk throughs. These techniques ensure that the added requirement is handled through correct channels, which are configuration management and project management, rather than through the system analyst, which may accept the added requirement and proceed to modify the system at a risk to schedule and budget.

These are three very strong reasons for going through the test technique selection process. The result will be that both real problems and potential problems are identified early and corrective action readily taken.

Test Case Development

Test cases are developed during the design phase also. Once the types of techniques are selected, the tests to be used throughout the life cycle need to be outlined, filled in, and reviewed. This activity ensures that the requirement as it is being satisfied by the design is testable and that thought has been given to the method for testing. Just as the overall selection of testing techniques initially determine what is valuable for an organization, the types of tests to be performed also influence the quality status of the system. For instance, when flowcharts and path testing are selected techniques, the type of test will logically be a technical design review. Path testing and transaction flows, on the other hand, would be applied during function tests, also referred to as black box testing. Data validation and syntax testing would most appropriately be applied during the coding phase as unit tests, string or thread testing. Whatever the technique, when testing begins, the testing team must keep sight of why the system is being developed in the first place. In other words, testers must map each test to the requirements being tested and be sure the test objective is consistent with the intent of these requirements.

Developed early enough in the development cycle, portions of test cases may be used by developers to test individual programs. More complete test cases may be used by team leaders to perform string testing. Having the test cases available to coders to use reduces risk and improves overall system quality in two ways. It ensures that programs are being constructed and tested to software requirements early enough in the cycle to minimize schedule and budget impacts, and it provides a method for exercising the test case and working out any flaws in the instructions provided to testers during quality system integration testing.

In constructing effective test cases, the test objective should be of primary focus. In doing this, a single test case may show compliance with a single or multiple requirements. The test case should reference each requirement by either statement or the requirements identification number from a requirements traceability matrix. Additionally, each test case should include a brief description of the test, and the expected results of the test.

Test Data Requirements

Test data is defined during the design phase and in conjunction with the development of test cases. Whereas test data can be identified before actual test cases are developed, the types of data identified must be checked thoroughly for both regular and exception data. The sources of data must then be identified and arrangements must be made to ensure that the test data is transferred to the test environment before the commencement of testing. Considerations in source identification and in bringing the test data into the test environment include determining the volume of data to be used in order to test the system adequately. The volume of data must be great enough to exercise the software for performance and accuracy.

THE CODING PHASE OF THE DEVELOPMENT AND TEST CYCLES

Gathering and Preparing Test Data

Test data is gathered and prepared for the test environment during the coding phase of the development effort. Once the decisions are made regarding the data, the data must be gathered and put on tape or in a directory. Source documents to be scanned or used for data entry need to be collected; these documents should be identified, numbered, and tracked throughout the testing process. The tracking of source documents is important in being able to predict test results and to accurately document the conditions of the test. The source document tracking list should become part of the test data baseline. Access to data items should be restricted to test team personnel.

Creating the Test Environment

Activities and tasks that ensure a test environment is ready for integration and system testing occur during the coding phase. In some organizations, an environment for testing is in place at all times, and for such organizations, preparing the test environment is a step that cannot be overlooked. The reason is that even though the existing system may well use the same hardware and system-level software as that for the system being developed, the equipment and version of software need to be assessed to ensure it will be adequate for the system under development or upgraded to handle the new system. This process takes time, too, and should be included in the schedule and in the budget to prevent unnecessary delays later on. To fully and correctly test the developed and integrated software, it is essential to have a controllable test environment. The test environment is the physical (i.e., facilities) and system (i.e., directories, types, and workstations) location and the rules governing access and use of these locations during testing.

The test environment needs to be established to be able to document the conditions under which testing occurs and to assess the integrity of the testing activities. Baselining, a function of configuration management, ensures that the software, the test data, and the test cases are the correct version for testing. The environment can be as elaborate as a separate facility with a system that is an exact duplicate development environment, where not only system access but testing facility access is restricted. The system may be as simple as baselined software being installed in the development environment during a certain time of each day reserved for testing. Restriction of the system to authorized test personnel is achieved in either case.

THE INTEGRATION PHASE OF THE DEVELOPMENT AND TEST CYCLES

Running Test Cases

When the designers and the coders decide the system is complete, the integration testing and system testing phase begin. The plan has been prepared at the end of the coding phase; it is implemented in the test phase of the development life cycle. Previously prepared, reviewed, and customer-approved test cases should provide the step-by-step information needed to test functionality and performance. Test management procedures and authorities should be in place. Test tools should have been installed and test data made available.

At this point, the test plan, which may include the test cases, a description of the test data, and a description of the test environment, must contain a schedule for conducting tests. This schedule indicates when tests are to be run but should also be accompanied by narrative giving the conditions under which the test will be performed and the methods to be used in recording the results of each test. Each test case should be run individually. When the test reveals a deficiency, the deficiency needs to be recorded and sent back to development with sufficient information for a fix to be made. When test cases have dependencies, the order in which tests are run may be affected by deficiencies found anywhere in the test path. When this is the case, the entire test path must be retested once a fix is made. The retest process is commonly and correctly called regression testing.

Capturing and Recording Test Results

Whether the test being performed is a walk through, inspection, examination, technical review, or transaction processing, the results of the test must be recorded. Documenting the results of each test is to be done whether the test passes the software as acceptable and compliant with requirements and system specifications or fails it because it does not meet its intended purpose. When a test fails, the reason for the failure needs to be explained in as much detail as possible. This documentation should include sufficient information to recreate identified problems, provide recommended solutions to problems, and indicate a priority for each identified problem. When no problems are identified, the test is considered as a pass, which is recorded along with the date of the test and the name of the person who performed the test.

SUMMARY

The decision to write and implement five basic procedures, three specific to test structuring and focus and two aimed at management control, can make a significant difference in the final quality of the product and validation of that quality by consumers. Building a thorough and comprehensive test approach positions a company to compete nationally and internationally by putting the procedures and processes in place that allows claims of quality to be audited and verified.

Chapter VIII-4
Software Testing to Meet Corporate Quality Goals

Polly Perryman

THE EFFECTS OF SATELLITE COMMUNICATIONS and worldwide Internet use in the business world are among the driving forces in today's software community. The pressure is on to beat the leading technological standards currently available. These pressures come into the world of software development from three distinct areas: business and industry demands, product quality, and world market competition. Each of these areas raises its own issues relative to testing. The result is that software developers and system integrators must alter their view of the work effort to ensure a more thorough and complete testing.

The perspective for a new view includes defining testing processes for the organization that not only overlap the development effort but also fully support the schedule and budgets of the project. These processes must address areas of testing that have traditionally been lumped into the part of the cycle where "a miracle occurs." Processes for planning, requirement mapping, change control, development tools, and testing tools are a few of the areas that are necessary to develop software and to integrate systems that satisfy the dimensions of twenty-first century technology. The development cycle may remain constant, but methods applied within the phases of the development cycle have become more sophisticated, and as a result, testing of these systems needs to be more thorough than when current systems were created.

Traditionally a problem area for containing costs and meeting schedules, testing processes are scrutinized in assessing the quality of a product and in selecting companies to develop software. More important, testing processes must meet the demands of business and industry for demonstrating that the software will meet the interoperability and reliability needed. Defining an approach to software testing that can be used on one or more software development projects can minimize problems previously prevalent throughout the software development community, but to accomplish this, it is necessary to start with a basic testing approach and to understand that there is a test cycle consistent with and complementary to the software development cycle. Once a basic approach for testing is

0-8493-9979-3/99/$0.00+$.50
© 1999 by CRC Press LLC

developed, it can in turn be customized to meet the organization's quality goals.

As competition increases on the international front, business and industry continuously identify greater areas of need. To meet these needs, they are raising an outcry for technological solutions, which in turn translates into systems that are more complex and more secure. As a result, innovative systems of the late twentieth century, such as bank ATMs, home shopping telephones, and nonrestricted scanners, are becoming substructures for twenty-first century technology. Routine, day-to-day tasks common to modern man are becoming automated, and the manual functions performed in corporations today are being reassessed for automation tomorrow. Even relatively simple systems for general business and financial applications must be integrated and perform at high speeds. To meet these technology-driven demands, software systems are becoming more complicated to design, construct, and test.

At every phase of the development effort, methods are needed for ensuring that new product specifications comply with the interface, interconnection, and interoperability requirements set for the software community, not only in the U.S. but the international marketplace. To test these systems adequately, testing processes must be well planned. Test objectives must be carefully defined. This is accomplished by accepting the changes that are already in process within the software community and in becoming knowledgeable about existing industry standards and those under development.

Whether the system to be developed is for corporate or home use, today's consumer expects the best. Corporate end users have, at a minimum, a fundamental knowledge of computer technology on which to base their purchasing decisions. They do their homework to find out which products, software developers, and system integrators offer the best value. What they are looking for is the highest level of usefulness and quality relative to cost.

An important starting place is an assessment of the philosophy and the testing processes already in existence within the corporation. This chapter proposes and discusses the following testing philosophy.

ESTABLISHING A TESTING STRATEGY

For the purposes of this article, a philosophy for testing is proposed to be the process for finding and fixing the inconsistencies and problems present in software and the process of identifying and developing procedural work around for those that are not easily fixed. The testing process is intended to help attain perfection rather than proving perfection.

In building a testing strategy to support that philosophy, it is important to establish a familiarity with testing terminology among developers and managers responsible for testing, because as software is developed and tests are designed to ensure quality, decisions need to be made whether white box testing or black box testing, or both, will be performed.

The term white box test is generally used to describe a controlled test or a series of controlled internal system tests that demonstrate what happens within the system under certain circumstances. Individual modules and strings or threads of code are generally tested using white box techniques. The unit or thread is executed and stopped at various points in the processing to determine what happens when it is stopped and to determine whether the processing that was intended to occur in fact did occur.

The term black box test refers to a test that validates the use and operations of a system with the internal processes of the system transparent to the testers. Black box tests generally consider the input and the output without regard to what is going on within the system. Black box testing of a GUI, for example, would be concerned with the human factors of the GUI, such as ease of use, correctness of the transportation through the system, and the response time of the displays.

Whereas these terms describe specific types of testing techniques, they do not represent or provide an overall strategy or approach for testing. A testing strategy is significant in being able to do one or more of the following:

- Show value (i.e., this product is better than the competition's product).
- Meet customer expectations (i.e., this product performs the functions needed with no failures).
- Contain costs (i.e., the problems are found as early as possible in the development cycle and fixed without exploding development budgets).
- Meet schedules (i.e., the defined processes used for development support better planning and execution).

In establishing a test strategy for single or multiple software development projects, five issues must be addressed: testing goals, pretest procedures, test methods and techniques, test cycle, and test activities.

TESTING GOALS

All organizations that are interested in finding ways to ensure the quality of their products through testing have a common goal, but the methods for achieving that goal employ many different testing methods and techniques. One way to determine if the methods and techniques meet the growing and changing technological advancements is to review what is being required in specific industries and for particular types of software. In the recently published book, *Software Engineering Standards and Specifications*,[1] 146 national and international standards development organizations are identified. These organizations are making headway in projecting the needs of software within particular industries and in general. The standards they are developing are affecting the future of software development in the areas of requirements definition, design, code, integration, project management, verification and validation, configuration management, quality assurance, and others. Forty-five of these organizations deal specifically with standards for software testing in some form.

A review of these standards points to specific testing requirements at various levels and for particular types of software. The standards provide valuable guidelines in industries in which safety is foremost, as it is in nuclear and air transport. They are also useful to organizations whose software products require accuracy and integrity but that may not be mission critical. The usefulness is in reviewing the standards, editing them to meet explicit needs in the organization, and then using them to customize a testing approach for independent corporate use and to meet the expressed quality goals of the organization.

PRETEST PROCEDURES

Creating testing procedures is an intricate part of having a defined testing approach. It does not have to be a painful experience, but it does require decision makers to document the steps that will be taken as each new development effort is begun.

Acceptance Criteria

At a minimum, a procedure should exist to ensure that the software acceptance criteria are put into place while system requirements are being defined. Defining the acceptance criteria for the software to be developed before the design work begins is one of the first steps in containing costs. The acceptance criteria sets the baseline standard on which testing will be conducted, by giving the high-level measurements against which compliance with requirements will be evaluated. This measurement is used to judge the completeness and usability of the software by the end user in deciding the acceptability of it for its intended purpose. For example, if a requirement states that the system must be available 99% of the time, the acceptance criteria must include those statements that explain precisely what constitutes 99% of the time. For example, does that mean 99% of a 40-hour work week or 99% of a 24-by-7 operation? If the requirement states that the system is to process 4 million documents annually, the acceptance criteria must clarify what constitutes a single document. For example, is a document a single sheet of paper, or is a document some number of related papers between 1 and 100?

[1]S. Magee and L.L. Tripp, *Software Engineering Standards and Specifications: An Annotated Index and Directory* (Global Professional Public Publications, 1994).

Test Methods and Techniques

Defining the minimum types of tests to be run before the development cycle begins is also critical. This procedure ensures that the testing approach put into place will consistently review individual software projects. It will make certain that scheduled testing activities meet the minimum level of testing needed for specific types of software, including, for example, the mission-critical software included in weaponry, information-processing software, such as tax returns and bank statements, and automation-processing software for automated teller machines and robots. The types of tests to be considered include reliability, usability, interoperability, accuracy, safety, performance, and stress testing.

Compiling a written list of the minimum types of test acceptable for the software to be developed provides a point of reference in analyzing software requirements during the requirements-definition phase of the development effort. A checklist may be included with the procedure. This procedure helps project managers understand the scope of testing needed for individual software projects, a key factor in ensuring that planned schedules and budgets are realistic from the beginning of the effort.

The Level of Testing Detail. Once the procedure specifying the types of tests is complete, guidelines are generated designating the level of detail that is needed for each type of test. The level of detail addresses both the technique and timing. The technique refers to the method to be applied, and timing states when in the development cycle the test will be conducted. Determining the level of detail needed to perform thorough testing for each type of testing means that planned testing techniques for a given project are identified and recorded before the development work commences.

Defining both the testing techniques and the type of testing establishes a clear testing picture, and the intended approach to testing becomes more definitive. For example, the technique for usability testing might be a peer review of flowcharts and decision tables during the design phase or path testing by the programmer or team leader during the coding phase.

Establishing the correct level of detail for testing in relationship to the complexity of the system enforces a definitive level of testing and precludes subjective testing decisions from being based solely on schedule issues. In other words, the approach not only reduces the risk that the software will be more grandiose than necessary or not usable at all, it also ensures that realistic schedules and budgets can be established and met. Just as important, in defining the level of testing, the level of understanding needed to meet quality goals is demonstrated.

By identifying criteria, defining which tests to use, and establishing a level of testing detail, an organization shows a commitment to quality. It also establishes the foundation for a repeatable testing approach and can reasonably establish a testing tool kit that can be reused from one project to another, effectively improving productivity during the testing phase of the development cycle.

TEST MANAGEMENT AND TEST AUTHORITY

An organization should also define how it will control all testing efforts and should identify, by position, the authority structure for every testing effort. The value of having these procedures in place as part of the organization's overall testing approach is threefold. First, they provide consistency, and consistency is, in today's market, translated into quality. This is highlighted by the growing requirement to demonstrate quality both internationally, through the ISO 9000 series of standards for quality management, and nationally, at least for government projects, through the Capability Maturity Model, created by the SEI at Carnegie Mellon University. (See Exhibit 1 for a more detailed discussion of ISO 9000 and SEI CMM.)

CONCLUSION

Because the test management procedures call out the way in which testing will be accomplished, it is essential that test authorities be established. This means that the positions or roles of a project are designated for test personnel, and assignments stating the responsibilities for each position, including who has signature authority to show successful test completion, are defined. When a project is staffed, a single individual could possibly fulfill the responsibilities of all the defined positions; however, having a clear understanding of what those responsibilities are could prevent untimely surprises — a skills shortage — from interfering with either the cost or schedule, or both.

Exhibit 1.   The Software Engineering Institute's Capability Maturity Model (CMM)and ISO 9000 Guidelines

The SEI CMM, initially developed and implemented in the United States for use by the Department of Defense, is now a feature of the commercial world, as the technology of today's businesses expand for greater and greater personal access and use in areas of finance and security. The SEI CMM quality guidelines were created specifically to measure and validate software development processes, and compliance results in a level rating somewhere between 1 and 5, with a rating of 5 being the highest. The SEI CMM rating is established though an assessment process defined and structured as part of the model. The SEI CMM is finding its way into the international software community via United States representatives working on international communities.

ISO 9000 is composed of a series standards and guidelines initially prepared to ensure that the processes used in the manufacturing of products met minimum criteria that could then be translated to assured quality of the product. Compliance with ISO 9000 is certified by registered ISO certification auditors. There are continuing efforts by representatives of ISO's subcommittee on software engineering and system documentation and by SEI CMM representatives to broaden the ISO 9000 quality-management guidelines in a manner that addresses software development quality issues.

SEI CMM and ISO 9000 are similar in that they both relate quality to process, both provide methods for validating the processes of an organization, and both result in recognized and accepted ratings or certification. Both the CMM and ISO 9000 seek to ensure consistency in the processes of an organization as part of the rating and certification assessments.

Second, consistency improves productivity by allowing personnel to do the job rather than trying to figure out how to do the job and how to get around personal agendas that can sabotage a project. These test management procedures also provide a baseline method from which process improvement can be attained and measured. Developers who work on one or more projects within an organization will find the snags in the process and be able to bring suggestions and recommendations for implementing day-to-day operations that support improvement of the procedure and ensure its smooth execution.

The third benefit is that an organization can correctly staff an upcoming development effort. Whether individuals are going to wear one hat or support multiple roles on a project, management must make several decisions before the project begins. It must define in advance how the testing effort is to be managed. Management must also determine what type of decision makers are going to be needed. By doing so, it minimizes the risk that the staffing process omits the skills necessary to complete the job on time and within budget. In other words, the planning can be more accurate and cost overruns can be minimized.

When establishing test management procedures, management must remember that the procedure will be the guidelines not only for managing staff, test environments, and schedules, but also for determining the test readiness of software. Consideration must be given to configuration management in terms of version control, problem reporting and tracking, and the overall integrity of the test environment.

Section VIII – Checklist
Testing Software Applications

1. Does your organization have a dedicated testing group? If not, who performs most of the application testing in your environment?
2. What conflicts do you think occur when programmers test their own software? How does this affect program quality?
3. Is your development environment conducive for testing? Does your organization support a formal testing methodology?
4. Are you more likely to delay a project due to needed testing or forego testing for timely project implementation? Is this true in all situations?
5. What benchmarks do you use when evaluating the benefits of software testing?
6. Should software testing be aimed at finding errors or confirming functionality or both? Are these issues factored into your test plans?
7. Could the testing process be outsourced in your organization?
8. What are the differences between software and data testing in your environment? Are these treated the same in importance?
9. Assuming that you acknowledge the importance of testing, when was the last time you reviewed the basic principles behind the software testing process?
10. What book, seminars, conferences, or outside sources have you utilized in your testing efforts? Have these been worthwhile?
11. To what extent have you automated testing functions? Does your organization use automated tools or procedures?
12. How would you describe the ideal test environment? Is this based on time, staff, or technical tools available to you?
13. When does testing become troublesome in your environment? Is testing considered during or after development?
14. Does your IS environment use various testing procedures based on platform, or other development paradigms?
15. Do you approach software testing as a necessary evil, or as part of the design and development of the system? What is the opinion of your co-workers?

Section IX
Quality and Productivity Initiatives

IMPROVING THE QUALITY AND PRODUCTIVITY of application development is a tenacious goal for most IS organizations. Few managers would debate the virtues of these objectives as related to overall programming efforts. Despite this fact, many organizations struggle in achieving the caliber of excellence that is often desired by the software industry. Some of the adversity can be attributed to lack of sufficient time and availability of resources. More often, however, there is uncertainty on defining the exact criteria for success. Perhaps the more realistic solution should be acknowledging that quality and productivity are continuous processes throughout the software life cycle. Finding a specific endpoint to these attributes is less important than incorporating diligent procedures in everyday software development. In either case, it is important that development managers understand and pursue the ongoing trends used successfully by the computing industry.

The movement toward quality management has become a necessary, if not fashionable, concept in the past decade. Based on competitive pressure from worldwide economics, many businesses are striving to improve quality objectives across all organizational departments. Quality initiatives in the IS environment have focused primarily on software development rather than other IS areas. This is understandable, since quality efforts in development may provide the most leverage to corporate computing. Chapter IX-1, "Producing Quality Software," examines the various issues that surround the drive in software quality assurance. This chapter provides an interesting viewpoint by presenting both the human and technological perspectives of quality.

Most IS professionals strive to develop software programs that meet functional goals without sacrificing execution performance. Unfortunately, not every program can meet both goals on equal basis. And in some cases, performance becomes a secondary goal to functional specifications. Typically, achieving the necessary performance criteria can occur from upgrades to the processing hardware. In lieu of this, however, programmers are forced to review the options inherent in specific programming languages or run time compiler settings. Chapter IX-2, "Measuring Program

Performance," provides suggestions for assessing the actual run time performance of deployed software applications. Although the examples are based on the C++ language, the concepts can be applied to other language environments. Development managers should encourage programmers to pursue a harmonious balance between program function and program performance in order to satisfy the overall goals of application systems. In a follow-up, Chapter IX-3, "Program Performance Improvement Techniques," delivers a series of recommendations that can be utilized within the C and C++ programming environments.

Chapter IX-4, "Improving Productivity Strategically and Tactically," presents an outline for a productivity program that can be utilized by large and small organizations. A case study using the Software Engineering Institute (SEI) productivity model is provided to the reader. There is no single methodology that can satisfy all productivity requirements. However, the information in this chapter offers development managers an opportunity to implement a plan on a larger strategic level as well as the detailed tactical level. This combined course of action can be beneficial in organizations where other forms of productivity improvement have yielded poor results.

Chapter IX-1
Producing Quality Software

Bernard S. Klopfer
Craig S. Mullins

TOTAL QUALITY MANAGEMENT, QUALITY INITIATIVES, ZERO DEFECT SOFTWARE, AND SIX SIGMA PROGRAMS are becoming familiar terms to software developers. The drive to software quality is in full throttle and there is no turning back. However, what are the overriding factors that a software manager must understand before embarking upon a quality program? Why is a quality program important? Even more to the point, have not systems developers been striving to produce quality software already? This chapter examines aspects of software quality from personnel and technological perspectives.

PERSONNEL AND QUALITY

Changes in business needs demand that software developers pursue quality. The concept of quality applied to software products and end-user applications has traditionally been defined as the reduction or absence of defects. This is no longer a sufficient definition. In *The Decline and Fall of the American Programmer*, Ed Yourdon suggested that the quality of software is defined by the development process but most importantly by the people that manage and are managed within the process.

The human element is the most frail component in the software quality process, because each individual has a unique set of concerns that affect the management of change. To manage software quality, a software development manager must first be able to manage the people that produce that software. A software developer must be familiar with three typical behaviors of software professionals that can impede the production of quality software. These are examined in the following sections.

The Super Genius

A typical super-genius developer would say, "I can develop a better system with more features, slicker algorithms, and fewer modules—each with no more than 256 lines of code." This type of excessive creativity often results in late and over-budget delivery of the system.

When a systems project does not meet deadline, perception of the system is lessened because one of the greatest quality concerns among end users is on-time delivery. A common user sentiment is: What difference does it make if the system will work wonders, if I cannot use it when I need it? Software development organizations should not define software quality on behalf of their users. Reigning in the free-wheeling attitude of the super genius programmer may be difficult but is mandatory if software quality is a major imperative.

Produce or Perish

Another typical behavior has resulted directly from today's precarious business conditions. With corporate downsizing, early retirement programs, layoffs, and the like, employees are apt to believe that if they do not give more than 100% they will be terminated. Programmers and managers that exhibit produce-or-perish behavior view applications development as a means of survival. This type of software professional focuses solely on a product's delivery and not on its development. The classic cartoon showing a room of developers with a manager saying, "Everybody start coding and I'll go find out what they want" reflects this type of behavior. When challenged with a short delivery time frame, this type immediately reacts by ignoring the methodology, if one exists, and starting to produce the application without regard to quality.

Methodologies exist for a reason. They provide a controlled approach to application development. Steps are delineated that result in the optimal production of the required application system. If a methodology cannot be used for typical application development needs, the methodology is flawed and should be replaced with a more appropriate methodology or the decision to subvert the methodology is flawed and should be reexamined.

The bottom line is not to let an overzealous developer hastily deliver an application by ignoring the process initiated to produce applications properly (i.e., the methodology). Methodologies are important, but they cannot be dogmatic and inflexible.

A Room Without a View

Sometimes software developers feel that they operate best in isolation. This occurs when application development becomes a finite project performed in a vacuum rather than as part of an ongoing process. Software developers often have the perception of being so busy that they are unable to see their work as part of a continuous process. Consequently, they do not take the time to apply techniques or lessons they have learned. When the opportunities for improvement have not been formalized and recorded, the successes that occur are more often than not due to chance.

It is important that everyone on a software development team act and be treated like part of a team. Failure to do so reduces quality. A successful approach to initiating an attitude of teamwork can be achieved by following the 3-C approach: communication, cooperation, and clarification. A systems development manager must communicate effectively at all levels within a group. Cooperation among project members must be stressed. No member of any team should be able to say, "That is not in my job description." Of course, cooperation should not be viewed as a synonym for off loading work to co-workers. A systems development manager should also clarify all matters that are confusing. All members of project team should not blindly attempt to develop what they do not understand. The 3-C approach can eliminate isolationist attitudes and heighten the possibility for quality software.

LACK OF PROCEDURAL APPLICATION

Many good software engineering principles and methodologies are well-known and well-established. However, these principles are not applied because the techniques and tools are seldom clearly defined and institutionalized. A study of software engineering practices at major companies conducted by the Software Engineering Institute (SEI) stated that a mere 1% of organizations have instituted a formalized software development process.

The goal for software development organizations should be to reach the point at which the development process is closely managed and measured quantitatively, with improvement fed back into the process. SEI reports that none of the companies surveyed had achieved this level of development in their software engineering.

As startling as these statistics seem, the most surprising aspect of software quality has been the level of tolerance by clients. Traditionally, it was widely accepted that an IS department or software vendor would typically over promise and under deliver. The effect of delivering low-quality products was generally negligible because IS departments and software vendors were the only game in town.

Satisfying Clients

Software users today are more sophisticated and demand more functions and ease of use than they did 10 years ago. They have become more savvy customers because they have gained broad experience with commercial PC software products. The current trend toward demanding quality is a direct by-product of the personal computer revolution. End users have become less tolerant of spending a lot of time or money to produce applications or receive software products, both in absolute terms and regarding predictability. The broad acceptance of client/server and departmental computing shows that end users have a great desire to participate in and control the software development process. It is not a far stretch to state that the broken promises and high costs of previous projects have caused this desire.

The key to establishing quality is defined by customers' satisfaction, and it does not matter if the customers are from a small or major account or a small or large department. In an environment of intense competition, customer satisfaction is the only definition of quality that matters.

INSTITUTING A FLEXIBLE METHODOLOGY

Software development productivity has improved during the past 20 years, but perceived software quality—customer satisfaction—has not kept pace. Software development must be guided by a comprehensive software quality improvement program.

Commercial methodologies incorporate idealized procedures and methods but have proven to be ineffective and are viewed as nuisances. Procedures and structure are crucial to the success of software development but the need for these is not generally reflected as part of a commercial product. Most important for adopting a methodology is an agreement on a basic philosophy that underlies and supports the motivational factors of a product group. Almost as important, a methodology must be flexible.

The rigorous methodologies that are in place within most organizations are not successful because of their rigor. Shifting the understanding of those who must adhere to the methodology is crucial. This shift cannot be achieved without accomplishing two objectives:

- *Making a methodology less stringent.* Most commercial methodologies are procedural in nature and require strict adherence to a specific sequence of procedures. By not following this sequence so closely, a software organization can customize a methodology to its own development tasks.

- *Informing developers about the methodology and its purpose.* Without a stated purpose, a methodology usually fails regardless of how flexible it is, because developers will view it as bureaucracy and a hindrance. With a stated goal, however, a flexible methodology has a chance to succeed.

STREAMLINING PERCEPTIONS

A management group whose mission is to improve quality must define quality that satisfies customers. This may appear at first to be a simple task, but how developers perceive quality often differs greatly from support personnel's perceptions as well as end users', managers', and analysts'.

For developers, quality is improved execution and efficient memory use, slick algorithmic solutions, and efficient code. If a program or product achieves these goals, a quality product is delivered. In fact, some developers have contests to see whose code best meets these goals, but the winning code is often complex and cryptic.

This is where support personnel's, end users', and developers' perceptions of quality diverge. Developers are not usually responsible for providing direct customer support of a software product, and therefore the perception of software quality is the individual developer's. However, the perception of quality by technical support staff or end users is quantified by the gross number of problem calls.

When quality becomes a corporate mission and everyone in the organization becomes involved in quality, then the perceptions of quality software begin to change. Quality reflects reliability, and quality software must be reliable. Reliability improves customers' opinions and satisfaction.

THE TEAMWORK RESOLUTION

To respond to the demands of software consumers, software developers and support personnel must have a definite and progressive procedural structure. The product and all its problems should be the responsibility of the entire development group. This shared responsibility can create an environment in which everyone works toward the common goal of reliability and quick problem resolution. Too often does each function blame the others in the software organization for a poor quality product.

Instilling a quality philosophy is not an easy task and most quality assurance methodologies and programs do little to establish an underlying philosophy. Quality programs or quality experts often recommend tools and procedures that reflect ideals, which are difficult to attain. Also, implementation of quality programs usually does not take into account such important factors as reeducation, philosophy change, and management buy-in.

Implementation of a successful quality program begins with two basics:

- Working to define what quality means.
- Establishing a philosophy of pride and ownership of a product.

Once these goals have been accomplished, a measurement process can be established to evaluate whether the product meets or falls short of the quality definition. Customers' requests for enhancement or the number of support calls can be used to measure customer satisfaction. Areas of lesser quality then become focal points of the individuals responsible for those areas and personal pride plays a key role in improving quality.

CORPORATE ACCEPTANCE OF THE QUALITY INITIATIVE

Sometimes the process of instituting quality measures is considered a waste of time. Of what value is a 50% decrease in defects if it comes at the cost of a 50% decrease in production? Has quality actually increased in this scenario?

These are reasonable concerns. However, they are not necessarily valid. The first approach to take when confronted with this argument is to ask the skeptic to define productivity. Too often, managers base their definition of productivity only on new development. If a quality program reduces productivity in terms of new development, it will most assuredly increase software maintenance productivity. Up-front quality measures always reduce post-implementation defects. However, the productivity of maintenance is rarely, if ever, measured. Productivity measurements must be taken for all software engineering activities. After all, what is new development but radical maintenance?

Any change such as the implementation of quality improvement is accompanied by a learning process that initially reduces output. If communication and a rigorous training program accompany the quality initiative, then the initial decrease in production can be lessened. Communication is as important as training in lessening production falloff. To achieve success, management must communicate the following messages:

- The quality initiative is not a reaction to the current quality of the systems being developed; instead it is a phase in the evolving field of systems development.

- The quality initiative is being instituted so the company can more effectively compete in the marketplace, which benefits everyone in the company. It is not a ploy to reduce staff, enforce overtime, or simply shake things up. In fact, it may have the opposite effect. When things are done properly the first time, less overtime will be required; defects as well as management's desire to shake things up will decrease.

Following a quality program makes developers feel better about their jobs. Just knowing that the project is being rigorously tested and measured should instill pride of authorship in the developers that further enhances overall software quality.

When everyone understands that the quality initiative is a new and better way of doing things rather than a punishment for past failures, initial acceptance increases, thereby minimizing the growing pains associated with the new methodology.

Of course, every developer who is to participate in the quality initiative must be trained. Ideally, this training should include all developers. This is where management buy-in to the quality objective is essential. Without management commitment there will be no training. How can developers deliver quality products according to the approved methodology if they have not been trained? As the quality program becomes accepted and its components become understood, production will rise to and eventually surpass past levels—but not at the cost of quality.

PROMOTING QUALITY WITHOUT MANAGEMENT BUY-IN

In reality, the vast majority of software organizations pay much lip service to quality. It seems that there is never enough time to do it right, but always enough time to do it over. Major commercial software development companies spend millions of dollars on product support, fix releases, and patches for their customers. Most corporate data processing shops have 24-hour application support for problems occurring after normal business hours. Although the actual percentage of total dollars spent on these activities cannot all be directly tied to problems that arise from faulty software, faulty software can cost significantly. This cost is associated with customer and end-user perception of commercial and corporate applications.

So what can be done? How can quality software be promoted without management cooperation? As with most solutions to problems, the answer lies with the individual. The individual, in this case, is the manager who can influence or direct his or her teams with relative autonomy. When an individual makes a decision to travel down a particular path for self-improvement, goals and milestones are set to accomplish that achievement. The same applies to improving software development. Following are some suggestions for instituting process improvements that require minimal effort and reap significant benefits:

- Implementing process improvements in small steps, procedural changes that provide more structure to existing processes.
- Empowering members of the project team with responsibilities associated with the implementation of the application of structure.
- Getting the team involved in the process.
- Establishing and using inexpensive project management tools to track tasks and resources associated with all or one particular phase of a project's life cycle. This establishes baseline statistics and improves estimates for future projects.
- Instituting task tracking by linking time reporting to task completion through the use of individualized task sheets or spreadsheet links to project management tools.
- Adopting metrics associated with establishing these techniques:

- — Establishing baseline measurement of an easily definable result of process (i.e., end user satisfaction qualified and measured by the number of problem reports).
- — Instituting structured techniques, then measuring and analyzing results of the process.
- — Sharing the measurements and results with the team.
- — Evaluating applied structure and improvement.
- — Establishing a consensus understanding of quality products and results.
- Encouraging ideas for improvements from the team. There is much to be said for pride of workmanship.

These steps enable the improvement of quality. In short, the success of any process improvement begins with its participants.

Enabling Quality

The most important tools that can be used to promote continuous improvement are quality metrics based on an organization's major quality issues. These measurements provide a benchmark, feedback from end users, and direction for improvement for software development teams.

Some attributes of quality that usually contribute most to customer satisfaction are predictability, business impact, appropriateness, reliability, and adaptability. Predictability means knowing and controlling the risk factors involved, such as delivery date, cost, and resources needed. The business impact of quality relates to whether an application provides a significant benefit to an organization, even if it is not technically elegant or efficient. An appropriate approach provides a solution that is suitable to the business and technical problems that end users want addressed. Reliability concerns whether a system will work for its users when they need it. Adaptability means that the system and support can be changed cost-effectively to meet the evolving needs of the end users and the users' customers.

By breaking each of these quality issues down into their key components and then formulating a measurement system based on those components, managers can begin to get a handle on the software development process. The key, then, to a software quality management program lies in whether an application development process can be measured. If a process cannot be measured, it cannot be understood, controlled, or improved.

There is a hidden danger when developing quality metrics for an organization. If the metrics do not truly reflect what is indicative of quality for an organization, quality will be ill-defined and difficult to achieve. For example, if metrics measuring satisfaction are absent, a key part of quality will be ignored. Quality must be defined by those who use the software. Yet, metrics that define customer satisfaction are difficult to obtain. Usually, one must be content with metrics (such as those previously listed) that measure portions of the customer satisfaction equation.

USING TECHNOLOGY TO IMPROVE QUALITY

Although much of this chapter may seem to be railing against technology, this is not its intent. Technology for technology's sake will never result in quality systems. However, appropriate technology can increase overall software quality. For example, the biggest selling point of object-oriented (OO) technology is increased reusability, which can improve quality. However, one must approach technological advances with caution. Simply adopting OO technology for new software development does nothing about current legacy systems that were written using many different approaches. Likewise, technology must not be approached as a silver bullet. The history of software development is characterized by a long list of panaceas.

SUMMARY

Software development managers cannot institute a quality process if they do not thoroughly understand what that process entails. They must not only understand the technological aspects of software development but also the people aspects as well.

To implement a quality program, a systems development manager must apply the following key concepts:

- Understanding the needs of customers and meeting them even if the development staff's goals are not the same as the customers' requirements.
- Understanding the needs of software developers and instituting policies to involve them in the quality initiative.
- The three types of developers.
- The 3-C approach: communicate, cooperate, and clarify. Without all three, a project is doomed.
- Informing, instructing, and empowering individuals to operate within the quality program.
- Being firm yet flexible. A methodology should not be so restrictive as to tie the hands of a developer. Yet, it must not be so lax as to be ineffective.
- Establishing metrics to gauge the effectiveness of the quality program.
- Incorporating technological advances into the quality framework. Technology alone is not the answer to all needs. No technological advance can replace a software developer's abilities, experience, and knowledge.

Chapter IX-2
Measuring Program Performance

Paul J. Jalics and Santosh K. Misra

PROGRAM PERFORMANCE IS OFTEN CONSIDERED SYNONYMOUS with the speed with which a program solves a specific problem. The speed, in turn, is influenced by a number of factors, some of which are programmer controlled and others that are dependent on the hardware and software environment of the program's execution. Whereas tuning all programs for performance efficiency may not be necessary, some programs do exist that are "critical," and such tuning is essential.

PERFORMANCE

Performance has received too little attention in the programming workplace. Reasons for the lack of emphasis include the not-as-yet-mature nature of the discipline and rapid performance gains realized through faster hardware. However, performance may be more of an issue in the future, because the desired performance of a program may not be completely realizable through hardware advances alone, given the increasingly complex software products. As in engineering, when performance standards are usually a part of a product's specifications, a program's performance may become an integral part of a matured software engineering process.

Speed of execution is only one of the dimensions of a program's performance. Other performance measures include issues such as memory usage, code portability, and readability. As will be shown in this chapter, tuning a program for improvement in the speed of execution can lead to compromises in other dimensions of performance.

Critical Programs

Speed of execution, referred to as performance hereafter, is not an primary consideration for all programs. For example, performance may be irrelevant if a program generates results faster than they can be used. For many other programs, using a faster hardware platform may be more cost effective than spending the effort required in tuning. There is, however, a

0-8493-9979-3/99/$0.00+$.50
© 1999 by CRC Press LLC

small percentage of programs, say 10%, for which performance is of some importance. This chapter calls these critical programs.

A program may be considered critical for a number of reasons, including:

- The user may need the output shortly after the input is available, in a situation in which a short delay can lead to economic or more serious loss. Many real-time operations fall into this category when sensor-generated data, as in process control and command and control systems, need to be analyzed and results fed back to an appropriate decision maker. Computer control of a car engine is a good example.
- The user's productivity is adversely affected if there is a wait for the interactive system's response.
- Systems are critical when hardware upgrades are not feasible because of economic or technical reasons and when the performance goals must be achieved within the existing configuration.

Critical Parts of a Program

The execution time is not uniformly distributed among a program's statements. The authors' experience shows that a small part (e.g., 10%) of a program largely determines its performance; therefore, most of the performance improvements are achievable by concentrating on that 10% and leaving the remaining 90% of the code alone. This 10%, for the purposes of this chapter, is called the critical parts of a program.

It is not the authors' intention to imply that noncritical parts of a program cannot be used to derive performance improvements. Such improvements are possible but would lead to diminishing returns on the labor invested; that is, disproportionate amounts of labor may be needed for small improvements in execution time.

A PROCEDURE FOR IMPROVING PERFORMANCE

Four steps can lead to improving program performance:

- Measuring the initial performance of the program
- Identifying the critical parts of the program
- Improving the performance of the critical parts
- Testing the modified program, remeasuring the performance, and comparing it to the initial performance. If the results do not meet expectations, Step 2 is repeated

Measuring the Program's Initial Performance

Measuring the execution time of a program can be as simple as using a stopwatch to note the start and finish time of a program. Though this is a very crude method, it may be adequate in some cases when the program executes long enough (e.g., 10 seconds or more) so that manual timekeeping does not lead to too much error in the calculated elapsed time.

A more precise technique is to let the program compute its own execution time by recording the start and finish time through calls to its host operating system. Elapsed times can be reported by all operating systems.

Identifying Critical Program Components

One can identify critical components of a program through manual inspection. For example, inner loops of a program may contribute more significantly to the execution time. However, proper identification of such code is difficult even for experienced programmers who know the program well. Correct identification would require the programmer to be aware of such details as the amount of work done by various statements and the relative frequency of data access from the input files.

What Is a Program Profiler? It is most practical to use special tools to profile the performance characteristics of a program; the profile can then be used to identify the critical parts. The authors used the Borland C++ profiler tool to identify the critical parts of the program. Such a profiler supports an executable program that was compiled with debugging options, so that the user can talk to the profiler, a separate utility program, using source line numbers, procedure names, and source module names. The profiler also supports a source code window, so the user can point to places of interest in the program. The user describes what areas of the program are to be profiled: any procedure, module, or individual source code lines.

The user specifies a profiling mode to be active or passive. Active profiling means that code is modified to intercept the execution of the areas of interest, whereas passive means that the profiler samples the program counter during execution and generates a table of how often the areas measured are sampled. The active mode has the advantage of collecting all the information, but it has the disadvantage of increasing execution time dramatically, sometimes by a factor of 5 to 1000, depending on what level of detail is measured. The test program is then run under control of the profiler, which collects information about the execution. Information includes the number of times a procedure or individual source code line is executed and the execution time spent on that module or code line.

First Profiling Results

Just two procedures, fsscan and symlkins, out of a total of 30 account for 55% of the execution time, excluding input and output. Exhibit 1 shows the initial performance profile (module level) of the program in the case study.

Exhibit 1.   Initial Performance Profile (Module Level)

Turbo Profiler Version 4.5 Fri Jan 12 14:56:00 1996
Program: C:\T\ASM990.EXE → CPU Execution Profile(by Procedures)
Total CPU Execution Time: 2.5 sec
Total Elapsed Time: 24.7 sec

fsscan	0.296 sec	36%	|**************************************
symlkins	0.140 sec	19%	|*********************
wrasl	0.044 sec	5%	|******
bchecksum	0.044 sec	5%	|******
oplook	0.034 sec	4%	|*****
pass2	0.033 sec	4%	|*****
getval	0.027 sec	3%	|****
bpackout	0.024 sec	2%	|***
p1alloc	0.021 sec	2%	|***
expreval	0.019 sec	2%	|**
evopnd	0.018 sec	2%	|**
optabinit	0.015 sec	1%	|**
wrasl1	0.014 sec	1%	|**
boutdata	0.014 sec	1%	|**
pass1	0.013 sec	1%	|**
refsym	0.011 sec	1%	|*

(<1%: wrasl2, poper, outext, bwrline, doarith, regchk, syminit, tss, pcomma, chksflgs, treedump)

A statement level profile of symlkins, illustrated Exhibit 2, shows that 3 out of a possible 39 statements account for 85% of the execution time of the procedure. Because symlkins accounts for 19% of the program's execution time, the three critical statements of symlkins contribute 16% toward the overall CPU execution time. Special profilers can not only identify such critical code but also guide the improvement efforts, which, for the following example, should be directed toward the three statements of symlkins.

Setting the Goal: CPU vs. Elapsed Time Measurements

To be useful in performance analysis, a program profiler should have the capacity to report not only overall elapsed time, as measured with a stopwatch from the beginning of program execution to the time the program is finished, but also the CPU execution time (CPU) at various levels of detail. The authors define CPU execution time as that part of a program's elapsed time in which the program is executing CPU instructions; CPU execution time does not include other activities, such as waiting for input/output(I/O) to complete, executing operating system calls, or running other processes.

Before discussing improvement experiments, this chapter must describe a goal for the improvements (i.e., should the goal be to seek to reduce the elapsed execution time of the test program or to reduce the CPU execution time of the program). The elapsed time can be measured with a

Exhibit 2.   Statement Level Profile of Symlkins

Turbo Profiler Version 4.5 Fri Jan 12 15:00:26 1996
Program: C:\T\ASM990.EXE module FS.C → CPU Execution Profile(Line-by-Line Profiling of symlkins Procedure)
Total CPU Execution Time:
  2.5 sec
Total Elapsed Time: 24.7 sec

293.	[symptr])>0)0.056 sec	35%	***
if((ret = strcmp(id,symname		
295. else	[symptr]:swit lr = 1;}0.055 sec	34%	***
if(ret<0){stmptr = slinkl		
296. else found = 1;	0.027 sec	16%	**************************
319.	0.005 sec	3%	****
if(debgdict)dbddum(sympt		
r);		
282. int symlkins(char *id,	0.004 sec	2%	***
int *symp)		
291. csymdepth++;	0.003 sec	1%	**
320. *symptr = symptr;	0.002 sec	1%	*
290.	0.002 sec	1%	*
for(csymdepth = 0,found = 0;		
found == 0 && symptr! = 0;)		
{		

(<1%: lines 294, 299,288, 313, 312)

stopwatch, as just described, but measuring CPU execution time is a bit trickier.

Most multiprogramming operating systems (e.g., UNIX) provide built-in services that can measure both elapsed and CPU execution time between any two points in the execution of a program. Microcomputer operating systems, such as Windows and MS-DOS, do not provide services to measure CPU time. However, most competent compilers, such as Microsoft Visual C++ and Borland C++, offer profilers as part of the compiler software, and the profiler can estimate CPU execution time.

The most straightforward performance measure is elapsed time. On a multiprogramming computer system with dozens of processes executing concurrently. It is, however, unwise to measure elapsed time, because when the CPU is shared, elapsed time depends on what work is being done for the other processes. In such a case, repeatable experiments can only be run if the system is running standalone, with no other processes active. CPU execution time, on the other hand, is repeatable under any load, because the operating system accumulates CPU time only when the CPU is executing the process's CPU instructions.

CPU execution time is important, because it is easily repeatable and also because it measures the amount of work done by the CPU for the program. CPU time does not include waiting for disk reads and writes, as this does not involve the use of the CPU. Further complicating the question is the fact that the most common machines, personal computers, cannot as yet measure CPU execution time. Unfortunately, elapsed time is what is important to the user. Very little other work is typically done by such a computer concurrently, and few users care about how busy or idle the machine is, since it is inexpensive.

TESTING THE MODIFIED PROGRAM

A modified program needs to be tested to verify that it continues to execute correctly and to verify that its performance has improved. If the execution time is not reduced, it will be necessary to back up to the premodification state of the program. Therefore, it is essential to retain older versions of the program until changes are successfully tested.

If the new performance improves without meeting the overall goals, the programmer should go back to Step 2 (identifying the critical parts of the program) to identify anew the critical parts of the modified program. The critical parts of the modified program may be substantially different from that of the previous version. For example, if the three statements that contribute 85% of the execution time of symlkins can somehow be eliminated, the procedure may no longer be in the critical part of the program at all.

REDUCING CPU EXECUTION TIME BY 50%

[Once the critical program components are identified, code changes can be implemented to improve performance. Discussion of these code changes appears in Chapter IX-3, "Performance Improvement Techniques."]

This section describes a test case that the authors used to demonstrate the process of performance improvement.

Asm990, a cross-assembler program for a TI 9900 microprocessor, was used as the case study program. It accepts assembler source code for the TI 9900 as input and produces an assembly listing and an object file as output. Asm990 is written in C with some emphasis on making it as efficient as possible. The source program for Asm990 is about 1660 lines of code and consists of five modules: bnc29c.c is the highest level main module; pass1.c scans the source; p1alloc.c allocates memory; expr.c evaluates the expressions; pass2 generates the object code and produces the listing file. The case-study uses a synthetically generated input file consisting of 2745 source lines.

The authors implemented nine rounds of improvements (Rounds A to I) on Asm990 with a goal of reducing its CPU execution time by 50%. They chose the reduction of CPU execution time as their goal because that is where they find most of the techniques in performance improvement that they wish to demonstrate. Furthermore, reducing CPU time also reduces elapsed time. Finally, the authors will focus on elapsed execution time reductions in the final round (Round J).

The experiments were carried out on a Pentium 75 with a Windows development environment, but program execution took place in an MS-DOS window, because the application is not a GUI Windows application. This platform used Borland C++ 4.5. Exhibit 3 presents the elapsed and

Exhibit 3. Elapsed and CPU for Ten Rounds

| IMPROVEMENT | PENTIUM 75 | | NATURE OF CHANGE |
	ELAPSED	CPU	
Round A	24.7	2.5	original program
Round B	24.0	2.0	hashing randomizing 1
Round C	23.2	1.8	hashing dispersion 2
Round D	22.5	1.6	hashing buckets → 500
Round E	22.7	1.1	macros for sprintf,strcpy
Round F	18.0	1.2	xgetc #def macro: buf = 8,192
Round G	18.4	1.3	xgetc #def macro: buf = 24,576
Round H	18.0	1.1	* → <<,setmem to init struct
Round I	18.0	1.0	-Ox max compiler optimization
Round J	5.8	2.6	setvbuf 32,767 byte buffering

CPU for each of the 10 rounds. The initial elapsed time for Asm990 on the Pentium is 24.7 seconds and the profiler estimated CPU time is 2.5 seconds.

A summary of the improvements is presented in the following sections. The improvements in the test program involve only a few of the many techniques that are possible.

The sequence of experiments described in the following sections, concerning Rounds A to J, reduced the CPU execution time by 60% on the Pentium (2.5 to 1.0). Thus, the user might expect a 60% reduction in elapsed time from 24.7 to 10 seconds. However, the actual elapsed time decreased from 24.7 seconds to 18 seconds, a savings of only 29%.

Round A. This is the initial program, the outputs of which are used later to verify that the modified versions still work correctly. A profile of the program, the first table shown in this chapter, indicates that 55% of the CPU execution time is being spent in two procedures: fsscan (36%), which is the lexical analyzer, and symlkins (19%), which is the symbol table search routine. These two procedures then clearly constitute the critical parts of the initial program, and they are targeted for improvement. The profiling report also indicates that the CPU execution time was only 2.5 seconds, so that 90% of the time was spent on waiting for I/O, system calls, and library functions.

Round B. The symlkins is a small symbol table insert procedure consisting of only 40 lines, so it was chosen for improvement. The hashing algorithm used in symlkins was changed, resulting in a 61% reduction in the CPU execution time used. The old algorithm did not distribute well, and most of the symbols fell into three buckets of the 27 alphabetics possible. Symlkins, which took 19% of the program's CPU execution time, now takes only 9%. The overall CPU execution time is down to 80% of the original, and the elapsed program time was also reduced by 3%. This change was limited to only five lines of source code.

Round C. The hashing algorithm still did not distribute well enough to the 27 buckets, so it was modified to include a weighted sum by character position of the symbol character values. This resulted in a fine distribution of the symbols into the 27 buckets and reduced symlkins execution time by another 4%, so that it ended at 13% of the original. This change only involved two source lines. The whole program CPU execution time is down to 72% of the original.

Round D. This iteration involved changes in the size of the hash table for the symbol table from 27 buckets to 500 buckets. The change in size resulted in a further 45% reduction in CPU time for symlkins, to a level of 9% of the original. The whole program CPU execution time is down to 64% of the original.

Round E. This iteration involved minor changes to some 95 source lines in a number of functions in the pass2.c source module. The general principle was to replace library routines, such as sprintf and strcpy, by user-written preprocessor macros that perform the required actions inline. The advantage is derived from avoiding the procedure call overhead of the C++/C library routines. Also for sprintf, the preprocessor macro takes advantage of the simple hex formatting required rather than the completely general formatting done by sprintf. The overall program Central Processing Unit time was reduced to 44% of the original.

Round F. At this time, the fsscan procedure accounted for 35% of CPU execution time, and the line profiling for this procedure indicated that a line with a getc library call took the most time. Thus this round focused on writing a preprocessor macro to substitute the getc routine of the library. A large buffer of 32,767 bytes was created, and fread filled it up with a single read. The xgetcmacro then picked out single characters from this buffer and replenished the buffer when it became empty. Total CPU execution time actually went up slightly (8%), but the elapsed time dropped from 22.7 to about 18 seconds, a decrease of 21%.

Round G. This was a continuation of the previous round. The data buffer for the user-written preprocessor xgetc macro was increased by a factor of three to 24,576 bytes. The change in CPU execution time was negligible, as was the elapsed time. Apparently a buffer larger than 8192 produced no additional benefit.

Round H. Still trying to reduce the CPU execution time in pass2.c, the authors replaced a loop zeroing out individual fields including an array of structures with a setmem library call that zeros out a range of memory cells. This reduced Central Processing Unit execution time to 1.1 seconds, and elapsed time stayed at 18 seconds.

Round I. This final try involved turning on all possible compiler optimizations. The previous tries were with the compiler defaults. This resulted in an extra 10% Central Processing Unit reduction to 1 CPU seconds. The total program time is now at 40% of the original. The authors have surpassed their goal by 10%.

Round J. This application is clearly I/O intensive, so the above CPU execution times are tiny when compared to the elapsed times. The only round that saw a significant reduction in elapsed time significantly was Round F, in which the I/O buffering for the source input file was improved. The authors realized that the program uses several files: source input, intermediate output then input, a list file output, and an object file output. Therefore, the code was changed to add a setvbuf library function after each open, and the I/O buffer was set to 32,767 bytes for each. This change is similar to the xgetc change, but it is better and simpler, and the normal getc, putc, fread, and fwrite functions work faster. This results in the elapsed time being reduced to 5.8 seconds, which is a 77% decrease from the original. Unfortunately, more time is spent on buffer management, so the Central Processing Unit execution time jumped to 2.6 seconds, to be slightly higher than the original. Nevertheless, this last change is very much worthwhile, as the user will see the program work four times as fast as in Round A.

REDUCING THE ELAPSED EXECUTION TIME

Another way of looking at the results is as follows: The CPU execution time of 2.5 seconds is only 10% of the total elapsed time of 24.7, so what the authors have done is reduce the 2.5 seconds to 1.0, and — all things being equal — the elapsed time should have decreased by only 1.5 seconds as well. Instead, it decreased 6.7 seconds! The explanation is that the changes have had a big impact on the time spent executing system calls, especially I/O-related ones. For example, the xgetc #define macro used in round F executed fewer freadlibrary calls by reading huge blocks of a file into a large 24K buffer, so the number of system calls was reduced by a factor of 100, and the I/O wait time was also reduced by doing fewer larger read system calls.

To reduce the elapsed time further, Round J was initiated to reduce the elapsed time further. Taking a lead from the xgetc experience above, the authors looked for a runtime library to improve I/O buffering on all four of the files the program accesses. The setvbuflibrary function allows the user to set the I/O buffer size.

The authors set the I/O buffer to its maximum of 32,767 bytes for all files in the program and reran the experiment, arriving at an elapsed time of 5.8 seconds, which is just 26% of the original. Unfortunately, the additional buffer management brought the CPU execution time back up to 2.6, which is slightly higher than the original.

CONCLUSION

The results of the experiments show that a program initially written with some attention to performance can still be improved substantially if it is analyzed systematically. The gain in performance would be even more dramatic if the original program were a typical C program (i.e., written without performance considerations in mind).

CPU execution time improvements should also reduce elapsed execution time. But in this case study, the real benefits came by actually increasing CPU time, which was a side effect of using the setvbuf library routine. The user was delighted because his 24.7-second execution time was reduced to 5.8. On a real multiprogramming system, such as UNIX, with 100 such assemblies executing at once, this change can be viewed as negative. Because it increased CPU execution time from 1.0 to 2.6, the throughput of the whole system might be reduced, and this could lead to slower program execution for an individual program.

In addition, the direction and magnitude of the improvements on one system, such as the Pentium 75, cannot be used to predict the improvements on another system, such as a HP9000 UNIX workstation. Some of the techniques yield similar results on all architectures, but others may vary substantially.

Chapter IX-3
Program Performance Improvement Techniques

Paul J. Jalics and Santosh K. Misra

NOT ALL PROGRAMS REQUIRE SPEED OF EXECUTION, referred to in this chapter as *performance*. There is, however, a small percentage of programs — roughly 10% — for which performance is of some importance. This chapter calls these *critical programs*. In addition, execution time is not uniformly distributed among a program's statements. The authors' experience shows that most performance improvements are achievable by concentrating on the 10% of a program that largely determines its performance and leaving the remaining 90% of the code alone. This 10%, for the purposes of this chapter, is called the critical parts of a program. These are the areas of concentration in this chapter.

A Procedure for Improving Performance

Chapter IX-2, "Measuring Program Performance," describes the four steps that lead to improving program performance:

- Measuring the performance of the initial program.
- Identifying the critical parts of the program.
- Improving the performance of the critical parts.
- Testing the modified program, remeasuring the performance, and comparing it to the initial performance. If the results do not meet expectations, Step 2 is repeated.

This chapter concentrates on Step 3, improving the performance of a program's critical parts, almost all of which can be used with C as well as C++. A number of these techniques are well known from the compiler design area. Some can be implemented by a programmer during coding; others depend upon special knowledge, such as the behavior of the compiler used, characteristics of the hardware, optimizing features of the compiler, and nature of the data being processed.

PERFORMANCE CHARACTERISTICS OF THE COMPILER

The authors started the performance improvement exercises by profiling the characteristics of the specific compiler and hardware combinations.

0-8493-9979-3/99/$0.00+$.50
© 1999 by CRC Press LLC

Exhibit 1.   CPU Execution Times

ID	Data-type	Pentium_75	HP9000	VAX-4000	Sun-Sparc4	DEC-Alpha
x1	int local	1.00	1.00	1.00	1.00	1.00
x2	long local	1.78	0.98	1.00	1.01	1.00
x3	char local	0.81	1.10	1.44	1.37	1.34
x4	bit-field auto	1.39	1.22	3.73	2.43	6.31
x5	int global	0.80	1.19	1.41	1.76	7.79
x6	int parameter	1.00	1.02	1.03	1.00	1.00
x7	int register	0.63	0.67	0.99	0.69	1.00
x8	int static	0.81	1.09	1.02	1.37	1.07
x9	int ele of struct	1.14	1.00	1.02	1.04	1.84
x10	int array[j]	1.61	2.11	1.30	2.29	3.62
x11	int via pointer	1.80	1.18	1.07	1.25	1.98
x12	int ptr>struct ele	1.75	1.19	1.02	1.28	2.67
x13	int ptr>ptr2>ele	2.90	1.58	1.59	1.77	6.46
x14	int array[i][j]	3.55	2.84	1.94	3.80	1.60
x15	unsigned int local	0.96	0.97	1.03	1.01	.55
x16	float local	1.81	0.72	0.50	0.96	1.00
x17	double local	1.98	0.77	0.68	1.08	1.52
x28	short local auto	0.91	1.08	1.48	1.48	1.33
x29	unsigned short auto	0.63	1.05	1.44	1.46	1.34

They used benchmark programs that can profile any C++/C compiler, measure the performance of various data types (i.e., procedure call overhead, I/O conversion overhead, library call overhead, and looping overhead), and allow determination of what is fast and what is not on a given hardware/software platform.

Extracts from the results of the benchmark programs run on the Pentium 75 are shown in the table in the next section. Though not shown in the table, these benchmarks were also run earlier on other systems, including DEC Alpha, which is a new 64-bit processor, DEC VAXs, a Sun Sparcstation 4, and an HP9000 UNIX system. The UNIX system test results will be used occasionally to gain a perspective into variations in performance on various computer systems.

A CHOICE OF DATA TYPES

A given data type performs differently on different computer systems. Exhibit 1 summarizes some of the results of CPU benchmarks for various data types on a variety of systems. Each column of this exhibit shows CPU execution times for identical tests run with different data-types. The individual values represent the performance relative to the base type of a local integer (int).

The results for the Pentium 75 show the following:

- Performance of local int, local short, and int parameter are all about the same.
- Unsigned short is 37% faster than the above, whereas global int, local char, and static int are about 20% faster than local int.
- Long is much slower than int at 178% of int.
- The register attribute on a declaration seems to have a substantial effect, saving 37% compared with int.
- Processing of the float floating-point is 181% of int, and double is just a little more, at 198% of int. Similar measurements on software emulated floating point are 66 times as slow. The Pentium is the worst of the systems by far for both float and double.
- Use of bit fields do not have a serious adverse effect on Pentiums, and they can be used efficiently when needed (39% extra overhead, as compared with int). Performance on the other systems is substantially worse with the DEC Alpha, taking over six times as long as int.
- Array subscripting is quite efficient, especially for one-dimensional arrays, with a penalty of about 60%. Subscripting in such cases is more efficient than dereferencing a pointer.
- Referencing a field of a record by a pointer to the record is as efficient as having a pointer to the record field directly.
- Integer multiply is four times as slow as addition, and integer division is 9 times as slow as subtraction. Multiplying by powers of two is twice as fast as shifting left (<<), and dividing by powers of two is 6 times as slow as shifting to the right (>>).
- Adding two numbers is nearly 7 times as fast as calling a procedure to do the same. On the DEC Alpha, the procedure call is only twice as much as the inline add.

Results for the DEC Alpha 64-bit processor indicate the following:

- The performance of int, long, param int, register int, int static, and float are about the same.
- Unsigned int is 45% faster than int, but unsigned short is the same as short (33% slower than int).
- Whereas float is as fast as int, double is 52% slower than float.
- Bit fields are very inefficient, at 637% times as much as int.
- Single subscript array access is very slow at 362% of int, but surprisingly double subscripting is only at 160% of int.
- Accessing a field of a record by a pointer is much slower than having a pointer to the field directly.
- Integer add, subtract, and multiply take about the same time, whereas division is 42 times as slow.

- Using multiply by powers of two is much faster than shifting left (<<), whereas dividing by powers of two is 13 times as slow as shifting to the right (>>).
- Adding two numbers using a procedure is only 267% as much as doing it inline. This procedure call overhead is very low on the Alpha.

A programmer often has a choice of the data-type to be used and therefore can influence the performance of a C++/C program from the knowledge of the behavior of a data-type on a given computer system. For example, on a 16-bit machine, such as the Pentium 75, the data types char, int, long, and unsigned are all integer types and can be used interchangeably depending on the range of values to be represented. However, use of a long to represent a value with a range of 0 to +100 would bring an additional 78% compared to an int'. On the other hand, similar use of long on an HP9000 is actually 2% faster than int. Also, it is more expensive to specify short signed and unsigned auto instead of long. Likewise, use of a float or double on a machine without floating-point hardware may take 66 times as much time, but it is actually faster on the HP9000 and the Sun Sparcstation 4. Performance tradeoffs among the following pairs should also be considered when either member of the pair can be used in a program:

- unsigned vs. signed
- global vs. local variables
- automatic vs. static memory allocation
- float vs. double precision floating point
- direct access vs. access through pointers
- subscripting vs. indirecting via a pointer

As this discussion shows, it is important to know the relative performance of various data-types to realize the maximum performance on a given system. On many occasions, changing of the data-type in an existing program can be a relatively easy way to improve performance.

C++ SPECIAL CONSIDERATIONS: PROCEDURE CALL OVERHEAD

One observation about object-oriented programs (OOP) in general and C++ in particular is that the OOP discipline tends to create many objects, each with several relatively small member functions (i.e., 30 to 100 lines). If most procedures are smaller in comparison to non-OOP programs, it seems logical that OOP programs will cross substantially more procedure boundaries in getting the same task accomplished as non-OOP programs. This factor increases the importance of procedure call overhead in C++ programs.

While the inline feature of C++ is intended to reduce this overhead, C++ compilers often give up or abort inlining because of procedure length or complexity. A good optimizing compiler should do such inlining as a

Exhibit 2.   Overhead Measurement Program Results

	Pentium	HP9000	SunSparc4	Vax4Alpha	Description of What Is Measured
1	0.20	0.90	0.19	.0012	Call normal function
2	0.05	0.83	0.22	.0012	Call inline member function
3	0.34	0.77	0.22	.0012	Call non-inline member function
4	0.05	0.82	0.22	.0017	Call virtual inline function
5	0.34	0.79	0.22	.0017	Call virtual non-inline function
6	0.05	0.89	0.22	.0012	Call overridden inline member function
7	0.34	0.82	0.22	.0012	Call overridden non-inline member function
8	0.05	0.80	0.22	.0018	Call overridden virtual inline function
9	0.34	0.83	0.22	.0018	Call overridden virtual non-inline function
10	0.35	0.80	0.20	.0011	Polymorphism base (ptr to simple member function)
11	0.47	1.18	0.39	.0110	Polymorphism of non-inline virtual array
12	0.48	1.16	0.39	.0111	Polymorphism of in-line virtual array
13	0.23	0.85	0.21	.0007	Call normal function with 1 param
14	0.23	1.04	0.26	.0004	Call normal function with 2 param
15	0.26	1.04	0.33	.0004	Call normal function with 3 param
15	0.28	1.11	0.45	.0004	Call normal function with 4 param
16	0.32	1.19	0.58	.0004	Call normal function with 5 param
17	0.33	1.15	0.66	.0004	Call normal function with 6 param
18	0.37	1.21	0.76	.0004	Call normal function with 7 param
19	0.39	1.27	0.84	.0004	Call normal function with 8 param
20	0.47	1.40	0.90	.0004	Call normal function with 9 param

standard feature, as do the Unisys 2200 C compiler or the IBM VS/COBOL II, which does inlining for up to two levels of nested PERFORMs.

The authors developed a procedure call overhead measurement program and learned the results shown in Exhibit 2.

A comparison of tests 1 and 3 indicates that in half the cases there is additional overhead of calling a member function, sometimes as much as much as 70%. One would expect a higher overhead for C++ member functions, because in calling member functions, C++ adds one hidden extra parameter, namely the pointer to the object being referenced. The actual increase in overhead for other systems has been measured to be from 4% to 35%. The authors do have an anomaly on the HP9000 in which the member function is actually faster.

Making a member function as inline (tests 2 vs. 3) often reduces the calling overhead from 45% to 85%. The best reduction, 85%, is on Borland C++ and may also be indicative of a relatively high procedure call overhead on the Pentium 75 when compared to DEC and Sun systems, which are relatively faster in procedure calls. The smallest reduction is on the DEC Alpha systems, on which the role of the procedure call overhead is lowest.

Another explanation of why inline on two of the systems makes no difference is that the C++ compiler may not do inlining or not do it well.

In addition, there is extra overhead of adding parameters one at a time (i.e., tests 1, 13 through 20). Whereas the additional overhead is fairly constant on the Pentium at about 15% for adding one parameter, the Sun Sparcstation 4 is the worst, with an average of 43% increase per parameter. The very best was the DEC Alpha; procedure overhead did not increase at all with the number of parameters.

On the Pentium the virtual member functions and overridden member functions do not have any performance penalties over other member functions when the compiler can figure out at compile time which function is to be called (i.e., tests 2 through 9). On the HP9000 and the DEC Vax 4000, however, the overhead is similar, with or without virtual. Finally, on the DEC Alpha, there is a 41% increase in execution time for all virtual functions.

When member function access is by a pointer (i.e., test 10), the performance does not seem to slow down at all on any of the systems. Also, specifying inline has no effect in these cases.

When polymorphism is involved (i.e., tests 11 through 12), the member function is accessed by pointers where the appropriate possibly inherited function needs to be decided on at execution time by a virtual array. The execution time for polymorphism increases more than when member function access is by a pointer — by 37% to 1000%, the least on Pentium and the most on the DEC Alpha system.

Recognition of such performance characteristics can guide a programmer not only during the initial design but also during improvement phases. For example, programs written for the DEC Alpha platform are less concerned with procedure call overhead, except in the case of polymorphism, than those written for the Pentium 75.

Strategies for Reduction in the Calling Overhead

The inline attribute can be used in declaring C++ class member; this will simply cause C++ to insert a copy of the machine instructions for a procedure where it is called. This means all of the procedure call/return overhead can be avoided at the price of a larger object program. If the member function is only called a few times, this additional memory size is insignificant.

Preprocessor Macro. One of the strategies to reduce call overheads is the use of a preprocessor macro instead of a procedure call. This option is open for both C++ and C. For example, the following code is in a program:

```
int sumtab(int tab[],int len)
        {int sum,i;
        for (sum = 0, i = 0; i < len; i++)
                sum += tab[i];
        return(sum);
        }
. . .
main( )
        {
        . . .
        tsum1 = sumtab(taba, 15);
        . . .
        tsum2 = sumtab(tabb, 128);
        . . .
```

Call overhead can be avoided by replacing sumtab by the preprocessor macro sumtable:

```
#define sumtable(tab,len,res) {int i; \
for (i = 0, res = 0; i < len; i++) res += tab[i];}
. . .
main( )
{
. . .
sumtable(taba,15,tsum1);
. . .
sumtable(tabb,128,tsum2);
. . .
```

Even though the interfaces of sumtable and sumtab are not identical, both sets deliver exactly the same function. Because sumtable is a preprocessor macro, the compiler replaces every call to the macro by its code at compile time, and hence there is no procedure call overhead. However, a penalty is paid through higher usage of memory and an increase in compile time, but these do not usually affect the execution performance, except when this is used extensively in demand paging systems. Higher usage of memory, in most cases, is not a matter of great concern, as the cost of memory continues to go down.

Preprocessor macros may not be feasible if the procedure's code volume exceeds compiler limits for preprocessor macros, typically 10 to 15 lines, or the volume and the number of calls are both large making code expansion at compile time undesirable. Converting a procedure to a preprocessor macro is not difficult to do manually; it is just a small headache.

Collapsing of a Procedure. In some cases, it may be desirable to collapse a procedure into its calling procedure. This is a desperate move that is worthwhile only if the function is called a very large number of times in a program, and is only called from one place.

Parameter Overhead. A decrease in procedure call overhead can be achieved by reducing the number of parameters passed. For example, the address of a record containing all the original parameters may be passed, instead of the parameters themselves. A large interface is also an indication of tight coupling between the caller and the procedure and is sometimes the result of poor module design. For such cases, redesign of the procedure would be the key to improving performance.

Executing Work Internally. It is also possible to reduce procedure call overhead by designing modules such that procedure boundaries are crossed as infrequently as possible. In this way, procedures can be designed to do a lot of work internally before exiting or calling other procedures.

Using C++ I/O Streams Versus C stdio

A number of measurements were undertaken to see if the new C++ I/O streams have a higher performance than the corresponding standards I/O in C. Results vary from system to system and measurements are needed to get a perspective of performance in this area on the programmer's system.

Using Class-Implemented Data Types in C++

One of C++'s most impressive features is the ability to create new data-types by creating a class to do so and can even make the operations overload the standard +, -, *, and/operators, for example. Measurements indicate that the performance of such new data types needs to be looked at carefully. For example, implementation of Int and Char were used in a Dhrystone benchmark instead of the standard data types, int and char, and the performance showed degradations from 43% to 93%. Also, the particular choices made in the implementation, including the use of inline, parameter passing by value vs. reference, and the use of virtual functions, can greatly affect performance.

Using C++ Container Class Libraries

The use of class libraries is one of the most important advantages of using C++. However, Jalics and Blake have found that the performance of such container-class libraries for lists, stacks, and arrays, is typically much slower than code written by the individual programmer to do such tasks (see Chapter IV-1, "Benchmarking C++ Performance," and Chapter IV-2, "Performance of Object-Oriented Programs: C++"). Factors of 5 to 1000 in worse performance are common. Again, such class library usage in critical parts of the program should be examined and perhaps replaced with the individual programmer's code or preprocessor macros.

ARITHMETIC PERFORMANCE

Arithmetic performance of the authors' Pentium Borland C++ compiler follows expected patterns; multiplication is about four times as slow as addition and subtraction. Division is about nine times slower than addition. A limited set of computation, specifically, multiplication and division by powers of two, can be improved by doing arithmetic shifts, because these operations are as fast as addition. Thus A = A * 8 can be replaced by A = A << 3. Round H (see Chapter IX-2, "Measuring Program Performance") of the authors' experiments replaced about a dozen such multiply expressions with left shifts to achieve a 15% CPU savings.

Elimination of Common Sub-Expressions

The subexpression $a*b+c$, calculated twice, is illustrated in the following statements:

```
sum1 = rating1 + (a*b+c) * result1;sum2 = rating2 + (a*b+c) * result5;
```

The code could be written as:

```
weighting = a*b+ c;
```

```
sum1 = rating1 + * weighting result1;
```

```
sum2 = rating2 + * weighting result5;
```

This would eliminate the duplication. Whereas a good optimizing compiler may do the above automatically, it is simple enough to do it manually in critical parts of a program.

Elimination of common subexpressions can yield substantial performance dividends provided these involve complex computations. For example, while working on a simulation program, the authors encountered the following critical code segment:

Line

```
1 Dx = v * cos (theta) – va;
2 Dy = v * (theta);
3 off_rail = y > = seat_hgt;
4 d = 0.5 * rho * cd * s * v * v;
5 if (off_rail)
6 {Dv = off_rail * (-d/mass-g*sin(theta));
7 Dtheta = off_rail*(-g*cos(theta)/v);
8 }else Dv = Dtheta = 0;
```

The authors changed the code by adding two lines at the beginning:

```
cosva = cos (theta);
sinva = sin (theta);
```

They also replaced cos and sin function calls in lines 1, 2, 6, and 7 above by cosva and sinva, respectively. This minor change decreased the execution time of the entire program, which is about 2800 lines, from 68.3 seconds to 55 seconds, a 19.5% reduction of the original time.

Equivalent Code Substitution

It is possible to improve arithmetic performance in some cases by substituting one set of code with another equivalent set. For example, in the simulation example referred to in the previous section, sinva = sin (theta); can be replaced by sinva = sqrt(1 – cosva*cosva); recognizing the trigonometric identity of the expressions. This change, in fact, was executed, resulting in the reduction of the program's run time to 52 seconds, a total reduction of 23.9% of the original. Equivalent code substitution should, however, be done cautiously. For example, the trigonometric identity can cause serious inaccuracy if cosva is near 1.

PERFORMANCE OF CONDITIONAL STATEMENTS

Performance benefits from conditional statements require some knowledge of the characteristics of the data being processed. Conditional statements can then be written to take advantage of those characteristics. The general strategy is to test for specific values that would eliminate most of the other testing.

Tests in a Sequence

In a case in which a sequence of tests is done to choose only one of the alternatives, the code should be written to test for the most likely value before the next most likely value. For example, if the probability of truth for conditional expressions boolean_1 through boolean_5 is known to be 3%, 15%, 1.8%, 80%, and 1.2%, respectively, then the tests should be ordered as follows:

```
if (boolean_4) {do_update( ); return(0); }

if (boolean_2) {do_new( ); return(0); }

if (boolean_1) {do_skip( ); return(0); }

if (boolean_3) {do_buy( ); return(0); }

if (boolean_5) {do_sell( ); return(0); }
```

This sequence will find the appropriate action in one or two tests for 95% of the cases. Notice that a test order of one through five would require about four tests to accomplish the same.

Repeated Testing of the Same Condition

In the following example, the same condition code_type == value is tested over and over even though code_type can have only one value.

```
if (code_type == 'A') sum += 10;

if (code_type == 'B') sum += 15;

if (code_type == 'C') sum += 20;

if (code_type == 'D') sum += 25;

if (code_type == 'E') sum += 30;
```

If we know that values A, B, C, D, and E occur at the rate of 5%, 10%,3%, 80%, and 2% of the cases, respectively, the set of tests could be reformulated as:

```
if (code_type == 'D') sum += 10;

else if (code_type == 'B') sum += 15;

else if (code_type == 'A') sum += 20;

else if (code_type == 'C') sum += 25;

else if (code_type == 'E') sum += 30;
```

Notice that the reformulated code not only takes advantage of the probability of test values but also avoids duplicate testing. This means that in 95% of the cases only one or two tests are made, as compared with exactly five tests for the original code.

In some cases, repeated testing is not done immediately afterwards, as in the following:

```
if (j == 'E' && k == 'C' && l == 'A') do_special( );

main_action( );

if (j == 'E' && k == 'C' && l == 'A') do_wrapup( );
```

Such cases can be handled by using a flag, as shown in the following example:

```
if (j == 'E' && k == 'C' && l == 'A')

    {ecaflag = 1;do_special( ); }

else ecaflag = 0;

main_action( );

if (ecaflag) do_wrapup( );
```

In other cases, the code can be packaged in a big ifstatement, such as:

```
if (j == 'E' && k == 'C' && l == 'A')

    {do_special( ); main_action( ); do_wrapup( ); }

else main_action( );
```

The latter example has the disadvantage of repeating a segment of the code. Therefore, the choice of using this strategy may depend on the length of the repeated code. The trade-off between code size and execution speed should be used to choose between the two strategies.

Compound Conditions

The knowledge of likely occurrence of a value can be gainfully used for testing logical ors and ands. For example, assuming the distribution of values shown in the repeated testing section earlier in this chapter, the following statement can be written in a descending order of likelihood:

```
if (j == 'A' || j == 'B' || j == 'C' || j == 'D' || j == 'E')
```

The descending order of likelihood would appear as follows:

```
if (j == 'D' || j == 'B' || j == 'A' || j == 'C' || j == 'E')
```

This order could be used instead of chronological or some other random order. Formulating the logical or in a descending order of likelihood allows the programmer to take advantage of the fact that the compiler will stop the tests as soon as the truth of the compound expression is established. Thus, the evaluation of the compound expression would stop for 80% of the cases after only one test, with a further 10% after two tests, and so on.

Similar approaches can be used for logical ands. However, unlike the ors, the ordering of logical ands has to be in the ascending order of likelihood, so that the most unlikely value can be checked first. For example, assume that each of the variables *j*, *k*, *l*, *m*, and *n* have the same distribution of values as above. Then if (j == 'D' && k == 'B' && l == 'A' && m == 'C' && n == 'E') will require more than 1 test 80% of the time, whereas the improved version, if (j == 'E' && k == 'C' && l == 'A' && m == 'B' && n == 'D'), will be evaluated to be false after only one test for 98% of the cases.

CASE STATEMENTS

Coding principles described for conditional statements apply in this case. An additional consideration is whether the case values are densely (i.e., 0,1,2,3,...) or sparsely (i.e., 12,52,97,...) packed, because many compilers generate faster code when the values are densely packed. The user can choose the values in some cases and can emulate dense packing by providing value clauses for all possible values. For most systems studied, densely packed case values lead to a better performance. On the Pentium 75, for example, the dense values in a switch statement reduce execution time by 79%. However, on the DEC Alpha, the results for the dense save only 3%.

LOOPS

There are no significant differences among the performance of various types of loops for most of the compilers studied. Therefore, unless a particular compiler implements a particular type of loop more efficiently, a programmer can be indifferent regarding the choice of a looping mechanism. The performance of loops can, however, be improved in some cases through a careful consideration of the loop's body.

Invariant Code in a Loop. Removal of invariant code, if any, from within an inner loop can lead to performance gains. The following is an example:

```
for (trip_cost = 0, i = 0; i < 15; i++)
    trip_cost += miles[i] * (price_per_gal/miles_per_gal);
```

The ratio of price_per_gal and miles_per_gal is invariant in the loop and could be calculated only once before the loop is entered.

Arithmetic Expressions Within a Loop. The statement in the previous section can be further optimized by noting that multiplication is slower than addition by a factor of about four on the Pentium 75. Therefore, for such a machine, the code could be rewritten as:

```
for (tot_miles = 0; i = 0; i < 15; i++)
    tot_miles += miles[i];
    trip_cost = tot_miles * (price_per_gal/miles_per_gal);
```

This reduces the computational overhead, because the multiplication is done once instead of 15 times.

Linearizing Loop Statements. In a few rare cases, a loop can be unrolled or linearized by repeating the contents of the loop for each time it needs to be executed. For example, if the miles table in the example mentioned earlier contained only 3 entries instead of 15, the loop could be eliminated:

```
trip_cost = (miles[0]+miles[1]+miles[2])*price_per_mile;
```

Minimizing the Iterations. The number of iterations can be minimized by terminating a loop as early as possible. An example is the zip code table for a given input:

```
for(this–0; this < 999; this++)
        if(ziptab[this]–inzip)
                zipptr–this;
```

The number of statements executed can be reduced by 50% on the average if the code is written as follows:

```
for(this = 0; this < 999; this++)
        if(ziptab[this]–inzip)
                { zipptr = this;
                break;
        }
```

Once the programmer finds the subscript for the correct entry, he or she does not need to continue trying the remaining entries.

INPUT/OUTPUT PERFORMANCE

The slowest activity during the execution of a program is its input and output (I/O). Some of the main conclusions regarding I/O are summarized in this section.

An I/O operation, such as getc/putc, is 3 to 200,000 times slower than a memory-based operation, such as an assignment (most calls are a factor of 3, but when the disk buffer needs to be replenished, the factor can be as high as 200,000). Use of getc/putc is generally as efficient as using fread/fwrite of large blocks of data.

In a typical printf statement with one variable to a disk file, the output conversion takes about 26% of the total elapsed time; the rest is waiting for the I/O to complete. Also, writing to the screen takes over 10 times as long as writing to a disk file.

I/O Buffer Size

The single most effective tool for improving I/O performance is increasing the I/O buffer size using the setvbuf library function. This reduces elapsed time dramatically for getc, putc, fread, fwrite, fprintf, and fscanf.

Most of the overhead associated with I/O is incurred each time a physical operation is started. The volume of data transferred during a given I/O does not affect the execution time as much as the number of I/O starts. Therefore, I/O routines that put data in large buffers and do actual physical I/O only when those buffers are full, or empty on input, have a dramatic effect on I/O performance. The authors experimented with buffering in case study rounds F, G, and J (see Chapter IX-2, "Measuring Program Performance").

The authors declared their own I/O buffer of 8192 bytes in Round F and wrote a xgetc preprocessor macro to execute block and character level input in fsscan:

```
#define xgetc(y) (sptr?)sinbuf[sptr++]:\

((slim=fread(sinbuf,1,8192,y)) <= (sptr=0)) ?EOF:sinbuf[sptr++])
```

However, this did not reduce the CPU execution, indicating that the authors' scheme was not any more efficient than getc, which is also preprocessor macro driven. However, elapsed time was reduced dramatically, by 21%. The authors' xgetc is probably faster simply because their buffer was bigger.

The buffer size was subsequently increased from 8192 bytes to 24,576 bytes in Round G, but this did not improve either CPU or elapsed execution time, because the 8192 buffer had already reaped most of the benefits available.

The authors' experience shows that user-written I/O procedures are not significantly beneficial in performance in comparison to library routines. This is so because the C I/O mechanisms getc, putc, fread, fwrite, printf and fprintf already use buffered data, and some of them are also efficient preprocessor macros. Buffer sizes of some of these macros can also be controlled with C library calls, such as the setvbuf library call used in Round J (see Chapter IX-2, "Measuring Program Performance"), which resulted in the most dramatic elapsed time improvement: A 68% reduction in elapsed execution time. Therefore, it is difficult to improve C++/C I/O performance because it is already good, and the remaining options include the programmer's doing I/O conversions and executing as few I/O calls as possible — with each transferring as much data as possible.

Reduction in I/O Volume

Eliminating I/O operations altogether is another strategy in controlling performance. Unfortunately, this can be applied only in a few cases. In one such case, I/O can be reduced by loading a table from a disk file at the start of the program and then, during program execution, data is accessed from the table rather than from the file, thus eliminating many calls to a disk file. An example is an invoicing system in an organization that has 100 stores. The system processes 50,000 orders and requires a random access lookup on the store placing the order. Because there are only 100 stores, the store records can be read into a table in memory and accessed from there for each of the 50,000 order records. Thus, the table loading takes 100 sequential reads and can save 50,000 random reads of the store file.

User-Written I/O Conversion Routines

In some cases, the speed of I/O can be improved through user-written conversion routines instead of relying on standard conversion facilities, such as sprintf. The benefit from such user-written routines is demonstrated in the case study in Round E (see Chapter IX-2, "Measuring Program Performance"). A segment of the critical code in wrasl contains a sequence of sprintf statements. These statements format binary values into four-digit hexadecimal ASCII for writing to the listing file. Because there is very little potential for improving the performance through such strategies as removal of statements, change of data-types, or the nature of the output lines, the authors decided to convert the series of sprintf statements into simpler and specifically tailored formatting routines. The authors wrote two preprocessor macros, hexem and sprintf4, to accomplish the conversion, as follows:

```
#define hexem(y) (y>9)?((y+'a'-10):y+'0')

#define sprintf4(x,y,z) x[0] = hexem((z>>12)&0xf);\

    x[1] = hexem((z>>8)&0xf); x[2] = hexem((z>>4)&0xf));\

    x[3] = hexem(z&0xf);
```

sprintf4 takes an unsigned int and converts it to a sequence of 4 ASCII characters. These changes, along with a few other preprocessor macros, resulted in savings of about 31% of the execution time for wrasl. The benefit comes for two reasons: (1) we do not incur a procedure call overhead on the preprocessor macros, and (2) our formatting is very specific and limited whereas the sprintf formatting is completely general.

POINTERS AND SUBSCRIPTS

Reduced address calculation is one option for improving performance. C++and C give the programmer the choice of subscripting through a table, as in the following example:

```
for (sum=0, i=0; i < 15; i++) sum += tab[i];
```

Another choice is to use pointers to access elements of the array, as follows:

```
int *ptr;

for (ptr = tab; ptr < &tab[15]; ptr++) sum+= *ptr;
```

The performance of these two techniques may vary significantly and is quantified by comparing the statements int array[j] auto and int via pointer in execution measurements of the C statements run in the Pentium_100Borland_4.5_CPU_Tests, as conducted by the authors. The performance differences may be even more pronounced if the item being accessed is a multidimensional array or a chain of pointers from one structure pointing to other structures. Performance can be improved by dereferencing the chain of pointers and calculating a pointer directly to the actual object, especially if this object is repeatedly accessed. For example, an object shock1 can be accessed through shock1p = &cust->car1->shock1 as *shock1p or alternatively as cust->car1->shock1. If shock1 is repeatedly accessed, the address calculation will save at least one memory access per reference to shock1.

Performance of Structure Elements. On some systems, it is more efficient to have a structure with several elements, whereas on others it is more efficient to have half a dozen variables that are freestanding and not part of a structure. For example,:

```
struct ctl_blk { int field1,field2 } rec1;

int f1,f2;

a: rec1.field2 = rec1.field1;

b: f2 = f1;
```

Statement a is 14% slower than statement b on the Pentium, and 84% slower on the DEC Alpha, but about the same in the other systems.

CONSIDERATION OF THE LIBRARY ROUTINES

C++ and C provide a large number of library routines. Some of these deliver system services and cannot be easily substituted. However, others, such as string handling routines (e.g., strcpy and strcmp), provide facilities for data manipulation. In general, these library routines are efficient but are implemented as general procedures and incur calling overheads for every invocation. In many cases, the significance of the overhead varies with the amount of data processed by the routine. Thus, the strcpy routine may be the most efficient when processing more than 10 characters when the calling overhead becomes negligible, but much slower than in-line code at string lengths of 1 to 4 characters.

A programmer can write tailored preprocessor macros to substitute library routine calls if the characteristics of the data being handled is known for the particular application. For example, consider case study Round E (see Chapter IX-2, "Measuring Program Performance"). Performance of Asm990 could be improved by substituting strcpy by the following

643

code for four-character strings and another similar preprocessor for two-character strings:

```
#define strcpy4(x,y) x[0] = y[0]; x[1] = y[1]; x[2] = y[2]; x[3] = y[3];
```

USE THE REGISTER ATTRIBUTE ON VARIABLES

C++ and C compilers have a register attribute that can be used on any data declaration. The compiler then tries to allocate a machine register to store that variable during program execution. This option is of interest especially on machines that have a large number of general-purpose registers, such as the RISC architecture machines. The user must investigate whether his or her compiler uses this feature, and if so, he or she must carefully place the register attribute on a very small number of declarations in a given procedure. These register declarations should be chosen only for the most frequently referenced variables. It is also useful to know whether the compiler allocates the first or the last variables in case more variables are declared than available registers.

COMPILER PERFORMANCE OPTIONS

Most compilers offer choices relating to various performance issues. These choices may include optimization for execution time, memory space, memory models, stack integrity checking during execution, and use of registers. Sometimes the implications of these options are not obvious from the documentation provided. The most direct approach is to do a little experimentation to see if a given feature has an impact on a specific situation.

MEMORY ALIGNMENT CONSIDERATIONS

While users do not usually have control of the memory alignment of the variables used, they do have control over the alignment of variables placed in a record or data structure. Each hardware architecture has certain favored memory alignments for structured data. For example, the Intel 80x86 processors use the following:

- ints (16-bit) should be word aligned and start at addresses 0, 2, 4, 6, 8, 10, and so on.
- longs, floats, doubles, and pointers should be double word aligned and start at addresses 0, 4, 8, 12, 16, and so on.

The Intel Pentium processor allows variables to be misaligned but may process unaligned accesses more slowly than aligned ones. Users can control the variables in a data structure by assuming that the record begins at a maximum alignment boundary, such as double-word aligned, and by assuming that variables are allocated in the order in which they are declared in the structure. For example, the following record has all the fields properly aligned:

```
struct good1 {
char field1;   /* starts at 0 bytes offset in record*/
char field2;   /* starts at 1 bytes offset in record*/
int field3;    /* starts at 2 bytes offset in record*/
long field4;}; /* starts at 4 bytes offset in record*/
```

The same fields can be written in a different order. As shown below, struct good1 is rewritten such that field3 and field4 are not properly aligned:

```
struct bad1 {
    char field1;     /* starts at 0 bytes offset in record */
    int field3;      /* starts at 1 bytes offset in record */
    long field4;     /* starts at 3 bytes offset in record */
        char field2;};   /* starts at 1 bytes offset in record
        */
```

field3 should start at an even address but starts at 1, and field4 should start at an address divisible by 4 but starts at address 3.

Some C++/C compilers will insert so-called "slack-bytes" to ensure that each field has the proper alignment. Sometimes there is a compiler option to control such slack-byte insertion.

ALGORITHMS USED

Choice of algorithms in a program is always a good prospect for performance improvement. For example, if the critical code of a program includes table searching, the performance can be improved by using binary search (i.e., order log2n) instead of a sequential search (i.e., order n). Similarly, memory sorts can be improved from order n2 for bubble sort to order nlog2n for merge-sort, for example. Changes in algorithms usually involve significant rewriting of a program, but such changes may not be too difficult in a well-designed modular program. The authors found that if Rounds B, C, and D are considered to be algorithmic changes (see Chapter IX-2, "Measuring Program Performance"), a 36% improvement in CPU execution time results from these improvements.

VIRTUAL MEMORY CONSIDERATIONS

If a program is to execute in a virtual memory system with demand paging, its performance can be improved by minimizing the use of page swaps. Code locality is generally one of the best strategies for minimizing page swaps. A simple example to reduce paging can be the scanning of a two-dimensional array or higher. Assuming that it is necessary to scan the array int matrix[100][100], paging can be minimized by accessing contiguous memory elements, as would occur from the following:

```
for (i= 0; i < ncols; i++)

for (j = 0; j; j++)

matrix [i] [j] = 0;
```

On the other hand, page swaps would increase if the statement in the inner loop above is changed to read matrix[j][i] = 0, slowing the execution time.

CONCLUSION

The authors' experiments in the case study show that the performance of a C++ or C program can be improved substantially using some of the techniques described in this chapter and Chapter IX-2, "Measuring Program Performance." The magnitude and effort required, however, depends upon the initial quality of the program from the performance perspective. Most programs are not written with performance in mind and are easily improved. For programs written with performance considerations, as in the case of Asm990, improvements are still possible. In either case, improvements can be continued so long as the performance analyst is able to identify the critical code of the program and effect tuning without excessive effort.

A critical factor governing performance analysis is the knowledge of what works on a specific machine architecture and the hardware/software platform. Also, the performance characteristics may change substantially from one release of a compiler to the next, so the measurement assessment of a compiler may need to be repeated with changes in the software and/or hardware platform.

The above assessment is necessary since all of the techniques described do not have a uniform effect on the execution speed across various machines and software systems. Also, some of the techniques may not be necessary because an optimizing compiler may already do the same automatically. It is also worth noting that many of the techniques described in the chapters do affect other quality parameters of the program, such as readability and portability, and in some cases trade space for time. However, when performance is essential, these limitations may be acceptable. In any case, the number of source lines affected by the changes are likely to be quite small, indeed.

Chapter IX-4
Improving Productivity Strategically and Tactically
Stanley H. Stahl

MANY SOFTWARE DEVELOPMENT ORGANIZATIONS have embarked upon improvement programs designed to improve product quality or development productivity. Some programs are general, following methodologies like those of the Software Engineering Institute (SEI) or more generic TQM-based programs. Others are specific, attempting, for example, to institute upper-CASE technology or implement a software metrics program. Unfortunately, failure among both these types of improvement initiatives is common.

Although there are several reasons for failure, one of the main causes is the failure to adhere to the simplest principle: "Think strategically—act tactically." All too often, in their zeal to get quick results, managers rush into action without carefully considering the strategic necessities appropriate to their cultural and environmental realities. Less frequently, but nevertheless still common, managers allow themselves to get wound around the strategy axle, allowing their improvement programs to die from analysis paralysis.

STRATEGY AND TACTICS

Successful productivity improvement programs have both a strategic and a tactical component. The strategic component, focusing on the big picture, combines a knowledge of the best practices in the industry with a deep awareness of the needs, opportunities, and constraints of the organization. The tactical component, focusing on the details, is used to translate the strategic component into the specific actions necessary for program success.

STARTING THE IMPROVEMENT PROGRAM

At the strategic level, an organization must begin its productivity improvement program by analyzing its business situation, processes, technologies,

0-8493-9979-3/99/$0.00+$.50
© 1999 by CRC Press LLC

and culture. In doing this analysis, software developers must consider such strategic questions as:

- How aligned is the development organization to the business needs of the company?
- How satisfied are users with the products of the development organization? Is product quality satisfactory?
- How satisfied are users with the development organization? Is product quality satisfactory?
- How satisfied are users with the development organization's time-to-deliver?
- How satisfied is senior management with the systems development process's cost structure?
- How good are the organization's current development processes?
- How do these compare with those of other development organizations?
- How advanced is the organization's product technology? How does it compare with those of other development organizations?
- How effective is the organization's use of CASE tools? How does it compare with those of other development organizations?
- How effective is the organization's training program?
- How open to change is the organization?
- How is employee morale?

Assessment Programs

Because the answers to these questions form the foundation of all subsequent improvement efforts, it is vitally important that software developers objectively assess their organizations, with respect to both current practices and the best industry practices. The assessment is a thorough examination and not a public relations opportunity. Because of the importance of the initial assessment and the difficulty of getting an accurate analysis, many organizations have found it valuable to have a consultant help with it.

Following the initial assessment, the second strategic step is to identify both the organization's goals and the constraints on achieving these goals. The result of this analysis may be, for example, a conclusion that the organization needs to improve product quality, and the primary constraints limiting quality are inadequate review and inspection processes and an inadequate training program. A more extreme example is the organization needs to improve product quality and delivery time, though it has no defined process, employee morale is low, and the organization is very resistant to change.

Proceeding with Caution

The next strategic step is to identify the key leverage points associated with achieving productivity improvement goals. This step requires an understanding of the organization, gathered in the initial assessment, with an understanding of the realities of productivity improvement. Organizations often err at this stage by attempting to implement a high capability method or tool without the needed infrastructure. Lots of companies, for example, have invested heavily in CASE tools only to see them underutilized. This often occurs because an organization lacked either the process discipline or the training capabilities needed to use the tools properly.

Developing an Action Plan

The final strategic step is to develop an action plan. The action plan acts as the bridge between the strategic and the tactical. Consequently, it must translate the strategic objectives and constraints into a workable plan for productivity improvement. Like any good plan, the productivity improvement action plan needs to lay out what is to be done, when it will be done, who is responsible for doing it, how it is to be tracked, and what resources are available for getting the job done. The plan should have a nominal two-year time horizon.

Implementing the program. After the action plan is developed, it must, of course, be implemented. There are several principles that underlie successful implementation of the productivity improvement action plan:

- Implementing improvement activities project by project.
- Providing lots of evaluative feedback for the productivity improvement process.
- Underpromising and overdelivering.
- Getting and maintaining the support of all stakeholders.
- Proactively managing the change process.
- Paying particular attention to employee morale.

A CASE STUDY

Hewlett-Packard Co. provided a case study of how to simultaneously think strategically and act tactically. The company needed to improve software quality, because it was finding that embedded software was becoming more and more critical to its product line. The next generation LaserJet, for example, has 1,000,000 lines of embedded code, 40 times more embedded software than the first generation LaserJet. More than 70% of Hewlett-

Packard engineers now work, either part-time or full-time, on software. Software has become the dominant factor responsible for the company's ability to generate more than $20 billion in annual sales.

Improving Productivity of Software Development

Recognizing the importance of software to its ongoing business success, Hewlett-Packard's management instituted several years ago a corporate software initiative program in partnership with its business groups. The objective was to use software to a competitive advantage. The results to date have been positive. One group has reduced its time-to-market from 50 months to 10. Another group has reduced the average time needed to correct a defect from 27 hours to 8. Overall, Hewlett-Packard's management believes that the implementation of inspections has saved $20 million per year and that this amount will grow to $100 million per year as software inspections become standard throughout the company.

Management of Strategy and Tactics

There are several factors that contributed to Hewlett-Packard's success at improving its software development productivity, but an important factor is the company's explicit management of both the strategic and tactical components to process improvement. Exhibit 1 shows a flowchart of how Hewlett-Packard identifies and implements productivity improvement through new and revised development processes.

Strategic component. The company starts its strategy cycle by identifying the productivity improvement efforts that are to be undertaken in support of identified business interests. This point is critical. Unless productivity improvement interests are tightly coupled to the business interests of the organization, they are irrelevant. And if they are irrelevant, it is difficult to generate and maintain the management commitment necessary for sustainable improvement.

Tactical component. On the tactical side, Hewlett-Packard makes a point of pilot-testing every new process before deploying it throughout the organization. Thus, early feedback on the process is available for the evaluation and fine tuning of the process before its deployment.

THE SEI PROCESS ASSESSMENT MODEL

Hewlett-Packard is not the only organization to have mapped a route to successful productivity improvement. The Software Engineering Institute

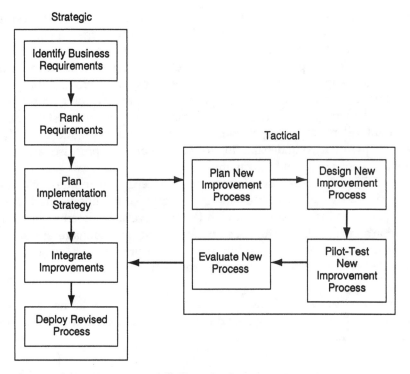

Strategic

Identify Business
Requirements

Rank
Requirements

Plan
Implementation
Strategy

Integrate
Improvements

Deploy Revised
Process

Tactical

Plan New
Improvement
Process

Design New
Improvement
Process

Evaluate New
Process

Pilot-Test
New
Improvement
Process

**Exhibit 1. Flowchart of How Hewlett-Packard Identifies and Implements
Productivity Improvement**

(SEI) has developed a very detailed program for productivity improvement
that focuses on improving the software development process. More than 100
companies in the US are using the SEI's model to improve their software
development processes.

SEI's process improvement model explicitly integrates the strategic with
the tactical. It commences with an organization's taking a strategic assessment of its current process capabilities. The output of the assessment is a set
of findings, designed to capture the needs, opportunities and constraints for
process improvement. These findings are then turned into an explicit action
plan that forms the bridge between the strategic and the tactical.

The Model's Framework

The foundation for the SEI model is for an organization to get basic management control over the development process. This means working on such
areas as project planning, project tracking and control, requirements man-

agement, subcontractor and supplier management, quality assurance, and configuration management. After establishing basic management control, an organization is then able to work on establishing an infrastructure for standardizing effective processes for all projects. Improvement activities at this stage include introducing peer reviews, working on improving intergroup coordination, beginning an explicit process focus, and working on the organization's training program. Next, an organization focuses on establishing a quantitative understanding of both its processes and its products. Finally, it uses its quantitative understanding to improve both its processes and products in a continuous and measurable way.

The SEI model uses a set of software engineering capabilities, which are divided into five levels. Organizations are supposed to improve productivity and quality as they progress through the five levels. To determine an organization's current level, SEI uses an assessment questionnaire and a five-point grading scheme. The grading scheme measures an organization's software development practices according to the five levels.

Level 1: Initial. The software process is characterized as ad hoc and occasionally even chaotic. Few processes are defined, and success depends on individual effort.

Level 2: Repeatable. Basic project management processes are established to track cost, schedule, and functional capabilities. The necessary process discipline is in place to repeat earlier successes on projects with similar applications.

Level 3: Defined. The software process for both management and engineering activities is documented, standardized, and integrated into a corporate-wide software process. All projects use a documented and approved version of the organization's process for developing and maintaining software. This level includes all characteristics defined for level 2.

Level 4: Managed. Detailed measures of the software process and product quality are collected. Both the software process and products are quantitatively understood and controlled using detailed measures. This level includes all characteristics defined for level 3.

Level 5: Optimizing. Continuous process improvement is enabled by quantitative feedback from the process and from testing innovative ideas and technologies. This level includes all characteristics defined for level 4.

Strengths and Weaknesses of the Model

One of the most valuable features of the SEI model is that it explicitly identifies a relative time-ordering for implementing process improvement activities. This time-ordering helps a developing organization strategically identify the steps it needs to take in improving its software development process capabilities. It is based on the premise that, much like building a skyscraper, it is necessary to build a strong foundation before attempting to build above ground.

A major strength of SEI's approach is that it carefully articulates a strategy model to help an organization develop a software process that is under statistical control. A limitation of the SEI model is that it explicitly focuses only on process improvement. Thus, the model provides little guidance to the organization from the perspective of business alignment, culture, and technology. A second weakness is that it puts off peer reviews and inspections until the second stage, though these activities are among the highest leverage processes for improving product quality and shortening development time.

SUMMARY

When senior management is pressed to provide quarterly results to shareholders, the result is, all too often, that the focus of productivity improvement is on adopting the latest and greatest whiz-bang technology. It is very important to avoid this temptation. Productivity improvement is a 26-mile marathon, not a 100-yard dash. The greatest opportunities for sustainable and meaningful productivity improvement occur by focusing on process and culture and by clearly aligning the development organization to business needs. Failure to pay proper attention to the strategic dimensions of process, culture, and business alignment too often consigns a productivity improvement program to failure.

Section IX – Checklist
Quality and Productivity Initiatives

1. Does your organization have a formal methodology for software quality? Does it work?

2. How are programmers in your environment educated about the quality process?

3. Is there a dedicated quality control group in your organization? If not, where are quality standards managed?

4. As a development manager, what steps do you take to ensure the quality of the software that is deliver to end users?

5. Do you consider quality management part of the software development process or part of the business development process?

6. Should software quality be reviewed during the testing phase of a project or during the design phase? How is it handled in your environment?

7. Does reduction in maintenance tasks reflect improvement in development quality or is it a function of application system complexity?

8. Can software quality improvements be measured accurately or is it too difficult to assess.

9. Has your organization ever halted implementation of a development project due to poor quality? If not, does this mean that quality is not important?

10. Are you familiar with software metric measurement techniques? If so, have you applied any metric measurement to development or support tasks?

11. Has your organization used software metric tools to establish a baseline complexity for all software programs in your installation? If not, is there a future opportunity for such activity?

12. Without the benefit of a formal measurement tool, would you estimate that your average software program is simple, moderate, or severe in complexity? Could you assess this based on maintenance effort?

13. Should productivity be measured in the number of written lines of code, the number of written programs, the ability to meet development schedules, or the quality of programming syntax?

14. What performance tools would be valuable to your efforts to improve program execution? Do these tools exist?
15. In your opinion, are "productivity" and "quality" textbook attributes that will never be achieved, or do you believe in pursuing these objectives as part of your professional commitment to the computing industry? Do other staff members share your opinions?

Section X
Leveraging Staff Resources

HARMONIZING THE DIVERSE NUANCES OF HUMAN BEHAVIOR with the technical complexities of application development can be strenuous as well as frustrating. Whether supervising computing professionals, communicating with end users, negotiating vendor contracts, or maintaining technical expertise, development managers must consider a myriad of personnel situations. This also includes career counseling, turnover, training, disciplinary action, motivation, and hiring. Unfortunately, few managers are fully prepared to embrace such a broad array of nontechnical skills. Nevertheless, within current business environments, the ability to persevere with all types of human resource issues is essential.

Attracting talented software professionals to accomplish development goals remains extremely challenging. Perpetual changes in technology have created fragmented pockets of skilled workers. And many of these workers vary in competence and ability. Additionally, the demands of business competition, including the Year 2000 crisis, has created a serious shortage of technical expertise. As a result, retaining qualified personnel has become a critical issue. Chapter X-1, "Fostering Loyal and Long-Term Employees by Raising Organizational Identification," offers valuable insight on the issues that can affect personnel stability. As turnover costs escalate, many organizations will need to find alternatives to cope with further shortages of programming talent.

Technical training has been an important and well recognized method for retaining software professionals. Training has also become a critical factor in reducing the shrinking labor pool. Many organizations are reeducating software professionals on newer technologies in an attempt to leverage existing business knowledge. Other organizations view training as an ongoing process that should be incorporated as part of the overall development life cycle. But training is not a panacea, nor is it as easy to implement as may be thought. Chapter X-2, "Training Options in a Technical Environment," and Chapter X-3, "Training and Hiring Systems Staff," both provide specific viewpoints on retaining skilled software professionals via training. The misconceptions and realities of retraining existing staff are closely examined with suggestions and guidelines that are practical. Development managers should establish a balanced plan that can attract needed professionals and ensure staff longevity.

Finding the time and the method for self-improving professional knowledge has been difficult for the vast majority of IS professionals. In particular, development managers may be most affected by the nature of their work. Supervising development staff may keep numerous managers from hands on technical expertise. Over time, the technical knowledge gap widens with added administrative responsibilities, and the continuous advancement of computing technology. Chapter X-4, "How to Stay Competitive Professionally," offers practical advice on methods and techniques for expanding professional expertise. Computer technology has, in itself, provided a rich environment for self-education. Automated software study packages, Internet-based instruction centers, and network-based research tools offer a wide array of learning opportunities. But these mechanisms are not effective without self-commitment. IS professionals still need to follow a disciplined approach to acquiring and maintaining professional knowledge.

Despite the advancements in software technology that enable business departments more autonomy with application development, there still exists a communication barrier between software professionals and end users. More often, communication problems have been the source of failed development endeavors and weak application deliverables. Chapter X-5, "Improving Communication Between End Users and System Developers," offers some valuable suggestions that can minimize difficulties between formal and less formal technical environments. Additional insight is given on methods that can improve relationships between IS staff and end-user professionals. Effective communication is an essential factor for applications that are codeveloped. Development mangers should strive to breakdown barriers that can possibly exist across departmental boundaries.

Chapter X-1
Fostering Loyal and Long-Term Employees by Raising Organizational Identification

Carl Stephen Guynes, J. Wayne Spence, and Leon A. Kappelman

THE INCREASED ORGANIZATIONAL RELIANCE on IT has led to the evolution of a group of highly technical IT specialists who display certain distinctive common characteristics. Among these common traits are

- High growth needs
- High professional identification
- Low organizational identification

IS professionals tend to like the change and challenge of their work and generally have high standards of professional conduct and performance.

Unfortunately for most employers, they also exhibit low organizational identification — that is, they do not exhibit a strong sense of identification or commitment to their current employer. Although there is little an organization can do about fostering the growth needs of its employees, and can have only a limited, albeit important, influence upon their sense of professionalism, an organization can take significant actions to foster their sense of identification. All too often, however, these actions are not taken, and organizations experience not only high turnover and all of its associated problems, but, more important and enigmatic, fail to optimally utilize their information assets.

This historical low organizational identification problem is now being manifested by other organizational members as more firms downsize; thus, the prescription for IS personnel may well have a wider context. The IS professional knows that since their skill set is in demand, if they become disenchanted with their current employer, they can find a suitable job with another firm by investing a minimum amount of effort. Perhaps because of

0-8493-9979-3/99/$0.00+$.50
© 1999 by CRC Press LLC

their employment flexibility coupled with the specialized nature of the work, it is not surprising to discover a peculiar cliquishness associated with small, specialized work groups such as that found in IS shops. This exclusiveness of interest and resulting camaraderie fosters a sense of functional identification among some IS staff members at the expense of organizational identification. But these are not mutually exclusive conditions and this does not have to be the case.

IS Employees' Concerns are Not Always the Company's

In many cases, these IS professionals are not really concerned about the organization. They have a job to perform, and it does not matter to whom they report. Organizational problems only secondarily affect them, and they are frequently indifferent regarding the nature of a problem. They do their job in much the same way regardless of whether they are working for a public sector organization or a large private corporation. The problems that they face may be different depending upon the particular organization they work for, but their approach to solving the problem is handled in a similar fashion.

In many instances, the organization's philosophy of management further contributes to the negative attitude held by these specialists. Organizational management often does not identify with its own personnel. Many managers do not understand the technical environment and have no desire to learn about them. These managers are often in a position where they must accept the use of the systems, but they do not try to understand them.

Low Loyalty and High Turnover

Organizational loyalty in IS sections is often minimal and the personnel turnover rate is frequently high. Many information systems managers try to explain this high turnover rate as simply a characteristic of technical personnel. Professional employees tend to stay with organizations and need more justification for making a change. It is generally felt that satisfied workers will not arbitrarily jump from one job to another. However, since some of these highly technical computer personnel do change jobs frequently, they are evidently not satisfied with their work environment. Yet, job-hopping is not a function of technical expertise, since engineers do not seem as prone to rapid employment change.

It is management's task to attempt to determine the source of employee discontent. This task can be extremely difficult when management must deal with technically oriented IS personnel, for it is difficult to make them feel that they are supplying a unique contribution to the organization. These employees must feel that they are part of the organization and not merely a separate group of people unrelated to the organization as a whole. The problem of satisfying the IS employees is, in many ways, similar to providing satisfaction for any type of specialized knowledge worker. It is common to find specialists, especially technical specialists, in any organization being treated similarly to IS personnel. It is, therefore, necessary for human resource management to look into the makeup of IS specialists in order to understand them in their peculiar situation.

WORK PROFILE OF IS PROFESSIONALS

IS professionals quite often feel a great degree of professionalism concerning their duties even though their superiors may not share these feelings, for they have acquired an impressive technical knowledge and talent for efficiency and technique within their own specialized area. Specialists must keep several important IS concepts in mind at all times and must be aware of the concept of change management. They must be prepared to install and maintain multiple systems while maintaining a certain level of efficiency, security, and reliability. IS specialists are rarely satisfied if a system simply works — it must possess the same degree of excellence that other craftsmen would devise. If they are not allowed to act as craftsmen, no personal pride can be attached to the work they completed.

The IS professional also tends to reject historical managerial control, which compounds the problem. Of particular importance is the dislike held for traditional auditing procedures and internal security measures. These procedures and measures are for the most part viewed as nuisances that keep the IS professional from doing the job efficiently and are often inadequate safeguards against error and invasion. It is common for such procedures to be rejected by the highly skilled IS personnel, because they perceive them to reflect upon the character of their immediate work group.

Lack of Organizational Identification

As mentioned previously, the lack of organizational identification can cause many of these problems. Therefore, a look at the IS specialists' profile could help to generate solutions to the problem. Although many IS personnel prefer not to become involved with the employing organization on a personal basis, the organization can emphasize that each individual is an integral part of the whole and does possess special talents worthy of notice. Such recognition of ability will surely help increase the employee's organizational identification.

In many cases, the IS professional feels that his or her contribution to the organization goes unrecognized. This is partly due to the nature of the work. When working on a system, the professional is immersed in the problems and daily activities of other organizational units. However, once the project has been completed, it is common that the IS professional has no idea of what has happened (is happening) to the system. Multiple levels of feedback are necessary to solve this problem.

FEEDBACK FOSTERS ORGANIZATIONAL IDENTIFICATION

Minimally, at least two forms of feedback are important. First, the IS professional needs feedback on how the system is working. This may be in the form of positive and negative information about system consequences. If the system is performing well, the IS professional receives personal satisfaction for a job well done, as well as an element of job closure. If the feedback is negative, the IS professional can use this information for product improvement and later system development. For the IS professional, not knowing how an employer uses and values information systems is a significant element of lack of organizational identification.

The second useful form of feedback is how a system contributes to the organization's bottom line. If IS employees can establish how their efforts are contributing to the overall organizational goals, they will feel more organizational identification.

Promoting Recognition. To amplify the impact of this feedback, recognition of contribution could be easily established. For example, a "best system of the year" award could be established to promote recognition of how individual systems and people are contributing to the organization. These awards would not even have to be monetary, but rather a plaque, certificate, or internal publication citation. The important factor is the recognition, not the form of the award.

COMMITMENT TO THE IS GROUP

However, organizational identification may be the wrong approach. Perhaps it is more important that the IS professional give his or her most significant allegiance to the IS function, even if there are problems. Within the IS function, individuals tend to work in project groups or teams. These groups are charged with the responsibility for completing the activities to which they are assigned. Yet, once the group discharges its responsibilities, the group is disbanded. Thus, any personal relationships with other individuals within the group or personal commitments to the group itself are severed when the group is disbanded. Thus, it is no wonder that the IS professionals feel no organizational commitment — they may not even feel any identification with the IS function within which they serve.

Tactical Teams

The solution to this problem is the creation of tactical work groups or teams rather than the more strategic nature of team development today. Tactical teams would by necessity have to be highly specialized and relatively small. However, the objective to be achieved is to have the individual member develop a sense of belonging and consequently commitment. In today's team environment, individuals often feel like interchangeable cogs in a machine. This feeling is the most significant reason for rapid job movement among IS professionals. There are, at present, few emotional reasons for staying put when another job around the corner has a few more dollars attached to it.

CREATING STRONGER ORGANIZATIONAL IDENTIFICATION BY PROMOTING EMPLOYEES

Many corporations now view IS professionals as potential managers. These employees have worked with many of the functional departments of an organization due to the nature of their work, and if they are knowledgeable concerning the procedures of each end-user department, they could be well equipped to view the organization as a whole. It is sometimes difficult to perceive an information systems analyst as a potential manager because of their seemingly technical role, a problem similarly experienced by engineers and scientists. However, many systems analysts are well suited to assume this type of position and seek the new challenges that a new role would afford.

This is not to say that a low-level IS specialist with a limited educational background is qualified to be a high-level manager. It does mean, however, that a qualified individual with a good educational background in business, who has a strong technical background and organizational experience, could excel at other responsibilities within an organization and have an understanding of an organization's aims and accomplishments. This person would be in a position to move into management and would, no doubt, have few organizational identification problems because of their more holistic perspective on the organization. It is, then, top management's responsibility to analyze the technically oriented computer personnel and consider their potential as management talent.

Managers who possess an information systems background should have the opportunity to follow a career path that is arranged in such a way that individuals that have potential managerial talent are recognized for that talent and can move along this the path. Many organizations have been well served by providing such opportunities (e.g., John Reed, CEO of CitiBank was once the CIO of the IS organization there). IS personnel who are not management-oriented should not be promoted into managerial positions merely because of seniority. The same people that do excellent network maintenance, for example, may not, by their technical nature, be qualified for advancement to top management levels. On the other hand, to stifle a valuable client/server analyst who is quite capable of being a manager is an excellent way to destroy any sense of organizational identification that may have existed.

Cultivating Talent

The lack of personnel planning has caused many bright IS professionals to become disenchanted with and disenfranchised from their organizations; thus they move on to other companies in hopes that they will be recognized as talented and will be, hopefully, more efficiently used. This lack of attention to planning may well extend into the realm of educational opportunities and other forms of job enrichment for the IS specialist. Many IS skills are indeed perishable — necessitating continued skill enhancements, and in some cases, altering the direction of new skill attainment. Thus, both the personnel function and the IS organization need to establish the skill sets that will best serve the overall organization in the future and establishing a training plan to achieve that goal. However, simply establishing the goal is insufficient — this goal must be communicated to the IS specialist, along with his or her place in achieving this goal. On a more personal level, this goal may be established in the sense of "we have a plan for your future" rather than dealing with the IS specialist as an indiscriminate entity within the organization.

MAKING IS PERSONNEL FEEL AS PART OF THE COMPANY

The fact that it often takes a large number of people to run a truly efficient information systems group poses a problem for some organizations. Unless cooperation and understanding are organizational characteristics, the IS group may not be working for the maximum good of the total organization. It is critical that the IS function be integrated into the overall organizational structure. The major way that management can integrate IS personnel activities into the organization is by the maximization of the employees' organizational identification. An employee must be made aware of where systems development fits into the overall organizational structure. IS personnel must also be familiarized with other areas of the organization and be included in meetings between the various department heads, or at least feel that they are represented at such meetings and be in communication.

Last, personnel should be encouraged to participate in informal meetings with personnel from other areas so that they might become acquainted with each other and feel less isolated in the area of the computer world. An accompanying solution would have the executives from throughout the organization visit the IS area to see what is being done relative to integrating departmental activities.

CONCLUSION — ORGANIZATIONAL RECOGNITION OF THE INDIVIDUAL

Any employee will become bored if left to stagnate in a job for a number of years. The high growth needs of IS professionals makes it unlikely that they would remain in an organization that allowed such a situation to exist.

IS personnel are a specialized group who possess characteristics exhibited by other specialists. If this personnel can be treated as professionals and be motivated by a challenge, business may be able to eliminate some of the organizational identification problems that currently exist among technical IS employees. If top management can create an environment that fosters employee well-being and promote loyalty to the organization, the organizational identification problem will eventually be minimized and more IS personnel will stay with the organization.

To retain IS personnel by fostering their sense of commitment and identification with an employer, this chapter recommends the following steps:

- Understand the profile of IS professionals.
- Recognize IS professionals' talents and contributions to the organization.
- Inform IS employees how they contribute to the organization.
- Create tactical teams in which each IS member is an integral part.
- Promote business-minded IS staff members to managerial positions.
- Offer training and education to enhance IS skills.
- Have IS personnel become more familiar and participate in other areas of the organization.

Chapter X-2
Training Options in a Technical Environment
Gilbert Held

THE ADVENT OF CLIENT/SERVER PROCESSING AND GROWTH in the use of open-system technology have resulted in most data centers using a wide mixture of hardware and software products. This, in turn, resulted in a dramatic change in the scope and depth of employee training requirements, as well as in options available to the data center operations manager (DCOM) to satisfy those requirements. By understanding the advantages and disadvantages associated with different training options, the DCOM can construct a training program that is best structured to meet the needs of the organization in a cost-effective manner. The objective of this chapter is to provide the DCOM with detailed information concerning viable training options that should be considered.

INTRODUCTION

Although there are literally hundreds of different types of training programs offered by thousands of vendors, these programs can be divided into six major categories. Major training method categories are listed in Exhibit 1, with the "technical seminar" entry further subdivided into two classifications that are discussed later in this article.

BOOK-BASED TRAINING

Even before vendors established formal training courses, they distributed equipment training manuals. Book-based training represents perhaps the oldest method used for training data center employees.

Since the 1950s, book-based training has significantly evolved, with formal "courseware" programs now being offered on a large number of topics. These programs allow employees to read the material at their own pace and usually include assignments that reinforce key topics. Some courseware programs are used by certification programs, which are described in the next section of this chapter. Other courseware programs may be developed by hardware and software vendors as instructional aids designed to enhance the ability of a person to use a specific product or to

Exhibit 1.   Training Method Categories

Book-Based Training
Certification Program
Computer-Based Training (CBT)
College/University Courses
Technical Seminars
Public
Vendor Developed
Video-Based Presentations

learn a specific subject (e.g., how to test a cable using the XYZ Corporation cable tester).

The key advantages of book-based training are its relatively low cost in comparison to other training methods and the fact that users can go through the material at their own pace.

The major disadvantages include the fact that it is usually necessary to obtain a set of manuals for each employee and the lack of assistance when an employee has a question that is not answered by the material. To help with this problem, some courseware developers now provide a limited amount of telephone consultation via a toll-free 800 number, while other courseware developers offer assistance via a 900 number, which results in additional charges that can rapidly mount up as employee questions increase.

CERTIFICATION PROGRAMS

The rapid expansion of local area network (LAN) technology resulted in the recognition that new areas of vendor-specific information were required by hardware and software users. Several vendors attacked this problem by establishing certification programs that require trainees to complete a core curriculum of courses and pass one or more tests to be certified as "proficient."

The earliest certification programs required trainees to attend courses conducted by a specific vendor. Recognizing that the rapid expansion of LAN technology required a more flexible training schedule and location availability than could be offered by hardware and software developers, vendors considerably expanded their certification programs. Today, many resellers and third-party training organizations are licensed by hardware and software vendors to provide a core series of training necessary for persons to obtain a particular type of certification.

Exhibit 2 lists popular certification programs currently offered by six hardware and software vendors. Fields of specialization are commonly offered within each program, which results in a varying designation of the

Exhibit 2. Popular Vendor Certification Programs

Vendor	Program
Banyan	Certified Banyan Engineer
Compaq	Accredited System Engineer
IBM	Certified LAN Server Engineer
	Professional Systems Engineer
Lotus	Certified Lotus Professional
	Certified Lotus Instructor
Microsoft	Certified Systems Engineer
Novell	Certified Novell Engineer (CNE)
	Master CNE

program. For example, Lotus Education, which is now part of the IBM Corporation, offers five Certified Lotus Professional (CLP) programs. Those programs include:

- *Applications Developer.* Focused on the construction of a Lotus Notes Database
- *Principle Applications Developer.* Focused on constructing applications that require meshed databases and linking to other tasks in and outside of Notes
- *System Administrator.* Focused on the installation, monitoring, maintenance, and operation of a Notes server
- *Principle System.* Focused on the integration of administrator-communication product technology.
- *Certified cc:Mail.* Focused on the installation and specialist-operation of cc:Mail across multiple networks and hardware platforms.

In addition to the five CLP programs, Lotus also offers a Certified Lotus Instructor (CLI) program. This is the program that enables more than 50 Lotus Authorized Education Centers operated by third-party training organizations to offer CLP certification programs. Thus, the Lotus CLI can represents a "train the trainer" program.

The key advantage of specialized certification programs is that they focus on a specific area or topic that is normally directly applicable to the training requirements of the organization. Other advantages include their availability and location. Most vendors have hundreds to thousands of authorized education centers located in most major metropolitan areas. This enables organizations to economize on travel costs. In addition, because of the popularity of many courses, they are offered frequently, so that organizations can rapidly upgrade employee skills.

The two primary disadvantages associated with certification programs are their cost and the fact that after completing a program, the employee will have new marketable skills and may choose to seek work elsewhere.

Even without factoring in the cost of travel or salaries while employees are working in an authorized education center away from their jobs, costs can run between $10,000 and $30,000 for courses and examinations required to obtain certification in a particular area.

Employee mobility is another significant issue. The completion of many vendor certification programs is considered to represent a passport to new employment opportunities. With more than 100,000 LANs being installed on an annual basis and each network requiring a manager or administrator, Novell and Microsoft, as well as their authorized education centers, are capable of teaching just a small fraction of the administrators that business, academia, and government seek. This fact is easily verified by scanning the Help Wanted columns in the Sunday paper, particularly the advertisements for LAN administrators, and noting the certification credentials required.

Although it is often difficult to retain trained and knowledgeable personnel under the best of circumstances, the completion of a certification program can make it more difficult. One method that data center managers may wish to establish is a career ladder, which works in conjunction with the completion of the various stages of most certification programs. As milestones are reached, the employee can be given added responsibility as well as an increase in compensation. In addition to this "carrot," DCOMs may wish to examine corporate policy concerning the investment of a large expenditure of funds for a certification program. Some organizations now require persons enrolled in a certification program being paid for by the organization to agree to remain employed by the company for a defined period of time. That period is typically one year from the completion of the certification program; if the employee should leave earlier, he or she must reimburse the company for the cost of training. Although this policy can be considered to represent a "stick," some organizations now mesh the "carrot" and the "stick" together, adding responsibility and periodically increasing the compensation level of employees as they successfully move through a certification program while requiring the employee to agree to stay with the organization for at least a year after the program is completed.

COMPUTER BASED TRAINING

The personal computer can be considered the guiding force for the development of computer-based training (CBT). Although a few vendors prior to 1981 offered mainframe- and minicomputer-based courses of instruction, when a large number of vendors could afford personal computers, a mass market opened for CBT products. Today, companies can obtain courseware covering mainframe, communications and networking, programming, and a variety of other topics for both mainframe and client-server technology.

The key advantages of CBT include its general ability to be reused by more than one employee and the fact that training can take place on a flexible schedule. Concerning the reusability of CBT courses, many vendors license a course for use either on one computer or as a network version. When licensed for use on one computer, the license allows the software to be removed and used on a different computer. Thus, it becomes possible to amortize the cost of the CBT course over several employees; however, only one can legally use it at a time.

When a network version of a CBT course is obtained, multiple persons can use the course at the same time. However, license restrictions for a network-based CBT course usually prohibit its removal onto a laptop for an employee to use at home. In comparison, it is perfectly legal for an employee to use a CBT course at work and then remove the diskettes and take them home to use during the evening or on a weekend. Another advantage associated with CBT courses is the fact that they can be taken on site so that it is unnecessary for employees to travel. This type of training is relatively economical in comparison to training that requires employees to leave the office.

Disadvantages associated with CBT courses include an inability to ask questions about the material, the fact that the structure of some courses makes them awkward to take, and the scope and depth of the material. Fortunately, many CBT development vendors provide demonstration diskettes that will give an indication of the structure of a course as well as the scope and depth of the material. Because of the significant differences in quality between courses on the same topic, time spent previewing demonstration diskettes is highly worthwhile.

COLLEGE/UNIVERSITY COURSES

Both continuing education as well as regular college and university courses represent an excellent source for employee technical training. Unfortunately, a majority of technical courses offered by colleges and universities may not be directly applicable to the operational environment of an organization. However, many educational institutions have recognized the training requirements of business organizations and government agencies by considerably expanding their continuing education programs to cover a variety of PC-related topics, such as word processors, spreadsheets, and database management programs.

Although there are many courses in programming, database design, and similar topics that can be very beneficial for employees to apply to their work environment, many training topics necessary for operating a data center usually cannot be obtained from educational institutions. A few examples of such topics in specialized or recently evolving technologies include Web server design, programming in HyperText Markup Language

(HTML), mainframe operations, and a variety of LAN topics ranging in scope from NetWare administration and Windows NT server setup to router and bridge configuration. Employees requiring this kind of specialized training may have to consider one or more of the other training methods listed in Exhibit 1.

Some additional advantages associated with courses offered by educational institutions include evening sessions that facilitate after-hours employee attendance, regular scheduling of courses, and a professional instructional staff. As far as course scheduling is concerned, many educational institutions now recognize the business potential obtained by developing specialized courses that better reflect the technical training requirements of industry. Recently, several universities established degree programs for such topics as data communications and database management.

Some of the disadvantages associated with training provided by educational institutions include scheduling and cost. For employees who travel frequently, it may be difficult to attend courses that meet on a defined schedule. As for cost, a three-credit course at some colleges now represents an expense of approximately $2,000 for tuition. For these reasons, many organizations have shown a greater willingness to send employees to public and vendor-developed technical seminars.

TECHNICAL SEMINARS

Technical seminars represent one of the best methods of obtaining information on narrowly defined or rapidly evolving topics. In the United States, there are more than 20 organizations that specialize in the development and presentation of technical seminars covering topics related to mainframes, PCs, and data communications. Such organizations range in scope from Amdahl and IBM Education Centers to Verhof, DataTech, Business Communications Review, The Learning Tree, and the American Research Group.

The major advantage associated with technical seminars is the fact that they often represent the only mechanism of obtaining training on rapidly evolving technology. Other advantages include their intensive presentation — typically over two, three, or four days — and the frequency with which they are offered plus the convenience of the training sites. It is often easier to send employees to a seminar and reschedule a portion of their work for part of a week than to attempt to modify their schedule so they can take a three- or four-hour class one day a week over the course of a semester. In addition, many seminar organizations schedule presentations in 10 or 20 major metropolitan areas, which can considerably reduce or eliminate travel expenses. This advantage can also represent the major disadvantage associated with technical seminars, since they are usually presented over a period of two or three months on a rotating schedule that results in the presentation in different cities on different dates. This means that to minimize travel expenses, an employee may have to wait several months until the seminar is presented in the city where he or she works. Other disadvantages associated with technical seminars include the fact that if an insufficient number of persons register for the seminar, it will be canceled. The cost of specialized seminars can also be prohibitive. Costs typically range between $1,000 for a two-day course to $2,000 for a four-day seminar. Travel expenses for attending several seminars in distant cities can rapidly deplete an organization's training budget.

RECOMMENDED COURSE OF ACTION

There is no one best method for obtaining technical training for employees. Instead, a mixture of the six major training methods should be considered by the data center operations manager. By carefully considering the advantages and disadvantages associated with each training method and comparing them to the training requirements of employees, the manager can select the best methods for each situation. Considerations include the size of the training budget, employee availability for training, subject matter, and the time period during which the knowledge should be acquired.

Although training is costly, when organizations consider the alternative, which can be the inability to correct problems in a timely manner, install new hardware or software, or support the organization's evolving data processing and data communications requirements, properly selected training can be a bargain.

Chapter X-3
Training and Hiring Systems Staff

C. Warren Axelrod

THE DOWNSIZING TRENDS OF RECENT YEARS have greatly altered the ratio of seasoned to inexperienced staff. The initial impact of such changes is a reduction in costs and a surge in development of systems incorporating the latest technologies. The longer-term effect, however, is just now beginning to raise its frightening head: Inadequate support of critical legacy systems—which somehow never quite got replaced during the downsizing years—and new systems that do not conform to traditional standards of quality, integrity, security, redundancy, recoverability, and documentation.

What is the answer? A growing realization among IS managers is that they perhaps need a mix of veterans and new recruits. Microsoft, for example, has set up a computer research laboratory into which it brought a group of proven veterans in addition to its usual coterie of young Turks hired directly out of engineering and computer schools.

RETRAINING

With information technology advancing in leaps and bounds and computers appearing on every desk, how are IS staffs responding? Are they adjusting enthusiastically to these new concepts or do they resist change?

A question echoing throughout business is: "What should I do with my long-time staff? They have been loyal employees for decades and know the business inside out, but they are not familiar with computer technologies."

In addition to suffering thorny personnel issues, organizations are feeling a general turmoil: The globalization of markets, the introduction of new products and services, and the push to increase worker productivity are all disruptive forces. This momentum of change is spilling over into and building in companies' technology departments, as they increasingly abandon mainframes and minicomputers in favor of workstations and client/server

0-8493-9979-3/99/$0.00+$.50
© 1999 by CRC Press LLC

architectures and adopt new forms of system development, such as object-oriented programming.

Competition in the marketplace has driven companies to seek an edge, often based on technology. The first one to market usually reaps most of the profits, and this need to implement the latest and greatest—often before it is ready—puts even greater pressure on technologists. At the same time, nontechnical staff must learn to use the new systems and incorporate them into their work functions. Often this requires nontechnical staff being able to assist others—particularly customers—in the use of an organization's new offerings.

STAFF ENHANCES THE IS DEPARTMENT'S ABILITY TO RESPOND

Technology departments have to be as productive as possible against shrinking time horizons. This need for responsiveness, as much as the push to reduce costs, is driving the newer client/server architectures and object-oriented programs, which may be more able to respond to today's interactive world than earlier technologies; however, despite these advances, technology's inability to meet unrealistic expectations is a cause of much turbulence.

Responsiveness to user needs implies well-trained, productive staff, and, unfortunately, a very limited pool of talent exists with the experience, maturity, and knowledge to design and write the new-wave systems, manage projects, and generally get the job done.

If organizations look to the academic world for help, they see that the college system is not producing graduates with the right set of skills, as stated by university IT manager Stephen Maloney in InformationWeek. The issue may well come down to having to train existing staff, but the question will be who and how much?

Minted Versus Seasoned Staff Members

Should IS departments bring in newly minted graduates (i.e., "new issues") who have a basic education in more recent technologies, albeit not fully adequate, and guide them through a period of acquiring on-the-job experience? Or should IS departments take "seasoned" individuals who know their way around mainframes and minicomputers and train them in the ways of client/server technology, communications networking, relational data bases, data warehousing, online analytical processing (OLAP), and object-oriented programming?

The answer is that it depends on the skills and attitudes of current staff, access to outside talent, and the nature of the projects to be embarked on.

The cost of training experienced staffers can be in the order of $40,000 to $80,000, according to the results of a *Computerworld* survey.

PERCEPTIONS, MISCONCEPTIONS, AND REALITIES

All too often, the temptation is to think of retrained individuals as "retreads," workable but not of the quality of "new issues." Such an attitude, however, diminishes the value of experience. If "seasoned professionals" are "reengineered" by being taught new skills, managers may well find that the end product is better than the sum of the parts.

"New issues" may dazzle with their knowledge of the latest technologies, particularly if the IS manager is not personally familiar with the newest buzz words, but new graduates may disappoint with their on-the-job performance. They may lack the structure, discipline, and knowledge required to build reliable, high-performance systems.

The Potential for Retraining

A common point of view is that mainframe and minicomputer professionals are obsolete, archaic, and set in their ways. This may be true for some, but certainly not for the many bright, hard-working, and enthusiastic individuals who just happen to be working on older systems. Interestingly, minicomputer staffers are often more adaptable to the new environments, because they are already familiar with flexible, interconnecting systems and with processing and data bases distributed over multiple processors.

The litmus test of potential for retraining, however, is attitude. It is not that hard to distinguish the Luddites from the Renaissance people. In fact, the systems manager probably already knows who is who. Characteristics that indicate whether a person is entrenched in existing technologies include self-development, work habits, scope, and attitude.

Self-Development. The trainable staff member keeps up with his or her field, asks to attend conferences, seminars, and courses, and subscribes to industry journals and magazines. He or she also belongs to professional groups and attends their meetings. The staff member who probably is not trainable only learns what is essential to do the job and needs to be forced to learn new concepts.

Work Habits. Another way to determine the trainable from the not trainable is by examining the employee's work habits. If he or she willingly puts in extra effort when required, does not need to be asked to perform a function as he or she recognizes the criticality of work, and frequently volunteers to help out, the manager quite probably has a trainable employee at hand. On the other hand, the employee who does only what is asked falls into the not trainable category. Also, if the person objects to overtime and weekend work, spends a lot of work time on personal matters, and does not volunteer even when assistance would obviously help, these are indications of a non-trainable staff member.

Scope. Behaviors the manager can identify for a trainable person are taking a broad perspective and desiring to know how his or her own activities fit into the overall picture. Not trainable staff take the narrow view and do not care about what else is going on in the department or the company.

Attitude. A can-do, positive approach, and trust that efforts will be rewarded in the future characterize the trainable person, whereas the nine-to-fiver who objects vociferously to requests by management for extra effort and looks for payback even before the task has been accomplished is probably not trainable.

Training resisters is throwing money away. Investment in the innovators, however, garners a surprisingly large return. Not only do the combination of experience and skills produce high productivity and quality systems, but these individuals also will be highly motivated because of the new lease on their careers.

The Value of Experience

Newer technologies are mostly extensions of earlier concepts. The basics of input, processing, and output remain the same, even though their specific implementations may have changed. The business world is moving from centralized to distributed data and processing. IS departments are enhancing the interface between humans and machines and are improving the access to, and availability of, information and the exchange and presentation of data. Beneath all this change, however, many concepts carry through. Such formulations relate to data structures, system integrity, reusable programs, security, recovery from errors and equipment and software failures, system and network performance, and network protocols.

Most knowledge of the basic concepts is best learned on the job; that is, the basic concepts can be taught in the classroom but the "tricks of the trade" cannot. Therefore, experience accumulated over 10 or 20 years counts in the kind of person who can bring this knowledge with him or her into the new world.

Selecting and ranking individual workers in a vacuum is not feasible, because the mix of experienced and newly minted workers depends almost entirely on what management expects them to do. After all, it makes no sense to tow a trailer with a Ferrari or put a tow truck on the race track.

System development projects are characterized by the complexity and innovativeness of the system and the end product's importance to the company. How should staff be matched to projects?

ASSIGNING THE APPROPRIATE STAFF TO PARTICULAR PROJECTS

Having determined who is trainable and who is not, information technology management must determine who should be assigned to which projects. After all, most firms still need to support older legacy systems, and that may be done best with those who are not suitable for training in newer technologies. Of course, such roles have a limited life span. At the other end of spectrum are the systems that will bring the firm up to date and take it into the future. With these systems, IS management must seek out the most dynamic and creative staff.

Before coming up with rules as to who should be assigned to specific types of systems development projects, certain categories of systems need to be defined. One way is by the type of activity supported. Another is by the orientation of the system, that is, whether it looks out to the user or inward on itself.

Types of Activity Supported

Systems and the processes they support can be characterized as operational, tactical, or strategic. Operational systems support the basic "bread-and-butter" activities of an organization, such as transaction processing and accounting. In general, operational systems comprise the much-maligned legacy systems running on central mainframes and minicomputers. Because they were the first types of process to be automated, they tend to have been developed using the programming languages of the time—predominantly COBOL or FORTRAN.

Tactical systems came later and were typically grafted onto existing legacy platforms, although some technical innovation began to appear with personal computers as front ends, larger color screens, graphical user interfaces, mouse support, and so on. Part of the motivation here was that the new audience (i.e., predominantly professional staff versus clerical staff) was less tolerant of the cryptic commands and awkward cybernetics of earlier systems and demanded greater ease of use. Tactical systems, by definition, extend beyond the day-to-day operational processes into support of such areas as trading, sales, and marketing, which need access to data bases and the ability to analyze data and present results.

Strategic systems generally provide some form of competitive advantage to a firm, either by performing an existing task in a different way through innovative adaptation of technologies or by creating a new business opportunity using technological developments. Major strategic developments are taking place in the use of communications networks and customer-oriented systems as well as in the search for advantage in trading analytics, incorporating such esoteric concepts as artificial intelligence, virtual reality, computer-aided design and multimedia video, animation, and voice. With strategic systems are embraced the adoption of newer technologies, such as workstations, client/server architectures, relational data base systems, and object-oriented programming. These technologies require speed and flexibility, and that usually means sophisticated development environments running on the latest in high-capacity equipment. Operational and tactical systems can be developed on this type of platform, as well; in fact, they increasingly are as the functionality of legacy applications have to be transported to newer platforms to provide additional needed capabilities and, importantly, to be able to be supported by a staff who can no longer modify or fix the older systems.

Orientation

System development generally falls into three categories: Under-the-hood systems, task-oriented systems, and user-oriented systems.

Under-the-hood systems generally are not visible to the end user. Projects in this category might include the modification of internal system software and equipment, updating the underlying technology, such as the operating system software that performs all the engine-room functions of the computers, and so on. Even though such efforts are crucial to the firm's ability to keep the systems viable, these activities are not well understood by nontechnical people and are certainly not directly noticeable.

Task-oriented systems are still the major segment of system development efforts. These systems are the workhorses of most securities firms; they take in orders and trades, customer information, security descriptions, market prices, processing and clearing transactions, managing inventories, and interfacing with other systems.

User-oriented systems are those seen through the window of the PC on the individual desktop. They frequently boast colorful, easy-to-use, flexible graphical user interfaces displaying text and pictures. These are the systems aimed at the professional staff and support their needs for information retrieval and analysis. These users frequently have to draw on information from the task-oriented systems, which are for the most part still the repositories of the firm's data.

Skill Requirements

The skills and backgrounds needed for these various orientations of systems vary. Under-the-hood, or internal, projects require skills belonging to specialized technical support analysts and system-software programmers. Business experience is not usually a requirement for these staffers.

Task-oriented systems generally follow the traditional form of systems analysis and programming, in which processes are analyzed, flow charted, and programmed in conformance with a formal system-development life cycle (SDLC). Consequently the need is for technical staff with predominantly long-standing experience in both business processes and system design and development.

The design of user-oriented systems requires a broader view of the business, so that users' needs can be fully understood and translated into technical form. Programming also has to be flexible and often iterative, requiring a more flexible technician and programming tools and platforms that allow for such flexibility and responsiveness.

For both tactical and strategic systems the business experience is most critical at the beginning and end of a development project. At the start, strong business credentials allows analysts to make their own determination as to what is actually needed from a system, versus what the users profess that they want. Toward the completion of the development stage and just before deployment, business knowledge is valuable in assuring that the functionality produced will meet the real needs of the user. Again, the user might try to push a change in design of the system after the fact unless the analyst understands the real requirements and can argue against such changes.

BRINGING THE SYSTEMS AND PEOPLE TOGETHER

This chapter has categorized the world of systems in two ways: One by type of activity (i.e., operational, tactical, and strategic), and the other by orientation (i.e., under-the-hood, task-oriented, and user-oriented). In general, these two sets of categories parallel each other. At one end of the spectrum, operational systems tend to need significant under-the-hood effort and are heavily task-oriented; at the other extreme, strategic systems tend to be user-oriented.

The relative effort by activity and orientation can be described as follows:

- Under-the-hood systems are highly operational, moderately to highly tactical, and only minimally to moderately strategic.
- Task-oriented systems are highly operational, highly tactical, and only moderately strategic.

681

- User-oriented systems are minimally operational, moderately tactical, and highly strategic.

Assigning the Appropriate Staff

In light of the first part of the chapter, technical staff can be divided into retreads, seasoned or retrained professionals, and new issues. The assignment of the most appropriate type of staff to project categories can be arranged as follows:

	Operational	Tactical	Strategic
Under the Hood	All Seasoned	Most Seasoned	Half Seasoned
		Some New Issues	Half New Issues
Task Oriented	Some Retreads	Some Retreads	Some Seasoned
	Some Seasoned	Some Seasoned	Mostly New Issues
	Some New Issues	Some New Issues	
User Oriented	Half Seasoned	Some Seasoned	Some Seasoned
	Half New Issues	Mostly New Issues	Mostly New Issues

In most cases, a blend of seasoned professionals and staff fully versed in newer technologies is recommended. The emphasis of the mix moves from the application of more experienced staff to the more operational systems and tasks with more technical orientation to staff with more current skills for strategic, end-user systems.

SUMMARY

With technologies changing too quickly for many people to keep up, management must select from its experienced staff those who can be trained effectively and mix them with newly minted entrants into the field. Project teams should be formed from individuals with business and technical experience and individuals with in-depth current training. The particular mix depends on the nature of the project, but all projects should be staffed with some mix rather than staff of all one type.

Chapter X-4
How to Stay Competitive Professionally

Douglas B. Hoyt

THE RATE OF CHANGE in the computer field is at a record-high pace, and systems development managers who do not constantly keep current could quickly fail to achieve their potential and lose the competitive advantage to others. Conversely, managers who demonstrate that they are equipped to lead in implementing new and effective systems are most likely to be given the authority to do so.

To stay on top professionally, however, takes time and effort, which adds to the work load at the office or, in many cases, may even impinge on the manager's personal life. Managers must carefully weigh the ways to advance their technical knowledge as well as their careers, select methods to reach their goals most efficiently, and work vigorously at the chosen approaches. The many options available are reviewed in this chapter.

AREAS TO WATCH

Areas in which to keep current include computer hardware and software, applications specific to the manager's industry or field, and business in general. Though identifying which systems will remain competitive is difficult, the systems manager can anticipate the future by looking at the developments that have evolved in the last decade.

Computer Developments

Recent computer direction changes include:

- From mainframes, minicomputers, and personal computers (PCs) to client/server technology, local area networks (LANs), wide area networks (WANs), and the Internet.

- From structured programming to computer-aided software engineering (CASE) tools and object-oriented programming.
- From COBOL and Fortran to C++ and other fourth-generation languages (4GLs).

Industry Innovations

In many industries, innovative computer applications have helped some companies achieve a competitive edge. Examples include:

- Reservations systems in the airline industry.
- Electronic data interchange (EDI) in manufacturing industries.
- Asynchronous transfer modes (ATMs) in the banking industry.
- Tracking systems in the trucking and package delivery business.

New Business Directions

In business and other organizations, managerial improvements have taken place with the help of computer systems. Business trends include:

- Downsizing.
- Restructuring.
- Quality improvement and control.

KEEPING UP TO DATE

The many possible ways to stay on top of technical and business developments include networking, joining associations and user groups, attending trade shows, and continuing professional education. The following sections discuss these and other paths to career competitiveness.

Networking

Networking is the cultivation of friends and acquaintances who may be of help in the future. Networking assumes reciprocity, or mutually beneficial relationships. It means engaging in conversations with people knowledgeable in the areas the systems manager has targeted for advancement.

Contacts can be friends, peers, subordinates, superiors, vendors, teachers, social acquaintances, and bulletin board users as well as people at association meetings, conferences, and trade shows.

Information is gained from these people by asking them about their experiences with and ideas on their areas of expertise. Paying close attention to the answers is critical, as is continuing the conversation with well-thought-out questions that display the manager's intellectual curiosity. Because people are generally flattered to be asked to explain things that they know about to an interested party, they usually respond willingly to such inquiries. They, in turn, gain from the opportunity to ask questions of their own about matters of interest to them.

Associations

A primary purpose of most professional associations is to help their members gain knowledge and generate ideas in their particular areas of expertise. This is done through monthly meetings, regional one- or two-day conferences, annual national or international conferences, technical journals, research, and traveling seminars.

Association meetings can be an important means for learning about technical developments from those who have specialized knowledge about them. As gatherings of people with similar concerns, they are an excellent source for developing networking contacts and discussing matters of mutual interest with them during function meals and social periods. Associations are also good places for developing and practicing leadership skills, as they offer volunteer positions that involve committee work and officer positions as well as opportunities to speak at and lead meetings.*The Encyclopedia of Associations* lists computer and related specialties associations.

User Groups

User groups are similar to associations in many respects; however, user group members are limited to people who use a specific vendor's products. These groups are organizationally and financially separate from the vendors, and vendors attend their gatherings only when invited. However, the vendors support the groups and may assist them when asked.

User groups offer the same benefits as associations: opportunities to network, learn the latest technical developments as well as anticipated releases, share experiences in problem solving, and practice leadership in the group's management and administration.

Trade Shows

Trade shows are usually annual events of several days' duration in convention center locations. In addition to offering seminars in the latest technology trends, these shows bring together representatives of such vendor groups as providers of networks, PCs, and imaging technology hardware and software. Competing vendors set up displays and booths where their sales people vigorously promote their products' beneficial features.

Trade shows are great places to develop a sense of what is new in the field, to get information about particular product features and plans, and to make contacts that may be useful in further investigations and research at a later time.

Vendors

Vendors are an outstanding resource for systems managers who need to know what is new and what is on the horizon as well as the pros and cons of various technology solutions. Because a vendor's success depends on developing effective methodologies, it is motivated to explain its products—as well as its competitors' products to highlight strengths, weaknesses, and features that set it apart. Even though vendors cannot ethically reveal proprietary information about their competitors, they often can indicate directions of competing companies in their particular industry.

The vendor also can discuss how its solutions can be implemented specifically in the systems manager's organization. To do this, the vendor's staff often visits the individual place of business and gives a demonstration of its products.

Systems managers should invite vendors in often to give presentations and proposals. Business lunches and vendor-sponsored seminars and announcements are also potential sources of information on how their products really work—information left "between the lines" in their promotional material.

Visits to Other Organizations

When another organization has developed or is known to be developing new technologies that might be applicable at the systems development manager's organization, a trip to that company to meet with project personnel is worthwhile. The systems manager can discuss the technology and observe the staff at work.

Sometimes the developer may be reluctant to discuss new projects, especially those contributing to competitive success. However, the staff involved is proud to display the innovations and are happy to benefit from the observations and input from outsiders. Such visits are further opportunities to broaden the systems manager's field of acquaintances and networking potential.

Magazines and Newspapers

Magazines are available in abundance, many covering quite thoroughly the very narrow areas of specialization in the computer and software fields. They are an essential resource for keeping current about present and future technology and products. These magazines discuss vendor product descriptions and what end users are saying about them; publications also contain editorial comments and opinions. Many describe customers' implementations, explain how they work, and list the successes and problems encountered.

Magazines are also a source for upcoming conferences, conventions, and trade shows. Many of these magazines are free to subscribers who are professionals in the magazine's area of specialization, because sufficient income is provided by the magazine's advertisers.

Newspapers are a primary source for coverage on managerial trends and technical developments as well as some activities of interest in individual industries.

Association Journals

Most professional associations publish journals that cover current technology issues and new directions. Content also includes case studies, which are articles detailing specific projects at real corporations: what went smoothly, what went wrong, and what the organization learned about how to surmount obstacles.

These journals are included in the membership fees but can be bought by nonmembers. One prolific source of material is the Association of Computing Machinery [(212) 626-0500], which publishes a particularly wide range of technical publications.

Books

Books evolve too slowly to be on the cutting edge of technology. They are an excellent source, however, for the systems manager who wants to build a solid foundation in a particular subject area, because books cover subjects more completely than periodicals. This is especially true of handbooks, because they are compilations of articles by various authors on related subjects. Structured for ready reference by their many headings, indexes, and detailed tables of contents, books are very accessible.

Newspaper advertisements, bookstores, and libraries are all sources of what books are available.

Libraries

Libraries are becoming increasingly efficient and easy to use. Computerized systems readily locate items by title, author, or key words or combinations of words. Small libraries have data bases of what neighboring libraries have; if material is found through the data base, the smaller library can request that material from the appropriate libraries. Larger libraries may have a variety of CD-ROMs with indexes to government data or other specialized fields of knowledge. Most library computerized reference systems print out selected reference data, and many print out abstracts of articles in periodicals.

One drawback to these electronic reference systems is they differ from library to library and CD-ROM to CD-ROM, so the systems manager who only uses them on occasion may need to invest a lot of time to become familiar with each new indexing system.

One advantage is library staff members are usually dedicated and willing to help. Their availability is also enhanced by the computerized reference systems that in turn have lessened the demands on their time.

Technical Publication Services

Technical publication services, such as those published by Auerbach Publications, cover fields by function with a practical, hands-on approach. Auerbach's lines include handbooks, which give comprehensive coverage of major areas of information management, loose-leaf services, and newsletters.

A main product is the Auerbach Information Management Series, which contains eight loose-leaf binder services that focus on information management, data base management, data center operations management, end-user computing management, data communications management, data security management, and EDP auditing. These services are supplemented bimonthly to keep subject coverage complete and up to date. These binders, which are also available on disk and CD-ROM, combine the benefits of books and periodicals; they cover the full range of a broad subject area, like books do, and reflect current facts and ideas more promptly than a book can. The electronic formats enable rapid searches by key words. This material can be downloaded readily for further analysis or presentations.

Colleges and University Courses

A great variety of college and university courses at the undergraduate and graduate levels are available, especially in urban areas. Some courses fulfill immediate learning needs, but more often such courses help form a foundation for reaching long-term career goals.

Business and computer courses can be taken evenings and weekends, and many can lead to degrees. Employers often pay part or all of the cost, particularly when the courses directly or indirectly support the job responsibilities of the employee.

Bulletin Boards and the Internet

Bulletin boards offer the latest in methods for networking and for finding people eager to exchange experience and ideas on subjects of common interest. Systems managers can secure answers that may not be readily found in literature or even among business associates and acquaintances, because there are a multitude of bulletin board users free to share information via electronic means. Information is gained efficiently because the bulletin board makes for networking without the bother of actually meeting the participants in person and making the small talk that such relationships usually entail.

Similarly, the Internet can be an effective means for securing information. The user, however, must first master the methodology for using the system and be aware of all the types of information available and where to get them.

The problem with these electronic sources is that bulletin boards and the Internet can be time-consuming diversions and lead to excessive search time.

Other commercial electronic data sources, such as America Online and CompuServe, also access business and technical information. Advantages include convenience and speed in securing articles and data from magazines, newspapers, encyclopedias, and other sources.

Certification

Some organizations have established certification programs to ensure adequate knowledge and experience in their fields. These programs provide training courses and review and preparatory materials to help certification applicants.

The Institute for Certification of Computing Professionals (ICCP) maintains a certification program to encourage and verify appropriate knowledge and competence in computer areas. The ICCP goals of continuing professional development are:

1. To maintain professional competence.
2. To update existing knowledge and skills.
3. To attain new or additional knowledge and skills.

The certification program also gives employers a competency guide when hiring computer staff members and assists computer specialists in evaluating their own skills.

Certification for Computing Professionals. To become a Certified Computing Professional (CCP) under ICCP, a practitioner must verify a minimum level of experience and pass a series of tests to validate competency in the field. Preparatory review courses and educational materials are available in audio cassette, computer disk, and workbook formats.

To remain certified, the CCP must demonstrate continued learning and professional activity by documenting attendance at seminars, conferences, university courses, and speaking and writing on computer topics. An alternative to this learning documentation is to retake the entrance tests after a three-year period. There are some 50,000 CCPs today.

The ICCP evolved from the combined efforts of associations that, some years ago, started to establish separate certifications. The ICCP today is run by 12 associations, each of which designates two ICCP board members.

An additional 12 affiliate societies support the program and are invited to board meetings but have no vote. Further information can be obtained from the Institute for Certification of Computing Professionals, 2200 East Devon Avenue, Suite 268, Des Plaines IL 60018-4503; (708) 299-4277; CompuServe 74040,3722.

Certification for Systems Security Professionals. The Institute of Information Systems Security (ISSA) joined with other organizations to establish a Certified Information Systems Security Professional (CISSP) designation. Further information about that certification program and its seminars can be obtained from the ISSA's overseeing organization, the International Systems Security Certification Consortium, Inc., at (508) 393-2296.

Certification for Systems Auditors. The Information Systems Audit and Control Association administers a Certified Information Systems Audit (CISA) program. Acceptance is based on experience requirements and the passing of an examination. Preparation and review material is available from the association at (708) 253-1545.

Some vendors, as well, give certificates for completing training programs related to their products.

DEMONSTRATING AND REINFORCING LEADERSHIP

Leadership can be practiced by volunteering for and accepting leadership work in associations and user groups. Another highly effective way for improving and displaying technical knowledge as well as leadership skills is developing speeches to be given at meetings and by writing articles for publication. Finally, taking the initiative in researching and developing innovative applications is the best way of all to offer proof of technical and business expertise.

Association and User Group Leadership

Most associations and user group chapters are eager to find members who are willing to work on projects—newsletters, membership programs, and conference planning, for example. Reliable members are often asked to become chairpeople and officers at regional, national, and international levels.

Though these activities and positions offer no salaries, costs of materials are normally reimbursed. The benefits for the systems manager include networking and learning; the most important value emphasized here, however, is the practice at performing leadership roles.

As people advance in these organizations, they must delegate responsibilities to others. This means they must use persuasion and encouragement to motivate others, because monetary rewards are not available as incentives. In paid positions at for-profit organizations, those who lead by persuasion and encouragement still get the best results; therefore, any managerial skills the systems manager develops in associations and user groups can foster managerial progress in the individual's career.

Speaking and Writing

Speaking and writing opportunities are easier to come by than many people think and have many benefits professionally. Members of associations or user groups can readily create opportunities to speak by offering to give a talk about an experience or know-how of interest to other members. After delivering the talk, the speaker can write up the session and send it to publications, which are often glad to receive material of interest to their subscribers. These publications usually pay modest honorariums for articles upon publication.

Benefits from speaking and writing include creating an image of authority in the field, which can lead to more offers to speak and write. Most important, public speaking enhances skills in explaining clearly and persuading an audience—talents that are of great importance in managing people on the job. These skills are also necessary when conducting meetings and managing subordinates.

A further benefit is the snowballing effect with the network process. People who have spoken at meetings and published are sought out by others who are looking for knowledgeable people with whom they can exchange experiences and views. Though the process of giving talks often starts with local association or user groups, these occasions can lead to presentations to larger groups at conferences, seminars, trade shows, and other gatherings.

Another by-product benefit is the feedback from audiences at such sessions. Often, during question-and-answer periods, audience members may explain their related experiences, challenge the speaker's premises, or bring to light important new aspects of the issues being discussed, all of which can further broaden the speaker's knowledge, as well.

Pioneering Research and Development Applications

When a beneficial new technology or methodology is on the horizon, systems managers can advise management that they would like to make a research analysis of the opportunities. Taking the initiative helps the manager become properly knowledgeable about emerging technology and shows management that the manager has a progressive point of view and intends to help the organization stay ahead in the future. Best of all, if the potential idea is developed successfully, it may produce an application giving significant competitive advantage to the organization.

RELATIONSHIP TO PERSONAL LIFE

Pursuing fully all the options discussed in this chapter while maintaining a nine-to-five job would require 48 hours a day—an impossibility, of course. Therefore, how much time is devoted to these self-training efforts depends on the demands of family and personal life, how much time and support the employer may give, and the intensity of the systems manager's desire to get ahead.

Most employers give at least nominal support to work with professional groups and to go to outside training. Attending conferences, seminars, and trade shows can often be done on company time, and the company may also pick up the cost of those activities as well as membership dues. Other activities that can be undertaken on company time are reading, writing letters, and making phone calls related to association activities.

Most professional and educational activities, however, cannot be done during the work day. Employers balk at supporting professional activities that take away from time ordinarily devoted to performing the primary responsibilities of the employee's position. Activities that must be undertaken outside of the normal work week are attending college and university classes, organizing talks and writing articles, and traveling to and attending committee meetings, conferences, and trade shows. These all take away from the time available for family matters and personal activities.

Because of the time considerations, therefore, the systems manager must consider carefully the options to meet career goals most effectively.

RECOMMENDED COURSE OF ACTION

These are the activities that maintain and advance professional knowledge, leadership, and stature:

- Participating in associations and user groups; attending presentations; accepting leadership positions; and offering to give talks.
- Mining for networking opportunities—on the job, with vendors, at association and user group gatherings, and at seminars and trade shows.

- Meeting with vendors, which use the opportunity to explain their current products and product plans; requesting presentations and proposals.
- Attending trade shows and comparing hardware and software products as to their features.
- Visiting other organizations to learn how they are using technological advances.
- Reading relevant books, magazines and association journals, newspapers, and technical publications.
- Taking college or university courses; pursuing certification when it is of value in reaching career goals.
- Strengthening leadership by accepting leadership roles in associations and user groups, and by offering to speak and write on technical and business subjects.
- Taking the initiative in researching and developing new technical opportunities on the job.

Systems managers can choose from these the most valuable approaches to reach their specific career goals, keeping in mind that they may need to modify personal advancement plans as their needs and circumstances change.

Chapter X-5
Improving Communication Between End Users and System Developers
Jack T. Marchewka

THE TRADITIONAL APPROACH TO INFORMATION SYSTEMS DEVELOP-
MENT (ISD) assumes that the process is both rational and systematic. Developers are expected to analyze a set of well-defined organizational problems and then develop and implement an information system (IS). This,
however, is not always the case.

The full extent of IS problems and failures may not be known, as most
organizations are less than willing to report these problems for competitive
reasons. However, a report by the Index Group indicates that 25 out of 30
strategic system implementations studied were deemed failures, with only 5
systems meeting their intended objectives. Moreover, it has been suggested
that at least half of all IS projects do not meet their original objectives.

Previous research suggests that a lack of cooperation and ineffective communication between end users and system developers are underlying reasons
for these IS problems and failures. Typically, the user--an expert in some
area of the organization--is inexperienced in ISD, while the developer, who
is generally a skilled technician, is unacquainted with the rules and policies
of the business. In addition, these individuals have different backgrounds,
attitudes, perceptions, values, and knowledge bases. These differences may
be so fundamental that each party perceives the other as speaking a foreign
language. Consequently, users and developers experience a communication
gap, which is a major reason why information requirements are not properly
defined and implemented in the information system.

Furthermore, differences in goals contribute to a breakdown of cooperation between the two groups. For example, the user is more interested in how
information technology can solve a particular business problem, whereas the

system developer is more interested in the technical elegance of the application system.

On the other hand, users attempt to increase application system functionality by asking for changes to the system or for additional features that were not defined in the original requirements specifications. However, the developer may be under pressure to limit such functionality to minimize development costs or to ensure that the project remains on schedule.

Subsequently, users and developers perceive each other as being uncooperative, and ISD becomes an "us versus them" situation. This leads to communication problems that inhibit the user from learning about the potential uses and benefits of the technology from the developer. The developer, on the other hand, may be limited in learning about the user's functional and task requirements. As a result, a system is built that does not fit the user's needs, which, in turn, increases the potential for problems or failure. Participation in the ISD process requires a major investment of the users' time that diverts them from their normal organizational activities and responsibilities. An ineffective use of this time is a waste of an organizational resource that increases the cost of application system.

The next section examines the conventional wisdom of user involvement. It appears that empirical evidence to support the traditional notion that user involvement leads to IS success is not clear cut. Subsequently, this section suggests that it is not a question of whether to involve the user but rather a question of how or why the user should be involved in the ISD process. In the next section, a framework for improving cooperation, communication, and mutual understanding is described. Within the context of this framework, the following section provides a classification of user and developer relationships. This is followed by a section that describes how to assess, structure, and monitor the social relationship between users and developers.

USER INVOLVEMENT AND COMMON WISDOM

The idea that user involvement is critical to the successful development of an information system is almost an axiom in practice; however, some attempts to validate this idea scientifically have reported findings to the contrary. Given the potential for communication problems and differences in goals between users and developers, it is not surprising, for example, that a survey of senior systems analysts reported that they did not perceive user involvement as being critical to information systems development.

Moreover, a few studies report very limited effects of user involvement on system success and suggest that the usual relationship between system developers and users could be described as one in which the IS professionals are in charge and users play a more passive role.

There are several reasons why involving the user does not necessarily guarantee the success of an information system. These include:

- If users are given a chance to participate in information systems development, they sometimes try to change the original design in ways that favor their political interests over the political interests of other managers, users, or system developers. Thus, the potential for conflict and communication problems increases.
- Users feel that their involvement lacks any true potential to affect the development of the information system. Consequently, individuals resist change because they feel that they are excluded from the decision-making process.

Despite equivocal results, it is difficult to conceive how an organization could develop a successful information system without any user involvement. It therefore may not be a question whether to involve the user, but how or why the user should be involved. More specifically, there are three basic reasons for involving users in the design process:

1. To provide a means to get them to "buy in" and subsequently reduce resistance to change.
2. To develop more realistic expectations concerning the information technology's capabilities and limitations.
3. To incorporate user knowledge and expertise into the system. Users most likely know their jobs better than anyone else and therefore provide the obvious expertise or knowledge needed for improved system quality.

While the more traditional ISD methods view users as passive sources of information, the user should be viewed as a central actor who participates actively and effectively in system development. Users must learn how the technology can be used to support their, whereas the system developer must learn about the business processes in order to develop a system that meets user needs. To learn from each other, users and developers must communicate effectively and develop a mutual understanding between them. This leads to improved definition of system requirements and increased acceptance, as the user and developer co-determine the use and impact of the technology.

COOPERATION, COMMUNICATION AND MUTUAL UNDERSTANDING

Earlier research suggests that effective communication can improve the ISD process and is an important element in the development of mutual understanding between users and system developers. Mutual understanding provides a sense of purpose to the ISD process. This requires that users and developers perceive themselves as working toward the same goal and able to understand the intentions and actions of the other.

To improve communication and mutual understanding requires increased cooperation between users and developers. As a result, many of the inherent differences between these individuals are mitigated and the communications gap bridged; however, the balance of influence and their goals affects how they communicate and cooperate when developing information systems.

The Balance of Influence

In systems development, an individual possesses a certain degree of influence over others by having a particular knowledge or expertise. This knowledge or expertise provides the potential to influence those who have lesser knowledge. For example, a system developer uses his or her technical knowledge to influence the design of the information system. If the user has little or no knowledge of the technology, the system developer, by possessing the technical knowledge needed to build the application system, has a high degree of influence over the user. On the other hand, the user has a high degree of influence over the system developer if the user possesses knowledge of the domain needed to build the application system. By carefully employing their knowledge or expertise, the user and the developer cultivate a dependency relationship. Subsequently, the balance of influence between the user and developer determines how these individuals communicate with each other and how each individual tries to influence the other.

Reconciling the Goals Between the User and Developer

Even though users and developers may work for the same organization, they do not always share the same goals. More specifically, the nature of the development process creates situations in which the user and developer have different goals and objectives. For example, the developer may be more interested in making sure that the IS project is completed on time and within budget. Very often the developer has several projects to complete, and cost/ schedule overruns on one project may divert precious, finite resources from other projects.

Users, on the other hand, are more interested in the functionality of the system. After all, they must live with it. A competitive situation arises if increasing the system's functionality forces the system to go over schedule or over budget or if staying on schedule or within budget limits the system's functionality.

In 1949, Morton Deutsch presented a theory of cooperation that suggests cooperation arises when individuals have goals linked in a way that everyone sinks or swims together. On the other hand, a competitive situation arises when one individual swims while the other sinks. This idea has been applied to the area of information systems development to provide insight as to how goals might affect the relationship between users and developers.

Cooperation arises when individuals perceive the attainment of their goals as being positively related (i.e., reaching one's goals assists other people in attaining their goals). Cooperation, however, does not necessarily mean that individuals share the same goals, only that each individual will (or will not) attain their goals together. Here the individuals either sink or swim together.

The opposite holds true for competition. In competition, individuals perceive their goals as being negatively related (i.e., attainment of one's goals inhibits other people from reaching their goals). In this case, some must sink if another swims.

Cooperation can lead to greater productivity by allowing for more substitutability (i.e, permitting someone's actions to be substituted for one's own), thus allowing for more division of labor, specialization of roles, and efficient use of personnel and resources. Cooperative participants use their individual talents and skills collectively when solving a problem becomes a collaborative effort. Conflicts can be positive when disagreements are limited to a specific scope, and influence tends to be more persuasive in nature.

Cooperation also facilitates more trust and open communication. In addition, individuals are more easily influenced in a cooperative situation than in a competitive one. Communication difficulties are reduced when persuasion rather than coercion is used to settle differences of viewpoints. Honest and open communication of important information exemplifies a cooperative situation. Competition, on the other hand, is characterized by a lack of communication or misleading communication.

The competitive process also encourages one party to enhance its power while attempting to reduce the legitimacy of the other party's interests. Conflict is negative when discussions include a general scope of issues that tend to increase each party's motivation and emotional involvement in the situation. Defeat for either party may be less desirable or more humiliating than both parties losing. In addition, influence tends to be more coercive in nature. Competitive individuals tend to be more suspicious, hostile, and ready to exploit or reject the other party's needs and requests. The cooperative process supports trust, congenial relations, and willingness to help the other party's needs and requests. In general, the cooperative process encourages a convergence of similar values and beliefs. The competitive process has just the opposite effect.

A CLASSIFICATION OF USER AND DEVELOPER RELATIONS

Exhibit 1 provides a classification scheme for viewing potential user/developer relationships based on the interdependency of goals and their

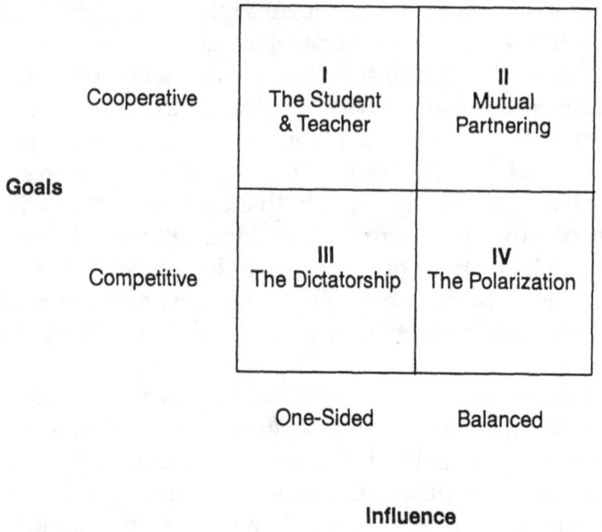

	One-Sided	Balanced
Cooperative	I The Student & Teacher	II Mutual Partnering
Competitive	III The Dictatorship	IV The Polarization

Goals

One-Sided   Balanced

Influence

Exhibit 1. Classification of User/Developer Relationships

---

balance of influence. Classification of relationships clarifies the social process of user involvement (i.e., how the user currently is involved or how the user should be involved) in ISD.

Quadrant I: The Student and Teacher

In this quadrant, the balance of influence is one-sided; however, the goals between the user and the developer are positively related. Subsequently, this relationship resembles a teacher/student relationship for two reasons.

First, because the balance of power is one-sided, the more experienced or knowledgeable individual most likely leads the ISD process. Because they both perceive their goals as being positively related, the less-experienced individual most likely follows the advice of the more influential individual.

The second reason has to do with a one-way model of learning. If the more influential individual leads the ISD process, he or she has more to offer in terms of being able to share his or her knowledge or expertise than the less-experienced individual. As a result, learning generally takes place in one direction as in a typical teacher/student relationship.

An example of this type of relationship is an experienced developer teamed with a novice user. The users' limited knowledge or experience may make it difficult to specify their requirements. The developer may then attempt to control or lead the ISD process, in which users contribute to the best of their knowledge or expertise.

Since these individuals perceive their goals as being positively related, the potential for resistance may be low. The user may view the development process as an opportunity to learn about the technology from the developer and may be easily influenced by the developer. An information system may be developed and viewed as successful; however, as the user becomes more experienced and familiar with the system, he or she may begin to request changes. Subsequently, these requests may result in higher maintenance costs later on.

Quadrant II: Mutual Partnering

In this quadrant the user and developer share the same degree of influence and have positively related goals. Here users play a more active role in the ISD process than a novice, as their knowledge and level of expertise is greater. Because the developer also is experienced and knowledgeable in ISD, the potential for a two-way model of learning exists.

Users, for example, learns how the technology supports their needs, whereas the developer learns about the business processes. Because the goals of these individuals are positively related, the potential for resistance is be low. Subsequently, a two-way model of learning suggests a higher degree of mutual learning and understanding where a system is be built successfully with lower maintenance costs later on.

Quadrant III: The Dictatorship

In the third quadrant the individuals exhibit more of a dictatorial relationship, in which the individual with the greater potential to influence leads the ISD process. Resistance is high, because the goals of these individuals are negatively related. If the developer has the greater potential to influence the user, for example, he or she may view the user as a passive source of information. Users may perceive themselves as lacking any real chance to participate and then subsequently offer a high degree of resistance. The developer may build a system that fits the developer's perception of user needs or wants, to attain his or her goals. As a result, a system is developed that does not meet the initial requirements of the user and ultimately exhibits high maintenance costs. The system might be characterized as a technical success but an organizational failure.

On the other hand, if the user has the greater potential to influence the developer, the user tries to increase, for example, the functionality of the system to attain his or her goals. As a result, the developer offers passive resistance when asked to comply with the user's requests to minimize what the developer perceives as a losing situation. Conflicts may be settled through coercion with limited learning occurring between these individuals.

Quadrant IV: The Polarization

The fourth quadrant suggests a situation in which both the user and developer have an equal balance of influence but negatively related goals. Mutual learning is limited or exists only to the degree needed by an individual to attain his or her goals. Settlement of conflicts are achieved through political means, and a high degree of resistance results if one side perceives themselves as being on losing side. Conflicts increase each individual's motivation and emotional involvement in the situation, making defeat less desirable or more humiliating than both parties losing. These individuals may become more suspicious, hostile, and ready to exploit or reject the other party's needs or requests. Subsequently, this type of relationship may potentially be the most destructive and could lead to the abandonment of the IT project if neither side is willing to capitulate.

STRUCTURING THE USER-DEVELOPER RELATIONSHIP

The framework presented in the previous section may be used to assess and structure the relationship between users and developers. A three-step process is now presented to assess, structure, and then monitor the social relationship between these individuals.

Assessment

Assessment of the user/developer relationship is useful for choosing project participants as well as for gaining insight during the project if problems begin to arise. Using the framework presented in the previous section, a manager may begin by determining the potential balances of influence. Examples of such factors that affect the balance of influence for both developers and users include:

- The level of technical knowledge.
- The level of domain knowledge (i.e., knowledge of the business processes or functions that are the core of the IS project).
- The years of experience in the company or industry.
- The prior involvement in system development projects.
- The rank or position within the organization.
- The reputation (i.e, how the individual's level of competency is perceived by others in the organization).

Other factors relevant to the project or organization can and should be used to assess the balance of influence among individuals. Subsequently, the manager should begin to get a clearer picture as to whether the balance of influence will be one-sided or balanced.

The next step is to assess individuals' goals. An easy way to make this assessment is to ask each individual to list or identify factors that are important to him or her. Examples include:

- What do you have to gain should the project succeed?
- What do you have to lose should the project fail?
- How would you determine whether the project is a success or failure?

After having both users and developers list what is important to them, a manager can compare these items to determine whether the individuals have potentially conflicting goals. End users and developers need not have exactly the same items of interest; these items need only not cause a win/lose situation. Asking the individuals to list how they would determine whether the project is a success or failure may uncover other potentially conflicting goals. For example, a manager may discover that users value functionality over cost, whereas the developer is concerned with ensuring that the project is developed by a specific date.

Structuring

A manager has several alternatives that can alter the balances of influence. The first alternative—choosing project participants—has the greatest impact. In an ideal situation, a manager can choose from a pool of personnel that includes both users and developers with varying degrees of skill, expertise, and knowledge. Unfortunately, if the pool is small, the number of possible combinations is reduced. As a result, training may prove to be a valuable tool for users becoming more knowledgeable about technology and developers becoming more knowledgeable about the business processes and functions.

As suggested in the framework presented, the goals of these individuals may be the most important factor in improving the social process of system development. For example, involving novice or less experienced individuals on a project is desirable when the project participants perceive their goals as positively related; however, serious communication problems arise if these same participants have negatively related goals.

To increase cooperation, then, the goals of the development team should be structured so that the individuals' goals are positively related. This may be accomplished in a number of ways.

Project Team Members Should Be Held Equally and Jointly Accountable. This may be in terms of a bonus or merit system under which each of the project team members is equally and jointly accountable for the success or failure or the information system. In other words, both the users and developers should both be concerned with such issues as the functionality of the system and with cost/schedule overruns.

Goals Should Be Made Explicit. Each individual involved in the development of the information system should have a clear, consistent perception that his or her goals are related in such a way that all sink or swim together. It is important not only that users and developers be held accountable using the same reward or merit system but also that they are aware that each is held accountable in the same way.

Management's Actions Must Reinforce Project Team Goals. It is important that management not allow project team members the opportunity to point fingers or assign blame. Subsequently, the actions of management must be consistent with the goals of the project team members. This is the most difficult challenge of all, because a change in values, attitudes, and possibly culture is required. For example, if goals are to be positively related, there can be no "us versus them" ideology. Instead, both users and developers should see themselves as part of the same team.

Monitoring

The goals and perceptions of the individuals may change over the course of the project. Just as the allocation of time and resources must be monitored during a project, the social process between the project participants should be monitored as well. Monitoring should be continual during the project to identify any problems or negative conflict before they adversely affect the project. Similar to assessment, a manager may want to look for warning signs. Examples of warning signs include:

Finger Pointing When Problems Arise. Project team members should fix the problem, not the blame.

Negative Conflict. Individuals focus on petty issues that do not move them closer to their goals but only serve one party at the expense of the other. However, users and developers should agree to disagree. Conflict can be positive, especially when developing innovative approaches or refining new ideas.

Lack of participation or interest. All members of the project should be involved actively. However, even when all members perceive themselves as having a cooperative relationship, some individuals may become less involved. This may occur when the balance of influence is one-sided. Too often systems developers take control of the IS project and attempt to act in the best interest of the users. Although the developers may mean well, they may attempt to develop a system that the user never asked for and does not want.

Assessment, structuring, and monitoring should be a cycle. If specific problems are identified, a manager should assess the balance of influence and goals of the project team members. Changes can be made to alter or fine-tune the balances of influence or goals among the members. By managing this social process between users and developers, a manager increases the likelihood that systems that meet the objectives originally envisioned are developed on time and within budget.

SUMMARY

This chapter suggests that even though users and developers may work for the same organization, they do not always share the same goals. Subsequently, problems in ISD arise, especially when the user is more interested in functionality and the developer is more interested in maintaining cost/time schedules.

Cooperation facilitates improved communication and leads to greater productivity, because individuals perceive their goals as being positively related. In addition, the goals of the individuals provide some insight as to how each party uses its influence in the development of an information system. This idea was presented through a classification of user and developer relationships that considered their interdependency of goals and their balance of influence. Using this framework, a manager can assess, structure, and monitor the social relationship between users and developers. Managing this social relationship may result in more systems being developed within budget and on schedule and that meet the needs of the user.

Section X – Checklist
Leveraging Staff
Resources

1. Which human resource issues are the most challenging to your IS environment?
2. Would you support licensing and/or accreditation programs for software professionals? If so, would this improve skills?
3. Do you think that managing today's IS professional is more difficult than ten years ago? If so, why?
4. Does your organization embrace newer methods for work, such as telecomputing, and flexible work weeks? If so, has this been successful?
5. Should IS professionals be given more latitude in their work based on the technology used in the IS environment?
6. What is your organization's turnover rate? Do you expect programmers to come and go or is that just a myth supported by employment agencies?
7. How much effort should an organization extend to retain qualified professionals? At what cost does this make business sense?
8. In your opinion, should an organization or an individual be responsible for the ongoing training of IS professionals?
9. Should organizations train staff members on future technology in order to build newer systems or train on current technology to extend the benefits of existing software?
10. How would you describe the communication between departments in your organization? Does this communication aid or inhibit software development?
11. Does your organization use methodologies such as joint application development (JAD) to help improve communication between end users and developers?
12. In your opinion, should IS staff learn to speak the business of the company in order to be effective? If so, how is that accomplished?
13. What steps does your organization take to improve overall communication between departments?

14. How do you plan to keep your technical and professional skills updated? Do you have an action plan?
15. Have you ever assessed your own technical skills or completed a skills inventory for yourself? If not, how do you decide which technical areas are important for you to continue learning?

Section XI
Supporting Existing Software

SUPPORT OF EXISTING SOFTWARE REMAINS AN ESSENTIAL PART of the application system life cycle. To dismiss program maintenance as merely software fixes would be impractical and unwise. Most reported maintenance activity, excluding the millennium date conversion, is not corrective in nature but rather modifications and/or enhancements that result from changes in business environments.

Enduring the demands of system support has been a hardship for many managers. Although some may argue otherwise, maintaining aging "legacy" systems is often perceived as an unrewarding and frustrating process. Even maintenance of newer systems, written in the microcomputer environment, poses a motivational challenge for programming staff. Justifying the true cost of support, either in savings or expense, has further added to the burden of maintenance efforts. Various approaches to the maintenance process, including management and technical techniques, continue to improve the success of overall support. However, rigorous challenges still exist and most organizations rely heavily on the maintainability of mission critical applications for business survival.

One of the significant maintenance challenges to affect most organizations has been the millennium date change. Although adequately covered in the trade press, there are many companies that have yet to address this issue. Additionally, there is still debate as to how serious the date problem will actually be to production systems. Chapter XI-1, "The Year 2000: Crisis or Opportunity," provides an interesting perspective on the impact that the millennium date conversion will have on computer-based organizations. Some organizations have already experienced problems due to projected date calculation routines. On the other hand, there may be opportunities for reviewing software inventories or analyzing systems for possible reengineering.

Given the pace of software and hardware advances, it should follow that programmer productivity has grown equally fast. This is not the case, because for many new applications being developed, there is one constraint — it must plug into an established world of corporate data and the processes that manage them. For many companies, the processes that manage their enterprise data were written at least 10 to 15 years ago. Rewriting legacy systems would solve the technology gap experienced today, but the cost and risks are usually too great. Chapter IX-2, "Interfacing Legacy Applications with RDBMSs and Middleware," outlines some options available for interfacing legacy systems with the latest technology, enabling a company to continue to compete in a rapidly changing field.

Extending the useful life of existing software applications is another option that is often prudent and economically wise. Unlike the necessary modification for the year 2000 dates changes, there can be beneficial reasons to keep mission critical systems in production. Chapter XI-3, "Improving Legacy Systems Maintainability," discusses the options and opportunities to invigorate the support process through various methodologies. Development managers may want to explore the many ways that these methods can help coalesce disparities between supporting legacy systems and new applications built with different technologies.

It is doubtful that software support will ever be eliminated from the list of responsibilities performed by IS departments. However, over time, the level of effort required to maintain any given application should diminish as older code is replaced with higher-quality programs. The current popularity of migrating long-standing applications to newer platforms and languages is a serious undertaking. In Chapter XI-4, "Critical Success Factors in Reengineering Legacy Systems," presents a comprehensive review of key elements for system redeployment. Consideration should be given for an integrated approach to reengineering that includes methodologies, procedures, and tools.

Another strategy to ease support efforts via improved development methods is presented in Chapter XI-5, "Moving Legacy Systems into the Future." Many IS environments fall prey to the redevelopment syndrome as the better method to lessen support overhead. In some situations, this approach is certainly warranted. But in many cases, application software is migrated to newer technologies without first assessing which technologies and alternatives provide the most return on investment. Development managers should be aware that the same issues for new development can be applied to redeveloping legacy systems.

Chapter XI-1

The Year 2000: Crisis or Opportunity?

Wayne R. Vincent

MANY COMPUTERS THROUGHOUT THE WORLD may cease to function properly on January 1, 2000, at 12:00:01 A.M. Referred to as the Year 2000 Challenge, or the Year 2000 Millennium Bug, the problem is this: Software applications that calculate, compare, sort, or perform computations on date fields will render incorrect responses if the applications are not year-2000 ready. Currently, many of the date fields stored in computer applications are in MM/DD/YY format. For instance, both November 21, 1905, and November 21, 2005 are stored, under the six-digit format, as 11/21/05, which is inconclusive as to which century the date indicates. Computers and users alike cannot properly compare or sort such dates in an intelligent, usable manner.

In addition, programming decisions were made decades ago that were appropriate at the time; however, these decisions are having implications today, with the year 2000 just around the corner, that are posing problems that may be hard to detect. For example, certain two-digit year values have been hard-coded into programs to indicate events, such as Interrupt, ,If year=00 or End-of-file, ,If year=99. Programs that incorporated these techniques will cause programs to hang or terminate prematurely, even before the turn of the century.

THE ORIGINS OF THE YEAR 2000 PROBLEM

Before the personal computer (PC) revolution in the early 1980s and the availability of off-the-shelf shrink-wrapped software solutions, the majority of computers in the world were mainframe and super-mini computers, most of which resided in the corporate sector. These were large systems that required a specially built, climate-controlled room, possessed limited RAM, and demanded optimized software functionality to obtain the fastest runtime and disk use. Large departments of internal programmers were hired to write business and scientific applications in various languages.

Given the prohibitive costs associated with using quantities of memory, internal programmers were trained to write software applications that contained algorithms for minimizing disk space, disk access, and RAM optimization. An obvious and simple way to minimize disk space was to store the year as two digits. Software applications were written to accommodate the two-digit year by implying the 20th century "19." This, in turn, led to substantial space savings in software applications that contained a date in every record. For example, insurance companies maintaining a database of accident claims in which 5 million records were stored would have saved 10 million bytes of disk by using this two-digit minimization, at a time when the price for disk space was approximately $5,000 per megabyte.

In spite of the pressures to produce the smallest, most efficient programs possible, one question arises: Why did programmers not anticipate the year 2000 in their design specifications? Many software departments were under constant pressure to deliver software according to an unrealistic time schedule created by upper managers, who were not always computer savvy. Supermini computers of the early 1980s ran with processors rated at 1.75 million instructions per second (MIPS), as opposed to today's UNIX workstations, for example, which execute at speeds in excess of 100 MIPS. (In fact, the MIPS measuring tool has since been superseded by SPECInts. SPEC, which stands for the Systems PerformanceEvaluation Cooperative, is made up of a number of computer system manufacturers that have developed a series of mutually accepted test programs to measure system performance. Ints represents a series of six C programs designed to measure system performance based exclusively on integer math. The resulting SPECInt number is a geometric mean of the elapsed time to complete each program. Therefore, large COBOL business applications commonly compiled for several hours, usually overnight. Errors in the code were corrected the following day and recompiled the following night—a long, tedious process. Older machines, dating from the 1960s and 1970s, ran with even slower processors and dramatically compound this problem.

There is one other reason why the problem could be easily ignored: Human nature. The majority of programmers never anticipated staying with an organization for 15 to 20 years, so the problem would ultimately be that of a successor.

THE SCOPE AND REACH OF THE YEAR 2000 SITUATION

Everyone in the IT industry is potentially affected by the turn of the century, if not directly, by internal computer resources, then indirectly, by outside vendors, partners, and other agencies that may either supply or request electronic data. A recent study by Olsten Corp. reported that nearly one in six North American senior executives surveyed were unaware of the year 2000 problem.

Another study performed by Gartner Group, Inc., a world leading provider of information technology advisory and market research services, has estimated that it will cost between $300 billion to $600 billion to correct the year 2000 problem worldwide (*Year 2000 Problem Gains National Attention*, at http://www.gartner.com/aboutgg/pressrl/pry2000.html). They have also estimated, with a probability of 0.7, that approximately 50% of the companies with the year 2000 problem may not become year 2000 compliant in time. Thus, all or part of their computer systems will render incorrect information or even shut down entirely on or after January 1, 2000.

The year 2000 problem exists in all organizations regardless of industry or product, in any of the following sites:

- In-house databases, where two-digit dates historically have been stored to save space.

- User interfaces, such as those requesting a range of search/sort dates from an operator for purposes of generating reports.

- Application logic, in all programming languages where dates are compared, sorted, or used in calculations.

- Electronic Data Interchange (EDI), where system receives electronic data feeds from around the world that contain dates. The problem is compounded by the fact that many of the American National Standards Institute (ANSI) Accredited Standards Committee (ASC) X12 EDI transaction sets in use today do not accommodate an eight-digit date or a century identification field.

- Operating systems, where library functions for date processing may cease to render correct results.

- Software licensing, when licenses based on the internal system date may render a false positive expiration.

- Password files, which may inadvertently expire.

Is Anyone Immune?

Companies that have stayed abreast of the leading-edge technologies and periodically reevaluated and upgraded their computer systems are less likely to be affected by the turn of the century, provided either of the following:

1. Internally written software has been rewritten with new data structures, and all data has been converted to handle the eight-digit date (i.e., mm/dd/yyyy).

Product Name	Date Limit	Date Format
Microsoft Access 95 (Assumed Date)	1999	Assumed "yy" Dates
Microsoft Access 95 (Explicit Date)	9999	Long Dates ("yyyy")
Microsoft Access (Next Major Version)	2029	Assumed "yy" Dates
Microsoft Excell 95	2019	Assumed "yy" Dates
Microsoft Excell 95	2078	Long Dates
Microsoft Excell 95 (Next Major Version)	2029	Assumed "yy" Dates
Microsoft Excell 95 (Next Major Version)	9999	Long Dates
Microsoft Project 95 (and Previous Versions)	2049	32 Bits
Microsoft SQL Server	9999	"Datetime"
MS-DOS® File System (FAT16)	2108	16 Bits
Visual C++® (4.x) Runtime Library	2036	32 Bits
Visual FoxPro	9999	Long Dates
Windows 3.x File System (FAT16)	2108	16 Bits
Windows 95 File System (FAT16)	2108	16 Bits
Windows 95 File System (FAT32)	2108	32 Bits
Windows 95 Runtime Library (WIN32)	2099	16 Bits
Windows for Workgroups (FAT16)	2108	16 Bits
Windows NT File System (FAT16)	2108	16 Bits
Windows NT File System (NTFS, which is good for about 28,000 years, starting from 1601 A.D.	Future Centuries	64 Bits
Windows NT Runtime Library (WIN32)	2099	16 Bits

Exhibit 1. The Last Year Handled by Current Microsoft Products

---

2. The computer system infrastructure is using third-party software that is year 2000 compliant.

Organizations that run primarily in a PC-networked environment with Microsoft applications are currently among the safest in the industry (see Exhibit 1). This does not include companies that connect their PCs to a mainframe computer as a remote client, whereby the mainframe's year 2000 shortcomings may adversely effect the PCs' processing environment.

DETERMINING AN ORGANIZATION'S RISK

Most organizations cannot afford down-time during normal business hours, so, with just under three years until the turn of the century, the time to begin evaluating whether an organization is year 2000 compliant is now. Another fact only emphasizes the point: As of January 1, 1997, there were 312 weekend days available for testing, redesigning, and implementation of a solution.

Corporations that use computers for business applications are not the only sectors at risk. Computers are used in thousands of businesses for tasks other than data processing, billing, accounting, and credit. For instance, mainframes are still used to drive machinery and equipment in:

- *Agriculture.* At risk are dairy farms and machines that process vegetation.
- *Industry.* Examples include paper mills, logging, and packaging plants.
- *Utilities.* The most obvious are nuclear power plants.

Exhibit 2 is a list of questions that has been designed to assist the systems development manager in identifying where to begin the evaluation of a computer system. Still other questions may be added as the research progresses.

The subsequent sections give a detailed explanation of each question and its implications.

Does the organization own all of the source code to the software used? Owning the source code to the software gives an advantage in testing and correcting those limitations within it. An in-house MIS department may perform the work, or it can be outsourced to a consulting firm. Modifications to a proven system is better than redesigning applications from square one.

How many total lines of code are there? Over the years, in effort to quantify programming costs versus efficiency, an average of $1.10 per line of code has been used. Ideally, IS staff does not have to visit every line of code within a program; however, modules that require modifications to correct flaws in date-specific calculations need to be quantified to build a business case for either repairing or reinventing the system.

Can IS staff compile the software on the organization's equipment? Does it own the compilers? Simply owning the source code is not enough. The company may own it because it was part of a contract with the consulting firm that provided the service, or it may have acquired the source code from an escrow account if the supplier of the software went out of business. In either case, IS requires a development system, proper compilers, and the library functions used in the application(s) to rebuild the organization's software infrastructure. This must be done whether the decision is to repair the existing system internally or through an outside service.

1. How many total lines of code are there?
2. Can the IS staff compile the software on the organization's equipment? Does it own the compilers?
3. Does the organization employ an MIS or software-development staff?
4. Is the software leased?
5. Was the software purchased from or written by an outside vendor?
6. Is that vendor still in business?
7. Do the warranties cover software-upgrade maintenance?
8. Is the software copyrighted by an outside company?
9. How many megabytes or gigabytes of data need to be converted to the new format?
10. Does the organization require additional hardware for the increased data size or for new development?
11. Which software applications could be eliminated by a change in business procedure?
12. Is EDI technology employed to transmit data to or from other organizations? Who are the trading partners?
13. What transactions take place? What applications are affected by this data?
14. Does the computer system's user manual indicate that the internal clock handles the year 2000?
15. Is the human resource department year 2000 compliant? Is payroll? Are the company's pension plans? What kind of commitment is there from the fund?
16. Is the organization publicly traded? If so, certain legal disclosures are reqired by the Securities and Exchange Commission.

Exhibit 2. Questions to Evaluate System Year 2000 Preparedness

---

Does the organization employ an MIS or software-development staff? If so, IS should create a year 2000 task force to evaluate and report on the current state of the technical infrastructure. The candidates for this task force should include the most experienced senior staff members. This is not an exercise in learning; rather, it is a strategic planning mission designed to identify the shortcomings of the business and implement a plan of correction for issues on the critical path.

Is the software leased? The company leasing the software may be obligated to address any year 2000 limitations within the software, as defined in the contractual agreement. Legal issues concerning services provided ensure they cannot limit, or impede, normal operating conditions. Nor can such services jeopardize the livelihood of the business. IS managers should contact the leasing agent and legal assistance to identify now how the millennium bug will be handled.

Was the software purchased from or written by an outside vendor? In many contracts the software vendor may stipulate that the software purchased is a one-time fee. Any additional software enhancements are billed as a premium to the base system.

Is that vendor still in business? Software companies and vendors that are no longer in business do not necessarily relinquish copyright ownership. However, because support is no longer an option, altering the product leaves the IS staff in no worse a position.

Do the warranties cover software-upgrade maintenance? Older contracts are unlikely to contain a clause that specifically mentions the turn of the century, but most contracts contain conditions by which the vendor must provide adequate support for inferiorities within their product. IS managers can contact the vendor to address the liabilities and consequences of flaws within their application. The real issue here is, does the corrective work fall under the guidelines of maintenance fees, or is it an additional cost?

Is the software copyrighted by an outside company? The issue here is copyright ownership. Software is copyrighted much the same way as literature; the author owns the rights for life plus 50 years beyond his or her death. For corporate authors, the number increases to 75 years. (Software copyright ownership applies only to computer software written after January 1, 1978.) Most software warranties are void if the user modifies the software beyond its intended use; therefore, executing software that modifies the purchased product may place an organization in a weaker position than if IS staff had consulted the original vendor first. The best advice is to seek legal guidance to protect the organization's interests.

How many megabytes or gigabytes of data need to be converted to the new format? The answer to this question gives an estimate for the amount of time required to convert the data to a structure that supports the new format, as in the case of accident claims.

Does the organization require additional hardware for the increased data size or for new development? Does the existing hardware infrastructure support 5M bytes, 10M bytes, 1G bytes of additional data? Many database applications require a fixed "BLOB" (Binary Large Objects) space. Will the addition of 2 bytes per record exhaust the existing area that has been allocated?

If IS will be rewriting and recompiling software applications, an off-line development system will be required. Mainframes that were designed with a wide databus were intended for interactive transaction updates. Compilers exhaust the minimal batch capacity of these systems, thus degrading the system below levels of productive use. Securing a development system is a must for parallel development and cost-effective reengineering.

Which software applications could be eliminated by a change in business procedure? IS staff should evaluate all applications and attempt to eliminate year 2000-affected applications by changing the workflow for a particular task. All should stay open minded and "think outside the box." Not all problems require a software solution, at least not immediately. If a workflow process can be restructured to eliminate the infected application, it will be one less task that demands valuable resources.

Is EDI technology employed to transmit data to or from other organizations? The data transmitted to other organizations must be year 2000 compliant for many legal reasons. The challenge here is to address a problem in which most of the ANSI ASC X12 EDI transaction sets in use today do not contain an eight-digit or century-switch field. Without a major overhaul of the interchange system, the problem cannot be solved.

How many vendors, platforms, and versions are currently in production? IS staff should compile a list of all vendors, platforms, and versions currently in use throughout the network, followed by a list of the shortcomings, limitations, and alternative solutions to address them.

Who are the trading partners? The IS manager should ask them whether they are or will be year 2000 compliant by the time it's necessary. Even if the organization's system is year 2000 compliant, trading partners' data may crash internal applications if it is not.

Preprocessing of received data may be an option, but Is managers should consider whether the organization ought to absorb the cost of implementing such processes.

What transactions take place? What applications are effected by this data? IS staff should identify which transactions are dependent on the received data and consider whether the transactions could paralyze the company's business.

Address	Organization
http://www.gartner.com	Gartner Group
http://www.year2000.com	Year 2000 Cosortium
http://www.microsoft.com	Microsoft
http://www.prairienet.org	Graduate School of Information and Library Science, University of Illinois at Urbana-Champaign
http://www.s390.hosting.ibm.com	IBM
http://www.dbss.com	Dun & Bradstreet

Exhibit 3. Universal Resource Locators of Interest to Year 2000 Bug Researchers

---

Does the computer system's user manual indicate that the internal clock handles the year 2000? Simply, IS staff should check the vendor manuals to determine whether the operating system and internal clock is capable of handling the turn of the century. The vendor can give this information if an answer cannot be determined from the manuals.

Is the human resource department year 2000 compliant? Is payroll? Are the company's pension plans? What kind of commitment is there from the fund to address year 2000 issues? Human resources, the bloodline to employees' benefits, must begin to validate the compensation system currently in place. Miscalculations in payroll, vacation time, and disability may create serious liability and legal repercussions. A company could risk to lose thousands, if not millions, of dollars in benefits, such as vacation time, as well as cause extreme confusion and penalties for overdrawn accounts. In addition, whether payroll is managed internally or outsourced, the system must be able to handle the new millennium. Repercussions include grossly overpaying or underpaying its employees.

IS managers should discuss how investments are selected within the organization's pension fund. Is the fund manager aware that many companies may declare bankruptcy shortly before, or shortly after, the turn of the century? Are the employees' interests protected?

Rumors are already circulating that the year 2000 will bring the next devastating stock market crash. Financial experts should be consulted, keeping in mind that employees closest to retirement may sustain loses that could never be recouped before their departure. The organization managing the fund should disseminate information showing the results of their research regarding the year 2000.

Is the organization a publicly traded company? If so, the organization may be required to disclose known problems regarding the Year 2000 Bug to the Securities and Exchange Commission. These disclosures will be enforced under various accounting standards, securities laws, and bank-examination policies. For example, under accounting standards that mandate disclosure exists a principle in Generally Accepted Accounting Principles (GAAP). This Principle, established by the Financial Accounting Standards Board (FASB) in 1984, is Statement of Financial Accounting Standards No. 5 (SFAS 5) "Accounting for Contigencies." This principle provides for contingencies which are reasonably possible, whether the amount can be calculated or estimated, must be disclosed in a note to the financial statements (*Legal Issues Concerning the Year 2000 "Millennium Bug,"* Jeff Jinnett, http://www.year2000.com/archive/legalissues.html). (Exhibit II-4-3 contains URLs of interest to year 2000 researchers.)

Chapter XI-2
Interfacing Legacy Applications with RDBMSs and Middleware
Dan Fobes

TODAY PROGRAMMERS HAVE A WIDE RANGE OF OPTIONS when developing applications. There is an endless number of tools and techniques associated with simply writing a program. Hardware advances deliver what used to be the power of a mainframe on a programmer's desktop. Given the pace of software and hardware advances, it should follow that programmer productivity has grown equally as fast. This is not the case, because for many new applications being developed, there is one constraint — it must plug into an established world of corporate data and the processes that manage them. For many companies, the processes that manage their enterprise data were written 10 to 15 years ago. These applications are also referred to as legacy systems. Rewriting legacy systems would solve the technology gap experienced today, but the cost and risks are usually too great. This chapter outlines some options available for interfacing legacy systems with the latest technology, enabling a company to continue to compete in a rapidly changing field.

CLIENT/SERVER AND DECENTRALIZED IS

In the 1970s and early 1980s IBM dominated IS with mainframes, and IS programmers wrote largely in COBOL. All programs were defined by users, then written by IS. As a result all mission-critical applications were coded by one group and executed on one machine. In the mid to late 1980s, the PC started to replace terminals as companies moved to empower the user with word processors and spreadsheet applications. Nontechnical users could move data from the mainframe to their desktop and do some additional client processing within a spreadsheet without the aid of IS. Network operating systems (NOSs) provided a means to connect PCs in a local area network allowing for users to share both the raw mainframe data and PC processed data. Hence the birth of client/server. As a result, companies had distributed their mission critical data processing from a centralized IS throughout the enterprise.

0-8493-9979-3/99/$0.00+$.50
© 1999 by CRC Press LLC

The Failure of Client/Server

All applications can be broken down into three groups of code (or tiers):

1. Presentation Tier — get user information.
2. Business Tier — process user information.
3. Data Tier — write processed information.

When applications were written by one group and run on one machine, these layers were usually intermixed. It was not uncommon for one programmer to write one program that contained all three. With the advent of modular programming, large programs could be broken down into a collection of shared modules, reducing both the time required to finish an application and the risk of writing entire applications from scratch. Unfortunately, the immediate IS benefit of reusing modules would often come at the expense of large modules with large numbers of parameters instructing them how to behave for different types of invocations. However, modular programming presented the opportunity to separate the presentation tier from the business and data tiers.

With client server applications, there is a requirement to distinguish between the presentation, business, and data tiers. There are two computers involved in client/server applications — the client and the server. The client application executes on the client PC, with all presentation input being received locally from the user. However, some data are read from and written to the server for the purpose of information sharing. As a result, unlike a mainframe application, a client/server application is separated from some of its data by a network — the slowest part of any computer.

For applications such as simple spreadsheet calculations the client/server model works fine. However, many corporations, lured by the low cost of client/server technology and a need to standardize, attempted to move all IS applications to a client/server architecture. After investing lots of time and money, many companies found that the tools enabled them to re-create the applications, but the client/server model made it impossible to implement them. No matter how fast the client and server hardware is, the network is a bottleneck. With the business tier executing on the client and saturating the network with file I/O requests, it was not uncommon to see a complex client/server application become unusable when 25 to 50 users begin to use it — something a mainframe could handle easily.

SUCCEEDING WITH DISTRIBUTED DATA PROCESSING

The scalability problem that exists with client/server applications has many proposing a return to mainframes and centralized IS. However, given that data is distributed throughout an enterprise and applications exist on various platforms, others would benefit if the data and the processes that manage them can be tied together. Currently available are several options that provide for both types of solutions:

- Relational Database Management Systems
- Remote Procedure Call
- Messaging

As stated above, most legacy mainframe applications contained all three tiers. Clearly the presentation must be rewritten for the PC. For each of the technical solutions above, consider a simple PC application, PCDEPOS, that collects user information such as an account number and amount of money to deposit. The goal is to have PCDEPOS call an existing COBOL program on a mainframe, MFDEPOS, which performs the transaction (i.e., it represents the business and data tiers only).

RDBMS

One solution to the fragmentation of mission-critical data and their processes is to centralize them to one or more relational databases. Data access through a relational engine can be much faster because data contained within files located across various platforms is moved under the control of a technology built to manage it. Files are moved to tables and selected columns within tables can be indexed. Furthermore, business logic, usually in the form of COBOL programs, can be recoded as SQL-based stored procedures that are compiled then executed within the RDBMS engine for optimal performance. Additionally, most databases support some form of replication whereby tables from one database can be replicated to others, facilitating information sharing. Finally, Transaction Processing (TP) monitors are available for most RDBMS. A separate product, TP monitors interface a client application to a RDBMS and increase performance where large numbers of users require data access. It does this by creating a pool of costly connections to the RDBMS and having the application use a connection from the pool only when necessary.

For the example application, PCDEPOS is created to collect information from the user using middleware, called an open database connectivity (or ODBC) driver, supplied by the RDBMS vendor to facilitate communication between the client and the server. Files that MFDEPOS wrote to and read from, or the data tier, must be moved into RDBMS'$ tables. There are two options for MFDEPOS'$ data processing logic (the business tier) — it can be rewritten as a stored procedure within the RDBMS or modified to perform I/O against SQL tables instead of files.

There are two problems with this solution. For one, it increases the cost and complexity of applications. An RDBMS requires the purchase of a RDBMS, additional server hardware, and one or more dedicated database administrators (DBAs) to install, design, tune, and maintain it. The other problem is risk. Simple applications may be easy to move to a RDBMS; however, no legacy application is simple. Many companies will be required to spend a large amount of resources normalizing or breaking up the data within records, as they move from files to RDBMS tables. This is because an RDBMS table has a limit of 255 columns and no row can exceed 2 kilobytes in size — legacy applications typically exceed this. Also, not all data maps over from a file to a table (e.g., dates), and for each of these, a translation is required. Time and staff must be allocated to not only normalize data and map data types, but also verify that existing data moves cleanly into the RDBMS. Part of the migration to an RDBMS is the modifications to the existing business tier code. In the example application, rewriting the MFDE-POS business tier as a stored procedure introduces significant risk because of the differences between the languages (a form of SQL and COBOL). The alternative of replacing file I/O within the COBOL program with RDBMS I/O is usually not feasible because of the scalability issues (requires the COBOL code to execute on the PC).

An RDBMS solution has many benefits, however the costs and risks associated with moving the data and recoding the business logic must be weighed.

REMOTE PROCEDURE CALLS

For most, there is a significantly smaller risk in tying together existing systems that work. What is needed is a form of interprocess communication (IPC) to have one process send and receive data to another. One form of IPC is Remote Procedure Call (RPC).

Using RPC a program calls a procedure that is executed on a different machine. There is always a one-to-one relationship, and the calling program blocks until the called procedure returns. This sounds simple enough, but since the applications are residing in different address spaces, the only data that each share are the parameters they pass, not global variables within the applications. For an RPC across different machines, data mapping must be addressed, because not all hardware supports the same byte-order (i.e., it stores numbers differently). Finally, either or both machines can crash at any point and recovery must be addressed.

Some vendors of development systems provide proprietary RPC mechanisms that address some of the above issues. There are also standards such as the RPC protocol used by the Open Group's Distributed Computing Environment (DCE). Additionally, third-party vendors provide Object Request Brokers (ORBs) for RPC services. The most common ORB is called CORBA. A standard created by the Object Management Group (OMG), CORBA facilitates RPCs across different machines. Unfortunately, the CORBA standard is just that — a standard. Because CORBA is similar to UNIX, each vendor has a slightly different implementation of that standard, and until very recently different CORBA implementations could communicate with each other. Microsoft has a competing technology called the Distributed Component Object Model (DCOM). Many vendors support both CORBA and DCOM as their RPC mechanism, and although both CORBA and DCOM are complex to program, they are options that should be considered when evaluating distributed processing via RPC.

MESSAGE-ORIENTED MIDDLEWARE

Another form of IPC is messaging. Vendors of message-oriented middleware provide a mechanism to send and receive messages asynchronously from one process to another. A message is simply a string of bytes the user defines. There are two approaches to messaging: message queues and publish/subscribe. In a message queue environment, an application sends messages to and receives messages from queues. In a publish/subscribe model, an application broadcasts and receives messages via a subject. The sender specifies the subject of the message and the receiver specifies the subject(s) it wants to get messages for. There are pros and cons to each; however, both are sufficient for most environments.

As stated above, a message is a user-defined string of bytes — there is no standard that needs to be followed. A typical messaging application sends and receives messages asynchronously across multiple platforms. The messaging subsystem handles the routing with most vendors supporting the concept of guaranteed and assured delivery (i.e., the message will get to the receiver and only once). One of the strengths of messaging, which differentiates it from RPC, is that the sender need not block, or wait until the receiver responds. Another strength is that one message may be delivered to multiple listeners.

For the example application, messages would contain the arguments to the MFDEPOS program. To facilitate messaging, a new server application called MFLISTEN is required, and the client application must be modified to send and receive messages to it. MFLISTEN listens for client messages and calls the server application with the arguments specified in the message. Once completed, MFDEPOS returns control back to MFLISTEN, which sends the arguments back to the client via a message.

Since there is no enforced message type, defining one that is flexible becomes a challenge. Different requests for different server applications will likely require a different message, and over time this may become unmanageable as each request begins to change. There are two ways to solve this problem: message versioning and self-describing messages.

To accomplish the deposit application using message versioning, a message could simply contain the linkage to MFDEPOS with each parameter separated by a delimiter (see Exhibit 1).

SUPPORTING EXISTING SOFTWARE

Exhibit 1. Message Containing Parameters with @@ as a Delimiter for MFDEPOS.

```
------------------------------------------------
| Parameter 1@@Parameter 2@@Parameter 3@@ ...
------------------------------------------------
```

Exhibit 2. Simple Message with Segments Supporting Message Versions.

| 4 bytes | 2 bytes | 2 bytes | 2 bytes | 2 bytes | ...

| MessageID | Segment Count | SegmentID | Segment Version | Segment Size | Parameter 1...

| SegmentID | Segment Version | Segment Size | Parameter 1...

Although this works, it requires a dedicated MFLISTEN program for each server program such as MFDEPOS. A more flexible approach would be to break up the message into multiple segments and then build a header to contain segment information (see Exhibit 2). Designing messages around segments is not new — a standard called Electronic Data Interchange, or EDI, is also based on segments.

Here MessageID represents the format of the message, Segment Count is the number of segments in the message, SegmentID is the start of the segment and represents the program name (e.g., 1 for MFDEPOS), segment version represents the format of the parameters (number, order, datatypes), and the parameters follow. The parameters can be delimited or fixed length — their layout is defined by SegmentID and Segment Version. The benefit to moving the program name and version down to the segment is that it allows for one MFLISTEN program to serve as an interface to multiple server programs. The only problem with this design is when MFDEPOS'$ linkage changes, the format of the segment changes and the segment version must be incremented. Sending applications such as PCDEPOS would need to be changed to send the new message. Receiving applications such as MFLISTEN would need to be modified to verify the new message version and call the updated version of MFDEPOS.

To accomplish the deposit application using self-describing data, the version number within the message is replaced by field descriptors. Specifically, each parameter value in the message is prepended with a field name that defines it (see Exhibit 3).

With self-describing data, the segment remains the same, but each parameter has two components: a descriptor and a value. These two components can be fixed length or delimited (they are fixed length in Exhibit 3). The benefit to this structure is that it automates the process of calling legacy

726

Exhibit 3. Segment Supporting Self Describing Data.

| 2 bytes | 2 bytes | 2 bytes | 8 bytes | ? | 8 bytes

| SegmentID | Segment Version | Segment Size | P1 Descriptor | P1 Value | P2 Descriptor | ...

applications. The best case scenario with versioning saw one listener program created to serve multiple server applications. However, the sending applications (PCDEPOS) and the listener application (MFLISTEN) require an update when there is any change to the server application's linkage (MFDEPOS). With self-describing fields, we can reduce this maintenance to a batch scan on the server. An application on the mainframe can be written to scan a COBOL program and extract the linkage to a table that contains each name and type. The sending applications would then use the names in the COBOL linkage to describe their data, followed by the value of that field. The MFLISTEN program, upon receiving a message, can extract the program name and map the linkage in the message to the linkage in the database automatically, then make the call. New versions of MFDEPOS can be scanned and the database updated. No changes are required to MFLISTEN or PCDEPOS in most cases.

Some message systems allow for field mapping within the message. This allows the MFLISTEN application to query the message for fields instead of parsing it directly. This simplifies MFLISTEN, and combined with self-describing data, which provides the optimal messaging solution.

Not all is golden with a messaging solution. Although guaranteed delivery insures a message gets to its destination, it may be possible that one transaction is composed of several messages. Additionally, one message may require the execution of multiple listener programs. In either case, a program would have to initiate a transaction locally, send the messages, subscribe to the responses, and roll back if any of them failed. Another possible issue with messaging is security. With messages traveling back and forth on a network, a hacker can easily listen in, make a change, and send messages back out. Here, encryption is required.

RECOMMENDED COURSE OF ACTION

The above technologies are not mutually exclusive, and in fact, it may turn out that a combination of all three is the best solution. For example, a client may communicate with a server using RPC, the server may use messaging to perform IPC with another server, and one or both of these servers may interact with an RDBMS.

In general, all programs should be separated into three tiers and corporate data should be managed by an RDBMS. Business logic should be coded in a high-level language such as COBOL, which calls a minimum of stored procedures for I/O intensive requests. Finally, the presentation should be coded in a rapid application tool that supports an RDBMS such as Visual Basic. For companies that require a high volume of transactions, middleware in the form of a transaction server or a TP monitor combined with an ORB should be considered.

Migrating an enterprise to this configuration involves many steps and differs for different companies. Avoid the all-or-nothing approach. Risk can be reduced by using a divide-and-conquer approach that targets subsystems. Below are some high-level steps for accomplishing such a migration:

1. Identify a logical subsystem of the enterprise.
2. Form a team composed of programmers who understand the subsystem and others who understand the target technology.
3. Identify the data of the subsystem.
4. Identify existing applications that manage the data, then tie them together using messaging. This will uncover redundant data and data processing within the subsystem.
5. Design the RDBMS solution (tables, stored procedures, etc.)
6. Create a listener program that listens to the messages created in step 4 and performs the requests on the RDBMS.
7. Once the RDBMS can service all of the messages of step 4, it can be phased in.
8. Go to step 1.

Some applications may span subsystems. Messaging supports this requirement well and should be used. Although most RDBMSs support replication, this usually requires one server to stream over tables of information to another server at scheduled intervals. Not only does this introduce a delay across servers, it does not scale for large databases — messaging the updates as they happen addresses both shortcomings.

When the RDBMS phase-in is complete, new applications should go directly against the RDBMS. Most new technology being introduced provides for access to RDBMSs. The legacy applications can continue using messaging, be modified for direct RDBMS access, or be rewritten.

Chapter XI-3
Improving Legacy Systems Maintainability
Young-Gul Kim

THE IS FIELD DEVOTES MUCH OF ITS HUMAN RESOURCES to software maintenance. When existing systems are difficult to understand, as is the case with many legacy systems, software maintenance becomes a time-consuming and challenging task. This chapter clarifies the features of legacy systems and the challenges the systems pose to IS managers and their staffs. It then presents improvement techniques geared toward specific types of legacy systems.

WHAT IS A LEGACY SYSTEM?

Despite its ubiquitous usage, the term "legacy system" suffers from ambiguity. Many people understand a legacy system to be a large and old piece of software that is hard to maintain. Others have defined legacy systems as large software systems that are vital to organizations but that staff have difficulty coping with.[1]

Although the word *legacy* implies some age, there is little agreement about how old a system needs be to qualify as a legacy system. Similarly, software size is not a readily applicable criterion for categorizing the legacy class.

For these reasons, it is more prudent and practical to define a legacy system as a software system in operation that is hard to maintain. Many such systems are old, having been built in the 1960s and 1970s. The majority of them are large batch-processing systems that handle an organization's high-volume business transactions on the mainframe.

The typical problems associated with such legacy systems are poor documentation, spaghetti code without an effective control structure, lack of knowledgeable personnel, and lack of performance and adaptability. Some of these problems result from a lack of proper management actions, whereas others stem from technical constraints.

0-8493-9979-3/99/$0.00+$.50
© 1999 by CRC Press LLC

Poor documentation and lack of modularity make the job of the maintenance programmer, who probably was not involved in the original development project, extremely difficult. Because many of these legacy systems were developed when main memory optimization and processing speed were key design considerations, they lack flexibility and user-friendliness and cannot exploit the features of today's vastly changed computing environment (i.e., cheap and huge main memory, optical storage, powerful graphics, and parallel processing architecture).

THE LEGACY DILEMMA

Legacy systems represent the years, and sometimes decades, of an organization's substantial investment in hardware, software, and human resources. The real value of a legacy system, however, lies in the years of accumulated business rules, policies, expertise, and know-how embedded the system. If corporate knowledge is defined as a company's organized experience and knowledge gained from problem-solving activities, a legacy system represents the corporate knowledge repository. It acts as an invisible but intelligent agent of the corporate problem-solving process.

On the other hand, because of their poor maintainability and technical obsolescence, legacy systems pose significant organizational burdens. As IS personnel invest their time and energy in understanding and maintaining legacy systems, increasing requests for new systems cause applications backlogs to increase further.

Because legacy systems reliably handle critical corporate transactions, giving them up or replacing them with new systems will not only incur huge financial burdens, but may create managerial chaos arising from user resistance and massive conversion of data, forms, and procedures. At the same time, today's legacy systems are too expensive to maintain and cause organizations to suffer from inflexible and unavailable IS services.

Assuming that giving up on a legacy system is not feasible for most organizations in the immediate future, the solution to the legacy dilemma appears to lie in improving legacy systems so that they become more maintainable.

CLASSIFYING LEGACY SYSTEMS

The definition of a legacy system as a software system in operation that is hard to maintain means that there are a variety of different legacy systems. Some were developed in the 1960s and others in the 1980s and 1990s. Some are enterprisewide batch transaction-processing systems and others are used within an end-user department for online analysis and reporting purposes.

Because of the variety of legacy systems in operation, it is futile to attempt to find a single legacy solution applicable to one class of system.

Instead, legacy systems should be classified into several types to which tailored approaches and techniques are applied.

First-Generation Legacy Systems

First-generation legacy systems were developed between the mid-1960s and late 1970s. Some of these systems were developed in machine language, but most of them were developed in assembly language or early versions of third-generation programming languages such as COBOL or FORTRAN.

Most first-generation systems are batch transaction-processing systems running on mainframes. They rarely have development or operational documentation, and no one in the organization fully understands their inner workings or the purpose of changes made over the years. First-generation systems have low modularization and suffer from a serious scalability problem in accommodating growing business demands.

Second-Generation Legacy Systems

Second-generation legacy systems were developed from the late 1970s throughout the 1980s. They differ from first-generation systems in many respects.

Unlike first-generation systems, many second-generation systems possess some level of modularity and development documentation. Many are used for online transaction processing (OLTP) tasks and run not only on mainframes but also on a diverse set of midrange computers. Although the majority were written in COBOL, some were written in fourth-generation languages and are based on early database management systems (DBMSs).

Despite these differences, second-generation systems share with first-generation systems the common symptoms of a legacy system: lack of documentation on changes, lack of knowledgeable maintenance personnel, and uncontrolled redundancy in data and functionality.

Third-Generation Legacy Systems

The origin and characteristics of third-generation legacy systems differ sharply from those of their first- and second-generation counterparts. Developed since the late 1980s, third-generation systems suffer or will suffer from even worse maintenance problems than their predecessors.

Many third-generation systems were developed using graphical user interface (GUI) development tools in the rapid application development (RAD) style. Because developers therefore skipped most of the conceptual- and logical-level modeling of data and processes, third-generation systems turn the clock of IS development back to the first generation. Only this time the maintenance nightmare is bigger, because new GUI development tool environments are far more diverse and are changing much faster in terms of functionality, structure, and, in some cases, existence than did their relatively stable COBOL counterparts.

Maintenance programmers of third-generation systems will soon become like the unfortunate end user lost in a sea of documents written in different versions of multiple word processing software without any indexing or document-type information. This problem is not limited to systems developed in-house. Companies that adopt popular enterprise resource planning (ERP) packages may find their state-of-the-art integrated client/server solution quickly turning into a third-generation legacy system if they customize it too much without care. One Korean firm, for example, recently customized 40% of its SAP R3 package without systematically documenting the changes.

IMPROVING LEGACY SYSTEMS

Improving a legacy system for higher maintainability involves understanding the following four software engineering techniques:

- Redocumentation
- Restructuring
- Reverse engineering
- Reengineering

These techniques differ from one another in terms of the tasks they perform and the level of abstractions they address.[2]

Redocumentation

Redocumentation is the creation or revision of a semantically equivalent representation within the same relative abstraction level. Adding program comment lines or reflecting changes of data definition in the original data model are examples of redocumentation efforts.

The goal of redocumentation is to reinforce the originally deficient documentation or keep it up to date by tracking changes made after initial development. Of the four legacy improvement techniques, redocumentation is the simplest and the oldest one with the least change impact. All three types of legacy systems can benefit from this technique.

Restructuring

Restructuring is the transformation from one representation form to another at the same relative abstraction while preserving the subject system's external behavior (i.e., functionality and semantics). Breaking a monolithic COBOL program with generic PERFORM statements into a set of more cohesive modules and CALL statements will be a common example of restructuring. Restructuring, however, is not limited to programs.

Normalization of relational database tables and the consequent redesign of COBOL's data divisions also belong to restructuring efforts.

The goal of restructuring is to achieve the benefits of modern programming (i.e., understandability) and data design (i.e., integrity) with minimal change effort at the syntactic level. Because of the unstructured nature of their processing logic and data design, first-generation legacy systems will benefit most from restructuring; second-generation systems may also benefit to some degree.

Reverse Engineering

Reverse engineering is the process of analyzing a subject system to identify system components and their relationships and to create representations of the system in another form or at a higher level of abstraction. Creation of a data model from the program's data descriptions or structure chart from the program's procedure division are examples of frequently performed reverse engineering tasks.

The purpose of reverse engineering is to ease the human user's understanding of the underlying semantics of the subject system by recovering them at a higher and therefore more user-friendly level of abstraction. Both first-generation and third-generation legacy systems, which are deficient of such high-level models, are ideal target systems for reverse engineering activities. Second-generation systems may also benefit from reverse engineering but mostly in the form of complementing the original models.

Reengineering

Reengineering is the examination and alteration of a subject system to reconstitute it in a new form and the subsequent implementation of the new form. Reengineering usually involves some form of reverse engineering, followed by either forward engineering or restructuring activities.

The main objective of reengineering is to lengthen the life of the target software system by modifying it to become more understandable to human users and more adaptable to changes in the business environment. Among the four legacy improvement techniques, reengineering is considered to have the most comprehensive scope and involve the most challenging change effort in terms of resource investment and project complexity. Although both first-generation and second-generation legacy systems may benefit from reengineering, cost/benefit considerations make second-generation systems the prime target of such initiatives. The enormous program understanding requirement and outdated development environment of first-generation systems require excessive resource investment for reverse and forward engineering activities.

Exhibit 1. Applicability of Legacy Improvement Techniques by Type of Legacy System

Types of Systems	Redocumentation	Improvement Restructuring	Techniques Reverse Engineering	Reengineering
First-Generation	**	**	**	*
Second-Generation	**	*	*	**
Third-Generation	**		**	

Key: **= Highly applicable
         *= Applicable

Exhibit 1 summarizes the match between the three types of legacy systems and the four legacy improvement techniques.

LEGACY FALLACIES

The widely differing perceptions and use of the term *legacy system* creates misconceptions that sometimes lead to critical investment errors. There are generally three common fallacies regarding legacy systems.

Fallacy 1: Symbols of Developers' Past Sins

Many people believe that legacy systems are the result of IS developers' lack of interest in documentation, structured programming, data modeling, and fourth-generation languages. Rather, the more fundamental problems of legacy systems result from management's inaction in setting realistic project deadlines, providing necessary tools and education, and establishing explicit and clear guidelines and procedures on handling changes in program codes and data definitions.

Legacy systems have persevered throughout the years of neglect and countless changes in business requirements. As systems that still handle the bulk of a company's business transactions, they ought to be seen as symbols of success and survival.

Fallacy 2: Replace as Soon as Possible

Against the backdrop of new GUI development tools and the movement toward distributed computing platforms, some IS professionals argue for the total and immediate replacement of their bread-and-butter legacy systems either by building new software or by purchasing an integrated, enterprisewide package. Proceeding without careful cost/benefit analysis of both replacement and improvement alternatives, however, will prove to be a critical and expensive mistake.

Moving from central host-based legacy systems to a distributed computing environment involves not only rewriting software in a new language, but also the nontrivial tasks of installing and managing networks, distributed databases, multiple servers, and from hundreds to thousands of personal computers. One major Japanese advertising agency, for example, that invested five years and over $100 million on replacing its mainframe legacy system with a client/server system of 40 servers and 900 clients is now suffering from unacceptably slow performance and high system management cost. In contrast, the U.S. Department of Defense's reverse engineering of data requirements and Boeing Corp.'s payroll-system reengineering project demonstrate the successful improvement of large-scale legacy systems.[3]

Fallacy 3: Automate Improvement with Tools

The emergence of several computer-aided software engineering (CASE) tools said to support reverse engineering or reengineering of legacy systems misleads IS managers into believing that running the codes through the tools will automatically recover higher level designs and generate the new system. This is not true, at least not yet.

Although many CASE tools support redocumentation and restructuring tasks to some extent, their support of reverse engineering and reengineering tasks remains at a basic understanding of the syntactic constructs and far from the automatic understanding of the program and data semantics required in such techniques. Design recovery as a core subset of reverse engineering must reproduce all of the information a person needs to completely understand what a program does, how it does it, and why it does it. Thus design recovery encompasses a far wider range of information than is found in conventional software engineering representations or code.[4]

THE FUTURE OF LEGACY SYSTEMS

General Douglas A. McArthur said, "Old soldiers never die, they just fade away." The same can be said of the millions of the legacy systems around the world. Although some of them will soon fade away, many of them, when properly improved, will survive the end of this millennium and continue to be the workhorses of their organizations well into the twenty-first century. Who said COBOL would be dead by the end of 1980s?

References

1. Bennet, "Legacy Systems: Coping with Success," IEEE Software 12, no. 1 (1995), pp. 19-23.
2. Chikofsky and J.H. Cross II, "Reverse Engineering and Design Recovery: A Taxonomy," IEEE Software 7, no. 1 (1990), pp. 13-17.
3. Aiken, A. Muntz, and R. Richards, "DOD Legacy Systems: Reverse Engineering Data Requirements." *Communications of the ACM* 37, no. 5 (1994) pp. 26-41; L. Markosian et al., "Using an Enabling Technology to Reengineer Legacy Systems," *Communications of the ACM* 37, no. 5 (1994), pp. 58-70.
4. Biggerstaff, "Design Recovery for Maintenance and Reuse," *IEEE Computer* (July 1989), pp. 36-49.

Chapter XI-4

Critical Success Factors in Reengineering Legacy Systems

Patricia L. Seymour

ARE ANY SOFTWARE MANAGERS today not concerned about the increasing cost of maintaining and migrating their legacy systems? Many find themselves on the firing line, unable to dodge the bullets, because they have few solutions for their legacy systems. The flush 1980s are gone but not the systems that were inherited.

However, some organizations did begin reengineering early, in the late 1980s. They have shown that reengineering can alleviate the organizational pressures caused by legacy systems. For example, Bruce Skivington of Aetna Insurance informed an audience at a conference on reengineering that Aetna had reengineered one major system and reduced its resource requirements by 60% from 1986 to 1988. The Aetna IS organization also standardized and rationalized data and thus reduced errors by 90%; such were the data complexities of its legacy systems.

Another reengineering success story comes from DST, in Kansas City MO, a processor of shareholder accounting and recordkeeping services for mutual funds. Estimates for a systems redesign and rewrite exceeded $50 million and three years for completion. The total cost was approximately $12 million, and the project was completed in 14 months

Because reengineering projects deliver often and early, organizations usually receive a return on investment quickly. Thus, scarce resources are made available for other projects.

WHAT IS REENGINEERING?

Over the years, various organizations that promote reengineering have emerged and undergone changes. So have various definitions of the term *reengineering.* Some still associate reengineering with code restructuring, and others associate it with a specific set of software tools. Still others include reverse engineering as part of reengineering.

The Systems Redevelopment Methodology (a trademark of James Martin & Co.) defines *software reengineering* as the use of tools and techniques to facilitate the analysis, improvement, redesign, and reuse of existing software systems to support changing business and technical information requirements. The IEEE has defined *reverse engineering* as "the process of analyzing a system to identify components and interrelationships and to create representations in another form or at a higher level of abstraction." The two processes often go hand-in-hand to deliver business solutions. For example, to understand data relationships in legacy systems and to extract business rules, data rationalization—a reengineering activity—must be performed, but the actual recovery and documentation of the business rules are considered reverse engineering activities.

REENGINEERING CRITICAL SUCCESS FACTORS

Why have not more companies followed the examples of Aetna and DST and embraced reengineering principles? Many organizations have approached reengineering with fragmented strategies because they believed that tools alone would solve the problems. What is needed for reengineering to be successful is an integrated approach.

The following sections examine 12 critical factors that must be addressed for reengineering to be successful. Failure to address these factors, which are also listed in Exhibit 1, often mean failure for the reengineering effort.

The Silver Bullet Syndrome

Many computer-aided software engineering (CASE) tools, workbenches, methodologies, and processes that organizations bought in the 1980s were bought because they seemed to make the transition from old to new systems as simple as pushing a button. More rigorous and disciplined reengineering concepts and strategies, which required rigor and discipline of IS organizations, struggled to compete with the many panaceas that were available. In fact, the slightest association with the word maintenance could doom a tool's or methodology's debut into the market. Continuing to budget for enhancements of legacy systems was often regarded as a waste of resources. Some organizations hired contract programmers to perform minimal maintenance on existing systems. These organizations spent the bulk of their resources on the latest and greatest state-of-the-art tools for building new systems.

There was one problem with this strategy. The old systems were poorly

- Silver bullet syndrome
- Technology driven
- Internal team
- Sponsorship
- Risk aversion and analysis paralysis
- Infrastructure support
- Ambiguous targets
- Integrated systems options
- Integrated tools
- Resistance to change
- Training and education
- Blueprint framework

Exhibit 1. Critical Success Factors in Reengineering

---

documented, and it seemed that the business rules required to create new systems could be found only in the existing source code. This was compounded by many organizations' downsizing and the forced early retirement of personnel. Those seemingly all-powerful tools, methodologies, and processes were finally seen as what they always were: silver bullets that could not deliver. It has been estimated that $16.5 billion is wasted annually on projects that never are delivered to the user.

Reengineering is not a panacea; it is not performed by pushing a button. It requires the proper set of tools and methods as well as resources and commitment. With these, reengineering can aid organizations in making a cost-effective transition from legacy to new systems that meet current and new business requirements.

Technology Driven

Reengineering began as a bottom-up technology. Programmers were toying with tools, debates about code restructuring began, and the rest is history. Rarely were strategic plans and business issues the motivation for systems reengineering. Attention was on code, and usually business sponsors were not involved. At one time, there was much trade press about whether code restructuring tools could even produce functionally equivalent code.

Such companies as Pacific Bell, Hartford Insurance, Aetna, and General Mills were some of the early pioneers that proved that code restructurers not only produced functionally equivalent code but facilitated reengineering strategies. When integrated into business strategies, these restructuring tools

- Create the team
- Understand the challenge
- Assess organization readiness and culture
- Identify stakeholders and create effective sponsorship
- Review and establish reward and recognition programs
- Market consultatively to the internal client
- Create, implement, and manage partenership agreements
- Communicate the change
- Provide for technology transfer
- Identify critical success factors for pilot projects

Exhibit 2. Steps in Human Factors Approach to Reengineering

---

would guide the migration to new systems. Some of these companies partnered with major reengineering software vendors to define requirements for data equivalency and modularization tools.

The technical debates over restructuring tools soon died, and many organizations rushed blindly to buy these tools. Without an integrated strategy for using the tools, these IS organizations soon found their shelves lined with unused copies of restructuring software.

The Need for an Internal Team

It soon became clear that reengineering required a different support structure than common, standalone maintenance tools did. Tool users lacked the skills to influence strategies of an entire IS organization and capture necessary funding and other resources. If reengineering were to survive, it would need a team approach.

Pacific Bell in San Ramon CA developed a team known as the Systems Renewal Group. Because reengineering was believed to be a technical problem, a technology group was formed. However, the group became greatly bewildered when it failed to influence peers on reengineering strategies. This resistance made the group reevaluate its approach. Exhibit 2 summarizes the approach that the group started to develop. It has been further refined by Technology Innovations of Danville CA.

After extensive training and applying the consulting and marketing skills they learned, the group successfully trained several other groups to perform software reengineering throughout the company. They attributed their success to having realized that their lack of understanding of organizational change rather than technology was at fault. Organizational change was found to be key in directing the reengineering methods and approach. Although the Systems Renewal Group was successful, its members have stated that it was a grass-roots effort with minimal sponsorship.

Sponsorship

The lack of IS and business sponsorship is probably the primary reason for failure with reengineering. Because software reengineering is usually started at the technical level, senior management may never become involved nor understand systems reengineering issues. One of the most frequently asked questions at reengineering conferences is, How can I sell reengineering to upper management and internal business clients and sponsors?

Usually, IS projects are approved and funded by business clients. In the last decade, a growing number of enhancements and changes to business applications have caused software to grow significantly more complex. Along with smaller IS staffs, this complexity has resulted in users' charging IS organizations with being unresponsive to their needs. This situation is exacerbated by new development projects that are delivered late or over budget or are never delivered. In many cases, friction has grown to the point that business users are hesitant to fund any project that does not directly support their needs.

When users are involved with every activity from training to reviewing reports and setting priorities, both users and IS staff better understand each other's needs. When business sponsors are able to get their back-log of requests attended to, they are more inclined to pay attention to the needs of IS.

Risk Aversion and Analysis Paralysis

Teams in large organizations frequently become frustrated when they attempt to create a reengineering environment. When considering new technologies, organizations seldom have teams complete necessary research, define their processes, and rank their projects and activities before they evaluate tools.

Often, new technology is considered when an individual or a group becomes interested in a tool and tries to evaluate or buy it. Without further investigation or analysis, the interested party does not have the data needed to influence management of the technology's value. One of two scenarios is usually played out at this point. Either the whole idea is dropped because there is no budgeting for it, or no one has the time to follow it up. Or, the business application has to be determined, standards resolved, and processes defined.

Vendors are continually confused by organizations' evaluation and procurement processes because they find the evaluations to be more expensive than the tools. Perhaps, less emphasis should be placed on the cost of the tool and more on the cost of implementing the tool.

When the United States Automobile Association (USAA), in San Antonio TX, became interested in reengineering technology, a few key reengineering sponsors and technicians visited Pacific Bell's Systems Renewal Group. Based on the data gathered from Pacific Bell, an industry survey was conducted by a small team at the USAA. The product of the survey was a comprehensive internal report, "An Industry Survey of Reengineering Theory and Practice," which discussed all phases of reengineering. The report focused on processes and implementation and not on tools.

Team members collected their information from masses of articles, journals, books, personal interviews, site visits, conferences, and training classes. After having issued the report and won the support of senior management, they formed a corporate team to define their processes and implementation strategies. Team members subsequently evaluated and purchased tools to support their processes.

They successfully avoided analysis paralysis. The project was carefully planned and managed to reduce risk. They completed the prerequisites for successful engineering.

Infrastructure Support

Occasionally, small application teams reengineer an insignificant number of programs without running into organizational policies and procedures. However, reengineering teams must address the following infrastructure support issues:

- Project management.
- Metrics.
- Development and redevelopment methodologies.
- Tools and support.
- Quality integration.
- Process improvement programs.
- Standards.
- Change management.

These issues are listed in Exhibit 3 and discussed in the following paragraphs.

Strong project management methods form the basis for improving an organization's processes; these methods turn chaos into repeatable processes. Reengineering projects are not an exception to this rule.

- Project management
- Metrics
- Development and redevelopment methodologies
- Tools and support
- Quality integration
- Process improvement programs
- Standards
- Managing change

Exhibit 3. Issues of Infrastructure Support

A written project plan with clear deliverables and defined roles and responsibilities is critical for success. Flaws in program logic are often discovered when code is restructured and data names are rationalized. Analysts and programmers instinctively want to fix incorrect logic. Although errors should be corrected, to do so without the proper project management can cause additional problems and increase the time and tasks required for testing. Instead, logic flaws should be documented and handled subsequently according to stringent project controls. This has caused more than a few reengineering projects to continue longer than they should have and management to believe that there was an insufficient return on their investment.

Data, coding, and testing standards must be in place before a reengineering project begins. Managers often underestimate the difficulty and necessity of this process. Without enforced standards, an organization stands little chance of improving its systems and processes. Strong data administration is also essential.

Most organizations today are involved in major quality and process improvement efforts. Reengineering teams need to unite these efforts and demonstrate that reengineering systems furthers quality and process improvement efforts already under way. For instance, reengineering systems to meet standards creates more flexibility for movement of resources as well as reducing the learning curve for new employees.

Metrics is another key infrastructure support issue. Organizations must develop a pro-metrics climate that fosters change. When performing technical analysis of an application, an organization must not use metrics for process improvement on the current individuals maintaining systems. These individual often maintain what they inherited. An application's metrics can give management an appreciation of its complexities. These metrics can be used to implement a logical plan for making systems improvements.

Ambiguous Targets

Frequently, organizations have a conceptual vision of their target environment but lack adequate models that enable mapping from the existing systems to the target environment. For example, organizations have tried to move their systems to a CASE environment. However, with only high-level models of what is wanted of the new environment and without detailed business area analysis and lower-level requirements completed, an organization cannot map business functions in the existing system to high-level models in the target system. Many organizations realized that they could port their legacy systems into CASE design-level tools. However, without the prerequisite reengineering and business area analysis, this porting most often produced only very large and flat action diagrams. An effective redevelopment methodology addresses this situation and provides the guidelines for functional mapping of the appropriate business area entities.

Integrated Systems Options

Because reengineering is a technology for transforming legacy systems, business scenarios may be altogether different for each project. The business object and legacy systems analysis dictates the reengineering process and methods—not the technology. Exhibit 4 shows a high-level framework for thinking about the integration of business needs, processes, tools, and technology. This framework is not intended to be all-inclusive but an example of how reengineering strategies add value to most systems options.

Organizations usually choose a systems option to the exclusion of all other options. An example is the redevelopment of an existing system. New development teams are created and usually start the traditional cycle of planning, requirements, design, coding, and implementation. Frequently, in doing a thorough job, IS project teams become so entrenched in their endeavor to discover and document business rules that the client loses patience or the budget is depleted before the requirements phase is completed or any deliverables are produced.

This often happens because:

- It is extremely difficult to determine when requirements are complete without exceeding the project's scope.
- The complexity of discovering business rules in legacy systems is often underestimated.
- Corporate downsizing has created a scarcity of subject matter experts and a subsequent lack of verbal documentation.

It can be determined what existing systems do not do, but it cannot be specified what they do do. The software assessment management framework

Business Analysis ⟶ Technical Analysis ⟶ Functional Analysis ⟶ Organizational Assessment

SYSTEM OPTIONS

Maintain	Replace	Enhance	Eliminate	Technical Migration	Develop New
Document • Process • Tools	Evaluate package • Process • Tools	Analyze alternative existing systems • Process • Tools	Determine system usage • Process • Tools	Implement standards • Process • Tools	Develop plan • Process • Tools
Implement quality control • Process • Tools	Rewrite application • Process • Tools	Implement quality analysis • Process • Tools	Phase out strategies • Process • Tools	Implement quality control • Process • Tools	New requirements • Process • Tools
Reengineer • Process • Tools	Package-rewrite combination • Process • Tools	Evaluate system function requirements • Process • Tools	Analyze existing systems • Process • Tools	Create regression tests • Process • Tools	Reengineer • Process • Tools
Outsource • Process • Tools	Analyze existing systems	Populate analysis workstation • Process • Tools	Outsource • Process • Tools	Technical analysis to manage portfolio • Analysis • Code restructuring • Rationalize and standardize data • Modularize code • Port personal computer/CASE	Reverse engineer • Process • Tools
Port to PC • Process • Tools					

Exhibit 4. Software Asset Management Framework

shown in Exhibit 4 is designed to guide the analysis required for determining how to reach a business goal.

It was once commonly held that reengineering was a systems option. The software assessment management framework, however, clarifies that reengineering is a horizontal strategy that should be applied in varying degrees according to business objectives analysis of existing systems. Redevelopment projects often fail because reengineering strategies are not considered and used as an element of the redevelopment life cycle.

Integrated Tools

Reengineering tools evolved from consultants' need to bid for and complete projects. Consultants played a major role in developing the reengineering tool set as they began to be able to perform repeatedly such activities as data name rationalization. Rarely was a project called reengineering. Instead, such terms as *language upgrades, platform migrations,* and *applications replacement* were used. Thus, consultants selected independent, standalone tools that they knew.

Integrated tool sets did not exist in the mid-1980s. Subsequently, a few vendors have built some quality tool benches. One vendor that has been a steady force in maintenance and reengineering is ViaSoft, Inc. ViaSoft has created an integrated set of quality tools, called Existing Systems Workbench, that supports most reengineering activities. This workbench provides metrics to analyze and guide reengineering projects and ongoing maintenance as well as integrated tools for performing mechanized reengineering.

When tools are evaluated, the cost of purchasing the tool should be considered secondary to the cost of implementing the tool. Better-integrated tool sets will require less support and be easier to implement.

Another consideration is choosing a vendor that will remain in the market. Vendors must understand legacy systems and have an overall reengineering vision. Many vendors have lacked this vision, and many tools have subsequently changed vendors several times. This raises support costs in organizations requiring new or revised processes. It is important to find vendors that continually enhance their products as well as their product lines. This information can be easily obtained by asking the vendor for the history of its product line. Vendors should also be asked for industry references. Independent consultants are also a good source of unbiased information about tools and vendors.

Resistance to Change

Organizations often underestimate the resistance to change, even change that is perceived to be good. Such was the case with the reengineering group at Pacific Bell. Projects managed and staffed by external consultants have faced this problem for a long time. External consultants, however, have the opportunity to finish the project and leave the organization. Internal teams do not have that opportunity and must continue to work against the resistance of colleagues. Therefore, it is important to start on the right foot.

Daryl Conner, an organizational development expert based in Atlanta, explains change in an interesting way. According to Conner, capabilities are always balanced against challenge. Status quo is when capability (i.e., ability and willingness) equals challenge (i.e., danger and opportunity). Positive change occurs when capability becomes greater than challenge, and negative change occurs when challenge becomes greater than capability.

Because of the fast pace of technological changes and the demanding nature of business changes, IS organizations, especially large ones, are confronted with employees who experience much change and consequent anxiety. On one hand, these employees want to continue to grow professionally (i.e., willingness); however, they fear that they will no longer be regarded as and rewarded for being experts if they allow their systems to be reengineered. Although these systems may be a complex mess, they are familiar with this mess.

Change requires training and time to assimilate new methods and concepts. The more employees are asked to change, the less time they have for learning and training. Thus, the perception of danger increases and so does resistance, which can lessen productivity.

Change begins at the sponsor level and requires adequate time and training. Unfortunately, few organizations are allowed this training and transition time because management does not really view the reengineered system as a different system. It is usually business as usual with the same or greater productivity expectations. With the proper support of senior management and training, change is not a painful and unpredictable process. The steps listed in Exhibit 2 are critical for successfully implementing change.

Education and Training

Although many companies have succeeded with reengineering, many still find that education is a critical issue. Because of constant corporate reorganizations, corporate decision makers are often unaware of the maturity of reengineering technology. They are unaware of the systems options that are possible through reengineering.

Industry experts are brought into the organization to deliver presentations for the purpose of educating and sharing success stories from other companies. In addition to methodology training classes, internal focus groups are another forum for sharing information on methods and processes. Because of the constant change in technology and business, education continues to be important.

Without proper education, internal teams cannot reengineer systems. Because reengineering can be applied to many business areas, specific training is needed to use the proper methods, processes, and tools as well as to understand the related changes.

Blueprint Framework

The method for creating a cost-effective strategy for making the transition from legacy systems is to understand business goals objectively and ask, How can the current system be used to meet these goals? Typically, organizations are reluctant to take the time to do an initial thorough inventory and analysis of their systems.

Metrics are often not kept on programs and systems. Without a set of comprehensive metrics, systems managers cannot measure the effects of new releases of systems and programs. Consequently, systems complexity and maintenance costs soar. With a portfolio of systems and program metrics, standards and software management methods can be enforced. The metrics can help management to see systems option alternatives, which are listed in Exhibit 4.

Legacy systems still exist because they do perform a business function. In most cases, the business rules still apply and major portions of the systems are salvageable. By combining the systems option of replacing and developing new (see Exhibit 4) systems, reengineers can extract reusable functions and code, thereby reducing project costs.

For organizations that simply want to decrease maintenance costs and improve maintainability, the 80/20 rule still applies; by improving the worst 20% of the system, 80% of the problems are solved. For example, one or two large, complex, critical path programs can be modularized to reduce complexity, eliminate redundant or dead functions, and improve architecture and processes. Multiple programmers can then work on new modules simultaneously to respond more quickly to user requests. In addition, productivity is increased, because smaller, less-complex modules require less time to analyze, change, and test, and the reliance on a few individual system experts is reduced.

Most companies have life cycle and development methodologies, but most lack a redevelopment methodology that guides the activities discussed in the previous paragraphs. Such organizations are unaware of the value of reengineering activities or how to plan such projects. These organizations can benefit from a redevelopment methodology, however, because at least 80% of all IS activity is related to existing systems.

A REDEVELOPMENT METHODOLOGY

A redevelopment methodology should be driven by business needs, provide flexible, robust processes, and integrate enabling technologies. The following sections give an overview of The Systems Redevelopment Methodology (TSRM), which was created by William M. Ulrich. This methodology is examined in depth in Chapter XI-5, "Moving Legacy Systems into the Future."

Business-Driven Scenarios

The scenario concept facilitates rapid analysis of specific IS situations and enables management issues to be matched to areas described in the scenarios. A scenario identifies a unique sequence of methodology activities to accommodate the project requirements. This is especially helpful to organizations that lack reengineering training or experience. The unique sequence ensures that all essential activities are addressed.

A few of the more common scenarios are the following:

- *Application replacement.* This scenario describes design recovery and component reuse processes that leverage application replacement efforts.
- *Infrastructure stabilization.* This is the most commonly applied scenario and is used to reduce maintenance costs and increase reliability and quality of legacy systems. It analyzes basic applications weaknesses, determines user requirements, and produces a detailed implementation plan to upgrade the system.
- *Package assimilation.* This scenario assumes that a package has been purchased and is now ready for implementation and integration into the IS environment. Step-by-step instructions are given for assessing the gaps between the existing system and the ideal target system (i.e., the package), ensuring that critical functions in the existing system are not lost in the implementation.

There are currently 11 such scenarios, with new ones being added with most product releases.

Inventory/Analysis

As shown in Exhibit 5, this phase consists of objective-setting tasks in which the reengineering team establishes the hypothesis and builds the plan that is to be followed for inventory and assessment activities. The technical assessment of environment, processes, and data is carried out with automated metrics that measure the quality and structure as well as assess the systems-level data use. Most of the quality metric tools have been integrated in the

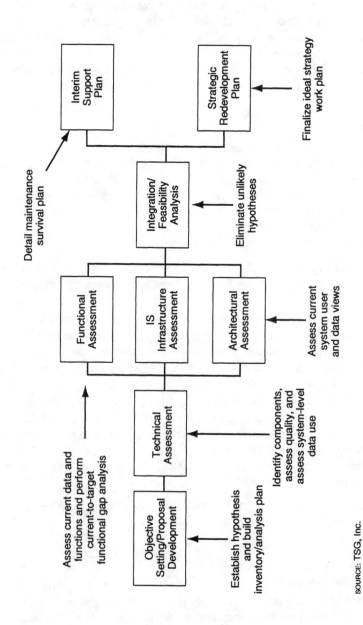

SOURCE: TSG, Inc.

Exhibit 5. Process Flow Summary for TSRM Inventory/ Analysis Phase

tasks and activities, thus alleviating much of the manual effort. As shown in Exhibit 5, once the initial inventory is complete, the technical assessment may be performed simultaneously with the other assessments.

The purpose of the functional assessment is to evaluate current data and functions and perform current-to-date functional gap analysis. In some scenarios, the user backlog is identified, categorized, and ranked during this assessment. The IS infrastructure assessment examines the organization and measures skill and experience levels, tool and methodology proficiency, and testing maturity. The architectural assessment appraises the current systems user and data views. Once all of the assessments have been completed, the metrics and other findings are summarized in the integration and feasibility component. At this time, unlikely hypotheses are usually eliminated, and the team focuses on one objective.

Some scenarios require an interim support plan, which is sometimes referred to as a maintenance survival plan, and others may require a strategic redevelopment plan. This is a long-term plan used to transform the system; transformation is the key component of any redevelopment initiative.

For each component, the methodology provides detailed objectives, entrance criteria, roles and responsibilities, input requirements, tool and technology support, task steps, deliverables, quality checks, metrics, and exit criteria. A team always knows exactly what is required for accurate planning and tracking.

Positioning

Until this phase, only assessments but no changes have been made. Exhibit 6 illustrates how the different activities that may occur are designated by the assessments in the prior inventory and analysis phase. Application staging is a support task used in all positioning tasks to ensure that the version control process operates properly. Language changes and upgrades may be as simple as a COBOL II upgrade or as complex as Assembler-to-COBOL conversion.

Code stabilization activities include restructuring accompanied by flaw analysis and removal. The lack of flaw analysis and removal has caused many restructuring projects to fail. Without this step, the quality of restructured code may be very poor.

Data definition and standardization involve multiple tasks that are aimed at improving the quality of existing data definitions across one or more systems and eliminating the redundant record groupings. Remodularization eases maintenance by decreasing complexity, realigning functions, and eliminating redundancies and facilitates transition architecture.

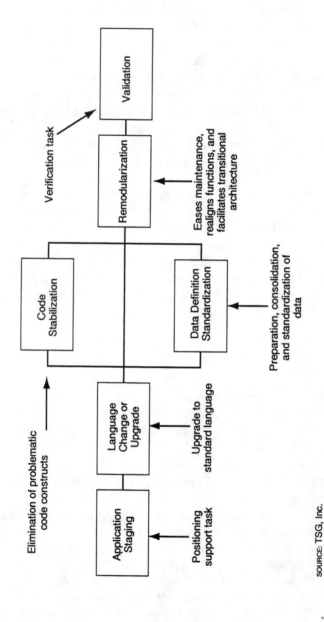

Exhibit 6. Process Flow Summary for TSRM Position Phase

SOURCE: TSG, Inc.

Validation is, of course, the process of verifying that source code improvements, as applied during the positioning tasks, do not introduce any functional changes to the code.

Transformation

The last phase of the methodology is depicted in Exhibit 7. In the transformation phase, software redevelopment models are created through the use of top-down and bottom-up analysis of current and target application. The goals of transformation are to specify the tasks required to view existing systems in the form of formal models and, if applicable, to use those models to assist in leveraging the development of a replacement system. Obviously, not all scenarios require this stage of the methodology.

ACTION PLAN

Successes and failures have been discussed throughout this chapter. For the most part, failures can be attributed to not meeting the reengineering critical success factors. Knowing and understanding the pitfalls before beginning a reengineering project can lessen risk factors significantly and increase project successes. Following are additional helpful hints:

- Always ensure that there is a real business need to reengineer. Reengineering can deliver significant value and return on investment if the application or system is of importance to the business.
- IS and business sponsors can form a powerful association. Encourage their continued involvement and support through constant education and project feedback.
- A trained team is essential to success.
- Technical skills are important, but a lack of organizational change skills can kill reengineering. It takes less energy to do the job right.
- The temptation to jump in with both feet is great. Do homework first.
- Assess infrastructure support. Scrutinize methods and standards. Standards should be developed and implemented before reengineering. Metrics education is essential to everyone involved.
- Overly ambitious targets may send reengineering efforts in circles.
- Research vendors as well as tools. The quality of vendor will probably be in business for years to come. Integrated tool sets are easier and less expensive to implement and maintain.
- Never underestimate the power of resistance to change. Remember to expect it, keep things out in the open, and stay constructive and nondefensive. Leveraging resistance can improve processes and products.

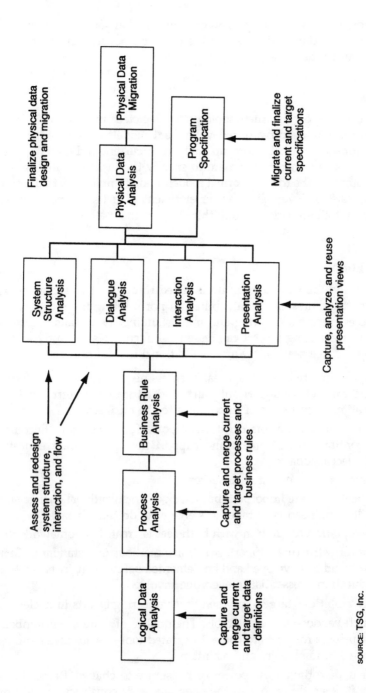

Exhibit 7. Process Flow Summary for TSRM Transformation Phase

SOURCE: TSG, Inc.

- Training and education are a constant and never-ending process. Reengineering conferences and user groups are sources for networking with those who have experience. Examine public courses and use industry speakers to influence internal sponsors, managers, and peers.
- Use the software assessment framework (see Exhibit 4) to maximize systems options. Remember, reengineering is a technology that has pragmatic strategies, techniques, and procedures, producing cost-effective solutions for many business needs.
- A methodology is essential to success. A flexible, project-oriented framework based on business requirements and integrated with supporting technologies ensures quality deliverables.
- Perhaps the most important point to remember is that there are no silver bullets.

Chapter XI-5
Moving Legacy Systems into the Future

William M. Ulrich

A STUDY POLLED senior software managers as to why key systems within their organizations had not been significantly updated or replaced. The most common answer, aside from "waiting on new technology," was the fact that key systems had "too many interfaces." The root cause of this is fairly simple. Standalone applications were built 20 to 25 years ago around organizational structures that are being dramatically reengineered today. For example, customer support may be dispersed across many disparate systems with data sharing limited to batch file interfaces. Business process redesign, driven by competitive pressure, requires that this and related architectural weaknesses be corrected in core business systems.

As inadequate as the original situation was, it has deteriorated even further in recent years. Core systems have had overlapping functions replicated in interfaces or in downstream systems that circumvent core processing rules. Additionally, data warehousing, graphical user interfaces (GUIs), and user-based systems have evolved around major systems to address data integration requirements that core systems cannot satisfy. Finally, replacement or package deployment efforts may have succeeded in partially replacing existing functions, but not to the point where legacy systems can be streamlined or eliminated.

One survey has indicated that over $16.5 billion is wasted annually on systems users never see. This will continue as long as piecemeal planning drives strategic IS projects. As new architectures emerge, it is clear that there is rarely a one-to-one correspondence between new systems and legacy counterparts. Within a transitional strategy to map legacy data and functions to target environments, such a simple issue as knowing which functions in which systems should be deactivated is, at best, guesswork. Functional synchronization during concurrent legacy maintenance and target design efforts in the same business area is another transitional challenge. The bottom line

0-8493-9979-3/99/$0.00+$.50
© 1999 by CRC Press LLC

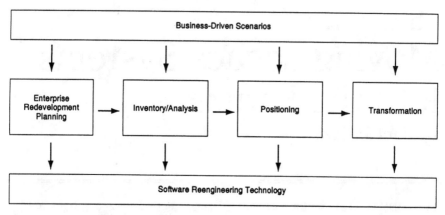

SOURCE: TSG, Inc. and James Martin & Co.

Exhibit 1. The Systems Redevelopment Methodology Framework

is that IS must establish an architectural transitional strategy that provides the purpose for migration, integration, acquisition, and replacement efforts of highly coupled legacy environments.

DEFINING A METHODOLOGY FOR ARCHITECTURE TRANSITION

The intent of this chapter is not to dictate how replacement efforts should be accomplished, even though traditional, top-down approaches have proven unsuccessful. This chapter does, however, use a formal redevelopment process to guide organizations through planning and implementing an architecture transition strategy. This process is defined in The Systems Redevelopment Methodology (TSRM), which is a registered trademark of James Martin & Co. The TSRM framework is shown in Exhibit 1. TSRM differs from traditional methodologies in its details analysis and incorporation of legacy systems as integral components to redevelopment efforts.

TSRM includes a collection of methodological and tool-related guidelines, organized into a cohesive, four-stage structure, driven by a variety of industry-standard, project-based scenarios. Enterprise Redevelopment Planning begins transition analysis at the organizational level. This stage maps legacy to strategic architecture requirements and recommends appropriate scenarios to executive redevelopment projects across various applications. Once a given business area defines a project requirement to redevelop one or more related systems, the remaining three TSRM stages are invoked.

The Inventory/Analysis Stage details application-specific analysis and planning tasks. The resulting plan details a phased transition to a target architecture for affected business areas. The Positioning Stage is comprised of code improvement tasks that stabilize current systems while preparing them for the architectural transition. The Transformation Stage applies reverse and forward engineering technology to support system redesign, respecification, and regeneration. This stage is based on the notion of phased transition and enables functions in target architectures as they are deactivated in legacy environments. The TSRM stages represent the collective set of redevelopment tasks required to make the transition from legacy IS environments to a variety of strategic architectures. Based on these tasks, project-oriented scenarios define the specific combination of tasks and steps required to plan and implement a variety of strategic IS projects.

ENTERPRISEWIDE ARCHITECTURE
TRANSITION STRATEGY

The first step in defining an architecture transition strategy is defining the target architecture. Many organizations have defined a target technical architecture but leave business and data architectures less defined. In this chapter, formal models are derived from the Information Engineering (IE) methodology. Under IE, the Information Strategy Plan (ISP) defines an information architecture, business architecture, and technical architecture. A variety of models and matrices are produced as a result. Regardless of the paradigm selected, organizations should use a formal, generally accepted set of models as a vehicle for mapping current-to-target architectures.

Elements of the transitional mapping process include data, functions, and technology. The ISP establishes information, business, and technical architectures by creating multiple models that define both target and existing systems. Enterprise Redevelopment Planning augments the ISP by mapping current-to-target data, function, and technological aspects of the enterprise. Exhibit 2 shows the TSRM Enterprise Redevelopment Planning task deliverable summary.

An enterprise assessment delivers an enterprisewide redevelopment strategy that augments the traditional ISP by focusing more intently on the role of legacy systems in the transition process. One result of this assessment is a recommended set of redevelopment scenarios that should be invoked on the basis of enterprisewide findings. Redevelopment scenarios address migration, integration, phased system shutdown, downsizing, and assorted stabilization projects for various application or business areas. The benefit of performing an enterprisewide assessment is that a comprehensive set of interdependent factors is taken into account before individual application area redevelopment projects are initiated.

Technical Architecture Assessment	Business Architecture Assessment	Data Architecture Assessment	Information Redevelopment Planning
• Current physical systems inventory • Current physical systems attributes and metrics • Current-to-target technical architecture variances	• Current systems summary • Current physical systems to current functions matrix* • Current physical systems to target functions matrix • Current systems inter-relationship data flow diagrams* • Functional mapping summary	• Current data stores description* • Current data stores to current systems matrix* • Current data stores to target entity types matrix • Data mapping summary	• Current-to-target enterprise architecture summary • Architecture transitioning and impact summary • Recommended redevelopment scenarios by application

Note:
• Derived from the Information Strategy Plan (ISP).

SOURCE: TSG, Inc.

Exhibit 2. Deliverables of Enterprise Redevelopment Planning

APPLICATION AREA ASSESSMENT AND IMPLEMENTATION PLANNING

Once an enterprise redevelopment strategy is in place, individual application areas may pursue migration and replacement plans. Although an enterprise-level analysis is recommended to define project scope, it is not essential. Application areas can select an appropriate scenario and begin transition planning by using the TSRM Inventory/Analysis Stage without benefit of enterprise-wide analysis. Scoping problems usually surface, however, in the absence of a comprehensive architecture transition strategy. Furthermore, certain enterprise-level matrices are useful for supporting interaction analysis relating physical data stores to legacy systems and target data models.

A redevelopment project plan is created by applying scenarios that define the sequence and applicability of various redevelopment tasks. To clarify the approach, an industry example is used in this chapter to outline a typical transition project. This example focuses on migrating multiple standalone mainframe systems into an integrated, client/server personnel application. The target client/server architecture is finalized through a combination of IE and client/server analysis and design models. The degree of legacy systems reuse within a given project varies, but in this example a sizable amount of legacy data and procedural components are reused.

Scoping is performed by identifying core systems that are affected by the business requirements driving the need for the project. Core systems are those systems that are actually being replaced in whole or in part. Interface systems pass or receive data from core systems and are documented during analysis but are not individually assessed. The assumption is that links to interface systems must remain essentially intact after implementation of the target application. Core systems in the personnel example include the payroll, pension, and insurance applications. Once core and interface systems are identified, the application area assessment plan can be created. This involves defining the technical, architectural, and functional assessment tasks required to complete the final project implementation plan.

Technical assessment tasks identify system components, document qualitative attributes, and capture metadata to support subsequent analysis. The architectural assessment documents systems flow, core system relationships, interface systems linkages, the user presentation layer, and the data access layer. Data access layer analysis is the baseline for distributed data base design as well as data migration and consolidation requirements. Screens and reports are assessed to determine the role of these components in a new GUI front-end design. Finally, the architectural assessment is a baseline prerequisite for the functional assessment.

THE FUNCTIONAL ASSESSMENT: BASIS FOR THE TRANSITION STRATEGY

In the functional assessment, the existing backlog, top-down models, and derived legacy models are linked to determine the specific role current systems play in the target architecture. This analysis extrapolates current functions from the presentation layer and links user interfaces to system components through a technique called reverse requirements tracing (see Exhibit 3). Results of this analysis, along with subject matter expert interviews, produce function hierarchy and dependency diagrams for each legacy system assessed. Exhibit 4 illustrates highlights of the mapping process that links legacy modules to existing functions and existing functions to related target functions.

In the example, basic pay functions, discovered in the payroll system, directly correspond to certain target pay functions. Other target functions, not defined in the existing payroll system, must be created from scratch. Still other functions, such as personnel management, are replicated across standalone payroll, pension, and insurance systems. Functional mapping identifies replicated functions in such different business areas as personnel management; baseline functions that are candidates for reuse, such as pay issuance; and legacy components that must be deactivated as the new system is deployed.

Transition management of data can be a more complex challenge than transition management of the functional component. Although functions can

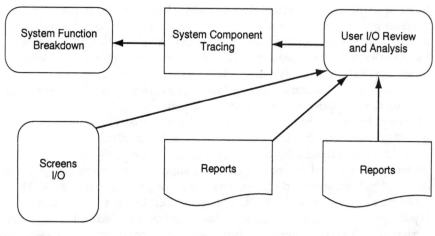

SOURCE: TSG, Inc.

Exhibit 3. Reverse Requirements Tracing Process

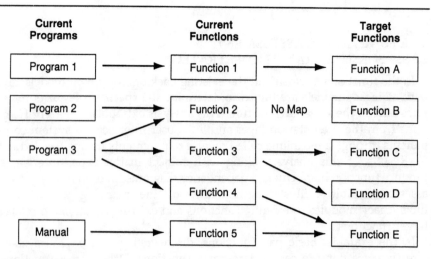

SOURCE: TSG, Inc.

Exhibit 4. Mapping Existing Programs and Functions to Target Functions

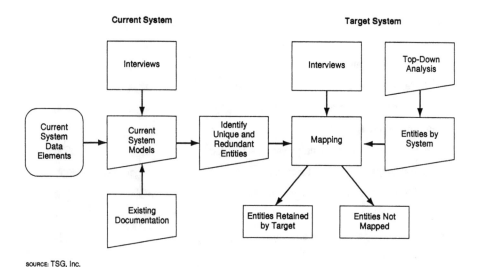

SOURCE: TSG, Inc.

Exhibit 5. Mapping Current System Entities to Target System Entities

be isolated to a degree, legacy data is coupled to the point of coexistence. The first step is to apply bottom-up modeling to capture logical views of legacy data in entity-relationship (ER) models for each system. These models are then merged into a single ER model and used to facilitate current-to-target gap analysis (see Exhibit 5). Gap analysis helps verify target data model integrity and completeness. This analysis, coupled with physical data store matrices developed during enterprisewide analysis, is key to establishing links between physical data stores and evolving architecture.

The mechanics of transition management are defined in the technology support section of this chapter. Once all functional assessment tasks are completed, feasibility analysis is used to select and finalize one of potentially many transition alternatives. In the personnel system example, the selected approach is turned into a transition work plan, which details the evolution from multiple, standalone mainframe systems to an integrated, client/server application. Exhibit 6 summarizes the plan recommended for the personnel system integration, client/server migration project. Implementation steps are outlined below.

LEGACY ARCHITECTURE PREPARATION

Legacy systems typically contain unstructured, monolithic models that have redundant and inconsistent data definitions. These issues, though not

Positioning Steps

Step 1. Code stabilization and restructuring

Step 2. Data name rationalization

Step 3. Redundancy reconciliation and reaggregation

Step 4. Client/server architecture finalization

Transformation Steps

Step 5. Redevelop personnel management subsystem

Step 6. Transform base payroll functions

Step 7. Transform base pension functions

Step 8. Transform base insurance functions

Step 9. Finalize target functions and deploy integrated system

SOURCE: TSG, Inc.

Legacy Architecture

Target Architecture

Exhibit 6. Plan for Migrating the Personnel Application to an Integrated Client/Server Architecture

necessarily as critical as legacy design problems, hinder analysis efforts. For example, it is difficult to extract data designs when customer data representations are inconsistently implemented. Similarly, identifying business rules in unstructured, monolithic source modules is extremely difficult. Such transition issues as decoupling legacy functions from monolithic models are further complicated by legacy system technical limitations.

Fortunately, technical problems found in legacy code can be corrected with reasonable effort. Exhibit 6 summarizes tasks typically used to prepare legacy systems for architecture transition. Although code restructuring and data name rationalization are common to most maintenance improvement and migration preparation projects, redundancy reconciliation, and reaggregation uniquely support architecture transition.

Restructuring and name rationalization facilitate remodularization efforts by eliminating the confusion created by nonsensical logic paths and cryptic naming conventions. In the personnel example, each standalone system has positioning tasks applied on the basis of the inventory/analysis transition plan. Code reconciliation and reaggregation, guided by functional mapping results, are applied to each standalone system. For example, redundant check processing tasks, discovered through functional analysis, can be isolated into subroutines and, optionally, consolidated. Isolated, cohesive models are much easier to examine when the situation demands that complex calculations or business rules be ported to the target architecture.

The consolidation decision hinges on the length of time all or part of the existing payroll system is to remain intact or on the intent to reuse legacy business rules under the target architecture. If the existing payroll system must remain in operation for more than two years, and regulatory changes are applied frequently to redundantly defined rules, consolidation is warranted. Similarly, if the potential for reuse is high because of the difficulty or inherent risk in recreating complex, yet required, business rules from scratch, consolidation of legacy-based rules is also warranted.

The approach used in this example does not assume that existing modules are to be moved intact into a client/server architecture. Although this is an option, intact legacy modules, even after remodularization, would likely corrupt a true client/server architecture. The approach outlined in this chapter focuses on selective reuse of legacy rules extracted from existing systems. The positioning tasks to be applied would be similar, but the level of code isolation and redundancy reconciliation can vary, if modules are to remain intact.

Redundancy reconciliation and reaggregation uses functional mapping, as illustrated in Exhibit 4, to map the physical location of redundant logic within legacy modules to related target functions. Code blocks are isolated using code slicing techniques that are based on computations or data supporting that function. Each isolated block is then consolidated, as a shared subroutine, into a single module. This process is repeated across each standalone system. Functions not to be ported to the new architecture are isolated through the same process. Similarly, functions to be imported during subsequent transformation phases, as illustrated in Exhibit 6, can be isolated into subroutines in anticipation of phased system shut down.

Physical data stores can be consolidated on the basis of the results from data name rationalization and existing data store analysis. The options for data are more limited in the legacy systems preparation phase, however, because any real change to legacy data structures forces redesign considerations. Redesign is a transformation-supported activity. Concurrent data management, for purposes of architecture transition, is discussed further during the Transformation Stage of the personal systems migration project.

It is important to note that positioning tasks have a direct effect on maintenance productivity by freeing senior analysts to assist with redesign efforts. In fact, improved versions of legacy systems may result in numerous, interim production releases based on the phased preparation plan. This is in keeping with the transition strategy. If funding is eliminated for subsequent phases of a redevelopment project, application areas still gain benefit from high-quality systems delivered as a result of applying various positioning tasks.

FINALIZING THE TARGET ARCHITECTURE

The Transformation Stage of a project depends, to a great degree, on solid top-down planning, analysis, and design. Some organizations do not emphasize this adequately. Client/server projects suffer inordinately from a lack of a clear design to manage distribution of functions, presentation interfaces, and databases. This is particularly true because of the number of client/server distribution options available. It is to be hoped that this trend will be reversed as client/server analysis and design paradigms gain acceptance within the industry. Exhibit 6 indicates how target architecture finalization must occur simultaneously with recommended positioning tasks.

The target architecture stems from basic IE methods with several variations. Architecture selection, driven by function, presentation, and data base distribution strategies, is an initial key step. Analysis includes object-relationship diagramming, an object-oriented data modeling technique, which produces a view of data that fits real world user views of objects. Process-dependency modeling is extended to encompass event-dependency diagramming.

Additionally, business rule definitions and process logic diagramming offer solid approaches to defining processing logic. Design-level issues include distribution, stability, and performance design, and construction includes network configuration and testing. Each of these development techniques have been defined in the Martin/Odell IEOO client/server methodology.

In the personnel system integration and client/server migration, finalization of top-down requirements, as well as the technical, data, and functional architectures, provide a baseline for transformation, which is the last major phase of the project. Once top-down efforts are completed, data model refinement, legacy system event analysis, presentation review, and business and process rule mapping can begin. From a timing standpoint, Exhibit 6 illustrates architecture finalization occurring concurrently with various positioning and architecture preparation tasks. This is refined in more detail in actual project work plans that vary based on a given application area's business requirements.

TRANSFORMATION: A PHASE IMPLEMENTATION APPROACH

The Transformation Stage deals with migration to client/server by using legacy components to leverage the effort. This involves examining or reusing data definitions, business rules, or presentation views of various standalone systems to validate the integrity of the target design while reducing the implementation window. This approach also facilitates collapsing redundant data, processes, and presentation views across legacy standalone systems, while shutting down legacy functions as new functions are activated under the target architecture. Finally, legacy and target data-store concurrency management is a key requirement that must be accommodated in a phased, transitional approach.

Legacy data analysis and design recovery are key components in the personnel transition example. This involves capturing rationalized data definitions from standalone systems, merging standalone data models into a top-down model, and refining this model according to legacy attributes. Data in the personnel system must be analyzed and merged into target data models and migrated to a distributed data base environment. Other approaches include reviewing existing models to refine the top-down model or building a target model based on integrated legacy views. The last approach is only recommended when no top-down model is available. Data store and data entity matrices, created during enterprise analysis, are used to establish mappings from legacy data stores to target data models and data stores.

Data model mapping begins at logical levels and continues throughout the distributed data design process. Exhibit 7 illustrates this mapping and the central repository that controls the mapping process. The mechanics, examined further in the section on technology support, involve maintaining relationships between interdependent legacy data stores and distributed data bases in the new client/server environment. If, as in the example, personnel management is the first function activated in the client/server environment, users would then begin updating this information through a client/server interface. Personnel data in legacy payroll, pension, and insurance data stores would be updated retroactively and on an ongoing basis using links maintained in the central repository.

Physical data migration, purification, and redundancy reconciliation use data store/target entity mappings created during prior analysis efforts. Redundancy mapping, begun during Enterprise Redevelopment Planning, continues throughout the final implementation and physical data migration phases of the project. If linkages are required to control target to legacy data store concurrency, they are maintained until a given legacy data store, and all other occurrences of that physical data, can be migrated to the new architecture. This process requires continuing synchronization of legacy data with the target system's distributed data bases as new functions in the target environment are activated.

Legacy presentation views, once captured through a variety of techniques, serve to support target system user presentation design. Presentation views may be captured and reused in their entirety or simply examined as input to distributed presentation design. Wholesale reuse of legacy screens or report layouts involves the use of certain technology to transform mainframe definitions into GUI-based representations. The personnel system example, where personnel management functions are embedded in different screens

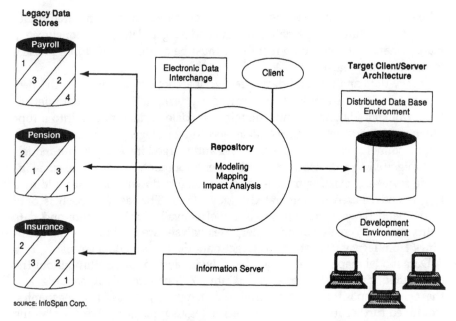

SOURCE: InfoSpan Corp.

Exhibit 7. Data Model Mapping with a Controlling Central Repository

used by disparate users across payroll, pension, and insurance business areas, does not lend itself to wholesale user view importation. Establishing legacy user views as a baseline, however, allows designers to smooth the transition for disparate users in different business areas.

Screen functions can be deactivated either through the presentation view itself or through elimination of update functions within the application code. In the first case, users would find various screens incapable of receiving update information related to personnel data in each legacy system. In the second case, users would get a message that personnel data update facilities have been deactivated in certain systems and be instructed to use the new client/server personnel management application.

Phasing of the migration from legacy environments to strategic architectures has the biggest impact on how functions are analyzed, consolidated, ported, and deactivated in current and target architectures. Implementation time frames are detailed in the inventory/analysis transition plan. In the personnel system example (see Exhibit 6), phasing involves consolidating and migrating personnel management functions, payroll functions, pension functions and, finally, insurance functions. Each set of functions is activated in the integrated client/server environment and deactivated in the appropriate legacy system. How well a given set of functions actually works in the absence of the remainder of the functional architecture is determined on a case-by-case basis.

As indicated previously, consolidation and importation of functions into a target architecture require that formal models be used to support the process. New client/server CASE tools, along with the evolution of traditional I-CASE products that support client/server development, facilitate this approach. Client/server functional models include event-dependency diagrams and business rule definition. Events occur in legacy environments, but triggers are not clearly defined. Architectural flow and process-dependency analysis of legacy environments allows designers to determine if legacy-based dependencies can provide input to the event design process. These are drawn from architectural flows of legacy system dependencies using data flow diagrams (DFDs) and other representations created during the architectural assessment.

Business-rule capture and importation is performed on legacy systems and uses defined models as the target. Business rules, in the client/server example, are invoked on the basis of event triggers. Rules consist of preconditions indicating situations that must be in effect before rule invocation and post conditions indicating action taken once a rule is enacted. Using prior functional mappings, analysts scan legacy modules using interactive analyzers to find condition and action logic that can be reused in the target architecture. A central repository maintains linkages to indicate where legacy rules were imported to the target architecture. This includes redundantly defined rules, such as legacy personnel management functions defined in the personnel example, that are being consolidated under a client/server architecture.

When legacy systems contain no functional equivalent to a target business rule, analysts must develop the rule from scratch. When redundantly defined rules conflict, analysts must resolve these conflicts and make a note that certain users must adjust to a new version of that rule. Reuse of legacy rules is an issue of semantics. If an analyst reduces development time by 50% by just reviewing legacy rules, versus building them from scratch, this is one form of reuse. If tools are used to capture a legacy rule and transform it into a rule format that can be put into a model, this is another form of reuse. A third form is code-to-code reuse. In any case, this process continues until a predefined component of the target architecture is completed on the basis of strategic requirements.

In the personnel system example, it is possible to move portions of the new architecture, such as personnel management functions, into production before activating remaining target system functions. Personnel management functions are then deactivated in legacy systems as discussed earlier in the functional assessment and architecture preparation sections of this chapter. Subsequent phasing of key functions is shown in Exhibit 6. Mechanics

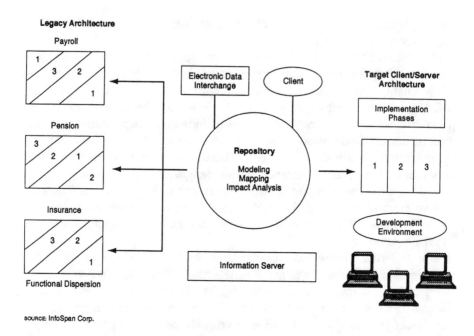

Legacy Architecture

Payroll

Pension

Insurance

Functional Dispersion

Electronic Data Interchange

Client

Target Client/Server Architecture

Implementation Phases

Repository

Modeling
Mapping
Impact Analysis

Development Environment

Information Server

SOURCE: InfoSpan Corp.

Exhibit 8. Phased Transformation of Legacy Functions

of this process are shown in Exhibit 8, where the number 1 represents personnel management functions spanning legacy and target architectures.

The transitional sequence of legacy-to-target functions is ranked by management requirements; for example, payroll functions must be activated under the target architecture quickly. Personnel management was deemed a baseline prerequisite to implementing other major target functions. Transformation completes the transition cycle begun during enterprisewide assessment and pursued through actual implementation of a new, integrated client/server system.

TRANSITIONAL TECHNOLOGY SUPPORT: THE ROLE OF THE REPOSITORY

Legacy-to-target functional mapping, integral to the transition process, is based on techniques detailed in the TSRM redevelopment methodology. Implementation of this process on a large scale depends on establishing and maintaining thousands of linkages across multiple views of legacy and target system metamodels. These linkages support reverse requirements tracing, reusability mapping, redundancy reconciliation, legacy deactivation analysis, phased target system implementation, and data concurrency tracking. A generally extensible repository, capable of maintaining multiple metamodels and related linkages, is the central implementation vehicle for this process.

The first component that must be defined is a legacy system metamodel (LTM). This requires defining an ER model that represents legacy system components, including JCL, jobs, steps, procedures, load/source modules, copy members, screen definitions, online tables, data definitions, and appropriate attributes and relationships. The LTM supports basic enterprise analysis, as well as application level reverse requirements tracing. The second requirement is a facility to load and refresh this model. Repository vendors may offer load facilities themselves or link to a number of commercially available environmental parsing tools. Continuous refreshing of legacy metadata is required as the system undergoes maintenance or related migration upgrades.

Commercial availability for this type of repository is currently limited. One vendor using a predefined LTM and also focusing on legacy-to-target metamodel mapping, is InfoSpan Corp. Such attributes as metrics indicating qualitative and quantitative features of a given object or object class should also be accommodated by the model. Occasionally, the parsers and loaders gather metric information but, in other cases, it may be left up to the repository itself to assign and track this information.

The next capability required in the LTM repository is the ability to represent a wide range of target objects that map directly to commercially available development paradigms. Examples include enterprise analysis matrices, ER models, function hierarchy/dependency models, data/process matrices, screen layouts, and other IE-related models. Client/server models include object relationship diagrams, event dependency diagrams, business rule definition, process logic diagrams, user interface models, and networking models. Target object requirements are dictated by the development paradigms and CASE tools used by the redevelopment team.

Once legacy environment and target architecture objects are customized in the LTM, linkages within the metamodel must be established and maintained. These relationships are highlighted in Exhibit 8. Linkages are driven by methodological requirements to map current legacy objects to target models, adjust these relationships during the architectural transition, and manage target-to-legacy data store concurrency. Two-way relationships are maintained between various legacy and target objects and are updated as legacy functions are remodularized or deactivated.

Data concurrency mapping ensures that, as target functions affecting legacy-related data are activated, data is updated in legacy data stores on a retroactive basis. In the personnel system example, an employee may be added to a distributed data base using personnel management functions of the new GUI-based, client/server system. The repository facility, which knows that this data is stored across multiple legacy multiple payroll, pension, and insurance data stores, can be used to invoke routines for updating selected data in those legacy systems. Exhibit 7 highlights the role of the repository in managing target and legacy data linkages.

This process continues until all data currently in legacy data stores is migrated to the target architecture. Although the methods define the mapping concepts and mechanics, the repository is the technology for supporting transition projects. TSRM defines and applies a baseline version of an LTM.

SUMMARY

The transitional approach facilitates phasing of legacy system shutdown, data structure migration, user training, and implementation of a radically different work environment (i.e., client/server). The ever-present risk of project cancellation is managed because implementation phases are grouped into relatively short time frames. An upgraded system is moved into production, whether under the existing or target architecture, on a regular basis. Users no longer must wait for years to see the results of development projects because value is delivered on a continuous basis throughout a project's life span.

It is unfortunate that the transitional strategy, as outlined in this chapter, will probably not be pursued by a majority of organizations near term. This is because the advent of new technology has made it much easier to look for such interim solutions as middleware, GUI facades, and a host of patchwork interfaces to legacy environments. Many of these solutions have value as long as they are viewed as stopgap activities. However, management often believes these approaches to be adequate and will be reluctant to make the intellectual investment required to truly address the systems architecture crisis. Until this occurs, the negative statistics quoted at the beginning of this article will probably continue to move in the wrong direction.

It is important to note, however, that a small but growing number of financial institutions, key US government agencies, and telecommunication companies have begun to utilize the redevelopment and transitional approach outlined here to achieve strategic information goals. These organizations are gaining an advantage over competitors that still believe outdated and unworkable development approaches hold the key to transforming decaying IS infrastructures into the strategic architectures of tomorrow.

Section XI – Checklist
Supporting Existing Software

1. How does your organization allocate resources to software support?
2. In your opinion, does system maintenance consume a high portion of staff time? How does this impact your responsibilities?
3. At which age would you define a legacy system? Would this classify most of your organization's systems as legacy?
4. What analysis has been performed to determine the scope of legacy applications? Does this cover multiple languages or just COBOL code?
5. Within an existing legacy application, has there been any effort to perform portfolio analysis to determine which programs are the most difficult to maintain? Does this apply to the library of all developed programs?
6. Has your organization estimated the cost of supporting existing applications vs. cost of replacement? If not, what effort would be required to make this determination?
7. Which methods has your organization applied to evaluate the pending millennium date changes?
8. In your opinion, is the Year 2000 Crisis a significant issue in your environment?
9. What is the ratio between support and development projects in your organization? Has anyone every calculated this ratio before?
10. What percentage of existing software is absolutely crucial to business survival? How are these systems supported?
11. What plans, if any, does your organization have toward reengineering older applications?
12. Has conversion of older systems been successful? If so, was this due to the use of methodologies, procedures, or tools?
13. Do you favor the use of software tools for reengineering or does it seem more practical to redevelop an application as if it were new? Are there advantages to this approach?
14. What steps has your organization taken to evaluate support beyond the year 2000 date change?
15. Would you support the use of newer technology, such as the Intranet, to extend the life of older systems? If not, how would keep legacy systems functioning longer?

Section XII
Postdevelopment Administration

THE PRESTIGE OF DESIGN AND DEVELOPMENT ACTIVITIES frequently over-shadows the subtle, but important, need of system administration. Typically, administrative tasks are neglected or ignored soon after the implementation process has ended. In turn, this can lead to long-term support hardships throughout the entire application system life cycle. Development managers in numerous IS environments struggle with the ongoing demands of administration duties. Larger organizations are often more successful due to dedicated staff resources. But smaller environments, which are prone to hectic development schedules, are less capable of keeping up with postimplementation requirements. In the latter situation, development managers should adopt practices that can minimize the overhead needed for system administration, especially in the area of data retention management.

As development of applications increase, the need for adequate procedures and resources to handle the volume of stored data becomes paramount. This should embrace all types of operating environments and hardware platforms, including those from mainframes, servers, and desktop workstations. Chapter XII-1, "File Retention and Backup," provides an overview on the fundamentals for adequate file control. Despite the obvious need for backups, many organizations do not have comprehensive backup procedures across all computing platforms. Usually, the realization of this fact comes to light only after a need for data restoration is required.

Organizations that store data in disparate repositories struggle with the variety of file structures that are used by software applications. But environments that use a formal database product may be better prepared and benefit from the inherent backup capabilities that are integrated into the product. Nevertheless, databases still need careful administration for effective recovery. Chapter XII-2, "Managing Database Backup and Recovery," delivers practical advice on the methods needed to maintain database integrity. These methods can even be used during the early stages of development so that preliminary data files are not lost or corrupted via software errors.

POSTDEVELOPMENT ADMINISTRATION

The need for administrative control of system enhancements is paramount to the longevity and efficiency of deployed applications. Communication between end users and programming groups should allow for an organized process to implement additional system functionality. In Chapter XII-3, "Change Control and Problem Tracking Systems," guidelines for establishing effective change control communication are reviewed. Although this aspect of system administration is often perceived as less appealing than development, it is nonetheless more common in organizations. The absence of well-defined change control procedures can severely affect staff time and available resources. Furthermore, there is more probability that end users will not obtain the full functionality of the application system. Development managers should strive for effective change control and tracking procedures that meet end-user needs and business objectives.

Chapter XII-1
File Retention and Backup
Bryan Wilkinson

WHEN DATA WAS STORED solely on paper, information was often duplicated and distributed to several locations. If one source of the information was destroyed, most of the data could be reconstructed from the alternative sources.

In a centralized data processing environment, an organization's current and historical data and the programs that process this data are stored on magnetic media in a central library. Although centralization offers certain advantages, it also exposes the organization to the risk of losing all its data and processing capacity in the event of a major accident. In addition, files stored on magnetic media are more susceptible to damage than are files stored on paper. For example, if a disk, reel, or cartridge is dropped, the data it stores could be destroyed; dropped papers require only resorting. In the event of fire, the glue binding ferrite particles to tapes, disks, and diskettes begins to dissolve at temperatures as low as 125° F; paper begins to burn at 451° F. Therefore, a fire-retardant vault designed for paper files provides only limited protection for magnetic media. Magnetic files are also susceptible to tape crimping or stretching, disk deformation, head crashes, viruses, and magnetic erasure.

Furthermore, when mainframes were the sole source of computer power, retention and backup procedures could be enforced. Copies of all files and programs could be conveniently kept in a central library. Copies of essential files and programs could be kept in a secure off-site location. Automated tape management systems were developed to facilitate proper file retention and backup.

Microcomputers and local area networks (LANs) have greatly complicated data storage and backup. Vital information is often stored on hard disks and diskettes that are scattered throughout an organization. The systems manager may have little or no authority or control over such distributed data. Furthermore, in environments in which data is transmitted by way of electronic data interchange, the data may reside only on magnetic media; there may be no input forms, no documentation, and no printed output. If a microcomputer's hard disk is damaged by physical accident or malicious mischief, the data is lost if the user has not followed proper backup procedures. If a diskette is lost or damaged through mishandling, the data is lost if no duplicates exist. This chapter explains how these problems can be minimized with proper file retention and backup procedures.

FILE BACKUP

The most common causes of file damage or destruction are operational errors, natural disasters, and sabotage. The proper backing up of files considerably lessens the adverse impact of such occurrences. The following sections discuss causes of damage and their effect on file integrity in both centralized and decentralized computing environments.

Operational Errors

In a centralized processing environment, more files are lost or damaged because of human error than for any other reason; the most common errors are probably unintentional scratches. Inadvertent scratches can occur when unlabeled tapes are being labeled, filed, pulled, and mounted. Labelling tapes does not necessarily prevent accidental scratches. Although most mainframe operating systems have an option that permits a retention date or period to be placed in the label, this capability is not always used, thereby making it impossible for the operating system to detect a tape that must not be scratched. With some operating systems, the operator can ignore the warning console message and write over a tape even when a retention period is specified in the internal label. An operator or user can also erase or incorrectly alter a file by entering a transaction that overwrites the file or by failing to save the file.

Updating the wrong generation of a master file can also destroy data. Both the operator and user are responsible for this error. The operator mounts the wrong generation of the file and ignores warning messages from the operating system; the user fails to notice the problem when reviewing the reports. If the error is not detected until after the transaction or the proper version of the master file has been scratched, it can be extremely costly and nearly impossible to correct. Additional updating problems can occur when an update period covers more than one transaction tape. A given tape can be used more than once or not at all. Without externally generated control totals, such errors are almost impossible to detect.

Unlike tape files, disk and diskette files have no automatic backup capabilities. A special operational procedure is necessary to copy the file. This problem is complicated by the update-in-place process used with disk and diskette files. If the system fails during an update, the operations manager must determine how much was accepted by the system to avoid duplicate updating. The use of a data base by several applications compounds the seriousness of losing a file.

Online systems present a special problem when input is not recorded on hard copy. If a file is accidentally destroyed, reconstruction may be impossible unless a tape or another disk copy was made during data collection. With online updating, transaction logs in the form of journal tapes can provide a valuable source of backup. Program, software, and equipment malfunctions can also destroy or alter data and therefore necessitate file reconstruction.

Another operational error is the improper handling of magnetic media. If, for example, an unprotected tape reel is grasped by the outer edge rather than at the hub, the tape can be crimped and made unreadable. Destroyed or degraded files must be restored, which requires file backup.

An automated tape management system can minimize some operational errors, especially if a computer center uses many tape files. Proper file retention and backup standards and procedures are other solutions to operational problems.

Microcomputer File Backup

An increasing amount of data is stored on microcomputers or downloaded from mainframes and then maintained on microcomputers. These computers are usually operated by people who are relatively inexperienced with data handling procedures. As a result, files have a greater chance of being lost or damaged. The systems manager should ensure that all microcomputer users know and understand the following basic precautions:

- If the microcomputer has a hard disk, the heads of the disk drive should be positioned over a nonsensitive area of the disk before the computer is moved—usually done by running a PARK routine. Many portable microcomputers also feature a headlock capability, which provides the same protection.
- If a large file is being created, it should be saved periodically during the creation process.
- Two files should not be created with the same name unless the older version is no longer desired—the new file will overwrite the old.
- File names should print in a standard location on output documents.
- Diskettes should be kept in protective envelopes and storage containers when not in use.
- No portion of the diskette's magnetic surface should be touched.
- Diskettes should not be bent or squeezed.
- Diskettes should be kept away from smoke, liquids, grease, motors,

779

magnets, telephones, display monitors, extreme temperatures and humidity, and direct sunlight.

- Diskettes should be removed from disk drives before the system is shut off.
- Only felt-tip pens should be used to write on 5 1/4-inch diskette labels.
- Paper clips and staples should not be used on diskettes.
- Diskettes should not be cleaned.

Natural Disasters

Operational errors usually destroy only a limited number of files; disasters can damage an entire library. Fire is the most common disaster threatening a data center. The data center environment creates its own fire hazards (e.g., high voltages and easily combustible paper dust). Fire melts or burns disk packs, diskettes, and tape cartridges and reels, as well as the glue that binds the ferrite particles to the medium. Media damaged by smoke are unreadable until cleaned. If water is used to extinguish the fire, the files must be dried before they can be used.

Microcomputers are vulnerable to such localized disasters as small fires, power surges, electrical shorts, or collapsing desks. This is reason enough for regularly backing up the hard disk by using diskettes, tape streamers, or Bernoulli boxes; by uploading to a mainframe; or by using another backup method.

Although other natural disasters—earthquakes, hurricanes, tornadoes, and floods—might not destroy the files, a medium is rendered unusable until it is cleaned, tested, and refiled. Magnetic files must be backed up and stored in a location that is not exposed to the same threat of natural disaster as is the central data library to ensure the organization's ability to recover these files in the event of a natural disaster.

Sabotage and Theft

Sabotage of files or programs can include magnetic erasure and physical abuse. In addition, programs can be altered to erase or modify files when a specified event occurs, and external tape labels can be interchanged, requiring the files to be reidentified. Anyone with physical, program, or online access can sabotage files and programs. An effective approach to protecting files from disaster and sabotage is off-site backup.

Microcomputer users should be warned about using bulletin board programs, programs obtained from friends, and programs purchased from people who do not have a well-established reputation in the computer industry. Such programs can carry viruses, worms, or Trojan horse programs that can wipe out or alter files or deplete a computer's resources. If the microcomputer is linked to a mainframe, there is the added hazard that the problem instruction set could be transmitted to the mainframe, where the problems it causes could be magnified and spread. It is recommended that someone well versed in programming review new microcomputer programs or that the programs be vetted by antiviral software before they are used.

In addition, microcomputers have increased the threat of file loss through theft. Microcomputer file libraries are usually not behind locked doors. Diskettes are easy to conceal. People steal diskettes, not only for the data on them but to use on their home computers. If the diskettes are stolen, the files are gone if no backups exist.

FILE-RETENTION REGULATIONS

The Internal Revenue Service, in Revenue Procedure 64-12, requires that adequate record retention facilities be available for storing tapes, printouts, and all applicable supporting documents. Because this procedure was issued in 1964, before the widespread use of disks, it refers only to tapes. Revenue Ruling 71-20, however, states that punched cards, magnetic tapes, disks, and other machine-sensible media must be retained for as long as their contents may be regulated by the administration of internal revenue law. If punched cards are used only as input and the information is duplicated on magnetic media, the cards need not be retained. The IRS has also developed audit programs that can be performed through the computer by using files retained on magnetic media.

There are about 3,000 federal statutes and regulations governing the retention of records. Not all the records covered by these regulations have been automated, but many have. A digest of these regulations, *Guide to Record Retention Requirements in the Code of Federal Regulations,* is available from the US Government Printing Office. These regulations can be grouped in the following categories:

- Accounting and fiscal.
- Administrative.
- Advertising.
- Corporate.
- Executive.
- Insurance.
- Legal.
- Manufacturing.
- Personnel.
- Plant and property.

- Purchasing.
- Research and development.
- Sales and marketing.
- Taxation.
- Traffic.

Although many of these records might not be automated, those that are can be retained economically on magnetic media. State-regulated organizations (e.g., banks and insurance firms) must also satisfy state file-retention requirements because audit software is used to expedite and expand state audits.

EDP AUDIT REQUIREMENTS

Electronic Data Processing (EDP) auditors must be able to verify that programs are operating properly and that magnetic file data is accurately represented by the tab listings for audit. In addition, they must confirm an organization's ability to recover from a disaster or an operational error. EDP auditors can impose retention and backup requirements on data processing by requesting that specific files—usually year-end files for important financial systems and transactions—be kept for testing.

Retention and Backup Standards

Generally, the absence of file-retention and backup standards means that the system designers probably decide which files are retained and backed up; consequently, too few or too many file generations may be retained. Each situation is costly and illustrates the need for file retention and backup standards. Standards should be established for local and disaster recovery backup and legal file-retention requirements (see Exhibit 1). The sources of information and approaches to file storage vary according to these requirements.

Local Recovery. The systems manager provides information about local recovery requirements. Responsibilities include detailing the types of operational errors that affect file or program integrity and documenting how and when a problem was detected and what steps were taken to restore file or program integrity. The causes and consequences of any situation in which integrity cannot be restored must be thoroughly investigated. Constraints on restoration should be listed, and steps that can simplify or improve restoration should be examined. When files are updated online or data is collected through communications networks, the individual most familiar with data

I. Purposes
   A. Retention
   B. Backup
II. Policies
   A. Existing files
   B. New systems and files
III. Standards
   A. Basic retention and backup schedules (time and location)
      1. Operating systems
      2. Software packages
      3. Application programs
      4. Master files
      5. Transaction files
      6. Work files
      7. Documentation
      a. System
      b. Program
      c. File
      8. Input documents
      9. Other material
   B. Retention and backup schedule approvals
      1. Retention
      2. Disaster backup
      3. Operational problems backup
   C. Security considerations
      1. Company private data and programs
      2. Government-classified data
      3. Customer files
   D. Use of retention periods in file header labels
   E. Storage location
      1. Backup
      2. Retention
   F. Transportation of files to and from off-site storage location
   G. Procedural Documentation
      1. For users
      2. For MIS
   H. Periodic tests of the usability of the backup and retained materials
IV. Appendix
The appendix should provide an item-by-item schedule of all material whose retention and backup schedules differ from the basic schedule.

Exhibit 1. Outline for Developing Standards

communications should provide the same type of information for communications failures.

Data Restoration. Users who prepare input should be questioned about the disposition of original input documents and data transmission sheets. This information is particularly important when data is entered online with no paper documentation for backup. The data entry supervisor should be questioned to determine the cost and time required to reenter the average quantity of input for one processing cycle (i.e., one transaction file).

The programming manager should be consulted about problems associated with restoring application programs and other software files. Particular attention should be paid to the recovery of packaged programs that have been modified in-house. It is important to determine the availability of procedural documentation needed to restore the programs. The programming manager should provide the same information for the operating system and its various subroutines.

Microcomputer users should be questioned about the types of data in their files. Such data is increasingly of the type usually stored on the mainframe and centrally maintained. If there is data of this type, the problems and costs associated with its loss must be considered.

Disaster Recovery. Some of the information needed to establish disaster recovery backup standards is collected during the local recovery survey. Additional data can be obtained from reviews of a file inventory that identifies the files of each department within the organization. Department managers should review the inventory on a file-by-file basis to specify which files are vital to operations and must be reconstructed, department documents from which files can be restored, and the maximum time limit for recreating each file (assuming that the disaster occurred at the worst possible time). The systems manager should review all application programs, software packages, and operating system files. If several departments maintain organizational data bases, it may be necessary to recreate data at the data element level of the file.

Although all this information may not be needed to develop retention and backup standards, it does provide justification for developing and enforcing the standards. The information can also be used to establish backup and recovery procedures.

Legal Requirements. Retention requirements are set by the IRS, other government regulatory agencies, and departments within the organization. The controller is generally responsible for meeting the legal requirements and therefore should be consulted when it is being determined which files must be retained and for how long. The IRS recognizes that not all magnetic files can be maintained for long periods because of cost and volume and therefore has found that the appropriate method of determining record-retention needs is to evaluate each system and current retention policies. If the IRS has not reviewed organizational retention policies, the controller should ensure that such an evaluation is made. If the IRS has identified what should be retained and for how long, this information should be incorporated into the retention standards. The retained files should be periodically inventoried to confirm that the standards are being followed.

Department managers must be familiar with the other federal and state guidelines that apply to their files. In addition, record-retention requirements established by users, senior management, EDP auditing, and other departments must be enforced. Differences between the requirements specified by the users and those deemed appropriate by the auditors should be resolved.

STORAGE LOCATIONS

For efficient operation, files are usually stored in the computer room or an adjacent tape library. Microcomputer users who back up their files usually store the backups near the microcomputer. As protection against disaster, sabotage, or theft, a duplicate copy of important files should be stored off site. Various facilities can be used for this purpose:

- *Commercial off-site storage facilities.* These are useful for an organization with hundreds of files to be stored.
- *Moving and storage companies.* Several of these organizations use part of their warehouses to store magnetic files.
- *Bank safe-deposit boxes.* The size and cost of safe-deposit boxes make them appropriate for only a small number of files. Access to safe-deposit boxes may be limited to banking hours.
- *MIS facilities of another organization.* This alternative provides an environment with proper temperature and humidity controls. Unauthorized access can be prevented by keeping the files in a locked facility that can only be opened by an employee of the customer organization.
- *Remote corporate buildings.* This approach is probably the least costly of this type of facility.

Off-Site Storage Selection

Several factors should be considered during the selection of an off-site storage location:

- *Availability.* Backup files should be available 24 hours a day. Bank safe-deposit boxes present accessibility problems.

- *Access.* File access should be limited to a few employees. Individuals outside the organization should not have file access.

- *Physical security.* Fire safeguards (e.g., heat and smoke detectors and automatic fire extinguishers) that will not damage the files should be installed. The storage facility should be located and built to minimize damage from disasters. On-site and off-site facilities should not be concurrently vulnerable to the same disaster.

- *Environmental controls.* The proper temperature and humidity should be maintained continuously, including weekends and holidays.

- *Identifiability.* If a storage facility is used that is not part of the organization, there must be a method of distinguishing and identifying the material that belongs to the organization. If this is not done and the storage company declares bankruptcy, the bankruptcy court will seize and hold the files.

- *Storage requirement flexibility.* A facility should be able to meet the organization's current and future storage needs. It must be determined whether increased storage requirements will require the organization to use different locations in the building, purchase additional equipment, or pay for remodeling.

- *Cost.* This factor should be considered only after all other requirements have been satisfied. Compared with the reconstruction of files, any form of off-site storage is a less expensive alternative.

Storage Contracts

If a commercial storage facility, bank, or warehouse is selected as a storage location, the proposed lease should be reviewed by legal counsel. The lease should specify the lessor's file protection responsibilities and the resource for appropriate indemnification of file damage or loss.

If the data center of another organization is used for storage, a written agreement should identify the legal owner of the file, stipulate access rights, and define the liability of the organization providing the storage facility (or its insurer) if the files are accidentally or deliberately destroyed while on its premises. Legal counsel should review the proposed agreement to verify its appropriateness and validity. If the other organization refuses to sign an acceptable written agreement, use of the proposed facility should be approved by the senior management of the organization wishing to obtain off-site storage.

Transportation Considerations

The method of transporting files to and from the off-site storage facility should be considered carefully. Because magnetic media can be damaged by excessive heat, jarring, and mishandling, files should be packed in protective containers. Logs of all material stored off site should be maintained, and if a commercial transportation service is used, a packing slip should accompany each file.

OPERATIONAL CONSIDERATIONS

Proper off-site backup can shorten disaster recovery time and simplify the process. Because backup takes time and costs money, the frequency of backup should depend on how long the organization can continue to function without up-to-date data. In some operations, the answer may be no time. In such cases, the data must be captured simultaneously on two or more remotely located computers. If the answer is one week, weekly backup of master files and daily backup of transaction files should be adequate.

Frequency of backup depends on the type of application. For example, most manufacturing companies first used computers for financial data. In such cases, the company could manage for a week or two without the usual computer-produced reports. Now, many production applications are running so that production lines are scheduled, material is bought, and product status is determined using online automated systems. Off-site backup is often needed in these situations.

A standard approach to backup is to require a minimum of three generations of each master file, with the oldest generation being off site. Transaction tapes needed to bring the off-site version up to current status would be taken off site daily, weekly, or monthly, depending on the frequency or volatility of the update. Some organizations maintain their permanent-hold (usually year-end) tapes at the off-site location if the off-site storage location is more secure or spacious than the organization's storage area.

In a VS1 or MVS environment, the system catalog should be backed up for off-site storage. When the catalog matches the tapes at off-site storage, recovery is much easier; it is unnecessary to modify job controls to specify volume and serial numbers or absolute generations. Instead, restore jobs can refer to the relative generation number with a symbolic parameter that is easily modified.

Many data centers use reel numbers instead of labels on tapes that are managed by a tape management software package. Even when external labels are on the tapes, finding a particular tape among hundreds or even thousands can be next to impossible. Therefore, it is strongly recommended that a complete listing of tapes to be sent to off-site storage be prepared just before pickup and that the list be sent off site with the tapes. The list should include the tape volume and serial number, the date and time that it was created, and the data set names of every file on each tape. Automated tape management systems can produce such a list quickly and easily, and the list is important enough to justify the labor of producing it manually if no tape management system is in use.

SPECIAL FILE ACCESS PROBLEMS

Special file access problems complicate file retention and backup procedures. For example, if customer, classified, trade-secret, and sensitive data are processed in an online environment, a security software package must limit file access. The following sections address other access considerations for such files.

Customer Files. If an organization performs processing for other entities, it must access their files and programs. Customer agreements should be reviewed to determine the organization's contractual liability. Standards and procedures should have safeguards that minimize the possibility of lost or altered files. The customer should agree in writing to proposed backup and retention schedules.

Classified Data. Files with a government security classification must be stored and transported according to government regulations. The systems manager and EDP auditor should review these limitations to verify their enforcement.

Trade Secrets. Trade secrets are programs, formulas, and processes that give an organization a competitive edge. Methods of handling and protecting trade secrets are specified by state law and therefore vary. Several requirements, however, are basic to maintaining trade secrets:

- A trade secret and its associated material must be physically secured and designated as company confidential.
- The information cannot be published or made available to the public.
- If the material must be disclosed to someone outside the organization, this individual must be advised of the trade secret and must agree to maintain its confidentiality.
- A permanent record should be maintained of the material's location when it is not in the usual storage location.

Senior management must designate which files or programs represent trade secrets, and the systems manager and EDP auditor should ensure that an organization's retention and backup standards and practices meet state and internal requirements. The standards and practices should be reviewed with legal counsel to ensure adequate control.

Sensitive Data. Financial, payroll, and similar accounting information is generally considered confidential, with access limited to specific employees. Such data may be found on both hard disks and diskettes. If the data is on hard disk, access to that computer must be limited. If the data is also on diskette and is not encrypted, the handling and storage of the diskette (including its off-site storage) must be controlled. The systems manager must determine which files contain sensitive information, who is permitted access to each of these files, and how such access is controlled. Access control should be specified in the appropriate standards and procedures.

BACKUP USABILITY

Although the proper files may be retained and backed up, procedures must be established to maintain and test backup file usability.

One problem occurs when files that are to be retained for several years are stored on tape. Unfortunately, gravitational pull usually deforms tapes that are unused for a year or longer. A standard technique to prevent this problem is to rewind unused backup tapes every 6 to 12 months. If this practice is not being followed, the readability of the older tapes should be verified through a tape-to-print program.

If there is no standard on file retention, or if the standard is not followed, the proper versions of files, transactions, and programs may not be retained. To detect this problem, the systems manager can inventory the files at the backup location and compare this listing to the standard. A more useful but difficult approach is to use the files and programs at the backup site (instead of those at the data center) to process one or more applications. This method determines whether the standards are adequate and are being adhered to and whether operators know the procedures for using the backup material. Even if this technique fails to make these determinations, the processing pinpoints unexpected problems that could arise in an actual emergency and reemphasizes the need for workable emergency procedures.

ACTION PLAN

To ensure effective file retention and backup, the systems manager should:

* Determine file exposure.

- Determine the government record retention requirements that affect the organization.
- Compare current record retention standards with exposures and requirements.
- Identify and evaluate local recovery problems and their solutions.
- Review the organizational understanding of potential problems, proposed solutions, and legal requirements for record retention.
- Inspect and evaluate off-site storage.
- Review off-site storage agreements.
- Inspect and evaluate the facilities used to transport files to the off-site location.
- Determine special file access restrictions.
- Evaluate the usability of backup files.
- Prepare recommendations based on reviews and evaluations.

Chapter XII-2

Managing Database Backup and Recovery

Michael Simonyi

MANAGEMENT OF THE CORPORATE DATABASE is arguably one of the most mismanaged areas in information technology today. Database technology has evolved from historical glass house foundations of the past into the point and click implementations that come right out of the box today. Where databases and systems were once carefully designed, implemented, and deployed, they are now installed, loaded, and deployed without regard to basic effective design. This chapter addresses the concepts necessary to formulate a method to protect, back up, and in the event of failure, recover, perhaps the most important aspect of a business, its database. Without proper preparation, planning, and testing an entire database infrastructure can become the target of lost devices, indices, degraded backup mechanisms, and corrupted data.

HIGH AVAILABILITY VERSUS RECOVERABILITY

There are important differences between database availability and recoverability. Database availability can be a driving factor to recoverability, but it does not guarantee recoverability. Database availability is the measurement of production uptime and physical access to production data in a networked environment. In contrast, database recoverability refers to the ability to successfully recover a database in its entirety. Recoverability is a measurement of how accurate and lengthy the process of recovering from partial or total failure can be. The difference lies in the application of backup tools used in conjunction with high-availability tools. The redundancy of high-availability systems in an environment can directly relate to a higher grade of successful backups for the database environment as well as the supporting systems. In this chapter, a database environment is defined as the database, connecting middleware, and application front end screens. These technologies are used to complement each other to offer accuracy, reliability, and stability.

METHODS OF DATA PROTECTION

The common methods of data production include the following: (1) Tape; (2) Mirroring (RAID 0); (3) Data Guarding (RAID 5); (4) Duplexing; (5) Partitioning; (6) Replication; and (7) Clustering. Each of these are explained further in this section.

Before investigating these different methods available for protecting a database environment, this chapter discusses the business requirements for data recoverability and availability. For example, should a database, in the event of failure, cause individuals to be placed into a life-threatening situation or force an organization into financial chaos and eventual closure? In such a case it is necessary to implement all available methods to become 100% fault tolerant. However, should a failure be merely an inconvenience, then a simple tape backup procedure may suffice. Most organizations seek the middle ground.

Tape Backup

Tape backup should form the foundation of a corporate backup strategy due to its ease of use and low cost. In order for the tape backup mechanism to be useful it must be well designed and tested regularly. At a minimum, backups should be performed on a daily basis and not less than weekly. If possible, the entire database(s) should be backed up on a daily basis. The database transaction logs should be backed up during and after business hours, or whenever feasible to minimize the risk of lost data.

Mirroring

Mirroring or RAID 0 provides for duplicate sets of data on two separate hard disk drives, a primary and a secondary. This is also known as a master/slave configuration. For each logical write operation there are two physical write operations to the hard disks. This scenario protects against an individual or set of drives from failure. If either the primary or secondary drive fails, the data on the surviving drive allows for system recovery. In most situations, this option is ideal for protection of the database transaction logs. However, it does not offer protection against multiple simultaneous failures.

Data Guarding

Data guarding or RAID 5 has the ability to stripe redundant data across multiple drives (minimum 3) in an array. The striping of data protects against a single drive failure in the array. When an array loses a drive, the system still functions by using the redundant data found on the surviving drives. There are two types of RAID 5 available today, namely software and hardware-based RAID 5. Hardware RAID is by choice the desired implementation method. This stems from the fact that RAID 5 was designed with drive failures in mind. Extending the tolerance level of a RAID 5 system can then be achieved by mirroring or duplexing drive arrays. This type of extension allows for whole drive arrays to fail without impacting the system

Duplexing

Duplexing is similar to mirroring except that in a duplexed configuration separate controller cards manage each drive or sets of drives. In essence, duplexing is Raid 0 with an additional layer or redundancy. The second disk controller cards removes a single point of failure that is exhibited in a standard mirroring (Raid 0) configuration.

Partitioning

Partitioning is the ability to deploy a database system across multiple servers where each server houses a different portion of the overall data-base. Should a server go down, only the component running on that server becomes unavailable. In this scenario the database can continue to function normally, provided applications are written to handle these types of situations. Additional protection can be achieved by employing RAID 0, 5 or duplexing to further minimize system down time.

Replication

Replication offers the ability to publish the contents (complete or portions thereof) of a database to another or multiple servers in an environment. The technique is similar to partitioning; however, to employ replication requires sophisticated application transaction logic in order to be used effectively. Replication allows for the mirroring of database transactions to be replicated in a secondary database at the central site or in a distributed location. Ideally all transactions should be processed at a central database and the transactions should be replaced to the other subscribing sites. This eliminates the difficulty that becomes inherent with transaction logic of the traditional two-phase commit that fails due to hardware failures.

Clustering

Clustering is the ability for a group of servers to share or cooperate with each other in using common resources. Clustering allows systems to monitor each other and in the event of failure, transfer processing to their counterpart. Clustering is a very reliable method for maintaining a fault-tolerant and highly available systems environment. However, vendors approach clustering differently. It is recommended that organizations examine their application architecture and processing requirements prior to selecting a clustering strategy and infrastructure.

Each of these individual methods can be used in tandem to build a graded level of fault tolerance and high availability. Again, as with any other technology, the system requirements dictate the configuration and detail that is ultimately required. In most cases the higher the required tolerance, the more methods that are included in the solution.

Batch Cycles

The size and complexity of the database environment determines the most suitable backup cycle. A small site can afford the luxury of daily full database and transaction log backups. A medium sized site must perform a mix of backups of full database and transaction log backups on daily and weekly cycles. A large site requires multiple staggered sets of backups and transaction logs on a daily basis with weekly and even monthly cycles backing up segments of the database to achieve a full database backup.

Transaction logs should be backed up at least once during the day. However, this depends on the transaction flow of the database. A low volume On Line Transaction Processing (OLTP) database may require only a single transaction log backup at the end of a business day, before or after any additional processing is enacted on the data. In the case of high-volume OLTP processing environments, the backup of the transaction log may require hourly backups. It will be necessary to gauge the transaction flow of the environment to determine the backup schedule of the transaction logs.

Sample backup schedules for small, medium and large sites are shown in the tables given in Exhibit 1.

With each scenario outlined above, the robustness of the hardware also impacts the backup schedule of an organization. Since most organizations cannot afford to replace hardware on an as needed basis, different backup schedules may need to be adopted over time, for different pieces of hardware.

ACCURACY OF BACKUPS

Although data backups are important, equally important is the need to determine the accuracy of the data prior to backup and the ability to guarantee the restoration of the contents of the backup into the original database or backup database system. The accuracy or consistency of the backup is paramount for recoverability. Should inconsistent data or data structures be stored onto the backup media, any attempt to restore them will most likely render the database inoperable, or worse, introduce inconsistent data into the production environment that may unknowingly place the organization at risk.

Most databases on the market today provide built-in tools that provide some level of data integrity checking that verifies that internal data structures are intact and tables, indices, and page linkage are consistent. Any warnings or errors reported for these utilities should be acted upon at

Exhibit 1.   Sample backup schedules for small, medium, and large sites.

Schedule for a Small Site for Database Less than 10GB

Time	Mon	Tues	Wed	Thurs	Fri	Sat	Sun
12am	DB Check	DB Check	DB Check	DB Chek	DB Check	DB Check	DB Check
1am		Full DB	Full DB	Full DB	Full DB	Full DB	
5pm	Tlog	TLog	Tlog	TLog	TLog		
9pm	Purge Log	Purge Log	Purge Log	Purge Log	Purge Log		

Times noted are for clarity only

Schedule for a Medium Site for Databases greater than 10GB but less than 100GB

Time	Mon	Tues	Wed	Thurs	Fri	Sat	Sun
12am	DB Check	DB Check	DB Check	DB Check	DB Check	DB Check	DB Check
1am						Full DB	
5pm	Tlog	TLog	Tlog	TLog	TLog		
9pm	Purge Log	Purge Log	Purge Log	Purge Log	Purge Log		

Times noted are for clarity only

Schedule for a Large Site for Databases greater than 100GB

Time	Mon	Tues	Wed	Thurs	Fri	Sat	Sun
12am	DB Check	DB Check	DB Check	DB Check	DB Check	DB Check	DB Check
1am	DB Seg 1	DB Seg 2	DB Seg 3	DB Seg 4	DB Seg 5	DB Seg 6	DB Seg 7
5pm	Tlog	TLog	Tlog	TLog	TLog	TLog	TLog
9pm	Purge Log	Purge Log	Purge Log	Purge Log	Purge Log	Purge Log	Purge Log

Times noted are for clarity only

DB Seg refers to a portion or segment of the database to be backed up. Each segment or portion of the database in conjunction with the transaction logs will provide for a full database backup at any point in time.

once. Failure to act on these messages can render a database inoperable and depending when the problem surfaced cause a loss of data. The following pseudo implementation provides an approach to handling a database backup.

Generic Backup Stream

1. Perform a data integrity check on the contents of the database.
    1.1. Have inconsistencies been found in the database?
        1.1.1. Send alert to DBA and Operations staff, write events to log file.
        1.1.2. Halt backup stream. (Problem resolution takes place at this point.)
        1.1.3. Reestablish backup stream after problem has been resolved.
    1.2. Be sure database is free of defects.
2. Begin backup stream.
3. Verify completion status.
4. Notify operations and DBA of backup completion.

Incremental Backups

Incremental backups are something that should be performed only if it is not possible to complete a full backup during the allotted timeframe or backup window. Incremental backups extend the period of time required for restoring the contents of a database in the event of a failure. Although unavoidable in huge database environments where incremental backups are the mainstay, they should still be staggered in such environments.

Backing Up in a Distributed LAN/WAN Environment

Backing up a distributed database in the LAN/WAN environment can be a nightmarish challenge. Time zones and production uptime in differing geographical areas can affect the ability of ensuring a reliable and accurate backup. If the data volumes are small and maintainable, it will be possible to coordinate backups and replication over the WAN. Some thought should be given to using redundant WAN links so as not to affect other communications over primary WAN Links. If data volumes are of an extremely high nature or the network spans the globe, it may become practical to build a hot site for this type of environment. Whether the site is built and maintained internally or through third-party vendors is purely academic. The rationale is to provide a site for conducting business transactions should the primary production facilities fail. The site should mirror the current production facilities at all times. It can be updated by replication or by the use of tape media. Such a site should also be tested on a regular basis to ensure accuracy and guarantee the ability to continue business if failure encroaches upon the production systems (see Exhibit 2).

Administration Tools

As mentioned previously, most products on the market ship with some sort of administration tool sets to maintain and administer database environments. These tools can be either GUI based or Command line based, and at a minimum the following tasks should be included in the process: user management, DDL scripting, data import and export, database consistency, device management, data recovery, and security utilities. Some database vendors also provide additional utilities in the areas of Hierarchical Storage Management (HSM), Database Cluster Management, and on-line statistics monitoring tools. If a database does not provide for a specific level of administration, there are many third-party products available on the market that can complement most database environments.

Areas to Protect

There are three basic areas of a database that must be protected. The data, of course, being the blood of the system, the catalogs, being the skeleton of the system, and the transaction logs, which are the heart of a database

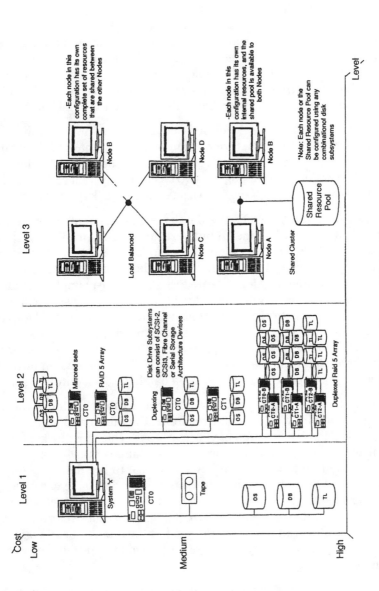

Exhibit 2. Types of Protection

as they detail all the events that have transpired against the data since the last full backup.

The transaction logs are considered paramount for any database system, especially after a database failure. Without the ability to maintain a readable copy of the transaction logs, any failure in the database places the data at extreme risk. For example, suppose a database is backed up fully once a week on Friday nights. During the week the transaction logs are written onto the hard disk. If the hard disk that holds the transaction log fails the following Thursday, and no prior backup of the transactions logs have taken place, the database will only be recoverable to the last point of a full backup.

The database catalog, as described above, acts as the skeleton for the database. It details the structure of the physical database. The catalogs must be rigorously maintained. Each and every change to the database modifies the catalog. The catalog has two facets, the system catalog and the user database catalog. Each has it own specialized backup requirements.

The system catalog defines the database environment, including the disk drives, database devices, configuration, logon privileges, tuning parameters, and device load points. This catalog must be backed up after every change because it affects the entire database environment. Any changes to the system catalog that are lost will seriously impair the ability to recover a database. In addition to having a backed up system catalog, a paper-based reproduction of the system catalog can be beneficial for audit purposes or if the need ever arises to restore an older database backup on a system prior to the installation of a new RAID array. As hardware is added to the system, database load points will vary. This can have undesirable effects when loading an older version of a database back onto the server.

The user database catalog on the other hand is the definition of the user database. It contains all the details regarding the tables and indexes used in the physical implementation of your database. This must be kept under strict observance. It should follow a strict change control process and must be backed up after each and every change to the database using a version control system. A failure to back up the database catalogs will result in loss of data if you are ever placed into a position of reloading the database from flat files. The database catalog, sometimes referred to as a schema, is the blueprint to your database. It is the foundation of your database. Keep it up to date and make sure you are able to retrace the path of its evolution.

The data, of course, being the lifeblood of the database and the reason for its existence, must also be safeguarded. The data should be backed up on a daily basis, if time permits, but not less than once a week. Backups should be restored from time to time to verify the validity of the backup

Exhibit 3. The Varying Levels of Database Recovery and Associated Costs

Method	Level	Cost	Down Time
Tape (mandatory)	Low	Low	Hours
Mirroring	Medium	Low	Minutes to hours
Duplexing	Medium	Low	Minutes to hours
Data Guarding	High	Medium	Minutes
Partitioning	Medium	High	Minutes to hours
Replication	High	High	Minutes
Clustering	Very High	Very High	Seconds to minutes
Hybrid Combinations	Extremely High	Extremely High	Seconds

and its state. There is no point in performing a backup if it is not tested periodically. What may have been restored last year may not be restorable now. Also be careful to test recoverability from tape backups.

Levels of Protection

Each of the individual methods provides a level of afforded protection. The base level of protection and last line of defense for a system failure should be a tape backup, the slowest of all methods to get the system back into operation when disaster strikes — the highest level being a hybrid system. Exhibit 3 demonstrates the varying levels of recovery and associated costs.

The application of each method will dictate the level of availability in the system and the degree of time required in recovering from a failure. For example, in a partitioned system the database is distributed between many separate servers. Should one of the servers go down, only a portion of the database becomes unavailable. Its cost is relatively high as there are many servers deployed and set up in a modular fashion. Each server then employs its own recovery mechanism.

In defining the level of protection to meet ones particular needs ask yourself these questions:

- Can I run the company without my database for an extended period of time?
- Do I risk my customer relationships if my database is unavailable?
- If the system becomes unavailable, is human life at risk?

If you answer yes to any of the above questions, you will need some form of high-availability solution to meet your needs. As mentioned previously, a tape backup should form the foundation of any backup strategy. Use the decision tree in Exhibit 4 to help guide the requirements for your backup strategy.

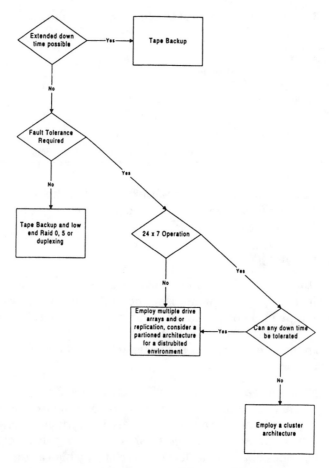

Exhibit 4.   Decision Tree for Selecting Desired Level of Protection

Virus Protection

Although a database system is usually well protected against direct virus attacks, you should make sure that the database is well secured from the rest of your computing environment. This usually means protecting the database by placing it on a dedicated system, making sure that the only way of reaching the system is via administrative tools, the deployed middleware, or operating-system-related administrative tools.

Even with a well-secured database, you will need to take similar precautions on the front end systems as well. Virus checking utilities should be deployed at the end-user client workstations and at any point in the environment where data will be fed into the database. Of course, this depends on the types of data being stored in the database. If Binary Large Objects

(BLOBs) are allowed to be inserted into documents, applications, or images that a virus can attach to, it may be necessary to implement additional levels of virus protection.

Internet and Intranet Firewalls

Database vendors are pursuing the ability to allow corporate data to become extensible to the Web if it is not already there. Most databases provide for this by using extensions to the middleware or database interface, providing extended datatypes in the database or providing plugins to the database.

This presents the problem of how to ensure that no one can gain direct access to a corporate database. By implementing hardware/software firewall combinations and proxies, it is possible to carefully segregate the database from the publicly exposed portion of a network. This allows construction of unidirectional paths into and out of the database that cannot be compromised easily.

CONCLUSION

In my experience, there is never too much protection, only too little. Having a well-thought-out backup and recovery procedure in place will save you time, money, and embarrassment when things go wrong. All of the topics examined within the body of this chapter detail methods that can be used to safeguard corporate databases or any other system. Pick and choose the pieces that best suit your needs when building your fail-safe environment.

Chapter XII-3
Change Control and Problem Tracking Systems
Thomas Fleishman

THE EXPLOSIVE GROWTH of information systems technology has been accompanied by an increase in the number of users whose daily activities are closely associated with and dependent on the IS function. In many cases, user activity involves complex online functions directly dependent on the availability of the computing resource. In the past, users seldom noticed such events as equipment changes, equipment outages, unsuccessful software installations, or untimely data. These events are now more visible to users than in the past, and they can cause significant service problems by interrupting online processing, which in turn disrupts the organization's business operation. Therefore, it is important to control such events to maintain the service levels required by users.

Determining baseline service levels and anticipating the effect that changes will have on these levels is one method of achieving user satisfaction. For example, the systems manager and the user community might agree that system availability at the terminal level is to be maintained at 98.5% for all online systems. If that level is barely maintained in a given period (e.g., a certain month), and if a major change is proposed that could reduce system availability below the baseline level during that period, that change (if not critical) could be postponed until the following month.

This chapter discusses the need for controlling changes and provides recommendations for implementing change control and problem tracking systems, usually referred to as systems management. These systems (i.e., as covered in this chapter) are not usable for controlling or tracking user requests for enhancements to production systems. It is assumed that such changes have been thoroughly tested before installation. The change control process begins when the tested enhancement is to be incorporated into the production environment. Initial requests for changes should be handled by some form of work request or project control process responsible for scheduling all projects and resources.

THE CHANGE CONTROL PROCESS

Experience in large, complex data centers has shown that a significant correlation exists between changes in the data center and subsequent interruptions or disruptions in service. A formal change control system—which identifies, evaluates, and coordinates required changes—can minimize such performance problems. The need for a change control system is reinforced by the following factors:

- *Volume of Changes.* As the size, complexity, and strategic importance of the computing environment increases, the number of required corresponding changes also increases—in some cases, proportionally; in others, exponentially. If uncontrolled, the volume of changes can quickly become unmanageable, resulting in a processing environment that is unstable and unable to meet the service levels required by and demanded by users.

- *Ranking of Changes.* As the volume of requested changes increases, so too will their scope and magnitude. A ranking process is recommended to help determine which changes must be installed and which can be deferred, combined, or eliminated to minimize the probability of service interruptions to users.

- *Visibility of Changes.* In an uncontrolled environment, certain systems or components are often the object of recurrent change. A change control system helps identify such systems or components and facilitates corrective action.

- *Coordination of Changes.* A change control system identifies changes that depend on other factors so that their installation can be coordinated.

- *Reduction of Impact.* A formal change control system can reduce the impact of required changes and help avoid serious problems and major outages.

- *Historical Records.* Formal change control procedures facilitate the maintenance of historical records, which help managers identify software systems and hardware components that require repeated changes. The records also help the systems manager institute problem tracking for added control by establishing such procedures as component failure impact analysis, which assesses the impact of failure in all identified components in the processing environment.

Definition of Change

The misconception that only major changes (e.g., migrating to a new operating system or installing a new online system) should be formally controlled prevents the fostering of effective change control management. Even such basic changes as installing an electrical outlet, moving a software module from a test to a production library, or increasing air-conditioning capacity should be monitored through the change control process because there is always a risk, however slight, that the change could disrupt service levels. In this context, a change is defined as any activity that can potentially degrade or interrupt service to users.

Step-By-Step Procedures

The change control process comprises a series of steps aimed at providing the user with maximum system stability and availability. These steps are initiation, review, approval, scheduling, coordination, implementation, and follow-up audit; they are described in the following sections.

Initiation. The first step of the change control process is initiation of the change request. Anyone who requests a change should be required to submit a formal request form that performs the following functions:

- *Communication.* This is to notify those concerned that a change is being requested.
- *Recording.* This is to provide documented input to a change history log.
- *Impact Analysis.* This is to determine the scope and expected impact of the proposed change.
- *Coordination.* This is to describe requisite and related activities that must be performed by other departments or personnel to implement the change.
- *Contingency Planning.* This is to describe specific contingency or back-up procedures to be invoked and how these will be managed if the change is unsuccessful.

Review. All change requests should be directed to a central committee where they are reviewed for clarity and completeness as well as for conformity with existing formats and standards. Exhibit 1 is an example of a typical change request form. This form is the major vehicle for the review process.

Approval. After the change request has been reviewed, it must be approved. The authorization or rejection of a proposed change should be the responsibility of a change control committee that represents the following groups:

- Application development.
- Software or technical support.

Date Received — M M / D D / Y Y

Date Required — M M / D D / Y Y

| 1 | 0 | | | | | | | | | | | | | | | | | | | | | |

Sub-Item Component

Unplanned
Fix   Problem/   Update
Y/N Work Request No. Y/N

Library   Documentation

Change Type
Hardware
H = Host
N = Network Software
A = Application
S = System Other
E = Environment
O = Operational

Risk Code
L = Low
M = Medium
H = High

Change Impact
1 = Cannot Reform Any Business Functions
2 = Cannot Perform Multiple Business Functions
3 = Cannot Perform Single Business Function
4 = Business Function Impacted
5 = Minor Change

Requester	Approved By	Implementor
0 2		

Change Description:
1 0
1 1
1 2
Reason:
2 0
2 1
2 2
Affected User(s): _____
Test Plan (Schedule): _____
Training Plan: _____
Recovery/Fall Back Procedure: _____

Source Names				Source Names		
Rename From	Level	Rename To		Rename From	Level	Rename To

Seq No.	Member Name	Library Type			Function			Compiles Only Procedure Name Used	Link Edit		CICS Rename Date Only
		Utility	Proce-dural	Source	Add	Re-place	Delete		Control Card Member	NCAL	

Exhibit 1. Sample Production System Change Request

- Communications (WANs, LANs, and data and voice).
- Production (or computer) operations.
- Production control.
- Users (in appropriate cases).
- Data base and data administration.

With the rapid growth of online systems as an integral and critical component of the daily operation of many businesses (including airlines, banks, brokerage houses, and medical care facilities, among others), a new function that affects the change control process has evolved in many of these organizations. This function is called service-level management, and its mission is to formally establish, track, monitor, measure, and report on information systems' service levels and the adherence of such service levels to the specified benchmarks. Representatives from this function are key members of the change control committee. If an organization's structure and size allow, the service-level management function should report to a neutral entity within the IS department, and a service-level management staff member should chair the change control committee.

Another major manifestation of the growth of strategic online systems and the organizational and technical changes that accompany such growth has been the emergence of the communications systems function and its convergence with the traditional IS department. The criticality of networks to support online systems and attendant business practices is readily evident and needs no substantive elaboration in this chapter.

The globalization of business, which is such a popular topic in many current business publications, requires an even greater dependence on networks in conjunction with providing computing resources to users in various parts of the world. Regardless of whether or not the communications systems function is part of the IS department, the communications function must have major representation on the change control committee because of its vital role in the maintenance of service levels to the entire user community.

Scheduling. After the change has been approved, it must be scheduled. By scheduling a change properly, the data center manager can ensure that:

- Several changes are not targeted for the same period.
- Adequate task planning can occur.
- All involved personnel can be notified of the proposed change.
- The resources required to effect the change can be made available at the required times.
- The change does not conflict with other activities outside of the change control area.

Coordination. The purpose of this step is to alert all involved or affected parties to the proposed change. Involved personnel should hold at least one meeting to:

- Fully discuss the change.
- Expose and resolve any conflicts and misunderstandings.
- Establish and agree on priorities.
- Develop a written change agenda for distribution to management and all areas potentially affected by the proposed change.

Implementation. After agreement has been reached concerning the change, a standard methodology should be used for implementation. For example, the methodology might state that nonemergency changes to financial applications can be made only on the second or fourth Tuesday of the month, and nonemergency changes to systems software (e.g., MVS, CICS, IMS, or TSO) can be made only on the first Sunday of each month. In addition, the implementation standards should explicitly state that only a specific group can implement production changes, thereby assigning accountability for the change process.

Follow-Up Audit. The last step of the change control process should be an audit to review changes that have been implemented. The audit function can:

- Compare the actual results of the change with the change request form and note any discrepancies.
- Aid in tracking changes made to production systems, systems software, and other modules, libraries, and utilities.
- Satisfy corporate internal audit requirements regarding changes in sensitive or proprietary data files.

Reporting Function

The reporting function is a key component of the change control process. For effective performance of this function, a change history file and some automated control over change-related data are necessary. The file should contain a composite list of all changes made to hardware, software, or the processing environment. The change history file may be archived, but it should not be destroyed.

In most installations, the volume of data that must be managed as part of the change control process is massive. If the data is handled manually, the results may be unsatisfactory and the personnel costs excessive or, in some cases, prohibitive. Therefore, some level of automation is necessary for effective data manipulation and storage.

Daily Change Control Reports

Report	Recipients	Purpose
Change activity	Change requestor, change coordinator	Feedback and activity summary for all changes in programs
Changes implemented	Managers, change coordinator	Daily log of implemented changes
Scheduled changes	Managers, change coordinator	Preview of changes scheduled for the next seven days

Weekly Change Control Reports

Report	Recipients	Purpose
Complete change schedule	Managers, change coordinator	Identification of changes approved and scheduled
Change summary (type)	Managers, change coordinator	Summary of changes by types (e.g., hardware, software)
Change summary (system)	Director, managers, change coordinator	Summary of changes made to applications and control software
Change summary (emergency)	Director, managers, change coordinator	Summary of all nonscheduled and emergency changes implemented

Monthly Change Control Reports

Report	Recipients	Purpose
Change summary	Director, managers, change coordinator	Summary of changes by type, requestor, system risk, and impact

Exhibit 2. Sample Change Control Reporting Structure

When the change control process is introduced, decisions must be made regarding the volume and level of reporting to be used. Exhibit 2 depicts a reporting structure currently being implemented in a large, multi-CPU installation supporting an extensive batch work load and an online user network with more than 10,000 workstations, terminals, and printers. Although the set of reports in Exhibit 2 is relatively small, the need for a complete change history file and an automated method for handling data and producing reports is clear.

This particular organization has created the position of change control coordinator as part of the service level management function. This employee plays a major role on the change control committee. The job description for this position is provided in Exhibit 3.

Overview of Responsibilities
- Analyzes each change request to ensure that no conflicts exist with other requests
- Interacts with IS personnel to develop a scheduled date for each change request
- Monitors all change requests to ensure timely implementation
- Is a member of, and reports any conflicts to, the change control committee
- Is responsible for the maintenance of change files and production libraries

Detailed Responsibilities
- Coordinates all changes in the production environment concerning online and batch systems through the use of appropriate forms
- Monitors and logs progress of changes to ensure that scheduled dates are met; if a scheduled date cannot be met, ensures that all affected areas are notified of any schedule changes
- Reviews all change requests to ensure that the requested dates are feasible; schedules requests that have little impact on the production environment; reports to the change control committee for scheduling of those changes that conflict with other requests or that significantly affect the production environment
- Maintains the change file to ensure that all historical data is correct and up to date
- Ensures that all change request entries are removed from the change file when implemented
- Provides special reports to the change control committee or management on request
- Moves all test programs to production libraries on the scheduled date and controls the production libraries' passwords
- Forwards to the change control committee all problem reports resulting from a previous change request
- Interacts with the technical standards group (if one exists) when a change request warrants a technical announcement or bulletin

Qualifications
- Ability to communicate and work effectively with all levels of IS, communications, and user personnel
- Strong oral and written communication skills
- Three to five years of experience in information systems, including at least one year of hands-on JCL experience
- Working knowledge of procedures for maintaining computerized files and data bases
- Understanding of the user community and its use of, and dependence on, computing services

Exhibit 3. Sample Job Description for Change Control Coordinator

---

IMPLEMENTATION CONSIDERATIONS

As an organization prepares to implement change control procedures, several additional considerations must be addressed. For example, any control procedure is effective only if it is applicable to the specific installation and organization. A procedure that is successful in one installation may be ineffective in another. Therefore, systems managers who wish to implement a change control system must be thoroughly familiar with the organization involved, the role of information technology in the organization, the nature and importance of the organization's automated systems, and the manner in which they support the organization.

The development of a change control system is a sensitive procedure that should not be undertaken without a detailed implementation plan. When implemented, the system will inevitably uncover weaknesses in various functions, systems, and departments involved in the process. Unless the systems manager is aware of this problem, the change control process can degenerate into a forum for accusations and recriminations that can disrupt data center and user operations. The issues that should be considered in the implementation plans are described in the following paragraphs.

Management Commitment. If management is not truly committed to the establishment, maintenance, and measurement of user service levels and to managing change, the systems manager should not try to implement a change control program. Management commitment must include an understanding of the philosophy behind change control and its potential impact on the various departments affected. In addition, management must recognize that effective change control requires significant resources in terms of time, hardware, software, and personnel.

Reporting Relationships. Organizational reporting relationships must be defined during the early stages of implementation. Although the change control function may report to the IS manager, the systems manager, or the technical support manager, it is advisable that a separate, neutral service-level management organization be established for this purpose. The definition of line reporting relationships depends on the size of the organization and the level of expertise, interest, and commitment of the personnel involved.

Change Committee Chairperson. Reporting relationships depend on who is selected as committee chairperson. In general, it is advisable to appoint a high-level staff member from the service level management organization as the chairperson.

Resource Requirements. The implementation plan should define the personnel resources required for the change control process, including meeting time, staff work, and management. In addition, if a software package is required for data collection and reporting, planners must decide who will develop the package, or if a package is purchased, who will install and maintain it.

Logistical Issues. If the organization is geographically dispersed, the impact on change control meetings, implementation of changes, delivery of reports, and management of the function must be determined.

PROBLEM TRACKING

The implementation of the change control process should be followed by the development and implementation of a problem tracking system. The change control process forms the foundation for problem tracking through the formalization of procedures and the compilation of data on changes in hardware, software, and the processing environment. Problem tracking is aimed at identifying and collecting detailed information on any occurrence that interrupts the computing resource at the user level.

The problem tracking system can be an automated system capable of tracking both changes and problems. A single center for trouble reporting should be established (e.g., the network control center). All hardware and software problems should be reported to network control, which is responsible for obtaining the essential descriptive details of the problem (e.g., terminal identification, hardware component serial number and address, application software system identification, transaction identification, or operating software system identification) along with any other information that can help identify and resolve the problem. After the data has been obtained, it is entered into the automated tracking system, and the problem is then assigned to the proper department for resolution.

The compilation of this data provides an invaluable tool for management. For example, the information can be used to:

- Control vendor performance.
- Evaluate the impact of changes to the computing environment.
- Track application software stability.
- Track operating system software stability.
- Monitor hardware component history.
- Assist in hardware maintenance control decisions.

Change control and problem tracking are logically linked and are needed for effective data center management.

Automated Systems. The availability of automated systems has improved during the past few years and has facilitated the implementation of change control, problem tracking and service-level management of both the IS and communications environments. The following software products are some examples of the availability of vendor-developed tools for systems management. This list is by no means exhaustive, nor should any endorsement be inferred; it is provided as a guide, and systems managers are encouraged to research these as well as other products to determine which best fit their organization's requirements:

- Change control and problem tracking:
  - Info Management/Info MVS—IBM Corp.
  - CA-Newman—Computer Associates International, Inc.
  - Network Management System 3—Peregrine Systems, Inc.
- Service level management:
  - Net Spy—Duquesne Systems.
  - Mazdamon—Computer Associates.
  - Infinet—Infinet.
  - Net Alert—Boole & Babbage, Inc.
  - System View Netview—IBM Corp.
  - Best-BGS Systems, Inc.

Because most available change control and problem tracking systems are currently mainframe oriented, and because of the consolidations among the software firms that address the mainframe utility software market, not many other automated tools are available. As the client/server architecture evolves and becomes a more extensive platform on which major production-level systems are developed, utility software for network management or security (to name a few) is likely to become more available and prevalent. Again, however, systems managers are encouraged to conduct a search for change control or problem tracking software for the specific computing platforms represented in their environments. Such a search is easily performed through any library or software vendor directory.

SUMMARY

The development and installation of change control, problem tracking, and service-level management systems is strongly recommended. To be successful, however, these tools must have both management and organizational commitment; in addition, planners must use detailed project plans (including estimates of required resources and specifications for reporting relationships) for development and implementation. When these issues are successfully addressed, change control and problem tracking can help maintain a high level of service to the user community.

Section XII – Checklist
Postdevelopment Administration

1. How does your organization manage the different system administration duties? Are there dedicated staff for the various functions?
2. Which administrative tasks are more likely to suffer from incompleteness in your environment?
3. Do you feel confident that postimplementation tasks receive the necessary attention for ongoing system support? If not, what steps have you taken to improve this?
4. Are system administrative projects scheduled as part of development or are these handled when time permits?
5. Is it your impression that programmers are more or less willing to complete administrative duties, such as documentation, and backup procedures? Is this due to lack of time, misunderstanding or other factors?
6. Should specialized staff be assigned to system administration functions? Would this improve the quality and the quantity of completed projects?
7. Has system security become more demanding in your environment? If so, could this be simplified with better technology, better procedures, or limited use of applications?
8. Does your organization have an enterprisewide file recovery procedure in place? If so, has it ever been tested?
9. What changes would you implement to improve the file retention and backup of the application systems in your organization?
10. Has your organization investigated the legal requirements for retaining files as it relates to your business goals?
11. How are end-user workstation files backed up in your environment? Is it done automatically, or voluntarily? Is it effective?

About the Editor

PAUL C. TINNIRELLO IS CHIEF INFORMATION OFFICER of a leading insurance information publishing organization and a consulting editor for Auerbach Publications. He is responsible for the development and support of financial software products in microcomputer and mainframe environments. He holds an MS in computer and information sciences as well as a BA in mathematics. Tinnirello has been a graduate and undergraduate adjunct professor at state and local colleges in New Jersey and is a founding member and past director of the Software Management Association, formerly the Software Maintenance Association. He has written and published numerous articles on the development and support process and has presented his material at various computer conferences throughout the country.

Index

Index

upgrading custom applications, 465
Windows 95 applications, 465
WITT, see Workstation Interactive Test Tool
Word processors, 671
Work
  breakdown structure, 8, 9, 25
  habits, 677
  processes, standardized, 12
Workbenches, 738
Working storage, 347
Workstation
  caching, 451
  files, end-user, 815
  Interactive Test Tool (WITT), 565
  upgrade planning for, 463
World Wide Web (WWW), 342, 545
Writing, benefits from, 691
WWW, see World Wide Web

X

X tests, 269
xref benchmark, 241, 254

Y

Year 2000 crisis, project management solutions for, 21–33
  closure, 32
  controlling year 2000 project, 32
  defining year 2000 project, 24–25
  four elements of project, 21–23
  leading year 2000 team, 24
  organizing, 31
  planning year 2000 project, 25–31
    calculation, 30–31
    resource allocation, 29–30
    time estimates, 28–29
    work breakdown schedule, 26–28
  project management for year 2000, 23–24
Year 2000, crisis vs. opportunity, 711–720
  determining organization's risk, 714–720
  origins of year 2000 problem, 711–712
  scope and reach of year 2000 situation, 712–714

Z

Zero defect software, 605